# Examining Wrongful Convictions

# Examining Wrongful Convictions
## Stepping Back, Moving Forward

Edited by

Allison D. Redlich

James R. Acker

Robert J. Norris

Catherine L. Bonventre

CAROLINA ACADEMIC PRESS

Durham, North Carolina

Library of Congress Cataloging-in-Publication Data

Examining wrongful convictions : stepping back, moving forward / edited by
Allison D. Redlich, James R. Acker, Robert J. Norris, Catherine L. Bonventre.
    pages cm
  Includes bibliographical references.
  ISBN 978-1-61163-252-1 (alk. paper)
  1. Judicial error--United States. 2. Judicial error--Social aspects--United States. 3.
Compensation for judicial error--United States. 4. Law reform--United States. I.
Redlich, Allison D., editor of compilation. II. Acker, James R., 1951- editor of compi-
lation. III. Norris, Robert J., editor of compilation. IV. Bonventre, Catherine L., editor
of compilation.
  KF9756.E93 2014
  345.73'0122--dc23

                        2014013622

Carolina Academic Press
700 Kent Street
Durham, North Carolina 27701
Telephone (919) 489-7486
Fax (919) 493-5668
www.cap-press.com

Printed in the United States of America
2016 Printing

# Dedications

*To my parents. If not for them and their insistence on being the best I could be, I would not be who and where I am today. I also dedicate this to the persons this volume is about: the innocents who languish in prison, who go unheard despite repeated cries for help, and whose unwanted sacrifice will hopefully pave the way so that others in the future will not endure what they have. Finally, I dedicate this volume to the attorneys, judges, journalists, policymakers, scientists, and others who work to right the wrongs of our criminal justice system.*

*—ADR*

*To Jenny, Elizabeth, Anna, Ethan, and Zoe; whether stepping back to reminisce about times past or moving forward in anticipation of times not yet revealed, I could not be happier than to be in such fine company. And let us all dedicate ourselves toward establishing a more perfect union in which justice carries the day.*

*—JRA*

*To my family, whose never-ending love and support in all that I do inspires me to keep going. And to Caitlyn, for her incredible patience with me, and for understanding when I have to work late nights or on weekends (even when it is her birthday). For those who have been wronged by the criminal justice system and those who work tirelessly on their behalf, I hope this volume can be but one small contribution toward making things just a little bit better.*

*—RJN*

*To my mom, my dad, and my stepdad; and to Vin, my brothers, and my stepsons. Thanks for expecting, demanding, and encouraging the best of me. And to Alan Newton, who I never met. A 2006* New York Times *article reported his exoneration and the loose-fitting designer suit, bought by a childhood friend, Newton wore when he was released from prison. That story, and the photos of him in that suit, broke my heart and solidified my commitment to help reduce the number of stories like his that must be told.*

*—CLB*

# Contents

# Acknowledgments

We first thank the good folks at Carolina Academic Press. Without exception, they all have been wonderful to work with. In particular, Beth Hall and Tasha Pippin have shepherded us through the process from beginning to end with enthusiastic and unwavering support. This is the first edited volume for three of the four editors, and Beth and her colleagues were always there to respond to our questions and concerns.

We also thank the authors who contributed to this volume. We have enjoyed working with you all and we so very much appreciate the time and thoughtfulness you put into your individual chapters. We consider ourselves lucky to be able to work with such fine colleagues.

—ADR
—JRA
—RJN
—CLB

# Examining Wrongful Convictions

# Chapter One

# Stepping Back—Moving Beyond Immediate Causes: Criminal Justice and Wrongful Convictions in Social Context

James R. Acker, *University at Albany, State University of New York*

Allison D. Redlich, *University at Albany, State University of New York*

Robert J. Norris, *University at Albany, State University of New York*

Catherine L. Bonventre, *University at Albany, State University of New York*

A person is innocent until proven guilty. This familiar maxim is of ancient origin and is widely observed. It is reflected in such venerable edicts as the Babylonian Code of Hammurabi, the laws of the Roman Empire, and English common law (Pernell, 1989; Quintard-Morenas, 2010). Although this nation also has long embraced this fundamental principle of law (*Coffin v. United States,* 1895), it has become apparent that a regrettable corollary is coupled with it: some persons are innocent even though they have been proven guilty.

More than 1,300 cases of wrongful convictions—involving individuals found guilty of crimes but later exonerated based on new evidence of innocence—have been identified in this country between 1989 and February 2014 (National Registry of Exonerations, 2014a). Well over 300—roughly one out of four—of the wrongful convictions were exposed with the assistance of DNA analysis (Innocence Project, 2014a; National Registry of Exonerations, 2014b). How many innocent people remain incarcerated or otherwise burdened by the stigma of wrongful conviction can only be the subject of guesswork. One authority has estimated that between 5,000 and 10,000 wrongful convictions occur *annually* in this country, including roughly 2,000 to 4,000 cases resulting in prison sentences (Zalman, 2010/2011; see also Gross, 2013).

Such miscarriages of justice produce multiple and deeply profound harms. The individuals wrongly convicted of crimes suffer the most. Those whose false convictions remain undetected will have no relief from punishment and will suffer the enduring stigma of a criminal record. Some may have been executed (Bedau & Radelet, 1987; Grann, 2009; Liebman, Crowley, Markquart, Rosenberg, White, & Zharkovsky, 2012). Those who ultimately were exonerated spent, on average, more than a decade in prison before securing release (National Registry of Exonerations, 2014c). Some of them (143, spanning 1973 through late February 2014) were erroneously convicted of capital murder and sentenced to death (Death Penalty Information Center, 2014). The years lost to wrongful conviction and incarceration almost inevitably spawn additional problems including broken familial relations, damaged physical health, lingering emotional trauma, and barriers to employment, social services, and compensation that endure well beyond release from custody (Grounds, 2004; Norris, 2012; Owens & Griffiths, 2011/2012; Westervelt & Cook, 2012).

Another harm, the inevitable companion of wrongful convictions, is the failure to bring the truly responsible criminal offenders to justice. When perceived as occurring with sufficient regularity, the twin evils of convicting the innocent and permitting the guilty to go free threaten to undermine public trust in the administration of justice (Findley, 2008; Huff, 2008; *In re Winship*, 1970). The more tangible consequences of allowing the actual perpetrators to remain at large while the innocent are erroneously convicted and punished can be devastating. The offenders who elude justice are often violent criminals who take advantage of their ill-gained continuing freedom to claim additional victims by committing repeat acts of murder, rape, and other serious crimes (Acker, 2012/2013; Conroy & Warden, 2011a). The associated financial costs of wrongful convictions are staggering, as well. The economic impact of the new crimes committed by the true perpetrators, combined with compensation from public funds paid to exonerees, runs well into the hundreds of millions of dollars (Acker, 2012/2013; Conroy & Warden, 2011b).

The substantial individual and social harms that wrongful convictions occasion underscore the urgency of understanding their causes and, to the greatest extent possible, preventing their occurrence, detecting those that have occurred, and providing redress to the innocent who have suffered them. Advancing theory, research, and policy initiatives directed toward these ends is the principal objective of this volume. Through the chapters presented, we have sought to broaden the disciplinary perspectives brought to bear in answering how and why justice miscarries in the form of wrongful convictions. At the same time, we have attempted to deepen our understanding of these issues by inviting exploration of the fundamental or root causes and consequences of wrongful convictions, rather than asking authors to focus on the circumstances that most immediately precipitate and result from them.

# Wrongful Conviction Scholarship and Activism: An Abbreviated History

A significant body of scholarship already has been devoted to miscarriages of justice. Edwin Borchard was among the earliest American writers to focus attention on wrongful convictions. His initial article, published more than a century ago while he served as the Law Librarian of Congress, was an impassioned call for the publicly funded compensation of innocent persons who had erroneously been convicted of crimes. It began: "In an age when social justice is the watchword of legislative reform, it is strange that society, at least in this country, utterly disregards the plight of the innocent victim of unjust conviction or detention in criminal cases" (Borchard, 1913, p. 684). Coincident with writing this article Borchard drafted a bill, which was considered by Congress but not enacted, to authorize federal compensation for persons wrongfully convicted of crimes (Little, 2008; McHenry, 1913). Two decades later, then a professor at Yale Law School, Borchard published *Convicting the Innocent: Sixty-Five Actual Errors of Criminal Justice* (1932). This seminal book is credited with transforming the question of "*whether* factually innocent individuals were wrongfully convicted in the American criminal justice system to the questions of *why* they were wrongfully convicted and *what could be done* to remedy the problem" (Leo, 2005, p. 203, emphasis added).

The following decades produced additional works which, using a format resembling *Convicting the Innocent*, reported on cases of known wrongful convictions, described the errors and missteps that contributed to the faulty verdicts, and then recommended reforms designed to avert future miscarriages of justice (Leo, 2005). As case histories, they represented compelling narratives involving individuals whose lives were turned upside down by accusations and convictions for crimes they had not committed. Journalistic in style, these writings typically were directed toward lay audiences and did not purport to be systematic or scientific analyses of the causes and consequences of wrongful convictions (e.g., Frank & Frank, 1957; Gardner, 1952; Radin, 1964). Some of the accounts were autobiographical while others involved case studies (e.g., Carter, 1974; Lassers, 1973; Zimmerman & Bond, 1964). Although offering insights about the factors commonly associated with wrongful convictions, and instrumental in harnessing public sympathies for the unfortunates who suffered them, works of this genre soon enough yielded diminishing returns with respect to offering new knowledge or proposing beneficial policy reforms.

The 1980s introduced dramatic changes, both in wrongful conviction scholarship and in technology that revolutionized how the natural sciences could be employed forensically to uncover and help prevent miscarriages of justice. In the former arena, Professors Hugo Adam Bedau and Michael Radelet (1987) published a groundbreaking article in the *Stanford Law Review* that systematically analyzed 350 cases which, in their assessment, involved the wrongful conviction of persons for capital or potentially capital crimes in this country between 1900 and 1985. Relying on the premise that the "failure by the authorities to acknowledge error is not very convincing evidence that errors have not occurred" (p. 25), Bedau and Radelet used a criterion to identify miscarriages of justice that did not depend on official recognition (such as through the reversal of a conviction or executive pardon) that an innocent person had wrongfully been convicted: "[T]he cases we have included ... are those in which we believe a majority of neutral observers, given the evidence at our disposal, would judge the defendant in question to be innocent" (p. 47). They detailed the contributing factors linked to the identified cases of wrongful conviction and classified them as being attributable to the police, prosecutors, witnesses, or other sources of error. Their methodology and conclusions inspired some disputation (Markman & Cassell, 1988; see also Bedau & Radelet, 1988), but their study focused renewed attention on errors of criminal justice and represented a significant departure from prior, primarily anecdotal accounts of wrongful convictions and their presumed causes.

The 1980s also heralded the forensic application of DNA analysis, a development that indelibly wrapped wrongful convictions within the legitimating mantle of science. Convictions for rape, murder, and capital murder increasingly came unraveled as laboratory analyses revealed that semen, blood, or other biological evidence left at crime scenes could not possibly have come from persons adjudged guilty of those offenses and sentenced to lengthy imprisonment or death. The publicized exonerations compelled recognition that wrongful convictions were real, as were the horrifying consequences for the innocent people who suffered them. The emergence of DNA profiling and its evidentiary use were not alone responsible for the heightened awareness among criminal justice officials and the American public that innocent people were at risk of wrongful conviction, but they were pivotal in stimulating and perpetuating the innocence movement (Baumgartner, De Boef & Boydstun, 2008; Cole, 2012; Findley, 2010/2011; Rosen, 2006; Zalman & Marion, 2014).

Organizations sprang up with missions of investigating cases of potential wrongful conviction and correcting miscarriages of justice. Centurion Ministries, founded in Princeton, New Jersey in 1983 by Reverend Jim McCloskey, was the first such prominent organization of the era (Centurion Ministries, 2013; Krieger, 2011; Stiglitz, Brooks, & Shulman, 2002). Nearly a decade later, in 1992, attorneys Barry Scheck and Peter Neufeld established the Innocence Project: "a national litigation and public policy organization dedicated to exonerating wrongfully convicted people through DNA testing and reforming the criminal justice system to prevent future injustice" (Innocence Project, 2014b). An expanding web of law schools and other clinics in this country as well as in Canada, Ireland, New Zealand, and the United Kingdom currently maintain innocence projects and are loosely connected through the Innocence Network (Innocence Network 2014; Findley & Golden, 2014; Ricciardelli, Bell, & Crow, 2011/2012). Northwestern University Law School's Center on Wrongful Convictions has been engaged in similar work since its inception in 1998 (Bluhm Legal Clinic Center on Wrongful Convictions, 2014). The Center commanded national attention by hosting a conference that year which brought together 31 exonerees who had been released from death rows following their erroneous convictions for capital murder (Warden, 2012).

The renewed public and scholarly attention to wrongful convictions, sustained and legitimated in part by the confirmatory science of DNA profiling, snowballed throughout the 1990s and into the new century. Illinois Governor George Ryan's decision in January 2003 to commute the death sentences of all 167 individuals on the state's death row and pardon four others captured national headlines. Those actions, taken as Ryan left office, were motivated by his profound doubts about the reliability of capital murder convictions in his state. Ryan noted that Illinois "had the dubious distinction of exonerating more men than we had executed, 13 men found innocent, [and] 12 executed" during the modern death-penalty era (*New York Times*, 2003; see also Marshall, 2004; Sarat, 2004). Eight years later, in 2011, Illinois repealed its capital punishment statute. The repeal was largely inspired by continuing concerns about the risk of executing innocent persons, a factor that has contributed to the recent abolition of the death penalty in other states and that also has helped significantly reduce the annual number of newly imposed death sentences throughout the country (Acker & Bellandi, 2014; Bowers & Sundby, 2009; Entzeroth, 2012; Jones & Wilson, 2013; Warden, 2012).

Research and scholarship devoted to miscarriages of justice continue to grow at an accelerating pace. Professor Samuel Gross and colleagues published a widely recognized study in 2005 that identified 340 individuals who were exonerated—officially pronounced not guilty—between 1989 and 2003 after they had been convicted of serious crimes (Gross et al., 2005). Their catalogue included both DNA and non-DNA exonerations, with the latter representing over half (196, or 58%) of the total. It excluded numerous "mass exonerations" involving "innocent defendants who were falsely convicted as a result of large scale patterns of police perjury and corruption" (p. 533). Professor Gross has since collaborated with others to compile a National Registry of Exonerations, where the ranks of exonerees had swelled by an additional 900 in the decade between 2003 and 2013 (National Registry of Exonerations, 2014a).

Attention naturally focused on the factors contributing to miscarriages of justice as wrongful convictions came under increased scholarly scrutiny. Noting that cases commonly "include a combination of" factors, the Innocence Project's analysis of the accumulating DNA-based exonerations resulted in its identification of "the most common causes of wrongful convictions" (Innocence Project, 2014c). This frequently replicated schematization includes the following sources of error:

- Eyewitness Misidentification
- Unvalidated or Improper Forensic Science
- False Confessions/Admissions
- Government Misconduct
- Informants or Snitches
- Bad Lawyering (Innocence Project, 2014c)

This list overlaps strikingly with factors that Professor Borchard identified several decades ago in the 65 cases he studied while compiling *Convicting the Innocent* (1932).

- "Perhaps the major source of these tragic errors is an identification of the accused by the victim of a crime of violence.... These cases illustrate the fact that the emotional balance of the victim or eyewitness is so disturbed by his extraordinary experience that his powers of perception become distorted and his identification is frequently most untrustworthy" (p. 367).
- "The unreliability of so-called 'expert' evidence is disclosed by eight striking cases" (p. 373).
- "In several of the cases ... a species of third degree or undue influence produced 'confessions' from the accused.... While confessions may often seem conclusive, they must be carefully examined. Persons charged with crime are not infrequently of defective or inferior intelligence, and, even without the use of formal third-degree methods, the influence of a stronger mind upon a weaker often produces, by persuasion or suggestion, the desired result" (pp. 371–372).
- "In a very considerable number [of cases], the zealousness of the police or private detectives, or the gross negligence of the police in overlooking or even suppressing evidence of innocence, or the prosecution's overzealousness was the operative factor in causing the erroneous conviction" (p. 369).
- "Cases in which the perjury of prosecuting or other witnesses ... was the main factor in the conviction are not inconsiderable...." (p. 369).
- "In the majority of these cases the accused were poor persons, and in many of the cases their defense was for that reason inadequate. The practice of assigning attorneys or the inability to engage competent attorneys makes it often impossible for the accused to establish his innocence" (p. 374).

The same essential grouping of sources of error has become firmly implanted in the extensive literature of wrongful convictions, offering a customary framework for explaining how and why innocent people are convicted. It provides a typical starting point for research studies and recommended policy reforms. Many important advances have clearly been made in both knowledge and official actions concerning the major factors linked to miscarriages of justice. The developments embrace issues of eyewitness misidentification (Clark, 2012; Wells & Quinlivan, 2009; Wells et al., 1998); unreliable science and overstated forensic testimony (Committee on Identifying the Needs of the Forensic Sciences Community, National Research Council, 2009; Garrett & Neufeld, 2009); false confessions (Garrett, 2010; Kassin et al., 2010; Lassiter & Meissner, 2012); misconduct and negligence of the police and prosecutors (Covey, 2013; Medwed, 2012; Simon, 2012,; Smith, Zalman, & Kiger, 2011); unreliable testimony of incentivized informants (Garrett, 2011; Natapoff, 2009); and deficient performance of defense lawyers (Acker & Bonventre, 2010; American Bar Association Criminal Justice Section, 2006; Garrett, 2011; Worden, Davies, & Brown, 2014). Further research contributions and additional policy implications are certain to follow. Still, so intensively have these familiar pathways been investigated that fresh theoretical and methodological perspectives are likely to hold greater promise for producing significant new insights about the causes and consequences of wrongful convictions (see Gould, Carrano, Leo, & Young, 2012; Gould & Leo, 2010; Leo & Gould, 2009).

Ironically, perhaps, in light of Borchard's (1913) initial focus on the inadequacy of compensation for wrongfully convicted persons, considerably less attention has historically been devoted to the aftermath of miscarriages of justices than to their precipitating factors. Signs of change have arisen in more recent scholarship and policy enactments. More intensive scrutiny has been given in academic writings to the debilitating psychological, physical, and social consequences of wrongful conviction that endure beyond exoneration and freedom from incarceration (Campbell & Denov, 2004; Grounds, 2004; Kleine, 2011/2012; Thompson, Molina, & Levett, 2011/2012; Westervelt & Cook, 2012). Critical analysis has been made of laws governing the compensation of wrongfully convicted individuals who have suffered the pains of imprisonment, including the often onerous barriers to damage awards and limitations on them (Bernhard, 2004; Kahn, 2010; Mostaghel, 2011; Norris, 2012; Owens & Griffiths, 2011/2012). As with the factors associated with the production of wrongful convictions, much has been learned and important reforms have ensued regarding the problems and challenges encountered by exonerees. Still, substantial potential remains for further advances to be made by broadening the research and policy perspectives applied to these issues.

The present volume originated with such considerations in mind.

# Wrongful Convictions: Stepping Back, Moving Forward

By definition, wrongful convictions occur in the courts of law that pronounce innocent persons guilty of crimes. The courts, in turn, are populated by individual actors—prosecutors, defense attorneys, judges, and juries—who perform their assigned roles subject to psychological, organizational, and institutional influences which operate at various strength and levels of awareness. The people, organizations, and institutions charged with dispensing justice, including law enforcement personnel, all function within a larger social context. Local communities reflect and help inculcate norms and attitudes that can alter conceptions of justice and its administration. The states, region, and the national society in which communities are embedded likewise can be expected to influence the perceptions and behavior of criminal justice actors. Within this broader domain, political values, economic considerations, attitudes about race, social class, gender, and countless additional variables coexist with and impinge on systems of justice and the actors within them. Wrongful convictions, thus conceived, are at the epicenter of a progressively widening series of concentric circles that represent multiple layers of influence—psychological, organizational and institutional, economic, sociopolitical, and more—relevant to miscarriages of justice and responses to them.

The essential premise of this book is that much of value can be learned by "stepping back" from the traditional focus on the direct or immediate causes and consequences of wrongful convictions and examining criminal justice systems, the actors in them, and the sociopolitical environments in which they operate to help explain how and why justice miscarries in the form of wrongful convictions. Multiple disciplinary perspectives address these fundamental issues, including some that are not customarily represented in this context. Contributors were invited to examine the underlying individual, institutional, systemic, and social or structural conditions that are likely to precipitate miscarriages of justice and also help explain impediments to preventing, detecting, and correcting them. We are hopeful that the resulting contributions to theory, methodology, and policy recommendations represented in the chapters will stimulate wrongful conviction scholarship to "move forward" by probing for the root causes of miscarriages of justice and for corresponding solutions and responses.

The volume is divided into three sections. In the first section, "Disciplinary Perspectives on Criminal Justice and Wrongful Conviction," contributors draw on diverse scholarly traditions to examine deep-seated factors that help shape systems of justice, the behavior of actors within them, and their relationship to miscarriages of justice. William Lofquist relies on sociological theory and constructs to identify factors that contribute to wrongful convictions in Chapter 2, "Finding the Causes in the Contexts: Structural Sources of Wrongful Convictions." The analysis discusses the imbalance of resources between the state and the accused and traces the roots of the "racialized punitiveness" of American criminal justice, which undergirds this asymmetry, to the Southern Strategy and the War on Crime. Keith Findley and Barbara O'Brien review cognitive and social psychological research to explore decision-making dynamics important to the production of wrongful convictions in Chapter 3, "Psychological Perspectives: Cognition and Decision Making." In Chapter 4, Cynthia Najdowski uses a psychological framework to examine "Interactions between African Americans and Police Officers: How Cultural Stereotypes Create a Wrongful Conviction Pipeline for African Americans." The influence of race is apparent throughout the system of criminal justice, but the relationship between race and wrongful conviction is vastly understudied. Najdowski draws on social psychological theory to examine how cultural stereotypes of African Americans can affect their encounters with law enforcement and thus their likelihood of being wrongly accused and convicted. In Chapter 5, "The Media's Muddled Message on Wrongful Convictions," Martin Yant enlists his perspectives as an experienced journalist to examine the media's role in helping shape public opinion by disseminating information about miscarriages of justice. He employs an historical perspective to describe a paradox of sorts, wherein the media can contribute to miscarriages of justice through their coverage of sensational crimes, yet often are instrumental in uncovering and remedying wrongful convictions.

Chapters in the volume's second section, "The Criminal Justice System: Producing, Detecting, and Remedying Wrongful Convictions," examine attributes of criminal justice actors and the incentive systems, organizational structures, and social contexts in which they function to explore their connection to the production, detection, and responses to wrongful convictions. The chapters in this section have a somewhat narrower focus than chapters in the preceding section. The section is divided into two parts: "The Production of Wrongful Convictions," and "Detecting and Remedying Wrongful Convictions."

Chapter 6, the first selection within "The Production of Wrongful Convictions," addresses "Wrongful Conviction, Policing, and the 'Wars on Crime and Drugs.'" Written by Hannah Laqueur, Stephen Rushin, and Jonathan Simon, it examines how law enforcement agencies and the policies they adopt can importantly influence miscarriages of justice. The two ensuing chapters address the roles of the courtroom advocates. Chapter 7, by Bennett Gershman, focuses on "The Prosecutor's Contribution to Wrongful Convictions." Although prosecutors are ethically bound to seek justice rather than convictions, Gershman discusses how they may inadvertently or intentionally impair the fact-finding process in ways that can help produce wrongful convictions, and he proposes measures designed to reduce such conduct. In Chapter 8, Ellen Yaroshefsky and Laura Schaefer analyze "Defense Lawyering and Wrongful Convictions." The vital role that criminal defense attorneys perform within justice systems in many respects has defied precise measurement and analysis. Yaroshefsky and Schaefer examine individual, structural, and legal factors that interact to influence defense lawyers' representation of their clients, emphasizing the increasing urgency for defense counsel to embrace science and scientific experts to help guard against miscarriages of justice.

Neil Vidmar and James Coleman examine the adversarial system of justice in Chapter 9 and explain how it differs in important respects from inquisitorial systems used in many other countries. They discuss how and why the adversarial system itself, which is the backbone of criminal justice administration throughout America, has the potential to influence actors and their decision-making in ways that can help spawn wrongful convictions. Chapter 10, by Stephanos Bibas, examines the important topic of "Plea Bargaining's Role in Wrongful Convictions." Vastly greater numbers of criminal convictions result from guilty pleas than contested trials. Bibas discusses how contemporary plea bargaining practices undermine the adversarial process and concomitant safeguards, thereby potentially helping manufacture wrongful convictions.

Two chapters follow that explore miscarriages of juvenile justice, focusing on the unique functions and procedures of juvenile justice systems and the characteristics of the adolescents whose cases are processed within them. In Chapter 11, Steven Drizin, Laura Nirider, and Joshua Tepfer analyze "Juvenile Justice Investigation: Narrative Contamination, Cultural Stereotypes, and the Scripting of Juvenile False Confessions." They describe how cultural stereotypes of juveniles—particularly, of the black urban superpredator and the white suburban loner—can lead to presumptions of guilt, false confessions, and wrongful adjudications. Chapter 12, by Barry Feld, critically assesses "'The Worst of Both Worlds': Adolescent Competence and the Quality of Justice in Juvenile Courts as a Prescription for Wrongful Convictions." Feld examines juveniles' competence to exercise their legal rights and the procedural safeguards in place to protect youths in the juvenile system, and discusses how current practices may be a recipe for wrongful adjudications.

Ensuing selections, presented in part two of this section, address issues pertaining to "Detecting and Remedying Wrongful Convictions." Chapter 13, by Nancy King, focuses on "Judicial Review: Appeals and Postconviction Proceedings." King highlights a number of doctrinal and practical obstacles that impede reviewing courts from discovering and correcting factually erroneous convictions, and recommends a number instructive reforms, including some that transcend the traditional judicial process. In Chapter 14, Kimberly Cook, Saundra Westervelt, and Shadd Maruna examine "The Problem of Fit: Parolees, Exonerees, and Prisoner Reentry." The authors draw on the extensive prisoner reentry literature, applying the lessons from this research to innocents returning home from prison. They discuss some of the shortcomings of existing reentry assistance and offer suggestions to provide more comprehensive support for exonerees returning to their communities. Frank Baumgartner, Saundra Westervelt, and Kimberly Cook then assess "Public Policy Responses to Wrongful Convictions" in Chapter 15. They demonstrate how increased recognition of the wrongful conviction problem has led states to restrict or abolish the use of capital punishment. Yet they note, paradoxically, that this widespread recognition has not led to corresponding increases in reforms designed to remedy individual victims of wrongful conviction. The last selection in this section, Chapter 16, is "Remedying Wrongful Convictions: Societal Obligations to Exonerees," by Elizabeth Griffiths and Michael Leo Owens. The authors examine the relationship between the incidence of exonerations and the quality of compensation statutes for wrongfully convicted individuals within states, and suggest that workers' compensation laws provide a model that could be better suited to compensating exonerees.

The chapters in Section III of the volume explicitly shift focus to address topics relevant to "Moving Forward: Advancing the Study of Wrongful Convictions." Marvin Zalman tackles the formidable task of "Theorizing Wrongful Conviction" in Chapter 17. He acknowledges the need for "greater theoretical sophistication" in the study of wrongful conviction but rejects the notion that one single theory will suffice given the diversity of agencies, actors, and processes involved. He proposes using a grounded theory methodology to develop an explanatory framework for error causation at the trial stage. Chapter 18, by Catherine Bonventre, Robert Norris, and Emily West, complements this perspective on theory by examining the methodologies used to study wrongful convictions. In "Studying

Innocence: Advancing Methods and Data," the authors take a hard look at the methods currently used to research miscarriages of justice, and offer novel ways to move the field forward. In the final selection, Chapter 19, Martin Killias offers lessons from countries beyond the United States in "International Trends and Developments: Perspectives on Wrongful Convictions from Europe." Wrongful convictions, of course, are not confined to the United States and its justice systems. Killias identifies several important issues related to the production of wrongful convictions that must be confronted in other countries, primarily in Europe, and explores their systemic underpinnings and calls for needed reforms.

The editors use the Conclusion, "Wrongful Convictions: Reflections on Moving Forward," to assimilate emergent themes from the collection of chapters and discuss their implications for further developing research, scholarship, and policies concerning miscarriages of justice. Much valuable work has been devoted to understanding how and why innocent persons are convicted of crimes and grappling with the many serious ramifications of wrongful convictions. Much more remains to be done. It is our hope that the insights and prescriptions reflected in these pages will advance these ends. We are indebted to each and every author for the thoughtful writings they have produced for this volume and for the contributions they have made while exploring issues of such fundamental importance to the scholarship of wrongful convictions.

# References

Acker, J.R. (2012/2013). The flipside injustice of wrongful convictions: When the guilty go free. *Albany Law Review, 76*, 1629–1712.

Acker, J.R., & Bellandi, R. (2014). Deadly errors and salutary reforms: The kill that cures? In M. Zalman & J. Carrano (Eds.), *Wrongful conviction and criminal justice reform: Making justice* (pp. 269–285). New York, NY: Routledge.

Acker, J.R., & Bonventre, C.L. (2010). Protecting the innocent in New York: Moving beyond changing only their names. *Albany Law Review, 73*, 1245–1356.

American Bar Association Section on Criminal Justice (2006). *Achieving justice: Freeing the innocent, convicting the guilty—report of the ABA Criminal Justice Section's Ad Hoc Innocence Committee to Ensure the Integrity of the Criminal Process.* Washington, DC: American Bar Association Criminal Justice Section.

Baumgartner, F.R., De Boef, S.L., & Boydstun, A.E. (2008). *The decline of the death penalty and the discovery of innocence.* New York: Cambridge University Press.

Bedau, H.A. & Radelet, M.L. (1987). Miscarriages of justice in potentially capital cases. *Stanford Law Review, 40*, 21–179.

Bedau, H.A. & Radelet, M.L. (1988). The myth of infallibility: A reply to Markman and Cassell. *Stanford Law Review, 41*, 161–170.

Bernhard, A. (2004). Justice still fails: A review of recent efforts to compensate individuals who have been unjustly convicted and later exonerated. *Drake Law Review, 52*, 703–738.

Bluhm Legal Clinic Center on Wrongful Convictions (2014). *About us.* Retrieved February 21, 2014 from http://www.law.northwestern.edu/legalclinic/wrongfulconvictions/aboutus/.

Borchard, E.M. (1913). European systems of state indemnity for errors of criminal justice. *Journal of the American Institute of Criminal Law and Criminology, 3*, 684–718.

Borchard, E.M. (1932). *Convicting the innocent: Sixty-five actual errors of criminal justice.* New Haven, CT: Yale University Press.

Bowers, W.J., & Sundby, S.E. (2009). Why the downturn in death sentences? In C.S. Lanier, W.J. Bowers, & J.R. Acker (Eds.), *The future of America's death penalty: An agenda for the next generation of capital punishment research* (pp. 47–67). Durham, NC: Carolina Academic Press.

Campbell, K., & Denov, M. (2004). The burden of coping with wrongful imprisonment. *Canadian Journal of Criminology & Criminal Justice, 46,* 139–163.

Carter, R. (1974). *The sixteenth round: From number 1 contender to number 45472.* New York: Viking Press.

Centurion Ministries (2013). *About us.* Retrieved November 3, 2013 from http://www.centurionministries.org/about/.

Clark, S.E. (2012). Costs and benefits of eyewitness identification reform: Psychological science and public policy. *Perspectives on Psychological Science, 7,* 238–259.

*Coffin v. United States* (1895) 156 U.S. 432.

Cole, S.A. (2012). Forensic science and wrongful convictions: From exposer to contributor to corrector. *New England Law Review, 46,* 711–736.

Committee on Identifying the Needs of the Forensic Sciences Community, National Research Council (2009). *Strengthening forensic science in the United States: A path forward.* Washington, DC: National Academy of Sciences. Retrieved November 8, 2013 from https://www.ncjrs.gov/pdffiles1/nij/grants/228091.pdf.

Conroy, J., & Warden, R. (2011a). The high costs of wrongful convictions: Human costs. Retrieved October 19, 2013 from http://www.bettergov.org/investigations/wrongful_convictions_human_costs.aspx

Conroy, J., & Warden, R. (2011b). The high costs of wrongful convictions: Financial costs. Retrieved October 19, 2013 from http://www.bettergov.org/investigations/wrongful_convictions_financial_costs.aspx.

Covey, R. (2013). Police misconduct as a cause of wrongful convictions. *Washington University Law Review, 90,* 1133–1189.

Death Penalty Information Center (2014). Innocence and the death penalty. Retrieved February 21, 2014 from http://www.deathpenaltyinfo.org/innocence-and-death-penalty.

Entzeroth, L.S. (2012). The end of the beginning: The politics of death and the American death penalty regime in the twenty-first century. *Oregon Law Review, 90,* 797–835.

Findley, K.A. (2008). Toward a new paradigm of criminal justice: How the innocence movement merges crime control and due process. *Texas Tech Law Review, 41,* 133–173.

Findley, K.A. (2010/2011). Defining innocence. *Albany Law Review, 74,* 1157–1228.

Findley, K.A., & Golden, L. (2014). The innocence movement, the innocence network, and policy reform. In M. Zalman & J. Carrano (Eds.), *Wrongful conviction and criminal justice reform: Making justice* (pp. 93–110). New York: Routledge.

Frank, J., & Frank, B. (1957). *Not guilty.* Garden City, NY: Doubleday.

Gardner, E.S. (1952). *The court of last resort.* New York: W. Sloan Associates.

Garrett, B.L. (2010). The substance of false confessions. *Stanford Law Review, 62,* 1051–1118.

Garrett, B.L. (2011). *Convicting the innocent: Where criminal prosecutions go wrong.* Cambridge, MA: Harvard University Press.

Garrett, B.L. & Neufeld, P.J. (2009). Invalid forensic science testimony and wrongful convictions. *Virginia Law Review, 95,* 1–96.

Gould, J.B., Carrano, J., Leo, R., & Young, J. (2012). *Predicting erroneous convictions: A social science approach to miscarriages of justice.* Retrieved November 8, 2013 from https://www.ncjrs.gov/pdffiles1/nij/grants/241389.pdf.

Gould, J.B. & Leo, R.A. (2010). One hundred years later: Wrongful convictions after a century of research. *Journal of Criminal Law and Criminology, 100,* 825–868.

Grann, D. (2009, Sept. 7). Trial by fire: Did Texas execute an innocent man? *The New Yorker.* Retrieved October 19, 2013 from http://www.newyorker.com/reporting/2009/09/07/090907fa_fact_grann.

Gross, S.R. (2013). How many false convictions are there? How many exonerations are there? In C.R. Huff & M. Kllias (Eds.), *Wrongful convictions and miscarriages of justice: Causes and remedies in North American and European criminal justice systems* (pp. 45–59). New York: Routledge.

Gross, S.R., Jacoby, K., Matheson, D.J., Montgomery, N., & Patil, S. (2005). Exonerations in the United States 1989 through 2003. *Journal of Criminal Law & Criminology, 95,* 523–560.

Grounds, A. (2004). Psychological consequences of wrongful conviction and imprisonment. *Canadian Journal of Criminology and Criminal Justice, 46,* 165–182.

Huff, C.R. (2008). Wrongful convictions in the United States. In C.R. Huff & M. Killias (Eds.), *Wrongful conviction: International perspectives on miscarriages of justice* (pp. 59–70). Philadelphia: Temple University Press.

*In re Winship* (1970) 397 U.S. 358.

Innocence Network (2014). *At the Innocence Network.* Retrieved February 21, 2014 from http://www.innocencenetwork.org/.

Innocence Project (2014a). DNA exonerations nationwide. Retrieved February 21, 2014 from http://www.innocenceproject.org/Content/DNA_Exonerations_Nationwide.php.

Innocence Project (2014b). About the Innocence Project. Retrieved February 21, 2014 from http://www.innocenceproject.org/about/.

Innocence Project (2014c). The causes of wrongful conviction. Retrieved February 21, 2014 from http://www.innocenceproject.org/understand/.

Jones, V.R., & Wilson, B. (2013). Innocence and its impact on the reassessment of the utility of capital punishment: Has the time come to abolish the ultimate sanction? *University of Miami Law Review, 67,* 459–476.

Kahn, D.S. (2010). Presumed guilty until proven innocent: The burden of proof in wrongful conviction claims under state compensation statutes. *University of Michigan Journal of Law Reform, 44,* 123–168.

Kassin, S.M., Drizin, S.A., Grisso, T., Gudjonsson, G.H., Leo, R.A., & Redlich, A.D. (2010). Police-induced false confessions: Risk factors and recommendations. *Law and Human Behavior, 34,* 3–38.

Kleine, R. (2011/2012). When justice fails: Collateral damage. *Albany Law Review, 75,* 1501–1508.

Krieger, S.A. (2011). Why our justice system convicts innocent people, and the challenges faced by innocence projects trying to exonerate them. *New Criminal Law Review, 14,* 333–402.

Lassers, W. (1973). *Scapegoat justice: Lloyd Miller and the failure of the American legal system.* Bloomington, IN: Indiana University Press.

Lassiter, G.D. & Meissner, C.A. (Eds.) (2012). *Police interrogations and false confessions: Current research and policy recommendations.* Washington, DC: American Psychological Association.

Leo, R.A. (2005). Rethinking the study of miscarriages of justice: Developing a criminology of wrongful conviction. *Journal of Contemporary Criminal Justice, 21,* 201–223.

Leo, R.A. & Gould, J.B. (2009). Studying wrongful convictions: Learning from social science. *Ohio State Journal of Criminal Law, 7,* 7–30.

Liebman, J.S., Crowley, S., Markquart, A., Rosenberg, L., White, L.G., & Zharkovsky, D. (2012). Los tocayos Carlos. *Columbia Human Rights Law Review, 43,* 711–1152.

Little, R.L. (2008). Addressing the evidentiary sources of wrongful convictions: Categorical exclusion of evidence in capital statutes. *Southwestern University Law Review, 37,* 965–985.

Markman, S.J., & Cassell, P.G. (1988). Protecting the innocent: A response to the Bedau-Radelet study. *Stanford Law Review, 41,* 121–160.

Marshall, L.C. (2004). The innocence revolution and the death penalty. *Ohio State Journal of Criminal Law, 1,* 573–584.

McHenry, W.H. (1913). Compensation for imprisonment of innocent persons in Wisconsin. *Journal of the American Institute of Criminal Law & Criminology, 4,* 285–287.

Medwed, D.S. (2012). *Prosecution complex: America's race to convict the innocent.* New York: New York University Press.

Mostaghel, D. (2011). Wrongfully incarcerated, randomly compensated—how to fund wrongful-conviction compensation statutes. *Indiana Law Review, 44,* 503–544.

Natapoff, A. (2009). *Snitching: Criminal informants and the erosion of American justice.* New York: New York University Press.

National Registry of Exonerations (2014a). Browse cases: summary view. Retrieved February 21, 2014 from http://www.law.umich.edu/special/exoneration/Pages/browse.aspx.

National Registry of Exonerations (2014b). Exonerations by year: DNA. Retrieved February 21, 2014 from http://www.law.umich.edu/special/exoneration/Pages/browse.aspx?View={B8342AE7-6520-4A32-8A06-4B326208BAF8}&FilterField1=DNA&FilterValue1=8_Y.

National Registry of Exonerations (2014c). The registry, exonerations and false convictions: Basic patterns. Retrieved February 21, 2014 from http://www.law.umich.edu/special/exoneration/Pages/learnmore.aspx.

New York Times (2003, Jan. 11). In Ryan's words: "I must act." Retrieved November 4, 2013 from http://www.nytimes.com/2003/01/11/national/11CND-RTEX.html.

Norris, R.J. (2012). Assessing compensation statutes for the wrongly convicted. *Criminal Justice Policy Review, 23,* 352–374.

Owens, M.L. & Griffiths, E. (2011/2012). Uneven reparations for wrongful convictions: Examining the state politics of statutory compensation legislation. *Albany Law Review, 75,* 1283–1327.

Pernell, L. (1989). The reign of the Queen of Hearts: The declining significance of the presumption of innocence—a brief commentary. *Cleveland State Law Review, 37,* 393–415.

Quintard-Morenas, F. (2010). The presumption of innocence in the French and Anglo-American legal traditions. *American Journal of Criminal Law, 58,* 107–149.

Radin, E.D. (1964). *The innocents.* New York: William Morrow.

Ricciardelli, R., Bell, J.G., & Crow, K.A. (2011/2012). "Now I see it for what it really is": The impact of participation in an Innocence Project practicum on criminology students. *Albany Law Review, 75,* 1439–1466.

Rosen, R.A. (2006). Reflections on innocence. *Wisconsin Law Review, 2006,* 237–290.

Sarat, A. (2004). Putting a square peg in a round hole: Victims, retribution, and George Ryan's clemency. *North Carolina Law Review, 82,* 1345–1376.

Simon, D. (2012). *In doubt: The psychology of the criminal justice process.* Cambridge, MA: Harvard University Press.

Smith, B., Zalman, M., & Kiger, A. (2011). How justice system officials view wrongful convictions. *Crime & Delinquency, 57,* 663–685.

Stiglitz, J., Brooks, J., & Shulman, T. (2002). The Hurricane meets The Paper Chase: Innocence projects new emerging role in clinical legal education. *California Western Law Review, 38,* 413–431.

Thompson, A.M., Molina, O.R., & Levett, L.M. (2011/2012). After exoneration: An investigation of stigma and wrongfully convicted persons. *Albany Law Review, 75,* 1415–1438.

Warden, R. (2012). How and why Illinois abolished the death penalty. *Law & Inequality, 30,* 245–286.

Wells, G.L. & Quinlivan, D.S. (2009). Suggestive eyewitness identification procedures and the Supreme Court's reliability test in light of eyewitness science: 30 years later. *Law and Human Behavior, 33,* 1–24.

Wells, G.L., Small, M., Penrod, S., Malpass, R.S., Fulero, S.M., & Brimacombe, A.E. (1998). Eyewitness identification procedures: Recommendations for lineups and photospreads. *Law and Human Behavior, 22,* 1–39.

Westervelt, S.D. & Cook, K.J. (2012). *Life after death row: Exonerees' search for community and identity.* New Brunswick, NJ: Rutgers University Press.

Worden, A.P., Davies, A.L.B., & Brown, E.K. (2014). Public defense in an age of innocence: The innocence paradigm and the challenges of representing the accused. In M. Zalman & J. Carrano (Eds.), *Wrongful conviction and criminal justice reform: Making justice* (pp. 209–225). New York: Routledge.

Zalman, M. (2010/2011). An integrated justice model of wrongful convictions. *Albany Law Review, 74,* 1465–1524.

Zalman, M., & Marion, N.E. (2014). The public policy process and innocence reform. In M. Zalman & J. Carrano (Eds.), *Wrongful conviction and criminal justice reform: Making justice* (pp. 24–38). New York: Routledge.

Zimmerman, I., & F. Bond (1964). *Punishment without crime: The true story of a man who spent twenty-four years in prison for a crime he did not commit.* New York: C.N. Potter.

# Section I

## Disciplinary Perspectives on Criminal Justice and Wrongful Convictions

Chapter Two

# Finding the Causes in the Contexts: Structural Sources of Wrongful Convictions

William S. Lofquist,[1] *State University of New York, College at Geneseo*

## Introduction: Standing in the Shadow of Injustice

The study and the list of wrongful convictions are dominated by capital and rape convictions. It makes sense that these cases receive so much attention; they are the most serious of crimes and most consequential of convictions, even matters of life and death. There are other reasons these cases receive so much scrutiny, though. Their dispositions are peculiarly subject to investigation because they involve trials and their attendant elements: carefully collected evidence, particularly DNA evidence, preserved written records, and motivated appellate attorneys, as well as long periods of time between conviction and ultimate disposition of the sentence.

This larger truth—that convictions are subject to exoneration based less on their reliability than on whether they were produced by a jury or a guilty plea—poses a problem that vexes the study of wrongful convictions. When we take one step back from known wrongful convictions and their immediate causes, we see that the circumstances through which wrongful convictions generally become knowable—trials, written records, and appellate processes—are nearly extinct in the routine operations of American criminal justice. Absent these circumstances, wrongful convictions exist, of course. Indeed, there is reason to believe that wrongful convictions are particularly likely to be produced by plea bargains (Dervan & Edkins, 2012), where the criminal justice assembly line moves fastest, is least transparent, and is least regulated. For these same reasons, they are also particularly likely to go undetected and unremediated.

There is a thus "dark figure" of wrongful convictions, generated by procedures that render them virtually invisible and unknowable: ubiquitous use of plea bargains, significant trial penalties, perfunctory access to defense counsel, and waivers of rights to trial and appeal and the written public records that they create. These unrecognized wrongful convictions stand alongside known cases as a kind of shadow, less clearly seen yet produced by a common if distant source.

---

1. *Author Note*: Correspondence concerning this chapter should be addressed to William S. Lofquist, Department of Sociology, 101 Sturges Hall, State University of New York College at Geneseo, Geneseo, NY 14454. E-mail: lofquist@geneseo.edu.

Take another step back and the common sources of wrongful convictions produced by trials and those produced by guilty pleas become visible. Aggressive policing of the disreputable behavior of overwhelmingly poor, non-white urban males, particularly through the War on Drugs, has become not just the focus of the criminal justice system but also the dominant urban policy of recent generations (Goetz, 1996; Beckett, 1997). Here, in the punitive control of the urban poor and in the larger enterprise of governing through crime (Simon, 2007), are the contemporary origins of wrongful convictions: a deeply racialized punitiveness that brings with it an unwillingness to invest in reliable convictions and an inability of defendants to enforce the promises of due process.

# Stepping Out of the Shadow of Wrongful Convictions

Samuel Gross, arguably the foremost active scholar of wrongful convictions (see Gross, 1996, 1998, 2000, 2008, 2011/12; Gross & O'Brien, 2008), examined all wrongful convictions identified between 1989–2003 and found that a remarkable 96% were murder and rape convictions (Gross, Jacoby, Matheson, Montgomery, & Patil, 2005). Without defending the integrity of violent felony trial proceedings, there can be no reasonable doubt that convictions produced as slowly, with as much due and adversarial process as these, are not representative of actual wrongful convictions. Yet here we are, increasingly aware that the study of wrongful convictions is caught in an empirical trap, studying what we know while knowing that what we study is not representative of the problem of wrongful convictions.

It is in this context that Huff (2006) notes that there is no "credible methodology" for measuring wrongful convictions and Gross and his colleagues observe that "[w]e can't come close to estimating the number of false convictions that occur in the United States" (2005, p. 551); the result is a "small, assorted, messy data set" (Gross, 2008, p. 176) of known cases. Without a reliably measured dependent variable—wrongful convictions—a more rigorous social science of the causes of those wrongful convictions is necessarily impeded. Yet, wrongful convictions are validated as such only through inherently arbitrary legal processes. Escaping this empirical trap is possible, however, as this chapter elaborates.

## The Remarkable Early Career of Wrongful Convictions

When the modern era of wrongful conviction research was launched with Bedau and Radelet's (1987) landmark *Stanford Law Review* article, wrongful convictions—as a scholarly issue and as a criminal justice concern—existed beyond the margins of debate. Bedau and Radelet changed that; they defined the field, they named names, and they placed wrongful convictions firmly in the death penalty debate (Radelet and Borg, 2000), even the criminal justice debate (Zalman, 2006). The scholarly, popular, and political responses to this article, some critical, most not, further elevated the significance of the issue (see Markman & Cassell, 1988; Bedau & Radelet, 1988; Gross, 1998; Kirchmeier, 2002; U.S. House of Representatives, 1994).

On the basis of Bedau and Radelet's first contemporary accounting of the scale of wrongful convictions, as well as a series of other accountings that followed (Radelet, Bedau, & Putnam, 1992; Radelet, Lofquist, & Bedau, 1996), the issue was quickly elevated to problem status. Developments in DNA technology (US Department of Justice, 1996; Scheck, Neufeld, & Dwyer, 2000), the formation of numerous innocence projects, a high profile wrongful conviction conference,[2] numerous high profile exonerations, and an exoneration-caused execution moratorium in Illinois, counterpoised with historically high rates of punitiveness, aggressive efforts to expand the use of the death penalty, and the presidential campaign of the nation's most active executioner, created a heady atmosphere among otherwise low profile scholars and practitioners.

Twenty-five years later, the study of wrongful convictions has reached a way station. After a generation of active scholarship and remarkable public and political responses,[3] there is growing concern that the social scientific study of wrongful convictions has stalled (Leo, 2005; Zalman, 2006; Gould & Leo, 2010). Escaping the empirical trap and moving beyond this initial burst of research and attention involves reframing the issue, not simply as one of wrongful (versus rightful) convictions, but rather as one of more reliable versus less reliable convictions. Viewed on this continuum, known wrongful convictions represent one end point—the least reliable of convictions. They also provide an empirical referent for developing insights into the larger population of wrongful convictions arising from the more routine operations of the criminal justice system.

## What We Know: The Social Dimensions of Wrongful Convictions

The paradigmatic known wrongful conviction is of an African American male capital or rape defendant (Gross, Jacoby, Matheson, Montgomery, & Patil, 2005; Gross, 2008; Harmon, 2004; Parker, Dewees, & Radelet, 2001) represented by indigent defense (Garrett, 2008; Harmon, 2001), convicted at trial, and exonerated more than a decade later (Gross et al., 2005). Indeed, exonerations in capital cases are twenty-five times more likely than in non-capital murder cases and 100 times more frequent than in all cases of imprisoned felons (Gross et al., 2005). The modal wrongful conviction, however, almost certainly involves an African American male charged with a felony property or drug offense who pleads guilty rather than face lengthy pretrial detention due to an inability to post bail (Gross & O'Brien, 2008). The differences—and the similarities—between these profiles are hugely instructive in thinking about the causes of wrongful convictions.

Analyses of known wrongful convictions have identified a "catalog of errors" (Zalman, 72; see also Huff, 2002; Garrett, 2008) common to these cases. Prominent among them are eyewitness misidentification, perjury, forensic science errors, flawed lineup procedures, false confessions, reliance on jailhouse snitches, inadequate defense, and prosecutorial misconduct (Gould & Leo, 2010). While these errors may leave their fingerprints most visibly on major felony trial convictions, they are no more the causes of these errant convictions than pulling the trigger causes a killing. A gun must be available, loaded, and aimed in order to kill, just as a suspect must be identified, arrested, and "convictable" in order to be wrongly convicted.

Consider the Central Park jogger case (see Smith, 2002; Burns, 2012). Four young African American males and a Latino were arrested in 1989 and convicted in 1990 in the

---

2. The first conference of its kind, the National Conference on Wrongful Convictions and the Death Penalty, was held at Northwestern University in 1998.

3. Public opinion research indicates that concern about wrongful convictions and the risk of executing an innocent person have figured prominently in declining support for the death penalty (Radelet & Borg, 2000; Unnever & Cullen, 2005).

rape of a white female after false confessions were coerced and videotaped, and with the assistance of prosecutorial overzealousness and misstatements (Gershman, 2003; O'Brien, 2009). Those confessions were gained within a day or so of the crime, without any serious consideration of alternative suspects or theories of the case, despite a known serial rapist active in the area, evidence, including DNA, that did not match the suspects, and confessions that did not match the evidence.

This description certainly fits what we know about the production of wrongful convictions, featuring as it does trials and numerous items from the catalog. It also illustrates the limitations of this approach, inasmuch as it does not address the larger contexts in which the case occurred. As Zalman (2008) rightly notes (see also Leo, 2005; Leo & Gould, 2009), the catalog of errors constitutes something less than a "social science theory of wrongful convictions" (p. 72). Yet, the catalog of errors and the Central Park jogger case provide a useful point from which to step back, in search of a "broader way of seeing the issues, one that involves a panoramic understanding of the criminal justice system" (Zalman, 2008 p. 87). By identifying the characteristics of cases and defendants most vulnerable to these types of errors, we may begin to develop a larger understanding of wrongful convictions.

Consider again the Central Park jogger case. That the defendants were young, poor, and non-white residents of Harlem in an era of historically high violent crime rates, the emergence and endemic trafficking and use of crack cocaine, and explosive racial politics made them the usual suspects.[4] That the crime occurred in Central Park, a refuge from the mean streets of the city and a place city authorities were particularly eager to protect, increased the pressure on police and prosecutors, as did the race of the victim and the nature of the crime. That the defendants were so young made them particularly vulnerable to false confessions (Rizer, 2003). That the police and prosecution were able to secure confessions, and to do so quickly, just as the case was making headlines, assured the most important objective: an apparently secure conviction, a win, if not the truth.

The defendants in this case were vulnerable to wrongful convictions. However, because their vulnerability was much more a product of who they were and the relationships between their community and the criminal justice system, than of the particular circumstances of their cases, understanding which of the catalog of errors occurred in this case does not lead toward a larger understanding of wrongful convictions. Indeed, it is telling that the young males who were ultimately convicted in this case were initially arrested on minor felony charges, crimes they deny involvement in, well before it was even known to police that a rape had occurred. They were the usual crime suspects well before they were the usual rape suspects.

## Beyond the "Catalog of Errors"

Finding the social structural causes of wrongful convictions thus involves identifying the larger contexts in which particular groups become vulnerable to being defined as suspects, to being arrested, and to having their arrests transformed into convictions,

---

4. The racial politics of the time could hardly have been more incendiary. Beyond the drug war and associated violence, there was a 1989 mayoral primary race between white incumbent Edward Koch, known for racially insensitive comments, and African American challenger David Dinkins; the 1989 racial killing of Yusef Hawkins by white teens; the just-concluded Tawana Brawley affair, in which Brawley and her advisors, led by Reverend Al Sharpton, publicly and wrongly proclaimed the 15-year-old African American girl had been raped and beaten by six white males; and the 1991 Crown Heights riot.

despite the absence of evidence to support that conviction in a reliable adjudicatory process. Though known wrongful convictions may be distant cousins to the much larger number of wrongful convictions likely produced by plea bargains, there is enough of a resemblance to be able to use the former to assist in developing this vulnerability profile.

Young African American male residents of heavily policed areas, particularly those in which high friction strategies such as stop-and-frisk practices, hot spots policing, and undercover drug operations are used, are at highest risk of arrest. Defendants regarded, whether by their race, their residency, or their record, as usual suspects, are also particularly vulnerable to arrest (Beckett & Herbert, 2008; New York Civil Liberties Union, 2012; Thompson, 1999). These same characteristics, particularly race, increase their vulnerability to eyewitness misidentification (Rizer, 2003). Further, arrests that occur under these circumstances, particularly drug arrests, are likely to lack the types of robust evidentiary circumstances that limit the risk of perjury and flawed lineup procedures.

Those represented by defense counsel with larger caseloads and fewer resources for independent investigation and expert witnesses are also more vulnerable to wrongful convictions. There is a racial component to this dynamic; according to Harmon (2004), police and prosecutors are more likely to pursue weaker cases against African American defendants, particularly in white victim cases. Likewise, white jurors are more likely to convict black defendants than similarly situated white defendants (Johnson, 1985). These circumstances are magnified by close investigative ties between police and prosecutors, statutes that provide prosecutors with significant trial penalties, wide-ranging charging discretion through which to maximize the leverage of these penalties, and badly underfunded indigent defense counsel; the net effect is an "adjudicatory asymmetry" that allows prosecutors to pursue and prevail in weak cases against weak defendants with weak representation (Givelber, 1997, 2001).

In summary, African Americans "face concentrated disadvantage—extreme levels of poverty concentration, joblessness, racial isolation, family disruption, and lack of residential mobility" (Parker et al., 2001 p. 127) that lock them in areas subject to aggressive policing and that deny them the resources—financial and reputational—to contest a wrongful arrest (Free & Ruesink, 2012; see also Rizer, 2003).[5] Seen in this way, vulnerability to wrongful convictions results from the accumulation of socio-economic and structural disadvantage and the exposure that this creates to superior state resources in defining criminals and processing criminal defendants.

# Stepping Back: The Social Contexts of Wrongful Convictions

Discussion of most issues associated with contemporary American criminal justice, be it stop-and-frisk police practices, life sentences for juveniles, marijuana decriminalization, or wrongful convictions, among issues recently in the news, must proceed from the recognition of three closely related and defining features of that system: that the United States has the largest penal system in history; that approximately 90% of all felony defendants are represented by indigent counsel; and that more than 95% of all felony convictions are produced by guilty pleas (Bureau of Justice Statistics, 2010).

---

5. The case of Erma Faye Stewart, detailed so effectively in the *Frontline* documentary, "The Plea," and featured in Alexander's *The New Jim Crow* (2010), fits well into this profile.

Pause to consider the systemic inequalities that those numbers conceal and reveal. Such a system, in which crime is nearly synonymous with poverty and convictions are produced in unprecedented numbers without trials, transforms poverty into crime and crime into punishment with brutal efficiency. That such a system has developed—one in which crime is regarded both as a serious criminal justice problem and as the near exclusive province of the poor—points toward the larger racial socio-economic inequalities around which crime and criminals are defined.

It is here that our inquiry turns: examining how the American criminal justice system became so large and focused so punitively on the problem behavior of the poor. From there, attention will turn to considering the ways in which the operations of the criminal justice system mediate the relationship between social inequalities and the problem behavior of poor urban males who populate that system. Wrongful convictions are a byproduct of these operations, a result of the expansive criminalization of problem behavior and the aggressive, asymmetrical enforcement of this governing strategy. In the language of the system, wrongful convictions are collateral damage in the war on crime (Stacy, 1991).

## The Birth of Mass Imprisonment

In the early 1970s, just after the Warren Court had modernized the operations of the American criminal justice system and just before the now recognized era of mass imprisonment had begun, there were fewer than 200,000 state and federal prisoners. The nascent drug war resulted in 300,000 or so annual arrests (Uniform Crime Reports, 1973). Forty years later, the drug war generates nearly 2 million arrests annually (Sourcebook of Criminal Justice Statistics, 2008) and the prison population exceeds 1.5 million, with half that many more in jails (Bureau of Justice Statistics, 2012). Reliance on plea bargaining, long a reluctantly accepted staple of the American criminal justice system (Alschuler, 1979; Friedman, 1979; Fisher, 2003), has become nearly complete and normalized, even as its use has become more abusive (McCoy, 2005).

How this happened is by now a well-told story (see, in particular, Beckett, 1997; Simon, 2007; Western, 2006; Wacquant, 2005). In broad outline, the tumultuous events associated with the Civil Rights and other progressive social movements produced a series of federal statutes (e.g., the Civil Rights Act, the Voting Rights Act), federal programs (e.g., Medicaid and Medicare), and federal agencies recognizing and protecting the rights of groups marginalized on the basis of race, class, gender, and national origin. With race now written out of the law and the skeletal New Deal social insurance system poised to become more robust and inclusive, a potent conservative political opposition developed.

Though often and understandably characterized as a white populist "backlash" against progressive racial and social policymaking, the organizing role played by Republican political strategists in developing their "Southern strategy"[6] suggests a more coordinated, less organic reality. The net effect of this "frontlash" (Weaver, 2007) was to refocus racial

6. The "Southern Strategy" has become the shorthand through which the transformation from New Deal governance to governing through crime is understood (Simon, 2007). This strategy of manipulating racial animus among previously core Democratic constituencies, particularly Southern white males, through racialized depictions of the criminal, the welfare dependent, and the beneficiaries of governmental support, provided the essential foundation for delegitimizing and defunding social welfare programs and directing those resources toward criminal justice.

animus around disproportionately non-white social groups still legitimately subject to social stigma and unequal legal treatment, particularly "criminals."[7] The War on Crime was underway. "Criminals" were the enemy and urban areas once the focus of renewal efforts were transformed into battlefields.[8]

The social construction of crime that developed in the late 1960s had multiple dimensions. Crime was constructed as a primary problem: a problem to be resolved through the direct application of policy resources, rather than also secondarily and indirectly, as a byproduct of investments in employment, community building, and education, as crime control had previously been understood (see, for example, President's Commission on Law Enforcement and the Administration of Justice, 1968). Crime was also constructed as a criminal justice problem, meaning that it was the criminal justice system spearheaded by the police, that was the state agency given primary crime control responsibility. Finally, crime was constructed as a serious and worsening problem, a problem requiring the maximum application of the state's punitive power.

## The Criminal Justice Consequences of the Southern Strategy

As this new era of punitiveness was emerging, the composition of the Supreme Court was changing in ways that would provide judicial endorsement of law and order politics. A pattern that would emerge over the next generation, in landmark cases from *Gregg* to *McCleskey* to *Whren*[9] and others, and that would come to define the Court's racial legacy, was its unwillingness to recognize the extent to which putatively neutral criminal justice practices operated in a racially patterned matter, reproducing racially biased results. In his remarkably prescient dissent in *Terry v. Ohio* (1968), a decision that is in the direct lineage of stop and frisk, Justice Douglas warned of precisely this risk, arguing that empowering the police to make warrantless stops and frisks absent probable cause represented "a long step down the totalitarian path" (392 U.S. 1, p. 38).

Armed with expanded legal powers, the vast statutory landscape of drug laws, high levels of public and political support, and generous federal financial support, the range of problem behaviors subject to policing and the powers of the police to act within that range were vastly expanded. In a society transitioning from the robust urban industrial economy and social welfare policy framework of Fordism to the post-union, neo-liberal, social control policy framework of post-Fordism (Wacquant, 2001), the criminal justice system replaced education, employment, and social welfare services as the state's most visible urban policy apparatus (Simon, 2007).

---

7. Alexander's observation that "[t]oday it is perfectly legal to discriminate against criminals in nearly all the ways it was once legal to discriminate against African Americans" (2010, p. 2) powerfully captures the consequences of this effort.

8. With characteristic flourish and insight, Wacquant (2002) refers to this transition as "a unique sociohistorical experiment: the incipient replacement of the welfare regulation of poverty and of the urban disorders spawned by mounting social insecurity and racial strife by its penal management via the police, courts, and correctional system" (2002, p. 19).

9. *Gregg v. Georgia* (1976), *McCleskey v. Kemp* (1987), and *Whren v. United States* (1996), are Supreme Court cases in which African-American criminal defendants alleged, among other causes, racially discriminatory treatment. In each case, the Court went to lengths to construct a "raceless" criminal justice system, in which racially disparate outcomes are viewed as the product of non-racial legally relevant considerations and in which claims of racial bias are subject to unreasonably demanding levels of proof.

Drug arrests exploded, increasing by 500%. Drug law enforcement, occurring as it does in the absence of a willing complainant, is driven overwhelmingly by the distribution of police resources. Those resources, in turn, are distributed where drug law enforcement is most viable: in poorer urban areas where drugs are used and sold most openly, where popular portrayals of predatory drug offenders are located, and where the political power to resist aggressive policing is limited (Beckett, 1997; Beckett and Herbert, 2008; Simon, 2009). As a result, those subject to arrest are disproportionately non-white, almost unbelievably so in the case of crack cocaine-related arrests. In 2006, for example, African Americans represented 82% of convicted crack offenders, while also experiencing higher rates of imprisonment and longer sentences than their white counterparts (Provine, 2011).

Tellingly, this expanded police authority to bring more offenders into the criminal justice system was not matched by a statutory or financial commitment to the full processing of these defendants. This is a two-fold problem. First judicial expenditures have failed to keep pace with police and correctional expenditures, reflecting and reproducing systemic pressure to efficiently transform large numbers of arrests into large numbers of inmates. In 2001, for example, local, state, and federal expenditures on police exceeded $75 billion and on corrections exceeded $70 billion, while judicial expenditures were approximately $40 billion (Bureau of Justice Statistics, 2001).

Second, within the courts, prosecutorial budgets far exceed defense expenditures. Though precise comparisons are made difficult by the different caseloads and responsibilities of prosecutors and indigent counsel (Mann, 2011), careful efforts to measure these spending disparities have been made. A recent analysis of prosecutorial and indigent defense spending in Tennessee, for example, concluded that indigent prosecution spending exceeded indigent defense spending by two to two-and-a-half times (Spangenberg et al., 2007). In California, the disparity is almost two to one, despite 90% of defendants being represented by indigent counsel (Benner, 2011a).

Perhaps the most visible consequence of these dual funding disparities is indigent counsel caseloads. National standards recommend that each fulltime attorney handle no more than 150 cases per year, a standard that is criticized as too high at the same time that it is not met by 75% of all indigent defense systems (Benner, 2011a, 2011b). Average caseloads now exceed 240 cases a year nationally (Farole, 2010), necessitating the full processing of more than one case per day. Caseloads in some locales are far higher. In Florida, felony caseloads exceed 500 cases a year (Benner, 2011a).

Felony defendants represented by indigent counsel are significantly less likely than those who retain counsel to meet with counsel until days or weeks after admission to jail. They also have far less contact with counsel overall, with 75% of all defendants represented by indigent counsel reporting three or fewer contacts with counsel prior to disposition (compared to approximately 40% among those represented by private counsel) (Bureau of Justice Statistics, 1997). Defendants represented by indigent counsel are also much less likely to be released from jail prior to case disposition, more likely to enter a guilty plea (Bureau of Justice Statistics, 1996a), and more likely to receive a prison sentence (Bureau of Justice Statistics, 1996b). All of these disadvantages are experienced racially, with African Americans significantly more likely than whites to be represented by indigent counsel regardless of offense type (Alexander, 2010).

This system, structured to produce convictions, has consequences for the integrity of those convictions. Without zealous advocacy by defense counsel and regular use of trials, adjudication becomes an *ex parte,* off the record proceeding. Plea bargains, negotiated at the point at which the financial, statutory, and ideological leverage of the state over the defendant is greatest, proliferate. Far removed from the adversarial ideal, police and prosecutorial practices adjust to this adjudicatory asymmetry by expanding the scope of their search, arrest, charging, and sentencing powers, unchecked by juries, public records, and the appellate process. The wheel turns and the state's leverage increases still more.

While wrongful convictions are only one of the excesses generated by these circumstances,[10] Leo echoes Justice Douglas's concern in noting that "to the extent we create rules and policies that give more freedom to police and prosecutors, we will have a higher rate of wrongful conviction; to the extent we make it more difficult for police and prosecutors to obtain convictions, we will have a lower rate of wrongful convictions" (2005, p. 214). Rattner (1988) offered perhaps the most compelling image, of an assembly line "without quality control" (p. 292). Whether the faulty products that result are excessive sentences, due process violations, or wrongful convictions, a miscarriage of justice has occurred.

# Moving Forward: Investing in Justice

Following this analogy, a line of wrongful conviction scholarship (see Lofquist, 2001; Doyle, 2010; Cole, 2012; Schoenfeld, 2005; see also Huff, 2002; Leo, 2005) analogizes wrongful convictions to unsafe products. Drawing on path-breaking work done primarily by organizational sociologists (see Perrow, 1984 and Vaughan, 1996, in particular) that focused on the role of organizational dynamics rather than individual actions in producing organizational harms, wrongful convictions are viewed as akin to unsafe products, produced as criminal justice personnel (employees) develop commitments to a particular theory of the case (product design) that lead them to discount contrary evidence. Similar to Vaughan's explanation of organizational error as an "incremental descent into poor judgment" (Vaughan, 1996), Gould and Leo (2010) refer to this approach as a "path analysis," (p. 840) in which early case processing errors put a case on a path that results in the routine production of an errant outcome.

The macro-level social structural analogy to this meso-level case-centered approach is that wrongful convictions may be viewed as resulting most fundamentally from the interaction of a large population vulnerable to official processing, with a political thrust toward the aggressive criminalization and punishment of problem behavior, with highly asymmetric investments in adjudicating arrests. Each of these conditions represents its own problem. In combination, particularly in the context of the elaborate choreography of "usual suspects," "normal crimes" (Sudnow, 1965), and "going rates" that substitutes for careful attention to the circumstances of individual cases, they create an environment in which high rates of disreputable behavior are aggressively policed and prosecuted, with limited personal or state resources available to defendants to protect their rights.

Investing in justice is the necessary corrective. At its most ambitious, this involves a long-term strategy of dismantling the vast carceral web and the crime-centered domestic social policy framework it buttresses. We know how to do this; models can be found in our own history and in the criminal justice systems of many of our peer nations. However, the political culture of punitiveness and the judicial culture that supports it are not undone in an election cycle or two. Budgetary considerations, rarely more acute than they are recently, may play a role in reducing punitiveness, particularly given the arrest discretion inherent in the War on Drugs and the prosecutorial discretion inherent in charging

---

10. Berman (2008) has been particularly emphatic in expressing the concern that recent attention to wrongful convictions may be obscuring attention to the larger problem of excess punishment that has become so much a part of American criminal justice.

decisions. However, Wacquant's (2005) argument that financial concerns would more likely work to erode justice than to scale down criminal justice is compelling.

More modestly, though certainly not easily, reform involves the development of a "culture of safety" (Doyle, 2010)—characterized by open communications and redundant safety protocols (Perrow, 1984). Note that this is precisely what is lacking in an environment of adjudicatory asymmetry and a reliance on plea bargains. While plea bargaining itself is too firmly established in American criminal justice to be wished or willed away, a reliable system for arresting, trying, and convicting offenders requires that there be some reasonable chance that the police and prosecutorial efforts that produced that arrest and charge be exposed to the public light of a jury trial. Fewer arrests, particularly of street level drug users and dealers and of technical violations of probation and parole, are probably the most effective way to reduce systemic pressures to plea bargain. Stricter public defense caseload standards, enforced by enhanced funding and by more meaningful (which is to say achievable) standards for demonstrating the ineffectiveness of counsel, are necessary corollaries.[11]

Most fundamental to a culture of safety, though, is the establishment of a system for enforcing the fundamental fairness that criminal justice decision making focus on the characteristics of the act rather than the actor. Proportionality review (see Bienen, 1996, for an overview), through which the actions of criminal justice decision makers from police to judges and juries are examined to determine whether race is affecting and infecting criminal justice processing, would seem to be well suited to this enforcement function. Public records of police stops and arrests (see Gelman, Fagan, & Kiss, 2007), charging decisions, plea offers and deals, and sentences, all readily subject to recording if not presently recorded, would serve as the empirical foundation of this culture. The first effect of this effort would be to increase the transparency of criminal justice decision making, with associated deterrent and remedial effects. The second effect would be to make possible remedies, modeled on the Racial Justice Act (Chemerinsky, 1995), to those defendants subject to disparate treatment. The net effect of these changes is to identify and protect those most vulnerable to wrongful processing.

# Conclusions: Stepping Back to Move Forward

That the academic study of wrongful convictions has blossomed in recent years is well known. It is increasingly acknowledged, though, that this effort has become stuck in an empirical trap, focusing largely on errors in investigatory and prosecutorial practices rather than on the larger social, racial, and organizational contexts in which these errors are embedded and must ultimately be understood.

This leaves wrongful conviction scholars with a choice. We can cede the field to those disciplines—journalism, law, and psychology among them—focused more on the dynamics of specific cases and immediate causes. Or, we can step back from the inhibiting yet still arbitrary practice of limiting the study of wrongful convictions to documented

---

11. The standards established by *Strickland v. Washington* (1986) are widely recognized as being so weak as to be of almost no use to defendants, no matter how demonstrably ineffective their counsel (Gabriel, 1986; Berger, 1990–91; Benner, 2011b)

exonerations and look more broadly at unreliable convictions and the criminal justice and social conditions from which they emerge.

This chapter has sought to provide an argument and a framework for this latter approach. By investigating the adjudicatory asymmetry that characterizes American criminal justice and the powerfully punitive politics of crime control that have installed and protected this asymmetry, we can gain insights into the characteristics of vulnerable defendants and the social structural and organizational dynamics of unreliable convictions. This approach holds the promise of opening the study of wrongful convictions—increasingly criticized as a kind of dilettantism divorced from the systemic injustices of contemporary criminal justice—to the larger currents of critical criminal justice and sociological scholarship.

# References

Alexander, M. (2010). *The new Jim Crow: Mass incarceration in the age of colorblindness.* New York: The New Press.

Alschuler, A. W. (1979). Plea bargaining and its history. *Law & Society Review, 13,* 211–245.

Beckett, K. (1997). *Making crime pay.* New York: Oxford University Press.

Beckett, K. & Herbert, S. (2008). "The punitive city revisited: The transformation of urban social control." In M.L. Frampton, I.H. Lopez & J. Simon (Eds.), *After the war on crime: Race, democracy, and a new reconstruction* (pp. 106–122). New York: New York University Press.

Bedau, H.A. & Radelet, M.L. (1987). Miscarriages of justice in potentially capital cases. *Stanford Law Review, 40,* 21–173.

Bedau, H.A. & Radelet, M.L. (1988). The myth of infallibility: A reply to Markman and Cassell." *Stanford Law Review, 41,* 161–170.

Benner, L.A. (2011a). Eliminating excessive public defender workloads. *Criminal Justice 26(2),* 1–11.

Benner, L.A. (2011b). When excessive public defender workloads violate the Sixth Amendment right to counsel without a showing of prejudice. *American Constitution Society for Law and Policy.*

Berger, V. (1990–91). The chiropractor as brain surgeon: Defense lawyering in capital cases. *NYU Review of Law & Social Change, 18,* 245–254.

Berman, D. (2009). Extreme punishment. In C.J. Ogletree & A. Sarat (Eds.), *When law fails: Making sense of miscarriages of justice.* New York: New York University Press.

Bienen, L. (1996). The proportionality review of capital cases by state high courts after Gregg: Only "the appearance of justice?" *Journal of Criminal Law and Criminology, 87(1),* 130–314.

Bureau of Justice Statistics. (1996a). *Survey of inmates in local jails.* U.S. Department of Justice.

Bureau of Justice Statistics. (1996b). *State court processing statistics.* U.S. Department of Justice.

Bureau of Justice Statistics. (1997). *Survey of inmates in state and federal correctional facilities.* U.S. Department of Justice.

Bureau of Justice Statistics. (2001). *Justice expenditure and employment in the United States, 2001.* U.S. Department of Justice.

Bureau of Justice Statistics. (2010). *Felony defendants in large urban counties, 2006.* U.S. Department of Justice.

Bureau of Justice Statistics. (2012). *Correctional populations in the United States, 2011.* U.S. Department of Justice.

Burns, S. (2012). *The Central Park Five.* New York: Vintage.

Chemerinsky, E. (1995). Eliminating discrimination in administering the death penalty: The need for the racial justice act. *Santa Clara Law Review, 35(2),* 519–533.

Cole, S.A. (2012). Forensic science and wrongful convictions: From exposer to contributor to corrector. *New England Law Review, 46,* 711–736.

Connors, E., Lundgren, T., Miller, N., & T. McEwen. (1996). Convicted by juries, exonerated by science: Case studies in the use of DNA evidence to establish innocence after trial. *United States Department of Justice Research Report.*

Dervan, L.E. & Edkins, V. (2012). The innocent defendant's dilemma: An innovative empirical study of plea bargaining's innocence problem. *Journal of Criminal Law and Criminology, 103,* 1–47.

Doyle, J.M. (2010). Learning from error in american criminal justice. *Journal of Criminal Law and Criminology, 100,* 109–147.

Farole, D.J. (2010). A national assessment of public defender office caseloads. *Bureau of Justice Statistics.*

Fisher, G. (2003). *Plea bargaining's triumph: A history of plea bargaining in America.* Palo Alto, CA: Stanford University Press.

Free, Jr., M.D. (2012). *Race and justice: Wrongful convictions of African American men.* Boulder, CO: Lynne Rienner Publishers, Inc.

Friedman, L.M. (1979). Plea bargaining in historical perspective. *Law & Society Review, 13,* 247–259.

Gabriel, R.L. (1986). The Strickland standard for claims of ineffective assistance of counsel: Emasculating the Sixth Amendment in the guise of due process. *University of Pennsylvania Law Review 134(5),* 1259–1289.

Garrett, B. (2005). Judging innocence. *Columbia Law Review,* 108, 55–142.

Gelman, A., Fagan, J., & Kiss, A. (2007). An analysis of the New York City Police Department's "stop-and-frisk" policy in the context of claims of racial bias. *Journal of the American Statistical Association, 102,* 813–824.

Gershman, B. (2003). Misuse of scientific evidence by prosecutors. *Oklahoma City University Law Review, 28,* 17–41.

Givelber, D. (1997). Meaningless acquittals, meaningful convictions: Do we reliably acquit the innocent? *Rutgers Law Review, 49,* 1317–1396.

Givelber, D. (2001). The adversary system and historical accuracy: Can we do better? In Westervelt, S.D. & Humphrey, J.A. (Eds.), *Wrongly convicted: Perspectives on failed justice* (pp. 253–268). New Brunswick, NJ: Rutgers University Press.

Goetz, E. (1996). The US war on drugs as urban policy. *International Journal of Urban and Regional Research 20(3),* 539–549.

Gordon, D.R. (1994). *Return of the dangerous classes: Drug prohibition and policy politics.* New York: Norton.

Gould, J.B. & Leo, R.A. (2010). One hundred years later: Wrongful convictions after a century of research. *The Journal of Criminal Law & Criminology, 100(3),* 825–868.

Gross, S.R. (1996). The risks of death: Why erroneous convictions are common in capital cases. *Buffalo Law Review, 44,* 469–500.

Gross, S.R. (1998). Lost lives: Miscarriages of justice in capital cases. *Law and Contemporary Problems, 61,* 125–152.

Gross, S.R. (2000). Still arbitrary, still unfair—But do we care? *Ohio Northern University Law Review, 26,* 517–527.

Gross, S.R. Convicting the innocent. *Annual Review of Law and Social Science, 4,* 173–192.

Gross, S.R. (2011/12). Pretrial incentives, post-conviction review, and sorting criminal prosecutions by guilt or innocence. *New York Law School Law Review, 56,* 1009–1030.

Gross, S.R. & O'Brien, B. (2008). Frequency and predictors of false conviction: Why we know so little, and new data on capital cases. *Journal of Empirical Legal Studies, 5(4),* 927–962.

Gross, S.R., Jacoby, K., Matheson, D.J., Montgomery, N., & S. Patil. (2005). Exonerations in the United States 1989 through 2003. *Journal of Criminal Law & Criminology, 95(2),* 523–560.

Harmon, T.R. (2001). Predictors of miscarriages of justice in capital cases. *Justice Quarterly, 18,* 949–968.

Harmon, T.R. (2004). Race for your life: An analysis of the role of race in erroneous capital convictions. *Criminal Justice Review, 29(1),* 76–96.

Harmon, T.R. & Lofquist, W.S. (2005). Too late for luck: A comparison of post-Furmanexonerations and executions of the innocent. *Crime & Delinquency, 51(4),* 498–520.

Huff, C.R. (2002). Wrongful conviction and public policy: The American Society of Criminology presidential pddress. *Criminology, 40,* 1, 1–18.

Huff, C.R. (2006). Wrongful convictions in the United States. In Huff, C.R. & Killias, M. (Eds.), *Wrongful convictions: International perspectives on miscarriages of justice* (pp. 59–70). Philadelphia: Temple University Press.

Kirchmeier, J. (2002). Another place beyond here: The death penalty moratorium movement in the United States. *University of Colorado Law Review, 73,* 1–116.

Leo, R.A. (2005). Rethinking the study of miscarriages of justice: Developing a criminology of wrongful conviction. *Journal of Contemporary Criminal Justice 21(3),* 201–223.

Leo, R.A. & Gould, J.B. (2009). Studying wrongful convictions: Learning from social science. *Ohio State Journal of Criminal Law 7(1),* 7–30.

Lofquist, W.S. (2001). Whodunit? An examination of the production of wrongful convictions." In Westervelt, S.D. & Humphrey, J.A. (Eds.), *Wrongly convicted: perspectives on failed justice* (pp. 174–196). New Brunswick, NJ: Rutgers University Press.

Lofquist, W.S. & Harmon, T.R. (2008). Fatal errors: Compelling claims of executions of the innocent in the post-Furman era. In Huff, C.R. & Killias, M. (Eds.), *Wrongful convictions: International perspectives on miscarriages of justice* (pp. 93–116). Philadelphia: Temple University Press.

Markman, S.J. & Cassell, P. (1988). Protecting the innocent: A response to the Bedau-Radelet study. *Stanford Law Review, 41,* 121–160.

Mann, P.E. (2011). Understanding the comparison of budgets for prosecutors and budgets for public defense. *National Legal Aid & Defender Association.*

McCoy, C. (2005). Plea bargaining as coercion: The trial penalty and plea bargaining reform. *Criminal Law Quarterly, 50,* 67–107.

New York Civil Liberties Union. (2012). *Stop and frisk 2011.* Available at http://www.nyclu.org/files/publications/NYCLU_2011_Stop-and-Frisk_Report.pdf

O'Brien, B. (2009). Recipe for bias: An empirical look at the interplay between institutional incentives and bounded rationality in prosecutorial decision making. *Missouri Law Review, 74,* 999–1050.

Parker, K.F., Dewees, M.A. & Radelet, M.L. (2001). Racial bias and the conviction of the innocent. In Westervelt, S.D. & Humphrey, J.A. (Eds.), *Wrongly convicted: Perspectives on failed justice* (pp. 114–131). New Brunswick, NJ: Rutgers University Press.

Perrow, C. (1984). *Normal accidents: Living with high risk technologies.* New York: Basic Books.

President's Commission on Law Enforcement and the Administration of Justice. (1968). *The challenge of crime in a free society.*

Provine, D.M. (2011). Race and inequality in the war on drugs. *Annual Review of Law and Social Science, 7,* 41–60.

Radelet, M.R. & Bedau, H.A. (1998). The execution of the innocent. *Law and Contemporary Problems, 61(4),* 105–124.

Radelet, M.R. & Borg, M.J. (2000). The changing nature of death penalty debates. *Annual Review of Sociology, 26,* 43–61.

Radelet, M.R., Lofquist, W.S. & Bedau, H.A. (1996). Prisoners released from death row since 1970 because of doubts about their guilt. *Cooley Law Review* 13, 907–966.

Rattner, A. (1988). Convicted but innocent: Wrongful conviction and the criminal justice system. *Law and Human Behavior 12(3),* 283–293.

Rizer, A.L. (2003). Justice in a changed world: The race effect on wrongful convictions. *William Mitchell Law Review 29,* 845–867.

Scheck, B., Neufeld, P. & Dwyer, J. (2000). *Actual Innocence.* New York: Doubleday.

Schoenfeld, H. (2005). Violated trust: Conceptualizing prosecutorial misconduct. *Journal of Contemporary Criminal Justice 21(3),* 250–271.

Simon, J. (2007). *Governing through crime: How the war on crime transformed american democracy and created a culture of fear.* New York: Oxford University Press.

Simon, J. (2009). Recovering the craft of policing: Wrongful convictions, the war on crime, and the problem of security. In Ogletree, C.J. & A. Sarat (Eds.), *When law fails: Making sense of miscarriages of justice* (pp. 115–139). New York: New York University Press.

Smith, C. (2002). Central Park revisited. *New York Magazine,* October 31.

Sourcebook of Criminal Justice Statistics. (2008). Available at www.albany.edu/sourcebook/pdf/t412008.pdf.

Spangenberg, R.L., Riggs, J.W., Desilets, R.A. & Saubermann, J.M. (2007). Resources of the prosecution and indigent defense functions in tennessee. The Spangenberg Group.

Stacy, T. (1991). The Search for truth in constitutional criminal procedure. *Columbia Law Review 91,* 1369–1451.

Sudnow, D. (1965). Normal crimes: Sociological features of the penal code in a public defender office. *Social Problems, 12,* 255–274.

Thompson, A.C. (1999). Stopping the usual suspects: Race and the Fourth Amendment. *New York University Law Review, 74,* 956–1013.

Uniform Crime Reports. (1973). *Crime in the United States.* Federal Bureau of Investigation.

Unnever, J.D. & Cullen, F.T. (2005). Executing the innocent and support for capital punishment: Implications for public policy. *Criminology & Public Policy, 4(1),* 3–38.

U.S. House of Representatives. 1994. Innocence and the death penalty: Assessing the danger of mistaken executions. *Subcommittee on Civil and Constitutional Rights, Staff Report. Washington, D.C.*

Vaughan, D. (1996). *The Challenger launch decision.* Chicago: University of Chicago Press.

Wacquant, L. (2001). Deadly symbiosis: When ghetto and prison meet and mesh. *Punishment & Society, 3(1),* 95–133.

Wacquant, L. (2002). Four strategies to curb carceral costs: On managing mass imprisonment in the United States. *Studies in Political Economy, 69,* 19–41.

Wacquant, L. (2005). Great penal leap backward: Incarceration in America from Nixon to Clinton. In Pratt, J. & Brown D. (Eds.), *Punitiveness: Trends, Theories, Perspectives.* Portland, OR: Willan Publishing, 3–26.

Weaver, V.M. (2007). Frontlash: Race and the development of punitive crime policy. *Studies in American Political Development* 21, 230.

Western, B. (2006). *Punishment and inequality in America.* New York: Russell Sage.

Zalman, M. (2006). Criminal justice system reform and wrongful conviction: A research agenda. *Criminal Justice Policy Review*, 17, 4, 468–492.

Zalman, M. (2008). The adversary system and wrongful conviction. In Huff, R.C. & Killias M. (Eds.), *Wrongful conviction: International perspectives on miscarriages of justice* (pp. 71–92). Philadelphia: Temple University Press.

# Chapter Three

# Psychological Perspectives: Cognition and Decision Making

Barbara O'Brien, *Michigan State University*
Keith Findley, *University of Wisconsin*

The most prominent individual sources of error in criminal cases are by now well known; the "canonical list," as Sam Gross has called it, includes eyewitness identification error; flawed or false forensic science; false confessions; perjury, especially perjury by jailhouse informants or "snitches"; prosecutorial misconduct; and inadequate defense counsel (Gross, 2008). But, as this book is designed to demonstrate, the problems that lead to wrongful convictions are much deeper and broader than that list of specific sources of error. Among the contributors to the problem that broadly affect all of these individual sources of error—and indeed, unavoidably affect everything in the criminal justice system (as in any human system)—are innate cognitive processes that can lead to decisional errors and what has broadly been called, in the criminal justice context, "tunnel vision" (Findley & Scott, 2006).

Given the nature of decision making in criminal cases, there is little wonder why such cognitive distortions are so ubiquitous and consequential. The criminal justice system requires individual and groups of decision makers to engage in a number of complex cognitive tasks. Police must interpret information and decide what leads to follow. Prosecutors decide when there is enough evidence to charge and then begin the task of case-building. Defense attorneys evaluate when and what to investigate and what kind of defense to present. Fact finders hear this evidence and decide whether it convinces them beyond a reasonable doubt that the defendant is guilty. Reviewing courts assess the series of decisions leading to conviction, with varying levels of deference depending on the precise issue before them. These decisions are not made independently, as each decision point is influenced by previous judgments.

In this chapter, we offer an overview of what social and cognitive psychological research can tell us about how people make these decisions, the factors that can undermine their reliability, and how these phenomena might contribute to wrongful convictions. Other chapters in this book go into greater detail about some of the phenomena at work with specific actors and stages of the criminal adjudication process. Our goal therefore is not to provide a comprehensive analysis of the psychological processes at work during each of these stages, but to offer a more general view of how they affect the fact-finding process as a whole.

In some areas, existing research provides clear evidence of the relations between the psychological phenomena at issue and a specific error. For instance, research on the fallibility of eyewitness identifications and the factors that can induce a false confession establish clear links between psychology and errors that can lead to false convictions. But there are other areas of psychological research that might also prove fruitful in understanding how decision makers get it wrong. We highlight some of these areas and suggest avenues of future research to test whether these psychological processes may contribute to false convictions.

Our review is necessarily quite cursory, and in many instances, the phenomena we discuss overlap. Some of the psychological processes we discuss do not fall squarely under the classification of cognitive biases, but they can affect decision making and thus shape the system that produces false convictions. Finally, a common thread in our discussion of all these processes is how they can cause decision makers to err inadvertently. Our focus is not on intentional wrongdoing; we assume that all the players in the system are generally trying to achieve an accurate and just result. Rather, we are interested in the ways honest and well-intentioned decision makers go astray, and how to counteract the common psychological tendencies that can undermine even the best intentions.

# Stepping Back: What Psychological Research Tells Us about the Limits of Cognition

The strategies we typically use to make judgments and form beliefs serve us well — most of the time. But a large body of scholarship demonstrates how decision making can fall short in predictable, systematic ways. In particular, people often cling to beliefs even when the evidence upon which they based those beliefs comes into question. They undervalue evidence that contradicts their theories, and seek out new information that tends to support them (see Burke, 2006, for a review). In this part, we discuss some commonly understood biases along with other psychological phenomena that can exacerbate them or undermine decision making in other ways.

## Confirmation Bias

The term "confirmation bias" is used to describe many phenomena (Klayman & Ha, 1987). Generally, confirmation bias refers to the tendency to seek, recall, and interpret information that supports rather than refutes an existing belief or hypothesis (Nickerson, 1998). People display confirmation bias when they test a hypothesis in a way that is likely to support it (Klayman & Ha, 1987), or search for new information in a biased manner (Friedrich, 1993).

Confirmation bias involves unwittingly selecting evidence and interpreting it so as to support a previously held belief (Nickerson, 1998). One does not set out to test a hypothesis deliberately to confirm it, but the strategies used tend to do so (Gibson, Sanbonmatsu, & Posavac, 1997). Thus, people interpret information, form questions, and search for additional evidence in a way that supports existing beliefs without even knowing that they are doing so. Once they form a hypothesis, people recall and search for new information that supports it rather than for information that might support an alternative (Klayman & Ha, 1987). That is, they unconsciously assume that the hypothesis in question is true, and search for evidence accordingly. This does not render them completely indifferent to inconsistent information, but assuming the truth of the focal hypothesis causes them to undervalue that evidence or to be less likely even to notice it. This can undermine accuracy by leading the hypothesis tester to overlook or undervalue evidence that the favored hypothesis is false or that an alternative is plausible (Jonas et al., 2001).

People have this tendency to look for confirming information rather than disconfirming information even when disconfirming information would be much more informative (Nickerson, 1993). If, for example, people formulate a hypothesis that a series of events, or numbers, or other outcomes—whatever it may be—is driven by a particular principle or pattern or cause, they will test that hypothesis by selecting events, or numbers, or other outcomes that are consistent with that hypothesis. But seeking such confirming evidence can only show that the tested item is consistent with the hypothesis; it can never conclusively prove that the hypothesis is correct or that it is the only principle that could be creating the observed outcomes. Testing the hypothesis by examining events or outcomes that are *inconsistent* with the hypothesis, by contrast, can conclusively *disprove* the hypothesis. In other words, without testing for outcomes that would disprove a hypothesis, people may never discover that their hypotheses were wrong and that they had merely proposed conditions that coincidentally fit the actual rule or principle at work. As any scientist knows, the inability to disprove a hypothesis is the closest one can come to proving the hypothesis to be true. But human beings do not naturally investigate hypotheses in this manner.

Confirmation bias also affects how people interpret information by causing them to assign too much weight to confirming evidence and too little to disconfirming evidence. This may happen because they notice confirming information more than disconfirming information (Gilovich, 1991). For example, in one study, teachers rated children's performance consistent with their expectations based on the children's socioeconomic status (Darley & Gross, 1983); in another, hypochondriacs perceived their symptoms to be consistent with the diseases they fear (Pennebaker & Skelton, 1978).

## Belief Perseverance

Related to confirmation bias is the phenomenon of belief perseverance, in which people cling to a belief even in the face of evidence that completely discredits it (Burke, 2006). In one study, for example, subjects were asked to distinguish between authentic and fake suicide notes. Subjects were then given feedback about how they were performing. The feedback was in fact independent of the choices they made; researchers randomly informed the participants that they were performing far above average or far below average. Even after the researchers debriefed the participants and explicitly revealed to them that the feedback had been false, predetermined, and independent of their choices, those who had received positive feedback continued to rate their ability much higher than those who had received negative feedback (Nickerson, 1998; Ross, Lepper & Hubbard, 1975).

## Hindsight and Outcome Bias

People also have a natural tendency to think, in hindsight, that an outcome was more inevitable, likely, or predictable than it actually was. This hindsight bias, or the "knew-it-all-along effect," operates as a means through which people project new knowledge—outcomes—into the past, without any awareness that the perception of the past has been altered by knowledge of the outcome (Hawkins & Hastie, 1990; Hoffrage, Hertwig, & Gigerenzer, 2000). Hindsight bias is a product of the fact that memory is a dynamic process of reconstruction. Memories are not drawn from our brains fully formed, but are assembled from little bits and pieces of information as we recall an event. Those little pieces of information about an event or situation are constantly being updated and replaced in our brains by new information. The updated information is then used each time we reconstruct a relevant memory, making the ultimate conclusion appear preordained, or more likely than we could have known at the outset. In much the same way that confirmation bias operates to emphasize information consistent with pre-existing hypotheses, hindsight bias results in a process in which evidence consistent with a known outcome is highlighted in our memory, and evidence inconsistent with that outcome is minimized or discounted. The result is that the ultimate outcome appears, in hindsight, to have been more likely or apparent than it really was before the outcome was known.

Closely related to hindsight bias is outcome bias. Like hindsight bias, outcome bias involves a process in which people project new knowledge — outcomes — into the past without awareness that the outcome information has influenced their perception of the past (Baron & Hersehy, 1998). Outcome bias differs from hindsight bias, however, in that outcome bias does not refer to the effect of outcome information on the judged probability of an outcome, but to its effect on evaluations of decision quality. In other words, outcome bias affects hindsight judgments about whether a decision was a good or bad one, rather than about how likely an event appears to have been. For example, subjects are more likely to judge the decision to perform surgery as a bad decision when they are told that the patient died during surgery than when told that the same patient survived the surgery (Baron & Hershey, 1988). While this might seem intuitively reasonable and rational, information acquired after a decision is made cannot affect the quality of the decision. Information that is not available at the time a decision is made cannot be the basis for improving decision-making in the future, before such information is available. Both hindsight bias and outcome bias are very hard to overcome. Even when people understand that outcome information should not be the basis for assessing either the likelihood of an outcome or the quality of a decision, they tend to exhibit such bias. The bias is present even when people seek to avoid it and think it has played no role in their assessments (Baron & Hershey, 1998).

## Mindset Theory

Research on mindset theory adds to our understanding about how people approach information gathering and interpretation (Gollwitzer et al., 1990). The task of choosing a course of action activates a different mindset than does the task of implementing it. Thus, people who are still deliberating on a goal process information differently than people who take the next step and begin to implement that goal (Gollwitzer et al., 1990; O'Brien & Oyserman, 2008). In particular, people in a deliberative mindset weigh information in a more even-handed and objective way than people in an implemental mindset, who tend to be more optimistic about their likelihood of success. This approach is rational. Attending to the pros and cons of a decision before committing to it allows one to choose the best course of action. After committing to that goal, second-guessing underlying decisions might slow progress. For instance, Nenkov and Gollwitzer (2012) found that after deciding to commit to a goal, study participants attended more to the pros than to the cons of their decision; in contrast, those who had not yet decided to commit to the goal showed the reverse pattern. But this defensive post-decision deliberation appeared to serve a useful end, in that it predicted how much time study participants spent in learning about ways to achieve that goal.

# Cognitive Dissonance

Cognitive dissonance refers to the discomfort people feel when their behavior is inconsistent with their beliefs. One way to alleviate that discomfort is to change one's beliefs, especially when there are external pressures not to change the behavior. Festinger and Carlsmith (1959) demonstrated this tendency in their classic study by asking subjects to engage in a tedious task, and then paying them either one or twenty dollars to tell another ostensible subject (a confederate) that the task was actually interesting. The subjects all completed the same task, but those who were paid a dollar to deceive the confederate rated their enjoyment of the task as higher than those paid twenty dollars. The task was the same, but the subjects' ratings varied depending on how much they were paid to say it was interesting. Festinger and Carlsmith argued that the conflict between the subjects' beliefs (that the task was dull) and their behavior (telling another that it was interesting) created dissonance only for those who did not have a clear justification for their behavior. Those paid twenty dollars knew why they were lying; those paid only a dollar had no good reason for the lie, and thus adjusted their perceptions of the task to reduce the discomfort the cognitive dissonance created.

In this section, we introduced some of the basic problems and vulnerabilities underlying human cognition. In the next section, we describe how cognitive bias can affect the criminal justice process. Moreover, we introduce other psychological phenomena and cognitive tendencies that may also serve to impede justice and produce wrongful convictions.

# Moving Forward: How Cognitive Biases Might Undermine Criminal Adjudications

A number of researchers have considered how these ubiquitous biases may undermine accuracy in the investigatory stage and thereby contribute to wrongful convictions. For instance, Charman, Gregory, and Carlucci (2009) found that investigators who got information implicating a suspect in a crime rated a facial composite of the perpetrator as more similar to the suspect than did those who did not receive the information. Ask, Rebellius, & Granhag (2008) found that police trainees shown various pieces of evidence of differing strength evaluated it differently depending on whether the evidence was consistent or inconsistent with their initial hypotheses about a suspect's guilt. When the evidence confirmed their hypotheses, they rated all three types of evidence as equally reliable. They rated the reliability differently (weak evidence less reliable than moderate, moderate less than strong) when the evidence disconfirmed their hypotheses, which suggests that they scrutinized the evidence more closely when it disconfirmed rather than confirmed their initial hypotheses.

The adversarial process itself may also influence the mindset of police. When police officers investigate a crime, they must first figure out what happened—who did it and how. But at some point in every case that ends in prosecution, they must shift from determining what happened to proving it. Once they have identified a suspect and developed a theory of what happened, investigators must gather evidence to allow the prosecutors to prove that case. This shift from investigating to building a case presents a risk that investigators will overlook or minimize new evidence that contradicts an early theory of a case. Evidence that points to another suspect or calls into doubt the suspect's guilt may not come to light until later in the process, after investigators have psychologically committed to a theory that the suspect is guilty (O'Brien & Oyserman, 2008).

Of course, the police are not the ultimate decision makers in a criminal case; a prosecutor must be sufficiently persuaded of a suspect's guilt to bring the case, a defense attorney must examine the evidence and determine what, if any, evidence to investigate and present at trial, and a jury must be convinced beyond a reasonable doubt to convict. Nevertheless, decisions made early in the process affect decisions made later, and bad decisions can taint the evidence. An investigator committed to a particular view of the case might convey information to others involved in the process, such as forensic analysts and eyewitnesses (Hasel, 2012). Dror and Charlton (2006) found that extraneous information about a case (such as that the suspect had confessed or was in custody on another charge at the time of the crime) influenced the conclusions of latent fingerprint experts. Eyewitnesses who learn of evidence corroborating the guilt of the suspect they identified become more confident in the accuracy of their memories (Hasel & Kassin, 2009). To the extent these cognitive biases affect early evidence gathering and processing, they can taint the entire process, making the evidence against the suspect look stronger than it actually is.

Confirmation and related biases, along with cognitive dissonance, may also help explain prosecutorial resistance to post-conviction claims of innocence (see Findley & Scott, 2006; Harris, 2012; Medwed, 2009). People are often reluctant to revisit their initial decisions that have been validated externally. A prosecutor whose case resulted in conviction and was affirmed on appeal may become even more convinced of its legitimacy and thus especially unreceptive to evidence suggesting innocence. In hindsight, the jury's decision to convict, and thus the prosecutor's decision to charge, appear wise (Findley & Scott, 2006). This perception reflects both hindsight bias (the outcome of the case seems more certain than it was at the outset) and outcome bias (the decisions to charge, prosecute, and convict appear to be qualitatively better decisions than they might have been prior to conviction and affirmance on appeal). The cognitive dissonance they likely experience when confronted with evidence that they convicted an innocent person might also explain resistance to post-conviction claims of innocence. Prosecutors and police who see themselves as honorable truth-seekers may find it hard to reconcile that self-concept with the notion that they might have contributed to a wrongful conviction. As a consequence, they are prone to attempts to resolve the dissonance by rejecting the notion that a person was wrongly convicted, even in the face of overwhelming evidence of innocence.

Such cognitive distortions affect defense lawyers as well. Defense lawyers enter cases after the initial police investigation has been completed and prosecutors have decided to charge. The evidence and the state's resources have coalesced around a narrative of guilt, which tends to frame the case, even for the defense lawyer. Moreover, defense lawyers, like prosecutors, quickly learn that most people charged with crimes are in fact guilty— or at least are convicted, whether by plea or trial. Defense attorneys thus begin their cases with powerful framing that renders them prone to confirmation bias and related cognitive distortions. While defense lawyers have countervailing institutional role pressures, the interplay between this framing and the various cognitive biases explored here might explain, in part, why research shows that defense lawyers conduct independent investigations in very few of even the most serious cases (McConville & Mirsky, 1986–87), and why in-effective assistance of defense counsel is a frequent contributor to wrongful convictions.

Judges reviewing cases either on direct appeal or on collateral post-convictions may also be influenced. Reviewing judges are confronted with scenarios that induce these biases in particularly stark forms. To a judge presented with a narrative that led to a guilty plea or a jury's judgment of guilt beyond a reasonable doubt, the guilt hypothesis is particularly strong. Confirmation bias can taint the judge's assessment of a defendant's postconviction claim of innocence and any evidence offered in support of that claim. Confirmation, hindsight, and outcome biases can have especially significant implications for appellate and postconviction review by judges who are called upon to apply legal doctrines such as harmless error, or the tests for evaluating newly discovered evidence, evidence favorable to the defense that was improperly withheld before trial by the government (*Brady v. Maryland*, 1963), or exculpatory evidence overlooked by defense counsel errors (*Strickland v. Washington*, 1984). In each such case, the reviewing court's task is to assess whether the new exculpatory evidence might have created a different trial outcome. But these cognitive distortions, together, should be expected to have an affirmance-biasing effect in post-conviction and appellate review. The outcome of the case—conviction—tends to appear, in hindsight, to have been both inevitable and a "good" decision, as well as the product of evidence that appears, through biased processing, to be overwhelmingly inculpatory (Findley & Scott, 2006).

Empirical data appear to support that conclusion, as reversals in criminal cases—even in cases where DNA testing subsequently proves the defendant was innocent—are quite rare (Garrett, 2008). Even where courts find error, they frequently forgive the error under the harmless error doctrine. With hindsight knowledge that a jury found the defendant guilty beyond a reasonable doubt, judges are likely to be predisposed to view the conviction as both an inevitable and sound decision, despite a procedural or constitutional error in the proceedings. Those biases are likely exacerbated by legal doctrines—like the *Brady* doctrine, which establishes an obligation on the prosecution to disclose to the defense material exculpatory evidence, the ineffective assistance of counsel doctrine, which provides a constitutional right to at least a minimally adequate defense attorney, and almost all state formulations of newly discovered evidence rules—that put the burden on the defendant of showing that evidence of innocence never heard by the jury might have changed the outcome (Findley, 2009). Cognitive predisposition to view the outcome as legitimate and well-supported is thereby reinforced by doctrines that tell courts to leave most judgments alone.

# Groupthink

Another psychological phenomenon that can distort the process is groupthink. Groupthink occurs when members of a close-knit group seek to reduce conflict and promote consensus at the expense of critically vetting ideas and questioning underlying assumptions. Groupthink may lead members of the group to stifle dissent and self-censor expressions of misgivings, to reject data that undermines the wisdom of the group's decisions or assumptions, and foster a general sense of righteousness (Tedlow, 2010). Detectives and members of a prosecutorial team might be especially vulnerable to groupthink, given their mission to punish criminals, adversarial roles, and camaraderie (Orenstein, 2011).

Groupthink can undermine accuracy in the criminal justice system by exacerbating existing biases and undermining critical thinking. Ideally, members of a group should check each other's biases and challenge dubious assumptions. But groupthink produces the opposite tendency, fostering tunnel vision and a sense of infallibility. This can lead the group's members to become especially resistant or even oblivious to information that conflicts with the group's shared beliefs. This phenomenon might contribute to an investigator's failure to follow leads that point away from a suspect's guilt, a prosecutor's decision not to hand over exculpatory evidence, or a group member's silence in the face of misconduct by a colleague.

# Fallibility of Human Memory

Of all the areas of psychological research relevant to wrongful convictions, research on the limits of human memory has been perhaps the most fruitful in explaining just how and why things go wrong. A substantial body of work about eyewitness identification has shown that even the most confident eyewitness can be wrong, and that subtle suggestions early in the identification process can supplant the witness's memory of an event (for a review, see, Davis & Loftus, 2012; Wells, 2003). These errors are likely among the biggest contributors to false convictions, as mistaken eyewitness identifications occurred in approximately three-quarters of known false convictions (Garrett, 2011; Gross et al., 2005).

The unreliability of eyewitness identification is compounded by the fact that the information jurors need to assess it is often itself unreliable. Witnesses are often quite bad at remembering details that bear on the accuracy of their identifications, such as distance from the perpetrator, duration of the encounter, and the witness's emotional state (Loftus, 2005). Studies that have examined mock jurors' abilities to assess the reliability of eyewitness testimony show that in the absence of expert testimony to guide them, they are unable to distinguish accurate from inaccurate witness testimony (see Loftus, 2005, for a review).

Human memory falls short in other ways as well. Though less studied than eyewitness memory, some evidence suggests that memory of conversations is also flawed. Like memory for visual events, conversational memory is malleable and poor, and the witness's confidence and consistency in the memory does not bear on its accuracy (see Duke, Lee, & Pager, 2007, for a review of the research). People are better at remembering the gist of a conversation than the precise words, but only slightly.

The implications of imperfect memories for criminal cases can be profound. In the eyewitness identification context, for example, confirming feedback offered by police after a witness picks out a suspect—feedback which itself might be based upon early errors or cognitive biases—can dramatically inflate not only the witness's confidence in the ultimate identification, but also the witness's assessment of the conditions surrounding the identification (Bradfield, Wells, & Olson, 2002; Wells & Bradfield, 1998). Hence, if an eyewitness had a poor view of a perpetrator or paid little attention to the incident at the time, the witness likely had a poor memory of the perpetrator. But if police then presented the witness with a clear image of a suspect in a photo spread or live lineup, the witness would likely replace the original, low-quality memory of the suspect with a clearer image from the identification procedure. Given that the witness really had a very poor memory of the perpetrator, the witness very well could be mistaken in the identification. But, bolstered by the confirming feedback, the witness might then draw on the cleaned-up image of the perpetrator together with the confirming feedback to overstate both the quality of the original viewing conditions and the confidence—the inevitability—of the ultimate identification. In hindsight, the identification might appear as if it was inevitable and based upon clear memories and an excellent opportunity to view the suspect (Bradfield, et al, 2002; Wells & Bradfield, 1998).

Likewise, a witness with only a general recall of the gist of a conversation or event, when presented with other biasing evidence (which itself might be the product of flawed investigations or biased evidence processing), might reconstruct her memory of the overheard conversation or observed event to generate memories of details or to interpret ambiguous data in ways that—perhaps incorrectly—coalesce with the guilt hypothesis created by the other biasing information. In this way, additional evidence gathered in a case, rather than acting as a check on flawed investigations and biased data interpretation, can to the contrary reflect and even amplify those initial errors.

# Credibility Determinations

Assessing whether someone is lying or telling the truth is an important part of the investigatory and trial process. Police must decide whether to believe a suspect's denial of guilt or to press on with an interrogation. Prosecutors must assess the credibility of a suspect's cellmate, who claims that the suspect made incriminating statements. And, of course, juries must determine whether to credit or reject witnesses' testimony.

The legal system places great confidence in the ability of its players to detect lies. Appellate courts expressly defer to juries and trial judges in credibility determinations, citing their unique position to observe the witness's demeanor (*California v. Green*, 1970). Police officers report great confidence in their ability to tell if a person is lying (Kassin, Meissner, & Norwick, 2005). Yet research demonstrates that most people—including police officers—are poor lie detectors (see Vrij, 2008, for a review of studies).

When poor lie-detection skills are combined with the kinds of cognitive biases that operate in criminal cases, the results can be disastrous. In interrogations, for example, police are trained to determine whether they believe a suspect is guilty, based in large part on their assessment of whether the suspect is being honest or dishonest in initial questioning (Inbau, Reid, Buckley, & Jayne, 2013). Research shows that when interrogators approach an interrogation with a firmly held presumption of guilt, they typically choose guilt-presumptive questions and use high-pressure tactics (Kassin, Goldstein, & Savitsky, 2003). At the same time, guilt-presuming interrogators are significantly more likely than those with innocent expectations to perceive suspect responses in incriminating terms. Indeed, research has shown that interrogators employ the most aggressive interrogation behavior when they are questioning actually innocent suspects, even when the innocent suspects tell denial stories judged plausible by neutral observers (Kassin, Goldstein, & Savitsky, 2003). Flawed deception detection, it turns out, means that actual innocence itself can put innocent suspects at risk (Kassin, 2005).

# Diffusion of Responsibility

People acting in groups tend to feel less responsible for their actions than those acting alone. This diffusion of responsibility can lead decision makers acting in groups to use less complex strategies and rely more on heuristics in making judgments (Tetlock & Kim, 1987). Decision makers in groups feel less responsible for the outcomes of their decisions than those acting alone, and therefore tend to make riskier and more polarized decisions (Sherman, 1994).

Jury decision making presents an obvious way in which diffusion of responsibility could undermine the accuracy of the criminal justice system. Capital jurors report difficulty accepting responsibility for deciding whether the defendant would live or die (Hoffman, 1995). Interviews with capital jurors reveal that many avoid a sense of responsibility for voting for a death sentence by assuring themselves that their verdict was merely a recommendation to the judge, or that the law dictated a particular result (Hoffman, 1995; but see Eisenberg, Garvey, & Wells, 1996, for evidence that most jurors do not believe their decisions will be reversed on appeal).

While this research involves capital sentencing, it is not hard to see how jurors faced with less-than-overwhelming evidence that the defendant committed a horrific crime might be tempted to minimize their own role in the process. If the defendant truly is guilty and they acquit, the defendant is free and may commit more such crimes in the future. If the defendant is innocent and they convict, however, at least there is an appeal to fix their error.

Likewise, diffusion of responsibility can affect other players in the system. Prosecutors faced with evidence of a wrongful conviction cite the jury's verdict to excuse any role they might have played in the error (Bandes, 2006). Reviewing courts defer to juries' findings of fact, placing great faith in their ability to discern the truth even in the face of questionable evidence For instance, in *Manson v. Brathwaite* (1977), the Supreme Court extolled "the good sense and judgment of American juries, for evidence with some element of untrust-worthiness is customary grist for the jury mill. Juries are not so susceptible that they cannot measure intelligently the weight of identification testimony that has some questionable feature" (see also Simon, 2012).

Legal doctrine in some ways amplifies the natural tendency for people to shift responsibility for their decisions away from themselves. Courts not only take natural comfort in deferring to jury fact-finding, but legal doctrine (which the courts themselves have largely constructed) guides them to defer to juries on factual determinations. Hence, while the Supreme Court has established that it violates due process for a jury to convict on the basis of evidence insufficient to meet the requirement of proof beyond a reasonable doubt (*Jackson v. Virginia*, 1979), the standard for assessing the sufficiency of the evidence is an extremely deferential one. Reviewing courts must construe all evidence in the light most favorable to the verdict, and to upset that verdict only if no reasonable fact-finder could have found guilt. Under this standard, the Supreme Court has affirmed convictions even while the justices expressed concerns themselves that the defendant might be innocent. In *Cavazos v. Smith* (2011), for example, the Court wrote: "Doubts about whether Smith is in fact guilty are understandable. But it is not the job of this Court, and was not that of the Ninth Circuit, to decide whether the State's theory was correct. The jury decided that question, and its decision is supported by the record."

And the empirical record supports the suggestion that such deference, regardless of its merits as a matter of legal doctrine, has a cost in terms of wrongful convictions. Garrett (2011) examined written appellate decisions available for 165 of the first 250 DNA exonerations—that is, cases in which post-conviction DNA testing proved that the defendant was actually innocent and wrongly convicted. He found that only 42% challenged on appeal the overall sufficiency of the evidence, and none received a reversal on that basis which was upheld on appeal. The courts in those cases ruled that the jury's verdict of guilt was due deference, even though the defendants, it turned out, were all innocent (Garrett, 2011).

## Stereotyping and Racial Bias

An extensive body of scholarship demonstrates the problem of racial discrimination at various stages of the criminal justice system process (see Kennedy, 1997; also, Najdowski, this volume). Discrimination need not be the product of overt racial animus, but may result from unconscious biases and stereotypes that affect how people perceive and remember information (Devine, 1989; Fiske, 1998). Stereotypes are categorizations that allow people to process information efficiently, and to generate hypotheses about how members of a particular group are likely to think and behave (McCrae, Milne, & Bodenhausen, 1994). This efficiency, however, comes at a cost in that it can lead perceivers to relegate their targets to caricatures, and these perceptions are often resistant to disconfirming information (Todd, Galinsky, & Bodenhausen, 2012).

Thus, people unconsciously seek and interpret information in a way that maintains existing stereotypes (Snyder & Swann, 1978). This tendency can undermine accuracy in the criminal justice system in several ways. Mock jurors are more likely to convict a defendant when the charged crime fits the stereotype of the defendant's group. For instance,

Jones and Kaplan (2003) found that mock jurors were more likely to find white defendants guilty of embezzlement than black defendants, and that the reverse was true when the charged crime was auto-theft. The mock jurors processed the evidence in a more superficial way and sought more confirmatory evidence when the charged crime was congruent with the stereotypes about the defendant's racial group than when it was not congruent (see Simon, 2012, for a review of similar findings).

In close cases (and cases that go to trial instead of ending in a guilty plea or dismissal are likely to be close), innocent defendants charged with a stereotype-consistent crime may be disadvantaged by these tendencies. Jurors may more readily accept evidence of guilt; witnesses may remember events in a way that conforms to the stereotype. But linking racial stereotyping to false convictions outside the laboratory is difficult for many reasons. There is evidence that racial minorities suffer false convictions disproportionately. For instance, one study of DNA exonerations found that exonerations for murder and sexual assault involving black defendants and white victims occur at a much higher rate than cross-racial crimes of that nature actually occur (Scheck et al., 2001; see also, Medwed, 2006, for a review of other studies). Despite this evidence, it is not clear whether stereotyping is the culprit.

While stereotyping might be involved, it is hard to assess what drives this disparity. Cross-racial eyewitness identification is particularly unreliable (Meissner & Brigham, 2001), for reasons that appear to be unrelated to stereotyping or racial biases, and this likely explains much of the over-representation of cross-racial crime among exonerations. But stereotyping might also undermine reliability in other ways that are more difficult to detect outside of the laboratory (see Taslitz, 2006). Police may be more easily convinced of a suspect's guilt when it conforms to their stereotypes, thus pursuing evidence that confirms rather than dispels their suspicions. They may be less inclined to believe a suspect's denial of guilt, and more inclined to employ interrogation tactics designed to pressure the suspect into confessing. Prosecutors may believe an informant's claim that his cellmate confessed (see Taslitz, 2008). Juries may be more likely to accept a narrative of the evidence presented at trial that is consistent with guilt, and thus convict on weaker evidence than would suffice to persuade them otherwise. But research on whether and precisely how these processes might contribute to wrongful convictions needs further development.

## Belief in a Just World and System Justification

Just world theory posits that people tend to believe that the world is fair and that people get what they deserve (Lerner, 1980). Relatedly, people tend to view the prevailing social order as fair and legitimate (Jost & Hunyady, 2002; Simon, 2012). These tendencies serve important psychological needs by allowing people to feel safe and assured that any role they played in the process was just.

This tendency can undermine accuracy by leading jurors to assume that the defendant must have done something to be on trial in the first place. It allows prosecutors and police to rationalize their roles in false convictions by minimizing the injustice the wrongly convicted defendant has suffered. Exonerees often report that they are still treated as criminals by the public, and officials sometimes publicly assert their personal belief in an exonerated defendant's guilt notwithstanding their exoneration (Medwed, 2004). As one scholar has noted, "[t]here appears to be an amorphous but widespread belief that those who are charged with crimes are probably guilty of something, regardless of the outcome of the trial" (Leipold, 2000).

Take, for instance, the notorious Central Park jogger case, in which five teenagers were convicted of raping and savagely beating a woman. No physical evidence tied them to the crime, but some had confessed after a prolonged interrogation. The defendants immediately recanted their confessions, claiming that they had been coerced, and DNA analysis later tied the crime to a serial rapist with no connection to the defendants. After their convictions were overturned, the lead prosecutor expressed certainty that defendants were guilty, noting that there was ample evidence that the young men had committed other crimes that night (Orenstein, 2011).

This tendency to believe that the system is just and fair may contribute to false convictions directly if it leads jurors to question the presumption of innocence, and by exacerbating prosecutors' resistance to post-conviction claims of innocence. It can undermine the system in indirect ways as well, by causing those with the power to fix it to deny the existence of problems in the first place (Simon, 2012).[1]

## Relationships and Reciprocity

For many important players in the system, their role is not a one-shot occurrence. Police, prosecutors, defense counsel, and judges often work together on many cases, and the relationships they develop extend beyond a particular case. Defense counsel need the trust of prosecutors to ensure favorable plea offers and a smooth discovery process. In a study of plea bargaining, Milton Heumann discussed how prosecutors can make life more difficult for defense attorneys who file too many motions or behave too zealously (Heumann, 1978). Prosecutors reward informal resolution of cases with access to informal discovery and acquiescence to requests to continue cases (Steman & Frederick, 2013). Judges are more likely to appoint defense counsel with a reputation of disposing of cases quickly, without filing excessive motions or seeking funds for experts or investigation (Brown, 2004).

A desire to maintain good working relationships can compromise defense counsel's zealous advocacy. Although this seems more likely to happen in low-level cases, the pressure to be a team player could undermine representation in more serious cases as well. Even in serious cases, defense counsel are conditioned to know that most of their clients are guilty and will be convicted, and that they usually can get better deals for their clients by not filing disruptive motions or fighting too hard. For example, defense counsel, even in a serious case, may be reluctant to accuse a prosecutor of withholding exculpatory evidence in violation of *Brady v. Maryland* (1963).

Moreover, even though we tend to think of false convictions as occurring in serious cases like rape and murder, it is likely that the pressure to be a team player contributes to false convictions in low-level cases as well. The perception that false convictions typically occur in serious cases may be due to the fact that we only learn of false convictions in the most serious cases. Defendants wrongfully convicted of less serious crimes are unlikely to find anyone willing to do the extensive legwork it takes to upset a conviction (Gross et al., 2005). It is entirely possible that wrongful convictions occur as frequently, or even more frequently, in more routine, less serious cases. In those types of cases, where the stakes are lower, defense counsel may be more susceptible to tempering her zealousness, particularly if she thinks that zealous representation will result in less favorable treatment of her other clients.

Prosecutors are subject to similar pressures in their relationship with police. A prosecutor who questions the integrity of a police investigation risks straining that relationship, to

---

1. Moreover, to the extent a belief in a just world affects the criminal justice system, it does not always work in favor of the prosecution. A substantial literature examines how this tendency can lead to blaming the victim, thus making it harder for the state to win a conviction (see Kleinke & Myer, 1990; Shen, 2011).

the detriment of future cases. Prosecutors with the reputation of being hard on the police can find it more difficult to get timely updates or accurate information (Levenson, 1994; Medwed, 2010). The desire to be a team player and cooperate with the police makes it difficult to question the thoroughness of an investigation or to take seriously claims of police misconduct, such as coercive interrogation tactics, withholding of exculpatory evidence, or evidence tampering.

## Power, Conformity, and Submission to Authority

Decision makers in the criminal justice system do not operate in isolation, but within groups, often with clearly defined hierarchies. This has advantages in that it allows input from multiple perspectives and keeps power from being concentrated in a few people. Ideally, the players influence each other's judgments and decision making for the better by sharing information and tempering each other's biases (see, e.g., *Ballew v. Georgia*, 1978, for a discussion of the benefits of group decision making by juries). But the power of social influence and the tendency to conform can have counterproductive effects as well, creating a cycle in which each player validates the others' work rather than examining it critically.

The desire to conform makes it hard to second-guess decisions of predecessors. This is especially true when one believes the initial decision maker had access to more information when he or she made the decision. If the initial decision makers are colleagues or superiors, second-guessing their decisions is even more difficult (Burkhardt, 2004). This reluctance can amplify confirmation bias, exacerbating any errors made earlier in the process (Findley & Scott, 2006). A prosecutor evaluating the work of investigators or other prosecutors has a strong incentive to accept their view of a case and not to suggest alternative hypotheses.

Jurors are not immune to the power of social influence either. Although, unlike repeat players, they need never work with their fellow jurors again, the pressure to achieve unanimity can lead a juror with doubts about a defendant's guilt to set aside those concerns in favor of consensus (Simon, 2012). The National Center for State Courts conducted a study involving interviews with over 3000 jurors, and found that in over half of juries that reached a verdict, at least one juror reported voting with the majority despite having reservations (Waters & Hans, 2009).

Jurors may also view the prosecutor's charging decision with some deference. Although, technically, the burden of proof means that the status quo in a criminal case is innocence, the decision to proceed with the case is a decision about the defendant's guilt. Though the prosecutor cannot assert his or her own personal belief about the defendant's guilt (see, e.g., *United States v. Smith*, 1993), the decision to charge makes clear that the prosecutor is quite convinced. If jurors see conviction as the default—despite instructions to the contrary—they might defer to the prosecutor more than they would have had they been presented with the information independent of a charging decision.

# Conclusion: Applying What We Know and Assessing What We Don't Know

An impressive body of research exists demonstrating how the ways in which people process and use information can produce errors in the criminal justice system. This research has taught us a lot about how to improve the accuracy of the system. Fortunately, some of that knowledge is beginning to be incorporated into improved criminal justice practices. Some legislatures, courts, and law enforcement agencies, for example, are mandating or incorporating social-science-based best practices for conducting eyewitness identification procedures, designed to minimize the effects that suggestiveness and bias can play in producing eyewitness evidence. (For a summary of the reform efforts, see Garrett, 2012.) In a smaller but growing number of jurisdictions, the social science research is leading to mandatory electronic recording of custodial interrogations of suspects as an antidote to some of the factors that can produce false confessions. (For a summary of the laws on recording of interrogations, see Sullivan, 2012.)

Unfortunately, however, these reforms are not universal, and players in the legal system have resisted the lessons of much of this research. Police departments continue to resist efforts to mandate recording of interrogations, for instance, or to implement best practices for line-up procedures. (For an analysis of some of the cognitive biases that prevent police and prosecutors from embracing the lessons from the social science research, see Harris, 2012.) Courts often refuse to allow expert testimony to aid jurors in understanding how to assess an eyewitness's credibility or why an innocent person might confess. Prosecutors faced with evidence that a person was wrongly convicted insist that they acted in good faith, failing to consider how ubiquitous cognitive biases may have affected their performance and contributed to the wrongful conviction. Forensic laboratories fail to follow basic scientific practices such as blind testing of samples.

Implementing the lessons from what we already know would likely reduce false convictions, though by how much, no one can say. Nevertheless, we see several areas that merit more research to further our understanding of how the system fails and what we might do to improve its accuracy. To what extent does diffusion of responsibility allow decision makers to pass the buck, assuming their errors will be corrected? Do prosecutors with relatively weak cases go forward with the belief that a jury will make the right decision, when in fact those jurors might be deferring to the prosecutor's decision to bring the charge? Do jurors believe that appellate courts will fix their errors, and would they behave differently if they were instructed about the appellate process and how factual judgments are largely left untouched? At what stage in the investigatory process do police shift from figuring out what happened to proving it? In other words, at what point do they shift from a deliberative to an implementation mindset? How might racial and other stereotypes affect how investigators, prosecutors, and jurors evaluate information that conflicts or confirms those stereotypes, and how might that interact with other cognitive biases to undermine reliability? Answering these questions would be difficult, but would significantly add to our understanding of how the criminal justice system errs.

# References

Ask, K., Rebelius, A., & Granhag, P. (2008). The 'elasticity' of criminal evidence: A moderator of investigator bias. *Applied Cognitive Psychology, 22*(9), 1245–1259.

Ask, K., & Granhag, P. (2007). Motivational bias in criminal investigators' judgments of witness reliability. *Journal of Applied Social Psychology, 37*(3), 561–591.

*Ballew v. Georgia*, 435 U.S. 223 (1978)

Bandes, S. (2006). Loyalty to One's Convictions: The Prosecutor and Tunnel Vision. *Howard Law Journal, 49*(2), 475–494.

Baron, J. & Hershey, J. C. (1988). Outcome Bias in Decision Evaluation, *Journal of Personality & Social Psychology, 54*, 569–579.

Bibas, S. (2004). Plea bargaining outside the shadow of trial. *Harvard Law Review, 117*(8), 2463–2547.

Bradfield, A. L., Wells, G. L., & Olson, E. A. (2002). The damaging effect of confirming feedback on the relation between eyewitness certainty and identification accuracy. *Journal of Applied Psychology, 87,* 112–120.

*Brady v. Maryland,* 373 U.S. 83 (1963).

Brown, D. K. (2004). Rationing criminal defense entitlements: an argument from institutional design. *Columbia Law Review, 104*(3), 801–835.

Burke, A. S. (2006). Improving Prosecutorial Decision Making: Some Lessons of Cognitive Science. *William and Mary Law Review, 47*(5), 1587–1633.

Burke, A.S. (2007). Neutralizing cognitive bias: An invitation to prosecutors. *New York University Journal of Law and Liberty, 2,* 512–530.

Burkhardt, S. (2004). The contours of conformity: Behavioral decision theory and the pitfalls of the 2002 reforms of immigration procedures. *Georgetown Immigration Law Journal, 19*(1), 35–98.

*California v. Green,* 399 U.S. 149 (1970).

*Cavazos v. Smith,* 132 S.Ct. 2 (2011).

Charman, S. D., Gregory, A. H., & Carlucci, M. (2009). Exploring the diagnostic utility of facial composites: Beliefs of guilt can bias perceived similarity between composite and suspect. *Journal of Experimental Psychology: Applied, 15(1),* 76–90.

Darley, J. M., & Gross, P. H. (1983). A hypothesis-confirming bias in labeling effects. *Journal of Personality & Social Psychology, 44(1),* 20–33.

Davis, D., & Leo, R. (2012). To Walk in Their Shoes: The Problem of Missing, Misunderstood, and Misrepresented Context in Judging Criminal Confessions. *New England Law Review, 46*(4), 737–767.

Davis, D., & Loftus, E. F. (2012). Inconsistencies between law and the limits of human cognition: The case of eyewitness identification (pp. 29–58). New York, NY, US: Oxford University Press.

Devine, P.G. (1989). Stereotypes and prejudice: Their automatic and controlled components. *Journal of Personality and Social Psychology, 56,* 5–18.

Duke, S. B., Lee, A., & Pager, C. W. (2007). A Picture's Worth a Thousand Words: Conversational versus Eyewitness Testimony in Criminal Convictions. *American Criminal Law Review, 44*(1), 1–52.

Eisenberg, T., Garvey, S. P., & Wells, M. T. (1996). Jury responsibility in capital sentencing: an empirical study. *Buffalo Law Review, 44,* 339–380.

Etienne, M. (2003). Remorse, responsibility, and regulating advocacy: making defendants pay for the sins of their lawyers. *New York University Law Review, 78*(6), 2103–2176.

Festinger, L., & Carlsmith, J. M. (1959). Cognitive consequences of forced compliance. *The Journal of Abnormal and Social Psychology, 58*(2), 203–210.

Findley, K. A. (2009). Innocence Protection in the Appellate Process. *Marquette Law Review, 93(2),* 591–638.

Findley, K. A., & Scott, M. S. (2006). The Multiple Dimensions of Tunnel Vision in Criminal Cases. *Wisconsin Law Review, 2006*(2), 291–397.

Fiske, S. T. (1998). Stereotyping, prejudice, and discrimination. In D. T. Gilbert, S. T. Fiske, & G. Lindzey (eds.), *The Handbook of Social Psychology* (4th Ed.) (pp. 357–414). New York: McGraw-Hill.

Freeman, N. J. (2006). Socioeconomic status and belief in a just world: Sentencing of criminal defendants. *Journal of Applied Social Psychology, 36*(10), 2379–2394.

Fujita, K., Gollwitzer, P. M., & Oettingen, G. (2007). Mindsets and pre-conscious open-mindedness to incidental information. *Journal of Experimental Social Psychology, 43*(1), 48–61.

Garrett, B. L. (2008). Judging Innocence. *Columbia Law Review, 108,* 55–142.

Garrett, B. L. (2011). *Convicting the innocent: Where criminal prosecutions go wrong* Harvard University Press, Cambridge, MA.

Garrett, B. L. (2012). Eyewitnesses and Exclusion. *Vanderbilt Law Review, 65,* 451–506.

Gibson, B., Sanbonmatsu, D. M., & Posavac, S. S. (1997). The effects of selective hypothesis testing on gambling. *Journal of Experimental Psychology: Applied,3*(2), 126–142.

Gilovich, T. (1991). *How we know what isn't so: The fallibility of human reason in everyday life*: NY, NY: Free Press.

Gross, S. R. (2008). Convicting the Innocent. *Annual Review of Law & Social Science, 4,* 173–192.

Gross, S. R., Jacoby, K., Matheson, D. J., & Patil, S. (2005). Exonerations in the United States, 1989 through 2003. *Journal Of Criminal Law & Criminology, 95*(2), 523–560.

Hafer, C. L., & Bègue, L. (2005). Experimental research on just-world theory: Problems, developments, and future challenges. *Psychological Bulletin, 131*(1), 128–167.

Harris, D. A. (2012). *Failed Evidence: Why Law Enforcement Resists Science.* New York & London: New York University Press.

Hasel, L. E. (2012). Evidentiary Independence: How Evidence Collected Early in an Investigation Influences the Collection and Interpretation of Additional Evidence.(pp. 142–158). New York, NY, US: Oxford University Press. Oxford Series in Neuroscience, Law and Philosophy.

Hasel, L. E., & Kassin, S. M. (2009). On the presumption of evidentiary independence: Can confessions corrupt eyewitness identifications? *Psychological Science, 20(1),* 122–126.

Hawkins, S. A., & Hastie, R. (1990). Hindsight: Biased judgments of past events after the outcomes are known. *Psychological Bulletin,107,* 311–327.

Heath, W. P. (2009). Arresting and convicting the innocent: The potential role of an "inappropriate" emotional display in the accused." *Behavioral Sciences & the Law, 27,* 313–32.

Heumann, M (1978). *Plea Bargaining: The Experiences of Prosecutors, Judges, and Defense Attorneys.* Chicago: The University of Chicago Press.

Hoffman, J.L. (1995). Where's the buck?—Juror misperception of sentencing responsibility in death penalty cases. *Indiana Law Journal, 70,* 1137–1160.

Hoffrage, U., Hertwig, R., & Gigerenzer, G. (2000). Hindsight bias: A by-product of knowledge updating?, *Journal of Experimental Psychology: Learning, Memory & Cognition, 26,* 566–581.

Inbau, F. E., Reid, J. E., Buckley, J. P., & Jayne, B. C. (5th ed. 2013). *Criminal Interrogation and Confessions.* Burlington, MA, USA: Jones & Bartlett Learning.

*Jackson v. Virginia,* 443 U.S. 307 (1979)

Jonas, E., Schulz-Hardt, S., Frey, D., & Thelen, N. (2001). Confirmation bias in sequential information search after preliminary decisions: An expansion of dissonance theoretical research on selective exposure to information. *Journal of Personality and Social Psychology, 80(4),* 557–571.

Jones, C. S., & Kaplan, M. F. (2003). The effects of racially stereotypical crimes on juror decision-making and information-processing strategies. *Basic and Applied Social Psychology, 25*(1), 1–13.

Jost, J. T., & Hunyady, O. (2002). The psychology of system justification and the palliative function of ideology. *European Review of Social Psychology, 13,* 111–153.

Kassin, S. M. (2005). On the psychology of confessions: Does innocence put innocents at risk? *American Psychologist, 60(3),* 215–228.

Kassin, S. M. (2008). False confessions: Causes, consequences, and implications for reform. *Current Directions in Psychological Science, 17*(4), 249–253.

Kassin, S. M., Bogart, D., & Kerner, J. (2012). Confessions that corrupt: Evidence from the DNA exoneration case files. *Psychological Science, 23*(1), 41–45.

Kassin, S. M., Goldstein, C. C., & Savitsky, K. (2003). Behavioral confirmation in the interrogation room: On the dangers of presuming guilt. *Law & Human Behavior, 27,* 187–203.

Kassin, S. M., Meissner, C. A., & Norwick, R. J. (2005). I'd Know a False Confession if I Saw One. *Law and Human Behavior*, 29(2), 211–227.

Kennedy, R. (1998). *Race, crime, and the law.* New York, NY: Vintage.

Klayman, J., & Ha, Y. (1987). Confirmation, disconfirmation, and information in hypothesis testing. *Psychological Review, 94,* 211–228.

Kleinke, C. L., & Meyer, C. (1990). Evaluation of rape victim by men and women with high and low belief in a just world. *Psychology of Women Quarterly, 14*(3), 343–353.

Lerner, M.J. (1965). *The belief in a just world: A fundamental delusion.* New York, NY: Plenum Press.

Leipold, A. D. (2000). The problem of the innocent, acquitted defendant. *Northwestern University Law Review, 94*(4), 1297–1356.

Levenson, L. L. (1994). The future of state and federal civil rights prosecutions: The lessons of the Rodney King trial. *UCLA Law Review, 41,* 509–608.

Luban, D. (1993). Are criminal defenders different?. *Michigan Law Review, 91,* 1729–1766.

Loftus, E. F. (2005). Planting misinformation in the human mind: A 30-year investigation of the malleability of memory. *Learning & Memory, 12*(4), 361–366.

Macrae, C.N., A.B. Milne, & G.V. Bodenhausen (1994). Stereotypes as energy-saving devices: A peek inside the cognitive toolbox. *Journal of Personality and Social Psychology, 66,* 37–47.

*Manson v. Brathwaite*, 432 U.S. 98 (1977).

McConville, M. & Mirsky, C. L. (1986–87). Criminal Defense of the Poor in New York City. *New York University Review of Law & Social Change.*

Medwed, D. S. (2010). Emotionally charged: The prosecutorial charging decision and the innocence revolution. *Cardozo Law Review, 31*(6), 2187–2213.

Medwed, D. S. (2009). The Prosecutor as Minister of Justice: Preaching to the Unconverted from the Post-Conviction Pulpit. *Washington Law Review, 84*(1), 35–66.

Medwed, D. S. (2006). Anatomy of a Wrongful Conviction: Theoretical Implications and Practical Solutions. *Villanova Law Review, 51*(2), 337–377.

Medwed, D. S. (2005). Up the river without a procedure: Innocent prisoners and newly discovered non-DNA evidence in state courts. *Arizona Law Review, 47*(3), 655–718.

Medwed, D. S. (2004). The zeal deal: prosecutorial resistance to post-conviction claims of innocence. *Boston University Law Review, 84*(1), 125–183.

Meissner, C. A., & Brigham, J. C. (2001). Thirty years of investigating the own-race bias in memory for faces: A meta-analytic review. *Psychology, Public Policy, and Law, 7*(1), 3–35.

Nenkov, G. Y., & Gollwitzer, P. M. (2012). Pre-versus postdecisional deliberation and goal commitment: The positive effects of defensiveness. *Journal of Experimental Social Psychology, 48*(1), 106–121.

Nickerson, R. S. (1998). Confirmation bias: A ubiquitous phenomenon in many guises. *Review of General Psychology, 2,* 175–220.

O'Brien, B., & Oyserman, D. (2008). It's Not Just What You Think, But Also How You Think about It: The Effect of Situationally Primed Mindsets on Legal Judgments and Decision Making. *Marquette Law Review*, *92*(1), 149–172.

Orenstein, A. (2011). Facing the Unfaceable: Dealing with Prosecutorial Denial in Post-conviction Cases of Actual Innocence. *San Diego Law Review*, *48*(1), 401–446.

Parker, K.F., DeWees, M.A., Radelet, M.L. (2003). Race, the Death Penalty, and Wrongful Convictions. *Criminal Justice*, *18*, 49–54.

Pennebaker, J. W., & Skelton, J. A. (1978). Psychological parameters of physical symptoms. *Personality & Social Psychology Bulletin*, *4(4)*, 524–530.

Perillo, J. T., & Kassin, S. M. (2011). Inside interrogation: The lie, the bluff, and false confessions. *Law and Human Behavior*, *35*(4), 327–337.

Ross, L., Lepper, M. R., & Hubbard, M. (1975). Perseverance in self-perception and social perception: biased attributional processes in the debriefing paradigm. *Journal of Personality & Social Psychology*, *32*(5), 880–892.

Scheck, B., Neufeld, P. J., & Dwyer, J., M. (2000). *Actual innocence*. New York, NY: Doubleday.

Shen, F. X. (2011). How we still fail rape victims: Reflecting on responsibility and legal reform. *Columbia Journal of Gender & Law*, *22*(1), 1–80.

Sherman, S. J. (1995). The capital jury project: The role of responsibility and how psychology can inform the law. *Indiana Law Journal*, *70*(4), 1241–1248.

Simon, D. (2012). *In doubt: The psychology of the criminal justice process*. Cambridge, MA, US: Harvard University Press.

Snyder, M., & Swann, W.B. (1978). Hypothesis testing processes in social interaction. *Journal of Personality and Social Psychology*, *36*, 1202–1212.

Spellman, B. A., & Tenney, E. R. (2010). Credible testimony in and out of court. *Psychonomic Bulletin & Review*, *17*(2), 168–173.

Steman, D. & Frederick, B. (2013). Rules, Resources, and Relationships: Contextual Constraints on Prosecutorial Decision Making. *Quinnipiac Law Review*, *31*, 1–83.

*Strickland v. Washington*, 466 U.S. 668 (1984).

Sullivan, T. P. (2012). A Compendium of Law Relating to the Electronic Recording of Custodial Interrogations. *Champion*, *36*, 22–24.

Taslitz, A. E. (2006). Wrongly accused: Is race a factor in convicting the innocent. *Ohio State Journal if Criminal Law*, *4*, 121–133.

Taslitz, A. E. (2008). Wrongly Accused Redux: How Race Contributes to Convicting the Innocent: the Informants Example. *Southwestern University Law Review*, *37*(4), 1091–1148.

Tedlow, R. S. (2010). *Denial: Why Business Leaders Fail to Look Facts in the Face—and what to Do about it*. New York, NY: Portfolio.

Tetlock, P. E., & Kim, J. I. (1987). Accountability and judgment processes in a personality prediction task. *Journal of Personality and Social Psychology*, *52*(4), 700–709.

Todd, A.R., Galinsky, A.D., & Bodenhausen, G.V. (2012). Perspective taking and stereotype maintenance. *Social Cognition*, *30*, 94–108.

*United States v. Smith*, 982 F.2d 681 (1st Cir. 1993).

Vrij, A. (2008). *Detecting Lies and Deceit: Pitfalls and Opportunities (2nd Ed.)*. New York, NY, US: John Wiley & Sons Ltd.

Waters, N. L. & Hans, V.P. (2009). A Jury of One: Opinion Formation, Conformity, and Dissent on Juries. *Journal of Empirical Legal Studies*, *6*(3), 513–40.

Wells, G. L., & Bradfield, A. L. (1998). "Good, you identified the suspect": Feedback to eyewitnesses distorts their reports of the witnessing experience. *Journal of Applied Psychology 83(3)*, 360–376.

Wells, G. L., & Olson, E. A. (2003). Eyewitness testimony. *Annual Review of Psychology, 54*, 277–295.

Wessel, E., Drevland, G. C. B., Eilertsen, D. E., & Magnussen, S. (2006). Credibility of the emotional witness: A study of ratings by court judges. *Law and Human Behavior, 30(2)*, 221–230.

# Chapter Four

# Interactions between African Americans and Police Officers: How Cultural Stereotypes Create a Wrongful Conviction Pipeline for African Americans

Cynthia J. Najdowski, Ph.D., *University at Albany, State University of New York*

## Introduction

Erroneous convictions are not as rare as one might expect, and when they occur, the wrongfully accused are more often African American than White: Of those who were wrongfully convicted and later exonerated in the last quarter century, 47% were African American (The National Registry of Exonerations, 2013), even though only 13% of the U.S. population is (Rastogi, Johnson, Hoeffel, & Drewery, 2011). Yet Gould, Carrano, Leo, and Young's (2013) recent analysis of miscarriages of justice indicated that race does not reliably differentiate between cases in which innocent defendants are wrongfully convicted as opposed to rightfully acquitted. They suggested that, rather than explaining what goes wrong at the plea or trial stage of the criminal justice process, race may be more important for understanding why innocent individuals erroneously enter the justice system in the first place. Indeed, every wrongful conviction can be traced back to the initial erroneous classification of an innocent person as guilty, the first of a series of mistakes made by the police and other criminal justice professionals (for review, see Leo & Drizin, 2010). The potential for race to lead to misclassification errors is demonstrated by the recent judgment in the class-action civil rights trial *Floyd v. City of New York* (2013). A federal judge determined that thousands of African Americans and Latinos had been illegally stopped, questioned, or frisked on the basis of discriminatory practices enacted by the New York Police Department (NYPD)—in fact, 90% of African Americans stopped by the NYPD in 2012 were innocent (New York Civil Liberties Union [NYCLU], 2013).

Disproportionate police contact with African Americans has been shown to result from socio-structural and institutional characteristics of communities and policing organizations (e.g., Beckett, Nyrop, Pfingst, & Bowen, 2005; Engel, Smith, & Cullen, 2012; Gelman, Fagan, & Kiss, 2005; Sampson & Raudenbush, 2004). The most common explanation for African Americans' overrepresentation in stops, searches, and arrests rests on the assertion that the criminal justice system at large, police departments' policies, and individual officers are racially biased (e.g., Coker, 2003). But racial disparities in criminal justice outcomes cannot be so easily explained, because, even absent any racial animus, a variety of social psychological processes contribute to an increased likelihood of mis-classification errors and subsequent wrongful convictions for African Americans as compared to White Americans. In this chapter I examine how cultural stereotypes that depict African Americans as criminals affect both African Americans' reactions to police officers and police officers' perceptions and judgments of African Americans.[1] My focus is on these police encounters because this is the step that sets the remaining chain of events in motion. That is, there are many subsequent steps in the criminal justice continuum at which racial disparities might appear (e.g., in charging decisions, jury voir dire, and verdicts), but it is the initial police interaction that creates these opportunities. Finally, I discuss how knowledge about these social psychological processes might be used to inform research and practice in the criminal justice system to improve racial equity.

# Stepping Back: Understanding How Stereotypes of African Americans Influence Police-Citizen Encounters

There is an abundance of scientific research evidencing the many harmful consequences that negative beliefs about African Americans produce. Particularly relevant for understanding the origins of racial disparities in wrongful convictions is the widely documented stereotype that depicts African Americans as violent and prone to crime (see, e.g., Oliver, 2003; Rome, 2004; Welch, 2007). Duru (2004) traced the roots of this stereotype to the sixteenth century, when European explorers first encountered and enslaved African men. Yet, modern studies show that this stereotype continues to be a part of our culture. For instance, aggressiveness and a tendency toward violence are identified as stereotypical attributes of African Americans by both White and African Americans (Kreuger, 1996; Madon et al., 2001) and criminality and hostility are among the features most commonly endorsed as stereotypic of African Americans by both high-prejudiced and low-prejudiced White Americans (Devine, 1989; Devine & Elliot, 1995). How does this stereotype bias African Americans' and police officers' expectations for their encounters with each other? What psychological processes explain how this stereotype puts African Americans at greater risk than White Americans of being misclassified as suspects and, ultimately, wrongfully convicted?

## How the Stereotype Influences African Americans' Reactions to Police Officers

Recent theory suggests that the negative cultural stereotype of African American criminality might actually cause African Americans to behave more suspiciously than White Americans when interacting with the police (Najdowski, 2011, 2012). The underlying premise of this work is that African Americans are concerned about being judged and treated unfairly by police due to the stereotype about their racial group — that is, African

---

1. I focus here on the impact of cultural stereotypes on police officers' encounters with African Americans as opposed to all or other minorities because most research to date has focused on African Americans. I expect, however, that the social psychological processes discussed herein generalize to other groups who are also stereotyped as criminals (e.g., Hispanics, Muslims).

Americans experience *stereotype threat* in police encounters. This is consequential because stereotype threat has been shown to have unintended effects on psychological functioning that inadvertently increase the likelihood that an individual will be perceived as confirming a stereotype about the group to which he or she belongs. For example, when the stereotype that African Americans are low in intelligence is salient, African American students underperform relative to White American students on standardized tests (Steele & Aronson, 1995). In the context of police encounters, stereotype threat could have detrimental consequences because threat and its psychological correlates (i.e., anxiety and arousal, self-regulatory efforts, cognitive load; see Schmader, Johns, & Forbes, 2008) produce nonverbal behaviors that are, ironically, the same as those that police commonly perceive as indicative of deception or guilt. For example, gay men who are primed to think of the stereotype that depicts them as child molesters and, thus, induced to feel stereotype threat, are perceived by observers as more anxious than non-primed, non-threatened gay men (Bosson, Haymovitz, & Pinel, 2004). And, in general, police believe that nonverbal cues to deception include social anxiety (Vrij & Winkel, 1992) and tense and nervous facial expressions and postures (Akehurst, Köhnken, Vrij, & Bull, 1996; Vrij, Akehurst, & Knight, 2006). In fact, there is considerable overlap between the nonverbal behaviors that are caused by stereotype threat and related psychological processes and those that the police associate with deception (for a review, see Najdowski, 2011). Given that innocent African Americans might experience stereotype threat and, in turn, behave in ways that are associated with lying (e.g., appear nervous, have more speech disturbances), police officers' beliefs about the ability of nonverbal cues to reveal deception might be inaccurate. As a result, police officers might misclassify more innocent African than White Americans as guilty.[2]

Considering that this theoretical process could have such serious consequences, it is critical to understand whether African Americans do, in fact, experience stereotype threat in police encounters. Preliminary support for this hypothesis can be garnered from studies showing that most African Americans are aware that they are stereotypically depicted as criminals. As noted previously, African Americans perceive that the cultural stereotype characterizes their racial group as prone to violence (Kreuger, 1996). In addition, Sigelman and Tuch's (1997) research on meta-stereotypes revealed that 82% of African Americans think they are perceived as violent by White Americans. African Americans, compared to White Americans, are also more likely to think that they are treated unfairly by police officers (Hagan & Albanetti, 1982; Hagan, Shedd, & Payne, 2005; Ludwig, 2003), and that racial profiling is widespread (Carlson, 2004; Ludwig, 2003).

---

2. It is worth noting that, although the racial discrepancy in wrongful conviction and exoneration rates has been found in cases involving rape, attempted murder, robbery, and drug crimes, the discrepancy is greatest in rape cases (The National Registry of Exonerations, 2013). Yet, one might argue that rape suspects comprise a minority of individuals affected by police-citizen encounters as described herein. However, many stops are initiated by police because a violent crime is suspected to have occurred and/or an individual "fits a relevant description"—these reasons, respectively, accounted for 11% and 17% of stops made by the NYPD in 2012 (NYCLU, 2013). Thus, it may be the case that, on occasion, African Americans are approached by police who are searching for suspected rapists, and that social psychological processes unfold in those cases as in any other. In fact, 60 stops made by the NYPD in 2012 resulted in arrests for rape and sexual offenses (NYPD, 2013). Although this constituted less than 1% of all arrests resulting from stops in that year and the actual guilt or innocence of the arrestees is unknown, it is also important to note that wrongful convictions, and racial disparities in rates, have likely been uncovered more often in cases involving rape as compared to other crimes. That is, rape exonerations primarily involve DNA identifications and no similar technique exists for proving innocence for other crimes that do not typically involve biological evidence (Gross, Jacoby, Matheson, Montgomery, & Patil, 2005).

More direct evidence that African Americans experience police-induced stereotype threat comes from two studies my colleagues and I conducted (Najdowski, Bottoms, & Goff, 2013). In the first study, we surveyed 49 African American and 184 White undergraduate students and found that African Americans were significantly more likely to agree with statements like, "I worry that police officers might stereotype me as a criminal because of my race." That is, as expected, African Americans were more likely to agree that they experience stereotype threat in police encounters than were White Americans. In the second study, we asked 38 African American and 96 White men to imagine what it would be like if, as they were walking down the street at night carrying a backpack, a police officer exited a store just ahead of them and then stopped and watched them as they approached. In response to an open-ended question about what they would think and feel in the imagined encounter, 33% of African American men, compared to only 2% of White men, spontaneously made statements that indicated they would experience stereotype threat (e.g., "I would think 'typical' cop. They always suspect the tall Black man."). African American men were also significantly more likely than White men to anticipate feeling both stereotype threat and concern that the police officer might accuse them of doing something wrong.

I extended these studies by conducting a third study in which 40 African American and 39 White men came face to face with a White security officer in an elaborate staged encounter (Najdowski, 2012). Each participant came to the laboratory individually. After completing a variety of control measures and demographic items, the participant read an article on a Kindle Fire. While he was reading, the experimenter made an excuse to leave the laboratory. The confederate security officer then approached a water fountain next to the laboratory, pretended to receive a call and talked into his cell phone, acted as though he noticed the participant, ended the pretend call, and then approached the participant. The extent to which the stereotype about African Americans and crime was relevant in the encounter was varied to examine whether stereotype threat manifests in only certain conditions or in any encounter with a law enforcement figure. In the high-stereotype-relevance condition, the officer noted that a woman had "just reported having her wallet stolen, and a little computer just like that," and asked several investigatory questions (e.g., "Is that tablet computer yours?"). In the low-stereotype-relevance condition, the officer asked for directions to a meeting. In both conditions, the officer next pretended to receive another call, said into his phone, "I think I'm just around the corner from there so I'll go check it out," and departed. The experimenter returned to the laboratory, and the participant completed more measures, including items assessing stereotype threat. Participants were surreptitiously videotaped during the encounter and their behavior was coded for a variety of nonverbal cues that police commonly associate with deception.

The results revealed that the stereotype threat effect found in my earlier studies generalized to a realistic encounter with a White security officer: Compared to White Americans, African Americans were significantly more concerned that the officer would be influenced by racial stereotypes and suspect participants of having committed a crime. Analyses revealed that race did not significantly influence the frequency with which participants averted their gaze, smiled, gestured, moved their heads, or shifted position. Compared to White Americans, however, African Americans used significantly fewer self-adaptors (movements involving touching and manipulating one's own body) and appeared significantly more nervous overall. Although the former effect is inconsistent with my hypothesis—law enforcement officers generally associate more self-adaptors with lying (Vrij & Semin, 1996)—the latter effect was predicted and in line with my hypothesis—as mentioned previously, police officers generally perceive tense and nervous expressions and postures as deceptive behaviors (e.g., Akehurst et al., 1996). As hypothesized, the main effect of race on nervous appearance was mediated by stereotype threat. Thus, expecting to be judged and treated unfairly due to the negative stereotype of African American criminality appears to cause African Americans to behave differently—more "suspiciously"—than White Americans in encounters with police-type figures.

Of importance, the main effects of race were not moderated by stereotype relevance (i.e., whether the officer was investigating a crime or asking for directions). It appears that situational factors that signal risk of being stereotyped might not influence African Americans' feelings and behavior above and beyond general beliefs about the extent to which the police are biased. Even so, high as opposed to low stereotype relevance did relate to significantly more stereotype threat as well as significantly more eye contact, less smiling, and more nervous appearance. Further, the last effect was also mediated by stereotype threat. That is, when the officer contact was investigatory versus not, participants were more likely to feel threat and, in turn, appear nervous. Thus, simply perceiving that one is being treated like a suspect increases the likelihood that one will indeed appear suspicious.

Taken together, these studies provide compelling evidence that African Americans do experience stereotype threat when they encounter police officers and that stereotype threat, in turn, translates into suspicious-looking nervous behavior. The significance of this finding cannot be understated because police often rely on suspect behavior when determining what actions to take, including whether to arrest or not (e.g., Stroshine, Alpert, & Dunham, 2008). Indeed, NYPD officers cited citizens' "furtive movements" as the reason for 52% of street stops in 2012 (NYCLU, 2013). Further, my own analysis of the NYPD stop-and-frisk data for 2012 (NYPD, 2013) revealed that furtive movements were used to explain stops significantly more often when citizens were African American (54%) rather than White American (44%), $\chi^2$ (1, $n = 334,595$) = 1,669.02, $p < .001$, $\psi = .07$.

# How the Stereotype Influences Police Officers' Perceptions and Judgments of African Americans

As it turns out, African Americans might be justified in their concerns about being perceived unfairly by police officers because of the African American criminal stereotype. A substantial body of social and social cognitive research has established that the cultural stereotype of African American criminality can have a subtle yet biasing influence on the way that people perceive individuals, process information, and form judgments, even absent any conscious bias on the part of the perceiver (e.g., Devine, 1989; Eberhardt, Goff, Purdie, & Davies, 2004). This means that the African American criminal stereotype can unconsciously and automatically influence what police officers see when they encounter African American citizens, how officers interpret what they see, and how they decide to act in response (for review, see Trope & Liberman, 1996). It does so by causing the concepts of race and crime to be inextricably and automatically linked, with thoughts of one leading to thoughts of the other, as illustrated in an elegant set of studies conducted by Eberhardt and colleagues (2004). In one study, the researchers subliminally primed participants with either African American or White faces by showing them pictures so quickly that they could not be consciously registered. Following the priming manipulation, participants were shown a series of initially degraded but increasingly clear images of crime-related objects (e.g., guns, badges) and non-crime-related objects (e.g., staplers, keys). Participants who had been primed with White faces identified objects just as quickly regardless of whether they were related to crime or not, but those who had been primed to view African

American faces identified the objects more quickly when they were related to crime than when they were not. As summarized by Richardson and Goff (2012), "the mere presence of Blackness made it easier to *see* crime than when Blackness was absent" (p. 303, emphasis as original).

Eberhardt and colleagues (2004) showed that the effect is reciprocal, too. In another study, police-officer participants were either subliminally presented with either crime-relevant words (e.g., violent, arrest) or not. Police officers then completed a dot-probe task, in which African American and White faces were presented on a screen simultaneously for less than one second, followed by a dot where one of the faces had been. Those who had been primed with crime-relevant words were able to find the dot more quickly when it was positioned behind an African American face than when it was positioned behind a White face. This result suggests that police officers who had been induced unconsciously to think about crime paid more visual attention to African American faces than White faces.

These stereotypic associations have the potential to disadvantage African Americans in police encounters in a variety of ways. To begin with, it can bias the way individuals are perceived in the first place. In yet another study by Eberhardt and colleagues (2004), police officers rated African American faces as looking more criminal than White faces. Hurwitz and Peffley (1997) found that White participants who reported more negative stereotypes were more likely to think that a hypothetical African American suspect accused of crime was guilty, prone to commit crime again in the future, unamenable to rehabilitation, and deserving of punitive outcomes. Graham and Lowery (2004) found similar results after experimentally manipulating the accessibility of stereotypes about African Americans prior to having police- and probation-officer participants read vignettes describing juvenile offenders accused of crimes. The race of the juvenile was never stated, but officers who were primed to think of stereotypes about African Americans via subliminal exposure to words such as "homeboy" and "ghetto" perceived the juvenile as more mature, violent, culpable, and deserving of punishment compared to officers who were primed with race-neutral words (e.g., toothache, summer).

In addition, the African American criminal stereotype might lead police officers to interpret the same actions differently based on whether the individual who carries them out is African American or White. For example, Duncan (1976) found that White participants characterized an ambiguous shove as more violent when the confederate actor was African American rather than White. Devine (1989) extended this finding by showing that White participants who were primed with African American racial labels or racially stereotypic words considered a race-unidentified actor's ambiguous behaviors to be more hostile than did participants who were not primed. Therefore, even if stereotype threat does not influence African Americans to appear more suspicious-looking than White Americans in police en-counters (Najdowski, 2012), it is likely that police will be biased to perceive African Americans' behaviors as more deceptive and criminal than White Americans' regardless.

Finally, the cultural stereotype can also influence police officers' decisions about how to act in encounters with African American citizens, including actions that have deadly consequences. Specifically, Payne (2001) found that subliminal exposure to an African American face caused non-African American undergraduates to mistakenly identify objects as weapons more quickly and more often than did exposure to a White American face. Further, using a videogame to simulate encounters with citizens who are holding either guns or other objects, Correll and colleagues have demonstrated repeatedly that participants who are instructed to shoot armed targets are quicker and more accurate in deciding to shoot armed targets who are African American rather than White American, and slower and less accurate in deciding to not shoot unarmed targets who are African American rather than White American (Correll, Park, Judd, & Wittenbrink, 2002; Correll, Park,

Judd, & Wittenbrink, 2007; Correll, Park, Judd, Wittenbrink, Sadler, & Keesee, 2007; Correll, Urland, & Ito, 2006). Correll et al.'s (2006) research indicated that the racial bias in shooting decisions results from both perceiving African American targets as more threatening than White American targets and the tendency to shoot being inhibited more by White American targets than African American targets. Thus, simply encountering an African American citizen rather than a White American citizen may increase the likelihood that police officers will see guns where there are none and decide to shoot in response. Studies such as these have been used to explain the 1999 wrongful shooting of Amadou Diallo, a 23-year-old African immigrant who was shot nineteen times by four New York Police Department officers who mistook his wallet for a gun. Even so, Correll, Park, Judd, Wittenbrink, Sadler, and Keesee (2007) found that, although police were just as likely as community members to exhibit racial bias in the time it took to decide whether to shoot a target, police were less likely to exhibit racial bias in the accuracy of their shooting decisions (i.e., they were less likely to mistakenly shoot an unarmed African American man or to not shoot an armed White American man), probably due to their training and expertise.

There is some evidence that the racial bias found in the studies reviewed herein might be stronger in those who have stronger automatic associations between race and crime. For instance, Donders, Correll, and Wittenbrink (2008) found that, the more participants automatically associated African Americans with the concepts of danger, crime, violence, and murder, the more quickly and longer they visually attended to African American versus White American faces in a dot-probe task. Also, Correll and colleagues (2002, 2006) found that the more participants reported that cultural stereotypes depict African Americans as violent, the more biased they were in their responses on the shooter task. Finally, Correll, Park, Judd, and Wittenbrink (2007) demonstrated that experimentally increasing the accessibility of the African American criminal stereotype (by having participants read newspaper stories about a African American versus White American criminal or exposing participants to more African American versus White American targets with guns) exacerbated racial bias in shooting decisions.

But it is important to note that one may be well aware of the ways that African Americans are negatively stereotyped without personally accepting or endorsing such beliefs (i.e., without being racially prejudiced; see Allport, 1954). For example, although Devine and Elliot (1995) found that 84% of high-prejudiced and 78% of low-prejudiced White Americans identified "criminal" as part of the cultural stereotype of African Americans, only 44% of high-prejudiced and 0% of low-prejudiced White Americans personally characterized African Americans as criminals (see also Kreuger, 1996). Indeed, many researchers have included measures of explicit racial prejudice in their studies to determine whether it leads to more negative responses to African Americans as compared to White Americans. The consensus seems to be that conscious or explicit racial prejudice does not explain bias beyond the effects of automatic stereotypic associations between race and crime (see Devine 1989; Donders et al., 2008; Correll et al., 2002, 2006; Eberhardt et al., 2004; Graham & Lowery, 2004). Correll et al. (2002) even showed that African American community-member participants were just as likely as White Americans to be racially biased in their response times and decisions on the shooter task.

Thus, it appears that police officers who are primed with the African American criminal stereotype, via either racial or crime-related cues, are probably automatically inclined to make stereotype-consistent inferences of criminality when they encounter African American citizens, whether officers are prejudiced or not. Considering the social psychological literature on confirmation bias in hypothesis testing, it is likely that the stereotype of African American criminality becomes the hypothesis that police officers unwittingly try to prove. This process involves increasing the likelihood that the hypothesis will be confirmed by assuming it is true, focusing attention on evidence that confirms the stereotype, and ignoring alternative explanations for such evidence. (For reviews, see Gilovich, 1993; Nickerson, 1998; Nisbett & Ross, 1980; Snyder & Stukas, 1999; Trope & Liberman, 1996.) As Nickerson (1998) stated, "once a person is convinced that members of a specific group behave in certain ways, he or she is more likely to seek and find evidence to support the belief than evidence to oppose it, somewhat independently of the facts" (p. 183). Indeed, police officers who are generally biased to presume guilt have been shown to engage in biased hypothesis testing in ways that are likely to lead to wrongful convictions (see, e.g., Ask & Granhag, 2005, 2007; Findley & Scott, 2006; Kerstholt & Eikelboom, 2007; Martin, 2001; Meissner & Kassin, 2002; O'Brien, 2009).

Confirmatory hypothesis testing could explain why African Americans are perceived as more "criminal" than White Americans (Eberhardt et al., 2004), and why the same behaviors are interpreted as more violent and more hostile when the actor is African American rather than White American (Duncan, 1976; Devine, 1989). That is, those who more strongly associate African American race with crime may attend more readily to features and characteristics that lead African Americans to be seen as stereotypical, including, for example, suspicious-looking nonverbal behavior. Stereotypic associations could lead police officers to focus on citizens' nonverbal behaviors in an effort to find evidence that they are behaving suspiciously. Considering that stereotype threat leads African Americans to appear nervous in police encounters, it is likely that police officers will see innocent African Americans as suspicious without considering alternative explanations for why they might be nervous. Because stereotype threat can produce the same nonverbal behaviors police associate with deception, police officers might make inaccurate suspicion judgments on the basis of evidence that has limited diagnostic value. Further, people require less evidence to judge that an individual has a trait when it is stereotype-consistent than when it is not (Biernat, Ma, & Nario-Redmond, 2008), so it may be easier for police to see African Americans as stereotypical criminals rather than innocent. Thus, the stereotype that depicts African Americans as prone to crime can directly influence police officers' and other law enforcement officials' perceptions in ways that lead them to mistakenly target innocent African Americans as criminal suspects and to make more misclassification errors and wrongful convictions of African Americans than White Americans.

# Moving Forward: Understanding How Stereotypes of African Americans Contribute to Wrongful Convictions

The social psychological science reviewed herein shows that African Americans are concerned that police officers will stereotype them as criminals, and this stereotype threat leads African Americans to be more likely than White Americans to behave in ways that could appear suspicious to police officers (Najdowski, 2012). And, indeed, simply by virtue of living in a culture in which African Americans are stereotyped as criminals, police officers are biased to see criminality more when they encounter African Americans as compared to White Americans (e.g., Eberhardt et al., 2004). Yet the source of racial disparities in criminal justice outcomes, including wrongful convictions, cannot be pinpointed to only African Americans' concerns and behavior in police encounters or police officers' unconscious but biased predispositions. Both African Americans and police officers approach their encounters with each other with biased expectations based at the broadest level of the cultural stereotype of African American criminality. Thus, these separate areas of research should be integrated in a dynamic process approach to understand how police-citizen encounters unfold and how the stereotype contributes to racial disparities in wrongful convictions.

For example, to understand more fully the impact that African Americans' stereotype threat has on police officers' perceptions and judgments, I will have police officers view videos of participants from the Najdowski (2012) study. In that study, as described above, African American participants in a staged encounter with a security officer reported experiencing more stereotype threat and behaved more nervously than did White participants. I propose that the degree to which participants experience stereotype threat will predict police officers' ratings of how suspicious the participants look and how likely the officers would be to initiate investigatory contact with the participants. I will also test whether the spontaneous cognitive accessibility of the African American criminal stereotype, priming of stereotype-related concepts, or personal endorsement of the stereotype increases the likelihood that police officers will perceive behavior as suspicious, engage in biased hypothesis testing, and/or initiate investigatory contact in response to videos of African American versus White participants. This future research will clarify the roles that stereotype threat, implicit race-crime associations, and explicit prejudice have in leading African Americans to be disproportionately more likely than White Americans to be targeted by the police as suspects. This is critical to understanding whether African Americans' stereotype-threat-induced nervous behaviors are misinterpreted by police officers as "furtive movements," and whether this initial erroneous classification of innocent African Americans as guilty sets the stage for wrongful convictions.

The threat of being accused of a crime not committed might lead African Americans to engage in nonverbal behavior that makes them appear nervous or suspicious before a police encounter even begins, but it is also important to understand how biased expectations influence African Americans and police officers *after* contact has been initiated. According to theories on self-fulfilling prophecies and behavioral confirmation (Gilovich, 1993; Nickerson, 1998; Snyder & Stukas, 1999), based on the hypothesis that the African American criminal stereotype is true, a police officer might approach African American citizens with the presumption of guilt. An innocent African American citizen might perceive that the officer believes he or she is guilty, and, inadvertently, respond by behaving in ways that the officer perceives as deceptive or suspicious. Research bears this out. For example, Hill, Memon, and McGeorge (2008), found that observers rated mock suspects as more nervous and defensive and their denials as less plausible when suspects were paired with an interviewer who asked guilt-presumptive questions versus neutral questions, and these effects tended to be stronger for suspects who were innocent than those who were guilty. Observers also rated Kassin, Goldstein, and Savitsky's (2003) mock suspects as more defensive when they were interviewed by an investigator who expected suspects to be guilty rather than innocent, regardless of suspects' actual guilt status. Further, when suspects are paired with a guilt-presumptive interviewer, they are more likely than other suspects to be judged guilty by not only third-party observers but also by the guilt-presumptive interviewers (Kassin et al., 2003; Hill et al., 2008). In addition, Kassin and colleagues found that interviewers who had high guilt expectations rather than low guilt expectations were perceived by others and also saw themselves as exerting more pressure on suspects and trying harder to get a confession, particularly when suspects were innocent rather than guilty. In fact, interviewers used more coercive techniques when questioning innocent suspects than guilty suspects. These kinds of effects are probably amplified for

African American citizens compared to White citizens because African Americans are already concerned about being misperceived as criminals and prone to exhibiting the kinds of behaviors that police officers interpret as evidence of guilt. Thus, self-fulfilling prophecies and behavioral confirmation might create a vicious cycle whereby police officers search for information in biased ways that confirm their presumptions of African Americans' criminality, African Americans then react in ways that officers perceive as confirming their presumptions, and officers, increasingly convinced of African American suspects' guilt, engage in increasingly adversarial tactics. All of this could serve to escalate tension between African Americans and police officers during their encounters. Taken together, these processes might increase the likelihood that innocent African Americans will enter the criminal justice system. Indeed, 3% of African Americans who were stopped by the NYPD in 2012 on the basis of furtive movements were arrested, even though they were not found to be carrying any contraband or weapons (NYPD, 2013). Although some of these individuals were certainly guilty of the crimes for which they were arrested, others may not have been.

Once in the criminal justice system, a series of checks and balances should prevent such innocent individuals from being erroneously convicted, but the cultural stereotype of African American criminality can also contribute to system failures. For instance, individuals who are thought to "fit a relevant description" might be presented to witnesses in lineups or photo spreads, a significant issue not only because mistaken identifications are one of the leading causes of wrongful convictions, but also because they occur most commonly in cases involving White American witnesses and African American suspects (The National Registry of Exonerations, 2013). This could be a particular concern for highly stereotypical African Americans (e.g., those with dark skin, broad noses) given that research has shown that highly stereotypical African American faces are perceived as more criminal than not only White faces but also less stereotypical African American faces (Eberhardt et al., 2004; see also Eberhardt, Davies, Purdie-Vaughns, & Johnson, 2006).

The stereotype of African American criminality could also increase the likelihood of wrongful convictions after innocent African Americans enter the system because of stereotype threat and related behavioral manifestations in evaluative contexts. For example, to the extent that stereotype threat leads African Americans to appear nervous, investigating officers, prosecutors, judges, and jurors might doubt their credibility when they assert their innocence (see Najdowski, 2011, 2012). In addition, the stereotype might provide a hypothesis that becomes the basis of confirmation bias and tunnel vision. That is, police and other legal decision makers might become so sure of an African American individual's guilt, because it is consistent with the stereotype, that they do not search for or believe facts that suggest the individual is innocent. In some cases, criminal justice players have even been found to withhold such exculpatory evidence (e.g., in Glen Edward Chapman's case, Chapman & Curry, 2010). Such tunnel vision has been linked to an increased likelihood for innocent individuals to be wrongfully convicted rather than have their charges dismissed or be acquitted (Gould et al., 2013).

It is easy to imagine how all of the dynamic psychological processes reviewed herein have the potential to increase the likelihood that innocent African Americans will erroneously enter the criminal justice system and, ultimately, be wrongfully convicted. But understanding these processes is key to being able to interrupt them. To the extent that African Americans' encounters with police officers create a gateway to wrongful convictions, it is important to find ways to close this gateway. In particular, it is necessary to ensure that African Americans do not have to live in fear that police officers will perceive them through the lens of the cultural stereotype, which fundamentally alters African Americans' experiences of police encounters, and also to prevent police officers from being biased by the stereotype, consciously or unconsciously, which fundamentally alters their perceptions of African Americans.

Interventions aimed at increasing police legitimacy may be one strategy for achieving this goal, given that beliefs about the degree to which the police are perceived as procedurally just influence the extent to which citizens attribute police decisions and actions to racial bias (Tyler & Wakslak, 2004). For example, police officers could make a point to communicate dignity, respect, and neutrality in their interactions with African Americans and perhaps, in turn, alleviate African Americans' concerns about being stereotyped as criminals. Evidence that such a strategy might be effective comes from Mazerolle, Antrobus, Bennett, and Tyler's (2012) recent study. Results showed that actual traffic stops in which police officers used a script that highlighted citizen participation, dignity and respect, neutrality, and trustworthy motives were perceived as more procedurally just than were "business-as-usual" stops. Further, receiving the script led individuals to perceive the police as more just in general. Surely some police officers do not require a script to achieve this goal, but other officers may benefit from having these interaction components routinized into customary procedure. Ultimately, this could create trust that police officers will be fair and equal in their treatment of African and White Americans.

Another way to increase fair and just contacts between African Americans and police is to implement community policing programs, which emphasize building trust and relationships with members of the public (see, e.g., Skogan & Hartnett, 1997). In fact, increasing non-investigatory police contacts with African Americans might have the added benefit of changing police officers' expectations about encounters, too. That is, increasing police officers' non-stereotypic contacts with African Americans may, over time, reduce the strength of officers' automatic associations between the concepts of race and crime, and in turn, officers' tendency to see African Americans' skin color as evidence of criminality (see Allport, 1954; Turner, Hewstone, & Voci, 2007; but see Henry & Hardin, 2006). Although the central aim of community policing programs is to reduce crime and disorder, research should test whether giving voice to African Americans in the community and increasing non-investigatory police contacts also reduce stereotype threat and the resulting racial differences in behavior in police encounters, police officers' tendency to unconsciously associate race and crime, and, ultimately, disparities in the misclassification of innocent African Americans as criminals. Evidence is needed to determine whether police departments should prioritize programs that bolster perceptions of police legitimacy and community trust in their agendas and budgets.

Other studies could focus on testing the effectiveness of training aimed at teaching police officers to suppress stereotypes and instead inform their judgments with appropriate situational and behavioral cues (see Lee, Bumgarner, Widner, & Luo, 2007). Indeed, education in prejudice and conflict has been shown to be effective at reducing negative implicit racial associations (Rudman, Ashmore, & Gary, 2001). Thus, it could be useful to train police officers about the ways that automatic racial bias can influence their perceptions and decisions, and that, regardless of how egalitarianly motivated they may be, nonbiased responses require the intentional inhibition of automatically activated stereotypes (Devine, 1989). It could also prove fruitful to train officers about how African Americans are affected by the cultural stereotype depicting them as criminals. Such training could remind officers to check and control unconscious processes and to consider alternative explanations for suspicious-looking nonverbal behavior throughout the course of their encounters with African American citizens.

# Conclusion

The automatic biasing effects of the cultural stereotype of African American criminality on African Americans' and police officers' experiences with each other are pervasive and serious. As outlined in this chapter, the stereotype affects social psychological processes that, in turn, increase the likelihood that innocent African Americans will enter the criminal justice system. To summarize, the stereotype affects police-citizen encounters in ways that create a pipeline for the wrongful conviction of innocent African Americans. Yet there is evidence that minor procedural changes can lead police to be perceived more positively by citizens (Mazerolle et al., 2012), and training may inoculate police officers against biased perceptions and judgments (Correll, Park, Judd, Wittenbrink, Sadler, & Keesee, 2007). Such interventions could affect African Americans' and police officers' expectations in ways that enhance the fairness and justness of their interactions, as well as the outcomes thereof. To be certain, progress will be slow, because citizens' preexisting attitudes shape the way that both personal and vicarious police encounters are perceived, and have more persistent effects than intervening experiences on future attitudes (Rosenbaum et al., 2005). But there is ample opportunity for research to shed light on ways to overcome the African American criminal stereotype and, and to make novel contributions to understanding racial issues related to actual innocence. As Nelson Mandela once noted, "It always seems impossible until it's done."

# References

Allport, G. W. (1954). *The nature of prejudice.* Reading, PA: Addison-Wesley.

Akehurst, L., Köhnken, G., Vrij, A., & Bull, R. (1996). Lay persons' and police officers' beliefs regarding deceptive behaviour. *Applied Cognitive Psychology, 10,* 461–471.

Ask, K., & Granhag, P. A. (2005). Motivational sources of confirmation bias in criminal investigations: The need for cognitive closure. *Journal of Applied Social Psychology, 37,* 561–591.

Ask, K., & Granhag, P. A. (2007). Motivational bias in criminal investigators' judgments of witness reliability. *Journal of Applied Social Psychology, 37,* 561–591.

Beckett, K., Nyrop, K., Pfingst, L., & Brown, M. (2005). Drug use, drug possession arrests, and the question of race: Lessons from Seattle. *Social Problems, 52,* 419–441.

Biernat, M., Ma, J. E., & Nario-Redmond, M. R. (2008). Standards to suspect and diagnose stereotypical traits. *Social Cognition, 26,* 288–313.

Bosson, J. K., Haymovitz, E. L., & Pinel, E. C. (2004). When saying and doing diverge: The effects of stereotype threat on self-reported versus non-verbal anxiety. *Journal of Experimental Social Psychology, 40,* 247–255.

Carlson, D. K. (2004, July 20). Racial profiling seen as pervasive, unjust. Retrieved from www.gallup.com/poll/12406/Racial-Profiling-Seen-Pervasive-Unjust.aspx

Chapman, G. E., & Curry, A. (2010). *Life after death row: The true story of Glen Edward Chapman.* Asheville, NC: Brave Ulysses Books.

Coker, D. (2003). Foreward: Addressing the real world of racial injustice in the criminal justice system. *The Journal of Criminal Law and Criminology, 93,* 827–880.

Correll, J., Park, B., Judd, C. M., & Wittenbrink, B. (2002). The police officer's dilemma: Using ethnicity to disambiguate potentially threatening individuals. *Journal of Personality and Social Psychology, 83,* 1314–1329.

Correll, J., Park, B., Judd, C. M., & Wittenbrink, B. (2007). The influence of stereotypes on decisions to shoot. *European Journal of Social Psychology, 37*, 1102–1117.

Correll, J., Park, B., Judd, C. M., Wittenbrink, B., Sadler, M. S., & Keesee, T. (2007). Across the thin blue line: Police officers and racial bias in the decision to shoot. *Journal of Personality and Social Psychology, 92*, 1006–1023.

Correll, J., Urland, G. R., & Ito, T. A. (2006). Event-related potentials and the decision to shoot: The role of threat perception and cognitive control. *Journal of Experimental Social Psychology, 42*, 120–128.

Devine, P. G. (1989). Stereotypes and prejudice: Their automatic and controlled components. *Journal of Personality and Social Psychology, 56*, 5–18.

Devine, P. G., & Elliot, A. J. (1995). Are racial stereotypes really fading? The Princeton trilogy revisited. *Personality and Social Psychology Bulletin, 21*, 1139–1150.

Donders, N. C., Correll, J., & Wittenbrink, B. (2008). Danger stereotypes predict racially biased attentional allocation. *Journal of Experimental Social Psychology, 44*, 1328–1333.

Duncan, B. L. (1976). Differential social perception and attribution of intergroup violence: Testing the lower limits of stereotyping of Blacks. *Journal of Personality and Social Psychology, 34*, 590–598.

Duru, N. J. (2004). The Central Park Five, the Scottsboro Boys, and the myth of the bestial Black man. *Cardozo Law Review, 25*, 1315–1366.

Eberhardt, J. L., Goff, P. A., Purdie, V. J., & Davies, P. G. (2004). Seeing Black: Race, crime, and visual processing. *Journal of Personality and Social Psychology, 87*, 876–893.

Eberhardt, J. L., Davies, P. G., Purdie-Vaughns, V. J., & Johnson, S. L. (2006). Looking deathworthy: Perceived stereotypicality of Black defendants predicts capital-sentencing outcomes. *Psychological Science, 17*, 383–386.

Engel, R. S., Smith, M. R., & Cullen, F. T. (2012). Race, place, and drug enforcement. *Criminology & Public Policy, 11*, 603–635.

Findley, K. A., & Scott, M. S. (2006). The multiple dimensions of tunnel vision in criminal cases. *Wisconsin Law Review, 2*, 291–397.

Floyd v. City of New York, 08 Civ. 2274 (SAS), U.S. Dist. LEXIS 113205, (S.D.N.Y., August 12, 2013).

Gelman, A., Fagan, J., & Kiss, A. (2005). An analysis of the NYPD's stop-and-frisk policy in the context of claims of racial bias. *Journal of the American Statistical Association, 102*, 813–823.

Gilovich, T. (1993). *How we know what isn't so: The fallibility of human reason in everyday life.* New York: The Free Press.

Gould, J., Carrano, J., Leo, R. A., & Young, J. K. (2013, March 1). *Predicting erroneous convictions: A social science approach to miscarriages of justice.* University of San Francisco Law Research Paper No. 2013–20. Available at SSRN: http://ssrn.com/abstract=2231777.

Graham, S., & Lowery, B. S. (2004). Priming unconscious racial stereotypes about adolescent offenders. *Law and Human Behavior, 28*, 483–504.

Gross, S. R., Jacoby, K., Matheson, D. J., Montgomery, N., & Patil, S. (2005). Exonerations in the United States 1989 through 2003. *The Journal of Criminal Law and Criminology, 95*, 523–560.

Hagan, J., & Albonetti, C. (1982). Race, class, and the perception of criminal injustice in America. *American Journal of Sociology, 88*, 329–355.

Hagan, J., Shedd, C., & Payne, M. R. (2005). Race, ethnicity, and youth perceptions of criminal injustice. *American Sociological Review, 70*, 381–407.

Henry, P. J., & Hardin, C. D. (2006). The contact hypothesis revisited: Status bias in the reduction of implicit prejudice in the United States and Lebanon. *Psychological Science, 17,* 862–868.

Hill, C., Memon, A., & McGeorge, P. (2008). The role of confirmation bias in suspect interviews: A systematic evaluation. *Legal and Criminological Psychology, 13,* 357–371.

Hurwitz, J., & Peffley, M. (1997). Public perceptions of race and crime: The role of racial stereotypes. *American Journal of Political Science, 41,* 375–401.

Kassin, S. M., Goldstein, C. C., & Savitsky, K. (2003). Behavioral confirmation in the interrogation room: On the dangers of presuming guilt. *Law and Human Behavior, 27,* 187–203.

Kerstholt, J. H., & Eikelboom, A. R. (2007). Effects of prior interpretation on situation assessment in crime analysis. *Journal of Behavioral Decision Making, 20,* 455–465.

Kreuger, J. (1996). Personal beliefs and cultural stereotypes about racial characteristics. *Journal of Personality and Social Psychology, 71,* 536–548.

Lee, Y.-T., Bumgarner, J., Widner, R., & Luo, Z.-L. (2007). Psychological models of stereotyping and profiling in law enforcement: How to increase accuracy by using more non-racial cues. *Journal of Crime and Justice, 30,* 87–129.

Leo, R., & Drizin, S. (2010). The three errors: Pathways to false confession and wrongful conviction. In D. Lassiter & C. Meissner (Eds.) *Interrogations and confessions: Current research, practice, and policy recommendations* (pp. 9–30). Washington, DC: American Psychological Association.

Ludwig, J. (2003, May 13). *Americans see racial profiling as widespread.* Retrieved from http://www.gallup.com/poll/8389/Americans-See-Racial-Profiling-Widespread.aspx

Madon, S., Guyll, M., Aboufadel, K., Montiel, E., Smith, A., Palumbo, P., & Jussim, L. (2001). Ethnic and national stereotypes: The Princeton trilogy revisited and revised. *Personality and Social Psychology Bulletin, 27,* 996–1010.

Mazerolle, L., Antrobus, E., Bennett, S., & Tyler, T. R. (2012). Shaping citizen perceptions of police legitimacy: A randomized field trial of procedural justice. *Criminology, 51,* 1–31.

Martin, D. L. (2001). Lessons about justice from the "laboratory" of wrongful convictions: Tunnel vision, the construction of guilt and informer evidence. *University of Missouri-Kansas City Law Review, 70,* 847–864.

Meissner, C. A., & Kassin, S. M. (2002). "He's guilty!": Investigator bias in judgments of truth and deception. *Law and Human Behavior, 26,* 469–480.

Najdowski, C. J. (2011). Stereotype threat in criminal interrogations: Why innocent Black suspects are at risk for confessing falsely. *Psychology, Public Policy, and Law, 17,* 562–591.

Najdowski, C. J. (2012). *Stereotype threat in police encounters: Why African Americans are at risk of being targeted as suspects.* (Unpublished doctoral dissertation). University of Illinois at Chicago.

Najdowski, C. J., Bottoms, B. L., & Goff, P. A. (2013). *Racial differences in experiences of police encounters: Effects on stereotype threat, psychological correlates, and anticipated behavior.* Manuscript in preparation.

The National Registry of Exonerations (2013, April 3). *Update: 2012: The National Registry of Exonerations.* Retrieved from https://www.law.umich.edu/special/exoneration/Documents/NRE2012UPDATE4_1_13_FINAL.pdf.

New York Civil Liberties Union (NYCLU). (2013). *NYPD stop-and-frisk activity in 2012.* Retrieved from http://www.nyclu.org/files/publications/2012_Report_NYCLU_0.pdf

New York Police Department (NYPD). (2013). *The stop, question and frisk data* [SPSS portable file]. Retrieved from http://www.nyc.gov/html/nypd/html/analysis_and _planning/stop_question_and_frisk_report.shtml.

Nickerson, R. S. (1998). Confirmation bias: A ubiquitous phenomenon in many guises. Review of General Psychology, 2, 175–220.

Nisbett, R. E., & Ross, L. (1980). *Human inference: Strategies and shortcomings in social judgment*. Englewood Cliffs, NJ: Prentice-Hall

O'Brien, B. (2009). Prime suspect: An examination of factors that aggravate and counteract confirmation bias in criminal investigations. *Psychology, Public Policy, and Law, 15,* 315–334.

Oliver, M. B. (2003). African American men as "criminal and dangerous": Implications of media portrayals of crime on the "criminalization" of African American men. *Journal of African American Studies, 7,* 3–18.

Payne, B. K. (2001). Prejudice and perception: The role of automatic and controlled processes in misperceiving a weapon. *Journal of Personality and Social Psychology, 81,* 181–192.

Rastogi, S., Johnson, T. D., Hoeffel, E. M., & Drewery, M. P. (2011). *The Black population: 2010*. Washington, D.C.: U.S. Census Bureau.

Richardson, L. S., & Goff, P. A. (2012). Self-defense and the suspicion heuristic. *Iowa Law Review, 13,* 293–336.

Rome, D. (2004). *Black demons: The media's depiction of the African American male criminal stereotype*. Westport, CT: Praeger Publishers.

Rosenbaum, D. P., Schuck, A. M., Costello, S. K., Hawkins, D. F., & Ring, M. K. (2005). Attitudes toward the police: The effects of direct and vicarious experience. *Police Quarterly, 8,* 343–365.

Rudman, L. A., Ashmore, R. D., & Gary, M. L. (2001). "Unlearning" automatic biases: The malleability of implicit prejudice and stereotypes. *Journal of Personality and Social Psychology, 81,* 856–868.

Sampson, R. J., & Raudenbush, S. W. (2004). Seeing disorder: Neighborhood stigma and the social construction of "broken windows." *Social Psychology Quarterly, 67,* 319–342.

Schmader, T., Johns, M., & Forbes, C. (2008). An integrated process model of stereotype threat effects on performance. *Psychological Review, 115,* 336–356.

Sigelman, L., & Tuch, S. A. (1997). Metastereotypes: Blacks' perceptions of Whites' stereotypes of Blacks. *The Public Opinion Quarterly, 61,* 87–101.

Skogan, W. G., & Hartnett, S. M. (1997). *Community policing: Chicago style*. New York: Oxford University Press.

Snyder, M., & Stukas, A. A. (1999). Interpersonal processes: The interplay of cognitive, motivational, and behavioral activities in social interaction. *Annual Review of Psychology, 50,* 273–303.

Steele, C. M., & Aronson, J. (1995). Stereotype threat and the intellectual test performance of African Americans. *Journal of Personality and Social Psychology, 69,* 797–811.

Stroshine, M., Alpert, G., & Dunham, R. (2008). The influence of "working rules" on police suspicion and discretionary decision making. *Police Quarterly, 11,* 315–337.

Trope, Y., & Liberman, A. (1996). Social hypothesis testing: Cognitive and motivational mechanisms. In E. T. Higgins & A. E. Kruglanski (Eds.), *Social psychology: Handbook of basic principles*, pp. 239–270. New York: Guilford Press.

Turner, R. N., Hewstone, M., & Voci, A. (2007). Reducing explicit and implicit outgroup prejudice via direct and extended contact: The mediating role of self-disclosure and intergroup anxiety. *Journal of Personality and Social Psychology, 93,* 369–388.

Tyler, T. R., & Wakslak, C. J. (2004). Profiling and police legitimacy: Procedural justice, attributions of motive, and acceptance of police authority. *Criminology, 42,* 253–282.

Vrij, A., Akehurst, L., & Knight, S. (2006). Police officers', social workers', teachers' and the general public's beliefs about deception in children, adolescents and adults. *Legal and Criminological Psychology, 11,* 297–312.

Vrij, A., & Semin, G. R. (1996). Lie experts' beliefs about nonverbal indicators of deception. *Journal of Nonverbal Behavior, 20,* 65–80.

Vrij, A., & Winkel, F. W. (1992). Social skills, distorted perception, and being suspect: Studies in impression formation and the ability to deceive. *Journal of Police and Criminal Psychology, 8,* 2–5.

Weitzer, R., & Tuch, S. A. (2002). Perceptions of racial profiling: Race, class, and personal experience. *Criminology, 40,* 435–456.

Welch, K. (2007). Black criminal stereotypes and racial profiling. *Journal of Contemporary Criminal Justice, 23,* 276–288.

# Chapter Five

# The Media's Muddled Message on Wrongful Convictions

Martin Yant

The media have long been a mass of contradictions when it comes to wrongful convictions. On the one hand, they contribute to them by either passively presenting the official version of a criminal case or actively spreading prejudicial misinformation about the accused. On the other hand—especially in recent years—they investigate old cases and help free innocent inmates who have often languished in prison for decades. When a new perceived criminal outrage surfaces, though, the media start the vicious cycle all over again with credulous coverage of the official version of what happened and who is responsible.

This chapter traces the media's involvement in miscarriages of justice from the 1800s to the modern DNA era, focusing both on cases in which they contributed to the conviction and those in which they uncovered errors. It concludes with a discussion of what the media can do to ensure more accurate and responsible coverage.

## Stepping Back: Covering Justice, Fostering Injustice

Warden (2002) notes that, "Throughout most of history, until quite recently, journalism generally was hostile to claims of innocence by those convicted or accused of serious crimes." Before trial, he says, sensational news stories often were "published in concert with police and prosecutors under pressure to convict someone without credible evidence." Afterward, coverage of new evidence of innocence "was subdued and devoid of any explicit suggestion that there might be systemic problems" (p. 2).

Contributions to exonerations by the press were usually inadvertent in the nineteenth century. Warden (2002) cites the example of the first documented wrongful conviction in the United States. Jesse and Stephen Boorn of Vermont were convicted and sentenced to death in 1819 for the murder of their brother-in-law, Russell Colvin, who had disappeared seven years earlier. When news of the Boorn brothers' conviction appeared in the *New York Evening Post*, however, the story piqued the interest of a traveler who knew a man named Russell Colvin in New Jersey who had told him he had previously lived in Vermont. The man eventually spirited a reluctant Colvin away to Vermont, where he was identified as the Boorns' supposedly murdered brother-in-law. Warden (2005) relates how publicity about the case made its way to England, where Wilkie Collins, in 1873, turned the tale into the novel, *The Dead Alive*.

*The Dead Alive* was not the first novel inspired by a wrongful conviction, however. That occurred in France, where Alexandre Dumas read a collection of intriguing tales about criminal cases written by Jacques Peuchet, a former archivist for the Paris police. One of the cases discussed (Peuchet & Bair, translator, 2011) was that of Francois Picaud, who was framed on charges of being an alleged British spy in 1807 by jealous acquaintances and spent seven years in prison. During his incarceration, Peuchet said, Picaud befriended a rich Italian priest who left him his fortune when he died. After his release from prison, Peuchet wrote, Picaud used his wealth and some elaborate disguises to befriend and then murder those who framed him. Dumas transformed Peuchet's story into the literary classic *The Count of Monte Cristo* in 1844.

But Dumas' cautionary tale of injustice based on the case of a man falsely accused of being a spy did not prevent Captain Alfred Dreyfus from being framed for being a spy in 1895. Dreyfus became a suspect when the French military learned that someone was leaking information to the German Embassy. Read (2012) documents how officials suppressed evidence that another officer was responsible for the leaks until the information reached famed literary lion Emile Zola, who became perhaps the first writer to expose a wrongful conviction. In a lengthy front-page letter in the Paris daily *L'Aurore* on January 13, 1898, boldly headlined, "J'accuse!" Zola accused top officials by name of anti-Semitism and obstruction of justice in the framing of Dreyfus and dared them to prosecute him for libel.

Zola got his wish. He was convicted a month later, but he fled to England rather than go to jail. Zola's impassioned recitation of the facts of the Dreyfus affair and his prosecution created such a furor that it helped spur the government's collapse in 1899 right after he defiantly returned to Paris. Dreyfus was freed and later fully exonerated by the French Supreme Court.

The power of the pen in the righting a wrong in the Dreyfus affair was an important precedent, but it was more of a recitation of facts uncovered by an officer, who got transferred to Africa for his efforts, rather than investigative journalism. It would be another famous writer across the English Channel to first perform that feat.

Sir Arthur Conan Doyle, creator of the famed private detective Sherlock Holmes, was overwhelmed with requests from around the world for Holmes' or his own help solving mysteries since the first Holmes story appeared in 1887. One letter caught his eye, in part because it included an intriguing article about the conviction of George Edalji for one of a string of bizarre mutilations of farm animals near Birmingham. Edalji, a young solicitor, was the son of an Indian immigrant who had married an Englishwoman and had served as a vicar of a small parish for over 30 years. Someone apparently did not approve of the family's mixed ethnic heritage, and the family started receiving anonymous threatening letters in 1895. The family was also the target of bogus newspaper ads.

The area's chief constable decided that Edalji was sending the letters and placing the ads himself to gain attention. He could not prove it, though, and no charges were filed. Then, in 1903, came a series of strange animal mutilations and anonymous letters accusing Edalji of being behind the attacks. With the help of an already discredited handwriting expert and possibly planted evidence, the chief constable was finally able to charge Edalji, who was convicted and sentenced to seven years in prison. The case was so weak and the evidence of bigotry so great that 10,000 people signed a petition demanding that Edalji be freed. The protests apparently worked, and Edalji was released after three years without explanation.

Symons (1979) and Oldfield (2010) recount how the mysterious nature of the anonymous letters, the strange animal mutilations and the offensive prejudice in the case struck a nerve with Conan Doyle. "As I read, the unmistakable accent of truth forced itself upon my attention, and I realized that I was in the presence of an appalling tragedy, and that I was called upon to do what I could to set it right," Conan Doyle later wrote (Symons, 1979, p. 76).

Conan Doyle worked 12 hours a day for eight months applying the principles of observation and deduction he had popularized in his Sherlock Holmes stories. When he was finished, Conan Doyle wrote two articles totaling 18,000 words for the *Daily Telegraph* that eviscerated the case against Edalji. Because Conan Doyle asked that the articles be published free of copyright, they were republished in newspapers and magazines around the world. The *Daily Telegraph* capitalized on the work with an editorial headlined, "Sherlock Holmes at Work." It was as if Sherlock Holmes, one of the most famous fictional figures in history, had suddenly come to life, and his millions of fans were thrilled. The legal establishment and law enforcement were not amused, however, and fought to preserve Edalji's conviction. Under immense pressure, Home Secretary Herbert Gladstone established a Committee of Enquiry. The committee cleared Edalji of the animal mutilation but ruled that, since he may have written the letters, which he was never convicted of, Edalji should not be compensated for his wrongful conviction. Conan Doyle was incensed. He said the finding was part of an effort "to admit nothing which inculpates another official … for offenses which have caused misery to helpless victims" (Symons, 1979, p. 78). Many members of Parliament were equally outraged. The resulting furor led to the creation of the Court of Appeal to review future questionable convictions.

Symons (1979) and Borchard (1932) detail how Conan Doyle reluctantly became involved in another apparent miscarriage of justice after Oscar Slater was convicted in Edinburgh of murdering a woman with a hammer and sentenced to death in 1909. Police claimed that Slater pawned a brooch stolen from the victim after the murder and then sailed to the United States under an assumed name. In an 80-page booklet, *The Case of Oscar Slater*, Doyle noted that the brooch Slater pawned did not match the victim's and that the hammer with which he allegedly beat her was too small to make the wounds on her body. He also argued that Slater had made reservations for his transatlantic trip before the murder and the reason he did not use his real name was that he was traveling with his mistress and did not want his wife to find out.

The press and officials were mostly hostile to Conan Doyle's efforts this time, though, and Slater remained in prison. But the case gained new traction in 1925, when William Park published a book called *The Truth About Oscar Slater* that confirmed Doyle's conclusions and added more evidence of Slater's innocence. The book revealed that, in 1914, a detective had discovered evidence that had been concealed from Slater's attorney. (For his diligence, the detective was fired and charged on trumped-up charges but eventually acquitted.) As criticism of the case grew, Slater was released in 1927. Conan Doyle and others then financed a legal effort to clear Slater's name, and he eventually was awarded compensation for his wrongful conviction (Borchard, 1932; Symons, 1979).

Journalists in the United States were slower to get on the exoneration bandwagon, and before they did they helped perpetrate a horrible injustice in the Leo Frank case in 1915. Van Woodward (1963) and Wade (1997) relate that a chief precipitator in the hysteria that led to Frank's dubious conviction for the 1913 murder of 13-year-old Mary Phagan and his subsequent lynching was Thomas E. Watson, publisher of *The Jeffersonian*, a populist weekly newspaper.

News of Phagan's murder set off heated competition between *The Atlanta Constitution* and *The Georgian*, during which photos were doctored and evidence stolen by reporters. When the investigation focused on Frank, a Jewish transplant from New York, news coverage took a decidedly anti-Semitic slant that helped spur his conviction. When the governor commuted Frank's death sentence to life in 1915, publisher Watson suggested that "lynch law … shows that a sense of justice lives among the people" (Woodward, p.

374). A short time later, Frank was abducted from prison and lynched. Afterward, Watson approvingly wrote that "the voice of the people is the voice of God" (Woodward, p. 445). Woodward says Watson's anti-Semitic slant on the case paid off. *The Jeffersonian's* circulation rose from 25,000 to 87,000 between the murder and Frank's lynching.

Warden (2002) and Borchard (1932) report that the first example of the U.S. press playing an active role in an exoneration occurred three years later, when an investigation by *The New York World* led to the release of Charles F. Stielow and Nelson L. Green. Based on confessions and ballistics evidence, the two farmhands were convicted in 1915 for the 1913 murders of their wealthy employer and his housekeeper. But *The World* and a private investigator it retained soon developed evidence that two other men had committed the murders. That prompted the governor to order a new investigation, which uncovered secret recordings that showed Stielow and Green never confessed to the murders and determined that the ballistics evidence against them was bogus. The governor pardoned both men in 1918.

The year 1932 began auspiciously for those who cared about miscarriages of justice with the publication of Edwin M. Borchard's seminal book, *Convicting the Innocent: Sixty-Five Actual Errors of Criminal Justice.* But Americans were in no mood to listen to such facts after the 20-month-old son of aviation hero Charles Lindbergh was kidnapped on March 1, 1932, and his body was found two months later. The press quickly assumed a prosecutorial tone with the arrest of German immigrant Bruno Richard Hauptmann in 1934. Regardless of his guilt or innocence, "The press veritably railroaded [Hauptmann] into the New Jersey electric chair in 1936" (Warden, 2002, p. 3). Hauptmann's conviction in "the trial of the century" set the standard for media excess. Kennedy (1996) notes that Hauptmann's ineffective lead counsel, the hard-drinking Edward Riley, was hired by newspaper publisher William Randolph Hearst in return for his reporters' exclusive access to the Hauptmann family.

Headlines routinely identified Hauptmann as the kidnapper and killer without qualification as soon as he was arrested. *The New York Journal* even turned random interviews with 12 people into a jury of Hauptmann's peers. The paper reported that its randomly selected jury "found [Hauptmann], on the basis of evidence deduced, guilty of both extortion and complicity in the actual kidnapping" (Warden, 2002, p. 4). Of course, the evidence on which the jurors based their verdict was highly slanted by the hysterical news coverage of the case.

The evidence the jury heard at Hauptmann's trial may not have been much more complete, arguably rendering Hauptmann's fate "a classic case of conviction based on an intricate web of circumstantial evidence, perjury, prosecutorial suppression of evidence, a grossly incompetent defense attorney, and a trial atmosphere of near-hysteria" (Bedau & Radelet, 1987, pp. 124–125).

The journalistic pendulum of justice swung to both extremes in Chicago in the 1940s. In the case of William G. Heirens, the pendulum swung strongly toward injustice. Heirens' problems started when *The Chicago Tribune* published a false story saying that the University of Chicago student had confessed to the murder and dismemberment of six-year-old Suzanne Degnan and the murders of Josephine Ross and Frances Brown, on whose bedroom wall police found the plea, scrawled in lipstick, "For heaven's sake, catch me before I kill more" (Warden, 202, p. 7). Reporters did their best to grant "the Lipstick Killer's" request that he be caught by possibly planting evidence and enhancing the writing on a ransom note found at Degnan's residence. "Chicago's five daily newspapers covered the case sensationally and irresponsibly in the manner immortalized by Ben Hecht and Charles MacArthur in *The Front Page.* The result was a lynch-mob atmosphere in which the Chicago police and Cook County state's attorney's office were under enormous pressure to solve the crime" (Warden, 2002, p. 7).

The July 29, 1946, issue of *Time* magazine reported that "Chicago's raucous dailies ... romped through the Heirens story like street urchins frolicking at an open hydrant....

He had not yet been charged with murder, but *The Tribune* airily convicted him: HOW HEIRENS SLEW 3" (see, http://content.time.com/time/subscriber/article/0,33009,776968, 00.html).

In addition to being the target of prejudicial publicity, Heirens was the victim of bad timing. According to Warden (2002), word that a convicted child molester had confessed in Phoenix to the murder of Degnan reached Chicago after police had already identified Heirens as the murderer. Officials had already been forced to drop charges against another man, and they were not about to do it a second time.

Desperate to save his life, Heirens' attorneys pressured the seventeen-year-old to agree to confess and plead guilty to avoid the death penalty, which he did after six days of questioning. But Heirens quickly recanted his confessions, which were later found to contain 29 inconsistencies with the known facts, and the evidence that surfaced over the next six decades backed his claim of innocence, as reported by Adam Higginbotham in *GQ* magazine in 2008:

> The fingerprints connecting him to the crime scenes may well have been planted. Independent experts have shown that his handwriting matches neither the Degnan ransom note nor the lipstick scrawl on the wall of Frances Brown's apartment; indeed, veteran newspapermen in Chicago say that the message of the Lipstick Killer wasn't written by the murderer at all but by a reporter who arrived at the scene before police and decided to add an extra twist to the story. In the meantime, the decay of physical evidence has placed the case far beyond the reach of DNA analysis (see, http://www.gq.com/news-politics/big-issues/200805/william-heirens-lipstick-killer-chicago).

But because of his experience with the press at the time of his convictions, Heirens always remained wary of journalists ("I think they're willing to sell out their mother if they could," he told Higginbotham) his case never got the kind of coverage it deserved. Heirens' appeals and petitions for clemency were routinely rejected, and he died in prison in 2012.

Ironically, the Chicago press' pendulum of justice had swung completely in the other direction the year before, when *The Chicago Times* reversed a wrongful conviction. Equally important, the case would be dramatized in a popular 1948 movie that suddenly made a journalist freeing innocent inmates a fashionable pursuit.

According to Warden (2002) and Howard (1946), the story started on October 10, 1944, when a classified ad ran in *The Chicago Times* that offered a $5,000 reward for information on who killed a Chicago police officer on December 9, 1932. When reporter James McGuire called the phone number listed in the ad, he ended up talking to Tillie Majczek, the mother of Joseph Majczek, who had been convicted in the murder along with his friend, Theodore Marcinkiewicz. Tillie Majczek told McGuire she had spent the past decade scrubbing floors to save up money for the reward. In a series of stories, co-written by McGuire and John J. McPhaul, *The Times* reported that the since-deceased judge who heard the case had expressed doubts about Majczek and Marcinkiewicz's guilt and that Vera Walush, whose testimony was the only evidence against Majczek and the primary evidence against Marcinkiewicz, had identified them as the killers only after being threatened with arrest. *The Times* also confirmed both defendants' alibis and discredited the testimony of two other witnesses. *The Times* then hired an attorney to represent Majczek, whose mother's devotion prompted the paper's interest, and he received a pardon in 1945. Marcinkiewicz was left to fend for himself, however, and his conviction was finally overturned in 1950. Majczek was later awarded $24,000 and Marcinkiewicz $35,000 in compensation. *Call Northside 777*, the movie about the case starring Jimmy Stewart and Lee J. Cobb, was released in 1948. The film was well received, and won an Edgar Award from the Mystery Writers of America for best motion picture.

Exonerating innocent inmates was suddenly becoming a popular pursuit. Even Perry Mason entered the fray in the 1940s in the person of the famed fictional attorney's creator, Erle Stanley Gardner. Yant (1991) tells how, in the 1940s, Gardner formed The Court of Last Resort, a panel of experts supported by *Argosy* magazine that reviewed and attempted to reverse wrongful convictions. In 1948, Gardner and his associates developed enough evidence to win the release of Clarence Boggie, who had been wrongly convicted of murder in 1935. In 1951, Gardner also persuaded the governor of West Virginia to stay the scheduled execution of Robert Ballard Bailey based on his group's investigation. After Gardner developed additional evidence, Bailey was released on a conditional pardon, which became unconditional in 1966. Gardner's expert panel's efforts became so popular that he published some of its success stories in the book *The Court of Last Resort* in 1952. A show with the same name appeared on NBC-TV in the 1957–1958 season. A similar British show, *Rough Justice,* appeared on the BBC from 1981 to 2007. It was credited with helping win the release of 18 wrongly convicted people.

*Inside Detective*, a pulp magazine similar to *Argosy,* also won the release of a man on Ohio's death row in 1957, when a woman in Texas read Bundy's wife's plea for someone to save her husband's life. The story reminded reader Norma Brajnovic of a conversation she had had with a man who looked like Russell McCoy, who was pictured in the article and identified as the key witness against Bundy. Brajnovic came forward to reveal McCoy had told her he had killed four people and was going to kill another one legally by implicating the man who told police he had committed two of the murders in the other two he had committed. Brajnovic's statement helped win Bundy a new trial, at which he was acquitted (Yant, 1991).

But Ohio courts and the news media were not nearly as friendly to another defendant in the 1950s, Dr. Sam Sheppard. Sheppard's ordeal began in the early hours of July 4, 1954, when he called police to report that he had found his wife, Marilyn, brutally beaten in her bed and that he had been knocked out by a tall, bushy-headed man as he fled. Coverage was neutral until rumors swirled about Sheppard's alleged affairs and aloofness. Then, Louis Seltzer, head of the *Cleveland Press*, threw down the gauntlet with a front-page editorial headlined, "Somebody is Getting Away with Murder."

At this time, newspaper circulation was beginning to decline, especially for the afternoon dailies, which were trying to remain relevant with more aggressive coverage. So it was not surprising that the afternoon *Cleveland Press* would ride a sensational murder case hard—especially with the hardboiled Seltzer at the helm. According to Neff (2001), Seltzer prided himself in being a man of the people.

"If ever a murder case was studded with fumbling, halting, stupid, uncooperative bumbling politeness to people whose place in this situation completely justified vigorous, searching, prompt and effective police work—the Sheppard case has them all," Seltzer fumed. He added that Sheppard "ought to have been subjected instantly to the same third degree to which any other person under similar circumstances is subjected." Another front page editorial asked, "Why Isn't Sam Sheppard in Jail?" Sheppard was arrested the same day (Neff, 2001, p. 84).

Sheppard's case was the first in which television news coverage was a factor. Investigators started pursuing every rumor and leaking lurid, often inaccurate, details to the press. The national media soon picked up on the case. By the time Sheppard went to trial, celebrity journalists like Dorothy Kilgallen and Walter Winchell, network correspondents and reporters from around the world were there to watch the show, which ended with Sheppard's conviction. It took 12 years for Sheppard's appeal to make it to the U.S. Supreme Court. The court rendered a scathing opinion on June 6, 1966, reversing a conviction for the first time because of prejudicial publicity. Writing for the majority, Justice Tom Clark said:

Much of the material printed or broadcast during the trial was never heard from the witness stand, such as the charges that Sheppard had purposely impeded the murder investigation and must be guilty since he had hired a prominent criminal lawyer; that Sheppard was a perjurer; that he had sexual relations with numerous women; that his slain wife had characterized him as a "Jekyll-Hyde" that he was "a bare-faced liar" because of his testimony as to police treatment; and finally, that a woman convict claimed Sheppard to be the father of her illegitimate child.…

Nor is there doubt that this deluge of publicity reached at least some of the jury. On the only occasion that the jury was queried, two jurors admitted in open court to hearing the highly inflammatory charge that a prison inmate claimed Sheppard as the father of her illegitimate child. Despite the extent and nature of the publicity to which the jury was exposed during trial, the judge refused defense counsel's other requests that the jurors be asked whether they had read or heard specific prejudicial comment about the case, including the incidents we have previously summarized. In these circumstances, we can assume that some of this material reached members of the jury (*Sheppard v. Maxwell*, 1966).

For once, the Sam Sheppard case was downplayed in Cleveland. *The Plain Dealer* buried its story about the landmark Supreme Court decision on page 7. *The Press* put the story on the front page, but there was no banner headline this time. The story only merited a small one-column headline. Prosecutors continued to claim that the Sheppard jury was not influenced by the press coverage of the case. But Neff (2001) learned otherwise when he interviewed the five surviving jurors. "Their opinions are eye-opening, even shocking.… Clearly, the jury had been contaminated by press accounts before the trial and perhaps during it" (Neff, 2001, pp. 166–167). The jurors repeated several accusations made in the press but not in court as reasons they found Sheppard guilty.

Coverage was remarkably restrained when Sheppard was retried in late 1966, and the jury returned a verdict of not guilty. Sheppard, however, was a broken man. He died four years later of liver failure caused by excessive drinking. But he left the legacy of a press that was a little more careful with how it covered criminal cases and a judiciary that sought to limit the effects prejudicial publicity.

Even before the Supreme Court's Sheppard decision, though, the news media had made a remarkable shift from the free-wheeling times of Sheppard's first trial. Journalists had become better-educated and better-mannered. They began to consider journalism a profession rather than a trade and took their role more seriously. American society had changed a lot as well. The civil rights and anti-war movements challenged authority in unprecedented ways. And the Sheppard decision was only one of a series of pro-defendant rulings by the U.S. Supreme Court that caused people to rethink their great deference to law enforcement and the courts.

Fittingly, one of the most popular TV shows from 1963 to 1967 was *The Fugitive*. Although the show's creators insisted it was not inspired by the Sheppard case, it had many similarities. The show's sole theme was prison escapee Dr. Richard Kimble's dogged pursuit of the one-armed man he saw fleeing his house, where he found his wife murdered—a crime for which Kimble would be unjustly convicted. Kimble was able to stay on the run only with the help of strangers who took risks to aid his quest for justice. When Kimble was exonerated after he caught up with the one-armed man in the show's final episode in August 1967, it was the most-watched show in television history (*Justice Denied*, 2007, pp. 25–26).

This jaundiced view of justice spilled over into the real world. In 1964, investigative reporter Edward Radin's book, *The Innocents*, highlighted 80 wrongful convictions. *Miami*

*Herald* reporter Gene Miller won the Pulitzer Prize in 1967 for investigations that led to the release of Joe Shea and Mary Hampton, both of whom had been convicted of murders they did not commit. Miller won a second Pulitzer in 1976 for his reporting on the case of Freddie Pitts and Wilbert Lee, who were wrongly convicted and sentenced to death in 1963 for the murders of two gas station attendants in Port St. Joe, Florida (Yant, 1991).

In 1975, *The Detroit News* spent an estimated $75,000 investigating the murder convictions of four Detroit-area motorcycle gang members who were sentenced to death in New Mexico in 1974 for the murder of man was also sodomized and had his penis amputated. The newspaper helped document that Thomas Gladish, Richard Greer, Ronald Keine and Clarence Smith were wrongly implicated by inaccurate polygraph exams, a witness police coerced into her identifications of them, and botched ballistics tests. The men were finally freed after a drifter and drug addict confessed to the crime (Bedau & Radelet, 1987). Even *Playboy* got into the act in 1980, when a senior editor and an investigator helped prove that Larry Hicks had been wrongly convicted of a double homicide in Indiana and sentenced to death, greatly because of his incompetent attorney's meager defense (Yant, 1991).

In 1983, Jim McCloskey founded Centurion Ministries, the first non-profit organization dedicated to vindicating wrongly convicted inmates. McCloskey became interested in the innocence claims of inmate Jorge De Los Santos while working as a student chaplain at Trenton State Prison in 1980 while working on his master's in divinity degree at Princeton University. When De Los Santos was exonerated and released in 1983, McCloskey knew he had found his calling. Centurion Ministries soon had many newsworthy successes. Two of its early cases, which led to the exoneration of Texas inmates Lenell Geter and Joyce Ann Brown after they were featured on the CBS television show *60 Minutes*, helped put both wrongful convictions and Centurion Ministries on center stage (Yant, 1991).

The stylish, innovative 1988 documentary *The Thin Blue Line* by director Erroll Morris about the shoddy investigation that put Ohio native Randall Dale Adams on Texas' death row won international acclaim and Adams' release in 1989. Morris did not set out to make a movie about Adams' case. He originally planned to make a movie about Dr. James Grigson, who had earned the moniker "Doctor Death" for his quick conclusions that almost every person accused of murder was a sociopath who would kill again if ever released. In the case of Adams, who had gone to work every day after the murder and had never been in trouble with the law, Grigson concluded that his perceived normality was proof of his lack of normal human emotions, which could cause him to "work all day and creep all night" (Yant, 1991).

Unlike the other inmates Morris interviewed, Adams proved to be so intelligent, well mannered and passionate in his claim of innocence that the former private investigator decided to dig into his case. Morris soon found that the case was built on a web of lies by witnesses who radically changed their stories over time. One of those witnesses was David Harris, who all but admitted to the murder in a dramatic interview at the end of the film. When Morris suggested in the film that Adams was innocent, Harris concurred. Asked how he could be so sure, Harris said, " 'Cause I'm the one that knows." Harris was never charged for the murder, however. He was already on death row for a murder he committed after the one he pinned on Adams. Harris was executed in 2004 (Yant, 1991).

If someone had bothered to interview Adams before Morris did a decade after his conviction, perhaps the whole tragedy could have been avoided. But that did not happen. "The Dallas news media convicted me within two days of my arrest.... They quoted the prosecutor about how I was a transient, which I wasn't, and how I signed a confession, which I had not. It wasn't until my trial several months later that one reporter bothered to interview me—for five minutes," Adams said (*The IRE Journal*, 1993, p. 5).

Despite all the positive publicity that increased public awareness of how easily innocent people could be convicted of serious crimes, the political climate slowly changed in the 1980s as the crack-cocaine-fueled crime rate rose (see generally, Alexander, 2010; Beckett, 1997; Garland, 2001). Some high-profile child abductions, especially the abduction and murder of Adam Walsh in 1981, led to exaggerated statistics about the number of abductions by strangers. These statistics were debunked by a Pulitzer Prize-winning series of articles in *The Denver Post* in 1985, but by then anxiety over children had segued into another media-fueled panic, this one over child sex abuse, often supposedly committed by satanic cults, that led to hundreds of wrongful convictions between the mid-1980s and the mid-1990s.

The epicenter was the McMartin Preschool scandal in Los Angeles, which started in 1983. Nathan and Snedeker (1995) show how, by the time the McMartin case was over in 1990 after the longest and most-expensive trial in American history resulted in no convictions, police, prosecutors and reporters had spread panic about non-existent sex-abuse cults throughout the country. Those accused of involvement in many of these supposed cults were not as lucky as the defendants in the McMartin case. Many were sentenced to hundreds of years in prison for crimes most later agreed never occurred.

The man most responsible for fanning the flames in the McMartin case was the late Wayne Satz, an investigative reporter for the local ABC affiliate who became intimately involved with the controversial therapist whose accusations and suggestive interview techniques fueled the hysteria. According to Nathan and Snedeker (1995), Satz should have been sensitive to how easy it is to make accusations about someone, since records were later submitted in court by defense attorneys showing that he had been accused in the 1970s of having "a penchant for deviant and forcible sex" and an obsession with the gruesome details in the Hillside Strangler case. But that did not stop Satz from reporting wild tales of rape, pornography production and animal slaughter taking place at McMartin and far beyond. Satz's heavily promoted stories prompted even wilder rumors and accusations. Nathan and Snedeker (1995, p. 88) note:

> In its rush to condemn the McMartin teachers, the media sided unstintingly with the prosecution. *People* magazine called McMartin "California's Nightmare Nursery." *Time* introduced its coverage with a one-word headline: "Brutalized." On ABC's *20/20* newsmagazine, host Tom Jarriel described the preschool as "a sexual house of horrors."

David Shaw of *The Los Angeles Times* documented how coverage of the McMartin case "exposed basic flaws in the way contemporary news organizations function" in his Pulitzer Prize-winning series on the coverage of the McMartin case. Shaw spared no one, including his own newspaper, in documenting how the media "plunged into hysteria, sensationalism, and what one editor call[ed] a 'lynch mob syndrome' " (Nathan & Snedeker, 1995, p. 88).

By then, though, the media were repeating this scenario across the country, often ignoring the same kind of conflicts of interest that Satz had. In New Jersey's Wee Care case, which led to the wrongful conviction of Kelly Michaels, the mother of one of Michaels' alleged victims was an editor at the Bergen County *Record,* the most influential newspaper in the area. According to Nathan and Snedeker (1995), that same editor was also a friend of a *Newsweek* writer who had been assigned to write an article about the case. The beleaguered defense hoped that a story about the absurd accusations in the case would result in offers of help, but the mother related in a book she later wrote under a pseudonym that she persuaded her *Newsweek* friend not to write it.

At the peak of the hysteria, journalists who questioned the validity of sex-abuse accusations had a hard time being heard (Nathan & Snedeker, 1995). Dorothy Rabinowitz's assigned story on the Michaels case was killed by *Vanity Fair* because of her conclusion that Michaels was innocent. (It was later published by *Harper's*.) Rabinowitz, who later won a Pulitzer Prize in part for her probing analysis of child-abuse hysteria, complained how "youngish journalists who prided themselves on their skepticism … were outraged by the merest suggestion that the state's charges against Kelly Michaels lacked credibility" (Nathan & Snedeker, 1995, p. 234). In addition, Nathan and Snedeker claim a reporter at *The Los Angeles Times* who questioned the accuracy of coverage provided by the reporter on the McMartin beat at its peak in the 1980s was disciplined for his criticism, and he resigned in disgust.

Media coverage of an investigation still underway often contaminated what the children said. In a 2013 affidavit, Dr. Maggie Bruck, a leading expert on the testimony of children, traced how when the first child to say she was abused saw a TV news report about a possible suspect in the 1993 Lorain, Ohio, Head Start molestation case, the child identified the previously unmentioned man as the molester. Then, Bruck noted, after this girl and her mother interacted with other children, those children also changed their stories to say the man was their molester. The children later changed their stories based on new information.

Child abuse hysteria ended almost as quickly as it started after a massive federally funded study (Goodman, Qin, Bottoms, & Shaver, 1994) concluded that rumors of satanic conspiracies had no basis in fact and that there was no widespread sex abuse in the nation's childcare system. Many of the people convicted during the mass panic eventually had their convictions overturned, but putting their lives and shattered families back together proved difficult (Nathan & Snedeker, 1995).

As the media and the nation began to weary of the frenzied coverage of satanic sex-abuse rings in 1989, they were able to divert their moral outrage to the vicious assault and rape of a white woman while jogging through New York's famed Central Park on the evening of April 20, 1989. The case set off a media frenzy in the crime-plagued city that soon spread across the United States after police announced that the five youths, all of them black or Latino, had confessed that they had committed the rape as one of a series of random assaults they and other teens committed in the park that night, a process they supposedly called "wilding."

In her book *The Central Park Five: A Chronicle of a City Wilding* (2011) and a similarly named documentary she produced with her father, Ken Burns, Sarah Burns shows how police jumped to conclusions and then manipulated and intimidated the five boys into highly inconsistent confessions that were greatly at odds with the facts. "Once the narrative about what happened was laid out within a few days of the rape, there was no turning back," Burns writes. "The few stories that were more balanced and less hysterical failed to make any difference in a city ready to believe the absolute worst about a group of poor black and Latino teenagers."

While coverage of the case by New York's *Post* and *Daily News* was particularly reprehensible, virtually all news coverage assumed that the New York Police Department's version of events was accurate when it was actually way off the mark. While the *Post* and *Daily News* were fanning racial and ethnic tensions with talk of the teens being a "wolf pack" bent on "savagery," *The New York Times* and minority-owned newspapers sought to examine the social factors that caused the boys to turn to such violence. Burns says the idea that the boys had not committed the rape at all did not seem to cross anyone's mind.

When the real rapist, Matias Reyes, finally came forward to say he committed the crime by himself in addition to the others in the area he had already been convicted of and DNA confirmed his guilt in 2002, the news media showed the same resistance to the truth that police and prosecutors do when confronted with evidence that they convicted an innocent person. Reporters did their best, Burns wrote, to link the boys to Reyes and suggest that they were all involved in the rape. To its credit, the district attorney's office admitted its mistake and moved to have the charges against the Central Park Five dismissed (Burns, 2011).

# Moving Forward: DNA and the Internet

Amid all the hype over the McMartin case and its progeny and the Central Park Five case in New York, the exoneration in Chicago of Gary Dotson in August 1989 did not get much attention. Warden (2002) notes that Dotson's conviction had been a source of publicity in 1985, when the woman who accused him of raping her in 1977, came forward to say she had made the story up to explain a feared pregnancy after having sex with her boyfriend. Cathleen Crowell Webb was subjected to considerable scorn and ridicule by prosecutors and some in the press, but the governor finally agreed to commute Dotson's sentence to time served. Then Dotson's attorney, Thomas M. Breen, read about a new test developed in Great Britain involving DNA that had been used to identify the man responsible for the rapes and murders of two teenage girls. If the test could be used to identify a perpetrator, Breen reasoned, it could be used to exclude someone, too. So he filed a motion for DNA testing on Crowell Webb's semen-stained underpants. The judge granted the motion, and when the tests excluded Dotson and said the semen was consistent with the DNA of Crowell Webb's old boyfriend, Dotson was cleared once and for all. The DNA exoneration revolution had begun (Yant, 1991).

Soon a few other inmates were cleared by DNA, and by 1992 Barry Scheck and Peter Neufield had formed the Innocence Project to use DNA testing to potentially clear inmates who claimed they had been wrongly convicted. Twenty years later, more than 300 people have been exonerated in the United States and millions of minds opened to the fallibility of the criminal-justice system. "The whole public has always viewed the criminal justice system through the optics of guilt," Neufeld told the newspaper, *The Missoulian* in 2013. "By developing all these wrongful conviction cases, and then people asking the question, 'What went wrong?' for the first time as a nation, we're starting to view the criminal justice system through the optics of innocence" (see http://missoulian.com/news/state-and-regional/sally-mauk-civil-rights-attorney-says-dna-has-changed-view/article_ce9d935a-c4ca-11e2-9977-001a4bcf887a.html).

Journalists were among those who were more willing to listen to claims of innocence, even when there was no possibility of DNA testing, which is true about 90% of the time. The Investigative Reporters and Editors group's *IRE Journal* published a cover story in 1993 on how journalists should do a better job of covering the courts and questioning dubious convictions. Reporters started digging into old cases across the country and some struck gold.

The innocence movement soon spread into television, books and the theater. *Actual Innocence: When Justice Goes Wrong and How to Make it Right* (2001), by Barry Scheck, Peter Neufield and journalist Jim Dwyer, became a best-seller. So did *The Innocent Man* (2006), the first non-fiction book by John Grisham, author of numerous legal blockbusters. *Conviction*, a movie starring Hilary Swank in the role of Betty Anne Waters, who overcame huge odds to prove that her brother did not commit the murder for which he was convicted, was released in 2010. A series of documentaries and investigative books, along with the support of celebrities, spurred the release in Arkansas of three men known as the West Memphis Three in 2011 who had been convicted in the murders of three boys in 1994. Americans seemed increasingly willing to accept that wrongful convictions occur. And legislators responded by enacting reforms to make mistakes less likely to happen, to permit DNA testing in old cases and to compensate the wrongly convicted when their innocence is proven.

The Internet aided the cause. Innocence projects across the country developed web sites to tell their stories. Informative websites like Truth in Justice and Justice Denied provided timely information on innocence-related issues. The Wrongful Convictions Blog, sponsored by the Center for the Global Study of Wrongful Conviction, posted reports on innocence issues from around the world. Web sites were created to advocate for individual cases, sometimes attracting support and donations. An early success story was www.freeclarence.com, started in 2003 in support of murder convict Clarence Elkins of Ohio. The site eventually raised $30,000 for DNA testing that freed Elkins and identified the actual killer.

But as the Internet fostered powerful unfiltered social media, prejudicial pretrial media coverage took an ominous turn. This became evident in the Amanda Knox murder case in Italy. Knox, an American exchange student, was charged in 2007 along with her Italian boyfriend, Raffaele Sollecito, with killing British roommate Meredith Kercher in an alleged sex game gone wrong. Within days, people in the blogosphere began declaring the two young defendants depraved and guilty. Most of the focus was on "Foxy Knoxy," an attractive 20-year-old college student who was portrayed as an evil vixen. In the e-book *Trial by Fury* (2013), Douglas Preston relates that he was shocked by what he saw being said about Knox on the web.

"The extreme viciousness of the anti-Amanda commentariage is startling," Preston (2013, Location 30) writes. "There are countless statements calling for the murdering, raping, torturing, throat-cutting, frying, hanging, electrocution, burning, and rotting in hell of Amanda, along with her sisters, family, friends, and supporters." Knox had online supporters, too, Preston found, but there were marked differences between them and her attackers. "The former were engaged in normal human behavior, the latter in something that felt pathological," he says (Preston, 2013, Location 82).

Preston began to see this power as the anti-Knox sites attracting millions of readers. Soon Preston saw their highly biased, poorly sourced posts about the case being relied on by major news organizations, particularly the BBC and *Newsweek/The Daily Beast*.

> The online furor was not just white noise. It drove public opinion against Amanda. It influenced coverage by legitimate journalists. For example, Barbie Nadeau, a Rome-based correspondent who covered the case for *The Daily Beast*, wrote a book about the case, *Angel Face: The True Story of Student Killer Amanda Knox*. While the book included no footnotes or bibliography, it appears to have used information sourced from anonymous bloggers—identifiable as such because it was incorrect. Tina Brown, editor-in-chief, contributed the foreword to the book. In it, Brown wrote that "a merciless culture of sex, drugs, and alcohol" led to Amanda's "descent into evil," and she wondered if Amanda's "pretty face" was perhaps only a "mask, a duplicitous cover for a depraved soul." To see statements like these come from the pen of the editor-in-chief of *Newsweek* shows how deeply the noise of the blogosphere had penetrated legitimate journalism (Preston 2013, Locations 134–138).

Preston says the anti-Knox invective soon invaded Wikipedia, whose neutral article on the case was continually re-edited by the Knox haters, finally forcing Wikipedia founder Jimmy Wales to enter the fray. When Wales ordered an all-new neutral article about the case, he was attacked as a sexual deviant who lusted for Knox. Preston says the anti-Knox group targeted contributors to the Wikipedia article they perceived as being pro-Knox by attacking them at their places of employment and posting personal details of their lives along with insults and threats.

The pro-Knox people finally retaliated. They revealed that Peter Quennell, creator of the anti-Knox "True Justice" site had once had a restraining order placed on him for harassing a New York ballet dancer. One of the Knox's most vicious critics was revealed to be on probation for attempting to strangle a female psychiatrist who had been treating him for drug and alcohol abuse. The millions of people who read their invective and formed opinions accordingly, of course, did not know this. Public opinion moved decidedly against Knox before her trial, at which she and Raffaele Sollecito, despite the paucity of evidence against them, were convicted. A higher court, after a more dispassionate review of the facts and new exculpatory DNA findings, later acquitted Knox and Sollecito, but another court has since ordered a new trial.

Another high-tech lynch mob formed in early 2013 over the Steubenville, Ohio, rape case of two members of the popular Steubenville High School football team. The alleged alcohol-fueled rape of an unconscious 16-year-old girl at a party while other boys supposedly watched and did nothing set off an international firestorm. The controversy was fueled by bloggers and hackers who contended that other boys should be charged in the case and that authorities were trying to cover up other wrongdoing by people associated with the football team.

Contrary to the narrative perpetrated in the cybersphere, however, law enforcement was not dismissive of the allegations. The alleged rape occurred on August 11, 2012. The girl's mother reported it to police on August 14. Charges were filed two weeks later and local authorities requested the assistance of the Ohio attorney general's office for additional investigation. But that was not good enough for some, particularly a purported member of the international hacker collective Anonymous who called himself KY Anonymous.

KY Anonymous released a lot of information (and misinformation) on his later-disbanded LocalLeaks web site. He also threatened to release the social security numbers and other personal information of people he believed had information on the rape if they did not come forward. As noted in the Wrongful Convictions Blog, this was a new frontier in media-fueled rushes to judgment. While some expressed concern about this new form of vigilante justice, many in the traditional media followed the social media's lead. What makes this particularly frightening was the instant worldwide distribution via social media of unproven allegations by a masked man who did not mind destroying the reputations of teenagers he called "psychopaths" who turned out to have nothing to do with the alleged rape.

To anyone who cares about the rights of the accused to a fair trial, CNN correspondent Gary Tuchman's interview with KY Anonymous should have been cause for concern. "We aren't the judge nor the jury, but it's fair to say we are the executioner," KY Anonymous said. The hacker added that, because some of the people have "incriminated themselves" in online tweets and postings, there is no real need to wait for the courts to decide on their guilt or innocence. "If you think they are guilty, that's because your conscience is telling you they are guilty," KY Anonymous said (see, http://wrongfulconvictionsblog.org/2013/01/09/vigilante-justice-goes-high-tech-in-ohio).

Although KY Anonymous and a local blogger took great credit for exposing a crucial photo of the rape victim being dragged from one room to another and other evidence, the county prosecutor told a Martins Ferry, Ohio, newspaper, *The Times Leader,* that police already had all that information before Anonymous hacked it. "They exposed what happened to the victim over and over and over," Jane Hanlin said of the video of a boy bragging about the rape and the photo of the girl being carried. "The video would have been seen by 50 people instead was seen by 500 million people. The victim's representative said that was not helpful to the victim. It was hurtful. It was pointless because it didn't bring anything to light that we didn't already have" (see, http://www.timesleaderonline.com/page/content.detail/id/546186/Hanlin-speaks-out-on-Steubenville-rape-case.html?nav=5010).

While many took delight in seeing a supposed football-crazed small town forced to abandon its alleged cover-up of an alleged rape of a 16-year-old girl by favored football players, Erika Christakis (2013), a time.com columnist, expressed concern.

> Our legal history is full of defendants tried in the court of public opinion and later found to be innocent. Cases such as the Central Park Five, a group of teenagers excoriated by the New York City press for a brutal gang rape in the 1980s and wrongly convicted, and the 2006 instance of three Duke University lacrosse players being falsely accused of the rape of a stripper suggest that media trial by fire can happen to people across the socioeconomic spectrum.
>
> But we need to worry about more than just the falsely accused. An equally important reason for caution is the potential harm to the *victim* from a public rush to judgment.... In Steubenville, lawyers for the accused are considering asking that the trial be moved, because not only have the defendants received threats, but so have the defense counsel and potential witnesses.
>
> These kinds of emotional responses erode the transparency so essential to the pursuit of justice. Even worse, they raise the chances that a guilty defendant will one day go free on appeal on the grounds of an unfair trial.

Alyce LaViolette, an expert witness, got a taste of what the social-media assaults can be like when she testified in the overheated Jodi Arias trial in Arizona in March 2013. LaViolette had been testifying in trials for many years and she more than held her own under questioning by the aggressive prosecutor about her belief that Arias was a victim of physical abuse by Travis Alexander, the man Arias was accused of killing. But LaViolette was no match for the tweets, emails, telephoned threats and vicious online reviews of her best-selling book that called her a fraud and a disgrace to her profession. People also called organizations to which LaViolette was scheduled to speak demanding that her appearance be canceled. As the onslaught continued, LaViolette ended up in the emergency room with an anxiety attack and palpitations. Some of the messages were deemed so threatening they were referred to police. "This is a logical extension of witness intimidation, taken to an extreme conclusion," Sree Sreenivasan, a journalism professor at Columbia University, told *The Arizona Republic*. "I imagine we will see it again" (see http://www.azcentral.com/community/mesa/articles/20130410arias-trial-witness-feels-social-medias-glare.html?nclick_check=1).

Then there is Nancy Grace. When J. Michael Flanagan was defending Conrad Murray, the doctor charged with causing the death of superstar Michael Jackson in 2011, he did not argue that Murray's right to a free trial was jeopardized by the usual media frenzy. He asked that the jury be sequestered during the trial for one reason: Nancy Grace. Here's how Tim Rutten (2011) described Grace in an op-ed piece in *The Los Angeles Times*.

> Grace is the former Georgia prosecutor who became a television legal commentator, first on Court TV and, more recently, on Turner Broadcasting's HLN cable channel. She's a snarling, angry presence whose habitual sneer is an epic chasm of contempt. Her view of the criminal justice system is flawlessly Manichean. There are good people — police officers and prosecutors — and evil people — defendants and their lawyers. Grace appears to have never met someone arrested who she believed should not be charged, nor anyone charged who should not be convicted.

It is hard to assess just how damaging the prejudicial pretrial publicity Grace generates has on jurors, but it is likely that it is far greater than potential jurors will admit. "Extensive research experimentation has indicated that only a fraction of the jurors who are actually prejudiced by pretrial publicity can articulate their bias and prejudice," says Richard Waites, a trial attorney and social psychologist. "Many research studies have indicated that most jurors who denied being influenced by pretrial publicity to which they were exposed voted in accordance with their reactions to the pretrial publicity. Most of the time, jurors are not aware that their perceptions of the case are being influenced or biased by pretrial publicity" (see www.theadvocates.com).

So while a few more innocent inmates are being freed in the DNA-testing era, many more are undoubtedly being convicted in the era of Nancy Grace and Internet hysteria.

# Conclusion: The Need for "Preventive Journalism"

Huff, Rattner and Sagarin (1996) conservatively estimate that almost 10,000 people are wrongly convicted every year. By contrast, the National Exoneration Registry (http://www.law.umich.edu/special/exoneration/Pages/about.aspx), which covers documented wrongful convictions from 1989, listed a mere 1,316 exonerations by February 2014. That means most wrongful convictions are missed.

It also means the media are not doing enough by occasionally exposing a particularly egregious wrongful conviction and ignoring thousands of others occurring on their watch. Nor is it adequate for them to back the reforms in police procedures that may help reduce wrongful convictions while ignoring reforms in journalistic procedures that could be equally beneficial.

Weinberg (2008) proposes just those kinds of reforms. He urges writers, editors and producers in all media to practice "preventive journalism rather than after-the-conviction, too-late journalism." Until journalists improve their coverage of the criminal-justice system, Weinberg argues, "far more innocent people will be imprisoned than the criminal-justice system seems likely ever to acknowledge" and "more criminals will continue to go unpunished, free to murder or rape or rob again" (see http://www.psmag.com/legal-affairs/innocent-until-reported-guilty-4231/).

Weinberg suggests that police and courthouse reporters and other staffers create a database to track every felony arrest and produce follow-up reports as needed. Although that might no longer be feasible in newsrooms with shrinking budgets and staffs, Weinberg's other suggestions are. They include reviewing the police file of each case, talking to the suspect, the victim, the prosecutor and the defense lawyer, and then tracking the case through the system and getting to know the people involved along the way rather than relying only on prosecutors and key detectives, as is the usual practice now.

For most of these reforms to happen and be effective, however, there would have to be some major changes in the attitudes of journalists and attorneys and in some restrictive laws. Reporters, in particular, need a wake-up call. Most police and courthouse reporters for metropolitan news organizations probably spend more time in police headquarters or the courthouse than they do the newsroom. They cultivate good relationships with the people they cover to get as much information as they can. In the process, they often become social acquaintances with their sources and sometimes come to reflect their values.

Entrenched beat reporters also can become lazy; they often take what is handed to them and look no further.

Paul Henderson, who won a Pulitzer Prize in 1982 for a series of articles in *The Seattle Times* that cleared a man of a wrongful rape conviction, says this type of one-sided coverage of criminal cases has long been endemic in American journalism. "I found it very difficult to interest my old newspaper in any type of criminal justice advocacy," he said (*The IRE Journal*, 1993, p. 5). As a result, Henderson eventually left the newspaper in frustration. He became a full-time investigator for Centurion Ministries in 1988.

Ironically, Henderson's old newspaper received an unprecedented rebuke from the independent Washington News Council for pro-prosecution bias in June 2013, when the panel determined that *The Seattle Times* inaccurately and unfairly represented the work of a forensic psychologist who testifies for defense attorneys in an investigative series on the state's sexually violent predator program. Relying on prosecution sources, the council said, reporter Christine Willmsen unfairly portrayed Richard Wollert as a hack who promulgated unorthodox theories in order to line his own pockets. Forensic psychologist and blogger Karen Franklin said Willmsen's claim that defense experts are paid more than prosecution experts was "patently false," yet it spurred the state to cap the fees of defense experts but not prosecution experts.

Unfortunately, reporters who follow Weinberg's suggestion that they get the other side of the story by talking to defense attorneys might find that it takes real effort. Many defense attorneys still cling to the rule that it does not pay to try a case in the press, which the American Bar Association has codified by stating that justice should be conducted "without distracting influences" (Warden, 2002, p. 25). Prosecutors get around this rule by leaking information favorable to their case while defense attorneys usually say nothing and tell their clients to do likewise. "We'll have our say in court," they state. But by then a lot of damage may have been done.

Warden (2002) notes that journalists are usually just as willing to accept information off the record from defense attorneys as prosecutors and that some potentially helpful witnesses who will not talk to a defense attorney or investigator might talk to a reporter. The most important benefit of cooperating with the media, he says, "is the potential the media have to foster a climate of favorable public opinion conducive to fairness and justice" (Warden, 2002, p. 25).

But more open-minded reporters still need facts, and facts are sometimes hard to come by both before and after trial. Most states restrict public access to police investigative files, sometimes for decades. Police usually have the option of releasing files at their discretion (except in Kansas, where releasing criminal records without a court order can be a criminal offense) but police are normally reluctant to release information that might hurt their case.

Even defense attorneys have trouble getting an entire investigative file, and prosecutors are often caught withholding exculpatory information in violation of the *Brady* rule. Some states are moving to a so-called open-file discovery process in which prosecutors supposedly make all reports available to the defense. But even if prosecutors abide by these rules—and some probably will not—the documents usually come with the caveat that the records cannot be released to third parties, including journalists.

Phillip J. Mause (2013), a prominent Washington, D.C., attorney, wrote about how the lack of transparency and the selective release of information "can distort the criminal law process and produce a situation in which a defendant may find it impossible to get a fair trial and may even be harassed and threatened after the trial is over." He continued:

> We have now had so many "media circus" cases that there is a corps of journalists
> specializing in the genre and attempting to identify and even generate new cases

on a full time basis. In some cases, media pressure may—rightly or wrongly—contribute to a prosecutor's decision to indict (that may be the case in the Trayvon Martin situation). In other cases, the media seems to have convinced the public of the guilt of the defendant so that even after acquittal, the defendant's life can become impossible (the Casey Anthony case).... In the O.J. Simpson case, witnesses paid by tabloids for interviews created credibility problems for the prosecution (see www.injustice-anywhere.org/MediaInfluence.html).

To avoid the sensationalism, misreporting and the selective release of facts about a case that frequently occurs, Mause recommended the creation of a "public file" in criminal cases. Here is how he explained it:

> The public file will be open to all reporters and to the public in general. The public file will contain all prosecution statements and press releases relevant to the case. The prosecution will refuse to favor any reporters with any information in addition to the public file. This will hopefully limit the ability of the prosecution to shape press coverage of a case by favoring sympathetic and "reliable" journalists with "inside information" about the case and using "leaks" to bargain for biased reporting (see www.injustice-anywhere.org/MediaInfluence.html).

James Madison would probably approve of Mause's idea. "A popular government, without popular information, or the means of acquiring it," Madison said, "is but a prologue to a farce or a tragedy or perhaps both." The U.S. criminal justice system proves that with every farcical and tragic wrongful conviction in which facts are withheld or misreported. Making that information available is the first step toward justice. Accurately disseminating it to the public is the second, equally important step, and the evolving media will have to prove that they are up to the task.

# References

Alexander, M. (2010). *The new Jim Crow: Mass incarceration in the age of colorblindness.* New York: The New Press.

Beckett, K. (1997). *Making crime pay: Law and order in contemporary American politics.* New York: Oxford University Press.

Bedau, H. A., & Radelet, M. L. (1987). Miscarriages of justice in potentially capital cases. *Stanford Law Review, 40,* 21-179.

Borchard, E. M. (1932). *Convicting the innocent: Sixty-five actual errors of criminal justice.* Garden City, NY: Doubleday.

Bruck, M. (2012). *Affidavit in State of Ohio v. Nancy Smith, Lorain County Common Pleas Court,* Case Nos. 93CR044489, 94CR045368.

Burns, S. (2011). *The Central Park Five: A chronicle of a city wilding.* New York: Alfred A. Knopf.

Christakis, E. (2013, January 8). Viewpoint: Don't rush to judge on Steubenville. *Time.* Retrieved from http://ideas.time.com/2013/01/08/viewpoint-dont-rush-to-judge-on-steubenville.

Franklin, K. (2013, June 4). *Newspaper unfairly maligned forensic psychologist, news council holds.* Retrieved from http://forensicpsychologist.blogspot.com/2013/06/newspaper-unfairly-maligned-forensic.html.

Gardner, E. S. (1952). *The court of last resort.* New York, NY: William Sloane Associates.

Garland, D. (2001). *The culture of control: Crime and social order in contemporary society.* Chicago: University of Chicago Press.

Goodman, G, Qin, J, Bottoms, B. L., & Shaver, P. R. (1994). *Characteristics and sources of allegations of ritualistic child abuse.* Washington, D.C.: National Center on Child Abuse and Neglect.

Higginbotham, A. (2008, May). The long, long life of the Lipstick Killer. *GQ.* Retrieved from http://www.gq.com/news-politics/big-issues/200805/william-heirens-lipstick-killer-chicago.

Huff, C. R., Rattner, A. & Sagarin, E. (1996). *Convicted but innocent: Wrongful conviction and public policy.* Thousand Oaks, CA: Sage.

Law, M. (2013, April 14). Hanlin speaks out on Steubenville rape case. The Times Leader. Retrieved from http://www.timesleaderonline.com/page/content.detail/id/546186/Hanlin-speaks-out-on-Steubenville-rape-case.html?nav=5010.

Masterson, M., & Yant, M. (1993). Presumed guilty: How negligent journalists contribute to wrongful convictions. *The IRE Journal,* March/April.

Kennedy, L. (1996). *Crime of the century: The Lindbergh kidnapping and the framing of Richard Hauptmann.* New York, NY: Penguin Books.

Kiefer, M. (2013, April 11). *Arias trial: Witness feels social media's glare.* Retrieved from http://www.azcentral.com/community/mesa/articles/20130410arias-trial-witness-feels-social-medias-glare.html?nclick_check=1.

Mauk, S. (2013, May 24). Civil rights attorney says DNA has changed view of justice system. *The Missoulian.* Retrieved from http://missoulian.com/news/state-and-regional/sally-mauk-civil-rights-attorney-says-dna-has-changed-view/article_ce9d935a-c4ca-11e2-9977-001a4bcf887a.html.

Mause, P. J. (2013). *Media influence on wrongful convictions.* Retrieved from www.injustice-anywhere.org/MediaInfluence.html.

Nathan, D. & Snedeker, M. (1995). *Satan's silence: Ritual abuse and the making of a modern American witchhunt.* New York, NY: Basic Books.

Neff, J. (2001). *The wrong man: The final verdict on the Dr. Sam Sheppard murder case.* New York, NY: Random House.

Oldfield, R. (2010). *Outrage: The Edalji five and the shadow of Sherlock Holmes.* Cambridge, England: Vanguard Press.

Peuchet, J. (2011). *The diamond and the vengeance: The true crime that inspired The Count of Monte Cristo* [Kindle version]. (J. Blair, Trans.). Retrieved from Amazon.com.

Preston, D. (2013). *Trial by fury: Internet savagery and the Amanda Knox case* [Kindle version]. Seattle, WA: Kindle Single. Retrieved from Amazon.com.

Read, P. P. (2012). *The Dreyfus affair.* New York, NY: Bloomsbury Press.

Rutten, T. (2011, July 23). The threat of Nancy Grace. *Los Angeles Times.* Retrieved from http://articles.latimes.com/2011/jul/23/opinion/la-oe-rutten-nancy-grace-20110723

*Sheppard v. Maxwell,* 384 U.S. 333 (1966).

Sherrer, H. (2007). The lost days of the fugitive. *Justice Denied, 35,* 25-26.

Symons, J. (1979). *Conan Doyle: Portrait of an artist.* New York, NY: The Mysterious Press.

Wade, C. W. (1997). *The fiery cross: The Ku Klux Klan in America.* New York, NY: Simon and Schuster.

Waites, R. (n.d.) *Reducing the prejudicial effects of pretrial publicity.* Retrieved from http://www.theadvocates.com/Reducing%20Prejudicial%20Effects%20of%20Pretrial%20Publicity.pdf.

Warden, R. (2002). The revolutionary role of journalism in identifying and rectifying wrongful convictions, *UMKC Law Review,* 70, 803-846.

Warden, Rob (2005). *Wilkie Collins's The Dead Alive: The novel, the case, and wrongful convictions.* Evanston, IL: Northwestern University Press.

Weinberg, S. (2008, September 23). Innocent until reported guilty. *Pacific Standard.* Retrieved from http://www.psmag.com/legal-affairs/innocent-until-reported-guilty-4231/.

Woodward, C. V. (1963). *Tom Watson, agrarian reformer.* Savannah, GA: The Beehive Press.

Wuxtry! Read all about it! (1946, July 29). Time. Retrieved from http://content.time.com/time/subscriber/article/0,33009,776968,00.html.

Yant, M. (1991). *Presumed guilty: When innocent people are wrongly convicted.* Buffalo, NY: Prometheus Books.

Yant, M. (2013, January 9). *Vigilante justice goes high-tech in Ohio.* Retrieved from http://wrongfulconvictionsblog.org/2013/01/09/vigilante-justice-goes-high-tech-in-ohio.

# Section II

## The Criminal Justice System: Producing, Detecting, and Remedying Wrongful Convictions

## Part One

### The Production of Wrongful Convictions

# Chapter Six

# Wrongful Conviction, Policing, and the "Wars on Crime and Drugs"

Hannah Laqueur, *University of California, Berkeley*
Stephen Rushin, *University of Illinois*
Jonathan Simon, *University of California, Berkeley*

Wrongful conviction ought to be an aberration for any system of criminal punishment tied to legal adjudication; certainly in a system such as we have in the United States, premised on the constitutional bedrock of requiring a jury to find guilt beyond a reasonable doubt (*Sandstrom v. Montana*, 1979). We suggest, however, that during the so-called wars on crime and drugs, wrongful convictions are no longer mere aberrations, any more than is holding to the end of hostilities captured members of an enemy army. Specifically, we hypothesize that these two "fronts" in two parallel national "wars" have transformed police practices in such a way that both homicide and drug crimes have become likely centers of concentration of some form of wrongful conviction.

In this chapter, we begin by discussing the war on crime and the war on drugs. We then discuss the ways in which these wars have transformed American policing and have served to promote wrongful conviction. We conclude the chapter by suggesting that we need political signals and institutional reforms, not just better methods and ad hoc individual correction. Only by clearly ending these wars—and their "state of emergency"-like signal to both frontline enforcers and citizens—can we restore the state of affairs in which wrongful conviction returns to being an aberration in our criminal justice system and a problem subject to effective technical and tactical solutions. Given that personal exoneration is neither practical nor likely for most individuals, we suggest broader policies are required.

## Stepping Back: The Wars on Crime and Drugs

The wars on (violent) crime and drugs, declared at the national level in the 1960s and revitalized several times since—under Reagan and Bush around drugs in the 1980s, and around policing and urban violence under Clinton in the 1990s—transformed the once relatively local culture of policing and prosecution in America (Feeley & Sarat, 1981; Stuntz, 2011). The consequences have been enormous for American law and society. Since the beginning of these publicly declared wars, the United States has seen incarceration skyrocket, and the gulf expand between frontline criminal justice enforcers and high-crime communities (see generally, Stuntz, 2011). Wrongful convictions, likely concentrated in those same communities, should ultimately be seen as another and integral consequence of the long war on crime.

The war on crime (as well as the war on drugs), as we discuss here, might be thought of as a metaphor "with teeth." Presidents asserting a war on crime never asserted they were using war powers in a constitutional sense, but by defining the national priority of combating crime as on an equal footing with war, politicians did more than invoke emotions and votes—they helped to cognitively reorganize the criminal justice field (Lakoff & Johnson, 2003; Simon, 2008); that is, rework the way frontline criminal justice agents had to intellectually operationalize their activity.

The war metaphor carries from its military source material into the criminal justice field three key implications. First, it marks territory as the key target of operations. Wars are won when the enemy finds itself completely denied freedom of operation in a territory. Thus the war on crime is brought into operation primarily against perceived "high crime" neighborhoods.

Second, wars mark race as a proxy and product of the war. All wars are, or tend to become, race wars in the sense that populations on the other side of the conflict come to be defined in racialized terms as permanently and dangerously "other" to the opposing race (whether, for example, Hutu and Tutsi, Arab and Jew, revolutionary and reactionary) (Foucault, 2003). A war on crime tends to become a war against those racialized as deviant and disaffected—in the United States, primarily African American and Latino youth, mostly in blighted urban centers, but increasingly in blighted rural and suburban areas as well (Pager, 2007; Western, 2008).

Third, all wars are preemptive. Once begun, war operations seek to neutralize enemy forces before they can be brought into effective action. The war is over when one side no longer has the capacity to produce new offensive operations or resist defensively. A war on crime becomes a preemptive war on those perceived to be involved in criminal lifestyles.

## Police and the Wars on Crime and Drugs

The cognitive remapping of the criminal justice field by the war on crime has had a number of profound effects on the incentives of policing in ways that we hypothesize encourage wrongful conviction. First, the war on crime minimizes the significance of individual guilt. An enemy combatant is not defined by acts but by other attributes. Enemies in the war on crime, as we have noted, are largely marked by race and territory. Second, the imperative of preemptive action gives precedence to crimes that are easily policed and prosecuted regardless of their direct relationship to violence. Third, the ease with which these crimes are "discovered" in territories marked for criminalization means that a large pool of "snitches" is always at hand, in prison or county jail. These snitches are potentially amenable to consideration from the prosecution in their own cases, irrespective of the quality of information they can actually provide. Due to the highly segregated nature of contemporary American cities, it is highly likely that the people they know well enough to snitch on will be the same race.

The impact of the federal war on crime on state and local policing has manifested in two important domains: homicides and drug law enforcement. The 1968 Omnibus Crime Control and Safe Streets Act, which is the foundational legal structure for the war on crime (Simon, 2007), was widely identified with the surging homicide rate and violent assaults associated with urban rioting. The specific measures in the federal law could do little to touch either directly, but instead attempted to bolster police effectiveness through a variety of methods. Similarly, the "war on drugs," declared by President Nixon in 1971 (Beckett, 1997), and extended by Presidents Reagan and Bush, placed the emphasis on drugs as a source of danger and ultimately violent death. The major thrust of these laws was to encourage police arrests through direct incentives (like sharing in federal forfeitures of drug crime assets) and to encourage longer sentences for drug criminals.

**The war on violent crime.** While the war on drugs often gets most of the attention, especially from critics, violent crime was clearly the first focus of national politics, beginning as early as the Goldwater campaign in 1964 (Beckett, 1997), and leading Lyndon Johnson to declare a war on crime in 1967, well before Nixon's emphasis on drugs in 1971 (Simon, 2007). While repressing violent crime has a clear legitimacy that the war on drugs often lacks, we point to crucial ways in which a "war on violent crime" can also create structural incentives for wrongful conviction.

*Homicide clearance rates and police misconduct.* Mounting evidence suggests that law enforcement agencies allocate a disproportionate amount of time and resources towards investigating homicides. In the era of modern policing in which agencies utilize accountability programs (such as Compstat; see below), on-the-ground detectives feel pressure to drive up their clearance rates, particularly for publicly visible crimes like murder. This pressure to solve homicide cases likely results in the apprehension of more guilty culprits. But emerging anecdotal and empirical evidence suggests that this pressure may also increase the likelihood of police misconduct, thus leading to wrongful convictions.

*Organizational pressure on homicide detectives.* American police departments have undergone major changes over the last few decades that may have contributed to heightened pressure during murder investigations. First, American society has ideologically reoriented to adopt what David Garland (2001, p.139) terms a "culture of high crime" in which crime fears are widespread and salient. Police departments have not escaped the pressure of this transformation. In major cities like New York, political leaders turned to police to reduce crime through aggressive urban policing tactics. High crime rates have seemingly reset the rules, expanding public support for aggressive policing tactics. Second, modern innovations in police department organization placed added stress on supervisors to get results. Police departments have rapidly professionalized over the last several decades. During this same time period, accountability programs like Compstat diffused across American law enforcement agencies. William Bratton popularized the use of Compstat when he implemented the system as New York City Police Commissioner. The term Compstat "refers to a 'strategic control system' developed to gather and disseminate information on the NYPD's crime problems and to track efforts to deal with them" (Weisburd et al., 2004, p. 2). One of the most visible components of the Compstat system is the use of weekly " 'crime-control strategy meetings,' where precinct commanders appear before several of the department's top brass to report on crime problems in their precincts and what they are doing about them" (p. 2). David Weisburd et al. found that by 1999, 32.6 percent of large departments implemented Compstat, with another 25.6 percent planning to in the immediate future. Mapping the trend in Compstat adoption over time, Weisburd et al projected that almost all large departments should have adopted some major elements of Compstat by 2007.

Admittedly, police departments across the United States have long fixated on murder clearance rates as a measure of overall effectiveness. Historical analysis demonstrates that, as far back as 1894, police responded more directly to murders than other felony offenses (Bijleveld & Monkkonen, 1991). But a bevy of contemporary studies have all verified that in the modern policing era, murder clearance rates have evolved into the "single most important quantified measure of police performance, despite questions of their adequacy as such" (Litwin, 2004, p. 331). And in the age of Compstat, the importance of homicide clearance leads to supervisors placing "unmistakable organizational pressure on homicide detectives" (331). In fact, it is not uncommon to find in the homicide office of a police department a score card showing the number of cases assigned to each homicide detective next to the number of cases the detective has cleared (Litwin, 2004; Simon, 1991). The conventional wisdom today is that increased performance can be tied to clearance rates[1] (Keel, Jarvis, & Muirhead, 2008).

Generally, "the pressure to solve homicides produces the intended results" (Gross 1996, p. 478). That is, this pressure results in clearance rates for homicide offenses that are substantially higher than all other felonies. In 2011, American law enforcement agencies reported clearing about 65% of all reported homicides, compared to only roughly 29% of robberies, 41% of rapes, 57% of aggravated assaults, and only 19% of property crimes (Federal Bureau of Investigations, 2011). In many ways, a police department's focus on homicides makes sense. Murders are the most dangerous felony offense, and they result in significant public outcry. At the same time, this understandable pressure may motivate some officers to cut corners, lie, or even manufacture evidence to justify an arrest and secure a conviction. Murder convictions — particularly in capital cases — represent a disproportionately high percentage of all known wrongful convictions (Gross, 1996). Various studies have reached this conclusion. For example, Arye Rattner (1988) found that of the 205 known wrongful convictions from 1900 onward, 45% were murder convictions, and 12% were death penalty cases. Keep in mind, homicide arrests "make up a fraction of 1% of all arrests in this country, and about 3% of arrests for crimes of violence" (Gross, 1996, p. 472).

In part, homicide cases and convictions receive more attention than the criminal processing of other offenses, and therefore a higher proportion of wrongful murder convictions are uncovered relative to other crimes (Gross, 2008). But Gross also identifies institutional and organizational pressure during the investigation process as key factors in explaining the disproportionately high number of individuals wrongfully convicted of murder offenses. A department's investigation of a murder "effectively establishes how the incident is to be remembered by the wider community" (Innes, 2003, p. 270). Detectives face political and organizational pressure to make arrests in unsolved murders (Davies, 2007). This pressure is particularly intense in the era of modern policing, where accountability programs like Compstat hold supervisors accountable for crime statistics and clearance rates. In light of this pressure, police sometimes take on the role of "moral entrepreneurs," willing to bend the rules and procedures to achieve what they view as a necessary outcome (Huff, Rattner, & Sagarin, 1986, p. 528). An officer may strongly believe that a suspect is guilty of a homicide, but lack sufficient evidence to bring the case to trial. When combined with intense political and social pressure to make an arrest, a well-intentioned officer may participate in misconduct to coerce or frame a criminal suspect.

There is ample anecdotal evidence to bolster the hypothesis that the political, organizational, and institutional pressures on detectives to make arrests may facilitate false convictions. We offer two particularly salient examples. The first comes from Gross's 1996 article. In 1983, an unknown criminal suspect abducted, raped and killed 10-year-old Jeanine Nicarico from Naperville, Illinois. For 13 frustrating months, the police failed to identify a solid suspect. Less than two weeks before the local prosecutor's reelection bid, Illinois indicted three suspects. On two separate occasions, a trial court in Illinois found two of the three suspects guilty and sentenced them to death. And after *both* convictions, the Illinois Supreme Court reversed the trial court's verdict. Finally, 12 years

---

1. It is worth noting that clearance rates for some homicide clearance rates have indeed fallen over the last several decades. We do not believe that this fact undermines our argument. Admittedly, this may bolster a claim that decreasing clearance rates would open up the opportunity for fewer wrongful convictions. No doubt this may be true. Conversely, we would argue that decreases in clearance rates may increase the pressure on police departments to clear cases and elevate these measures.

later, during the third trial against the two criminal suspects, a police officer admitted to lying under oath. According to Gross (1996), "under intense pressure, the police convinced themselves that they knew who killed Jeanine Nicarico, and they manufactured evidence to convince the prosecutors and to use in court" (p. 478).

Another case originating in the 1980s involved two Florida men incarcerated, one on death row, one for life, for rape-murders committed by serial killer Eric Mosely in Fort Lauderdale. Simon (2010) describes Mosely's crimes and the failures of Fort Lauderdale Sheriff's Department and the Broward County prosecutors to convict him. The two men convicted represented targets of opportunity, known to law enforcement and with significant vulnerabilities (one was mentally disabled, one was on parole for a murder committed in his youth). In both cases there were significant failures on the parts of police and prosecutors to turn over evidence that would have been helpful to the defense.

Although the Nicarico and Mosely cases seem to represent jarring examples of misconduct in response to possible organizational pressures, it does not appear to be particularly unique. The recent allegations surrounding former Brooklyn Detective Louis Scarcella provide another poignant example. Detective Scarcella worked in New York City during the crack cocaine epidemic of the 1980s and 1990s. New evidence uncovered by the *New York Times* has cast doubt on the validity of many of his arrests. Scarcella apparently relied on the same crack-addicted prostitute as a primary eyewitness in multiple murder cases. Scarcella's supervisor told the *Times* that Scarcella would regularly pay prostitutes $100 for information. Scarcella also allegedly testified in court about confessions he obtained from suspects who often claimed to have told him nothing. The *Times* learned that Scarcella obtained identifications not through the use of a photo gallery, or in-person lineup, but instead through showing witnesses a single photo and allowing witnesses, "to mingle together while making an identification" (Robles, 2013, p. A1). Although this case is still under investigation, there is preliminary support that the prosecutor, as in the Nicarico case, potentially facilitated the alleged misconduct — as Brooklyn District Attorney Charles Hynes "has [allegedly] for years aggressively fended off appeals and denied public records requests from inmates who believe they were wrongfully targeted by Mr. Scarcella" (Robles, 2013).

**The war on drugs.** The rise of stringent sentencing statutes for drug law offenses is perhaps the most transparent and widely cited dimension of the punitive and racially disparate effects of the so-called war on drugs. But the drug war has also had a profound impact on law enforcement activity at the local, state and federal level. It has dramatically expanded the scope, intensity, and stringency of police efforts to detect drug manufacture, sale, and use. The result has been not only a rise in drug law policing, but also a transformation of the tactics and nature of on-the-ground police practices. "Buy and busts," "jump outs," the use of informants, wiretaps, and even paramilitary tactics, as well as the broader expansion of pretextual stops and searches and low-level arrests, have produced an increasingly aggressive, intrusive and indiscriminate form of policing that falls disproportionately on low-income communities of color (e.g. see Alexander, 2012; Balko, 2006; King, 2008; Lynch, 2012)

In 1971, President Richard Nixon called for "a new, all-out offensive" to fight "America's public enemy number one" (Nixon, June 17, 1971). Two years later, he declared "an all-out global war on the drug menace," and issued an Executive Order creating the Drug Enforcement Agency (DEA) within the Department of Justice to consolidate and coordinate the federal government's drug control activities (Administration, 2008, p. 13). The dramatic and unprecedented expansion of drug law enforcement efforts began in earnest, however, in the early 1980s under the Reagan administration. The federal budget for drug control increased almost six-fold during the decade: from $1.5 billion in fiscal year 1980 to $6.7 billion in 1990 (Reuter, 1992).[2] Between 70 and 80 percent of this federal spending was devoted to enforcement efforts. State and local level drug enforcement expenditures are generally subsumed within department budgets and are therefore harder to quantify; nonetheless, estimates suggest such spending is at least as much and likely exceeds federal expenditures. Reuter (1992) estimated, for example, that roughly $14 billion was spent on state and local drug control enforcement (police, courts, and corrections) in 1990.

*The quantitative change: Rise in drug arrests.* The number of drug arrests in the United States has grown steadily and dramatically since the early 1970s. In 1970, there were under a half million state and local arrests for drug offenses; by 2006, the number of arrests for drug offenses reached a peak close to two million (UCR, BJS 2012). While drug arrests have uniformly risen, the composition of these arrests has changed over time. During the 1980s, while arrests for both possession and distribution grew, distribution arrests increased at a higher rate, accounting for 27 percent of all drug arrests in 1990 as compared to 18 percent in 1980. As Figure 1 shows, since 1991, the rise in arrests for drug offenses has been exclusively for possession charges (Bureau of Justice Statistics, 2010). Roughly 80 percent of the drug arrests made today are for possession.[3]

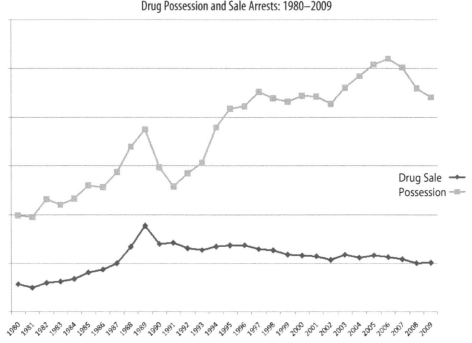

Drug Possession and Sale Arrests: 1980–2009

Source: Bureau of Justice Statistics Figure 41. Drug sale/manufacture arrest rates.

2. The DEA budget was $74.9 million in 1973, the year the Drug Enforcement Administration was created. It increased to $140.9 million in 1975; $362.4 million in 1985; $769.2 million in 1990.

3. In 1980 the absolute number of arrests was much lower than today, but the composition was similar to the composition of drug arrests today: 70 percent of all drug arrests in 1980 were for marijuana and 82 percent of all drug arrests were possession offenses. In 1990, the composition changed and marijuana arrests comprised only 30 percent of all drug arrests and the percent of arrests for the distribution of drugs increased from 18 to 27 percent. By 2011, drug arrests again primarily involved possession offenses (80 percent), and marijuana sale and possession arrests comprised 49 percent of all the arrests. (Federal Bureau of Investigation, 1980–2011)

The aggregate rise in drug arrests at the national level holds across states and localities. An analysis of 43 of the nation's largest cities shows, for example, that between 1980 and 2003, in all but three cities, drug arrest rates grew, with increases ranging from 13 to 887% (King, 2008). This variation underscores the highly discretionary nature of drug law policing. Drug crimes, like all "victimless" crimes, are rarely reported to police. Drug arrests are therefore in large part the product of enforcement priorities and proactive targeting rather than changes in drug supply or use.

*Federally driven changes.* While the war on drugs triggered a significant expansion in federal policing, to a great extent, the "war" has been fought at the state and local level. Federal investments, in the form of grants, equipment, training, and the extension of asset forfeiture laws, helped to facilitate this reorientation of state and local police priorities and resources directed towards drug law enforcement. These investments, in combination with police organizational and institutional incentives, and the wide discretion officers have been afforded by the courts, has resulted in the proliferation of aggressive and widespread street-level drug policing throughout the United States.

*Grants.* The first authorization of direct federal aid to state and local governments for the purpose of combating drug-related crime was authorized under the 1986 Anti-Drug Abuse Act. Two years later, Congress extended and expanded the federal aid program, re-named the Edward Byrne Memorial State and Local Law Enforcement Assistance Program after a New York City officer who was shot dead by drug dealers while in the line of duty protecting a drug case witness (Administration, 2008). The Byrne program was designed to emphasize "the reduction of violent and drug-related crimes" and to foster "multijurisdictional efforts to support national drug control priorities" (BJS, 2002). The largest share of Byrne funding has gone towards multijurisdictional narcotics task forces, which, often quota driven, loosely supervised, and without strict guidelines, have been rife with corruption and misconduct (Blakeslee, 2006). The Tulia case, among the most publicized of the countless cases of wrongful incarceration associated with Byrne task forces, involved a Byrne-funded narcotics officer in the Texas Panhandle who set up dozens of individuals, most of them black, for allegedly dealing cocaine. After a four-year legal battle, Governor Rick Perry pardoned the wrongfully convicted; by that time, the 38 Tulia defendants had cumulatively spent over 70 years wrongly imprisoned in Texas jails and prisons (Sherrer, 2003).

*Asset forfeiture.* The "equitable sharing" provisions of the asset forfeiture laws have provided another important source of income for local drug law enforcement. Authority to seize criminally acquired profits and assets was first granted under the 1970 Comprehensive Drug Abuse, Prevention and Control Act (Miller & Selva, 1994).[4] The Act was amended in 1978 to permit *civil* forfeiture, which permitted the government to seize and retain assets even in cases where the criminal charges were dismissed and reduced the burden of proof. By 1985, 47 states had passed laws resembling the federal model (Miller & Selva, 1994).

*Police organizational/institutional incentives.* In addition to the federally driven incentives described above, organizational and institutional features of police departments have encouraged the proliferation of aggressive street-level drug policing. Arrests numbers are a commonly used metric of officer productivity. The increasingly statistics-driven model of law enforcement, and relative ease of targeting drug users and low-level street dealers has made drug arrests an attractive way for officers to appear productive and

---

4. The law was directed towards fighting organized crime, and this included individuals operating trafficking organizations.

advance their career (Moskos, 2008). In many departments, officers are additionally incentivized to focus on easy drug arrests rather than on solving serious crimes, because the arrests, particularly if made at the end of a shift, can provide guaranteed and effortless overtime pay in the time required to fill out paper-work and appear in court (Levine & Small, 2008).

In the context of fighting the war on drugs, the courts have consistently granted the police broad discretion with respect to their stop, search, seizure and arrest practices (Alexander, 2012). Justice Stevens made this point in his widely cited dissent in *California v. Acevedo* (1991), which ruled the police do not need a warrant to search a container, package or compartment within an automobile provided they have probable cause to believe contraband or evidence is contained within the vehicle: "No impartial observer could criticize this Court for hindering the progress of the war on drugs. On the contrary, decisions like the one the Court made today will support the conclusion that this Court has become a loyal foot soldier in the Executive's fight against crime" (*California v. Acevedo*, 1991).

The drug war is now widely discredited as a way to reduce crime overall or the particular social problems associated with drug addiction, but its larger effects on the culture of policing, courts and prosecution have yet to be reckoned with and may linger long after the federal incentives to pursue it cease.

# Moving Forward: How the Wars on Crime and Drugs Promote Wrongful Convictions

As the intense politicization of crime policy discussed above has begun to wind down in many respects, it has become possible to open up a broader policy discussion of how our crime fighting choices have compromised some of our core legal and political values and to seek ways to rebalance the system. We lay out our main hypotheses about the links between crime wars and wrongful convictions, before offering suggestions for a path forward.

## The Hypothesized Link Between Homicide Policing and Wrongful Conviction

Admittedly, it is impossible to know exactly how often our justice system wrongfully convicts individuals for murder, or any offense. Nevertheless, the available evidence suggests that wrongful convictions for murder are more prevalent than other miscarriages of justice (Gross, 1996). And misconduct by police, even if well intentioned, appears to play a significant role in this phenomenon. Previous attempts to conceptualize the links between policing and wrongful convictions have focused on the micro-level processes that contribute to these injustices — coercive confessions, faulty lineup procedures, and undue reliance on questionable eyewitness testimony (e.g., Kassin, et al., 2010; Wells, et al., 1998). No doubt each of these micro-processes facilitates police-induced wrongful convictions, as noted by Borchard (1932) some 80 years ago. The Supreme Court has also attempted to address these concerns. For example, in *Miranda v. Arizona* (1966) and subsequent cases, the Court has taken steps to limit the coerciveness of interrogations. Similarly, in *Simmons v. United States* (1968), the Court clarified some of the limitations on lineup procedures. These micro-processes are, however, mere symptoms of a broader shift in American policing over the last several decades, largely associated with the national war on crime. New organizational models have increased the demands for accountability in police agencies. Cultural and social trends have put pressure on police departments to reduce crime and respond rapidly to particularly gruesome crimes like homicides. It is in this cultural, social, and organizational environment that police officers sometimes turn to misconduct which can result in wrongful convictions.

## The Hypothesized Link Between Drug Policing and Wrongful Convictions

The series of incentives discussed above that have been built into contemporary policing by the war on drugs (e.g., federal grants, asset forfeitures) may have had the unintended consequences of wrongful conviction.

**Police corruption.** By the end of the 1980s there was growing evidence of the pervasiveness of police corruption in connection with drug law enforcement efforts (Carter 1990). While there are no systematic data quantifying the full scale of drug-related police corruption, there have been numerous cases in cities across the U.S. including Atlanta, Chicago, Cleveland, Detroit, Los Angeles, Miami, New Orleans, New York, and Philadelphia (Office & Division, 1998).[5] Investigations have found officers engaged in overt criminal acts for private gain—taking bribes, or stealing drugs or money, for example—as well as the more pervasive problem of illegitimate means used in the pursuit of drug crime— unconstitutional searches and seizures, officers providing false testimony or false crime reports, entrapment of suspected of drug offenders, and planting drugs in drug raids.

A number of features of drug law enforcement make it particularly prone to corruption. Drug law offenses can often involve large sums of money, creating the opportunity for criminal private gain (Newburn, Webb, & Britain, 1999). More generally, the widespread and "victimless" nature of drug use and drug sales makes arrests practices highly discretionary and subject to minimal managerial scrutiny. Further, the consensual nature of drug exchanges has meant officers are "required" to secure information from close to the market. This may mean officers buy or use drugs in the course of their work, or rely on informants to secure information, a practice police have increasingly come to depend on despite the fact that the evidence provided by informants is often highly unreliable (Natapoff, 2009). The rise of mandatory minimums and augmented sentences for drug offenses has increased the incentives for individuals arrested for drug crimes to serve as "snitches" irrespective of the quality of information they may have; and the surge in the sheer number of drug arrests produces an expanded pool of potential informants. Unlike high-profile informant cases, the use of drug informants by local and state police is largely

---

5. Numerous media reports of drug-related police corruption began to proliferate in the late 1980s. Cater (1990) cites reports in cities including Kansas City, Detroit, Miami, New York City: "DEA Agents Suspected in Theft of Heroin." Kansas City Times (19 December 1988:A-3); "Seven Ex-Police Officers Indicted in Philadelphia," Kansas City Times (20 July 1988:A-2); "125 Detroit Officers Suspected of Crack Ties." Detroit Free Press (5 May 1988: 1A); "Drug Corruption Claims Growing Number of Miami Cops," Law Enforcement News (8 December 1987: I); 400 Cases Will Be Dropped Because D.C. Cops Stole Drugs," WA Today (17 September 1987:3A); "13 New York Cops Charged With Shaking Down Drug Dealers," The State News (7 November 1986:2)

unregulated. Finally, the "war" rhetoric itself, in pushing a mentality that demands results at all costs, likely encourages officers to engage in unlawful, dishonest, and unreliable practices.

**"Policing for profit."** Civil asset forfeiture has been implicated in numerous police abuse scandals, and, more generally, critics argue, corrupts police interests such that they actually come to have a stake in maintaining the perpetual existence of the war on drugs (Alexander, 2012). Asset forfeiture distorts police priorities by incentivizing police departments to devote manpower to drug crimes rather than serious or violent crimes. Further, there is evidence that it directly shapes how and when police make arrests. For example, Miller and Selva (1994) found officers would orchestrate drug busts in order to maximize profit by waiting to arrest suspected dealers until the end of the day when they would have depleted their drug supplies and be flush with cash. Similarly, former New York City Police Commissioner Patrick Murphy testified before congress in 1992 admitting officers routinely imposed roadblocks on southbound rather than northbound lanes to increase the probability of confiscating cash rather than drugs: "seized cash will end up forfeited to the police department while seized drugs can only be destroyed" (Blumenson & Nilsen, 1998; Roberts, 1993).

In addition to the perverting influence of asset forfeiture on police behavior, the practice serves a punitive function before there has been a determination of guilt or formal punishment. The vast majority of civil forfeiture actions—upwards of 90 percent according to some estimates (Hyde, 1995)—are not accompanied by criminal prosecution.[6] Given the majority of targeted individuals are low income and, if the criminal case is dropped, do not have state provided counsel, most forfeitures, approximately 80 percent, are uncontested (Alexander, 2012).

**Aggressive and intrusive policing.** The war on drugs has not only provided growing opportunities for police misconduct and distorted law enforcement priorities, but, more broadly, it has institutionalized increasingly intrusive and aggressive forms of policing practices and tactics. This aggressive face of drug law enforcement is exemplified by the proliferation of paramilitary police units across urban, suburban, and even small town police departments (Balko, 2006). The police use of "Special Weapons And Tactics" (SWAT) teams began in Los Angeles in the 1960s, and spread to police departments throughout the country in the 1970s. But their initial use was reserved for highly volatile and unusual circumstances, such as cases involving hostages or hijackings. In the 1980s, the federal government began to provide local jurisdictions with surplus military equipment and federal grants to develop military-style operations for the specific purpose of conducting drug raids (Balko, 2006). SWAT teams and the use of "no-knock" and "quick-knock" drug raids became increasingly common. Even after the violence associated with drug markets had long receded, military-style policing persisted and even escalated in cities across the United States. In 1972, there were a few hundred paramilitary drug raids per year, by the early eighties there were 3,000 annual SWAT deployments, an estimated 30,000 in 1996, and by 2001, an estimated 40,000 raids (Balko, 2006; Kraska, 2005). The most common use of SWAT teams today is to serve narcotics warrants, usually by forced and unannounced entry. In some jurisdictions drug warrants are *only* served by SWAT teams or similar paramilitary units (Balko, 2006).

The enforcement of drug laws has also provided a pretext for the dramatic expansion of stops and searches. The pretense of "suspected drug activity" has allowed officers to broadly target suspects, who, in most cases, have done nothing wrong. Stops are often

---

6. Until the 2000 Reform Act, the burden of showing that property or money seized was legitimately earned was the responsibility of the owner.

based not on specific suspicious behavior or evidence, but rather around geographic areas or racial profiles. With few exceptions, the Court has consistently made it easier for the police to establish grounds to stop and search motorists and pedestrians. The police have thus undertaken countless searches with barely probable cause; and the great majority of those stopped and searched are young men of color.

**Proliferation of low-level violations.** Many have argued the police practices developed and encouraged by the drug war have distorted the nature of police work itself (Simon & Burns, 1998). Officers do not need to learn to conduct investigations or follow procedures in an environment in which street sweeps can easily turn up arrests. And even if drugs are not found, other low-level violations such as loitering or disorderly conduct can often be charged. As a result, groups of individuals are broadly and collectively punished irrespective of their individual culpability. Recent reports on the conduct of the New York City police, for example, have established the widespread practice of wrongful trespassing arrests of young men of color found in or near low-income housing projects (Gross, 2008). Many individuals are arrested in these housing projects simply because they do not have identification to present to the police when entering a building, or they are paying an unannounced visit to a friend (Fabricant, 2011). The incidents of police officer dishonesty with respect to these trespassing arrests is pervasive: officers frequently file boilerplate complaints stating the defendant told the officer he was in the building to purchase marijuana (Gross, 2008). As reported by *The Village Voice,* a judge, in hearing one of these trespassing cases, recognized the duplicity: "This court does not credit the testimony that the defendant disclosed to a person wearing a badge that he was going to buy marijuana. [That] does not make sense" (Fabricant, 2007, p. 1). Many of these defendants, despite being innocent, end up pleading guilty to avoid the cost and risk associated with proceedings. The NYPD maintains that the practice of patrolling the buildings keeps drugs and drug dealing out of low-income housing. But whatever its impact on drug trafficking activity, in the process, many innocent people are arrested, charged and convicted (Fabricant, 2007; Gross, 2008).

## Solutions: End the Wars on Crime and Drugs

In this chapter we have offered a historically grounded, theoretical account of how the federally mobilized long war on crime (1967– present) has substantially distorted police incentives in such a way that has likely increased the number of wrongful conviction in our contemporary criminal justice system. This distortion of incentives may well have overwhelmed improvements in representation and professional standards during the same period. Two considerations emerge from this, one relevant to political institutions and one relevant to policy.

Political scientists and punishment and society scholars have debated whether America's punitive turn in policing and imprisonment is best seen as a consequence of the extreme degree of decentralization, or instead as a consequence of the interference of the federal government in local affairs through the war on crime and drugs (Garland, 2010; Lacey & Soskind, forthcoming; Stuntz, 2011). The model of wrongful conviction incentives that we have outlined suggests that the combination of the two is problematic. The federal "war on crime" has both promoted local crime politics but also helped disable traditional political checks on local criminal justice by overriding local budgeting (forfeitures) and jury trials (severe fixed sentences).

Legal scholars and criminologists have developed a strong evidence-based body of knowledge about investigative techniques that present a high risk for wrongful convictions. These scholars have also made various recommendations on procedures and techniques to help avoid these risks. An inventory of risk factors can obscure, however, the extent to which wrongful convictions are the logical result of the war on crime and the ethos and incentives it entails; not simply the product of individual failures. Furthermore, states have shown remarkable resistance to adopting even these limited protective measures, an enduring result of politics that came out of the war on crime. Given states' resistance, the federal government may hold a key role in ending the war on crime and the wrongful convictions it produces. There is a recent precedent for such a federal role: President Obama's Spring 2013 speech to the Naval Academy suggesting the war on terror is now over.

A political decision to end the wars on crime and drugs, whether at the presidential level or at the state and local level, should include several elements if it is to help remove the incentives for wrongful conviction that we have discussed in this chapter.

1. An end to the state of emergency ethos around violent and drug crime. Even the worst crimes can be handled through traditional criminal justice methods with a focus on solving individual crimes and prioritizing the presumption of innocence.

2. A revision of sentences extended recklessly during the past several decades in an effort to incapacitate our way out of a period of high crime. This should be retroactive. Prisons remain overcrowded throughout the country, including thousands of men in their fifties and sixties (or older) convicted of murders or other violent crimes who have now served sentences that would meet retributive purposes around the world (20 years or more of imprisonment). Some of these are indubitably wrongfully convicted but due to features of their case or blind luck, there will never be a clear opportunity for exoneration. We need broad amnesty aimed at prisoners who have served more than twenty years (mostly without disciplinary problems).

3. Going forward we need an improved commitment and respect for the humanity and dignity of all prisoners, premised on the realization that some of them will inevitably be wrongfully convicted. The only realistic way to achieve this against the ongoing pressure of populist crime fears (a genie that will not go back into the bottle no matter how terrible the consequences of its emergence in the eyes of legal elites) is through constitutional change. The Supreme Court's recent *Brown v. Plata* (2011) invoked dignity as a determinative value in the Eighth Amendment, a trend in jurisprudence last in vogue in the period 1948–1972, but largely missing since the war on crime came to dominate American policy and politics (Simon, 2014). And while *Brown v. Plata* (2011) suggests a growing judicial readiness to protect human dignity against the pressures of populist punitiveness, the degree of inhumanity revealed in that case suggests that something legally stronger would be appropriate. Ultimately a constitutional amendment adopting Article 5 of the Universal Declaration of Human Rights ("No one shall be subjected to torture or to cruel, inhuman or degrading treatment or punishment") would be the best way to empower courts and public officials to reverse the pattern of deference to both populist driven state penal policies and dubious claims of state penal expertise that characterized the past quarter century of law and policy.

# Conclusion

This chapter has sought to analyze the contributions made by the historic transformations in penal policy known popularly as the "war on crime" and the "war on drugs" to the problem of wrongful conviction. We offered hypotheses tracing the incentives that these broad political initiatives have created within the administration of justice that can produce wrongful convictions. Although we do purport to test these hypotheses, satisfying tests may not be possible given the absence of a control sample of police departments or prosecutorial offices not affected by the broad national trends we have summarized. But if our hypotheses capture important dynamics unleashed by the wars on crime and drugs, then technical solutions to the problem of wrongful conviction are unlikely to address the full scope of the problem. We recommend instead that political solutions, including a formal renunciation of the "wars" on crime and drugs, and proactive efforts to deliver relief on a systemic basis to long serving prisoners through parole consideration, clemency and retroactive reductions in sentences for whole categories of offenses where incentives to wrongful conviction were particularly strong.

# References

Administration, U.S. Drug Enforcement. (2008). *Drug Enforcement Administration: A Tradition of Excellence, 1973-2008*: Drug Enforcement Administration. Haiti Trust Digital Library. Retrieved June 1, 2013, from http://catalog.hathitrust.org/Record/005952023

Alexander, M. (2012). *The new Jim Crow: Mass incarceration in the age of colorblindness.* New York: The New Press.

Balko, R. (2006). Overkill: The latest trend in policing. *Chicago Daily Law Bulletin, 6.*

Benson, B. L., Rasmussen, D. W., & Sollars, D. L. (1995). Police bureaucracies, their incentives, and the war on drugs. *Public Choice, 83,* 21-45.

Beckett, K. (1997). *Making crime pay: Law and order in contemporary America.* New York, NY: Oxford University Press.

Bijleveld, C. C. J. H., & Eric H. Monkkonen. (1991). Cross-sectional and dynamic analyses of concomitants of police behavior. *Historical Methods, 21,* 16-24.

Blakeslee, N. (2006). *Tulia: Race, cocaine, and corruption in a small Texas town*: New York, NY: Public Affairs.

Blumenson, E. D, & Nilsen, E.S. (1998). Contesting government's financial interest in drug cases. *Criminal Justice, 13,* 4.

Borchard, E. M. (1932). *Convicting the innocent: Sixty-five actual errors of criminal justice.* Garden City, NY: Garden City Publishing Inc.

Bureau of Justice Statistics (2010). U.S. Department of Justice. Washington, DC: Bureau of Justice Statistics. Retrieved June 1, 2013, from http://www.bjs.gov/

*California v. Acevedo,* 500 U.S. 565, 1991.

Davies, H. (2007). Understanding variations in murder clearance rates: The influence of the political environment. *Homicide Studies, 11,* 133-150.

Ehlers, St. (1999). Policy briefing: asset forfeiture. *Washington, DC: The Drug Policy Foundation.*

Fabricant, M C. (2007). Rousting the cops: one man stands up to the NYPD's apartheid-like trespassing crackdown. *Village Voice.*

Fabricant, M C. (2011). War crimes and misdemeanors: Understanding 'zero-tolerance' policing as a form of collective punishment and human rights violation. *Drexel Law Review, 3,* 373-414.

Feeley, M. & Sarat, A. (1981). *The Policy Dilemma: Federal Crime Policy and the Law Enforcement Assistance Administration, 1968-1978.* Minneapolis: University of Minnesota Press.

Federal Bureau of Investigation. 1980-2011. Uniform Crime Reports for the United States. Retrieved May, 2013, from http://www.fbi.gov/about-us/cjis/ucr/ucr

Foucault, M. (2003). *Society must be defended: Lectures at the College d' France, 1975-6.* New York, NY: Picador.

Fyfe, J. J. (2004). Stops, frisks, searches, and the constitution. *Criminology & Public Policy, 3,* 379-96.

Garland, D. (2001). *The Culture of Control: Crime and Social Order in Contemporary Society.* Chicago: University of Chicago Press.

Gross, S. R. (1996). The risks of death: Why erroneous convictions are common in capital cases. *Buffalo Law Review, 44,* 469-500.

Gross, S. R. (2008). Convicting the innocent. *Annual Review of Law and Social Science, 4,* 173-192.

Huff, R, Rattner, A. & Sagarin, E. (1986). Guilty until proved innocent: wrongful conviction and public policy. *Crime and Delinquency, 32,* 518-544.

Hyde, H. J. (1995). *Forfeiting Our Property Rights: Is Your Property Safe from Seizure?:* Cato Institute.

Innes, M. (2003). *Investigating Murder: Detective Work and the Police Response to Homicide.* Oxford: Oxford University Press.

Keel, T. G., Jarvis, J. P., & Muirhead, Y. E. (2008). An exploratory analysis of factors affecting homicide investigations examining the dynamics of murder clearance rates. *Homicide Studies, 13,* 50-68.

King, R. S. (2008). *Disparity By geography: The war on drugs in America's cities.* Washington, DC: The Sentencing Project.

Kraska, P. (2005). Researching the police-military blur: Lessons learned. *Police Forum, 14,* 1-12.

Lakoff, G. & Johnson, M. 2003. *Metaphors we live by.* (2nd ed.). Chicago, IL: University of Chicago Press.

Levine, H, & Peterson, D. S. (2008). *Marijuana arrest crusade.* New York, NY: New York Civil Liberties Union.

Litwin, K. J. (2004). A multilevel multivariate analysis of factors affecting homicide clearances. *Journal of Research in Crime and Delinquency, 41,* 327-351.

Lopez, A. B. (2001). Racial profiling and when: searching for objective evidence of the fourth amendment on the nation's roads. *Kentucky Law Journal, 90,* 75.

Lynch, M. (2012). Theorizing the role of the 'war on drugs' in US punishment. *Theoretical Criminology, 16,* 175-99.

Miller, J. M., & Selva, L. H. (1994). Drug enforcement's double-edged sword: An assessment of asset forfeiture programs. *Justice Quarterly, 11,* 313-35.

Moskos, P. (2008). *Cop in the hood.* Princeton, NJ: Princeton University Press.

Murgado, A. (September 5, 2012). Drug interdiction for patrol: know what to look for on traffic stops to make an impact on the drug trade. *Police Magazine.* Retrieved from, http://www.policemag.com/channel/patrol/articles/2012/09/drug-interdiction-for-patrol.aspx

Myers, H. L., & Brzostowski, J. P. (1981). *Drug agents' guide to forfeiture of assets, first edition.* Washington, D.C.: U.S. Department of Justice.

Natapoff, A. (2009). *Snitching: Criminal informants and the erosion of American justice:* New York, NY: NYU Press.

Natapoff, A. (2012). Misdemeanors. *Southern California Law Review, 85,* 101-163.

Newburn, T., & Webb, B. (1999). *Understanding and preventing police corruption: Lessons from the literature*: Home Office, Policing and Reducing Crime Unit, Research, Development and Statistics Directorate.

Nixon, R. (June 17, 1971). Remarks about an Intensified Program for Drug Abuse Prevention and Control. In G. Peters & J. T. Woolley (Eds.), *The American Presidency Project.* http://www.presidency.ucsb.edu/ws/?pid=3047.

Office, US Government Accountability, and General Government Division. (1998). Law Enforcement: Information on Drug-Related Police Corruption. *No.: GAO/GGD-98-111, 46.*

Pager, D. (2007). *Marked: Race, crime and finding work in an era of mass incarceration.* Chicago: University of Chicago Press.

Rattner, A. (1988). Convicted by innocent: wrongful conviction and the criminal justice system. *Law and Human Behavior, 12,* 283-293.

Reuter, P. (1992). Hawks ascendant: the punitive trend of American drug policy. *Daedalus, 121,* 15-52.

Roberts, P. C. (Nov. 1 1993). Forfeiture Laws Let Government Take Property From Innocent People. *Deseret News.* Utah.

Robles, F. (May 11, 2013). Review of 50 Brooklyn Murder Cases Ordered. *The New York Times.*

*Sandstrom v. Montana,* 442 U.S. 510 (1979)

Sherrer, H. (2003). *Travesty in Tulia, Texas: Frame-up of 38 innocent people orchestrated by a county sheriff, prosecutor and judge.* Retrieved from, http://www.forejustice.org/wc/tulia_travesty.htm

Simon, D. (1991). *Homicide: A year on the killing streets.* Boston: Houghton Mifflin.

Simon, D., & Burns, E. (1998). *The corner: A year in the life of an inner-city neighborhood.* New York, NY: Broadway.

Simon, J. (2007). *Governing through crime: How the War on Crime transformed American democracy and created a culture of fear.* New York, NY: Oxford University Press.

Simon, J. (2008). War on! Why a war on cancer should replace our war on crime (and terror), *European Journal of Cultural Studies, 11,* 351-369.

Simon, J. (2014). *Mass incarceration on trial: California's inhuman prisons before the Constitution.* New York. NY: New Press.

Smith, S. D. (1988). Scope of real property forfeiture for drug-related crimes under the Comprehensive Forfeiture Act. *University of Pennsylvania Law Review, 137,* 303.

Weisburd, D., Mastrofski, S. D., Greenspan, R. & Willis, J. J. (April 2004). The growth of Compstat in American policing. *The Police Foundation Reports.* Retrieved from, file:///C:/Users/ar148255/Downloads/growthofcompstat.pdf.

Western, B. (2006). *Punishment and Inequality in America.* New York. Russell Sage Foundation.

Zimring, F. E. (2011). *The city that became safe: New York's lessons for urban crime and its control.* Oxford: Oxford University Press.

# Chapter Seven

# The Prosecutor's Contribution to Wrongful Convictions

Bennett L. Gershman, *Pace University*

## Introduction

A prosecutor is viewed by the public as a powerful law enforcement official whose responsibility is to convict guilty people of crimes. But not everybody understands that a prosecutor's function is not only to win convictions of law-breakers. A prosecutor is a quasi-judicial official who has a duty to promote justice to the entire community, including those people charged with crimes. Indeed, an overriding function of a prosecutor is to ensure that innocent people do not get convicted and punished. The Supreme Court observed in the famous passage in *Berger v. United States* (1935) that a prosecutor's dual responsibility is that "guilt shall not escape or innocence suffer" (p. 88).

Despite the heavy burden placed on prosecutors to ensure that justice is afforded to all accused, empirical and anecdotal evidence strongly demonstrates that prosecutors — by overt misconduct, exercise of bad judgment, or simple carelessness — have been responsible for causing the convictions of hundreds, perhaps thousands, of innocent persons. The media regularly report stories of innocent people being released after spending many years in prison for a crime they did not commit. In many of these instances, there is powerful evidence that the wrongful conviction was attributable directly, or indirectly, to errors or misconduct by prosecutors. According to the National Registry of Exonerations (as of September, 2013), 1,162 defendants in the U.S. have been exonerated since 1989, and prosecutorial misconduct has been a significant factor in more than one-third of these erroneous convictions.

It should be intuitively obvious that given the preeminent role played by the prosecutor in the U.S. criminal justice system, the heaviest responsibility for ensuring that only guilty people are convicted lies with the prosecutor. More than any other government official, a prosecutor possesses the greatest power to take away a person's liberty, reputation, and even a person's life. The irresponsible use of this power, as noted above, can have tragic results.

A prosecutor is constitutionally and ethically mandated to promote justice. The prosecutor is even considered a "Minster of Justice" who has a constitutional, statutory, and ethical duty to ensure that a defendant is convicted on the basis of reliable evidence in proceedings that are fair. Nevertheless, some prosecutors deviate from these rules and engage in conduct that distorts the fact-finding process and produces erroneous convictions. Indeed, if a prosecutor is motivated to zealously win a conviction by any means, and engages in conduct that either intentionally or carelessly undermines the integrity of the fact-finding process, the prosecutor inescapably will bring about the conviction of a defendant who is actually innocent.

# Stepping Back: A Brief Historical Perspective

Prosecutors historically have exercised enormous power with very little oversight or accountability over the use of that power. The absence of significant checks has created broad opportunities for abuse. Commentators have routinely bemoaned the frequency and flagrancy of misconduct by prosecutors. Dean Roscoe Pound (1930) more than eighty years ago decried the "number of new trials for grave misconduct of the public prosecutor" and the "abuse and disregard of forensic propriety which threatens to become the staple in American prosecutions" (p. 187). The legal literature over the years has contained titles such as "Improper Conduct of Prosecuting Attorneys," "Remarks of Prosecuting Attorney as Prejudicial Error," "Appeals to Race Prejudice by Counsel in Criminal Cases," and "Shall Prosecutors Conceal Facts."

The most famous documentation of misconduct by prosecutors was contained in the 1931 Report by the National Commission on Law Observance and Enforcement, popularly known as the Wickersham Commission, which systematically documented widespread abuses by U.S. prosecutors and the adverse impact of the misconduct on the administration of criminal justice. Examples of the misconduct committed by prosecutors, and the consequences to the fair administration of justice, are described in the sections below. Perhaps the most serious consequence of the misconduct, according to the Report, is "the conviction of the innocent."

Indeed, the question at the time of the Report, and thereafter, as to whether innocent persons were convicted of crimes was neither abstract nor hypothetical. The well-known study by Professor Edwin M. Borchard (1932), *Convicting the Innocent*, documented sixty-five cases of convictions of innocent defendants drawn from a much larger number of erroneous criminal convictions of innocent people. The most prominent causes of erroneous convictions, Borchard found, and this is similar to the findings today, were mistaken identifications and witness perjury.

Moreover, there is little doubt that the Supreme Court's famous articulation of the prosecutor's special obligation to ensure that "justice shall be done" in the 1935 *Berger* decision was influenced by then-Canon 5 of the Canons of Professional Ethics of the American Bar Association (1908), which stated: "The primary duty of a lawyer engaged in public prosecution is not to convict, but to see that justice is done. The suppression of facts or the secreting of witnesses capable of establishing the innocence of the accused is highly reprehensible." Nevertheless, despite legal and ethical norms designed to encourage prosecutors to pursue justice rather than convictions, empirical studies since 1935 have documented serious and pervasive misconduct by prosecutors. And while courts have continued to bemoan their inability to make prosecutors play by the rules, there is little evidence that courts, lawmakers, or professional disciplinary bodies have demonstrated a willingness or capacity to impose sanctions on prosecutors for committing misconduct.

# Significance of a Prosecutor's Mental Culpability

In analyzing the nature, extent, and reasons for a prosecutor's wrongful or negligent conduct, it is often unclear whether a prosecutor is motivated by a good faith desire to convict a person the prosecutor honestly believes is guilty, or a bad faith desire to win a conviction at all costs regardless of whether the defendant is actually guilty. Prosecutors often argue that even if they may have deviated from a rule, the violation was not willful, but attributable to mistake, inadvertence, or the pressure of the trial. Courts usually do not address whether a prosecutor's violation of a rule was deliberate or inadvertent; nor do courts typically ask whether a prosecutor was motivated to bring about the conviction of a person whom the prosecutor believed may have been innocent. These questions almost always are incapable of resolution. First, trying to divine a prosecutor's intent or motivation is virtually impossible. Moreover, seeking to discover a prosecutor's intent to engage in misconduct, or her indifference to the truth, is in fact irrelevant. As one court put it, "It hurts the defendant just as much to have prejudicial blasts come from the trumpet of the angel Gabriel" (*United States v. Nettl*, 1941, p. 930).

It is also noteworthy that a prosecutor's conduct in causing an innocent person to be convicted does not require a finding that the prosecutor engaged in any misconduct. Some violations, as noted below, have a considerable bearing on whether an innocent defendant may be found guilty. To be sure, conduct that distorts the fact-finding process and manipulates the fact-finder's evaluation of the proof frequently plays a significant role in the conviction of an innocent person. But even absent any wrongful conduct, a prosecutor's conduct may contribute to an erroneous conviction merely by the prosecutor's failure to scrutinize carefully the quality of his proof and to examine closely the reliability and credibility of his witnesses. Thus, even absent wrongful conduct, a prosecutor may be exercising poor judgment in allowing a tenuous case to go forward to trial. Indeed, if a prosecutor after closely examining his proof is not morally certain of a defendant's guilt, then the prosecutor has abdicated his responsibility to protect innocent persons from being wrongfully convicted and punished.

With respect to a prosecutor's mindset in preparing to go to trial, every prosecutor probably believes that the defendant is guilty and probably has assembled what he believes to be sufficient evidence to prove the defendant's guilt. However, it is not unusual that given an intensive investigation of a case, there may be evidence in the prosecution or police files that contradicts the defendant's guilt, or at least raises a significant doubt. How should a prosecutor view this contradictory proof? Studies show that a prosecutor predisposed to believe in the defendant's guilt and seeking to win a conviction may likely view contradictory evidence as false, irrelevant, or unreliable, and certainly not sufficient to cause the prosecutor to rethink the theory of prosecution or cause the prosecutor to hesitate to take the case to trial. Experts in cognitive psychology maintain that prosecutors ordinarily make professional decisions based on their personal beliefs, values, and incentives, and these psychological forces may lead a prosecutor to make decisions, even unintentionally, that are inconsistent with promoting justice (Findley & Scott, 2006). These studies question whether prosecutors are able to maintain the neutrality and objectivity that is needed to protect innocent persons against a wrongful prosecution, and suggest that these psychological biases impede rational decision-making.

A prosecutor seeking to win a conviction is likely to overestimate the strength of her case and underestimate the probative value of evidence that contradicts or undermines her case. For example, studies show that too many prosecutors exhibit a so-called "tunnel vision" whereby they ignore or dismiss evidence that might contradict the defendant's guilt (Bandes, 2006); a "confirmation bias" that credits evidence that confirms the prosecution's theory and discounts evidence that contradicts that theory (Burke, 2006); "selective information processing" that weighs evidence that supports one's belief more heavily than evidence that contradicts those belief; "belief perseverance" that describes a tendency to adhere to one's chosen theory even though new evidence comes to light that completely undercuts that theory's evidentiary basis; and "avoidance cognitive dissonance" under which a person tends to adjust her beliefs to conform to her behavior.

# Impairing the Integrity of the Fact-Finding Process

The prosecutor dominates the fact-finding process in several ways. First, the prosecutor has a virtual monopoly of the proof, superior access to and knowledge of the facts that are used to convict a defendant, and the ability to shape and present those facts to the fact-finder in the most persuasive way. To be sure, as a legal and ethical matter a prosecutor must have confidence in the reliability of his evidence before bringing charges, and before presenting the evidence to a jury. However, as noted above, a prosecutor typically is confident in the accuracy of his evidence, whether or not that confidence is justified. Moreover, as the representative of the government, the prosecutor before the jury is cloaked with considerable prestige and respect, and therefore has a unique power to affect a jury's evaluation of the facts. Juries may view the prosecutor as a "Champion of Justice," a heroic figure who can be trusted to use the facts and make arguments in a fair and responsible manner.

The types of conduct by prosecutors that contribute to wrongful convictions usually fit into several well-recognized categories. They include concealing evidence that may prove a defendant's innocence, presenting evidence of an identification witness that is unreliable, eliciting testimony from an accomplice, informant, or jailhouse "snitch" that is false, offering testimony by a police witness that is false and inaccurate, presenting testimony in child sexual abuse cases that is untruthful or exaggerated, and presenting scientific evidence that is fraudulent or erroneous.

The following sections describe examples of misconduct by prosecutors that distort the fact-finding process and interfere with the jury's ability to decide a case fairly and rationally.

**Prosecutors' suppression of favorable evidence.** A prosecutor's failure to disclose favorable evidence to the defense that may either exculpate a defendant or undermine the truthfulness or reliability of prosecution witnesses is one of the leading causes of wrongful convictions (Garrett, 2011). Under the landmark case of *Brady v. Maryland* (1963), a prosecutor's failure to disclose favorable evidence that is material to guilt or punishment, regardless of the reason, and regardless of the prosecutor's good or bad faith, violates due process. The kinds of proof that are principal bases for wrongful convictions — erroneous eyewitness identifications, cooperation deals with witnesses, and flawed scientific evidence — often have been suppressed by prosecutors and only many years later have been discovered. For example, after an exoneration based on DNA evidence, it may be revealed that the identity of the real perpetrator was known to the police from the beginning but never disclosed to the defendant. The U.S. Supreme Court has ruled in several cases that prosecutors were guilty of suppressing material evidence, and it is reasonably clear in some of these cases that the defendant was wrongfully convicted.

It is difficult to estimate the number of defendants who have been wrongfully convicted because of a prosecutor's suppression of exculpatory evidence. It appears that apart from errors relating to incompetent defense counsel, the most frequent basis for wrongful convictions has been prosecutorial suppression of exculpatory evidence. According to one study, out of 133 known exonerations that resulted in a written decision by a court, 14 defendants, or just over 10%, resulted in relief based on a violation of *Brady* (Garrett, 2008). A study of all exonerations in Massachusetts shows that 12 of 33 cases, or over 36%, involved a *Brady* violation (Fisher, 2002).

Cases involving mistaken eyewitness identifications are perhaps the most dramatic examples of the impact of a prosecutor's violation of *Brady* on the conviction of an innocent person. Suppressed evidence by the prosecutor showing that the witness may have been mistaken ranges from evidence that the police initially suspected another person committed the crime, to an eyewitness's initial failure to identify the defendant, to an eyewitness's positive identification of someone else as the perpetrator. Most recently, in *Smith v. Cain* (2012), the Supreme Court reversed a murder conviction because the prosecutor suppressed a police officer's notes revealing that the only eyewitness initially told the police that he could not identify any of the perpetrators, did not see their faces, and "would not know them if he saw them."

Suppression of exculpatory scientific evidence has resulted in the conviction of innocent persons. For example, in the widely reported Texas case of Michael Morton, an innocent man who was wrongfully convicted of murdering his wife in 1987 and who spent 26 years in prison, the prosecution suppressed evidence of a bloody bandana discovered behind his home on the day of the murder which contained DNA that would have excluded Morton and identified the real killer. In *Connick v. Thompson* (2011), a wrongful conviction of murder in which the defendant spent 18 years in prison, the prosecution failed to disclose to the defense that a scientific analysis of a piece of the victim's clothing stained with the perpetrator's blood showed that it did not match the blood type of the defendant.

Suppression of evidence that could be used to impeach prosecution witnesses is commonplace. Prosecutors are notorious for failing to disclose immunity deals with key witnesses that would suggest to a fact-finder that the witness was giving false or misleading testimony as a quid pro quo (Garrett, 2011). Prosecutors have failed to reveal that a witness's incriminating testimony came about only after the witness was hypnotized. Prosecutors also have failed to disclose recorded statements of key witnesses indicating that they planned to frame the defendant.

**Prosecutors' use of unreliable testimony.** Some witnesses are indispensable to secure convictions of guilty persons, such as eyewitnesses, children, cooperating witnesses, and scientific experts. By the same token, however, these witnesses are notorious for skewing the fact-finding process and causing erroneous convictions, not necessarily because of a prosecutor's misconduct, but because a prosecutor has not carefully vetted the witness's story. Too often police and prosecutors interview these witnesses with insufficient attention to details, contradictions, and inconsistencies. Moreover, these witnesses may be unusually vulnerable to coercive or suggestive interviewing techniques. It is often unclear whether these witnesses have actually been "coached" to give a false or exaggerated account of the event, or through subtle interviewing techniques have shaped their stories to accord with what they believe the police and prosecutors want to hear.

*Identification witnesses.* Identification witnesses are among the most unreliable witnesses. Misidentification is the single largest source of error in wrongful conviction cases (Garrett, 2011). Many prosecutors do not appreciate the dangers associated with eyewitnesses, and the difficulties associated with retrieving a witness's memory of an event and reconstructing that memory. Prosecutors in interviewing such witnesses and preparing them for testifying may assist the witness in remembering the event and retrieving a truthful recollection. But a prosecutor's actions also may distort a witness's underlying memory and produce a false recollection. A prosecutor in preparing an eyewitness's testimony has the ability to influence a witness to remember facts and fill in gaps that may be inaccurate, but which the witness may come to believe are the truth. Moreover, because of the prosecutor's special status, he is often viewed by the witness as an expert who is highly knowledgeable of the facts, and will use the facts responsibly. Indeed, some witnesses may even try to shape their stories to what they believe may accord with the prosecutor's expectations.

Some prosecutors may even attempt to adjust the testimony of eyewitnesses to strengthen the impact of their identification, and an erroneous conviction. For example, in *Kyles v. Whitley* (1995) a capital murder case, the prosecutor presented testimony from the key eyewitness who gave an extremely detailed account of the killing. However, in a statement the witness gave to the police shortly after the killing, the witness gave a vastly different account of the crime (which the prosecution never disclosed to the defense), stating he did not see the actual killing, nor did he remember many of the details that he testified to at trial. The Supreme Court reversed the conviction based on the prosecutor's nondisclosure, but implied that the witness's account had been "adjusted" by the prosecutor for the trial, and that the prosecutor had "coached" the witness's new story. Other instances of eyewitness memory adjustments by prosecutors reasonably lend themselves to procuring wrongful convictions.

*Child witnesses.* The testimony of child witnesses is especially vulnerable to manipulation by prosecutors. A familiar instance is the testimony of young children in sexual abuse cases. Indeed, numerous instances of wrongful convictions are attributable to the testimony of child witnesses (Garrett, 2011). Courts have increasingly scrutinized the testimony of young children for coercive or suggestive conduct by interviewers in preparing these witnesses for trial. For example, in *Idaho v. Wright* (1990), the Supreme Court found that a child's accusation of sexual abuse was based on leading and suggestive questioning by an interrogator who had a preconceived idea of what the child should be disclosing.

Prosecutors in seeking a conviction may present the testimony of children without sufficient scrutiny of the truth of their stories and the techniques used to elicit their testimony. Prosecutors have often failed to carefully probe the accuracy of the accounts of child witnesses, and have not been sufficiently attentive to factors that might shed light on the truthfulness of the child's account, such as the absence of spontaneous recall, the bias of the interviewer, the use of leading questions, multiple interviews, incessant questioning, vilification of the defendant, ongoing contact with peers and references to their statements, and the use of threats, bribes, and cajoling. Courts have also criticized the prosecutor's failure to videotape or otherwise record the initial interview session.

*Cooperating witnesses.* Cooperating witnesses are probably the most dangerous prosecution witness of all. No other witness has such an extraordinary incentive to lie. No other witness has the capacity to manipulate, mislead, and deceive law enforcement officials. No other witness is capable of lying so convincingly and yet be believed by the jury. Wrongful convictions are replete with instances in which cooperating witnesses gave false testimony that was critical to the verdicts (Garrett, 2011).

A prosecutor has a powerful incentive to seek out and accept a cooperator's account uncritically. Moreover, as noted above, a prosecutor often has a predetermined view of the facts of a case that may inhibit the prosecutor from scrutinizing the cooperator's account objectively. If a prosecutor has a theory of the case that has been developed from other evidence, or from the opinions of the investigators, the prosecutor is more apt to accept the cooperator's version uncritically. If the cooperator deviates from the prosecutor's theory, the prosecutor may conclude that the cooperator is lying or withholding information.

Cooperators are manipulative people, and their testimony may impair the integrity of the fact-finding process to such a degree that innocent persons are caught in the web of the cooperator's lies. Some prosecutors have a mindset that serving justice means putting people in jail and may tend to rely heavily on the cooperator's account. Moreover, some prosecutors are easily manipulated by cooperators, and therefore do not examine the co-operator's account objectively. If a prosecutor neglects to probe a cooperator's story or background sufficiently to uncover inconsistencies or outright lies, then the cooperator's testimony may be perjury, and help produce an unjust conviction. Also, some cooperators may not even know the difference between truth and untruth, and a prosecutor who fails to intensively probe the cooperator's story invites false testimony. Cooperators often come from environments of crime and deceit that may make an understanding of truth ambiguous. Cooperators may not have a prosecutor's concern with exact facts, and may use language in a loose and non-literal fashion that encourages them to make exaggerated assertions that they may believe are the truth.

*Scientific and forensic experts.* Prosecutors' use, and misuse, of scientific evidence has been one of the principal causes of wrongful convictions, particularly in death penalty cases (Garrett, 2011). Prosecutors may present—through the testimony of an expert witness whom the prosecutor claims to be trustworthy—an opinion linking the defendant to the crime, when in fact the proof may be erroneous or fraudulent. Prosecutors in many cases have concealed from the defense evidence that would have discredited the expert's opinion, and distorted the evidence to make it appear reliable, often with tragic results. Prosecutors have elicited fraudulent testimony, erroneous and prejudicial conclusions without any factual basis, and opinions that appear to be based on a valid scientific theory but are really the expert's speculation and conjecture. They also have attempted to bolster the expert's credibility by exaggerating the expert's background and experience, and by giving the jury personal assurances that the expert is credible and reliable.

Prosecutors know that juries ordinarily view experts with heightened respect, and give considerable weight to their opinions. In contrast with other types of witnesses, the expert is usually viewed by the jury with an aura of special reliability and trustworthiness. Moreover, the expert usually possesses impressive credentials that reinforce the jury's trust in the expert's opinion. Further, the expert is usually adept at presenting his or her testimony skillfully and persuasively, and in language that jurors can understand. Finally, the expert's conclusions almost always interlock with other evidence in the case and reinforce and corroborate the prosecution's theory of guilt. More than any other witness, the expert probably has the greatest capacity to mislead the jury. And in tandem with a prosecutor who aggressively seeks a conviction, the expert can provide the testimony that virtually secures that conviction.

Fraudulent and erroneous scientific evidence has included fingerprints planted at the scene of the crime, faked autopsies in death penalty cases, fabricated breathalyzer readings in intoxicated driving cases, and perjured testimony by experts making hair and blood comparisons. Prosecutors have also presented as trustworthy the testimony of scientific experts that contained false, exaggerated, and erroneous conclusions that lacked a scientific basis. Numerous instances of so-called "junk science" have been presented by prosecutors as reliable and used to win convictions. Some of these pseudo-experts are notorious for promoting bogus opinions.

Moreover, because of the secretive nature of pre-trial preparation, the manner in which a prosecutor is able to shape, manipulate, and even manufacture the expert's testimony is virtually impossible to prove. It is intuitively obvious, however, that the relationship between prosecutors and their experts is mutually reinforcing often not in the service of truth but to win a conviction. Many experts display a pro-prosecution bias, especially those employed by law enforcement agencies (Giannelli, 1997). Many of these experts are notorious for manufacturing testimony to fit the prosecution's theory of guilt. By the same token, prosecutors routinely seek out experts who will support the prosecution's theory of guilt, and reject experts who might display more independence (Faigman, et al., 2002).

# Manipulating the Jury's Decision-Making

A prosecutor has a special duty not to mislead the fact-finder or attempt to manipulate a jury's ability to review the evidence fairly and dispassionately. The opportunity for a prosecutor to mislead the fact-finder and manipulate the verdict inheres in virtually every phase of the criminal trial. Misleading conduct can even rise to the level of a due process violation when it involves the knowing use of false evidence, or when the prosecutor's conduct renders the trial fundamentally unfair. The risk that an innocent person may be convicted because of such tactics is evident.

**False, misleading, and inflammatory tactics.** The prosecutor's deliberate use of perjured testimony violates due process, may result in an unfair trial, and may even result in the conviction of an innocent person. Even non-deliberate conduct that elicits perjured testimony is a due process violation if the prosecutor should have known about the perjury. A prosecutor also commits misconduct when she uses fraudulent physical evidence or creates false impressions from the evidence, such as asking questions without a factual basis, or insinuating that the defendant has a criminal background and a propensity to commit crimes.

A prosecutor also undermines the integrity of the trial and risks convicting an innocent person by referring to matters outside the record and misrepresenting the record. Thus, courts have rebuked prosecutors and in some cases reversed convictions for allusions to private conversations with witnesses or the defendant; references to evidence that had been excluded; insinuations that issues of fact have previously been authoritatively determined; or comments that dilute reasonable doubt and the presumption of innocence.

Prosecutors can also misrepresent the record by making false or exaggerated claims that can mislead the jury into convicting. In the well-known case of *Miller v. Pate* (1967), a prosecutor committed reversible misconduct by misrepresenting in a rape and murder trial that undershorts belonging to the defendant were stained with the young victim's blood, when the prosecutor well knew that the stains were paint. Prosecutors have also made false assertions that an object in the defendant's possession was the murder weapon, that the defendant's fingerprints were found at the crime scene, and that the defendant failed an intoxication test.

In addition, appeals by prosecutors to a jury's fears, passions, and prejudices are a common tactic to manipulate the fact-finder and may produce an erroneous verdict. Such conduct often appears deliberately calculated to impair a defendant's right to a fair trial. For example, prosecutors have introduced inflammatory physical evidence, have elicited inflammatory testimony containing irrelevant racial and sexual innuendos, and have engaged in other inflammatory conduct designed to prejudice the jury.

Prosecutors are forbidden to use arguments calculated to inflame the passions and prejudice of the jury. However, they also know that such arguments are much more effective than restrained and objective remarks, and some may be willing to assume the risk that an appellate court will find the conduct not severe enough to warrant a reversal when the remarks are viewed in black and white in the appellate record. Thus, prosecutors use a litany of colorful and abusive rhetoric to denigrate the defendant, and some courts give the prosecutor considerable latitude in such disparaging comments. Prosecutors also make arguments calculated to incite among jurors feelings of fear, anger, and revenge. Exhortations to join the War on Crime, predictions of the dire consequences if jurors do not convict, and exploitations of the jury's sympathy for the victim to incite feelings of anger and retaliation can sufficiently inflame a jury to result in the conviction of an innocent person.

Prosecutors use other tactics to inflame, such as insinuating that the defendant has murdered, threatened, and bribed potential witnesses. Appeals to a jury's prejudices and stereotypes also may undermine the accuracy of a verdict, such as appeals to racial, national, religious, gender, wealth, and patriotic biases. Prosecutors can also make other arguments that can mislead a jury into convicting, such as comments on a defendant's failure to testify, call witnesses, and engage in other constitutionally protected activity. Finally, a prosecutor can mislead the jury when she makes a personal endorsement of the strength of the case, the credibility of witnesses, and the defendant's guilt.

**Unfair attacks on defendant's character.** Prosecutors in many of the cases in which innocent persons were wrongfully convicted sought to prejudice the jury's assessment of the evidence by attacking the defendant's character. This tactic usually works. The prejudicial impact of a defendant's criminal or sordid background on a jury can be devastating. Studies show that when a defendant's criminal record is known and the prosecution's case is weak, the chances of acquittal are far less likely (Kalven & Zeisel, 1966). Prosecutors are well aware of the prejudicial effect on jurors, and even though courts attempt to confine such evidence to a proper purpose, prosecutors often find ways to expose a defendant's bad character to the jury.

For example, prosecutors in cross-examining a defendant might use a defendant's criminal record not for the proper purpose of showing untruthfulness but to insinuate guilt by suggesting a predisposition to commit crimes. Prosecutors violate rules regulating cross-examination by including inflammatory details in their questions, especially when the prior crimes are for violent acts, or by portraying the defendant as a dangerous, sinister, or undesirable person. However, if a defendant does not take the witness stand, a prosecutor is forbidden to introduce evidence of the defendant's criminal record. Prosecutors use a variety of tactics to circumvent this prohibition by introducing evidence that the defendant used aliases, was pictured in police "mug shots," had police criminal identification numbers signifying a prior arrest, and through other ways that depict the defendant as a sinister character. Prosecutors also try to prove a defendant's guilt by showing that the defendant may have associated with other criminals and courts sometimes have reversed convictions because of this tactic.

**Unfair attempts to bolster credibility.** A prosecutor can mislead a jury into giving a witness's testimony greater believability by artificially inflating the credibility of that witness before it has been attacked. This technique is referred to as bolstering, and its use may obstruct a juror's rational analysis of the facts and the witness's credibility, and potentially result in an erroneous verdict. Prosecutors do not know whether a witness is giving truthful testimony, yet they might either expressly or impliedly assure jurors that a witness is telling the truth. The personal endorsement of a witness's credibility by a prosecutor is improper, first, because of the exalted position a prosecutor occupies in the eyes of the jury and the weight a juror may give to the prosecutor's assurances, and second, because it may create the impression that the prosecutor possesses other information outside the record of the trial that supports the assertion that the witness is telling the truth.

Prosecutors also subvert this anti-bolstering rule by eliciting testimony from witnesses, particularly experts, to endorse or validate the credibility of other witnesses, who may be victims or eyewitnesses. The danger, of course, is that jurors often rely heavily on the testimony of experts. Thus, if an expert offers an opinion that validates a witness's truthfulness, or implicitly endorses the witness's truthfulness by suggesting that the witness is a member of a class of persons who are trustworthy, or asserting directly that the complainant has in fact been victimized, the jury may give that witness's testimony added weight. Appellate courts monitor this practice, and convictions in child sexual abuse, domestic violence, rape, and drug prosecutions have been reversed because of improper testimonial interference by experts.

Prosecutors employ other tactics to enhance a witness's credibility. Prosecutors have attempted to bolster the credibility of police officers by pointing to awards for heroism; referring to witnesses successfully passing a polygraph test; eliciting testimony that an informant has always been truthful; suggesting that a cooperation agreement with a witness was prepared only after the prosecutor believed the witness; giving the jury the misleading impression that the prosecutor is monitoring the cooperating witness to make sure he tells the truth; deliberately introducing inadmissible and prejudicial hearsay to support a witness's testimony; manipulating a witness's invocation of a privilege; instructing a prosecution witness to testify while holding a Bible; and having a child witness sit on the prosecutor's lap while testifying.

# Moving Forward

As we have seen, prosecutors by overt misconduct or the failure to scrutinize with sufficient care the quality of their evidence and the reliability of their witnesses do in fact contribute to the conviction of innocent persons. Assuming, quite properly, that prosecutors seek to avoid such miscarriages of justice, what actions can prosecutors take to prevent the conviction of an innocent person? There are several ways that prosecutors' offices can reduce the risk that an innocent person will be convicted.

First, prosecutors' offices should implement ongoing education and training programs that identify the best practices to insure against wrongful convictions. Such programs should emphasize the best practices for interviewing, assessing, and presenting in court the testimony of the kinds of witnesses who have been most responsible for erroneous convictions — eye-witnesses, children, cooperators, and experts. This training might focus on issues such as problems of misidentification, how to deal with inconsistent and contradictory statements, how to evaluate alternative perpetrator evidence, how to deal with uncharged criminal conduct, how to deal with drug, alcohol, or medical issues that might interfere with a witness's accurate accounting, and any bias or interest that the witness may have.

Education and training should emphasize compliance with *Brady v. Maryland* (1963) and *Giglio v. United States* (1972), including the use of checklists to review the various types of evidence that need to be closely scrutinized for possible exculpatory and impeachment information, such as prior inconsistent statements, cooperation agreements, criminal background evidence, and evidence bearing on a witness's motive to lie. Prosecutors' offices should also be trained on working with police departments and individual police officers who might be in possession of information that may need to be disclosed to the defense. Some police officers might not be aware of their constitutional obligations under *Brady-Giglio,* and prosecutors should be trained to assist the police in understanding their constitutional obligations and carrying out their duties properly and effectively.

Second, prosecutors' offices should adopt policies to enhance the reliability of the fact-finding process. One such policy would be to maintain an "open file" discovery system whereby the entire file of a case is routinely made available to the defense well in advance of trial. Under such an open-file approach, materials that are critical to defense discovery, including a list of prosecution witnesses, statements of these witnesses, summaries of statements made by witnesses, and relevant police reports, are turned over to the defense early in the case. Moreover, an open file policy that discloses every relevant item in the prosecution's case to the defense may offer a better chance of the prosecutor complying with his *Brady-Giglio* disclosure obligation than a more restrictive discovery approach.

Indeed, by using an open file discovery system, a prosecutor would not have to assume the risk of making a mistake in evaluating the materiality of certain evidence. Under an open file policy, the evidence would be disclosed regardless of materiality. Additionally, an open file system would protect the integrity of the process in the event a new prosecutor who may be unfamiliar with the evidence enters the case and needs to make a relatively quick decision on whether to take a plea, go to trial, or seek a dismissal. Finally, an open file discovery policy would enhance a prosecutor's reputation for transparency and fairness, and foster in judges and defense lawyers a sense of trust and reduce occasions for contentious discovery litigation.

Third, prosecutors' offices should also create databases for identifying and tracking *Brady* and *Giglio* information relating to key witnesses such as informants, police, and experts who may have testified for the government in the past and may testify in future cases. For example, if a prosecutor intends to call as a witness a police officer, the prosecutor could enter his name in the database, locate previous cases in which he may have testified, or previous investigations in which he may have been involved, to see if he has been cited for false or erroneous testimony, or other questionable conduct. The same type of vetting could be done with informants, expert witnesses, and virtually any other witness, including even eyewitnesses. Indeed, some eyewitnesses have testified in several different and unrelated prosecutions, raising serious questions about their reliability.

Fourth, prosecutors' offices should establish programs to investigate post-conviction claims of actual innocence. Indeed, several prosecutors' officers have created "Conviction Integrity Units" or "Second-Look" bureaus to investigate such claims of actual innocence in closed cases. The creation of these bureaus is consistent with a prosecutor's ethical duty to "do justice." Procedures could be established to assess claims critically based on the kinds of allegations made. For instance, claims with strong indicia of actual innocence might be given investigative priority, such as claims of misidentification, perjury by informants and cooperators, witness recantations, and allegations of newly discovered evidence. The standard for reviewing claims of actual innocence should not be unduly restrictive, but should allow for flexibility in deciding which cases to investigate, especially where a claim is made that is plausible and contains specific factual allegations that can be investigated.

Finally, to reduce the risk of wrongful convictions prosecutors should establish protocols with police department to become involved in the investigation earlier to assist police in protecting the integrity of the investigation from mistakes, especially constitutional mistakes. Prosecutors should work with police departments to establish training and education programs in the areas that are most often cited as causes for wrongful convictions — false confessions, use of informants, and *Brady* and *Giglio* disclosure violations. Indeed, since *Brady* violations occur when police fail to disclose exculpatory information to prosecutors, it is important for prosecutors to educate police on the nature of *Brady* information and the importance of disclosing such information. Prosecutors could also educate police on best practices for videotaping confessions, and using identification procedures to protect against misidentification, such as double-blind lineups, where the officer conducting the lineup does not know the identity of the suspect, and sequential lineups, in which persons are presented to the witness one at a time rather than all at once.

# Conclusion

Prosecutors have a constitutional and ethical obligation to ensure that innocent people do not get punished. A prosecutor is a minister of justice with virtually unlimited discretion to charge a person with a crime, and advocate for that person's conviction and punishment. As the number of exonerated defendants continues to grow, however, it becomes increasingly clear that prosecutors, either by affirmative acts of misconduct, or a failure to carefully and responsibly scrutinize the quality of the evidence, sometimes do contribute to defendants' wrongful convictions.

However, reining in prosecutorial excesses that produce wrongful convictions is a difficult task. Prosecutors typically believe that defendants are guilty, and aggressively seek to convince juries to return guilty verdicts. Most prosecutors would probably claim that they never convicted an innocent person. But such a claim is not surprising. Studies show that a prosecutor's personality and mindset may lead him or her to discount evidence supporting the defendant's innocence as erroneous or unreliable. This attitude of denial simply reinforces the possibility that a prosecutor may pursue a conviction against an innocent person even though substantial evidence points away from guilt. Unless prosecutors become more sensitive to the perilous situation facing defendants who are actually innocent, and to the kinds of dangerous witnesses and ambiguous evidence that have been responsible for producing miscarriages of justice, and unless they are able to discipline themselves to be skeptical and open-minded regarding the sufficiency of the proof, the likelihood is that many more innocent people routinely will be convicted.

# References

American Bar Association (1908). *ABA canons of professional ethics.* Chicago, IL: American Bar Association. Retrieved from http://www.americanbar.org/content/dam/aba/migrated/cpr/mrpc/Canons_Ethics.pdf-17k-2013-03-02.

American Bar Association (1993). *Standards for criminal justice: Prosecution function and defense function* (3rd ed.). Chicago, IL: American Bar Association.

Bandes, S. (2006). Loyalty to one's convictions: The prosecutor and tunnel vision. *Howard Law Journal, 49,* 475–494.

Bedau, H. A. & Radelet, M. L. (1987). Miscarriages of justice in potentially capital cases. *Stanford Law Review, 40,* 21–90.

*Berger v. United States,* 295 U.S. 78 (1935).

Borchard, E. M. (1932). *Convicting the innocent: Errors of criminal justice.* New Haven, CT: Yale University Press.

*Brady v. Maryland,* 373 U.S. 87 (1963).

Burke, A. S. (2006). Improving prosecutorial decision-making: Some lessons of cognitive science. *William and Mary Law Review, 47,* 1587–1633.

Cassidy, H. M. (2013). *Prosecutorial ethics* (2nd ed.). St. Paul, MN: West Academic.

Center on the Administration of Criminal Law (2002). *Establishing conviction integrity programs in prosecutor's offices: A report of the Center on the Administration of Criminal Law's Conviction Integrity Project.*

*Connick v. Thompson,* 131 S. Ct. 1350 (2011).

Faigman, D. L., Kaye, D. H., Saks, M. J., Sanders, J. (2002). *Science in the law: Forensic science issues.* St. Paul, MN: West Group.

Findley, K. A. & Scott, M. S. (2006). The multiple dimensions of tunnel vision in criminal cases. *Wisconsin Law Review, 2006,* 291–397.

Fisher, S. Z. (2002). Convictions of innocent person in Massachusetts: An overview. *Boston University Public Interest Law Journal, 12,* 1–72.

Garrett, B. L. (2008). Judging innocence. *Columbia Law Review, 108,* 55–142.

Garrett, B. L. (2011). *Convicting the innocent.* Cambridge, MA: Harvard University Press.

Gershman, B. L. (1998). Mental culpability and prosecutorial misconduct. *American Journal of Criminal Law, 26,* 121–164.

Gershman, B. L. (2001). The prosecutor's duty to truth. *Georgetown Journal of Legal Ethics, 14,* 309–354.

Gershman, B. L. (2002). Witness coaching by prosecutors. *Cardozo Law Review, 23,* 829–863.

Gershman, B. L. (2003). Misuse of scientific evidence by prosecutors. *Oklahoma City University Law Review, 28,* 17–41.

Gershman, B. L. (2012–2013). *Prosecutorial misconduct* (2nd ed.). Eagan, MN: Thomson Reuters.

Giannelli, P. C. (1997). Essay: The abuse of scientific evidence in criminal cases: The need for independent crime laboratories. *Virginia Journal of Social Policy & the Law, 4,* 439–478.

*Giglio v. United States,* 405 U.S. 150 (1972).

*Idaho v. Wright,* 497 U.S. 805 (1990).

Joy, P. A. & McMunigal, K. C. (2009). *Do no wrong: Ethics for prosecutors and defenders.* Chicago, IL: American Bar Association.

Kalven, Jr., H. & Zeisel, H. (1966). *The American jury.* Boston, MA: Little, Brown and Company.

Kamisar, Y., LaFave, W. R., Israel, J. H., King, Nancy, Kerr, O. S., & Primus, E. B. (2012). *Modern criminal procedure* (13th ed.). Eagan, MN: West.

*Kyles v. Whitley,* 514 U.S. 419 (1995).

Medwed, D. S. (2012). *Prosecution complex: America's race to convict and its impact on the innocent.* New York, NY: NYU Press.

*Miller v. Pate,* 386 U.S. 1 (1967).

National Commission on Law Observance and Enforcement (1931).

Pound, R. (1930). *Criminal justice in America.* New York, NY: Henry Holt and Company.

Simon, D. (2012). *In doubt: The psychology of the criminal justice process.* Cambridge, MA: Harvard University Press.

*Smith v. Cain,* 132 S. Ct. 627 (2012).

*United States v. Nettl,* 121 F.2d 927 (3d Cir. 1941).

Weinberg, S. (2003). *Breaking the rules: Who suffers when a prosecutor is cited for misconduct?* Center for Public Integrity. Retrieved from http://www.publicintegrity.org/2003/06/26/5517/breaking-rules.

Yaroshefsky, E. (1999). Cooperation with federal prosecutors: Experiences of truth telling and embellishment. *Fordham Law Review, 68,* 917–964.

# Chapter Eight

# Defense Lawyering and Wrongful Convictions

Ellen Yaroshefsky, *Benjamin N. Cardozo School of Law, Yeshiva University*
Laura Schaefer, *Postgraduate Fellow, Federal Defenders for the Southern District of New York*

## Introduction

Between 1989 and August 2013, 311 people were exonerated based upon DNA evidence that proved them to be innocent of the crimes for which they were convicted (Innocence Project, 2013a). While most were wrongly convicted following a jury trial, 28 of the 311 DNA exonerees actually pled guilty to the charges against them (Innocence Project 2013b). In each case, the verdict was upheld on direct appeal, and the defendant served time in prison for a crime he did not commit (Innocence Project 2013a). These exonerations also have something else in common: each wrongfully convicted defendant was represented by defense counsel.

This chapter focuses upon the defense lawyering in those cases and considers what lessons can be learned to reduce the likelihood of future wrongful convictions. It draws upon the research on DNA and non-DNA wrongful conviction cases as well as research and literature about defense lawyering, primarily in state courts. It surveys the law regarding defense attorneys' obligations to their clients and the existing ethical standards for defense lawyers, and then examines the extent to which criminal justice systems adhere to such standards. Finally, it highlights one contributing factor to wrongful convictions that the research reveals defense attorneys must be prepared to confront more robustly: the State's reliance on forensic evidence to secure a conviction. As we will explain, the research demonstrates that improper or false forensic evidence contributed to wrongful convictions in about 50% of the known wrongful conviction cases currently surveyed. The chapter closes by drawing certain conclusions about what constitutes effective defense lawyering today, in light of the increasing awareness surrounding the causes leading to wrongful convictions.

## Stepping Back: Understanding the Problem

Any discussion about defense lawyering and wrongful convictions necessarily has limitations. First, the actual number of individuals who have been wrongfully convicted is impossible to know. According to the National Registry of Exonerations, a joint project between the University of Michigan and Northwestern University law schools, "there is no way to estimate the overall number of false convictions from these reported exonerations, but it is clear that there are many more false convictions than exonerations" (National Registry of Exonerations, 2012). Exonerations typically are only possible in certain types of cases, such as where dispositive physical evidence is available for testing, or where new information comes to light that persuasively suggests a defendant's innocence.[1] The National Registry of Exonerations notes that numerous convictions are reversed on procedural grounds or due to revelations of misconduct or the discovery of new and potentially exculpatory information.[2] In some cases where defendants were exonerated on procedural grounds, the evidence of the defendant's innocence was also overwhelming, even if the court did not make such a finding (Innocence Project, 2012).

Second, the data set for the examination of ineffective defense lawyering is limited. Research is in the early stages of understanding the interaction among contributing factors to wrongful convictions. Some of the causes of wrongful convictions are better understood than others. The greatest contributing factors to wrongful convictions—faulty eyewitness identification, false confessions, so-called "bad" science, and police and prosecutorial misconduct—have been analyzed to greater and lesser extents, and are the focus of different sorts of reform efforts (Innocence Project, 2013c). Untangling the various factors that contribute to a wrongful conviction is exceptionally difficult, especially because the universe of wrongful convictions is impossible to know. Nevertheless, the currently available data allow us to draw certain conclusions regarding the causes and circumstances common in wrongful conviction cases. Perhaps unsurprisingly, research shows that *multiple* factors –including bad lawyering—typically play a part in an innocent defendant's conviction (Innocence Project, 2013a). Invalid or improper forensic testimony is seen in more than half of known wrongful conviction cases, while eyewitness misidentification contributes to wrongful convictions in more than 70% of cases (*id.*). In many wrongful convictions involving improper or invalid forensic science evidence, therefore, eyewitness misidentification is also likely to have played a role. Twenty-five percent of exoneration cases involve false confessions, and jailhouse snitch testimony played a role in wrongful convictions in 16% of cases (Findley, 2013). The research also shows that government misconduct was at play in 18% of wrongful conviction cases.[3] Most commonly among the government misconduct cases, a failure to disclose exculpatory or impeaching evidence—and in many of those cases "bad lawyering"—is cited as a contributing cause to the conviction (Innocence Project, 2013d, 2013e). In other words, effective lawyering may have prevented some of the

---

1. For example, George Allen was exonerated after serving 35 years in prison. His conviction was overturned on the basis of exculpatory evidence that was not disclosed to the defense. While the Missouri court that exonerated him did not reach his claim of "actual innocence" in the decision vacating his conviction, the judge who decided his case nevertheless concluded that the withheld evidence strongly suggested his factual innocence (Innocence Project, 2012).

2. The National Registry of Exonerations (2013) has identified 1,196 exonerations between 1989 and August 30, 2013. The National Registry of Exonerations (2012) defines exoneration as the process through which "a person who has been convicted of a crime is officially cleared based on new evidence of innocence." According to the National Registry's statistics, exculpatory DNA test results account for roughly one-third of currently documented exonerations, while new evidence of innocence or state misconduct accounts for the exonerations in the remaining two-thirds of cases (*id.*).

3. One frequently cited phenomenon is "tunnel vision," or the inability of police or prosecutors to properly credit exculpatory information when they already are convinced of a suspect's guilt. It stands to reason that in cases where the wrong person has been arrested, law enforcement may have fumbled various aspects of the investigation or relied on false information or evidence to become convinced of the suspect's guilt (Findley, 2013).

other errors in these cases, such as the failure to bring exculpatory evidence to light. Had the defense attorneys in those cases argued for greater access to discovery, for example, or challenged an eyewitness's identification or a client's confession more robustly, they may have uncovered exculpatory evidence which would have changed the outcome of the trial.[4]

Third, it is also important to acknowledge that wrongful convictions can and do occur in cases where the defense lawyer was competent and may have provided excellent representation in spite of the wrongful result. In some cases, police or prosecuting attorneys intentionally withheld exculpatory evidence despite defense counsel's repeated requests for full access to significant case information. For example, Michael Morton served nearly 25 years in prison for the murder of his wife before being exonerated in 2011 based upon DNA evidence that was in the State's possession, which linked a convicted rapist to the crime. After Morton's exoneration it came to light that in 1987, prosecutor Ken Anderson—who later became a sitting judge—intentionally hid evidence of Morton's innocence and disobeyed a court order requiring him to disclose such evidence. In addition to the dispositive DNA evidence of Morton's innocence, Anderson failed to disclose a transcript of a police interview with exculpatory information, a police report pointing to another man, and notes and documents from the lead detective. Trial counsel was diligent and conscientious in seeking to obtain such information, but was repeatedly informed by the prosecuting attorney that no such exculpatory information existed. In 2013, a Texas Court of Inquiry Commission examined this case and issued arrest warrants for Anderson for tampering with physical evidence, concealing physical evidence, and tampering with a government record. There was little more that Morton's defense lawyer could have done to prove his client's innocence when faced with such egregious conduct by the prosecutor (Innocence Project, 2013f).

## The Right to Counsel: A Brief Overview

The overall quality of defense lawyers in state and federal court must certainly frame the discussion of lessons to be learned from the wrongful conviction cases. Sadly, the state of representation of indigent clients in the United States leaves much to be desired.

Fifty years ago in *Gideon v. Wainwright* (1963), the Supreme Court held that the Sixth Amendment guarantees a right to court-appointed counsel to defendants in serious criminal proceedings. While *Gideon* only established the right to counsel in felony cases, the Court extended its ruling in subsequent decisions to include a right to defense counsel in misdemeanor trials that result in incarceration (*Argersinger v. Hamlin*, 1972); juvenile delinquency proceedings (*In re Gault*, 1967); and at arraignments (*Rothgerry v. Gillespie County*, 2008). Today, the constitutional right to counsel is understood to attach as soon as formal charges are filed against the defendant, and this right remains in place until the trial proceedings and any direct appeals of the conviction or sentencing are resolved.[5]

---

4. As this chapter will explore in greater depth, while the expectation may be that a competent defense lawyer is able to expose or challenge such errors or misconduct, the current state of criminal prosecutions is such that highly effective lawyering is not always possible. Unfortunately, research on the contribution of "bad lawyering" to wrongful convictions is the least advanced in the analysis of this question so far and warrants further development.

5. While defendants are constitutionally guaranteed counsel through trial and direct appeal, the majority of states do not recognize a constitutional right to counsel for post-conviction proceedings—the stage at which most wrongful convictions are uncovered.

*Gideon* requires all states to ensure that indigent criminal defendants receive cost-free representation, regardless of the state's resources—or political will—to provide them with counsel.[6] In the five decades since *Gideon*, states have established various initiatives to comply with its mandate. Depending on the jurisdiction, an indigent defendant may obtain a lawyer through a state-run defender program, a court-appointed counsel program, or on an ad hoc basis. In some court-appointed attorney systems, lawyers may also represent private clients while handling indigent defendants' criminal cases (Lefstein, 2010). Understandably, such systems run the risk of affording defendants distracted or insufficiently motivated attorneys.

Despite the letter of the law solemnized in *Gideon*, indigent criminal defense across the country is consistently described as an unfulfilled promise; many agree that it seemingly is in a state of perpetual crisis. Criminal defendants increasingly are indigent and thus unable to procure counsel independently. Until the 2013 "budget sequester," the federal courts generally have provided adequately funded systems of defense representation, as have a few cities and states (Cohen, 2013). By and large, however, representation of indigents is shockingly inadequate. As the American Bar Association (ABA) has long decried: "the disturbing conclusion is that thousands of persons are processed through America's courts every year either with no lawyer at all or with a lawyer who does not have the time, resources, or in some cases, the inclination to provide effective representation" (Bright & Sanneh, 2013, quoting American Bar Association, 2004). As Stephen Bright, President and Senior Counsel of the Southern Center for Human Rights, notes:

> Most states, which are responsible for more than 95% of all criminal prosecutions, have treated the *Gideon* decision as an unfunded mandate to be resisted. They have little incentive to provide competent lawyers to represent the people they are trying to convict, fine, imprison or execute. Many focus on minimizing costs, awarding the defense of poor people to the lowest bidder, compensating lawyers at meager rates and underfunding public defender programs. This facilitates pleas, speeds up cases and heightens the chances of conviction for anyone accused of a crime. (Bright & Sanneh, 2013)

Moreover, the law makes it difficult to reverse a conviction on grounds of constitutionally inadequate defense counsel even where a lawyer has provided little—if any—assistance to the client. Even where the defense lawyer is incompetent by any professional or legal standard, unless the defendant is able to show "prejudice"—that is, a reasonable probability that the outcome of the proceeding would have been different *but for* the defense attorney's deficient performance—the case will not be reversed on appeal. This standard to reverse a conviction was established in *Strickland v. Washington* (1984), where the Supreme Court held that to succeed on a claim of ineffective assistance of counsel the defendant must show that the outcome of the case was "prejudiced" by the defense attorney's performance. Prejudice "requires showing that counsel's errors were so serious as to deprive the defendant of a fair trial, a trial whose result is reliable" (*Strickland v. Washington*, 1984, p. 687).

As the Court explained further, "the purpose of the effective assistance guarantee of the Sixth Amendment is *not* to improve the quality of legal representation, although that is a goal of considerable importance to the legal system. The purpose is *simply to ensure*

---

6. "Prisoners are not a sympathetic minority; certainly in this country, there are few places where a politician will win votes by standing up for the rights of prisoners. [ ... ] Few prisoners have any substantial wealth with which to influence elections or even public policy debates, and their ability to communicate with their fellow citizens, the primary alternative means available to influence public policy, is obviously severely limited" (*Kane v. Winn*, 2004, pp. 175–176).

*that criminal defendants receive a fair trial*" (*Strickland v. Washington*, 1984, p. 689, emphasis added). The Court defined effective representation as that which does not fall below "an objective standard of reasonableness," noting that reviewing courts must afford significant deference to the judgment of defense attorneys at the time of trial (*Strickland v. Washington*, 1984, p. 688). A number of individuals who were eventually exonerated by DNA testing initially raised claims of ineffective assistance of counsel on direct and collateral appeals and lost (Garrett, 2011). In these cases, courts concluded that significant evidence of guilt precluded a finding of prejudice to the outcome. The sad irony is that a competent defense lawyer might have been able to bring evidence to light challenging the seemingly "overwhelming" evidence of guilt—but precisely because defense counsel was *not* competent in many of these cases, the evidence available to the appellate court upon review appeared to confirm the trial court's verdict.

Thus, the *Strickland* standard, subject to longstanding and extensive criticism, rarely results in reversals of convictions, even in cases where the lawyer slept during trial or otherwise performed abysmally below any accepted understanding of competent counsel (Burns, 2012; Guggenheim, 2012; Hughes, 2013). "*Strickland* tolerat[es] systemic conditions that structurally preclude effective representation" (Dripps, 2013, p. 888). Moreover, the Supreme Court in *Harrington v. Richter* (2011) made it even more difficult to challenge effective assistance of counsel in habeas cases by "doubly deferring" to state court decisions even where the state court did not specify whether it denied the ineffective assistance of claim (O'Brien, 2012). Since most challenges to effective assistance of counsel occur in habeas proceedings and not on direct appeal, reversal is highly unlikely even in instances of egregiously poor lawyering. Scholars' arguments that the Court should adopt a standard that *presumes* prejudice for many ineffective assistance of counsel claims—given that it is nearly impossible to prove what should have been uncovered, but as a result of poor lawyering, was not—have fallen on mostly deaf ears (Parmeter, 2003).

# Wrongful Convictions and Defense Practice in Context

**Individual instances of defense misconduct.** As we have just discussed, many known cases of wrongful convictions involve egregious examples of "bad lawyering." These practices include fundamental failure on the part of defense attorneys to investigate, prepare for, and ultimately defend their clients' cases. The 1984 capital murder trial of Earl Washington, Jr. is well known as one of the most extreme examples of bad lawyering in a wrongful conviction case. According to Brandon Garrett, a leading scholar on the causes and consequences of wrongful convictions, "the entire [Earl Washington, Jr.] defense case occupied only forty minutes" (Garrett, 2011, p. 146). Despite the fact that (well-defended) death-penalty cases typically require months of preparation and involve putting on a multitude of defense witnesses and experts to rebut the State's case, Washington's trial lasted a total of five hours and involved a total of two defense witnesses (Garrett, 2011). Although Washington initially was represented by a public defender, his family subsequently retained private counsel—presumably on the assumption that in so doing, they would receive better representation—but the defense attorney they were able to hire was woefully ill prepared and had never defended a capital case.

In cases like Washington's, it is relatively easy to assess the incompetency of defense counsel, and to identify what a qualified, diligent defense attorney should have done when faced with a similar set of circumstances. At the very least, adequate defense representation in a capital murder trial would have involved following the carefully delineated standards for representation of a client accused of a capital crime (American Bar Association, 2003).

These standards require defense attorneys to take sufficient time to prepare for the case, interview and adequately consult with the defendant, interview and subpoena witnesses, request discovery, file pretrial motions, investigate the physical evidence, anticipate the State's theory of guilt at trial, and diligently prepare mitigation evidence. Washington's defense attorney's representation clearly fell short of these professional standards of practice. Nevertheless, the lawyering in his case withstood scrutiny on review; Washington was exonerated on the basis of his innocence, established in part by DNA evidence, and not due to concerns that his Sixth Amendment right to the effective assistance of counsel may have been violated by his attorney's performance.

Even in stepping back to consider cases as troubling as Washington's, however, there are lessons to be learned regarding the role of defense attorneys and the prevalence of wrongful convictions today. First, the legal standard to reverse a conviction based on ineffective assistance of counsel set forth in *Strickland* shields many defense attorneys from scrutiny. In practice, the prejudice prong of *Strickland* fails to take into account that if defense counsel were, in fact, ineffective, the trial record may suggest the inevitability of a guilty outcome—but only because of the attorney's poor performance. In relying on the trial record to determine whether a defendant was prejudiced by ineffective assistance, appeals courts have no real way of knowing what other information affecting the outcome of the case might have been drawn out by a more diligent and competent attorney.

Oftentimes, even if the defense attorney undertook no considerable effort to investigate or defend his client's case, there is little risk of counsel being found constitutionally ineffective precisely because the prejudice prong of the standard is so difficult to meet. Because *Strickland* mandates that as long as defense counsel went through the cursory motions of attorney practice, and the record on appeal suggests that a guilty verdict was likely on the weight of the prosecution's evidence alone, deficient defense representation, while not encouraged, is at the very least not adequately proscribed by current Sixth Amendment jurisprudence. Because it is so unlikely that an appellate court will find defense attorneys who fail to exert reasonable effort in representing their clients to be ineffective, the professional incentives to avoid such a finding may be diminished. Moreover, even where an appellate court finds ineffective assistance of counsel, incompetent defense attorneys rarely receive censure for their unprofessional performances. While that is not to say that simply disciplining ineffective defense attorneys will reduce wrongful convictions, it nevertheless stands to reason that when the law itself does not require reversal of a conviction for egregiously poor defense practice, competent lawyering is not sufficiently incentivized.

Personal or professional biases also may play a role in diminishing defense attorneys' zeal for representing clients. After years of law practice, some defense attorneys become jaded—skeptical not only of a client's claimed innocence, but also about the likelihood of securing an acquittal. Some attorneys fail to develop a relationship of trust with clients; after years of representing clients accused (and frequently found guilty) of brutal crimes, they may no longer care about the fate of their client, even if they once did. Some have described such defense attorneys as lawyers who might as well "just phone it in." These lawyers are the antithesis of a zealous advocate and unfortunately constitute some portion of the defense bar. There is no firm research to suggest that lawyers with such attitudes were involved or overrepresented in the universe of known wrongful conviction cases, but simply reviewing the trial transcripts of many of these cases suggests that a lawyer's lack of competence and diligence may stem from a lack of motivation.

Nevertheless, there is no doubt that other important factors played a role in those unjust outcomes, as well. Not least among these other considerations are the structural inequities currently in place in our system of indigent defense. To understand the relationship between defense attorney practice and wrongful convictions, it is crucial to take into account the hurdles faced by public defenders in providing quality representation to their numerous clients.

**Structural inequities and wrongful convictions.** As much research suggests, the quality of defense lawyering is varied and dependent on a host of factors. This chapter concentrates on cases handled by public defenders — attorneys employed full-time by state or local governments to represent indigent criminal defendants. Roughly seven out of every 10 (70%) of the 311 wrongfully convicted individuals exonerated by DNA through August 2013 were represented by public defenders or court-appointed counsel (Innocence Project, 2013a).

Extensive literature describes overwhelming caseloads and the lack of resources hindering defense attorneys' ability to properly investigate and defend their clients' cases. In an increasingly overburdened criminal justice system, public defenders often lack the time, money, and information needed to "zealously" advocate on behalf of their clients. In a significant work surveying the burdens facing public defender systems, Norman Lefstein described one defense attorney with a caseload of over 300 active cases. Regardless of attorney competence, diligence, or motivation, it would be practically impossible to provide effective counsel to each of those 300 clients (Lefstein, 2011).

As U.S. Attorney General Eric H. Holder Jr. said in marking the 50th anniversary of the historic decision in *Gideon*, "public defender offices and other indigent defense providers are underfunded and understaffed. Too often, when legal representation is available to the poor, it's rendered less effective by insufficient resources, overwhelming caseloads and inadequate oversight." In short, Holder said, "the basic rights guaranteed under *Gideon* have yet to be fully realized" (Walsh, 2013). No doubt, the hurdles faced by public defenders that are rooted in the indigent defense system itself contribute to wrongful convictions.

> The resources of the justice system are often stacked against poor defendants. Matters only become worse when a person is represented by an ineffective, incompetent or overburdened defense lawyer. The failure of overworked lawyers to investigate, call witnesses or prepare for trial has led to the conviction of innocent people. (Walsh, 2013)

It has become increasingly apparent that even ordinarily diligent defense attorneys are unable to defend clients successfully in the face of staggering caseloads, insufficient resources, enhanced prosecutorial discretion, and the use of increasingly complex (and often untested) scientific evidence in courts. Adding a lazy, unethical, or unmotivated attorney to an already overburdened system of indigent defense may all but guarantee a conviction.

Statutory restrictions on discovery often hinder defense attorneys' ability to prepare their cases adequately, as well. While discovery guidelines vary widely from state to state, there are few jurisdictions in which defense attorneys are entitled to review all of the information relevant to their clients' cases prior to trial (Roberts, 2004). In some cases, defense lawyers describe the experience of going into court in jurisdictions with limited access to discovery as "trial by ambush," stating that they are entering into trial "blind." unaware of the key facts and witnesses that the State will present until the very last minute.

And, while prosecutors are constitutionally obligated to provide the defense with material evidence that is either exculpatory or impeaching (*Brady v. Maryland*, 1963), the significance of the failure to disclose such information to the production of wrongful convictions is the subject of ongoing controversy. To date, prosecutorial misconduct — which encompasses both prosecutors' and law enforcement's failure to turn over exculpatory information — has played a part in 18% of the DNA exonerations documented by the Innocence Project (Innocence Project, 2013d). Diligent lawyering through repeated requests for discovery may result in more disclosure of exculpatory evidence, but it will not help in cases involving intentional misconduct (Uphoff, 2006).

Overwhelming caseloads and lack of resources should not excuse poor or unprofessional defense performance (even if they may help to explain it). And while a lazy, unethical, or unmotivated defense attorney certainly increases an innocent client's chances of being wrongfully convicted, other aspects of defense practice today must also be considered to understand how the unjust outcomes occur in these cases.

**The "plea-mill," misdemeanors, and deficient defense resources: factors beyond defense control.** There is widespread consensus that one of the greatest barriers to effective defense representation is the fact that the overwhelming majority of cases never go to trial: plea bargains now account for roughly 95% of criminal adjudications (Devers, 2011; Reimer, 2012; Weinstein, 2003). Public defenders face overwhelming caseloads, making it all but impossible for them to resolve the majority of their cases other than through a plea. And while defense attorneys are obligated to advise clients of their rights to reject a plea-deal and proceed to trial, in many cases defense caseloads are too great to pursue this option. Even though public defenders are (or should be) aware that pressuring their clients to accept guilty pleas simply for the sake of expedience is unethical, the fact remains that if the majority of cases are not resolved through pleas, our current system of criminal representation and adjudication would crumble.

Significantly, for most defendants, the perceived costs of going to trial may far outweigh the benefits. Overwhelmingly, criminal defendants are poor, facing misdemeanor charges, and primarily interested in the quick resolution of their cases (Reimer, 2012). For these defendants—who comprise the *vast majority* of defendants in all criminal cases—accepting a plea may be the best option.

Other defendants may enter a guilty plea because their trial lawyer has convinced them to accept the plea offer even though that lawyer has not performed minimal investigation or otherwise provided a competent and diligent defense (Weinstein, 2013). In some (hopefully rare) instances, a prosecutor may intentionally fail to disclose exculpatory evidence and then offer the defendant a significantly reduced prison sentence to obtain a guilty plea—without the exculpatory evidence ever coming to light. Innocent defendants have pled guilty under such circumstances. It is not possible to know the number of innocent people who have pled guilty to crimes to avoid lengthy prison terms, but studies in recent years have established that the phenomenon occurs with greater frequency than once imagined (American Bar Association, 2005).

In Chris Ochoa's case, for example, police went so far as to point to the vein where lethal injection would be administered if Ochoa did not confess to a rape-murder he did not commit, and implicate another man—Richard Danziger—in the crimes as well. After writing and signing a full confession and testifying against Danziger, Ochoa pled guilty to the crimes. He spent more than twenty years in prison before being exonerated when DNA evidence established that another man—already serving a third life sentence—was the perpetrator of the crime. Danziger also was exonerated after serving an equally lengthy prison sentence (Yaroshefsky, 2004).

"[T]he incentives for defendants to plead guilty are greater than at any previous point in the history of our criminal justice system...." Moreover, "the incentives to bargain are powerful enough to force even an innocent defendant to falsely confess guilt in hopes of leniency and in fear of reprisal" (Dervan, 2012, p. 58). "Taken as whole, deficiencies in indigent defense services result in a fundamentally unfair criminal justice system that constantly risks convicting persons who are genuinely innocent of the charges lodged against them" (American Bar Association, 2005).

**Defense attorneys as scientists: forensic evidence and its implications for effective defense practice.** According to the Innocence Project (2013g), invalidated or improper forensic evidence has contributed to wrongful convictions in just over half of the DNA-based exonerations. As prosecutors are becoming increasingly reliant on forensic science in criminal cases, defense attorneys must now be skilled in the use of forensic science at trial as well. In proceedings where the State's case relies upon forensic evidence and expert testimony, the need for defense attorneys to understand the nature and implications of such evidence cannot be overstated.

The "CSI" effect has become well known. Jurors in criminal cases not only commonly expect forensic evidence, but often are willing to trust such evidence whole cloth without properly understanding its actual implications. Discrediting such evidence or ensuring that its probity is properly contextualized is essential to ensuring a fair trial and outcome. In addition, before achieving greater awareness about the role that faulty forensic evidence and scientific testimony have played in contributing to wrongful convictions, many defense attorneys may have been swayed by the assumed infallibility of forensic evidence, as well. Nevertheless, we now know that much of this evidence cannot be trusted. The research into wrongful convictions shows that in many instances, either the *science relied on by the prosecution is itself* unreliable, or that testimony regarding the *significance of the scientific evidence* has been vastly exaggerated. In either case, the scientific testimony offered by the prosecution in support of guilt constitutes "invalid" forensic evidence.

Suggestions that the roles and responsibilities of defense attorneys must expand and transform in light of the growing awareness about wrongful convictions place a heavy burden on the defense bar, particularly in light of existing funding shortages, heavy caseloads, and other obstacles. Nevertheless, advocating such a transformation may be necessary to ensure just outcomes in criminal cases. In order for a defense attorney to properly litigate a case where forensic evidence is relevant, that defense attorney must be responsible for understanding the science, including the extent to which it can be trusted and the parameters of its accuracy in any given case.

An influential study of the use of forensic science in the trials of 232 defendants later exonerated by DNA testing found that a high percentage of forensic evidence was empirically false or inaccurate (Garrett & Neufeld, 2009). Moreover, flawed forensic testimony was not limited to one area of forensic science or to a single class of experts. Rather, 72 forensic scientists "employed by 52 laboratories, practices, or hospitals from 25 states" presented this invalid and unsupportable testimony (p. 9). Upon analyzing the data, Garrett and Neufeld concluded that the prevalence of invalid forensic testimony admitted at trial was not just the consequence of "a few 'bad apples'" being permitted to testify, but rather reflected an inability of the "adversarial system" to "police this invalid testimony" (pp. 23-24). The shortcomings included the performance of defense attorneys, who either did not develop the necessary expertise in the forensic science at issue at trial, employ a defense expert to validate the State's forensic assertions, challenge the admissibility of the evidence in pre-trial motions, or effectively examine prosecution experts. The rules governing the admissibility of forensic science in the courts no longer constitute an adequate bulwark against the introduction of unreliable or false testimony at trial — indeed, many judges themselves apparently did not know or understand the science behind many experts' testimony. The onus to learn fully about these forensic disciplines now falls on defense attorneys so they can prepare adequately for their clients' defense.

As an initial matter, a defense attorney may not be familiar with the significant difference between so-called "junk science," which refers to forensic evidence that is *inherently* unreliable, and testimony which misstates the significance of the science at issue ("improper" testimony) (Garrett & Neufeld, 2009, p. 12). Although junk science and improper forensic testimony may overlap, they present separate problems when they arise at trial. They are both invalid forensic testimony.

"Junk science" refers to certain forensic disciplines, such as hair microscopy and bite mark comparison, which the research on wrongful convictions shows to be consistently unreliable. That is, hair microscopy and bite mark comparison evidence is so frequently disproven by DNA evidence that the reliability of these disciplines on the whole is at issue. For example, by examining two hairs under a microscope—hair microscopy—an analyst cannot opine to a scientific certainty that the two hairs "match" without additional evidence, such as mitochondrial DNA. To the extent that the State tries to put on evidence that microscopic hair analysis reveals that hairs from the defendant "match" hairs found on the victim, for example, defense attorneys need to be aware of the limitations of the *discipline as a whole*, and ensure that the jury understands those limitations as well. The problem with "junk science" is that it involves a purportedly "scientific" discipline that has not undergone sufficient research and testing to be trusted by courts and defense attorneys. In every stage of the trial process where the State seeks to introduce bite mark or hair comparison testimony, a defense attorney needs to be prepared to 1) challenge the admissibility of the testimony based on the mounting research showing its unreliability; 2) have the evidence examined and discussed by a defense expert; and 3) cross-examine the State expert not only on her conclusions regarding the evidence, but on the reliability of the discipline upon which those conclusions are based.

Identifying improper forensic testimony, on the other hand, is more difficult for a defense attorney because it involves understanding not only the science at issue, but also the conclusions being drawn from that science and offered as evidence of guilt. In cases where misleading forensic evidence has been identified as a contributor to the wrongful conviction, it is not always the scientific *discipline* that is at issue: rather, it is the assertions that were made *about* that evidence which are erroneous. For example, if a serologist—a blood expert—states that both the perpetrator and the defendant have Type O blood, and Type O blood is only seen in 5% of the Caucasian population (when the real rate is between 35% and 45%), such testimony is not based on junk science but is nonetheless invalid (American Red Cross, 2013). So, while serology itself is not "junk science," it can nevertheless be employed improperly in a trial setting. The wrongful convictions research teaches us that the defense lawyer must know that when the State seeks to introduce forensic testimony, both the science involved and the conclusions drawn based upon that science must be scrutinized carefully.

While not all of the defense attorneys involved in wrongful conviction cases lacked diligence or professionalism, review of the data on DNA exonerations nevertheless suggests that the majority of defense attorneys have been woefully inadequate in challenging the presentation of invalid forensic testimony in court (Garrett, 2011). In significant measure, this is a failing of the adversarial system—and not that of the defense lawyer alone—in keeping flawed science out of the courts.

It is increasingly clear that the use of forensic evidence in criminal cases has evolved faster than defense attorneys' abilities to learn about or contest its use. Our current knowledge about the prevalence of invalid forensic testimony in criminal trials is limited; it is largely based upon DNA testing that conclusively has disproven forensic experts' testimony. Challenges to the admissibility of forensic evidence long accepted in courts— such as bite mark, fingerprint, or ballistics evidence—are fairly new and will be made in a context where the case law governing the admissibility of forensic evidence shows a general trend toward greater inclusion of such testimony (Bizzaro, 2010).

Since 1993, the federal courts and many state courts have admitted forensic evidence once the "trial judge … ensure[s] that any and all scientific testimony or evidence admitted is not only relevant, but reliable" (*Daubert v. Merrell Dow Pharmaceuticals, Inc.*, 1993, p.

589).[7] In assessing reliability under the *Daubert* standard, courts consider a range of factors, including whether the scientific theory or technique had been tested, subjected to peer review, has a known or discernible error rate, and whether it is "generally accepted" within the relevant scientific community (*Daubert*, 1993, p. 584). In 2000, the Federal Rules of Evidence were revised to allow the admission of expert testimony if such testimony "a) ... will help the trier of fact to understand the evidence or to determine a fact in issue; b) ... is based on sufficient facts or data; c) ... is the product of reliable principles and methods, and; d) the expert has reliably applied the principles and methods to the facts of the case" (Federal Rules of Evidence, 2013, Rule 702). To contest the admissibility of forensic evidence on the ground that such criteria are not met, the defense lawyer must be knowledgeable about the discipline in question and the standards governing the admissibility of evidence in the jurisdiction.

As the legal standards regarding the admissibility of forensic science have evolved, so too has forensic science itself. For example, DNA evidence was only first admitted in criminal trials in the late 1980s (Barr, 1989). In 2009, the National Academy of Sciences published a comprehensive report on the use of forensic science in criminal cases, largely in response to the growing number of wrongful convictions shown to have relied on improper forensic testimony. This report, *Strengthening Forensic Science in the United States: A Path Forward* (hereinafter "NAS Report") commended advances in DNA science to assist law enforcement in identifying criminals accurately and efficiently (National Academy of Sciences, 2009). It also found that unlike DNA, however, a number of the scientific disciplines frequently relied on in courts did not meet the same standards for accuracy and reliability.

> Over the last two decades, advances in some forensic science disciplines, especially the use of DNA technology, have demonstrated that some areas of forensic science have great additional potential to help law enforcement identify criminals.... Those advances, however, also have revealed that, in some cases, substantive information and testimony based on faulty forensic science analyses may have contributed to wrongful convictions of innocent people. This fact has demonstrated the potential danger of giving undue weight to evidence and testimony derived from imperfect testing and analysis. (National Academy of Sciences, 2009, p. 5)

The report continues: "Imprecise or exaggerated expert testimony has sometimes contributed to the admission of erroneous or misleading evidence" (National Academy of Sciences, 2009, p. 5). Thus, although the legal standards regarding the admissibility of scientific evidence have broadened, and the science in certain areas, such as DNA testing, has advanced, many areas of forensic science nevertheless are not yet sufficiently reliable to offer dispositive evidence of guilt.

Given the extent to which forensic evidence is regarded as particularly convincing evidence of guilt, and keeping in mind the overall deference that juries and judges give "expert" witnesses, defense attorneys' failure to properly grapple with invalid forensic testimony is of particular significance in understanding wrongful convictions. While in some documented wrongful conviction cases the prosecution's forensic expert consciously misled the jury regarding the probity of certain evidence, improper forensic evidence presented by the State oftentimes reflects a misunderstanding that could have been corrected

---

7. Some jurisdictions adhere to the pre-1993 standard for the admission of expert testimony, governed by the decision in *Frye v. United States* (1923), which determined that scientific evidence cannot be introduced in court unless it is "generally accepted" in the relevant scientific community.

through effective cross-examination or countered through the testimony of a competent defense expert.

> Most of the invalid forensic testimony involved evidence presented as inculpatory. In just 2 of the 82 cases with invalid testimony, the analysts testified that all of the forensic evidence was non-probative or inconclusive; in fact that evidence was exculpatory. The forensic testimony would have played a reduced role in many more of the 82 cases had forensic analysts accurately presented the evidence. (Garrett & Neufeld, 2009, p. 15)

Invalid scientific evidence presented to the jury as proof of the defendant's guilt in the 82 exoneration cases where such evidence was introduced could have been challenged if the defense attorneys had the resources, knowledge, instinct, or willingness to do so. However, only in roughly 30% of the wrongful conviction cases did attorneys introduce expert testimony in their clients' defense (Garrett, n.d.). While funding for experts may be denied defendants by the courts, it is nevertheless incumbent upon a defense attorney to file motions and litigate the necessity of being afforded a defense expert where forensic evidence is crucial to a case.

At the same time, however, it bears repeating that defense attorneys are not to blame for failing to challenge forensic evidence in every case where such evidence contributed to a wrongful conviction. Current research shows that in some wrongful conviction cases, the prosecution offered forensic evidence in support of guilt that at the time was not known to anyone to be faulty or unreliable. In Cameron Todd Willingham's case, for example, the common consensus among forensic experts is that the State relied on forensic evidence that was based on scientific assumptions now known to be false (Grann, 2009). Willingham was convicted of arson and murder in Texas after being accused of setting the house fire that killed his three children. He was sentenced to death and, despite numerous appeals challenging the validity of the evidence used against him, was executed by Texas in 2004 (Innocence Project 2013h). The evidence presented against him continued to unsettle criminal justice advocates as well as members of the scientific community, however, and years after his execution his case was reinvestigated. Following a complete re-investigation of the charges against him, the state investigative committee assigned to review his conviction ultimately determined that the science—arson evidence—used to convict him was unreliable (Innocence Project, 2013).

Research challenging scientific disciplines such as arson investigation has only emerged relatively recently. Thus, courts, attorneys, and forensic analysts themselves may not have been on notice that these areas of forensics could not be trusted at the time they were offered in criminal trials as evidence of guilt. In the case of ballistics analysis, for example, many diligent defense attorneys assumed that forensic experts could be relied on when they reported that they were able to match a bullet fired to a defendant's gun. More recently, however, evidence has come to light disputing the reliability of such analysis. In a detailed exploration of the many problems inherent to such evidence, Adina Schwartz (2005, p. 1) writes, "firearms identification, often improperly referred to as 'ballistics identification,' is part of the forensic science discipline of toolmark identification. Despite widespread faith in 'ballistics fingerprinting' [ ... ] because of systemic scientific problems, firearms and toolmark identifications should be inadmissible across-the-board." Because the research about "junk science" has evolved and is now widely available with the exercise of diligent trial preparation, defense attorneys can be expected to know of—and challenge—such assertions. In many wrongful conviction cases relying on misleading scientific testimony, however, defense attorneys could not reasonably have been expected to know that the science was unreliable.

Nevertheless, we also know that in many wrongful conviction cases, forensic testimony was misstated or exaggerated at trial, and could have been challenged had the defense attorney exercised proper diligence in mounting a defense. Garrett and Neufeld's data indicate that in many wrongful conviction cases, forensic experts provided testimony which improperly bolstered the State's case by simply misstating its significance, with no challenge from the defense or the court (Garrett & Neufeld, 2009). This science was not unknown or unknowable at the time, and a diligent defense attorney should have been able to point out the flaws in such testimony. In such cases, a failure to do so can be imputed to the defense attorney.

To emphasize this point, Garrett and Neufeld's study documents a number of cases in which defense attorneys should have been able to dispute serology testimony offered by the prosecution. Expert testimony was false or overstated in 57% of the 100 wrongful conviction cases in which serological evidence was presented (Garrett & Neufeld, 2009). Serology can help determine the blood type of an individual responsible for depositing certain physical evidence in connection with a crime (such as semen, saliva, or skin cells) (Garrett & Neufeld, 2009). Prior to DNA testing, serological evidence frequently was offered to suggest guilt, where the blood type in physical evidence collected at the crime scene matched the blood type of the defendant.

However, a serological "match" without more distinctive DNA markers is never conclusive evidence of guilt. No matter how rare, no blood type is unique to a single individual. A serological "exclusion," on the other hand, can be exculpatory—to the extent that the evidence is uncontaminated and analysis of it was performed correctly, no one can deposit bodily fluids inconsistent with his or her individual blood type. That is to say, in a single perpetrator rape case, where the victim is alive and was conscious at the time of the attack and knows that only one perpetrator was involved, if the defendant's blood type is inconsistent with the blood type of the semen deposited, this inconsistency—known as an "exclusion"—is dispositive proof of innocence. In contrast, if the defendant's blood type is consistent with the blood deposited at a crime scene, this alone is not sufficient to prove guilt. Such evidence would only serve to establish that the defendant—along with everyone else in the population with that particular blood type—could be the source of the blood found at the crime scene and thus might have perpetrated the crime.

Therefore, while serological evidence can be dispositive, it is nevertheless subject to limitations that an effective defense attorney must be prepared to address. In many cases where invalid serology testimony was discovered, experts "failed to accurately provide the relevant statistic regarding the included population. These analysts instead offered invalid, reduced frequencies (a rarer event) that appeared to further inculpate the defendant" (Garrett & Neufeld, 2009, p. 47). This information is available to the diligent and competent defense attorney, who is able to educate him or herself on the relative frequencies of blood type and expose any misleading statements by prosecution experts on cross-examination.

# Moving Forward

Defense attorneys unquestionably must be skilled and knowledgeable about forensic science. Case investigation increasingly utilizes various forensic disciplines, and it is therefore incumbent upon an attorney to work competently within the scientific arena. This may be outside of the comfort zone of many defense attorneys, who had little expectation that criminal defense lawyering would require such a level of engagement with science.

Today, the lawyer must *know* what disciplines are subject to challenge, and be able to properly explain to a court why evidence based on such disciplines may be unreliable or unduly prejudicial to the defendant. An effective defense attorney must be able to recognize when an independent expert should vet forensic evidence and otherwise must be knowledgeable regarding the implications of the science presented. Competent attorneys will diligently file pretrial motions challenging the presentation of forensic evidence that is based on invalid science and will utilize their own experts in pretrial admissibility hearings and during trial for cross examination of the prosecution's expert and other witnesses.

To the extent that the court chooses to admit potentially invalid forensic evidence over defense objection, the defense attorney must be prepared to cross-examine the State's expert on the reliability of the scientific discipline at issue and highlight for the jury the proper weight that such evidence should be assigned. Moreover, it may be necessary to seek introduction of the testimony of a defense expert who can convincingly speak to the problems of reliance upon invalid forensic testimony, even where a court has determined that the evidence is admissible. Defense attorneys also must be on notice that even if the science at issue is "good," the expert's conclusions may be incorrect. In some cases, paying close attention to the statistics offered and the probative weight assigned to such statistics may be sufficient to identify the error in the expert testimony.

Thus, not only must the effective defense lawyer establish a relationship of trust with and effectively counsel the client; thoroughly investigate the case; file necessary pretrial motions; seek to hire necessary investigators and experts; negotiate appropriate disposition with the prosecution; prepare for trial; carefully select a jury; conduct witness examinations; make opening and closing statements and appropriate motions; prepare for and conduct sentencing; and be knowledgeable about collateral consequences of convictions; but the attorney must also pay particular attention to the state of scientific knowledge that may have an impact upon the case. Moreover, the successful defense attorney today must be knowledgeable about the predominant causes of wrongful convictions and be prepared to do what is necessary to avoid future wrongful convictions.

How can the already overburdened indigent criminal justice system ensure that defense lawyers achieve such a level of skill, knowledge, diligence and competence? A multifaceted approach is essential.

First, any viable and respected criminal justice system must cope with longstanding structural impediments. Adequate funding and lowered caseloads are essential if defense lawyers are to be expected to undertake additional responsibilities and be competent in forensic science. Second, when forensic science is involved in a case, courts must authorize expert services for the defense without delay or undue burden on the defense lawyer. The judiciary needs to assist in ensuring that counties or states adequately fund forensic experts. Third, training institutes and programs are essential to ensure that defenders around the country receive adequate instruction and training on all aspects of forensic sciences. The training should begin in law schools where criminal justice courses and concentrations assure that science is part of fundamental preparation for the profession. Law schools could partner with graduate schools to provide interdisciplinary courses for future lawyers and scientists alike.

In addition, a functional system for effective assistance of counsel cannot focus solely on the defense lawyer. Trial and appellate judges and prosecutors need to assume significant responsibility for the flaws that lead to wrongful convictions. The standard for reversal set forth in *Strickland* has ensured that systemic ineffectiveness has little consequence.

The judiciary should closely examine the *Strickland* standard in light of teachings from wrongful conviction cases. What needs to change when courts repeatedly deny ineffective assistance of counsel claims because there was no showing of prejudice and the individual later is proved to be innocent? At the very least, a presumption of prejudice should become the standard where the lawyer's performance is significantly below that of reasonably competent counsel (the first prong of the *Strickland* standard). Certainly, failing to address forensic science adequately in a case, whether through lack of investigation, failing to engage an expert, or effectively challenge invalid forensic testimony, should presumptively be prejudicial. A court's failure to appoint a defense expert when it is reasonably required also should presumptively be prejudicial. Judicial decisions in such a direction could change defense practice significantly.

# Conclusion

Cases of wrongful conviction are powerful validation of the need to provide greater resources to public defenders and court-appointed attorneys so the Sixth Amendment's right to effective assistance of counsel can be realized. To the extent that funding and quality services are lacking, indigent defendants, without diligent, competent, zealous defense lawyering, will continue to stand an especially great chance of a wrongful conviction. This fundamental point cannot be overstated.

The task for defense lawyers has become even more complicated and demanding whenever the prosecution's case is based, in whole or in part, upon forensic science. The evolution of scientific knowledge about a range of disciplines—traditionally accepted as valid science in courtrooms throughout the country, but now identified as "junk sciences"—requires defense attorneys to become expert in each of these disciplines so they can persuasively challenge such evidence or, where the science may be valid but nevertheless subject to limitation, so they can effectively cross-examine prosecution experts.

More often than not, however, the only way for a defense attorney to ensure that the State's expert is not offering false or flawed testimony is to enlist an independent expert to review that testimony. To the extent that the science being offered is fairly nuanced or complex, neither the judge, nor the jury, nor the defense attorney can be expected to assess the expert's methods without assistance. This is no small task, especially in financially strapped counties and cities where many judges are loath to expend funds to permit the defense lawyer to employ an independent expert.

Finally, the role of the defense lawyer in wrongful convictions cannot be examined in a vacuum. The roles of the prosecutor and the court must be part of any calculus in deriving lessons from wrongful convictions. A system in which 95% of defendants plead guilty and in which it is not mandatory for prosecutors to disclose potentially exculpatory information to the defense prior to a defendant entering a guilty plea is fraught with the potential to produce wrongful convictions. Similarly, for the small percentage of cases that go to trial, a lack of robust discovery increases the chances of wrongful convictions. The prosecutor, the court, and the defense lawyer each share the responsibility to ensure a process that facilitates the fair exchange of information. Without changes in disclosure policies and practices, an innocent client may still be convicted, even with the most diligent and competent defense lawyer.

# References

Alexander, M. (2012, March 12). Go to trial, crash the system. *New York Times: Sunday Review*. Retrieved August 4, 2013, from: http://www.nytimes.com/2012/03/11/opinion/sunday/go-to-trial-crash-the-justice-system.html.

American Bar Association (2005). House of Delegates Resolution 107. Retrieved August 4, 2013 from http://www.americanbar.org/content/dam/aba/migrated/legalservices/downloads/sclaid/indigentdefense/20110325_aba_res107.authcheckdam.pdf.

American Bar Association (2003). Guidelines for the appointment and performance of defense counsel in death penalty cases. Retrieved August 4, 2013 from http://www.americanbar.org/content/dam/aba/migrated/2011_build/death_penalty_representation/2003guidelines.authcheckdam.pdf.

American Red Cross (2013). Blood types. Retrieved August 4, 2013 from http://www.redcrossblood.org/learn-about-blood/blood-types.

*Argersinger v. Hamlin*, 407 U.S. 25 (1972).

Barr, J. J. (1989). The use of DNA typing in criminal prosecutions: A flawless partnership of law and science? *New York Law School Law Review, 34*, 485–530.

Bizzaro, A.L. (2010). Challenging the admission of forensic evidence. *Wisconsin Lawyer, 83* (Sept.), 12–15, 68–70.

*Brady v. Maryland*, 373 U.S. 83 (1963).

Bright, S. B. & Sanneh, S. (2013). Violating the right to a lawyer. *The Los Angeles Times* (March 18). Retrieved August 4, 2013, from http://articles.latimes.com/2013/mar/18/opinion/la-oe-bright-gideon-justice-20130318.

Burns, A. K. (2012). Insurmountable obstacles: Structural errors, procedural default, and ineffective assistance. *Stanford Law Review, 64*, 727–764.

Cohen, A. (2013) How the sequester is holding up our legal system. *The Atlantic Monthly*, July 12, 2013. Retrieved August 6, 2013 from: http://www.theatlantic.com/national/archive/2013/07/how-the-sequester-is-holding-up-our-legal-system/277704/.

*Daubert v. Merrell Dow Pharmaceuticals, Inc.*, 509 U.S. 579 (1993).

Dervan, L.E. (2012). Bargained justice: Plea-bargaining's innocence problem and the *Brady* safety valve. *Utah Law Review, 51*, 64–96.

Devers, L. (2011). *Plea and charge bargaining*. Washington, DC: Bureau of Justice Assistance, U.S. Department of Justice.

Dripps, D. A. (2013). Why *Gideon* failed: Politics and feedback loops in the reform of criminal justice. *Washington & Lee Law Review, 70*, 883–925.

Findley, Keith A. (2013). Understanding failed evidence. *Criminal Justice, 28* (Spring), 66–69.

*Frye v. United States*, 293 F. 1013 (D.C. Cir. 1923).

Garrett, B. (n.d.) The defense case at trial. *University of Virginia Law School*. Retrieved August 4, 2013, from: http://www.law.virginia.edu/html/librarysite/garrett_innocenceontrial.htm.

Garrett, B. L. (2011). *Convicting the innocent: Where criminal prosecutions go wrong*. Cambridge, MA: Harvard University Press.

Garrett, B.L. & Neufeld, P. (2009). Invalid forensic science testimony and wrongful convictions. *Virginia Law Review, 95*, 1–96.

*Gideon v. Wainwright*, 372 U.S. 335 (1963).

Grann, D. (2009). Trial by fire: Did Texas execute an innocent man? *The New Yorker* (Sept. 7), retrieved October 21, 2013 from: http://www.newyorker.com/reporting/2009/09/07/090907fa_fact_grann.

Guggenheim, M. (2012). The people's right to a well-funded indigent defender system. *N.Y.U. Review of Law & Social Change, 36*, 395–463.

*Harrington v. Richter*, 131 S.Ct. 770 (2011).

Hoffmann, J. & King, N. (2008). Envisioning post-conviction review for the twenty-first century. *Mississippi Law Journal, 78*, 433–451.

Hughes, E. (2013). Investigating *Gideon's* legacy in the U.S. Courts of Appeals. *Yale Law Journal, 122*, 2376–2393.

*In re Gault*, 387 U.S. 1 (1967).

Innocence Project (2013a). DNA exoneree case profiles. Retrieved August 4, 2013, from http://www.innocenceproject.org/know/.

Innocence Project (2013b). When the innocent plead guilty. Retrieved August 4, 2013, from http://www.innocenceproject.org/Content/When_the_Innocent_Plead_Guilty.php.

Innocence Project (2013c). Fix the system: Priority issues. Retrieved August 4, 2013 from http://www.innocenceproject.org/fix/Priority-Issues.php.

Innocence Project (2013d). Government misconduct. Retrieved August 4, 2013 from http://www.innocenceproject.org/understand/Government-Misconduct.php.

Innocence Project (2013e). Bad lawyering. Retrieved August 4, 2013 from http://www.innocenceproject.org/understand/Bad-Lawyering.php.

Innocence Project (2013f). Michael Morton. Retrieved August 4, 2013 from http://www.innocenceproject.org/Content/Michael_Morton.php.

Innocence Project (2013g). Unreliable or improper forensic science. Retrieved August 30, 2013 from http://www.innocenceproject.org/understand/Unreliable-Limited-Science.php.

Innocence Project (2013h). Cameron Todd Willingham: Wrongfully convicted and executed in Texas. Retrieved August 4, 2013 from http://www.innocenceproject.org/Content/Cameron_Todd_Willingham_Wrongfully_Convicted_and_Executed_in_Texas.php.

Innocence Project (2012). Missouri Appeals Court clears way for George Allen's exoneration. Retrieved August 4, 2013, from http://www.innocenceproject.org/Content/Missouri_Appeals_Court_Clears_Way_for_George_Allens_Exoneration.php.

*Kane v. Winn*, 319 F. Supp.2d 162 (D. Mass. 2004).

Kirchmeier, J. L. (1996). Drink, drugs, and drowsiness: The constitutional right to effective assistance of counsel and the *Strickland* prejudice requirement. *Nebraska Law Review, 75*, 425–475.

Lefstein, N. (2011). *Securing reasonable caseloads: Ethics and law in public defense.* Chicago, IL: American Bar Association.

Model Rules of Professional Conduct: 1.1. *The American Bar Association.*

National Academy of Sciences (2009). *Strengthening forensic science in the United States: A path forward.* Washington, DC: The National Academies Press. Retrieved August 30, 2013 from https://www.ncjrs.gov/pdffiles1/nij/grants/228091.pdf.

National Registry of Exoneration (2013). Exonerations by year: DNA and non-DNA. Retrieved August 30, 2013 from https://www.law.umich.edu/special/exoneration/Pages/Exoneration-by-Year.aspx.

National Registry of Exonerations (2012). Exonerations in the United States, 1989—2012. Retrieved August 8, 2013 from http://www.law.umich.edu/special/exoneration/Documents/exonerations_us_1989_2012 summary.pdf.

O'Brien, D. J. (2012). Heeding Congress's message: The United States Supreme Court bars federal courthouse doors to habeas relief against all but irrational state court decisions, and oftentimes doubly so. *Federal. Sentencing Reporter, 24*, 320–328.

Parmeter, K.C. (2003). Dreaming of effective assistance: The awakening of *Cronic's* call to presume prejudice from representational absence. *Temple Law Review, 76*, 827–882.

Reimer, N. (2012). After half a century, *Gideon's* promise remains elusive. *The Champion, 36* (Feb.), 7– 8.

Roberts, J. (2004). Too little, too late: Ineffective assistance of counsel, the duty to investigate, and pretrial discovery in criminal cases. *Fordham Urban Law Journal, 31,* 1097–1154.

*Rothgerry v. Gillespie County,* 554 U.S. 191 (2008).

*Strickland v. Washington,* 466 U.S. 668 (1984).

Uphoff, R. (2006). Convicting the innocent: Aberration or systemic problem? *Wisconsin Law Review, 2006,* 739–842.

*United States v. Frazier,* 387 F.3d 1244 (2004).

*United States v. Hines,* 55 F.Supp.2d 62 (D. Mass. 1999).

Weinstein, I. (2003). Don't believe everything you think: Cognitive bias in legal decision making. *Clinical Law Review, 9,* 783–834.

Yaroshefsky, E. (2008). Ethics and plea bargaining: What's discovery got to do with it? *American Bar Association Criminal Justice Magazine, 23(3).* Retrieved August 4, 2013 from: http://www.americanbar.org/content/dam/aba/publishing/criminal_justice_section_newsletter/crimjust_cjmag_23_3_yaroshefsky.authcheckdam.pdf.

# Chapter Nine

# The American Adversary System: Sources of Error in the Criminal Adjudication Process

Neil Vidmar, *Duke University*
James E. Coleman, *Duke University*

## Introduction

An examination of research and writing about wrongful convictions indicates that errors may occur not only at any stage of the criminal justice process, but in fact many are system errors that are cumulative (Gould & Leo, 2010). A significant portion of the errors result from incentives and biases that arise out of the American adversarial system of adjudication. This is not to claim that the American adversary system, derived from English common law, is necessarily inferior to the inquisitorial systems used in most European countries and, indeed, most other countries throughout the world. The adversary system has many strengths and recent findings suggest that countries with inquisitorial systems also produce erroneous convictions (see Huff & Killas, 2010). However, a brief discussion comparing the two procedural systems is helpful in highlighting sources of potential error in the American criminal justice process. Additionally, even within an adversarial system, two sets of somewhat competing values, namely "crime control" versus "due process," may influence the ways that criminal matters are handled. A very brief, indeed truncated, overview of adversarial versus inquisitorial criminal justice systems, including the influence of roles and role demands and their cumulative effects, provides a perspective on potential sources of error in the American criminal justice system.

## Stepping Back: Understanding Adversarial Versus Inquisitorial Modes of Criminal Procedure

There are two principal forms of criminal justice systems, those using *adversarial* rules of procedure and those using what are generally labeled *inquisitorial* forms of procedure. A number of writings (e.g., Damaska, 1986; Frankel, 1975) have described and compared the two systems. In an inquisitorial system, once a crime is brought to the attention of authorities, regardless of the source, one or more neutral judges, acting on behalf of the state, takes control of the investigation, directing the prosecutors and police as they attempt to uncover the circumstances of the alleged crime. Under the judge's supervision, witnesses are located and questioned, forensic tests are made, and other forms of evidence are gathered. If expert witnesses are required, the judge finds and hires those witnesses on behalf of the state. With some significant exceptions, there are typically no separate witnesses for the defendant. Although the defendant is entitled to legal representation, the defense lawyer's role is primarily limited to raising questions about the investigation or charges and making suggestions about witnesses or other relevant sources of evidence to the investigating judges. Much of the evidence is recorded in document form for the trial. Depending on the seriousness of the charges, as many as three judges may preside at the trial. In some countries, a small panel of laypersons, as many as seven but typically fewer, sits with the judges at trial (Hans, 2003; Jackson & Kovalev, 2006). Recently, some countries (e.g., Japan, South Korea, Taiwan) have attempted to introduce modified forms of the jury system, but usually these "juries" do not have the final say on the verdict, which is left to the judges (see, e.g., Huang & Lin, 2013). Another component of inquisitorial system proceedings is that, in contrast to the American adversary system, on appeal the total set of proceedings is subject to review by a higher court, and not just alleged errors on specific points of law brought forth by the parties. European and many Asian systems of criminal justice are generally based on this inquisitorial model.

In contrast, the American adversarial system, derived from England's common law system, places a great deal of responsibility for the trial outcome in the hands of the contending parties, that is, the prosecutors and the defense lawyers (and ultimately the laypersons who form the jury). Police investigate an alleged crime and bring the evidence to the prosecutor's office. One or more prosecutors compile the evidence, depending heavily on the police to gather that evidence against the defendant. For serious crimes, after the initial evidence is gathered, the next step is to present the evidence to a grand jury. The grand jury is composed of citizens, ranging in size from six or seven persons up to 20 or more, who vote under a majority rule and on the balance of probabilities as to whether there is sufficient evidence to render an indictment allowing the prosecution to file charges and take the case to trial. At this stage, only the state actively participates in the proceedings, and the grand jury's decision is greatly influenced by what the prosecutor discloses or fails to disclose, and ultimately by what the prosecutor asks the jurors to do. At some point in this process, either a defense lawyer will be hired by the defendant or a public defender will be appointed to handle the defense. Even before charges are formally laid, there may be some preliminary, informal discussions between the prosecution and defense regarding the nature of the evidence against the defendant, possible charges, and even about a possible plea bargain.[1] From this point, the prosecution and defense proceed more or less independently to gather evidence in support of their respective positions, depending on inclination and resources.

During the early stages of the American criminal justice process, the prosecution has momentum in gathering evidence. This includes not only interviewing witnesses but gathering forensic evidence, which usually is analyzed by a forensics crime laboratory. The defense may also collect evidence, but often its position is mostly reactive to the prosecutor's evidence. Under *Brady v Maryland* (1963) the defense is entitled to obtain any material evidence gathered by the prosecution, either incriminating, exculpatory, or that may impeach the state's case. However, often there are disputes about full disclosure by the prosecution, requiring intervention by a judge to resolve the dispute. Both prosecution and defense may hire their own experts in an attempt to make an affirmative case to re-

---

1. Preliminary field research by the authors and several colleagues, also at Duke University Law School, has begun to document this process.

fute—or at least offset—the conclusions reached by the other side's experts. As discussed in more detail below, while the rationale behind the adversary system is based on an assumption that both sides have equal resources and are roughly comparable, often the prosecution has a significant advantage, not only because it is funded by the state, but also because it has an ongoing relationship with police and crime laboratory personnel. In *Convicting the Innocent,* Brandon Garrett (2011, Chapter 6) concluded that the vast bulk of evidence put forth in trials resulting in wrongful convictions was presented by the prosecution. In contrast, the defense in many instances, whether funded by the government or privately, has fewer resources—a topic discussed below.

Another very significant difference between an inquisitorial system and an adversary system involves the role of the judge. While inquisitorial system judges, as described above, are active at every phase of the criminal justice process, adversary judges are put in the role of neutral referees between the prosecution and defense. To be sure, adversary judges may be asked to tender rulings in relatively early stages of the process with respect to disputes about such matters as the prosecution withholding evidence. However, in theory, and mostly in practice, the judge does not actively engage in the investigative stages of a prosecution but merely rules on disputed matters (though see Frankel, 1975).

This neutral role of the judge as referee also applies if the case goes to trial. Although some cases are tried by a judge sitting alone, trials of major offenses are usually by jury. The trial judge is an umpire between the opposing parties. Formal rules of evidence and procedure guide how the jury is chosen, what evidence it is allowed to hear at trial, and which decision rules the jury is to use when deciding on guilt or innocence. This is not to say that the judge is unimportant in the adversarial proceedings. There is a degree of flexibility in judicial rulings and often appeals of rulings or verdicts are made based on how the judge applied, or failed to apply, legal rules. Rather, the point is to emphasize the lesser power of the judge in an adversary system versus the power of the judge in an inquisitorial system. Similarly, while the adversarial judge makes decisions about evidence and instructs the jury, it is the jury that makes the ultimate decision on guilt or innocence. The assumption about the jury verdict is that the jury followed the law as instructed by the judge and applied the law to the facts exclusively brought out at trial.

Finally, there is another matter regarding judges in an adversary system, namely the standards of appellate review after the jury reaches a verdict. In reviewing a conviction, most of the time judges in an adversary system tend to focus on procedural and substantive errors of law rather than errors involving fact interpretation. Great deference is ordinarily given to the trial court's decisions, both with respect to judicial rulings and jury verdicts. As Garrett (2011, pp. 182–183) has pointed out, by the time that a conviction reaches appellate review, the appellate court judge (or judges) recognize that the jury and the trial judge saw and heard the evidence first-hand and ordinarily assume the appeals court would be second-guessing the evidence indirectly and over the distance of time. This is not to say that appellate judges have no power to assess evidence, but in relative terms their main role is to ensure that proper procedure was followed and that rulings on evidence and instructions to the jury conformed to legal precedent.

None of the above summary comparison of adversarial versus inquisitorial modes of criminal legal procedure discussed here is intended to evaluate the overall merits of one system over the other. Indeed, it is a great simplification of differences between the two systems. However, the summary helps to set the stage by sensitizing the reader to the effects of adversary system role demands on lawyers, witnesses, trial judges, juries, and appellate judges. We now turn to select examples of the effects of the adversary process.

# Prosecutorial Discretion

Prosecutors have virtually unlimited discretion to decide whether to file charges and, if so, the nature of those charges. They also decide such matters as the nature and quantum of the evidence brought forward, whether to accept a plea bargain, trial strategy, including jury selection, the theory on which the defendant's guilt is based, the nature of the sentence requested if the accused is found guilty, and a series of other matters. Looking at any single case, once some of these decisions are made, prosecutors may be biased by escalating commitment to prior decisions, tunnel vision, and other psychological traps in decision making.

A study by the Center for Public Integrity (2013), hereinafter "Center Report," relying on a number of case studies, identified several prosecutorial decision points that resulted in erroneous convictions. The Center concluded that a central problem arises because of the fact that there is typically an ongoing relationship, often extending over many years, between prosecutors and the same group of police officers, forensic scientists, and expert witnesses (and even judges in front of whom they make frequent appearances). Prosecutors must, of necessity, rely on these other professionals to build their cases, but heavy case loads, public pressures to convict, including those stemming from the victim or the victim's family, and the fact that many accused persons have prior convictions or at least unsavory reputations, may result in blind spots that lead to short cuts in analysis and thinking. Indeed, even the base rate accuracy of the prosecution's prior convictions in other cases probably adds to the tendency toward what is commonly labeled "tunnel vision."

The 2013 Center Report describes a number of elements that may take place in the prosecutorial process. Premature conclusions on the part of investigators may point to an innocent person as the perpetrator. Charges may be brought despite a lack of solid evidence. Judicial review during early stages of charging is absent or nugatory. Grand jury testimony leading to a criminal indictment does not permit defense input, and in many jurisdictions there is no duty to disclose potentially exculpatory evidence to the grand jurors. Prosecutors sometimes do not skeptically evaluate police reports, eyewitness testimony, or testimony from "incentivized" jail house informants and other "snitches." The Center Report also documents instances of uncritical reliance on scientific and forensic experts. Finally, the Report discusses instances in which prosecutors withheld exculpatory evidence or evidence otherwise favorable to the defendant (and in some cases destroyed evidence), *Brady v. Maryland* (1963) notwithstanding.

In addition to the above structural elements built into the prosecutorial process, there is often a complicating political factor. In most states, in contrast with the federal system, district attorneys are elected officials who are sensitive to their voting constituencies. Being charged by one's electoral opponent as being soft on crime is an implicit concern of prosecutors and empirical evidence suggests that these concerns result in changes in prosecutors' decisions, including whether to take cases to trial or accept plea bargains. Bandyopadhyay and McCannon (in press), for example, found that in years in which incumbent prosecutors in North Carolina were facing reelection, the number of felony cases taken to trial, as opposed to being resolved through plea bargains, increased. Moreover, the effect was larger if the incumbent was facing a political challenger for his or her office. Subsequently, McCannon (2013) investigated whether election cycle pressure might have an effect on errors in the prosecutorial process. Using a sample of appealed cases from western New York, he found that six months prior to a reelection bid, the number of cases that were eventually overturned or modified by an appellate court increased. The reasons for modifying the trial court decisions included inaccurate sentences and wrongful convictions. In short, McCannon's research suggests that prosecutors' political concerns and consequent decisions are sometimes correlated with conviction errors.

One example of the adversary system's occasional tendency to bias prosecutorial behavior can be found in litigation involving North Carolina's 2009 Racial Justice Act (see generally, Coleman and Vidmar, 2014; *State v. Golphin et al.*, 2012; Vidmar, 2012). The Racial Justice Act (before it was amended[2]) applies to individuals who have been found guilty of murder and sentenced to death. The Act allows any person on death row, black, white, or of another race, to appeal his or her death sentence (though not the verdict of guilt, which automatically carries a sentence of life imprisonment) on the ground that prospective jurors of African American heritage were systematically excluded from serving on their jury, thereby evading the Supreme Court ruling in *Batson v. Kentucky* (1986) forbidding peremptory challenges based on race or ethnic membership. Based on the empirical research of Grosso and O'Brien (2012) plus testimony and trial documents from prosecutors, a judge in Cumberland County overturned the sentences of the three defendants in *Golphin et al.* The evidence unequivocally showed that North Carolina prosecutors involved in these cases had taken part in seminars in which "cheat sheets" on how to avoid *Batson* challenges were distributed to participants. Moreover, notes of prosecutors in the trials clearly showed that they had followed the suggestions in the "cheat sheets." This kind of behavior is not confined to North Carolina (see, e.g., Center Report, 2012, p. 20). The importance of *Golphin et al.* and similar cases (see *Miller-El v. Dretke*, 2005) for purposes of the present discussion is not to condemn the prosecutorial process generally—defense lawyers also take professional seminars in which they are taught how to gain an advantage over the prosecution during jury selection. However, the *Golphin et al.* cases clearly demonstrate how the adversary system creates conditions whereby adversarial role pressures sometimes result in unethical or even illegal behaviors, and more generally creates conditions leading to tunnel vision and a tendency to place winning over the desired goal of impartial justice.

Consistent with the North Carolina cases, a study for the Equal Justice Initiative (see Bellin & Semitsu, 2011) examined all federal and state published and unpublished decisions involving *Batson* claims from 2000 through 2009. Those authors concluded that *Batson* was easily avoided, primarily by prosecutors using race-neutral explanations similar to those uncovered in the *Golphin et al.* cases. Another study by the Equal Justice Initiative (2010) examined jury selection practices in eight southern states: Alabama, Arkansas, Florida, Georgia, Louisiana, Mississippi, South Carolina, and Tennessee. Similar prosecutorial biases were documented. For example, in Houston County, Alabama, from 2005 through 2009, prosecutors used peremptory strikes to remove 80 percent of African American jurors. In 2003 in Jefferson Parish, Louisiana, despite the fact that 23 percent of the county was African American, there was no effective representation of that segment of the population in jury trials. In one Georgia county, where African Americans constituted 34 percent of the population, prosecutors exercised 83 percent of their peremptory strikes against that racial group. In a sample of cases from Dallas County, Alabama, prosecutors used 76 percent of their strikes against African Americans. Similar to the findings in *Golphin et al.* in North Carolina, the Equal Justice Initiative report found evidence that prosecutors were explicitly trained to mask racially biased decisions for their strikes.

This discriminatory behavior is not located only in southern states and only in death penalty cases. An empirical study by Baldus et al. (2001) found that Philadelphia prosecutors

---

2. In 2012 the North Carolina legislature effectively rescinded the Act but the more than 100 inmates who filed appeals while the Act was in force may still appeal under the original Act. The North Carolina Supreme Court has not ruled on litigation under the Act (see, e.g., Severson, 2013).

were more than four times as likely to use a peremptory challenge on black venire members as on non-black venire members. The only variable that better predicted a prosecutorial peremptory challenge was a juror's expression of discomfort with imposing a death sentence.

Experimental research involving samples of prosecutors is consistent with the archival findings reported above. A study by Hayden et al. (1978) involving 20 Massachusetts prosecutors found that race of the juror was considered more important in a hypothetical case involving a black defendant as opposed to a white defendant. Kerr et al. (1991) conducted an experiment in which attorneys assigned the role of prosecutor in mock proceedings were five times more likely to strike black prospective jurors than jurors of other races.

## Defense Lawyer Behavior (and "Ineffective Assistance of Counsel")

Another tenet of the adversary system is that a defendant is entitled to effective legal representation (*Gideon v. Wainwright*, 1963; *Strickland v. Washington*, 1984). Implicit in *Strickland* is the assumption that a defense lawyer will have the ability, the motivation, and the financial resources to counter the charges brought by the prosecution. Yet the study of wrongful convictions suggests that this assumption is often an ideal rather than what actually occurs before, during, and after trial. For example, Garrett (2011) reported that ineffective assistance of counsel (IAC) was one of the most frequently raised claims during post-conviction appeals. A study of *habeas* claims by the National Center for State Courts (Flango, 1994) found that ineffective assistance of counsel claims were part of appeals in almost half of the cases.

The Innocence Project (West, 2010) conducted a study of the first 255 exoneration cases involving DNA analyses that were appealed to a higher court. That study revealed that IAC claims were made in 54 cases, that is, about one case in five. The claims involved such matters as failure to present defense witnesses, failure to seek DNA testing, failure to object to prosecutor arguments, failure to object to prosecution evidence or to cross-examine witnesses, and failure to file an appeal following conviction. Most of these appeals were rejected by the higher court on the ground that overturning a conviction requires a high standard of proof; but the facts alleged in the appeals raise serious concerns about the performance of defense lawyers.

While considering the defense counsel component of the adjudicative process, it is important to recognize that there are three main types of defense lawyers: privately retained lawyers, public defenders, and individually appointed lawyers. Controversy constantly arises about the effectiveness of private lawyers versus public defender offices. Defendants often prefer a private lawyer if they have the resources to hire one. However, an early, in-depth study by Skolnick (1966, 1967) examined the relative performance of private defense lawyers versus public defenders. Skolnick drew attention to the fact that public defenders and private attorneys typically had different clients, with private lawyers representing clients who had sufficient personal or family resources to afford lawyer fees. There was also a generally held perception among defendants that private lawyers were better advocates than public defenders. Skolnick, however, pointed out that better outcomes may have been due to the fact that having the funds to hire a private lawyer often meant that the accused person could make bail and then assist in his or her own defense by seeking out witnesses and other evidence. Moreover, defendants with a public defender were less trusting and cooperative than defendants with a private lawyer. Some public defender clients believed that since their lawyers were paid by public funds they had a "tie in" with the police and the district attorney. Skolnick's research also drew attention to the fact that despite defendants' perceptions that private lawyers were smarter and worked harder because they were being directly paid by their client, many private lawyers were single practitioners or worked in two- or three-person law firms and thus had the liability of office overhead and other expenses. As a consequence, financial pressures frequently caused them to present a less vigorous defense than would be ideal. In contrast, public defender offices had the advantage of having multiple lawyers. To be sure, some public defender offices frequently treated many of their clients as "files" or "cases," but for more serious cases, public defender offices could bring more resources to bear on the defense than many private lawyers.

Contemporary research on wrongful convictions also explores the basic issues associated with ineffective assistance of counsel. Much of the controversy about IAC involves heavy caseloads (see Lefstein, 2011; Schulhofer & Friedman, 2010). Similar to Skolnick's earlier writings, Schulhofer and Friedman (2010) drew attention to three types of legal counsel for persons accused of a crime: privately retained lawyers, public defenders, and assigned lawyers. The latter group involves willing lawyers in private practice who are assigned to defend a case by a judge or a court administrator. In addition, a fourth option in some jurisdictions involves a private organization which contracts with the government to provide attorneys for indigent defendants. Schulhofer and Friedman argued that public defenders often have extremely heavy caseloads. In one Tennessee county, for example, the public defender office had only six lawyers to handle more than 10,000 misdemeanor cases. In Missouri, individual case loads of public defenders averaged 395 per year. Not all of these statistics apply to serious felony cases, but time and resources available to both private and public defense lawyers nevertheless are often inadequate. The result is that such lawyers may have inadequate resources to thoroughly investigate the charges, hire experts, and thoroughly prepare for trial (see also Garrett, 2011). Schulhofer and Friedman (2010) pointed out that even in serious felony cases lump sum payments for some appointed counsel are the norm and these sums are often inadequate for a proper defense. Those authors cited one survey completed in 2007 that found that many jurisdictions paid assigned lawyers only $40 or $50 per hour. In June 2007, the maximum total fee for a non-capital felony in New Mexico was $650 and in Illinois it was $1,500. In Virginia the maximum payment was $445 for felonies carrying a sentence of up to 20 years; for potential sentences exceeding 20 years, the maximum allowed was $1,235.

In summary, while the American adversary system assumes equal resources between the prosecution and the defendant, in reality defense lawyers often have inadequate resources.

# The Judicial Role in the Adversary Process

As discussed earlier in this chapter, both trial judges and appellate judges in an adversary system are assigned the primary role of referees for the litigation between prosecution and defense. Nevertheless, even in early stages of the adjudication process, the judge may play an important role in case outcomes. Consider the fact that after a person is arrested, he or she may be released on bail or kept in detention. This decision is made by a judge  and may have a major impact on the degree to which an accused person can assist in his or her own defense. Further, a judge rules on pre-trial motions, presides over the jury selection process, including ruling on peremptory challenges as well as challenges for cause, decides disputes about the admissibility of evidence at trial, instructs the jury on the appropriate law or laws, renders final approval of the jury's verdict, and decides the sentence. If the jury verdict or sentence is appealed, a panel of judges rules on whether the trial judge appropriately applied the law or otherwise incorrectly supervised the trial process.

Despite their legal training, judges are susceptible to biases in decision-making, sometimes rooted in ideology—such as being "tough on law and order"—which may affect even the very early stages of the criminal justice process. McIntyre and Baradaran (2013), for example, conducted a representative sampling of state court processing of felony defendants to determine how judges made decisions about pretrial release. They found that there was an 11 percent racial difference in rates of pretrial detention. As discussed earlier, pretrial detention can negatively affect the ability of a defendant to aid in his or her defense. However, controlling for the probability that a defendant will be rearrested prior to trial caused the racial gap to disappear.

The role of judges in the adversary process is discussed at greater length in Guthrie et al., 2001; Klein & Mitchell, 2010; Schauer, 2010; and Vidmar, 2011.

## Expert Witnesses

Expert witnesses play a crucial role in many criminal trials. For literally centuries, such witnesses have been called upon to provide testimony that is critical to a finding of guilt or innocence. As already discussed, in an adversarial system each side is responsible for calling its own expert witnesses. What impact does partisan selection of these witnesses have upon evidence that gets before a trial's fact finder, whether that be a judge or a jury? Although the "battle of experts" is most often discussed in the context of civil litigation, it applies equally to criminal trials. Both prosecutors and defense lawyers seek expert testimony that will support their adversarial position, with respect to plea bargaining, trial, and sentencing. Indeed, they often seek experts with reputations, justified or not, that they favor the prosecution or the defense (see, e.g., Bernstein, 2008; Mnookin, 2008).

Expert witnesses can be variously classified, but for present purposes we consider two general categories: those who provide testimony about physical evidence, and those who provide testimony about medical conditions and mental or cognitive states.

Crime laboratories provide critical evidence about a large number of types of physical evidence related to a crime investigation, including fingerprints, DNA, blood spatter patterns, gun residue, bite marks, and fiber analyses. In addition, coroners' offices provide forensic evidence bearing on cause of death. The most well-known labs are those run by the FBI, but each state also has a government-sponsored laboratory and there are also some privately run laboratories. Crime laboratories are generally regarded as being independent of the contending parties. However, the reality is that most of the requests for analyses and testimony come from the prosecution, and on-going professional relationships develop between prosecutors' offices and laboratory personnel, raising suspicions that results may sometimes be slanted in favor of the prosecution.

In recent years, for example, the North Carolina State Bureau of Investigation has been embroiled in controversy over the pro-prosecution biases of some of its employees. Indeed, several convictions have been overturned as a result of the misbehavior of one of its agents (Locke & Blythe, 2010; Neff, 2012), and there are suspicions about biases of other personnel (see Gianelli, 2012; Swecker & Wolf, 2011). Despite the fact that the SBI laboratory is supposed to be neutral, its close ties to prosecutors appears to have tainted the prosecutorial process.

Analogous concerns arise with respect to expert witnesses and their psychological assessments of persons charged with criminal offenses. For example, Murrie and his colleagues (2009) investigated a sample of cases in which there was expert disagreement on standardized and widely accepted psychological scales used to assess the degree to which a defendant has tendencies toward sexual violence. Their findings were mixed, but overall the data raised concerns that adversarial selection, or alternatively, allegiance toward the side that hired the experts, produced results favoring the side that paid them and called them to testify.

To further investigate these archival findings Murrie et al. (2009) followed up with an experiment involving 108 forensic psychologists and psychiatrists who were trained on scoring widely used scales and subsequently were paid to examine and score four case files. All participants reviewed the same offender case files. However, some were told they were assessing the files for prosecutors while others were led to believe that they were making assessments for defense lawyers. In each condition they met with a person who portrayed himself as a defense lawyer or a prosecutor, but in fact the same person played both roles. There were substantial differences in scoring between the two conditions: assessors who believed they were working for the defense produced scores relatively favorable to the defense, while those who believed they were working for the prosecution produced scores favorable to the prosecution. Murrie et al. (2009) drew attention to the fact that their experimental manipulation of the role favoring prosecution or defense was relatively weak. The psychologists and psychiatrists met with the "lawyer" for only about 15 minutes, in contrast to the real world where far more time may be spent with legal counsel discussing the case and preparing for testimony.

The Murrie et al. findings likely have relevance beyond psychological assessments. They should be considered in the context of other forms of evidence, including "hard" forensic evidence, such as fingerprint matching and blood spatter. Bias is especially problematic if the financial and personnel resources of the defendant are limited. In such cases, the jury may only hear the prosecution's expert and have to draw conclusions about the merits of that testimony based on cross-examination by the defense and whatever cautions about expert testimony that the trial judge conveys (see generally, Garrett, 2011).

## Role Bias Effects on Civilian Witnesses' Testimony

To what extent does being called to testify for the prosecution or the defense potentially affect the nature of that witness's testimony? Sheppard and Vidmar (1980) conducted an experiment to test effects of role assignments in an adversary versus inquisitorial system. Introductory psychology students unexpectedly observed a media presentation involving a fist fight between two males in a bar. They were then interviewed by senior students who were ignorant of the circumstances of the event, but who had been assigned to the role of a "lawyer" for either of the two parties involved in the fight or they were assigned to a role as a neutral lawyer. Each "lawyer" then interviewed his or her witness. A week later, the witness was asked to testify about the fight in a formal "hearing" before a neutral "judge" dressed in judicial garb. An analysis of the witnesses' testimony revealed that those persons who had been interviewed by a "lawyer" representing either the plaintiff or the defendant gave testimony that was slanted toward the position of that lawyer's client. The effects were subtle, often involving nuances of language, such as "he hit" versus "he slugged" the other person. In contrast, witnesses who were interviewed by a neutral lawyer did not exhibit such biases.

A possible criticism of the Shepard and Vidmar study is that the students assigned to the role of lawyers did not have training in neutral interviewing of witnesses. Consequently, Vidmar and Laird (1983) repeated the experiment but eliminated the lawyer role. The student witnesses saw the same fight and were randomly assigned to the role of testifying on behalf of the plaintiff, the defendant, or they were assigned a neutral role to testify as to what they had seen. Strikingly, the results were similar to the earlier research: being assigned to testify for one side or the other versus testifying as a neutral witness significantly biased the testimony in the direction of the party to whom the witnesses were assigned. The neutral "judges" who heard the testimony, but were blind as to the witnesses' assignments, rated the testimony as favoring the side for whom the witness was testifying.

Subsequent research on eyewitness identification also points to adversary effects on witness memory consistent with these earlier findings (Bradfield et al., 2002). Equally important is the possibility that the preparation of witnesses for depositions and trial testimony in non-eyewitness identification matters produces similar effects, but that possibility will not be explored further here.

## Incentivized Jail House Informants and Fabricators

Jail house "informants" and "snitches" are special types of civilian witnesses. They often play an important role in the American adversary process. Garrett (2011) concluded that in his study of 250 cases of erroneous convictions, 21 percent involved outside informants, many of them having been in the jail with the defendant, while others involved co-defendants and still others involved "confidential" informants. These witnesses came forward after initial interrogation of the defendant. Many issues concerning the reliability of these informants are discussed in Garrett's research, but for present purposes, the important point is to place them in the context of the adversary process, and to consider how such information drives prosecutions and is sometimes the primary source of evidence against the defendant. Garrett's research suggests that such informants played an especially important role in murder cases. Moreover, most of these informants testified that they had had no contact with law enforcement personnel until after they had independently heard or seen the incriminating information. Further, the informants asserted facts that were crucial to the prosecution's case, which prosecutors and police had been unable to prove by other means. These findings about jail house informants should be considered within the context of the adversarial approach to adjudication. The LaMonte Armstrong case in North Carolina, discussed next, is a prime example.

## Cooperation in the Criminal Litigation Process: A Case Study of the Exoneration of LaMonte Burton Armstrong

A brief synopsis of the erroneous conviction and eventual exoneration of LaMonte Burton Armstrong through Duke Law School's Center for Criminal Justice and Ethical Responsibility helps to illustrate cumulative errors in the prosecutorial process, but also the eventual willingness of prosecutors to aid in correcting the injustice.[3] Armstrong's case is especially instructive because it is a non-DNA case.

LaMonte Armstrong, a man of African American descent, had graduated from North Carolina A&T State University in Greensboro, North Carolina, with a B.S. in Physical

---

3. Defendant's Motion for Appropriate Relief, in *State of North Carolina v. LaMonte Burton Armstrong*, General Court of Justice, Superior Court Division, No. 94 CRS 38153. (Professors Theresa Newman and James E. Coleman of Duke Law School directed the research for the Motion for Appropriate Relief.)

Education and Recreation. He had been a basketball player, a member of the marching band, and a fraternity member at that institution. After graduation, Armstrong taught school in New York, but he eventually moved back to Greensboro, where he also taught in several schools. However, in the early 1980s Armstrong began using heroin, which led to his conviction for a number of drug-related offenses.

In July 1988, Ernestine Compton, a long-time faculty member at North Carolina A&T, was found murdered in her home in Greensboro. An autopsy concluded that she had been both stabbed and strangled. Ms. Compton was well liked by her friends and neighbors. Moreover, she frequently loaned small amounts of money to persons who needed it. She kept a list of the loans on her refrigerator. Armstrong knew Ms. Compton and lived in her neighborhood.

Armstrong's name surfaced in the police investigation of the Compton murder following a Crime Stopper's tip two weeks after the murder. A police detective contacted Armstrong by telephone. Armstrong admitted knowing Ms. Compton for 23 years but stated that he had not been inside her house for several years. Three and a half months later police interviewed Armstrong again. This time, the interview was conducted in person by two detectives. Armstrong stated that he had never borrowed money from Ms. Compton, although she had paid him for odd jobs such as mowing her grass. He also told the detectives that a casual acquaintance, Charles Blackwell, had started calling him about the case in August. Unknown to Armstrong, Blackwell's calls were initiated by the Greensboro police. Armstrong agreed to take a lie detector test, but his lawyer from a previous drug charge advised him to not do so—typical advice under such circumstances—and he declined to participate.

There were no further developments in the case and little investigation except for a test of latent fingerprints in 1992, which did not result in any identification.

In March 1994, however, the Greensboro police began to review the unsolved case and centered on Charles Blackwell, who was then incarcerated for a felony in another county. The prosecutors decided to charge Blackwell, who was facing criminal charges in other matters, as a participant in the Compton murder. Authorities in the other cases returned him to Greensboro. As part of a plea arrangement, Blackwell then agreed to testify against Armstrong and identify him as someone to whom Ms. Compton had loaned money. In April 1994, Armstrong was charged with the Compton murder. Protesting his innocence, Armstrong rejected a plea agreement involving a sentence of up to 20 years. The case went to trial in 1996, and the jury convicted Armstrong of Compton's murder. The judge sentenced him to life in prison. This background information is important to understanding Armstrong's conviction. At trial, the State's theory of the case was that Armstrong owed Ms. Compton money; they argued about the loan, and he killed her. However, no physical evidence linked Armstrong to the killing. As noted above, early in the Compton investigation Charles Blackwell had named Armstrong in the hope of receiving reward money from "Crime Stoppers." Blackwell subsequently received small amounts of money from the police for cooperating in the investigation. Police did not give Blackwell a polygraph test because he was such a "habitual liar" that they believed the test would be meaningless. Police also threatened to accuse Blackwell as the murderer. In the face of such threats and relying on detailed newspaper accounts of the murder and multiple meetings with police, Blackwell provided a number of versions of how the crime occurred, each with Armstrong as the killer. The alleged motive was Armstrong's need for money to buy drugs. In one iteration, Blackwell told of driving Armstrong to a location near the victim's home and waiting 45 minutes for him; Armstrong subsequently appeared, breathing heavily and with an amount of cash. When police expressed skepticism about the story, Blackwell revised the account, adding more detail. Eventually police reduced one of these accounts to writing and Blackwell signed the document. However, the police apparently did not believe the story was sufficiently credible and nothing happened for the next two years.

The Compton case became active again when several incarcerated fabricators surfaced. In 1994 an inmate in a correctional institution, Timothy McCorkle, wrote to the Greensboro District Attorney that he had information about the Compton murder. He subsequently said that he had seen both Armstrong and Blackwell coming out of the victim's house on the night of the murder. McCorkle's story differed in substantial ways from the one told by Blackwell. Moreover, McCorkle had been convicted of another crime largely on the basis of testimony by Armstrong's brother. Nevertheless, the prosecution subsequently called McCorkle as a witness at Armstrong's trial. Three other witnesses also came forward. Each claimed that Armstrong had confessed the crime to them. One witness, A. Dwight Blockem, had been in jail awaiting trial on a drug charge. Learning of the Armstrong case and probably hoping for some favors, he recounted an alleged conversation with Armstrong and Blackwell while all three were in a holding cell at another jail. In trial testimony McCorkle claimed that Armstrong had talked in detail about the interior of Ms. Compton's house. Another habitual criminal and frequent police informant, William Earl Davis, also testified against Armstrong. Davis testified that while he and Armstrong were incarcerated together, Armstrong had admitted to killing Ms. Compton.

At trial, Armstrong testified in his own defense and denied any involvement in the killing. The defense called a number of witnesses who testified that the main witness, Blackwell, had admitted to them that he was lying and that the police had provided him with crucial information about the killing. Nevertheless, the jury convicted Armstrong and he was sentenced to life in prison.

Despite the verdict, LaMonte Armstrong continued to insist on his innocence, and eventually the North Carolina Center of Actual Innocence took up his case. The Center referred the case to Duke Law School's Wrongful Conviction Clinic, a component of Duke's Center for Criminal Justice and Professional Responsibility. From the beginning, the Clinic's team of law students interviewed many witnesses and poured over countless numbers of documents. It is worth noting that during their investigative efforts, the students and their faculty supervisors worked cooperatively with the Greensboro District Attorney's office and the Greensboro Police Department.

After several years, the Clinic's investigation uncovered the many iterations of the crime that chief accuser and witness, Charles Blackwell, gave police, raising questions about his veracity. More importantly, Blackwell subsequently recanted his trial testimony and admitted that Armstrong was innocent. The Greensboro police detectives, who had led the criminal investigation and who revealed the many iterations of Blackwell's story to the Duke students, conceded that in their view, nothing Blackwell said could be believed. The two other jailhouse fabricators (often erroneously called "snitches") who had testified at Armstrong's trial were also discredited. The Duke investigation also uncovered multiple witnesses from Ms. Compton's neighborhood who testified that they had seen her alive two days after the alleged date that she was killed, strongly suggesting that the date pointing to Armstrong as the killer of Ms. Compton was incorrect. The investigation further revealed that the jury which convicted Armstrong did not know that key witness Blackwell had received payments from the Greensboro Police Department. Moreover, surreptitious recordings that police had made of Armstrong denying his involvement in the murder were never revealed to the defense, nor were other favorable recordings of statements made by Blackwell. A central part of the State's case was the alleged motive for the murder; that Armstrong owed money to Ms. Compton and that he and she got into a deadly argument over the debt. However, when the Duke students discovered the notes, they found that the police had recovered eight lists of loans from Ms. Compton's home, but none were presented at trial. Strikingly, Armstrong's name did not appear on any of the lists. Additionally, the State withheld other critical evidence, including evidence bearing on a viable alternative suspect.

A key new piece of evidence was discovered in 2012 by the Greensboro police. A handprint that had been examined in 1992 was re-examined and a suspect was identified. That suspect's name did appear on Ms. Compton's list of debtors. In addition the alternative suspect had been convicted of killing his father months after Ms. Compton was murdered. The Greensboro police were now convinced that this man was likely the real killer.

As a result, in 2012, following a hearing uncontested by the prosecution and after he had spent 16 years in prison, LaMonte Armstrong was freed. He was granted a full pardon of innocence shortly before Christmas 2013 by North Carolina Governor Pat McCrory.

The Armstrong case illustrates the many errors that are common in wrongful conviction cases. Despite the lack of physical evidence or credible witnesses, police and prosecutors felt public pressure to find and convict Ms. Compton's killer. Unreliable, incentivized witnesses were used to build the case against Armstrong. Alternative suspects were ignored. Armstrong's lawyer did not have the resources to conduct a thorough investigation, and the State suppressed critical evidence. The trial judge's limited oversight role was passive and not designed to identify and correct such problems. As a result, the prosecution presented a case that was fabricated and the jury verdict was based upon a fictional account of the murder.

# Moving Forward: Remedial Steps for Avoiding Erroneous Convictions

In concluding this brief overview of the adversary system and its potential effects on erroneous convictions, it is important to step back and view the prosecutorial process from the general perspective of organizational psychology. Research has long demonstrated that initial commitments to one course of action cause the actors within that organization to remain committed to that decision, and in fact sometimes escalate that commitment, even when there are cues strongly suggesting that original assumptions were wrong and the course of action may be in error (see, e.g., Staw & Ross, 1989). The Armstrong case should be viewed not only from the perspective of the adversary process, with its competitive "win mentality," but also with understanding of organizational pressures within both police and prosecutors' offices. Prosecutors and police are at the frontline viewing often horrible human events. They not infrequently are under great pressure to solve crimes and bring perpetrators to justice. Initial findings may cause them to center on a suspect, interpret evidence as pointing to the suspect, and proceed with their initial assumptions. They talk with colleagues who often lend support to their assumptions with no one playing devil's advocate. Additionally, although lack of resources may be one element in many ineffective assistance of counsel claims, researchers should not ignore the possibility that similar biases in the other direction sometimes affect defense counsel, causing them to ignore alternative strategies. Judges, too, may place too much faith in the adversary system as they adjudicate disputes.

In some states attempts have been made to correct deficiencies in the prosecutorial process. For example, the District Attorney's Association of the State of New York (2012) produced a booklet entitled "The Right Thing," providing guidelines for prosecutors. Among other matters, that document draws attention not only to the victim of a crime and the victim's family, but also to the defendant and his or her family. It emphasizes the right to a fair trial and the consequences of unethical conduct and summarizes rules of fairness and ethical conduct.

Recently, the International Association of Chiefs of Police (2013) held a "National Summit on Wrongful Convictions" involving 75 subject matter experts who attempted to address points at which errors can occur at the various stages of the criminal justice process and suggested means through which errors can be avoided.

There are also lessons for empirical research on wrongful convictions. It is important to view the criminal justice process from all perspectives. Field research, including systematic interviews with all sides, systematic observations of the processes, and archival research are necessary to gain a full understanding of why and how wrongful convictions occur.

# References

Baldus, David D. C., Woodworth, G., Zuckerman, D., Weiner, N.A., & Broffitt, B. (2001). The use of peremptory challenges in capital murder trials: A legal and empirical analysis, *University of Pennsylvania Journal of Constitutional Law, 3,* 171–274.

Bandyopadhyay, S., & McCannon, B. (In press). Prosecutorial election: Signaling by trial. *Journal of Public Economic Theory.*

*Batson v. Kentucky* (1986) 476 U.S. 79.

Bellin, J., & Semitsu, J.P. (2011). Widening *Batson's* net to ensnare more than the un-apologetically bigoted or painfully unimaginative attorney. *Cornell Law Review, 96,* 1075–1131.

Bernstein, D. (2008). Expert witnesses, adversarial bias and the (partial) failure of the *Daubert* revolution. *Iowa Law Review, 93,* 451–489.

Bradfield, A., Wells, G., & Olson, E. (2002). The damaging effect of confirming feedback on the relation between eyewitness certainty and identification accuracy. *Journal of Applied Psychology, 87,* 112 –120.

*Brady v. Maryland* (1963) 373 U.S. 83.

Center for Public Integrity (2013). Anatomy of misconduct. Retrieved from http://www.publicintegrity.org/2003/06/26/5524/anatomy –misconduct.

Coleman, J.E., & Vidmar, N. (2014) Amicus curiae brief for North Carolina Conference of the NAACP in *State of North Carolina v. Golphin et al.*, No. 139PA13 –1, Supreme Court of North Carolina.

Damaska, M. (1986). *The faces of justice and state authority: A comparative approach to the legal process.* New Haven, CT: Yale University Press.

District Attorney's Association of the State of New York (2012). "The right thing": Ethical guidelines for prosecutors. Retrieved from http://www.daasny.org/Ethics%20 Handbook%209.28.2012%20FINAL.pdf.

Equal Justice Initiative (2010). Illegal racial discrimination in jury selection: A continuing legacy. Retrieved from http://www.eji.org/files/EJI%20Race%20and%20Jury%20 Report.pdf.

Flango, V. (1994). Outcomes in state and federal court, from habeas corpus in state and federal courts. Retrieved from https://www.ncjrs.gov/App/Publications/abstract. aspx?ID=149663.

Frankel, M. (1975). The search for truth: An umpireal view. *University of Pennsylvania Law Review, 123,* 1031–1059.

Garrett, B. L. (2011). *Convicting the innocent: Where criminal prosecutions go wrong.* Cambridge, MA: Harvard University Press.

Gianelli, P.C. (2012). The North Carolina Crime Lab scandal. *Criminal Justice, 27.* Retrieved from http://www.americanbar.org/content/dam/aba/publications/criminal_justice_magazine/sp12_sci_evidence.authcheckdam.pdf.

*Gideon v. Wainwright* (1963) 372 U.S. 335.

Grosso, C., & O'Brien, B. (2012). A stubborn legacy: The overwhelming importance of race in jury selection in 173 post-Batson North Carolina capital trials. *Iowa Law Review, 97,* 1531–1559.

Hans, V.P. (2002). Introduction: Lay participation in legal decision making. *Law & Policy Quarterly, 25,* 83–92.

Hayden, G.J., & Siegel, L. (1978). Prosecutorial discretion in peremptory challenges: An empirical investigation of information use in the Massachusetts jury selection process. *New England Law Review, 13,* 768–791.

Huang, K., & Lin, C. (2013). Rescuing confidence in the judicial system: Introducing lay participation in Taiwan. *Journal of Empirical Legal Studies, 10, 542–569.*

Huff, C.R., & Killias, M. (Eds.). (2010). *Wrongful conviction: International perspectives on miscarriages of justice.* Philadelphia, PA: Temple University Press.

International Association of Chiefs of Police (2013). National summit on wrongful convictions: Building a systematic approach to prevent wrongful convictions. Retrieved from http://www.theiacp.org/Portals/0/documents/pdfs/Wrongful_Convictions_Summit_Report_WEB.pdf.

Jackson, J.D., & Kovalev, N.P. (2006). Lay adjudication and human rights in Europe. *Columbia Journal of European Law, 13,* 83–123.

Kerr, N.L, Kramer, G. P., Carroll, J. S., & Alfini, J. J. (1991). On the effectiveness of voir dire in criminal cases with prejudicial pretrial publicity: An empirical study. *American University Law Review, 40,* 665–701.

Klein, D., & Mitchell, G. (Eds.). (2010). *The psychology of judicial decision making.* New York: Oxford University Press.

Lefstein, N. (2011). Securing reasonable caseloads. Retrieved from http://www.americanbar.org/content/dam/aba/publications/books/ls_sclaid_def_securing_reasonable_caseloads.authcheckdam.pdf.

Leo, R., & Gould, J. (2009). Studying wrongful convictions: Learning from social science. *Ohio State Journal of Criminal Law, 7,* 7–30.

Locke, M., & Blythe, A. (2010), SBI to review old lab cases. *Raleigh News & Observer* (Feb. 28). Retrieved from http://www.newhaven.edu/53517.pdf.

McCannon, B. (2013). Prosecutor elections, mistakes and appeals. *Journal of Empirical Legal Studies, 10,* 696–714.

McGonigle, S., Becka, H., LaFleur, J., & Wyatt, T. (2005). A process of juror elimination: Dallas prosecutors say they don't discriminate, but analysis shows they are more likely to reject black jurors. *Dallas Morning News* (Aug. 21), at 1A.

McIntyre, F. & Baradaran, S. (2013). Race, prediction and pretrial detention. *Journal of Empirical Legal Studies,* 10, 741–770.

*Miller-El v. Dretke* (2005) 545 U.S. 231.

Mnookin, J. (2008). Expert evidence, partisanship, and epistemic competence. *Brooklyn Law Review, 73,* 587–611.

Murrie, D.C., Boccaccini, M.T., Guarnera, L.A., & Rufino, K.A. (2009). Are forensic experts biased by the side that retained them? *Psychological Science, 15,* 19–33.

Neff, J., & Locke, M. (2010). Forensic groups' ties raise concerns. *Raleigh News & Observer* (Oct. 13). Retrieved from http://www.newsobserver.com/2010/09/26/703376/ forensic-groups-ties-raise-concerns.html.

North Carolina Racial Justice Act (2009). N.C.G.S. § 15A-2010.

Schauer, F. (2010). Is there a psychology of judging? In Klein, D.E., & Mitchell, G. (Eds.). *The psychology of judicial decision making* (pp. 103–120). New York: Oxford University Press.

Schulhofer, S., & Friedman, D. (2010). Reforming indigent defense: How free market principles can help to fix a broken system. Retrieved from http://www.cato.org/ ... / *reforming-indigent-defense-how-free-Principles Can Help to Fix a Broken System.*

Severson, K. (2013). North Carolina repeals law allowing racial bias claim in death penalty challenges. *New York Times* A13 (June 6).

Sheppard, B. & Vidmar, N. (1980). Adversary pretrial procedures and testimonial evidence: Effects of lawyers' role and Machiavellianism. *Journal of Personality and Social Psychology, 39,* 320–332.

Skolnick, J. (1966). *Justice without trial: Law enforcement in a democratic society.* New York: John Wiley & Sons.

Skolnick, J. (1967). Social control in the adversary system. *Journal of Conflict Resolution, 11,* 52–70.

*State of North Carolina v. Golphin, et al.* (2012). 97 CRS 47314-15 (Dec. 13); Motion to prohibit the State from seeking the death penalty. Retrieved from http://www.ncids.org/ Motions%20Bank/RacialJustice/MotionToProhibitDP.pdf.

Staw, B., & Ross, J. (1989). Understanding behavior in escalation situations. *Science, 246,* 216–220.

*Strickland v. Washington* (1984) 466 U.S. 668.

Swecker, C. & Wolf, M. (2011). An independent review of the SBI Forensic Laboratory. Retrieved from http://www.ncids.com/forensic/sbi/Swecker_Report.pdf.

Vidmar, N. & Laird, N. (1983). Adversary social roles: Their effects on witnesses' communication of evidence and the assessments of adjudicators. *Journal of Personality and Social Psychology, 44,* 888–898.

Vidmar, N. (2011). The psychology of trial judging. *Current Directions in Psychological Science, 20,* 59–62.

Vidmar, N. (2012). The North Carolina Racial Justice Act: An essay on substantive and procedural fairness in death penalty litigation. *Iowa Law Review, 97,* 1969–1983.

West, E. (2010). Court findings in ineffective assistance of counsel claims in post-conviction appeals among the first 225 DNA exoneration Cases. Retrieved from http://www.innocenceproject.org/docs/Innocence_Project_IAC_Report.pdf.

# Chapter Ten

# Plea Bargaining's Role in Wrongful Convictions

Stephanos Bibas,[1] *University of Pennsylvania*

## Introduction

Lists of wrongful convictions are dominated by convictions after trial. But those lists should not breed complacency about the plea-bargaining system, which disposes of roughly 95% of adjudicated criminal cases (Maguire, tbls. 5.24.2008, 5.46.2006). Though it seems hard to believe, innocent defendants do confess and plead guilty; we have DNA exonerations to prove it (Garrett, 2011). And wrongful convictions produced by plea bargains are far less likely to come to light. That is partly because guilty pleas waive most claims, and often appeals and collateral attacks as well, and partly because trials generate fuller records and so are easier to second-guess. Moreover, the overwhelming majority of cases involve no DNA, similar indisputable forensic evidence, or exposures of law enforcement corruption, so many more injustices are hidden. We have no way of knowing how much of the iceberg is submerged beneath the exposed tip.

One way to approach the problem is to do empirical work analyzing and reasoning inductively from the dozens of wrongful convictions after guilty pleas that scholars have documented (Garrett, 2011). A difficulty with that approach, however, is that we have no way of knowing how representative these few dozen cases are. Instead, I analyze the problem from the other end, using the forces and flaws exposed by the plea-bargaining literature to explain where and how plea bargaining is vulnerable to error.

In a nutshell, the basic problem is that plea bargaining short-circuits the adversarial protections of a criminal pretrial process and trial. In effect, it treats a defendant's willingness to concede guilt as conclusive proof, even though plea discounts and threats can sometimes coerce even the innocent to plead. And it gives free rein to the agency costs, psychological pitfalls, and structural flaws that plague our overworked, underfunded criminal justice system. Plea bargaining lets harried police, prosecutors, defense counsel, and judges jump to conclusions, putting efficiency ahead of accuracy. Solutions must reverse this trend, at least in part, building more vigorous investigation, defense, and careful screening into the system. But given the volume of cases and scarcity of funding, that approach is far easier said than done.

---

1. *Author's Note*: The author thanks Brandon Garrett, Nancy King, David Rudovsky, and the editors of this volume for helpful comments on an earlier draft. Correspondence concerning this chapter should be addressed to Stephanos Bibas, University of Pennsylvania Law School, 3501 Sansom Street, Philadelphia, PA 19104. E-mail: stephanos.bibas@gmail.com.

Other chapters in this volume deal with reforms that could improve all cases, including but not limited to those by guilty plea, such as procedures for eyewitness identifications, interrogations, and the like. Chapter 13, on appeals and post-conviction review, tackles after-the-fact review, including the problems caused by plea-bargained appeal waivers, DNA waivers, and retrospective review of ineffective assistance of counsel during bargaining. Other retrospective remedies include conviction integrity units within police and prosecutors' offices, and relaxed limits on withdrawal and reopening of pleas, particularly based on new evidence. By contrast, my focus here is prospective, on features of plea bargaining specifically that lead to wrongful convictions in the first place.

# Stepping Back: The Plea-Bargaining Mindset, Pressures, and Temptations

Defenders of plea bargaining admit that innocent defendants may plead guilty. But they defend that result as a design feature rather than a bug, a rational way for innocent defendants to avert the risk of a higher punishment after a wrongful conviction at trial (Easterbrook, 1983). That response ignores the callous message sent by endorsing wrongful convictions, and it erroneously deflects attention to flaws elsewhere in the system. Many attributes of the plea bargaining system itself exacerbate the innocence problem.

## The Mindset

To understand plea bargaining, one must first see criminal justice the way that busy, jaded insiders do: as an assembly line speeding huge numbers of guilty defendants along to almost inevitable convictions. Harvard law professor and defense attorney Alan Dershowitz (1982, p. xxi) famously characterized criminal justice as a "game" whose key rules begin with:

Rule I:     Almost all criminal defendants are, in fact, guilty.

Rule II:     All criminal defense lawyers, prosecutors and judges understand and believe Rule I.

Some observers might quibble with the modifier "[a]lmost all" or note that the grade of offense is sometimes in question, but few would dispute Dershowitz's basic point. Once police have arrested and prosecutors have charged a suspect, a conviction of some sort is the norm. Fewer than 10% of federal defendants, for instance, have their charges dismissed, and fewer than 1% are acquitted (Maguire, tbl. 5.24.2008). The question is not so much *whether* a defendant is guilty and will be convicted than *what* charges and *how much* of a sentence he will receive. Overwhelmed insiders, aware of those facts, find it hard to keep looking assiduously for innocent needles in haystacks.

## The Insiders' Incentives

Next, one must understand criminal justice insiders' own incentives and interests. Most criminal justice professionals want to do justice, but that sense of justice is influenced and colored by various self-interests and outlooks as well.

**Police.** Police officers are evaluated based in large part on their arrest statistics. Their self-interest, therefore, is in making enough arrests and doing just enough investigative work to persuade prosecutors to charge their cases. The word of an eyewitness or two, resemblance to a suspect, a nervous or defensive response to questioning, or a shaky alibi may convince police of a suspect's guilt. That generates a sort of tunnel vision (see Findley & O'Brien, this volume). Once police officers have decided a suspect is guilty, they have little incentive to turn over every stone, particularly because they know most defendants plead guilty and many confess, so there will be little need to prepare for trial.

**Prosecutors.** Prosecutors want to prosecute only guilty suspects, but they have no way of knowing guilt apart from the results of police investigation. Every defendant, whether guilty or innocent, has strong incentives to claim innocence. Guilty and innocent defendants thus pool together, so prosecutors must discount their self-serving claims of innocence. Thus, the main filters for innocence are the pre-charge investigation and the trial (Scott & Stuntz, 1992). But plea bargains bypass the latter check.

Prosecutors are evaluated based primarily on their conviction statistics. They care much more about the certainty of conviction than the severity of punishment (Alschuler, 1968; Bibas, 2004a; Heumann, 1978). They can thus offer very large sentence discounts to buy off the risk of acquittal (odds bargaining) and save the work of going to trial (costs bargaining). They receive no extra pay for putting in the extra work needed to secure a conviction at trial. Moreover, modern criminal codes are broad and overlapping, offering prosecutors a broad menu of options for charging (Stuntz, 2001; 2004). Some of these charges carry heavier sentences than others, particularly where mandatory minimum sentences or sentencing guidelines are in play. And, in many prosecutors' offices, the same prosecutor decides on the charges and the plea offer. Prosecutors thus have every incentive to charge high, to stack up plea-bargaining chips, and then bargain low, to ensure convictions in exchange for reduced punishment. Once they have decided on a suspect's guilt, they have the carrots and sticks needed to induce a plea.

The fear of loss should steer police and prosecutors away from defendants who may well be innocent, but prosecutors' overwhelming power to induce pleas dampens the power of that incentive (Bibas, 2004a). "[I]nstead of allowing juries to air and wrestle with the hard, troubling cases, plea bargaining lets prosecutors protect their reputations and win-loss records by hiding close cases from view" (Bibas, 2004a, p. 2473). For instance, if "prosecutors bargain away most cases involving dubious confessions, they avert public scrutiny of police interrogation tactics. If they buy off credible claims of innocence cheaply, they cover up faulty investigations that mistakenly target innocent suspects" (Bibas, 2004a, p. 2473). Prosecutors presumably believe that their defendants are in fact guilty, or else they would not pursue them. But post-charge tunnel vision may lead them to discount proof problems that might otherwise flag possible innocence, and plea bargaining facilitates that blindness.

**Defense counsel.** Most defense lawyers have multiple incentives to plea bargain as well. First, there is the matter of stingy compensation. Four-fifths of felony defendants are indigent and so represented by appointed defense counsel, paid for by the government (Harlow, 2000). There are three categories of appointed counsel: a) public defenders, who are paid flat salaries; b) appointed private lawyers, who are paid flat fees or low hourly rates subject to low caps; and c) contract attorneys, who receive a fixed payment (often the lowest bid in a competitive auction) in exchange for handling an entire category of cases. In other words, appointed counsel receive few financial rewards for investing more work to take a case to trial instead of bargaining it away. On the contrary, private appointed attorneys can earn more by pleading a larger volume of cases out than taking a smaller number to trial (Bibas, 2004a). Underfunding also makes it harder to retain experienced, talented counsel, who are often lured to other work by the promise of higher pay for their marketable skills and experience (Bibas, 2004a).

Second, the relationship between defendants and their counsel is plagued by mistrust. Defendants habitually distrust their appointed lawyers, in part because defense lawyers are paid by the government and not their clients (free advice seems worth the money paid for it) and in part because overworked lawyers have little time to spend building rapport or investigating their clients' cases. Defense lawyers may even press their clients to plead guilty right after meeting them, which hardly inspires clients' confidence in their lawyers' willingness to fight the prosecution. To inspire their lawyers to fight harder, many defendants falsely deny their guilt, and defense lawyers come to assume their clients' guilt and distrust most of what they say (Bibas, 2012; Heumann, 1978).

Third, most defense lawyers have few other resources. There is little funding for private investigators, forensic scientists, psychologists, and other professionals who are often needed to mount a vigorous defense. Without these tools, many defense lawyers cannot credibly challenge the prosecution's case or stand up to prosecutors' plea-bargaining offers. Even a defense lawyer who had the time and money to investigate thoroughly would often find it hard to do so, particularly when the crime happened well before the appointment of counsel. Often, he must depend on the contemporaneous police investigation.

Fourth, many appointed counsel are overworked. Many public defenders juggle hundreds of cases per year. Such workloads far exceed American Bar Association standards, which recommend a maximum of 150 non-capital felony cases per lawyer per year (American Bar Association, Criminal Justice Standards Committee, 1992, § 5-5.3 cmt.). They must plead out case after case to keep moving cases along, without taking the time to dig up exculpatory evidence and possible defenses. And because prosecutors know that these lawyers must plead everything out, their threats to take cases to trial ring hollow and do not force prosecutors to take a second look (Bibas, 2004a).

**Judges.** Like prosecutors and defense counsel, judges have incentives to encourage plea bargaining as well. Even though judges' jobs are generally secure, judicial culture often emphasizes "moving the business" to improve case disposition statistics. In the absence of trials, judges know much less about the defendant's guilt than the parties do, making it easy to rubber-stamp the proposed plea and hard to learn the facts or second-guess guilt. That is especially true because most cases contain no disputes that judges think merit a trial, and most defendants admit guilt at a scripted plea colloquy. And when judges go along with proposed plea bargains, as they usually do, the parties are unlikely to appeal (indeed, they may waive the right to appeal), avoiding the prospect of embarrassing appellate reversals (Heumann, 1978).

The bottom line is that all of the repeat-player professionals in criminal justice have interests in encouraging guilty pleas and face pressures to do so. Collectively, these insiders form a courthouse workgroup, developing norms and habits of disposition that expect most cases to plead out for substantial discounts in exchange for a minimum of fuss or investigation. Though the adversarial system presupposes that defense lawyers, judges, and juries will scrutinize police investigations and evidence, run-of-the-mill cases rarely involve vigorous probing or adversarial testing. In lieu of zero-sum adversarial combat, the parties expect and reward collaboration in moving cases ahead to preordained convictions, which serves each professional's interests and resource constraints.

**The jury.** The missing actor is the jury. The whole point of plea bargaining is to bypass juries, which serve as neutral fact-finders and checks on police and prosecutors. In a world of plea bargaining, the defendant's admission of guilt substitutes for the jury's au-thoritative finding. But given the strong pressures and incentives to plead guilty, one cannot automatically credit a guilty plea as if it were a sincere and contrite admission of guilt. That, however, is what our system of plea bargaining effectively does.

# Structural Constraints

Other factors that exacerbate pressures to plead are bail, discovery, plea, sentencing, parole, and clemency rules. Though many defendants charged with minor crimes are released on bail pending trial, some do not have enough money to make bail or are detained in jail without bail. In such cases, the pretrial detention can approach or even exceed the punishment that a court would impose after trial. Prosecutors may offer to let these defendants plead guilty in exchange for a sentence of time already served. A guilty plea thus means immediate freedom, whereas fighting to vindicate one's innocence necessarily means a longer wait for a trial and potential freedom. Even an innocent defendant may find such a deal, and the prospect of immediate release, irresistible. Moreover, pretrial detention hampers a defendant's ability to track down witnesses, meet with his lawyer, and in general mount his defense (Bibas, 2004a; Bowers 2008).

Discovery rules likewise hobble innocent defendants. Guilty defendants usually know that they are guilty and have a sense of the likely evidence against them. But innocent defendants may have no idea about what evidence the prosecution would use at trial to prove their guilt. While prosecutors must turn over known exculpatory and impeachment evidence, most incriminating witness testimony and statements are immune from disclosure until trial in most states (Bibas, 2004a). Prosecutors may thus say little about their cases in plea bargaining, or even bluff, as long as they do not lie or misrepresent the facts. And because they would often like to protect their informants' and witnesses' identity and spare them the ordeal and danger of testifying, prosecutors apply more plea bargaining pressure to obviate trial testimony.

Plea rules make matters worse. In order to dispose of stubborn defendants without trial, most jurisdictions are willing to waive the requirement that defendants who plead guilty must admit guilt. Defendants may plead no contest (neither admitting nor denying guilt) or enter *Alford* pleas (protesting innocence while agreeing to plead guilty and be sentenced as if guilty). Anecdotal evidence suggests that the main users of these pleas are defendants who are guilty but in denial to others or even to themselves. But *Alford* and no-contest pleas may also grease the wheels for innocent defendants to plead guilty to avert possibly heavier sentences after trial (Bibas, 2003).

Sentencing rules also contribute to the innocence problem. Many drug and gun crimes carry mandatory minimum penalties. About the only way around these stiff sentences is to confess and cooperate fully with the police. Admission of guilt is also a substantial factor in, if not a prerequisite to, earning a discount of one-third or more for pleading guilty and accepting responsibility (Bibas, 2004a; *see, e.g.,* U.S. Sentencing Commission, 2012, § 3E1.1). These substantial rewards tempt innocent defendants to admit guilt falsely.

Parole and clemency boards may likewise be unwilling to parole or commute the sentences of inmates who persist in denying their guilt. For guilty defendants, these rules may help to break down denial mechanisms and induce remorse and repentance. But innocent defendants who maintain their innocence look just like guilty defendants who remain stubbornly in denial and so unworthy of leniency. Once an innocent defendant admits guilt, however, his wrongful conviction is even less likely to come to light.

# Psychological Influences in Plea Bargaining

Various psychological biases and heuristics may contribute to wrongful convictions. At the most general level, both insiders and the public believe that the system works and that police arrest, prosecutors charge, and juries convict only guilty people. They also find it hard to believe that innocent defendants would ever plead guilty. That faith in the system may be exaggerated and may reduce actors' vigilance in preventing, or retrospectively recognizing and correcting, wrongful convictions.

The faith in the adversarial system is exacerbated by the psychology of overconfidence. People are consistently overconfident in their own abilities and accuracy; like the citizens of Lake Wobegon, most think they are better-than-average drivers (Bibas, 2004a). People are also inordinately influenced by first impressions and jump to conclusions. Thus, police and prosecutors' focus on a suspect breeds tunnel vision, leading them to spin other evidence in ways consistent with their initial impressions instead of taking a fresh look at potentially contradictory facts. Even defense lawyers may take seemingly overwhelming evidence for granted. And once a defendant is convicted, the "inevitability bias" makes the actual result seem to have been inevitable all along. That is certainly true of police and prosecutors, who, as public servants dedicated to doing justice, can find it hard to admit that they have unwittingly perpetrated an injustice. Reviewing courts, on appeal or post-conviction habeas corpus challenges, also find it hard to see weaknesses in seemingly inevitable convictions, particularly ones resulting from guilty pleas with no trial record (Bibas, 2004b; 2006). Of course, as Chapter 13 discusses, many claims are waived by the fact of a plea or by an express plea waiver or appeal waiver. But some claims, such as ineffective assistance of counsel, may survive in theory but be hard to prove in practice.

Innocent defendants may plead guilty in part out of risk aversion. Citizens who have committed no crime may be more risk averse than guilty suspects, who are more likely to be risk-seeking types (Bibas, 2004a). And threats of the death penalty or life imprisonment may scare even innocent defendants into pleading guilty.

Certain categories of innocent defendants face particular psychological and social challenges. We know that defendants who are mentally retarded, mentally ill, or are juveniles are especially likely to confess falsely (Kassin et al., 2010). Once a defendant has falsely confessed, he faces tremendous pressure to plead guilty; even his own lawyer is unlikely to believe a later recantation and protestation of innocence. These same attributes, as well as difficulty speaking and understanding English and drug or alcohol addiction, can also impair credibly showing one's innocence, understanding a plea offer, and weighing it carefully.

# Moving Forward: Fixing a Broken System

At this point, many critics throw up their hands and recommend waving a magic wand to abolish plea bargaining. That will not happen. And if it did, abolition would deluge courthouses and abbreviate trials, re-creating the innocent needle and haystack problem there (Scott & Stuntz, 1992). The second-best solution would be to increase substantially indigent defense funding and change the compensation structure, to reward aggressive representation through and beyond plea bargaining. That too is unlikely. Voters have little appetite for spending more tax dollars to defend criminals in the hopes of sifting out a few innocents, and only a small (but growing) number of courts will order increased funding.

# Institutional Reforms

Nevertheless, there are ways to shave off or soften some of the worst features and most troubling incentives plaguing the plea bargaining system today. Reforms should begin with the structures and incentives that shape the key actors' incentives.

**Police.** As earlier chapters of this book discuss, police need to do more to document their evidence during investigations, by for example recording identification procedures, interrogations, and details of work with confidential informants. They also need better information technology and flow of information, to ensure that they share all their information with prosecutors and provide legally required discovery to the defense. Police should not terminate investigations as soon as they have probable cause to arrest one suspect, secure in the belief that the suspect will probably plead out and not require additional evidence of guilt.

**Prosecutors.** Prosecutors should demand more evidence before charging cases; they should first question key witnesses and ask police to explore alibis and alternative culprits. (They cannot do so effectively if police have not documented their investigations and shared their evidence.) Prosecutors' offices should assign experienced prosecutors to make these intake decisions as part of an elite charging and screening unit, as the New Orleans District Attorney's Office once did. Doing so would guard against prosecutors' jumping to conclusions on the second-hand information relayed by police. It would also ensure that the prosecutor who charges a case will not try it or bargain it, removing the self-interested incentives to overcharge to coerce plea bargains (Wright & Miller, 2002).

Once prosecutors decide to file charges, cases take on a forward momentum of their own; prosecutors often strike bargains to deal with troublesome weaknesses in the evidence instead of dismissing entire cases outright. Rigorous screening up front greatly increases the fraction of cases that prosecutors decline to charge in the first place (Wright & Miller, 2002). Many of the screened-out cases are declined because of weak evidence, which indicates that the defendant may well be innocent. Thus, more rigorous screening leads prosecutors to decline cases against potentially innocent defendants who prosecutors would otherwise charge and have to bargain down. The result should be fewer wrongful plea bargains. In addition, the cases that are charged will be based on stronger evidence, so prosecutors will not need to bargain down charges.

Prosecutors can also do more to gather, consider, and disclose possibly exculpatory evidence (called *Brady* material) and impeachment evidence (called *Giglio* material). Internal databases would help to gather such evidence from police and link it across cases by name of witness, informant, officer, or the like. Document retention policies would also help. So would ethical rules, internal guidelines, and training for police and prosecutors on how to recognize, gather, and disclose *Brady* and *Giglio* material in time for discovery and internal plea decisions. (Symposium: New Perspectives on *Brady* and Other Disclosure Obligations, 2010).

Relatedly, prosecutors could provide more discovery, to give innocent defendants a better idea of why the government erroneously believes in their guilt. In particular, though the constitutional right to disclosure of exculpatory evidence may not kick in until trial, rules and procedures could require or encourage prosecutors to turn it over in plenty of time for plea bargaining (Bibas, 2006). Rules or policies could also authorize greater disclosure of impeachment and incriminating evidence except where witnesses are at risk of intimidation or tampering, which is more of a danger in many violent-crime cases.

Supervisory prosecutors could also review the evidence again before approving plea bargains, to take a second look if any new evidence came to light. That procedure could promote later dismissals when new evidence came to light. Unfortunately, tunnel vision, the inevitability bias, and the like hamper fresh second looks. What matters more is getting the first look right. But when wrongful arrests, charges, and convictions do come to light, police and prosecutors' offices need conviction integrity processes, to audit what went wrong, and feedback loops, to prevent systematic errors from recurring.

Police and prosecutors' incentives also need to change. Rewarding and promoting police and prosecutors based in part on arrest and conviction statistics encourages promiscuous charging, regardless of cases' weaknesses or the deals struck. At least one prosecutor's office has reframed its focus from the raw conviction rate to the as-charged conviction rate, encouraging prosecutors to file sustainable charges and not to bargain them down (Wright & Miller, 2002). In tandem with the hard screening discussed above, that approach encourages police and prosecutors to pursue only those cases that can be proven at trial beyond a reasonable doubt, not just any case with probable cause to arrest and charge. One could imagine other limits on the size of the discounts that prosecutors may offer, but it is hard to come up with enforceable ways to limit discounts without first limiting initial charging discretion and incentives. (Otherwise, prosecutors can simply bargain before filing formal charges.) One might at least forbid prosecutors to use the death penalty as a terrifying bargaining chip to induce pleas, requiring them to decide up front whether to seek capital punishment or not.

**Judges.** Making judges a meaningful check on possibly wrongful pleas is harder. Judges know little about cases at the time of plea colloquies and receive their information from parties who have strong incentives to support a deal. One could imagine turning plea colloquies into mini-trials. It would, however, be hard to make those mini-trials meaningful without all but abolishing the advantages of plea bargaining, though Philadelphia's use of bench trials is a possible model (Schulhofer, 1984). At the very least, judges (or rules of criminal procedure) could reject *Alford* and no-contest pleas, where the defendant's unwillingness to admit guilt signals the risk of a wrongful conviction. They could also require somewhat more detailed allocutions from defendants about what they did, to air any discrepancies. While defense lawyers typically script their clients' allocutions, follow-up questions could elicit defendant's own versions of events.

Another prospective judicial reform would be for judges to require prosecutors to disclose their plea offers to the court. If a prosecutor offered a very low sentence but threatened a high one after trial, the court would learn of the large discrepancy and be less willing to impose the threatened sentence after trial. Knowing that, prosecutors would be less willing to offer low sentences in the first place, reducing their ability to counterbalance a large chance of acquittal with a large sentencing differential. (Prosecutors could still use mandatory minimum and maximum sentences or guidelines to tie judges' hands, to an extent.) Defendants facing weak cases would be more likely to persist in seeking acquittal at trial and thus less likely to be charged in the first place. That would disproportionately benefit innocent defendants, by insulating them from extreme odds bargaining.

At bail hearings, judges could also increase their use of electronic ankle bracelets and similar substitutes for money bail. That would reduce pretrial detention of non-dangerous suspects and so alleviate the pressure to plead guilty in exchange for time served.

**Defense counsel.** Assuming a fixed pot of money for indigent defense, states should prefer public defender systems to appointment and contract-attorney systems. Public defenders specialize in criminal work, gaining more experience and expertise. They enjoy economies of scale in employing attorneys and support staff, so offices can support private investigators and the like. Their offices' size allows for greater training and supervision, which can help line defenders to make credible claims of innocence. They can allocate more of their time and money to potentially innocent defendants in their triage. They can also cultivate credibility with judges and prosecutors to convince them to take second looks at potentially innocent defendants. True, public defenders can become jaded by the large volume of cases and false protestations of innocence, but that problem is probably offset by public defenders' greater ideological commitment to fight for their clients (Bibas, 2004b). Recent empirical evidence confirms, for example, that public defenders' clients charged with murder are more likely to plead guilty to lesser charges than similarly charged clients of private appointed counsel (Anderson & Heaton, 2012).

## Psychology

Unfortunately, it is far easier to identify psychological biases and heuristics than to guard against them. Simply telling someone about a bias is inadequate to protect against it, nor does telling him to try harder or offering him more money to get it right (Bibas, 2004a).

What does work is to force a decision-maker to consider the opposite — here, the possibility that the defendant is innocent (Bibas, 2004a). That is what full-blown adversarial trials are meant to do. At trial, defense lawyers make juries confront the inconsistencies and contrary evidence, suggesting that the government got the wrong man. The disappearance of that check may be the most troubling thing about our world of guilty pleas.

In a world without trials, the main decision-maker is not the jury but the prosecutor, who needs to consider whether the police (who work closely with the prosecutor) got it wrong. The charging and screening prosecutor should explore that possibility upon intake. A supervisory prosecutor should do the same before authorizing a trial or plea. Both supervisory and line prosecutors should confront that possibility when defense lawyers point out conflicting evidence. And a closed-cases unit needs to grapple with new evidence of innocence even after conviction.

More radically, one could aspire to change the conviction mindset of partisan police and prosecutors who count the notches on their belts. America could abandon its adversarial system for a more inquisitorial joint search for truth, as in much of continental Europe. A truly nonpartisan mindset, however, would be fundamentally at odds with American legal traditions, structures, and expectations. It would be all but impossible to implement here, at least in criminal cases (Bibas, 2006). Nevertheless, greater supervision by judges and supervisory prosecutors, as suggested above, could take our system at least a few steps toward the inquisitorial model.

# Conclusion

America's adversarial system is supposed to ensure a defendant's guilt beyond a reasonable doubt, but our plea-bargaining assembly line short-circuits these elaborate safeguards. Plea bargaining is not a carefully planned system for adjudicating factual guilt, but an improvised shortcut that assumes the defendant's guilt. Documented erroneous convictions show that in an unclear fraction of cases, the system fails. Sometimes, criminal justice professionals jump to mistaken conclusions and do not vigorously investigate and challenge the assumption of guilt. Their overwork, underfunding, incentives, self-interests, and tunnel vision contribute to the problem. Solutions need to change professionals' incentives and plea procedures, to counteract the power of tunnel vision, the assumption of guilt, and the pressures to plead. That is far easier said than done. But better discovery, better documentation, and more rigorous screening are important, practical steps in the right direction. Perhaps the momentum of the innocence movement will help these much-needed reforms to spread.

# References

Alschuler, A. W. (1968). The Prosecutor's Role in Plea Bargaining. *University of Chicago Law Review, 36*, 50–112.

American Bar Association, Criminal Justice Standards Committee (1992). *ABA Standards for Criminal Justice: Providing Defense Services*, 3d ed. Washington, DC: Author.

Anderson, J. M. & Heaton, P. (2012). How Much Difference Does the Lawyer Make? The Effect of Defense Counsel on Murder Case Outcomes, *Yale Law Journal, 122*, 154–214.

Bibas, S. (2004a). Plea Bargaining Outside the Shadow of Trial. *Harvard Law Review, 117*, 2463–2547.

Bibas, S. (2004b). The Psychology of Hindsight and After-the-Fact Review of Ineffective Assistance of Counsel. *Utah Law Review, 2004*, 1–11.

Bibas, S. (2006). The Story of *Brady v. Maryland*: From Adversarial Gamesmanship Toward the Search for Innocence? In C. Steiker (Ed.), *Criminal Procedure Stories* (pp. 129–54). New York, NY: Foundation Press.

Bibas, S. (2012). *The Machinery of Criminal Justice*. New York, NY: Oxford University Press.

Bowers, J. (2008). Punishing the Innocent. *University of Pennsylvania Law Review, 156*, 1117–1179.

Dershowitz, A. M. (1982). *The Best Defense*. New York, NY: Random House.

Easterbrook, F. H. (1983). Criminal Procedure as a Market System. *Journal of Legal Studies, 12*, 289–332.

Garrett, B. L. (2011). *Convicting the Innocent: Where Criminal Prosecutions Go Wrong*. Cambridge, MA: Harvard University Press.

Harlow, C. W. (2000). *Defense Counsel in Criminal Cases*. (Bureau of Justice Statistics, Special Report No. NCJ 179023). Retrieved June 25, 2013 from Bureau of Justice Statistics: http://www.bjs.gov/content/pub/pdf/dccc.pdf.

Heumann, M. (1978). *Plea Bargaining: The Experience of Prosecutors, Judges, and Defense Attorneys*. Chicago, IL: The University of Chicago Press.

Kassin, S. M., Drizin, S., Grisso, T., Gudjonsson, G. H., Leo, R. A., & Redlich, A. D. (2010). Police-Induced Confessions: Risk Factors and Recommendations. *Law and Human Behavior, 34*, 3–38.

Maguire, K. (Ed.). *Sourcebook of Criminal Justice Statistics Online*. Albany, NY: University at Albany, Hindelang Criminal Justice Research Center. Available: http://www.albany.edu/sourcebook/ [June 3, 2013].

Schulhofer, S. J. (1984) Is Plea Bargaining Inevitable? *Harvard Law Review, 97*, 1037–1107.

Scott, R. E., & Stuntz, W. J. (1992). Plea Bargaining as Contract. *Yale Law Journal, 101*, 1909–1968.

Stuntz, W. J. (2001). The Pathological Politics of Criminal Law. *Michigan Law Review, 100*, 505–600.

Stuntz, W. J. (2004). Plea Bargaining and Criminal Law's Disappearing Shadow. *Harvard Law Review, 117*, 2548–2569.

Symposium: New Perspectives on *Brady* and Other Disclosure Obligations: What Really Works? (2010), *Cardozo Law Review, 31*,1943–2256.

U.S. Sentencing Commission (2012). *Guidelines Manual.* Washington, DC: Author.

Wright, R., & Miller, M. (2002). The Screening/Bargaining Tradeoff. *Stanford Law Review, 55*, 29–118.

# Chapter Eleven

# Juvenile Justice Investigation: Narrative Contamination, Cultural Stereotypes, and the Scripting of Juvenile False Confessions

Steven Drizin, *Northwestern University*

Laura Nirider, *Northwestern University*

Joshua Tepfer, *Northwestern University*

Many wrongful convictions begin as hunches gone wrong: as suspicions that are followed down the rabbit hole until they transform from theories into real-world injustices. In the world of juvenile justice, as in many other arenas, these wrong hunches are often based on pervasive cultural stereotypes concerning the ways that teenagers act and the kinds of things that "bad kids" do. Unfortunately, these stereotypes can drastically affect the way police investigate even serious crimes, despite their sometimes dubious reliability.

When crimes involving juveniles are investigated, these stereotypes can play particularly prominent—and problematic—roles. This chapter considers how juvenile wrongful convictions and, in particular, juvenile false confessions from the 1980s and 1990s were built on then-common cultural stereotypes concerning "bad" teenagers. First, we step back to examine the development of certain juvenile cultural types in the 1980s and 1990s, including the black urban super-predator and the white suburban loner. Next, we examine the use of these stereotypes to script the false confessions of black and white youth, respectively—a process we call *narrative contamination*—and the resulting power of those confessions, through their culturally resonant storylines, to bring about the wrongful convictions of factually innocent juveniles. We conclude by proposing ways to ensure that confessions will be "authentic, compelling, and self-corroborating" not because they incorporate culturally potent "bad kid" stereotypes, but because they constitute reliable evidence of guilt (Leo, 2009, p. 168).[1]

---

1. The examples we have identified are not the only stereotypes that underpin false confessions. We hope this chapter interests other researchers in examining narrative contamination and the use of cultural tropes in both false confessions and wrongful convictions more generally.

# Stepping Back: The Development of Teenage Character Tropes in 1980s- and 1990s-Era Popular Consciousness

From the late 1980s through the 1990s, at least two cultural types concerning youth criminals began to emerge in the American consciousness. The first type discussed here is that of the black urban teenage "super-predator" — a remorseless, amoral, animalistic black youth who engages in violent crime sprees for the fun of it. While its roots lie deep in the filth of centuries of racism (Burns, 2011), this particular stereotype gained popular traction in the 1990s after New York's Central Park Jogger case, now widely acknowledged to have involved five juvenile wrongful convictions. The second trope, in contrast, is that of the angry white suburban loner — an isolated, bullied, misanthropic white youth who exacts violent revenge on his peers. This type, too, has deep roots, but acquired new relevance after a wave of school shootings — apparently perpetrated by such types — rippled across America in the 1990s. Both types were disturbing enough to grasp the American popular imagination for the better part of a decade and continue to surface to this day (Abcarian, 2013).

## African-American Youth, the Central Park Five, and the Age of the Super-Predator

In the late 1980s and early 1990s, the American public was introduced to what academic John DiIulio later termed the "super-predator" (DiIulio, 1995a, 1995b, 1996).[2] Predicting a "horrific" nationwide surge in violent youth crime, DiIulio published a series of articles warning that "the next 10 years will unleash an army of young male predator street criminals" consisting of "tens of thousands" of "black inner-city males" (1995b, p. 23). Those "juvenile super-predators," he claimed, were "hardened, remorseless" youth who were "perfectly capable of committing the most heinous acts of physical violence for the most trivial reasons" (1995b, p. 23). DiIulio characterized the super-predators as different than previous generations — they would make "even the leaders of the Bloods and the Crips ... look tame by comparison" — such that they were not "merely unrecognizable but alien" (DiIulio, 1995b, 1996). DiIulio explained that the super-predators had been born "out of wedlock" in blighted urban centers and raised by "deviant, delinquent, and criminal adults" who abused their children and "failed to teach them right from wrong" (as cited in Schiraldi, 2001, p. A19). Even more frighteningly, these ultra-vicious black juveniles, he claimed, traveled in "wolf packs" that targeted not only other kids, but adults too.

DiIulio's deeply racialized vision of the "morally impoverished juvenile super-predator" fast became a potent stereotype that affected the public, members of law enforcement, and policymakers alike for many years (1995b, p. 23). By the latter half of the 1990s, one

---

2. Although John DiIulio of Princeton coined the term "super-predator," he was not the only social scientist to predict a crime wave by urban black youths. Northeastern University Professor James Allan Fox and University of California Los Angeles Professor James Q. Wilson, among others, also foretold the coming of the "super-predator."

in three young African-American males were put under criminal justice control; and at decade's end, the number of adults and juveniles locked up nationwide topped the two million mark (*Youth Violence*, 2001).

The super-predator stereotype has its roots, at least in part, in one of the most infamous juvenile confession cases in American history: the Central Park Jogger case. In April 1989, five youths—four blacks and one Latino, all between fourteen and sixteen years old—confessed to brutally raping a white female jogger and beating her nearly to death in New York City's Central Park (Burns, 2011). All five boys were tried, convicted, and sentenced to lengthy prison terms (Burns, 2011). The vicious attack was particularly brazen—it happened in a busy public park—and occurred with no apparent purpose other than to terrorize and injure. Accordingly, the media's intense coverage of the case was a near-perfect presentation of the super-predator trope. Reporters pilloried the five charged boys as symbols of a new breed of urban teenager who raped and killed without remorse. Screaming newspaper headlines described them as an animalistic "wolf pack" engaged in "wilding" (Burns, 2011). Business magnate Donald Trump even ran a full-page newspaper ad calling for the reinstatement of the death penalty, and commentator Patrick Buchanan demanded that the boys be publicly lynched or flogged (Burns, 2011; Buchanan, 1989).[3] This case introduced the public to the juvenile super-predator type with a vengeance—and the public responded with outrage and hysteria.

Indeed, the power of the super-predator narrative fast resonated far beyond New York. Soon, super-predator language was being used to describe other cases involving black youth around the nation. The Chief of the San Diego District Attorney's Division described a new phenomenon involving "kids who have never been socialized properly ... real predators," (Pertman, 1996, p. A1), while Professor Linda J. Collier contrasted the "truants, vandals, and petty [juvenile] thieves of a different era" with the "violent juvenile offender of today" (Collier, 1998, p. C01). But it was in Chicago that the super-predator stereotype took perhaps its firmest hold.

Only a month after the Jogger defendants were arrested, the *Chicago Tribune* cited the Jogger case when reflecting on residents' fear of teenage violence in two local public housing projects (Ogintz, 1989). The story quoted high-ranking Chicago police officers as saying that "more kids do things with less reason" and that the new generation of juveniles is "more vicious.... Maybe they're meaner kids" (Ogintz, 1989, p. 1). Four years later, the super-predator trope resurfaced after five-year-old Chicagoan Eric Morse was killed by two boys aged ten and eleven, who dropped him out of a fourteenth-floor window while Morse's eight-year-old brother watched—supposedly because Morse had refused to steal candy for them (Kuzka & McRoberts, 1994). A *Chicago Tribune* editorial called the alleged killers "dead souls" and "the most frightening of beings: the amoral child" ("What Eric," 1994). President Clinton even referenced the case in a speech, using language that bespoke a coming wave of morally depraved, remorseless children:

> What we have to worry about is wave upon wave upon wave of these little children who don't have somebody both good and strong to look up to; who are so

---

3. Buchanan stated:

How does a civilized, self-confident people deal with enemies who gang-rape their women? Armies stand them up against the wall and shoot them; or we hang them, as we did the Japanese and Nazi War Criminals. If the eldest of that wolf pack were tried, convicted, and hanged in Central Park, by June 1, and the 13- and 14-year-olds were stripped, horsewhipped, and sent to prison, the park might soon be safe for women.

vulnerable that *their hearts can be turned to stone by the time they're 10 or 11 years old* ("Clinton cites need," 1994).

A few months later, an eleven-year-old black boy was convicted of binding, beating, and stabbing an eighty-three-year-old white woman named Anna Gilvis in her Chicago apartment in October 1993. Detective James Cassidy, who obtained the boy's confession, wrote an opinion piece in the *Chicago Tribune* describing his confrontation with the boy:

> The manifestation of hate filling up in his young face sent me reeling back like nothing I had ever experienced or probably ever will. Yes, the kid did it to me, a homicide detective who has stared into the faces of hundreds of murderers through the years and never let any of them get through to me, never. This time it was different. This kid was different. He wasn't like any of the other killers I had dealt with in the past.... The murderer was just a kid, an 11 year old baby-faced boy who could be living next to anyone, anywhere. But something made him different. While only 10 years old, he chose to commit a brutal murder (Cassidy, 1994).[4]

Detective Cassidy predicted a future "onslaught of juvenile crime" and pleaded with the public to "lock away" today's violent youths (Cassidy, 1994). That same year, the *Tribune* invoked super-predator language in its coverage of eleven-year-old Chicago gang member Robert "Yummy" Sandifer, who shot a young girl named Shavon Dean to death only to have two teenage members of his own gang kill him in response (Gibbs, 1994). The next year, the *Chicago Tribune* gave full-page treatment to DiIulio and his super-predator theory, quoting Cook County State's Attorney Jack O'Malley as saying: "It's Lord of the Flies on a massive scale. We've become a nation terrorized by our children" (Annin, 1996, p. 57).

The tale of the super-predator trope, however, has an important epilogue. More than thirteen years after their arrests, the five teens convicted in the Central Park Jogger case — in a sense, the first "super-predators" — were exonerated in December 2002 after DNA evidence pointed to a man named Matias Reyes. Reyes was an infamous serial rapist and murderer who attacked several women near Central Park both before and after his attack on the jogger (Burns, 2011). Those five boys, in short, were no wolf pack; rather, they had been sacrificial lambs. And in a fascinating parallel, we now know that contemporaneous predictions of a generation of juvenile super-predators were similarly baseless — little more than urban legends. In 2001, the United States Surgeon General issued a report declaring the super-predator nothing more than a myth (*Youth violence*, 2001). In 2012, DiIulio himself admitted in a brief filed before the U.S. Supreme Court that his predictions about super-predators had been wrong (Miller, 2012). Laudably, he stated that he had never intended for children to be incarcerated as adults and began urging a halt to prison-building (Schiraldi, 2001). Reflecting on the media's role in fueling the super-predator myth, one astute reporter has referred to the entire episode as "super-scapegoating" (Templeton, 1995). Sadly, however, the story does not end here; even today, media coverage of a mythical epidemic in which African-American youth attack innocent white passersby in so-called "Knockout Games" continues to contribute to the "ongoing demonization of black teenagers" (Abcarian, 2013, p. 1).

---

4. The post-script to this case is that the boy's conviction was overturned by the federal courts, because, among other reasons, his confession had been coerced (A.M. v. Butler, 2004).

# White Adolescent Males, the School Shooting Cases, and the Angry Teenage Loner

In addition to the super-predator myth, the 1990s gave rise to a second culturally resonant type that also surfaced repeatedly in media coverage of youth crime: that of the angry white teenage loner. The misanthropic adolescent is, of course, a familiar character that long predates the 1990s. It is a cultural type that has emerged repeatedly throughout the history of American pop culture, from Holden Caulfield to James Dean to countless other examples. But in the later 1990s, a more particularized — and violent — version of this cultural type began to emerge in the wake of several highly-publicized school shootings which appeared to have been committed by the same type of person: angry, isolated, adolescent boys — invariably white — who sought revenge on the world for being picked on, bullied, or ignored by their peers.

One of the first school shootings to grab the national spotlight was a 1996 shooting at Frontier Junior High School, in Moses Lake, Washington. On February 2nd of that year, fourteen-year-old Barry Loukaitis dressed up as a Wild West-style gunslinger, complete with a black "duster" or trench coat (Tizon, 1997). He brought a deer rifle and two handguns to school, where he killed his algebra teacher and two students during a fifth-period math class — announcing to his horrified classmates "This sure beats algebra, doesn't it?" — before being subdued by a gym teacher. In the days that followed, it emerged that the skinny, white Loukaitis was an unpopular honor student who had been bullied by his classmates and called a "dork," "gay lord," and "faggot" (Greenya, 2005; Tizon 1997). One of his victims was a student who Loukaitis claimed had teased him.

The Moses Lake killing, however, was only the first in a string of school shootings that were depicted in the media as eerily repetitive. On October 1, 1997, sixteen-year-old Luke Woodham — an "overweight and bookish" white student whom the *New York Times* later deemed a "misfit on the fringes of [high school] society" — shot two students and injured seven others at his high school in Pearl, Mississippi (Sack, 1997). Like Loukaitis before him, he wore a trench coat during the shootings. Minutes before he started his rampage, Woodham gave a message to a friend which stated, in part, "I am not insane, I am angry. I killed because people like me are mistreated every day. I did this to show society, push us and we will push back.... All throughout my life, I was ridiculed, always beaten, always hated." Woodham explained that he resented "watching Johnny football player get the glory when in actuality he does nothing" (Sack, 1997b, p. A10).

A similar story was repeated only two months later on December 1, 1997, in West Paducah, Kentucky. There, fourteen-year-old Michael Carneal opened fire on a group of praying students at Heath High School, killing three and injuring five more. The *New York Times* reported that Michael's essays and short stories indicated that he had "struck out in anger at the world" because he felt weak and picked on; apparently, it claimed, he had been "teased all his life" (Bragg, 1997, p. A26). For its part, *Time* magazine described Carneal and his predecessors, including Woodham, as "lonely or teased" boys who "seem to share a deep-seated ... sense of rage" (Cloud , 2001).

Over the following months, several additional school shootings happened — nearly all of which were described in the media as following the same pattern. On May 21, 1998, fifteen-year-old Kip Kinkel killed two students and wounded twenty-five others in a shooting spree at his high school in Springfield, Oregon. Kinkel, who suffered from mental illness, had been bullied as a child and was a lonely teen with few friends, in contrast to his popular older sister Kristen (Kinkel, 2000). And perhaps the most widely publicized school shooting of all, occurred on April 20, 1999, at Columbine High School in Littleton,

Colorado. There, eighteen-year-old Eric Harris and seventeen-year-old Dylan Klebold—clad in the black trench coats that have come to be associated with them—notoriously committed a twenty-minute-long killing spree using a handgun, a rifle, two shotguns, and more than thirty homemade bombs. They succeeded in killing one teacher and twelve students and wounding twenty-three others before they turned their own weapons upon themselves. In the resulting media storm, Harris and Klebold were widely described as bullied, angry misfits who sought the ultimate revenge (Frymer, 2009; James, 2009). Indeed, Eric Harris' journal entries, which frequently seethed with anger at his classmates, appeared to support this theory: "Everyone is always making fun of me because of how I look, and how fucking weak I am and shit. Well, I will get you all back: ultimate fucking revenge here.... That's where a lot of my hate grows from" (Harris, 1998).

As these stories built over time, it became apparent that the cultural type that came to be associated with the perpetrators—the angry teenage loner—was confined largely to suburban and rural white America. Indeed, some media outlets openly acknowledged the whiteness of this new breed of violent teen. Months after the Columbine shootings, the *Daily Oklahoman* reported that school shooters are "often from white, middle-class families with many social and economic advantages" (Tatum, 1999). More indirectly, the *Atlanta Constitution* quoted a local pastor as saying "[t]his is supposed to happen in New York City or Atlanta," suggesting that stories of violence were common—even expected, perhaps—in urban areas. Now, however, "the stories about teen violence are coming out of towns like Pearl and Paducah, where people have long believed the slower pace and the firmer rooting in traditional values somehow made them immune" (Williams, 1997). Such a message carries with it an easily rooted-out racial overtone, contrasting urban areas—which, of course, were being shot up by young black "super-predators"—with the traditional peacefulness of predominantly white rural and suburban America.

To what, then, could this sudden apparent explosion of rage-driven violence among white adolescent males be attributed? For its part, the media was quick to identify a common culprit among many of the school shooters: the influence of violent video games, movies, and books. Barry Loukaitis, the *Washington Post* reported, got ideas from the book *Rage*—written by Stephen King under an assumed name—and the movie *Natural Born Killers*, which depicts a high school student taking a gun to school and killing two teachers ("Teen Convicted," 1997; "Stephen King," 1996). Even Loukaitis' words during his shooting spree—"This sure beats algebra, doesn't it?"—were said to be quoted directly from *Rage*. Michael Carneal, too, reportedly had read *Rage* before his rampage; indeed, Stephen King requested that the book be removed from shelves when he was told that it might have contributed to Carneal's actions (King, 2013). For his part, Luke Woodham was said to have listened to the music of so-called "goth rocker" Marilyn Manson, who sometimes wore a black trench coat on stage and whose lyrics *Time* magazine described as part of a genre "lush with nihilism" (Cloud, 2001). The *New York Times* stated that Woodham also participated in role-playing games in which he could act like the "bad guy" ("Revenge" 1998). Similarly, Michael Carneal reportedly told detectives that he got the idea for his shooting spree from a movie called "The Basketball Diaries," which featured a short dreamlike scene in which teenage gunmen terrorize their school (Williams, 1997). Perhaps most famously, Eric Harris and Dylan Klebold's actions were widely attributed in the press—at least in part—to their fascination with violent video games, including ultra-realistic shooting games like Quake and Doom (Johnson & Brooke, 1999). Indeed, just a few years earlier, Michael Carneal had also said he enjoyed playing the same two video games (Cloud, 2001). This media-driven theory regarding cultural influences became so pervasive, in fact, that the United States House of Representatives held hearings a month after the Columbine massacre investigating whether "the kids who were harassed" at school had a "culture that gave them permission—whether it's through Doom or whether it's through the lyrics of music—that gave them permission to turn that rage and that depression against others" (U.S. Representative Michael Castle (R-DE) Holds Hearing on School Violence, 1999).

Notably, these efforts to blame pop culture for white teen violence—at least in part—contrasted greatly with the super-predator myth. The super-predator myth described a generation of unsalvageable black children who comprised an inherently amoral wolf pack, little better than animals and deserving to be treated as such. In contrast, white teenage perpetrators of violence were frequently described as "troubled" and "disturbed"—victims, in essence, of external influences including toxic music, movies, books, and video games which had displaced their essential goodness—who needed help and intervention (Drizin, 1999). But in spite of this difference—or perhaps because of it—the angry teenage loner trope became just as firmly affixed in the popular consciousness.

While the super-predator trope has been debunked—it was founded on theories that have been repudiated and, in part, on five convictions that turned out to be wrongful—a debate continues today as to the validity of the angry teenage loner trope. Certainly the school shootings discussed in this article cannot be called wrongful convictions; unlike the Central Park Five, the guilt of the individuals responsible for those crimes has never been seriously disputed. But does that mean that the angry teenage loner trope—derived from the likes of Loukaitis, Woodham, Carneal, Harris, and Klebold—has some legitimacy? The answer to that question, it turns out, is still being answered. In 2009, *USA Today* ran an article suggesting that the Columbine shooters were not bullied after all, faulting mental illness for their actions (Toppo, 2009). Similarly, the *New York Times* ran an article a year after Columbine suggesting that cultural influences were less to blame for the shootings than mental health issues ("A Closer Look," 2000). But some neuroscience studies suggest that violent cultural influences can, in fact, be traced to an increase in violent behaviors (Wang et al., 2009). The authors will not weigh in on this debate here, which falls well beyond the scope of this chapter. We simply point out that, empirically valid or not, the angry teenage loner trope is just as pernicious a source of narrative contamination as the super-predator myth—and, as we will now discuss, it may be just as likely to spawn wrongful convictions.

# Moving Forward: Examining the Use of Cultural Stereotypes to Script Teenage False Confessions

## Juvenile False Confessions Generally

To date, 312 individuals have been exonerated on the basis of DNA testing after having been convicted of crimes that they did not commit. Approximately one-quarter of those individuals falsely confessed under police interrogation to the crimes in question (False Confessions, n.d.).[5] Such false confessions result in large part from the pressures of custodial interrogation, which have been discussed elsewhere at length. Indeed, the United States

---

5. This statistic does not include false confessors who have been exonerated on the basis of non-DNA evidence or false confessors who have yet to be exonerated. To date, scholars have uncovered at least 250 false confessions made over the last twenty years, and there are likely a great many more individuals who have falsely confessed whose stories are simply not known (Leo, 2009).

Supreme Court has twice recently acknowledged that "there is mounting empirical evidence that these pressures [associated with custodial police interrogation] can induce a frighteningly high percentage of people to confess to crimes they never committed" (*Corley v. United States*, 2009; *J.D.B. v. North Carolina*, 2011).

Authorities ranging from the U.S. Supreme Court to the International Association of Chiefs of Police, further, agree that juveniles are particularly likely to give false or involuntary statements during police questioning (International Association of Chiefs of Police, 2012; *J.D.B. v. North Carolina*, 2011). In *J.D.B. v. North Carolina*, the Supreme Court found that the risk of false confession is "all the more acute" when a young person is the subject of custodial interrogation. Several studies of wrongful convictions have borne this conclusion out, noting that juveniles' rate of false confession is much higher than that of adults (Gross, Jacoby, Matheson, Montgomery, & Patil, 2005; Tepfer, Nirider, & Tricarico, 2010). Juvenile false confessions, however—like false confessions generally—do not simply happen; they are made. It is to the process of manufacturing juvenile false confessions, and the role of cultural stereotypes in that process, that we now turn.

# False Confessions and Narrative Contamination

When a defendant's confession is introduced in court, police and prosecutors often characterize that confession as a spontaneous, get-it-off-my-chest outburst, made freely by a defendant who needed minimal persuasion from interrogators (*A.M. v. Butler*, 2004). But the work of scholars like Richard Leo and Saul Kassin has proven otherwise (Leo, 2009, p. 168). According to Professor Kassin, a confession is like a "Hollywood drama— scripted in accordance with the police theory of the case, rehearsed during hours of unrecorded questioning, directed by the questioner, and ultimately enacted on paper, tape, or camera by the suspect" (Kassin, 2008, p. 1309, 1318). This is doubly true for false confessions, in which the defendant's statement is truly a work of dramatic fiction that is taken from concept to production by police interrogators.

Although confession-making occurs in both true and false confessions, the process of constructing false confessions requires interrogators to engage in the most active level of scripting. One common type of scripting has already been identified by Professor Brandon Garrett, who found that an overwhelming 95% of confessions proven false by DNA still managed to include accurate, non-public details about the crime that were only known to police investigators and the true perpetrator (Garrett, 2011). The only possible explanation, he concluded, is that interrogators "contaminated" the confession by using leading questions, showing photographs of the crime scene, and otherwise disclosing facts about the crime to the suspect (Nirider, Tepfer, Drizin, 2012).[6]

While Garrett and others have focused on the incorporation of accurate facts into provably false confessions—what we term *fact contamination*—it is important to note that false confessions also often include highly persuasive contextual "facts" that can be neither proven nor disproven by the evidence left at the crime scene. These details could include, for instance, menacing words supposedly said during the crime or instances of remorseless behavior after the crime. Such contextual details are critical: they fill out the storyline of the confession, defining the defendant as a "bad guy" more fully than a mere

---

6. Contamination can also occur from exposure to detailed media accounts of the crime or from the suspect's own innocent knowledge of crime scene facts, which can be obtained by visiting the crime scene before the crime, finding the victim's body, or hearing about the crime from the neighborhood gossip mill. Police fact-feeding, however, is likely the most common culprit.

recitation of the who-what-where-when facts. In this way, these contextual details contribute to the construction of an "authentic, compelling, and self-corroborating" narrative (Leo, 2009, p. 168). We refer to the incorporation of such details into a confession as *narrative contamination*.

With specific respect to juvenile confessions, the process of narrative contamination can cause an innocent juvenile's confession to contain vivid—though often unprovable— details that are consistent with preconceived stereotypes of how "bad kids" behave. In the juvenile confession cases discussed in the next two sections, narrative contamination resulted in the incorporation both of easily recognizable super-predator stereotypes into false confessions made by black youth and, similarly, of angry teenage loner stereotypes into false (or likely false) confessions made by white juveniles.

**Super-predator narrative contamination and confessions of black youth.** Cook County, Illinois—a metropolis of more than five million residents which includes Chicago and some surrounding suburbs (United States Census Bureau, 2012)—has spawned at least eighteen known juvenile false confessions.[7] This is more than any other jurisdiction in the United States (Drizin & Leo, 2004; Pitts, 2012). Each of these false confessions occurred during the mid-1990s, in the heart of the super-predator era. Each of these false confessions, moreover, involved black youth, and some cases involved multiple false confessions to the same crime. But a close examination of the false confessions in two representative cases, as set forth below, reveals a strikingly familiar story: those confessions were structured and scripted in a way that unmistakably defined the accused juveniles not only as criminals, but as remorseless and depraved super-predators.

*The Dixmoor Five.*[8] On December 8, 1991, the body of fourteen-year-old Cateresa Matthews was discovered in a well-trodden field near Interstate 57 in a small suburb of Chicago called Dixmoor. Naked from the waist down, she had been raped and then shot in the mouth point-blank. Cateresa had been reported missing almost three weeks earlier, after she had failed to arrive home from school at her usual time.

For almost a year, law enforcement's efforts to find Cateresa's rapist and killer were unsuccessful. In October 1992, however, investigators received a tip that she had last been seen with a group of boys, including two fourteen-year-olds named Robert Veal and Robert Taylor. A week later, the police interrogated Veal and Taylor, then fifteen years old, both of whom ultimately confessed to participating in a group attack on Cateresa. Both Veal and Taylor also implicated fourteen-year-old Jonathan Barr, Barr's sixteen-year-old brother James Harden, and a sixteen-year-old friend named Shainne Sharp. Two days later, Sharp—now seventeen years old—also confessed under police interrogation.

---

7. The Cook County juvenile false confessors, with their crimes, ages at the time of the confession, and the year of their alleged crimes in parentheses, include Harold Hill (murder/rape, 16, 1990); Peter Williams (murder/rape, 17, 1990); Daniel Taylor (murder, 17, 1992); Robert Taylor (15, murder/rape, 1992); Robert Veal (15, murder/rape 1992), Shainne Sharp (17, murder/rape, 1992); Lafonso Rollins (17, multiple rapes, 1993); Terrill Swift, (17, murder/rape, 1995); Vincent Thames (18, murder/rape, 1995), Michael Saunders, (15, murder/rape, 1995), Harold Richardson, (16, murder/rape, 1995); Jerry Fincher (18, murder/rape, 1995), Mario Hayes (17, murder, 1996), Don Olmetti (16, murder, 1997); Eric Kittler (15, murder, 1997); Eddie Huggins (15, murder, 1998); Unnamed Juveniles (7, 8 murder/rape, 1998). There may be, of course, undiscovered juvenile false confessions or others that are unknown to the authors. In making this claim, the Authors adopt earlier criteria defining a "proven" false confession to include only confessions in which 1) the defendant confessed to a crime that never occurred; 2) it was physically impossible for the defendant to have committed the crime (for instance, he was incarcerated at the time of the crime); 3) the true perpetrator is reliably identified; or 4) scientific evidence conclusively proves that the confession is false (Drizin & Leo, 2004.)

8. The information for this section was taken from Tepfer, Cooley, & Thompson (2012), or pleadings and documents on file with the authors.

Taken together, the three confessions painted a horrifying picture of unrestrained group violence. According to those confessions, the five boys picked up Cateresa while driving around and took her to a field near the interstate. The boys then supposedly winked at each other and began to beat Cateresa, tied a scarf over her mouth to silence her, and raped her one by one as the others held her down. According to one of the boys, Harden announced that "he was fittin' to fuck the bitch" before he assaulted her and even taunted her during the assault, "kissing her and slapping her and asking if she was gonna give him some pussy." Once the assault was complete, Harden calmly took out a small black gun, stood over Cateresa, and shot her in the face.

The confessions, however, did not end here. All three statements went on to incorporate additional details that portrayed the boys as particularly vicious and remorseless. After the incident, for instance, Sharp's statement indicated that he went to a friend's house and "shot dice," apparently unaffected by what had just occurred. Similarly, Robert Veal went to a "candy store." The confessions also seemed to blame Cateresa for the attack; one called her "a tease" and "a flirt that made guys want it from her."

After these confessions, the Cook County State's Attorney's Office filed sexual assault and murder charges against all five boys. As their investigation continued, however, the results should have raised some red flags. First, the crime scene was relatively undisturbed, displaying no evidence of the frenzied struggle one would expect in a sexual assault case involving five attackers. Further, several of the boys were only passing acquaintances—indeed, some of them were outright enemies—and none of them had backgrounds suggesting that they were capable of such depravity. And finally, there was one piece of evidence that should have been truly unignorable: the DNA left on Cateresa's body, it turned out, belonged only to a single unknown male. It did not belong to any of the five accused teenagers.

None of these red flags, however, caused prosecutors to back away from a narrative of the case that evoked and exploited the super-predator trope, which was then exploding onto the national consciousness. Consider the rhetoric employed by prosecutors during closing arguments at the jury trial of Robert Taylor and Jonathan Barr:

> When Cateresa Matthews walked out of her grandmother's house she walked out of her world and into the world of Robert Taylor, Robert Veal, James Harden, Shainne Sharp, and Jonathan Barr. And their world is a little different from Cateresa Matthews' world. Their world is a world of savagery, of ruthlessness, and of violence. It was a world that fourteen-year-old Cateresa Matthews couldn't even begin to comprehend. It was a world where so-called friends would turn into a pack of jackals hunting down their prey and then when they were done with it killing it for sport.

This is a narrative of unhinged violence by a "pack" of predatory, "savage" black youth; unmistakably, it is a super-predator narrative. It embraces the same animal imagery prevalent in the national media's earlier coverage of the Central Park Jogger case, in which five black youths were deemed little more than a "wolf pack." It also evokes the same frightening soullessness borne so vividly of DiIulio's imagination, describing a group of teens engaged in intentional murder merely "for sport." Unsurprisingly, all five boys were convicted; three were sentenced to the equivalent of life in prison.

It was not until almost twenty years later that the DNA found on Cateresa's body was finally identified as that of a man named Willie Randolph. At the time of the crime, Randolph was a convicted rapist and serial violent offender in his early thirties. He also had no connection to any of the convicted teens. At long last, the Dixmoor Five—who had, by now, become men who had spent most of their lives behind bars—were exonerated. The three confessions—and the powerful super-predator imagery that underpinned both the confessions and the prosecutions—were revealed to be nothing more than worthless pieces of fiction.

*The Englewood Four.*[9] Three years after the disappearance of Cateresa Matthews, another Chicago-area woman was raped and murdered—this time in an impoverished neighborhood known as Englewood. In the early morning hours of November 7, 1994, the body of a drug-addicted sex worker named Nina Glover was found in a Dumpster; she had been sexually assaulted and strangled.

The investigation into Glover's death was led by Chicago Police Detective James Cassidy—the same officer who had just published an op-ed in the *Chicago Tribune* describing a new crop of remorseless juvenile killers who were somehow different, not like "any of the other killers I had dealt with in the past" (Cassidy, 1994). In March 1995, Detective Cassidy's investigation got a big break: According to police, an eighteen-year-old Englewood resident named Jerry Fincher walked into a police station and offered to trade "information" he knew about Glover's murder for some help for a recently-arrested friend. After he was held two days in custody, Fincher's "information" was revealed to be a confession to Glover's murder, handwritten by law enforcement officers and signed by Fincher. In his confession, Fincher implicated himself as "security," or the lookout, while four teenage members of the Blackstone gang—Michael Saunders, Terrill Swift, Harold Richardson, and Vincent Thames—viciously gang-raped and murdered Glover over a drug debt. In the days that followed, each of the other four boys eventually made similar confessions during police interrogations. Detectives wrote out statements for Thames and Saunders to sign; a detective and a Cook County prosecutor together obtained Richardson's oral statement; and Swift confessed during a prosecutor-directed question-and-answer session transcribed by a court reporter.

These confessions depict a group of ruthlessly violent black boys concerned solely with gangs, drugs, and money. At the start, each of the confessions names the boys as members of the Blackstone gang and identifies them using supposed gang nicknames like "The Undertaker" or, together, the "Mos." The confessions go on to assert that Nina Glover, who owed the boys $400 for drugs, met all five of them on the street and requested an additional "bag" of drugs. According to Fincher's confession, Richardson (whose nickname was "Mo Mike") replied that he would give her a "bag" if she "suck[ed] the Mos dick." Glover supposedly agreed and followed all five teenagers to the basement of Vincent Thames' house. Before entering the basement, Richardson was said to have ordered Fincher to "do security" because "the Mos are gonna change this bitch." The confessions themselves explain that "to change a bitch" means to kill a woman.

According to the gruesome confessions, the five boys—much as in the Dixmoor case—supposedly took turns punching, kicking, and raping Glover while the others held her down. During the assault, two of them—"Mo Mike" and "The Undertaker"—supposedly screamed "you stole my work," later explained as a reference to the drug debt. "Mo Mike" then choked the victim with his bare hands while the others beat her with a metal shovel until she collapsed in a pool of blood, foam dripping from her mouth. The teenagers were then said to have cleaned up after themselves, mopping up the blood, wrapping the victim in a sheet, and carrying her body two blocks down the street before discarding it in the Dumpster.

Like the Dixmoor confessions, the Englewood confessions described in vivid detail horrible acts of uncontrolled violence perpetrated by groups of amoral youths—a theme certainly evocative of the super-predator trope. Also like the Dixmoor confessions, the

---

9. The information for this section was taken from Tepfer, Cooley, & Thompson (2012), or pleadings and documents on file with the authors.

Englewood confessions also include extraneous details that appear to have been included simply to illustrate the perpetrators' total want of remorse. Thames' confession asserts that after the attack, he went home, listened to the radio, talked to his cousin on the phone, and went to bed. For his part, Swift supposedly went on to visit his girlfriend, then headed home and went to sleep.

Again, based on these confessions, the Cook County State's Attorney's Office charged all five teenagers with the murder and sexual assault of Nina Glover. But like the Dixmoor case, the Englewood case soon presented a number of red flags. Once again, the supposed accomplices either did not know each other or were only passing acquaintances. And once again, it was discovered that the DNA of only a single man had been left on the victim's body. Just as in the Dixmoor case, that DNA had been left by an unknown man and did not belong to any of the charged boys. Regardless, prosecutors again clung to the gang-rape narrative and pursued the boys with a vengeance, ultimately securing the convictions of Richardson, Thames, Swift, and Saunders under a theory of the case that was steeped in the super-predator narrative. Only Fincher, whose confession was suppressed by a Cook County judge, avoided this fate. Without his confession, prosecutors were forced to drop all charges against him and he was freed after serving more than three years in jail pending trial.

Two decades later, the remaining four—who became known as the Englewood Four— were finally exonerated when their confessions were revealed to be works of pure fiction. Just as in the Dixmoor case, the male DNA found on Glover's body was identified as that of an adult named Johnnie Douglas—a seven-time accused rapist and convicted murderer with a history of targeting drug-addicted prostitutes.[10] Douglas had no links to any of the five charged boys.

In this way, the super-predator narrative underpinning the Englewood confessions was utterly belied. Nina Glover was not victimized by a "pack" of black juveniles, but by a lone adult serial rapist and killer. The ruthless and vengeful dialogue described in the confessions had never been actually spoken; nor had the remorseless actions after the attack ever actually occurred. In all probability, such details were plucked directly from law enforcement's imaginings of how teenage super-predators would have acted. Due to the resonance of the confession narratives, however—based on persuasive, stereotype-driven imagery of violent black gang members—these imaginings were long mistaken for reality.

*Other Chicago cases.* The Dixmoor and Englewood defendants were not the only black youths whose false confessions appear to have been contaminated by the super-predator narrative. Sixteen year-old Don Olmetti falsely confessed to the murder of a Chicago Public School teacher in April 1997. At Olmetti's bond hearing, a Cook County State's Attorney testified that Olmetti "showed no signs of remorse for the shooting and took the bus home afterward to take a nap and watch cartoons" ("Bond," 1997). Two years later, the charges against Olmetti were dropped (Hill, 1999) when it was proven that Olmetti could not have murdered the teacher because at the time of the crime, he had been sitting in his own classroom.

The nadir, however, was the July 1998 rape-murder of an eleven-year-old girl named Ryan Harris that, once again, involved a false confession commandeered by Chicago Police Detective James Cassidy. This time, Cassidy obtained a confession from a seven-year-old boy who also implicated his eight-year-old friend. The confession unraveled before trial,

---

10. Douglas was also identified as being at the scene at 7:00 a.m., watching as police lifted Nina Glover's body from the Dumpster. In fact, Detective Cassidy spoke to Douglas at the time who lied when he told Cassidy and a partner that he did not know Glover.

however, after DNA evidence linked a neighborhood adult sexual predator to the crime (Kotlowitz, 1999). According to the confession, one of the boys supposedly rode his bike home after the crime and watched cartoons, just like Olmetti (Greene, 1996).[11] The image of such young killers watching cartoons in the immediate aftermath of brutal killings undoubtedly evokes powerful images of utter depravity inspired by and exemplified in the super-predator myth.

The exoneration of the two young boys in the Ryan Harris case marked the beginning of the end of the super-predator myth. In hindsight, it is striking that both the case that gave birth to the super-predator myth — New York's Central Park Jogger case — and the case that helped to fast-track its demise, at least in Cook County — the Ryan Harris case — were both false confession cases involving multiple black children accused of rape-murders. As the Dixmoor and Englewood cases demonstrate, however, there were other such cases in Cook County during the super-predator era that did not penetrate the national consciousness to the same extent as these. And there is good reason to think that there are still other juvenile false confession cases in Cook County from this era that were influenced by the young, black super-predator myth that have yet to result in exonerations.[12]

**"Angry loner" narrative contamination and confessions of white youth.** Just as the super-predator myth formed the script for the false confessions of black urban youth, the angry teenage loner trope provided the plotline for several confessions taken from white teenage boys. Two such examples can be found in the confessions of Michael Crowe of California and Thomas Cogdell of Arkansas.

---

11. Is it just a coincidence that two false murder confessions from children both contained references to the fact that the killers went home to watch cartoons after committing a murder? Perhaps — but there's another equally plausible explanation. A year before Olmetti's confession, Bob Greene, a popular columnist for the Chicago Tribune, wrote a column on juvenile super-predators. In that column, Greene highlighted a number of cases from around the country to demonstrate that today's teenage criminals were remorseless. One of those cases he described as follows:

In San Jose, Calif., in 1992, an 8-year-old 3rd grader named Melvin Ancheta stayed home from elementary school one day because he had a cold and a fever. According to police, three neighborhood teenagers who knew Melvin and his family came to the door. He told them that he wasn't supposed to let anyone in. They persuaded him that it was all right.

They beat Melvin, hacked at him with a butcher knife and a meat cleaver, marched him from room to room, stuffed a sock into his mouth, wrapped tape around his face, put him on a couch while they looked for items to steal—*then watched a cartoon show on TV* as Melvin lay bleeding. They left the house with a hand-held video game and a portable telephone. Melvin's brother Ryan, 14, came home from school and found Melvin dead. His eyes were wide open, brown plastic tape was wrapped over his mouth, a cord was twisted around his neck (Greene, 1996).

Were Cassidy and other members of the Chicago Police aware of this story? Did they use this trope as a source for their confession narratives? It would be interesting to see whether the notion of post-murder cartoon-watching appeared in any other confessions — true or false — during the age of the super-predator.

12. One such case worth particular mention involves a December 1995 double murder and robbery at a used car lot. Teenagers Charles Johnson, Larod Styles, Lashawn Ezell, and Troshawn McCoy each signed confessions written by law enforcement and littered with gang terminology. Detective James Cassidy was again involved, obtaining the first confession from McCoy, which became the basic script for the other three confessions. Recently, multiple fingerprints from two different crime scenes miles apart were matched to an offender that was not named by the teens and whom they do not know. Because of the location of the prints — on cars on the lot and on the adhesive side of a sticker peeled off of the stolen cars — and the fact that the stolen car was abandoned a block away from the man whose fingerprints were a match, an Illinois appellate court has ordered a hearing on innocence (*People v. Johnson*, 2013).

*Michael Crowe.*[13] Even as school shootings were unfolding across the country in the late 1990s—sometimes as frequently as once every few months—a different tragedy was unfolding in Escondido, California. On the night of January 20, 1998, twelve-year-old Stephanie Crowe was stabbed to death in her bedroom inside her family's Escondido home. She was found by her grandmother the next morning; after the authorities arrived, the police checked all of the house's doors and windows and found no signs of forced entry, although two doors and one window had been left unlocked. Police brought Stephanie's parents, ten-year-old sister Shannon, and fourteen-year-old brother Michael (all white) to the police station hours after Stephanie's body was found, where they were questioned. During questioning, Michael's father gave the police a description of the family's everyday life. He described Stephanie as outgoing, popular, and well-liked and Michael as a child who loved video games. Police later found several video games in Michael's room that bore names like *Underground, Final Fantasy, Gauntlet,* and *Double Dragon,* along with a handmade booklet referring to the role-playing video game *Dungeons and Dragons* that contained the sentence "Many have entered, none have left alive."

For his part, Michael told the police that he had awoken at 4:30 that morning with a headache, so he had gone to the kitchen—half-asleep and in the dark—for some Tylenol. He reported that all the bedroom doors had been shut in the hallway and that he had seen nothing strange. Police, however, believed that Stephanie had been killed before 4:30 and that her body was lying in her bedroom's doorway at that time; for that reason, Michael's account raised their suspicions.

Acting on those suspicions, police subjected Michael to three additional interrogation sessions. As part of one session, he underwent a so-called "computer voice stress analyzer" test, the results of which supposedly indicated that Michael was lying. Police also falsely informed him that they had found scientific evidence incriminating him, including Stephanie's blood in his bedroom. Michael reacted with horror: "God. God. Why? Why? Why? Oh, God. God. Why? Why? I don't deserve life. I don't want to live. I can't believe this. Oh, God. God. Why? Why? How could I have done this? I don't even remember if I did it."

Over the course of his interrogations, Michael came to believe what his interrogators were suggesting to him: that he—or rather, a side of him called "Bad Michael"—had killed his sister and that "Good Michael" had blocked the memory out. Eventually, on videotape, Michael falsely confessed to killing his sister. As part of his confession, he claimed that he was extremely jealous of his sister, who was friends with all the popular girls. "Every time I was going to be in the spotlight," he told police, "she grabbed it away from me.... She made me feel worthless." He said he hated his family and escaped to his room as often as he could, where he would become absorbed in a fantasy world of video games and books. In that fantasy world, Michael said, he would become an evil person named "Odin"—a name that appeared in several popular role-playing video games. He concluded that Stephanie had died, therefore, because "Odin came out to play." Michael told police that he couldn't remember details of the killing, but he did remember acting out of "pure rage." Eventually, Michael's friend Joshua Treadway was also subjected to lengthy interrogations by police. Joshua, too, eventually falsely confessed to participating in Stephanie's murder, giving police a statement based in part on his knowledge of *Dungeons and Dragons.*

To the horror of the Crowe family, Michael and his friend Joshua were charged with Stephanie's murder, along with a third youth whom Joshua had implicated named Aaron

---

13. The information for this section was taken from Warden & Drizin (2009), and *Crowe v. County of San Diego*, 2010.

Houser. However, the charges against them were dismissed after DNA testing revealed the presence of Stephanie's blood on both a sweatshirt and an undershirt that belonged to a local, mentally ill transient named Richard Tuite. Tuite was subsequently convicted of killing Stephanie and sentenced to thirteen years in prison.[14]

Importantly, Michael Crowe—and, to an extent, Joshua Treadway—ended up telling a false story that fit in almost every respect to the narrative of the angry teenage loner. The story was replete with the jealousies of a misfit child who sought a violent outlet for his pent-up rage, inspired by and practically living in a dark fantasy world. In this sense, the fit between Michael's confession and the trope of the angry teenage loner—a cultural type that was then exploding into the national consciousness in the wake of the Moses Lake, Pearl High, and West Paducah school shootings—cannot be coincidence. Instead, it is in all probability an example of narrative contamination, one that would have resonated with jurors if Michael or Joshua had gone to trial. Indeed, had Stephanie's DNA not been found on Tuite's clothing, Michael's confession—built on the foundational trope of the angry teenage loner—would probably have led to his wrongful conviction.

*Thomas Cogdell.*[15] Several years later, in Camden, Arkansas, a different murder led to a different juvenile confession built on the angry teenage loner trope—a confession whose reliability has been widely questioned, though it has never been proven false as definitively as that of Michael Crowe (Phil, 2012). In that case, eleven-year-old Kaylee Cogdell was found dead in the morning of August 7, 2006, in the rural Arkansas home she shared with her mother Melody Jones and her twelve-year-old brother Thomas Cogdell, all of whom were white. Melody and Thomas found Kaylee's body lying on her bed, where she had been asphyxiated with two Wal-Mart bags and tied up with a dog leash and seamstress tape. Melody's wallet, moreover, was found in the back yard.

Just as in the Crowe case, police did not suspect an outside intruder, despite the wallet's location. Instead, they focused almost immediately on twelve-year-old Thomas as their prime suspect. Thomas was an honor student—one reporter described him as a "reclusive bookworm"—who spoke with a speech impediment and had only one close friend. He was going through a "Gothic stage," according to his mother, and like Michael Crowe enjoyed role-playing video games such as *Final Fantasy*. Kaylee, on the other hand, was described to police as a popular girl who was like a "little ray of sunshine." In the words of their mother, Kaylee was Tigger while Thomas was Eeyore.

When Melody Jones told police during her interview that Thomas enjoyed role-playing video games, the investigators immediately seized on that theory: "Do you think that they may have started maybe doing some role playing and it got out of hand maybe?" one officer asked Melody. When she responded that Kaylee's death couldn't have been accidental because she had been tied up, the officer responded that the tying up "may have been [from] some of the books that he had been reading lately or some of the, I don't know what that Final Fantasy thing is, that thing does."

After developing this theory during Melody's interview, investigators next turned to Thomas. While police video-cameras rolled, he described the night before her death, when he and his mother had gone to church to watch Kaylee star in a play. After the play, Kaylee and Melody had gone off to have "girl time" together, leaving Thomas at home. Thomas reported that he had played *Fantasy 10* when they left, and described his familiarity

---

14. Tuite's conviction for voluntary manslaughter has since been overturned, but Escondido authorities have indicated an intent to retry him due to "the seriousness of the crime and public safety" (Stickney, 2012).

15. The information in this section, unless otherwise noted, is taken from *T.C. v. State and Warren*, 2012.

with it and other similar role-playing video games like *Dungeons and Dragons*. After he finished playing *Fantasy 10*, he continued, he stayed up much of the night, reading a spooky book from the popular children's series *Goosebumps*. Thomas fell asleep on the couch and never heard anything suspicious.

Investigators pressed him, however, to describe a role-playing scenario between himself and Kaylee that got out of hand, resulting in her death. At investigators' prompting, Thomas acknowledged that he was occasionally resentful of his sister, but he insisted he never took part in her killing. Police told him that no one had broken in and that if he hadn't killed her, his mother must have done it. After denying involvement more than three dozen times, Thomas broke down in hysterical tears and incoherent mumbling. Telling Thomas to "cut this crap out," the investigators turned off the video-camera, which remained off for the next three hours.

When the camera was turned back on, a very different Thomas could be seen glibly reciting a confession to his sister's murder. According to that confession, Thomas had been playing his video game and was about to win when he heard a noise from Kaylee's room. Thomas asked her to keep quiet, but Kaylee refused, calling Thomas "just a little boy" and slamming the door in his face. Annoyed at the loss of his game and fuming at the disrespect his sister showed him, Thomas tried to read his dark-themed books, but his "frustration kept on building and building." Eventually, he said, he returned to his sister's room, smothered her with two WalMart bags until she passed out, and tied her wrists and ankles up. He claimed he threw the wallet in the back yard in order to preoccupy his mother and buy enough time for his sister to resume consciousness. He didn't realize that Kaylee had died, he told police. His intent had only been to "teach her a lesson not to disrespect people."

After giving the police this statement on videotape, Thomas was allowed to see his mother. With cameras still rolling, Thomas whispered to his mother not to worry—that his confession was not true and that he would not be convicted because police would not find any of his fingerprints at the crime scene. Despite his misplaced confidence—and despite the strange three-hour gap in his interrogation—Thomas was convicted of Kaylee's murder in juvenile court. His conviction was later overturned by the Arkansas Supreme Court because of errors in the administration of his *Miranda* rights. While his confession has never been officially disproven, many commentators, including the authors of this chapter, suspect that it is false.

Just like Michael Crowe's confession, the Camden police appear to have relied greatly on the angry teenage loner cultural type not only in scripting Thomas' confession, but also in choosing how to direct their investigation. They apparently became convinced of Thomas' guilt after his mother described him as "Gothic" and interested in role-playing fantasy games. Predictably, therefore, his confession features all the main points of the angry teenage loner trope, including misfit status, escapist video game-playing and book-reading, and resentfulness towards a more popular person. Indeed, Thomas' confession was likely all the more compelling because of this narrative contamination and its common cultural resonance.

# Conclusion

Whereas past articles on the problem of police contamination in false confessions have focused on fact contamination, in which the suspect incorporates true facts about the crime into his or her confession after police disclose those facts during interrogation, we have identified in this chapter what might be called a subset of this problem: narrative contamination. Under this type of contamination, law enforcement officers rely on common cultural stereotypes of youth to construct fictionalized details in false confessions that are neither proved nor disproved by the objective crime scene facts. These details and the tropes upon which they are based often demonize the defendants, making their confessions more persuasive to jurors and increasing the chances that jurors will convict them.

One important way to prevent both types of contamination is to require that all interrogations of suspects be electronically recorded in their entirety. Without a recording, there is simply no way for a fact-finder to spot contamination. When cases go to trial, the interrogators who took the confession inevitably claim that the suspect provided the details that only the true perpetrator could have known while the suspect invariably claims that the details were fed to him by the police. In the absence of a recording, judges and jurors are left to resolve these swearing contests and typically side with the police witnesses. In cases of proven false confessions, that result is simply wrong.

The existence of narrative contamination, however, makes the need for electronic recording even more compelling. Narrative contamination involves much more than the often inadvertent disclosure of facts to a suspect; it is the scripting of an entire false story, one that often relies on cultural stereotypes about why a certain type of person commits crimes. If fact contamination gives a confession the ring of truth, narrative contamination can elevate a confession to the realm of gospel truth. Electronic recording of the entire interrogation is an important way to enable jurors to separate true confessions from those that are, in reality, little more than pieces of pulp fiction.

# References

*A.M. v. Butler*, 360 F.3d 787, 793-94 (7th Cir. 2004).

Abcarian, R. (2013). Blurring reality stokes fears, raises ratings. *Los Angeles Times*. Retrieved from: http://www.latimes.com/local/la-me-abcarian-knockout-20131126,0,7313576.story?page=2#axzz2mKdgQYm6.

Annin, P. (1996). Superpredators arrive. *Newsweek*, p. 57.

Bond in teacher slaying. (1997, April 5). *Chicago Tribune*. Retrieved from: http://articles.chicagotribune.com/1997-04-05/news/9704050094_1_shooting-death-don-olmetti-sonia-hernandez.

Bragg, R. (1997, December 4). Theories but no answer in school shooting. *The New York Times*, p. A26.

Buchanan, P. (1989, April 30). The barbarians are winning. *New York Post*.

Burns, S. (2011). *The Central Park Five: A chronicle of a city wilding*. New York, NY: Knopf.

Cassidy, J. (1994, December 28). The ugliness of being a kid of the '90s: toughen laws for kids who commit vicious crimes. *Chicago Tribune*.

A closer look at rampage killings. (2000, April 13). *New York Times*, p. A30.

Clinton cites need for role models. (1994). *Chicago Sun Times*, p. 3.

Cloud, J. (2001, June 24). Of arms and the boy. *Time*. Retrieved from: http://content.time.com/time/magazine/article/0,9171,139492,00.html.

Collier, L. (1998, March 29). Adult crime, adult time, outdated juvenile laws thwart justice. *Washington Post*, p. C01. Retrieved from: http://www.washingtonpost.com/wp-srv/national/longterm/juvmurders/stories/adultcrime.htm.

*Corley v. United States*, 129 S. Ct. 1558, 1570 (2009).

*Crowe v. County of San Diego*, 608 F.3d 406 (9th Cir. 2010).

DiIulio, J. J. (1995a, December 15). Moral poverty: the coming of the super-predators should scare us into wanting to get to the root causes of crime a lot faster. *Chicago Tribune*, 3.

DiIulio, J. J. (1995b, November 27). The coming of the super-predators. *The Weekly Standard*, 23. Retrieved from http://cooley.libarts.wsu.edu/schwartj/criminology/ dilulio.pdf.

DiIulio, J. J. (1996). My black crime problem and ours. *City Journal*. Retrieved from http://www.city-journal.org/html/6_2_my_black.html.

Dr. Phil. (2012, August 8). Did he or didn't he? Inside a murder confession. Retrieved from, http://drphil.com/shows/show/1843/.

Drizin, S. A. (1999). Race, class, religion, politics cloud juvenile justice. *Chicago Sun Times*, 31.

Drizin, S. A., & Leo, R. A. (2004). The Problem of False Confessions in the Post-DNA Age. *North Carolina Law Review, 82*, 891-1007.

False confessions. *Innocence Project*. Retrieved from http://www.innocenceproject.org/ understand/False-Confessions.php.

Frymer, B. (2009). The Media Spectacle of Columbine: Alienated Youth as an Object of Fear, *American Behavioral Scientist*, 1387-1404.

Garrett, B. L. (2011). Convicting the innocent: where criminal prosecutions go wrong. Cambridge, MA: *Harvard University Press*.

Gibbs, Nancy. (1994, September 19). The short violent life of "Yummy" Sandifer: so young to die, so young to kill. *Time*.

Greene, B. (1996, April 29). When right and wrong are words without meaning. *Chicago Tribune*, 1.

Greenya, J. (2005, February 4). Bullying. *CQ Researcher, 15*, 101-124. Retrieved from http://library.cqpress.com/cqresearcher/.

Gross, S. R., Jacoby, K., Matheson, D. J., Montgomery, N., & Patil, S., (2005). Exonerations in the United States, 1989 through 2003. *Journal of Criminal Law and Criminology, 95*, 523-560.

Harris, Eric. (1998, November 12). Eric Harris' Journal. Retrieved from http://acolumbine site.com/eric/writing/journal/journal.html.

Hill, J. (1999, May 21). Youth jailed for 2 years goes home. *Chicago Tribune*. Retrieved from, http://articles.chicagotribune.com/1999-05-21/news/9905210254_1_weapons-charges-don-olmetti-cook-county-jail.

International Association of Chiefs of Police (2012). *Reducing Risks: An Executive's Guide to Effective Juvenile Interview and Interrogation*. Washington, DC: Office of Juvenile Justice and Delinquency Prevention.

*J.D.B. v. North Carolina*, 131 S.Ct. 1394, 1401 (2011).

James, S.D. (2009, April 20). Surviving Columbine: What We Got Wrong. *ABCNews*.

Johnson, D., & Brooke, J. (1999, April 22). Terror in Littleton: the suspects; portrait of outcasts seeking to stand out. *The New York Times*.

Kassin, S. M. (2008). Confession evidence: commonsense myths and misconceptions. *Criminal Justice and Behavior, 35*, 1309-1322.

King, S. (2013, February 1). Stephen King: Why the US Must Introduce Limited Gun Controls. *The Guardian*.

Kinkel, K. (Interviewee). (2000). *Frontline* [Interview transcript]. Retrieved from Frontline's webpage for the episode "The Killer at Thurston High": http://www.pbs.org/wgbh/ pages/frontline/shows/kinkel/kip/kristin.html.

Kotlowitz, A. (1999, February 8). The unprotected. *The New Yorker*.

Kuzka, S., & McRoberts, F. (1994). 5 year-old was killed over candy: boy refuses to shoplift and is dropped 14 floors to his death police say. *Chicago Tribune*, 1.

Leo, R.A. (2009). Police interrogations and American justice. Cambridge, MA: *Harvard University Press*.

Meyer, J. R., & Reppucci, N. D. (2007) Police practices and perceptions regarding juvenile interrogation and interrogative suggestibility, *Behavioral Sciences and the Law, 25,* 757-770.

*Miller v. Alabama*, 10-9647, 10-9646, Brief of Jeffrey Fagan et al. as *Amici Curiae* in Support of Petitioners (2012).

Moriearty, P. L., & Carson, W. (2012). Cognitive warfare and young black males in America. *Journal of Gender, Race, & Justice, 15,* 281-313.

Nirider, L. H., Tepfer, J. A., & Drizin, S. A. (2012). Combating contamination in confession cases: convicting the innocent: where criminal prosecutions go wrong. *The University of Chicago Law Review, 79,* 837-49.

Ogintz, E. (1989, May 24). Wounded childhood: many youngsters don't need TV to show them the face of war. *Chicago Tribune*, 1.

*People v. Johnson*, No. 1-12-0201, 2013 IL App (1st) 120201-U (March 29, 2013).

Pertman, A. (1996, April 11). States Racing to Prosecute Young Offenders as Adults. *Boston Globe*, 1.

Pitts, Byron (correspondent) (2012, December 9) Chicago: The False Confession Capital. [*60 Minutes*]. Rosen, I. & Schonder G. (Producers), New York, New York: CBS News.

Revenge of the Krath. (1998, January 18). *The New York Times*. Retrieved from: http://www.nytimes.com/1998/01/18/magazine/sunday-january-18-1998-crime-revenge-of-the-krath.html.

Sack, K. (1997a, November 13). Youth held as cult killer places blame on a friend. *The New York Times*, A14.

Sack, K. (1997b, October 15). Grim details emerge in teen-age slaying case: a manuscript tells of a cult bent on killing. *The New York Times*, A10. Retrieved from: http://www.nytimes.com/1997/11/13/us/youth-held-as-cult-killer-places-blame-on-a-friend.html.

Schiraldi, V. (2001, February 5). Will the real John DiIulio please stand up. *Washington Post*. Retrieved from: https://www.commondreams.org/views01/0205-02.htm.

*School Violence: Views of Students and the Community*: Hearing before the Subcommittee on Early Childhood, Youth, and Families, *House of Representatives*, 106th Cong. 1 (1999). Retrieved from http://commdocs.house.gov/committees/edu/hedcew6-42.000/hedcew6-42.htm.

Stephen King plot played out in school shooting. (1996, April 12). Associated Press: *Telegraph Herald (Dubuque, IA)*.

Stickney, R., Heaslet, M, Shin, T. & Garske, M. Richard (2012, Oct. 24) Richard Tuite Returns to Court. *ABC7 San Diego*. Retrieved from, http://www.nbcsandiego.com/news/local/Stephanie-Crowe-Richard-Tuite-Hearing-San-Diego-Escondido-Girl-175602071.html.

Tatum, L. (1999, December 19). Common threads found in school shooters: narcissism, rage can be a deadly combination. *The Daily Oklahoman*. Retrieved from: http://newsok.com/common-threads-found-in-school-shooters-narcissism-rage-can-be-a-deadly-combination/article/2679339.

*Taylor v. Rednour*, No. 11-3212 (7th Cir. Oct. 25, 2011).

Teen convicted in murder of teacher, classmates. (1997, September 25). *Washington Post*, A02.

Templeton, R. (1998): Superscapegoating: teen superpredator hype set stage for draconian legislation. *Extra!*. Retrieved from http://www.fair.org/index.php?page=1414.

Tepfer, J. A., Cooley, C. M., & Thompson, T. (2012). Convenient scapegoats: juvenile confessions and exculpatory DNA in Cook County, Illinois. *Cardozo Journal of Law and Gender, 18,* 631-684.

Tepfer, J. A., Nirider, L. H., & Tricarico, L. (2010). Arresting development: convictions of innocent youth. *Rutgers Law Review, 62,* 887-941.

Tizon, A. (1997). Scarred by killings, Moses Lake asks: what has this town become? *Seattle Times*. Retrieved from: http://community.seattletimes.nwsource.com/archive/?date=19970223&slug=2525360.

Toppo, G. (2009). 10 years later, the real story behind Columbine. *USA Today*. Retrieved from http://usatoday30.usatoday.com/news/nation/2009-04-13-columbine-myths_N.htm.

United States Census Bureau, Cook County, population, 2012 estimate. Retrieved from http://quickfacts.census.gov/qfd/states/17/17031.html.

Wang, Y., Mathews, V.P., Kalnin, A.J., Mosier, K.M., Dunn, D.W., Saykin, A.J., Kronenberger, W.G. (2009). Short term exposure to a violent video game induces changes in frontolimbic circuitry in adolescents. *Brain Imaging and Behavior, 2,* 38-50.

Warden, R. & Drizin, S. A. (2009). *True stories of false confessions*. Chicago, IL: Northwestern University Press.

What Eric Morse's heroism teaches. (1994). *Chicago Tribune*. Retrieved from: http://articles.chicagotribune.com/1994-10-19/news/9410190235_1_eric-morse-moral-core-killers.

What is pulp fiction. (1996). *The Vintage Library*. Retrieved from http://www.vintage library.com/pulpfiction/introduction/What-Is-Pulp-Fiction.php.

Williams, M. (1997 December 7). Violence goes to high school. *Atlanta Constitution*.

Youth Violence: A report of the Surgeon General (2001). Retrieved from http://www.surgeongeneral.gov/library/youthviolence/chapter1/sec2.html#myths.

# Chapter Twelve

# "The Worst of Both Worlds": Adolescent Competence and the Quality of Justice in Juvenile Courts as a Prescription for Wrongful Convictions

Barry C. Feld, *University of Minnesota*

## Introduction

Nearly fifty years ago, the Supreme Court observed that "the child receives the worst of both worlds: ... he gets neither the protections accorded to adults nor the solicitous care and regenerative treatment postulated for children" (*Kent v. United States*, 1966, p. 556). Juveniles today continue to receive "the worst of both worlds" because two competing images of youth influence juvenile justice policies. Policy makers sometimes describe young people as vulnerable children who need special safeguards to protect themselves from their own immaturity. At other times, they characterize youths as mature and responsible and treat them just like adults. They pick and choose between these competing images, but decline to recognize the developmental characteristics of youths that would warrant greater procedural safeguards. Rather, they treat juveniles just like adults when formal equality results in practical inequality and endorse juvenile court procedures that provide delinquents with less effective protections than those enjoyed by adult criminal defendants. Relying on these competing constructions of adolescents raises questions about the adequacy of juvenile court procedures and juveniles' competence to exercise legal rights. This, in turn, affects the reliability of evidence and the accuracy of judicial fact-finding and increases the potential for wrongful convictions.

This chapter examines research on youths' ability to exercise rights and its implications for juvenile court practice. It addresses youths' competence to stand trial, police interrogation of juveniles, pretrial screening processes, access to counsel, and the right to a jury trial. It argues that the diminished competence of juveniles and the less stringent procedural safeguards of juvenile courts are a prescription for wrongful convictions. The first section of the chapter "steps back" to review the adjudicative process and assess the ability of juveniles to navigate it. The second section "moves forward" by offering policy recommendations to address juvenile courts' chronic procedural deficiencies which can heighten the risk of wrongful convictions.

# Stepping Back: Adolescents' Competence in the Juvenile Justice System

The competence of adolescents to navigate the many facets of the juvenile justice system has long been a topic of social scientific and legal scholarship. This section will review the research, providing background on why the juvenile justice system may be prone to producing erroneous convictions. The section is split into seven parts. Part one briefly reviews juvenile justice policy-makers' conflicted conception of juveniles' competence to exercise rights. Part two then reviews developmental psychological research on adolescents' competence and their ability to exercise rights. Part three assays youths' competence to stand trial. The fourth part analyzes juveniles' ability to exercise *Miranda* rights, contrasts the legal standards with psychological research on juveniles' competence, and highlights their vulnerability in the interrogation room. Part five considers informal "gate-keeping" decisions at the front of the juvenile court which may result in erroneous diversions and collateral consequences. Part six examines juveniles' competence to waive counsel, the impact of waiver on delivery of legal services, and appellate courts' inability to review delinquency convictions. Finally, part seven examines the denial to juveniles of a constitutional right to a jury trial, which undermines accurate fact-finding and makes it easier to convict delinquents than adult criminal defendants.

## Competing Conceptions of Juveniles' Competence and Procedural Rights

A century ago, juvenile courts separated children from adult offenders, treated them rather than punished them, and rejected the procedural safeguards of criminal prosecutions. Progressive reformers gave juvenile court judges broad discretion to make dispositions in a child's "best interests." They characterized children as irresponsible and incompetent. Because delinquency proceedings focused primarily on a child's background and future welfare rather than proving the facts of a criminal act, juvenile courts dispensed with formal procedures such as lawyers, juries, and rules of evidence (Feld, 1999; Tanenhaus, 2004).

In 1967, the Supreme Court in *In re Gault* (1967) began a "due process revolution" that substantially transformed the juvenile court from a social welfare agency into a more formal, legal institution (Feld, 1984; 1988a; 1999; Scott & Steinberg, 2008). Among other safeguards, *Gault* granted delinquents a right to counsel and the Fifth Amendment privilege against self-incrimination, and initiated a procedural convergence between juvenile and criminal courts (Feld, 1984). Although Progressive reformers characterized young people as immature and irresponsible to reject procedural safeguards, *Gault* viewed youths as competent to exercise legal rights in an adversarial process. Subsequent decisions further emphasized the criminal nature of delinquency proceedings. *In re Winship* (1970) held that the state must prove delinquency "beyond a reasonable doubt" rather than by the lower "preponderance of the evidence" standard in civil cases. *Breed v. Jones* (1975) posited a functional equivalence between delinquency and criminal trials and held that the Fifth Amendment's double jeopardy clause barred criminal re-prosecution of a youth after a judge had adjudicated him delinquent. However, *McKeiver v. Pennsylvania* (1971) declined to give delinquents all criminal procedural safeguards and denied a constitutional right to a jury trial. The absence of a jury affects administration of evidentiary issues, the accuracy of fact-finding, and the presence and performance of counsel (Feld, 1984). These procedural differences increase the likelihood of erroneous fact-finding and wrongful convictions in juvenile courts (Drizin & Luloff, 2007; Feld, 2003a).

Macro-economic and racial demographic changes in American cities during the 1970s and 1980s contributed to an increase in black youth homicide rates in the late 1980s and early 1990s as the crack cocaine epidemic spurred gun violence (Feld, 1999; 2003b; 2007). By the end of the twentieth century, states adopted harsh, get tough policies that equated the crimes and culpability of adolescents with those of adults — "adult crime, adult time." In the early 1990s, states revised laws to transfer more and younger juveniles to criminal courts, and to punish more severely delinquents who remained in juvenile courts (Torbet et al., 1996). These changes replaced the view of children as immature and irresponsible with one in which the law regarded them as responsible and adult-like offenders (Feld, 2003b). The increased punitiveness of both the juvenile and criminal justice systems' responses to offending youth raise urgent questions about their competence to exercise legal rights, the accuracy of juvenile justice administration, and the consequences of erroneous adjudications.

## Adolescent Competence and Procedural Justice

Despite developmental differences between adolescents and adults, the Court and most states do not provide youths with additional procedural safeguards to protect them from their immaturity and vulnerability. Instead, states use adult legal standards to gauge juveniles' competence to stand trial, to waive *Miranda* rights, and to relinquish the right to counsel. Because developmental immaturity impairs youths' competence to exercise rights, formal legal equality results in practical inequality. By contrast, when states have the option to provide delinquents with procedural safeguards comparable with criminal defendants such as a jury trial, they use less effective juvenile court procedures that provide the state an advantage and make it is easier to convict a youth (Feld, 1984; 2003a).

Created in response to the get tough policies of the 1990s, the John D. and Catherine T. MacArthur Foundation sponsored a decade-long interdisciplinary network on Adolescent Development and Juvenile Justice (ADJJ) to study juveniles' decision making, judgment, adjudicative competence, and culpability (Scott & Steinberg, 2008; http://www.adjj.org). Research on competence focused on how adolescents think, their decision-making capacities, and how their limitations affect their ability to work with counsel and participate in the justice systems. The ADJJ research reported a disjunction between youths' cognitive abilities and mature judgment (Feld, 2008; Scott &Steinberg, 2008). The research reports that by age sixteen or seventeen, adolescents possess cognitive abilities similar to adults, but their judgment and self-control does *not* correspond with that of adults until their twenties. Moreover, younger and mid-adolescent youths exhibit substantial deficits in understanding and judgment which affect their competence to stand trial, their ability to exercise or waive *Miranda* rights, and their ability to assert their right to counsel and work with an attorney. These deficits in judgment and competence increase their likelihood to make erroneous decisions — *e.g.*, to confess falsely or to relinquish counsel at trial — and increase their risks for wrongful convictions.

**Children are different: Law and developmental psychology.** In 2005 the Supreme Court, in *Roper v. Simmons* (2005), barred states from executing youths for crimes committed prior to eighteen years of age. *Roper* reviewed changes in state statutes and jury practices and found a national consensus against executing juveniles. The justices conducted an independent proportionality analysis and concluded that youths' immature judgment, susceptibility to negative peer influences, and transitory personality development reduced their culpability and barred the most severe sentence. In 2010, the Court in *Graham v. Florida*, (2010), extended *Roper's* diminished responsibility rationale and prohibited states from imposing life without parole (LWOP) sentences on youths convicted of non-homicide offenses. Two years later, the Court in *Miller v. Alabama*, (2012) used *Roper's* and *Graham's* diminished responsibility rationale to bar *mandatory* LWOP sentences for youths convicted of murder. All three decisions affirmed that "children are different" from adults and do not deserve as harsh punishment for their crimes. They shared the same developmental premises that immature judgment and impaired self-control cause youth to act impulsively and without full appreciation of consequences, reduce their culpability, and compromise their competence. Deficits in judgment and self-control and greater susceptibility than adults to social influences also affects youths' understanding of and competence to exercise legal rights. The Court's decisions rested, in part, on the MacArthur Foundation's developmental research.

The ADJJ research distinguishes between youths' cognitive abilities and their maturity of judgment (www.adjj.org; Feld, 2008; Scott & Steinberg, 2008). By mid-adolescence, most youths can distinguish right from wrong and reason similarly to adults (Scott and Steinberg, 2008; Steinberg & Cauffman, 1999). For example, youths and adults make informed consent medical decisions similarly (Morse, 1997). But the ability to make good choices when provided with complete information in a laboratory differs from the ability to make good decisions under stressful conditions with incomplete information (Cauffman & Steinberg, 1995; Spear, 2000; Steinberg & Cauffman, 1996). Emotions influence youths' decision-making and researchers distinguish between choices made under conditions of "cold cognition" and "hot cognition" (Aronson, 2007; Dahl, 2000; 2004).

Even though adolescents by about sixteen years of age exhibit cognitive abilities comparable with adults, they do not develop mature judgment and self-control until their early-twenties (Feld, 2008; Scott, Reppuci, & Woolard, 1995; Scott & Steinberg, 2003). Youths' immature judgment results from differences from adults in risk perception, appreciation of future consequences, capacity for self-management, and experience with autonomy (Morse, 1997; Scott &Steinberg, 2003). Youths' poorer decisions reflect differences in knowledge and experience, short-term versus long-term time perspectives, attitude toward risk, and impulsivity which are normal features of adolescent development (Scott & Grisso, 1997; Scott, Reppucci, & Woolard, 1995; Scott & Steinberg, 2003). To a greater extent than adults, adolescents underestimate risks, use a shorter time-frame in their calculus, and emphasize gains rather than losses (Furby & Beyth-Marom, 1992; Grisso, 2000; Scott, 2000). Adolescents possess less information and consider fewer options than do adults (Scott, 2000). Younger teens act more impulsively than do older adolescents or adults. Youths' risk perception actually *declines* during mid-adolescence and then gradually increases into adulthood—sixteen and seventeen year olds perceive fewer risks than do either younger or older research subjects. They are more present-oriented and discount future consequences. They weigh costs and benefits differently than do adults and apply different subjective values to outcomes to their choices (Scott & Steinberg, 2008). Youths view *not* engaging in risky behaviors differently than do adults (Scott, 1992; Scott & Steinberg, 2003; 2008). They crave excitement and heightened sensations—an adrenaline rush (Scott & Grisso, 1997; Spear, 2000). These differences in judgment, self-control, and appreciation of consequences cause youths to make more impulsive legal decisions which increase their risk of wrongful convictions.

**Neuroscience: Judgment and impulse control.** The human brain does not mature until the early twenties, and the differences that social scientists observe in youths' and adults' thinking and behavior reflect these developmental features (Dahl, 2000; 2004; Maroney, 2009; Scott & Steinberg, 2008; Sowell et al., 1999; 2001 Spear, 2000). Adolescents do not have the physiological capacity of adults to exercise mature judgment or control impulses (Dahl, 2004; Gruber & Yurgelun-Todd, 2006). Two neurobiological systems underlie youths' propensity for risky behavior. The prefrontal cortex (PFC) of the frontal lobe of the brain is responsible for judgment and impulse control, and the limbic system is responsible for emotional and reward-seeking behavior. The PFC operates as the Chief Executive Officer to control executive functions such as reasoning, planning, anticipating consequences, and controlling impulses (Aronson, 2009; Kandel et al., 2000).

The limbic system—the amygdala—controls instinctual behavior, such as the fight-or-flight response (Kandel et al., 2000). Adolescents rely more heavily on the limbic system and less heavily on the PFC than do adults (Scott & Steinberg, 2008). During adolescence, the two systems are out of balance as limbic system activity increases while the prefrontal regulatory system lags behind. Pleasure-seeking and emotional reward responses develop more rapidly than does the system for self-control and self-regulation (Arrendondo, 2003). The neuroscience helps to explain adolescents' impulsive behavior and susceptibility to social influence.

**Adolescents' competence and legal standards.** Contemporary delinquency proceedings are much more procedurally formal than those envisioned a century ago. Progressive reformers assumed that children lacked competence to exercise rights and posited a procedurally informal court that acted in the child's best interests. *Gault* granted delinquents the right to counsel and Fifth Amendment privilege against self-incrimination, made delinquency proceedings more formal and complex, and required youths to make difficult legal decisions. Developmental psychologists question whether younger juveniles possess competence to stand trial and whether adolescents have the cognitive ability, maturity and judgment necessary to exercise *Miranda* rights during interrogation, or to waive counsel at trial. The developmental research reviewed previously—impaired judgment, poor self-control, skewed risk-calculus, short-term time perspective, and impulsive decisions—convincingly indicates that younger and mid-adolescent youths exhibit substantial deficits in understanding and competence compared with adults. Despite clear developmental differences between youths and adults, the Court and most states do not provide additional procedural safeguards to protect juveniles from their own immaturity and vulnerability and thereby increase the likelihood that youths' limitations will produce erroneous outcomes.

# Competence to Stand Trial

As juvenile court proceedings have become more formal and punitive, analysts increasingly question juveniles' ability to function in complex legal settings with significant penal consequences. To be competent to stand trial, a defendant must have "sufficient present ability to consult with his lawyer with a reasonable degree of rational understanding [and have a] rational as well as factual understanding of the proceedings against him," and have the capacity "to assist in preparing his defense" (*Dusky v. United States*, 1960, p. 402; *see also Drope v. Missouri*, 1975). Competence to stand trial hinges on a defendant's ability to understand proceedings; to provide, receive, and understand information from counsel; and to make reasonable choices (Bonnie & Grisso, 2000; Grisso, 2000).

Developmental psychologists contend that adolescents' immaturity produces the same deficits of understanding, impairment of judgment, and inability to assist counsel as does severe mental illness or mental retardation (Grisso, 1997; 2000; Scott & Grisso, 2005). These generic developmental limitations adversely affect their ability to understand proceedings, to make rational decisions, and to consult with and assist counsel (Grisso, 1997; Scott & Grisso, 2005). Research on competence reports significant age-related developmental differences in understanding and judgment (Grisso et al., 2003). Most juveniles younger than thirteen or fourteen years of age exhibited impairments similar to adults with severe mental illnesses and lacked the ability to assist or to participate in their defense (Bonnie & Grisso, 2000; Grisso et al., 2003). A significant proportion of juveniles younger than sixteen years of age lacked competence to stand trial and many older youths exhibited substantial impairments (Grisso et al., 2003). Juveniles with below average intelligence— a characteristic of many delinquents—exhibited greater impairment than did either low-intelligence adults or juveniles with normal intelligence (Grisso et al., 2003). Even formally competent adolescents made poorer decisions than did young adults because they emphasized short-term over long-term outcomes and sought peer approval (Bonnie & Grisso, 2000; Scott & Grisso, 1997; Steinberg & Caufman, 1999). The Court in *Graham* noted how these characteristics adversely affected juveniles' ability to exercise procedural rights and impaired their defense representation:

> [T]he features that distinguish juveniles from adults also put them at a significant disadvantage in criminal proceedings. Juveniles mistrust adults and have limited understandings of the criminal justice system and the roles of the institutional actors within it. They are less likely than adults to work effectively with their lawyers to aid in their defense. Difficulty in weighing long-term consequences; a corresponding impulsiveness; and reluctance to trust defense counsel seen as part of the adult world a rebellious youth rejects, all can lead to poor decisions by one charged with a juvenile offense. These factors are likely to impair the quality of a juvenile defendant's representation (*Graham v. Florida*, 2010, p. 2032).

Thus, adolescents' questionable adjudicative competence impairs their ability to assist counsel in preparing a defense, increases the risk that legitimate defenses will go unrecognized or undeveloped, and compounds the likelihood that youths may enter false guilty pleas.

About half the states address juveniles' competency to stand trial in statutes, court rules of procedure, or case law and conclude that delinquents have a fundamental right not to be tried while incompetent (Feld, 2013b; Scott & Grisso, 2005). Even after states recognize juveniles' right to a competency determination, they differ over the appropriate standard to apply. Some courts apply the adult competency standard in delinquency and criminal prosecutions because both proceedings may result in a child's loss of liberty. Other jurisdictions opt for a more-relaxed competency standard in delinquency than in criminal proceedings, because juvenile hearings are less complex and the consequences less severe than criminal proceedings (Scott & Grisso, 2005). However, courts do not routinely initiate competency evaluations even for very young offenders and many delinquents may face charges without understanding the legal process or the ability to work with counsel (Feld, 2013b). Their lack of adjudicative competence and inability to assist counsel undermines the justice system's ability to provide a fundamentally fair trial or to assure the factual accuracy of guilty pleas.

# Juveniles and Police Interrogation

The Supreme Court has decided more cases about interrogating youths than any other issue in juvenile justice (Feld, 2013a). Although the Court repeatedly cautioned that youthfulness adversely affects juveniles' ability to exercise *Miranda* or make voluntary statements, it has not required special procedures to protect young suspects. Rather, it endorsed the adult waiver standard — "knowing, intelligent, and voluntary" — to gauge juveniles' *Miranda* waivers (*Fare v. Michael C.*, 1979).

**Interrogating juveniles: "Law on the books."** In the decades prior to *Miranda*, the Court adopted a protectionist stance and cautioned judges to examine closely how youthfulness affected voluntariness of confessions (Feld, 1999; 2013a). *Haley v. Ohio* (1948) emphasized that a fifteen-year old boy's youth and inexperience increased his vulnerability and rendered his confession involuntary. *Gallegos v. Colorado* (1962) found that age was a special circumstance that rendered a fourteen-year-old boy's confession involuntary. *In re Gault* (1967) reiterated that youthfulness undermined the reliability of juveniles' statements and granted the privilege against self-incrimination in delinquency proceedings. Although some analysts advocate relaxed procedural safeguards in juvenile courts to foster a rehabilitative or preventive mission (Scott & Grisso, 2005), *Winship* and *Breed* recognized juvenile courts' criminal aspects and *Gault* highlighted their adversarial character.

The Court in *Miranda v. Arizona* (1966) required police to warn suspects of their right to remain silent and to counsel in order to dispel the coercive pressures of custodial interrogation. *Fare v. Michael C.* (1979) held that the test used to evaluate adults' *Miranda* waivers — "knowing, intelligent, and voluntary" under the totality of the circumstances — governed juveniles' waivers as well. *Fare* reasoned that *Miranda* provided an objective basis to evaluate waivers, denied that youths' developmental differences required special procedural protections, and required children to assert rights clearly (Feld, 2013a). *Miranda* provided that if police question a suspect who is in custody — arrested or "deprived of his freedom of action in any significant way" — they must administer a warning. The Court in *J.D.B. v. North Carolina* (2011) considered "whether the *Miranda* custody analysis includes consideration of a juvenile suspect's age," and reasoned that age was an objective fact that would affect whether a young person felt restrained.

Most states use *Fare*'s totality framework for juveniles and adults (Feld, 2013a). Trial judges consider characteristics of the offender — age, education, I.Q., and prior police contacts — and the context of interrogation — the location, methods, and length of questioning — when they evaluate *Miranda* waivers. Appellate courts do not assign controlling weight to any factor and the totality approach provides no meaningful check on trial judges' discretion (Feld, 2000; 2006a). Judges find valid *Miranda* waivers by children as young as ten years of age with no prior police contacts, with limited intelligence, and without parental assistance (Feld, 2000; 2013a).

About ten states provide additional safeguards beyond the "totality" approach endorsed by *Fare* (Feld, 2006a; 2006b). They require the presence of a parent or other interested adult at a juvenile's interrogation as a prerequisite to a valid *Miranda* waiver. They presume that most juveniles lack competence to exercise *Miranda* rights and require an adult's assistance. They assume that a parent's presence will enhance juveniles' understanding of their rights, mitigate the dangers of unreliable statements, provide an independent witness of what occurs, and reduce police coercion. As juvenile justice has become more punitive, youths need additional procedural safeguards to achieve functional parity with adult defendants (*State v. Presha*, 2000]). Moreover, parents are the practical means by which juveniles can secure their *Miranda* right to counsel. While parents may have greater understanding than their children, their knowledge is incomplete, especially about tactics that police may use during interrogation (Woolard et al., 2008). Commentators endorse parental-presence safeguards, even though reasons exist to question the validity of the assumptions (Feld, 2013a).

**Juveniles' ability to exercise rights: Developmental psychology.** Developmental and social psychologists question whether juveniles have the cognitive capacity or maturity to make "knowing, intelligent, and voluntary" waivers. Research by Thomas Grisso reports that many juveniles do not understand a *Miranda* warning well enough to make a knowing and intelligent waiver of rights (Grisso, 1980; 1981). The language and concepts contained in a *Miranda* warning require reading levels and understanding beyond that possessed by most delinquents (Feld, 2013a). Juveniles most frequently misunderstood that they had the right to consult with an attorney and to have a lawyer present when police questioned them (Grisso, 1980; 1981). Similarly to research discussed earlier on juveniles' adjudicative competence, youths fifteen years of age and younger exhibited significantly limited understanding of *Miranda*'s words and concepts (Grisso, 1980). Although older juveniles exhibited a level of understanding comparable with adults, substantial minorities of both groups failed to grasp some elements of the standard warning.

Juveniles often fail to appreciate the significance of rights or to understand that they can exercise them without adverse consequences (Grisso, 1997; Grisso, et al., 2003). This confirms *Graham*'s observation that they are less competent defendants. Juveniles view a right as something that authorities allow them to do but that they may unilaterally retract or withhold (Feld, 2013a). They misconceive the attorney role and client confidentiality. *Roper* and *Graham* emphasized youths' susceptibility to social influences as a factor that reduced culpability and diminished competence. Lower social status and expectations of obedience to authority make children more vulnerable than adults in the interrogation room. The *Miranda* Court characterized questioning in an interrogation room as an inherently coercive environment, and juveniles are especially susceptible to waive their rights and to tell their interrogators what they think they want to hear, even if untrue (Drizin & Luloff, 2007; Feld, 2013a). Youths respond more passively and acquiesce more easily to police suggestions. Adolescents' impulsivity and immaturity may cause them to confess falsely in order to end an interrogation, rather than to consider the long-term consequences. *Fare* requires juveniles to invoke *Miranda* rights clearly and unambiguously, but this expectation conflicts with the normal responses and verbal styles of most youths.

To summarize, developmental psychological research spanning decades consistently indicates that adolescents as a class are at a significant disadvantage in the interrogation room. For youths fifteen years of age and younger, these disabilities are clear and substantial. While juveniles sixteen and seventeen years of age exhibit some degree of impairment, they function comparably with adults. Because of developmental differences, using the same legal framework to judge juveniles' and adults' waivers of rights puts youth at a considerable disadvantage.

**Juveniles in the interrogation room: "Law in action."** Three decades of research reports that about 80 percent of adults and 90 percent of juveniles waive *Miranda* rights (Feld, 2013a; Goldstein &Goldstein, 2010; Grisso, 1980; Grisso & Pomiciter, 1977; Leo 2008). The largest empirical study of juvenile interrogations reported that 92.8% of youths waived *Miranda* (Feld, 2013a). Juveniles' higher waiver rates may reflect their lack of understanding or inability to invoke *Miranda* effectively, *i.e,.* vulnerability to coercion (Feld, 2013a). Once officers secured a juvenile's *Miranda* waiver, they use the same two-pronged strategy employed with adults to overcome suspects' resistance and to enable them more readily to admit responsibility (Feld, 2013a; Kassin, 2005; Kassin et al., 2010; Kassin & Gudjonsson, 2004). Maximization techniques intimidate suspects and impress on them the futility of denial, and minimization techniques provide moral justifications or face-saving alternatives to enable them to confess (Feld, 2013; Kassin, 2005; Leo, 2008). Despite youths' heightened susceptibility, police do not incorporate developmental differences into the tactics they employ (Owen-Kostelnik et al., 2006). Techniques designed to manipulate adults — aggressive questioning, presenting false evidence, and leading questions — may create unique dangers when employed with youths (Redlich & Drizin, 2007; Tanenhaus & Drizin, 2002). Police did not report receiving special training to question juveniles (Feld, 2013a) and used the same tactics they employed with adults (Feld, 2006b; Leo, 1996). Juveniles responded to those tactics, cooperated or resisted, and provided incriminating evidence at about the same rate as did adults.

As noted above, some states require a parent to assist juveniles in the interrogation room (Farber, 2004). However, analysts question whether they can provide practical protection (Feld, 2013a; Grisso, 1981; Grisso & Ring, 1979). Parents — as adults — may have somewhat greater understanding of *Miranda* than do their children, but both share fundamental misconceptions about police interrogation practices (Woolard et al., 2008). Parents did not provide children with useful legal advice, increased pressure to waive their rights, and urged them to tell the truth (Feld, 2013a). Parents may be emotionally upset or angry at their child's arrest, believe that confessing will produce a better outcome, or think that children should respect authority or assume responsibility (Feld, 2013a). Juveniles rarely spontaneously request a parent for a variety of reasons: estrangement from their parents, feeling that they cannot provide meaningful assistance, embarrassment or shame about their crime, or hope that their parents will not learn of their arrest (Feld, 2013a). If a parent is present, police either enlist them as allies in the interrogation or neutralize their presence. Officers tell parents that the role of police is to learn the truth and try to recruit parents as collaborators to learn the truth so as to better enable them to help their child. If parents do attend their child's interrogation, police try to render them as passive observers by seating them behind the child and instructing them not to intervene (Feld, 2013a). In the vast majority of interrogations at which parents were present, they did not participate after police advised them of the child's *Miranda* rights, sometimes switched sides to become active allies of the police, and played a protective role in only two (8%) interviews (Feld, 2013a).

Research on false confessions underscores the unique vulnerability of younger juveniles (Drizin & Leo 2004; Garrett, 2011; Gross et al., 2005). In one study, police obtained more than one-third (35 percent) of proven false confessions from suspects younger than eighteen (Drizin & Leo, 2004), and younger adolescents are at greater risk to confess falsely than older ones (Tepfer et al., 2010). In another study, false confessions occurred in 15% of cases, but juveniles accounted for 42% of all false confessors and among the youngest juveniles — those aged twelve to fifteen — more than two-thirds (69%) confessed to crimes they did not commit (Gross et al., 2005). Significantly, exonerated juveniles who confess falsely involve only the small population of youths whom states prosecuted as adults. This reflects the greater seriousness of their crimes, the greater pressure on police to solve them, and the longer period available to youths and their attorneys subsequently to correct the errors.

Developmental psychologists attribute their overrepresentation among false confessors to reduced cognitive ability, developmental immaturity, and increased susceptibility to manipulation (Bonnie & Grisso, 2000; Redlich et al., 2004). They have fewer life experiences or psychological resources with which to resist the pressures of interrogation (Redlich et al., 2004). Juveniles are more likely than are adults to comply with authority figures, tell police what they think they want to hear, and respond to negative feedback (Gudjonsson, 2003). Their impulsive decision-making and greater desire to obey and please authority figures heightens their risk. *Miranda* is especially problematic for younger juveniles who may not understand its words or concepts (Grisso, 1980; Grisso et al., 2003). The stress and anxiety of interrogation intensify their desire to extricate themselves in the short-run by waiving and confessing (Goldstein & Goldstein, 2010; Owen-Kostelnik et al., 2006). Developmental immaturity and diminished competence heighten juveniles' suggestibility. Police can more easily pressure, persuade, or manipulate them to make statements— including false ones— than they can adults. The generic vulnerabilities of youth multiply when coupled with mental illness, mental retardation, or compliant personalities. Juveniles' immature brains contribute to impulsive decision-making and limited ability to consider long-term consequences heighten their risk and increase their vulnerability to confess falsely (Gruber & Yurglin-Todd, 2006; Maroney, 2009). These cumulative risk factors heighten susceptibility to give false confessions (Feld, 2013a).

# Preliminary Screening Procedures: Intake and Diversion

A number of individuals make "front-end" decisions that affect the processing of youths. Police officers may refer youths to juvenile court intake for formal processing as well as decide whether to place a youth in a pretrial detention facility. Probation officers in a juvenile court's intake unit may refer a youth to the juvenile court for formal adjudication or dispose of the case through informal supervision or diversion to a program run by the juvenile court or some other social services or community agency (Mears, 2012). The intake function may be administered by the juvenile courts' probation department and/or the prosecutor's office. About fifty-five percent of all delinquency referrals are handled formally with the filing of a petition (Mears, 2012).

Of the cases handled informally, if intake does not dismiss the case—typically about one-fifth of all referrals—then the youth may "voluntarily" agree to informal sanctions or conditions for a period of time. These conditions may be outlined in a written agreement such as a "diversion contract" or "consent decree." The decision whether to divert a youth or impose informal probation typically occurs during an interview in an office with a probation officer, the juvenile, and a parent. Because intake evaluations occur prior to the filing of a formal petition, counsel will not be present. The intake decision involves both legal factors—the offense alleged—and social factors—the child's "best interests," problems, and needs. However, probation officers rely almost exclusively on police reports and a child's admission to establish the circumstances of the offense (Mears, 2012). Moreover, probation officers may have more of a social welfare orientation and tend to emphasize a child's "needs" rather than deeds (Mears, 2012). "The absence of legal training on the part of intake officers ... has often led to unrepresented youngsters' accepting terms of informal probation ... without anyone's having scrutinized the legal sufficiency of the case. Competent evaluation of the legal correctness of police interrogation or search and seizure practices should not be expected of intake officers ..." (Rubin, 1980, p. 308). Analysts have noted that, "The juvenile court traditionally has proceeded as if this situation—one where officers of the court render a legal assessments or decisions even though they lack legal training—were not a problem" (Mears. 2012, p. 581).

Referral to a diversion program may subject a factually and legally innocent youth to some type of informal supervision or intervention. Critics note that,

> there are cases where, at least some of the time, prosecutors would fail to adjudicate a youth as delinquent if the youth challenged the case. Such cases then would be dismissed. By admitting guilt and accepting an informal sanction, youths essentially close off any possibility of a dismissal. In addition, they create a situation where their case may appear worse—because of the admission of guilt and a record of violating the agreed-upon sanction—than if the original petition were challenged. In these cases, youths may face stiffer penalties, including placement in secure confinement (Mears 2012, p. 591).

Moreover, prosecutors and judges may consider a previous diversion—even if factually erroneous—when they charge or sentence a youth for a subsequent offense (Feld, 2013b).

## Juveniles' Competence to Waive Counsel or Plead Guilty

*Gault* compared a delinquency proceeding to a felony prosecution and granted juveniles the right to counsel. *Gault* relied on the Fourteenth Amendment Due Process Clause rather than the Sixth Amendment which guarantees criminal defendants' right to counsel (*Gideon v. Wainwright*, 1963), and did not order automatic appointment of counsel. Instead, *Gault* only required a judge to advise a child and parent of a right to counsel and to have counsel appointed if indigent. *Gault* ruled that juveniles could waive counsel and most states do not use any special measures to protect delinquents from their own improvident decisions, such as mandatory, non-waivable appointment of counsel (Feld, 1984, 1993). As with *Miranda* waivers, formal equality produced practical inequality—lawyers represent delinquents at much lower rates than they do adult criminal defendants (Burrus & Kempf-Leonard, 2002; Feld, 1988b, 1993; Harlow, 2000; Jones, 2000). Despite statutes and court rules of procedure that apply equally throughout a state, juvenile justice administration varies with urban, suburban, and rural context and produces "justice by geography" (Bray et al., 2005; Burrus & Kempf-Leonard 2002; Feld 1991, 1993; Feld & Schaefer 2010a, 2010b; Guevara et al., 2008). Lawyers appear more frequently in more formal, bureaucratized, and due-process-oriented urban courts (Burrus & Leonard, 2002; Feld, 1991, 1993). In turn, more formal courts tend to hold more youths in pre-trial detention and to sentence them more severely. Rural courts tend to be procedurally less formal (Burrus & Kempf-Leonard, 2002; Feld, 1991, 1993). Finally, a lawyer's presence appears to be an aggravating factor when judges sentence delinquents. After controlling for legal variables, judges sentence youths who appear with counsel more severely than they do those who appear without an attorney (Burrus & Kempf-Leonard, 2002; Feld, 1988b, 1991; Feld & Schaefer, 2010a). Several factors contribute to this consistent finding: lawyers who appear in juvenile court may be incompetent and prejudice their clients' cases; judges may pre-determine sentences and appoint counsel when they anticipate out-of-home placements; or judges may punish delinquents for exercising procedural rights (Feld, 1989, 1993; Feld & Schaefer, 2010a).

**Presence of counsel in juvenile courts.** When the Court decided *Gault*, lawyers seldom appeared in juvenile courts (Note 1966). Although states amended their juvenile codes to comply with *Gault*, the "law-in-action" lagged behind changes of the "law-on-the-books." Evaluations of initial compliance with *Gault* found that most judges did not advise juveniles of their rights and the vast majority did not appoint counsel (Canon & Kolson 1971; Ferster et al., 1971; Lefstein et al., 1969; Stapleton & Teitelbaum, 1972). Studies in several jurisdictions in the 1970s and early 1980s reported that juvenile courts failed to appoint counsel for most juveniles (Aday, 1986; Bortner, 1982; Clarke & Koch, 1980). Research in Minnesota in the mid-1980s reported that most youths appeared without counsel (Feld, 1988b, 1989, 1993), that rates of representation varied widely between urban, suburban and rural counties (Feld, 1991, 1993), and that nearly one-third of youths whom judges removed from their homes and about one-quarter of those whom they confined in institutions were unrepresented (Feld, 1989, 1993). A decade later, about one-quarter of juveniles removed from home were unrepresented despite law reform efforts to eliminate the practice (Feld & Schaefer, 2010a, 2010b). A study of delivery of legal services in six states reported that only three of them appointed counsel for a substantial majority of juveniles (Feld, 1988b). Studies in the 1990s described juvenile court judges' failure to appoint lawyers for many youths who appeared before them (Burruss & Kempf-Leonard, 2002; GAO, 1995). In 1995, the General Accounting Office (1995) confirmed that rates of representation varied widely among and within states and that judges tried and sentenced many unrepresented youths. Research in Missouri found urban, suburban and rural variation in rates of representation and reported that an attorney's presence increased a youth's likelihood to receive out-of-home placement (Burruss & Kempf-Leonard, 2002). Race, gender, and type of representation influenced sentencing severity in different court settings (Guevara et al., 2008).

In the mid-1990s the American Bar Association published two reports on juveniles' legal needs. The first reported that many children appeared without counsel and that the lawyers who represented youth lacked adequate training and often failed to provide effective assistance (ABA, 1993; Bishop & Farber, 2007). The second focused on the quality of defense lawyers, again reported that many youths appeared without counsel, and concluded that many attorneys failed to appreciate the challenges of representing young clients (ABA, 1995). Since the late 1990s, the ABA and the National Juvenile Defender Center have conducted more than a dozen state-by-state assessments of juveniles' access to and quality of counsel. These studies report that many, if not most, juveniles appear without counsel and that lawyers who represent youth often provide substandard assistance because of structural impediments to effective advocacy—heavy caseloads, inadequate resources, and the like (*see, e.g.,* Bookser, 2004; Brooks & Kamine, 2004; Celese & Puritz, 2001; Drizin & Luloff 2007; Puritz & Brooks, 2002; Puritz et al., 2002). Overburdened attorneys conduct fewer and less thorough investigations and provide less adequate representation. Poor investigations coupled with juveniles' lesser competence to assist counsel increase the likelihood of false guilty pleas and wrongful adjudications.

**Waivers of counsel and guilty pleas in juvenile court.** Several factors account for why so many youths appear in juvenile courts without counsel. Public-defender legal services may be inadequate or non-existent in non-urban areas (ABA, 1995). Judges may give cursory advisories of the right to counsel, imply that a rights colloquy and waiver are just legal technicalities without substance, and readily find waivers to ease courts' administrative burdens (ABA, 1995; Berkheiser, 2002; Bookser, 2004; Cooper et al., 1998). If judges expect to impose a non-custodial sentence, then they may dispense with counsel (Burrus & Kempf-Leonard, 2002; Feld, 1984, 1989; Lefstein et al., 1969).

The most common explanation why so many juveniles are unrepresented is that they waive counsel (ABA, 1995; Berkheiser, 2002; Cooper et al., 1998; Feld, 1989). As with *Miranda* waivers, judges in most states use the adult standard—knowing, intelligent, and voluntary—to gauge juveniles' waivers of counsel (Berkheiser, 2002; *Fare v. Michael C.*, 1979; *Johnson v. Zerbst*, 1938). They consider the same factors—age, education, I.Q., prior police contacts, or experience with delinquency trials—as those in *Miranda* waivers to decide whether youths understood and voluntarily waived counsel (Feld, 1984, 1989, 2006a). Many juveniles waive counsel without consulting with either a parent or an attorney (Berkheiser, 2002). Although judges are supposed to conduct a colloquy to determine whether a child has the ability to understand and exercise rights and to represent herself (*In re Christopher H.*, 2004; *In re Manuel R.*, 1988), judges frequently failed to give delinquents any counsel advisory, often neglected to create a record, and readily accepted waivers from manifestly incompetent children (Berkheiser, 2002; Drizin & Luloff, 2007). The research on juveniles' adjudicative competence and exercise of *Miranda* rights reviewed earlier applies equally to their ability to make knowing, intelligent, and voluntary waivers of counsel and to plead guilty, a much more frequent outcome. Many juveniles simply do not understand the meaning of a *Miranda* warning, counsel advisory, or a plea colloquy and cannot exercise their rights effectively (Grisso, 1980, 1981, 2000). Even youths who understand a *Miranda* warning or a counsel advisory may not appreciate the importance of the right or the collateral consequences of relinquishing counsel (ABA, 1995; Grisso 1980, 1997; Grisso et al., 2003). Juveniles' diminished competence, inability to understand legal proceedings, and judicial encouragement to waive counsel results in larger proportions of youth without lawyers than criminal defendants (Feld, 1988b; Harlow, 2000). These disabilities become even more consequential for the vast majority of unrepresented juveniles who then plead guilty without understanding or appreciating the consequences.

Like adult criminal defendants, nearly all delinquents plead guilty and proceed to sentencing (Feld 1993). Because most states deny juveniles the right to a jury trial (*McKeiver v. Pennsylvania*, 1971), delinquents have very little plea bargaining leverage (Rosenberg, 1993). Juvenile court judges resist sentencing bargains that enable prosecutors and defense counsel to restrict their discretion (Sanborn, 1993). Even though pleading guilty is the most critical decision a delinquent makes, states use adult legal standards to evaluate juveniles' competence and ability to enter a plea (Sanborn, 1992, 1993; Singleton 2007). A valid guilty plea requires a judge to conduct a colloquy on the record in which an offender admits the facts of the offense, and establishes the youth understands the charges and potential consequences (Singleton, 2007). Because appellate courts seldom review juveniles' waivers of counsel (Berkheiser, 2002), scrutiny of pleas made without counsel receive even less judicial attention (Sanborn, 1992, 1993). Analysts contend that guilty pleas by factually innocent youths occur because attorneys fail to investigate cases, assume their clients' guilt especially if they have already confessed, and avoid adversarial litigation, discovery requests, and pretrial motions which conflict with juvenile courts' cooperative ideology (Drizin & Luloff, 2007). Juveniles' emphasis on short-term outcomes rather than long-term consequences, immature judgment, and dependence on adult authority figures increases their likelihood to enter false guilty pleas (Drizin & Luloff, 2007).

**Counsel as an aggravating factor in sentencing.** Historically, juvenile court judges discouraged adversarial representation and organizational pressures to cooperate impeded effective advocacy (Blumberg, 1967; Bortner, 1982; Clarke & Koch 1980; Feld, 1984; Stapleton & Teitelbaum, 1972). Lawyers in juvenile courts may disadvantage their clients at sentencing (Bortner, 1982; Burrus & Kempf-Leonard, 2002; Feld 1988b, 1989; Feld & Schaefer, 2010a). Research that controls for legal variables—e.g., present offense, prior record, and pre-trial detention—consistently reports that judges removed from home and incarcerated delinquents who appeared with counsel more frequently than they did unrepresented youths (Bortner, 1982; Burrus & Kempf-Leonard, 2002; Clarke & Koch, 1980; Duffee & Siegel, 1971; Feld, 1989, 1993; Feld & Schaefer, 2010a; Guevara et al., 2004). Law reform efforts to improve delivery of legal services actually increased the aggravating effect of representation on sentences (Feld & Schaefer 2010a, 2010b).

Several factors may contribute to the negative impact of counsel at sentencing. First, juvenile defenders may be incompetent and prejudice their clients' cases (Cooper et al., 1998; Knitzer & Sobie, 1984; Lefstein et al., 1969; Stapleton & Teitelbaum, 1972). Public defender offices may assign their least capable or newest attorneys to juvenile court to gain trial experience (Flicker, 1983; Handler, 1965). Lack of funding for juvenile defender services may preclude adequate investigations which increase the risk of wrongful convictions (Drizin & Luloff, 2007). Court-appointed lawyers may place a premium on maintaining good relations with judges who assign their cases rather than to vigorously defend their oft-changing clients (Feld, 1989; Flicker, 1983). Despite the due process revolution, juvenile courts' "best interests" ideology discourages zealous advocacy and may engender adverse consequences for an attorney or her client (Ainsworth, 1991; Drizin & Luloff, 2007). Most significantly, conditions under which many defense attorneys work constitute a structural impediment to quality representation (ABA, 1995; Cooper et al., 1998; Jones, 2004). Observations and qualitative assessments in several jurisdictions consistently report adverse working conditions—crushing caseloads, penurious compensation, lack of support services, inexperienced attorneys and inadequate supervision—that detract from or even preclude effective representation (Brooks & Kamine, 2004; Celeste & Puritz, 2001; Jones, 2004; Puritz & Brooks, 2002; Puritz et al., 2002). Ineffective assistance of counsel, for whatever reasons, is a significant factor in about one-quarter of cases of wrongful convictions (Drizin & Luloff, 2007).

Judges may appoint lawyers when they expect to impose more severe sentences (Aday, 1986; Canon & Kolson, 1971). Court decisions prohibit "incarceration without representation" (*Scott v. Illinois*, 1979), and judges' efforts to comply with that requirement may explain the relationship between initial decisions to appoint counsel and subsequent decisions to remove youths from their homes (Feld & Schaefer, 2010a). In most jurisdictions, the same judge presides at a youth's arraignment, detention hearing, adjudication, and disposition and may appoint counsel if they anticipate a more severe sentence (Feld, 1984). If judges appoint counsel at all, it typically occurs at the arraignment or detention hearing. How would a judge know at the beginning of formal proceedings that he or she intends to incarcerate a youth later? Can an attorney provide an effective defense if the judge has already pre-judged the case (Burrus & Kempf-Leonard, 2002; Feld & Schaefer 2010a; Guevara et al., 2008)?

Finally, judges may sentence delinquents who appear with counsel more severely than those who waive because the lawyer's presence insulates them from appellate reversal (Burrus & Kempf-Leonard, 2002; Duffee & Siegel, 1971; Guevara et al., 2004). Juvenile court judges may sanction youths whose lawyers invoke formal procedures, disrupt routine procedures, or question their discretion in ways similar to the harsher sentences imposed on adults who demand a jury trial rather than plead guilty (Engen & Steen, 2000).

Heavy caseloads and inadequate resources preclude effective pretrial investigations. Courtroom cultures that that discourage zealous advocacy and appointed counsel systems that make lawyers dependent on judges for future clients impede the filing of motions and factual testing of the state's case. Waivers of counsel encourage many short-sighted youths to plead guilty at their arraignments or to avoid detention, even if they have valid legal defenses. And appointment of counsel who meet with their clients for the first time at their adjudicatory hearing create a system conducive to wrongful convictions (Drizin & Luloff, 2007).

**Appellate review.** Regardless of how poorly lawyers perform, appellate courts cannot correct juvenile courts' errors (Berkheiser, 2002). Juvenile defenders rarely, if ever, appeal adverse decisions and often lack a record with which to challenge an invalid waiver of counsel or trial errors (Berkheiser, 2002; Bookser, 2004; Crippen, 2000; Harris, 1998; Puritz & Shang, 2000). Adult defenders appeal criminal cases about ten times as frequently as do juvenile defenders (Harris, 1998). Juvenile court culture, even among public defenders, may discourage appeals as an impediment to a youth "assuming responsibility" and beginning the process of rehabilitation (Harris, 1998). Overwhelming juvenile defender caseloads make appellate divisions a luxury few offices can afford. High rates of guilty pleas also waive the right to appeal which prevents review. Juveniles who already waived counsel at trial will be less aware of or able to pursue their right to appeal. The relatively short length of most juvenile dispositions renders many appealed cases moot if the child is released before the case is reviewed. Against this backdrop, the observation of the Alaska Supreme Court is telling—"We cannot help but notice that the children's cases appealed to this court have often shown much more extensive and fundamental error than is generally found in adult criminal cases ..." (*RLR v. State*, 1971, p. 38).

# Right to Jury Trial: Accurate Fact-Finding and Collateral Consequences

As reviewed above, states treat juveniles just like adults when formal equality produces practical inequality—e.g. competency assessments, waivers of *Miranda* rights, and the right to counsel. Conversely, when states have an opportunity to treat juveniles at least as well procedurally as adult criminal defendants, such as the right to a jury trial, they use juvenile court procedures that provide *less* effective safeguards. *McKeiver v. Pennsylvania* (1971) declined to grant delinquents all the procedural safeguards of criminal trials. Although *Duncan v. Louisiana* (1968) previously gave adult criminal defendants the right to a jury trial in state criminal proceedings, *McKeiver* (1971, p. 541) insisted that "the juvenile court proceeding has not yet been held to be a 'criminal prosecution,' within the meaning and reach of the Sixth Amendment, and also has not yet been regarded as devoid of criminal aspects merely because it usually has been given the civil label." The plurality reasoned that fundamental fairness in delinquency proceedings emphasized accurate fact-finding which a judge could satisfy as well as a jury. *McKeiver* invoked the imagery of a sympathetic, paternalistic judge, disregarded delinquents' need for protection from state over-reaching, and rejected concerns that informality could compromise accurate fact-finding (Feld, 2003a; McCord et al., 2001; Poe-Yamagata & Jones, 2000). The Court feared that jury trials would interfere with juvenile courts' informality, flexibility, and confidentiality, make juvenile and criminal courts procedurally indistinguishable, and could lead to their elimination (Feld, 2003b).

The dissent in *McKeiver* insisted that once the State charged a youth with a crime for which it could incarcerate her for a term of years, then the delinquent should enjoy the same right to a jury trial as an adult defendant (Feld, 2003a). It asserted that the rationale of *Gault* and the punitive consequences of delinquency adjudications—criminal charges carrying the possibility of confinement—required comparable criminal procedural safeguards. It feared that juvenile courts' informal procedures could contaminate the accuracy of judicial fact-finding. The vast majority of delinquents, like adult criminal defendants, plead guilty rather than have their cases decided by juries. But the possibility of invoking a jury trial provides an important check on prosecutorial over-charging, on judges' evidentiary rulings, and the standard of proof beyond a reasonable doubt in marginal factual cases (Ainsworth, 1995; Feld, 2003a). The possibility of a jury trial also increases the visibility, accountability, and performance of lawyers and judges. The jury's checking function may be even more important in discretionary, low-visibility juvenile courts that deal with dependent youths who may be unable effectively to protect themselves.

A few states give juveniles a right to a jury trial as a matter of state law (*e.g.*, Feld, 2003a; *In re L.M.*, 2008), but the vast majority do not. Significantly, in the decades since *McKeiver*, every state has revised its juvenile code, adopted get-tough provisions, fostered a punitive convergence with criminal courts, and eroded the rehabilitative rationale for less effective procedures in delinquency trials (Feld, 1988b; Torbet et al., 1996). Despite these substantial changes in juvenile court jurisprudence and sentencing practices, state courts generally reject juveniles' claims that they should enjoy a right to a jury (*see e.g.*, *In re. D.J.*, 2002; *In re. J.F. and G.G.*, 1998; *State v. Hezzie R.*, 1998).

*McKeiver* assumed that states do not need to provide juries to assure accurate fact-finding because judges could do so as well. By contrast, *Winship* reasoned that the seriousness of proceedings and the potential consequences for a defendant, whether juvenile or adult, required proof beyond a reasonable doubt to avoid convicting innocent people. *McKeiver*'s rejection of jury trials undermines factual accuracy and creates the strong probability that outcomes will differ in delinquency and criminal trials because juries and judges evaluate testimony and decide cases differently. Although judges and juries agree about defendants' guilt or innocence in about four-fifths of criminal cases, when they differ, juries acquit more often than do judges (Greenwood et al., 1983; Kalven & Zeisel, 1966).

Fact-finding by judges and juries is intrinsically different, because the former may preside over hundreds of cases annually while the latter may hear only one or two cases in a lifetime (Ainsworth, 1991; Kalven & Zeisel, 1966; Saks, 1997). Because judges hear many cases, they sometimes become less meticulous when they weigh evidence, more casual when they evaluate facts, and apply less stringently the reasonable doubt standard than do jurors (Guggenheim & Hertz, 1998). Judges hear testimony from police and probation officers on a recurring basis and develop settled opinions about their credibility (Feld, 1984; Guggenheim & Hertz, 1998). Similarly, judges may have an opinion about a youth's credibility, character, or the merits of the case from hearing earlier charges against her or presiding at her detention hearing. The informality of delinquency proceedings compounds the differences between judge and jury reasonable doubt and places delinquents at a disadvantage. When juvenile court judges preside at detention hearings, they receive information about a youth's offense, criminal history, or social circumstances. This non-guilt-related evidence increases the likelihood that a judge will convict and subsequently institutionalize her (Feld, 1984). The youthfulness of a defendant is another factor that elicits jury sympathy and accounts for some of the differences between jury and judge trial outcomes. Indeed, juvenile court judges may be more predisposed to find jurisdiction that criminal court judges or juries in order to "help" an errant youth. Finally, the absence of a jury enables juvenile courts to adjudicate many juveniles without the assistance of an attorney which further prejudices the accuracy of fact-finding (Cooper et al., 1998; Feld, 1993). It is easier to convict a youth in a juvenile court trial than to convict a person in a criminal proceeding with a jury (Drizin & Luloff, 2007; Greenwood et al., 1983).

**Suppression hearing.** The absence of a jury enables judges to conduct suppression hearings immediately before or during trial, exposes them to inadmissible evidence and prejudicial information about youth, and further increases the likelihood of erroneous conviction (Feld, 1984; Guggenheim &Hertz, 1998). A judge may know of a youth's prior delinquency involvement from presiding at a detention hearing, prior adjudication, or disposition, or at the trial of a youth's co-offenders. Similarly, a judge who suppresses an inadmissible confession or illegally seized evidence may still be influenced by that excluded evidence in her subsequent determination of guilt. Whenever a judge knows information that is inadmissible at trial, but is prejudicial to a defendant, the impartiality of tribunal is open to question. The presumption against evidentiary "seepage" is particularly troublesome in juvenile court proceedings because the same judge typically handles the same case at different stages. For example, at a detention hearing, a judge may be exposed to a youth's social history file and prior record. When the same judge subsequently rules on the admissibility of evidence in a suppression hearing and the guilt of the juvenile in the same proceeding, the risks of prejudice become almost insuperable. Whereas an adult defendant can avoid these risks by choosing a jury trial, delinquents have no corresponding ability to avoid the cumulating risks of prejudice in a bench trial (Drizin & Luloff, 2007; Feld, 1984). The vast majority of states deny juveniles a right to a jury trial and most delinquents plead guilty—with or without the assistance of counsel. As a result, states may obtain delinquency convictions that would not have resulted in convictions or pleas if defendants had received adequate procedural safeguards (Feld, 2003a).

# Moving Forward: Reforming Court Procedures to Prevent Wrongful Convictions

Recent developmental psychological and neuroscience research has taught us scientifically much more than we previously knew about how children think and act and how their thought processes differ from adults. The research findings reinforce the historic recognition that youths' legal competence is less than that of adults and support the rationale for a separate juvenile justice system (Scott & Steinberg, 2008). The decades since *Gault* have witnessed a procedural as well as substantive convergence between juvenile and criminal courts which place greater demands on juveniles' competence to exercise rights. The greater procedural formality and adversarial nature of delinquency proceedings reflects juvenile courts' shift in emphases from rehabilitating offenders to protecting public safety and punishing offenses. Despite these changes, most states do not provide delinquents with procedural safeguards that provide formal or functional protections comparable to those of adult criminal defendants (Feld, 1984, 2003a). Juveniles waive their *Miranda* rights and right to counsel under a standard—"knowing, intelligent, and voluntary" under the "totality of circumstances"—that is unlikely to discern whether they understand and are competent to exercise the rights they relinquish.

The Court has recognized youths' vulnerability to police questioning and distinguished between younger and older youths. Developmental psychologists corroborate their differing abilities. Younger juveniles' incomplete understanding and heightened vulnerability warrant greater assistance—a non-waivable right to counsel—to assure voluntariness of a *Miranda* waiver and statement. The Court in *Haley*, *Gallegos*, *Gault*, *Fare*, and *J.D.B.* excluded statements taken from youths fifteen years of age or younger and admitted those obtained from sixteen- and seventeen-year-olds. That line closely tracks what psychologists have found about youths' ability to understand the warning and concepts. Policy makers should formally adopt that functional line and provide greater protection for youths fifteen and younger. Analysts advocate that juveniles younger than sixteen years of age "should be accompanied and advised by a professional advocate, preferably an attorney, trained to serve in this role" (Kassin et al., 2010, p. 28). Juveniles should consult with an attorney, rather than to rely on parents, before they exercise or waive constitutional rights (American Bar Association, 1980; Bishop & Farber, 2007; Farber, 2004). Requiring a child to consult an attorney assures an institutionalized legal services delivery system and an informed and voluntary waiver (Farber, 2004). If youths fifteen years of age or younger consult with counsel prior to waiver, it will limit somewhat police's ability to secure confessions. However, if younger juveniles cannot understand and exercise rights without a lawyer, then to treat them as if they do enables the state to exploit their vulnerability.

States also use the adult waiver standard — "knowing, intelligent, and voluntary" — to gauge juveniles' waivers of counsel, although many youths are incapable of meeting it. The high rate of waiver of counsel is an indictment of the juvenile justice system because assistance of counsel is the essential prerequisite to the exercise of other procedural safeguards (Drizin & Luloff, 2007; Guggenheim & Hertz, 1998). Youths require and deserve safeguards which only lawyers can effectively invoke to protect against erroneous and punitive state intervention (Feld, 1988a, 1999, 2003b). The direct consequence of delinquency convictions — institutional confinement — and the use of prior convictions to sentence recidivists more harshly, to waive youths to criminal court, and to enhance adult sentences makes effective assistance of counsel imperative (Feld 1988a, 2003a). Because of the high rates of delinquency convictions obtained without the assistance of counsel, the dubious competence of most juveniles to waive their rights, and the inability of appellate courts subsequently to assess the validity of their waivers of counsel, only mandatory and non-waivable appointment of counsel can prevent erroneous convictions and the collateral use of those adjudications which compound injustice. A non-waivable right to an attorney can only safeguard youths if they receive the effective assistance of counsel. This requires adequate resources, enhanced training, and zealous advocacy.

The denial of jury trials calls into question the factual accuracy, validity and reliability of delinquency adjudications both for initial dispositions and for collateral use such as sentence enhancements (Feld, 2003a). States do not provide juveniles with special procedural safeguards to protect them from their own immaturity and vulnerability nor do they provide them with the full panoply of criminal procedural safeguards to protect them from punitive state intervention. Instead, juvenile courts assure that youths continue to "receive the worst of both worlds" — treating juvenile offenders just like adult criminal defendants when formal equality redounds to their disadvantage and providing less effective juvenile court procedures when they provide an advantage to the state.

# References

Aday, D. P., Jr. (1986). Court structure, defense attorney use, and juvenile court decisions. *Sociological Quarterly, 27*, 107–119.

Adolescent Development and Juvenile Justice. John D. and Catherine T. MacArthur Foundation, available at www.http//adjj.org.

Ainsworth, J. E. (1991). Re-imagining childhood and reconstructing the legal order: The case for abolishing the juvenile court. *North Carolina Law Review, 69*, 1083–1133.

Ainsworth, J. E. (1993). In a different register: The pragmatics of powerlessness in police interrogation. *Yale Law Journal, 103*, 259–322.

Ainsworth, J. E. (1995). Youth justice in a unified court: Response to critics of juvenile court abolition. *Boston College Law Review, 36*, 927–951.

American Bar Association, Institute of Judicial Administration. (1980). *Juvenile justice standards relating to pretrial court proceedings.* Cambridge, MA: Ballinger.

American Bar Association. (1993). *America's children at risk: A national agenda for legal action.* Washington, DC: American Bar Association Presidential Working Group on the Unmet Needs of Children and their Families.

American Bar Association. (1995). *A call for justice: An assessment of access to counsel and quality of representation in delinquency proceedings.* Washington, DC: American Bar Association Juvenile Justice Center.

Aronson, J. D. (2007). Brain imaging, culpability and the juvenile death penalty. *Psychology, Public Policy and Law, 13*, 115–142.

Aronson, J. D. (2009). Neuroscience and juvenile justice. *Akron Law Review, 42*, 917–929.

Arrendondo, D. E. (2003). Child development, children's mental health and the juvenile justice system. *Stanford Law & Policy Review, 14*, 13–28.

Berkheiser, M. (2002). The fiction of juvenile right to counsel: Waiver in the juvenile courts. *Florida Law Review, 54*, 577–686.

Bishop, D. M. & Farber, H.B. (2007). Joining the legal significance of adolescent developmental capacities with the legal rights provided by *In re Gault. Rutgers Law Review 60*, 125–173.

Blumberg, A. S. (1967). The practice of law as a confidence game: Organizational cooptation of a profession. *Law & Society Review, 1*, 15–39.

Bonnie, R., & Grisso, T. (2000). Adjudicative competence and youthful offenders. In T. Grisso & R. G. Schwartz (Eds.), *Youth on trial: A developmental perspective on juvenile courts.* Chicago: University of Chicago Press.

Bookser, S. M. (2004). Making *Gault* meaningful: Access to counsel and quality of representation in delinquency proceedings for indigent youth. *Whittier Journal of Child & Family Advocacy, 3*, 297–328.

Bortner, M. A. (1982). *Inside a juvenile court: The tarnished ideal of individualized justice.* New York: New York University Press.

Bray, T., Sample, L. L., & Kempf-Leonard, K. (2005). Justice by geography: Racial disparity and juvenile courts. In D. Hawkings & K. Kempf-Leonard (Eds.), *Our children, their children: Confronting racial and ethnic differences in American juvenile justice.* Chicago: University of Chicago Press.

*Breed v. Jones,* 421 U.S. 519 (1975).

Brooks, K. & Kamine, D. (2003). *Justice cut short: An assessment of access to counsel and quality of representation in delinquency proceedings in Ohio.* Washington, DC: American Bar Association Juvenile Justice Center.

Burruss, G. W. Jr. & Kempf-Leonard, K. (2002). The questionable advantage of defense counsel in juvenile court. *Justice Quarterly, 19*, 37–68.

Canon, B. C. & Kolson, K. (1971). Rural compliance with *Gault*: Kentucky, a case study. *Journal of Family Law, 10*, 300–326.

Cauffman, E. & Steinberg, L. (1995). The cognitive and affective influences on adolescent decision-making. *Temple Law Review, 68*, 1763–1789.

Celeste, G., & Puritz, P. (2001). *The children left behind: An assessment of access to counsel and quality of legal presentation in delinquency proceedings in Louisiana.* Washington, DC: American Bar Association Juvenile Justice Center.

Clarke, S. H. & Koch, G. G. (1980). Juvenile court: Therapy or crime control, and do lawyers make a difference? *Law & Society Review, 14,* 263–308.

Cooper, N. L., Puritz, P., & Shang, W. (1998). Fulfilling the promise of *In re Gault*: Advancing the role of lawyers for children. *Wake Forest Law Review, 33,* 651–679.

Crippen, G. L. (2000). Can the courts fairly account for the diminished competence and culpability of juveniles? A judge's perspective. In T. Grisso & R. Schwartz (Eds.), *Youth on trial: A developmental perspective on juvenile justice.* Chicago: University of Chicago Press.

Dahl, R. E. (2000). Affect regulation, brain development, and behavioral/emotional health in adolescence. *CNS Spectrums, 6,* 60–72.

Dahl, R. E. (2004). Adolescent brain development: A period of vulnerabilities and opportunities. *Annals of the New York Academy of Sciences, 1021,* 1–22.

Drizin, S. A. & Leo, R.A. (2004). The problem of false confessions in the post-DNA world. *North Carolina Law Review, 82,* 891–1007.

Drizin, S. A. & Luloff, G. (2007). Are juvenile courts a breeding ground for wrongful convictions? *Northern Kentucky Law Review, 34,* 275–322.

*Drope v. Missouri,* 420 U.S. 162 (1975).

Duffee, D. & Siegel, L. (1971). The organization man: Legal counsel in the juvenile court. *Criminal Law Bulletin, 7,* 544–553.

*Duncan v. Louisiana,* 391 U.S. 145 (1968).

*Dusky v. United States,* 362 U.S. 402 (1960).

Engen, R. L. & Steen, S. (2000). The power to punish: Discretion and sentencing reform in the war on drugs. *American Journal of Sociology, 105,* 1357–1395.

Farber, H. B. (2004). The role of the parent/guardian in juvenile custodial interrogations: Friend or foe? *American Criminal Law Review, 41,* 1277–1312.

*Fare v. Michael C.,* 442 U.S. 707 (1979).

Feld, B. C. (1984). Criminalizing juvenile justice: Rules of procedure for the juvenile court. *Minnesota Law Review, 69,* 141–276.

Feld, B. C. (1988a). The juvenile court meets the principle of offense: Punishment, treatment, and the difference it makes. *Boston University Law Review, 68,* 821–915.

Feld, B. C. (1988b). *In re Gault* revisited: A cross-state comparison of the right to counsel in juvenile court. *Crime & Delinquency, 34,* 393–424.

Feld, B. C. (1989). The right to counsel in juvenile court: An empirical study of when lawyers appear and the difference they make. *Journal of Criminal Law & Criminology, 79,* 1185–1346.

Feld, B. C. (1991). Justice by geography: Urban, suburban, and rural variations in juvenile justice administration. *Journal of Criminal Law & Criminology, 82,* 156–210.

Feld, B. C. (1993). *Justice for children: The right to counsel and the juvenile courts.* Boston: Northeastern University Press.

Feld, B. C. (1999). *Bad kids: Race and the transformation of the juvenile court.* New York: Oxford University Press.

Feld, B. C. (2000). Juveniles' waiver of legal rights: Confessions, *Miranda*, and the right to counsel. In T. Grisso & R. Schwartz (Eds.), *Youth on trial: A developmental perspective on juvenile justice.* Chicago: University of Chicago Press.

Feld, B. C. (2003a). The constitutional tension between *Apprendi* and *McKeiver*: Sentence enhancements based on delinquency convictions and the quality of justice in juvenile courts. *Wake Forest Law Review, 38,* 1111–1224.

Feld, B. C. (2003b). Race, politics, and juvenile justice: The Warren Court and the conservative 'backlash'. *Minnesota Law Review, 87,* 1447–1577.

Feld, B. C. (2006a). Juveniles' competence to exercise *Miranda* rights: An empirical study of policy and practice. *Minnesota Law Review, 91,* 26–100.

Feld, B. C. (2006b). Police interrogation of juveniles: An empirical study of policy and practice. *Journal of Criminal Law & Criminology, 97,* 219–316.

Feld, B. C. (2007). A century of juvenile justice: A work in progress or a revolution that failed? *Northern Kentucky Law Review, 34,* 189–256.

Feld, B. C. (2008). A slower form of death: Implications of *Roper v. Simmons* for juveniles sentence to life without parole. *Notre Dame Journal of Law, Ethics, & Public Policy, 22,* 9–65.

Feld, B. C. (2013a). *Kids, cops, and confessions: Inside the interrogation room.* New York: New York University Press.

Feld, B. C. (2013b). *Cases and materials on juvenile justice administration* (4th ed.). St. Paul, MN: Thomson Reuters.

Feld, B. C. & Schaefer, S. (2010a). The right to counsel in juvenile court: The conundrum of attorneys as an aggravating factor in dispositions. *Justice Quarterly, 27,* 713–741.

Feld, B. C. & Schaefer, S. (2010b). The right to counsel in juvenile court: Law reform to deliver legal services and reduce justice by geography. *Criminology & Public Policy, 9,* 327–356.

Ferster, E. Z., Courtless, T., & Snethen, E. (1971). The juvenile justice system: In search of the role of counsel. *Fordham Law Review, 39,* 375–412.

Flicker, B. (1983). *Providing counsel for accused juveniles.* New York: Institute of Judicial Administration.

Furby, L. & Beyth-Marom, R. (1992). Risk-taking in adolescence: A decision-making perspective. Washington, DC. Carnegie Council on Adolescent Development.

*Gallegos v. Colorado,* 370 U.S. 49 (1962).

Garrett, B. L. (2011). *Convicting the innocent: Where criminal prosecutions go wrong.* Cambridge: Harvard University Press.

General Accounting Office. (1995). *Juvenile justice: Representation rates varied as did counsel's impact on court outcomes.* Washington, D.C.: U.S. General Accounting Office.

*Gideon v. Wainwright,* 372 U.S. 335 (1963).

Goldstein, A. & Goldstein, N. E. S. (2010). *Evaluating capacity to waive Miranda rights.* New York: Oxford University Press.

*Graham v. Florida,* 560 U.S. 48, 130 S.Ct. 2011 (2010).

Greenwood, P. W., Abrahamse, A., & Zimring, F. E. (1983). *Youth crime and juvenile justice in California: A report to the legislature.* Santa Monica, CA: Rand Corporation.

Grisso, T. (1980). Juveniles' capacities to waive *Miranda* rights: An empirical analysis. *California Law Review, 68,* 1134–1166.

Grisso, T. (1981). *Juveniles' waiver of rights: Legal and psychological competence.* New York: Plenum Press.

Grisso, T. (1997). Juvenile competency to stand trial: Questions in an era of punitive reform. *Criminal Justice, 3,* 5–11.

Grisso, T. (2000). What we know about youths' capacities s trial defendants. In T. Grisso & R. Schwartz (Eds.), *Youth on trial: A developmental perspective on juvenile justice.* Chicago: University of Chicago Press.

Grisso, T. & Pomicter, C. (1977). Interrogation of juveniles: An empirical study of procedures, safeguards and rights waiver. *Law & Human Behavior, 1,* 321–342.

Grisso, T. & Ring, M. (1979). Parents' attitudes toward juveniles' right in interrogation. *Criminal Justice and Behavior, 6,* 211–226.

Grisso, T., Steinberg, L., Woolard, J., Cauffman, E., Scott, E., Graham, S., Lexcen, F., & Reppucci, N. D. (2003). Juveniles' competence to stand trial: A comparison of adolescents' and adults' capacities as trial defendants. *Law & Human Behavior, 27,* 333–363.

Gross, S. R., Jacoby, K, Matheson, D.J., Montgomery, N, & Patil, S. (2005). Exonerations in the United States: 1989 through 2003. *Journal of Criminal Law & Criminology, 95,* 523–560.

Gruber, S. A. & Yurgelun-Todd, D. A. (2006). Neurobiology and the law: A role in juvenile justice. *Ohio State Journal of Criminal Law, 3,* 321–340.

Gudjonsson, G. H. (2003). *The psychology of interrogations and confessions: A handbook.* New York: John Wiley & Sons.

Guevara, L., Spohn, C., & Herz, D. (2004). Race, legal representation and juvenile justice: Issues and concerns. *Crime & Delinquency, 50,* 344–371.

Guevara, L., Spohn, C., & Herz, D. (2008). Race, gender, and legal counsel: Differential outcomes in two juvenile courts. *Youth Violence and Juvenile Justice, 6,* 83–104.

Guggenheim, M. & Hertz, R. (1998). Reflections on judges, juries, and justice: Ensuring the fairness of juvenile delinquency trials. *Wake Forest Law Review 33,* 553–593.

*Haley v. Ohio,* 332 U.S.596 (1948).

Handler, J. F. (1965). The juvenile court and the adversary system: Problems of form and function. *Wisconsin Law Review, 1965,* 7–51.

Harlow, C. W. (2000). *Defense counsel in criminal cases.* Washington, DC: Bureau of Justice Statistics, U.S. Department of Justice.

Harris, D. J. (1994). Due process vs. helping kids in trouble: Implementing the right to appeal from adjudications of delinquency in Pennsylvania. *Dickinson Law Review, 98,* 209–235.

*In re Christopher H.,* 596 S.E.2d 500 (S.C. App. 2004).

*In re. D.J.,* 817 So. 2d 26 (La. 2002),

*In re Gault,* 387 U.S. 1 (1967).

*In re. J.F. and G.G.,* 714 A.2d 467 (Pa. Super. 1998).

*In re L.M.,* 186 P.3d 164 (Kan. 2008).

*In re Manuel R.,* 207 A.2d 719 (Conn. 1988).

*In re Winship,* 397 U.S. 358 (1970).

*J.D.B. v. North Carolina,* 131 S. Ct. 2394 (2011).

*Johnson v. Zerbst,* 304 U.S. 458 (1938).

Jones, J. B. (2004). *Access to counsel.* Washington, DC: Office of Juvenile Justice and Delinquency Prevention.

Kalven, H. Jr. & Zeisel, H. (1966). *The American jury.* Chicago: University of Chicago Press.

Kandel, E. R., Schwartz, J., & Jessell, T. (2000). *Principles of neuroscience* (4th ed.). New York: McGraw Hill.

Kassin, S. (2005). On the psychology of confessions: Does innocence put innocents at risk? *American Psychologist, 60,* 215–228.

Kassin, S. & Gudjonsson, G. H. (2004). The psychology of confessions: A review of the literature and issues. *Psychological Sciences in Public Interest, 5*, 33–69.

Kassin, S. M., Drizin, S. A., Grisso, T., Gudjonsson, G.H., Leo, R.A., & Redlich, A. D. (2010). Police-induced confessions: Risk factors and recommendations. *Law & Human Behavior, 34*, 3–38.

*Kent v. United States*, 383 U.S. 541 (1966).

Knitzer, J. & Sobie, M. (1984). *Law guardians in New York State: A study of the legal representation of children.* Albany, NY: New York State Bar Association.

Lefstein, N., Stapleton, V., & Teitelbaum, L. (1969). In search of juvenile justice: *Gault* and its implementation. *Law & Society Review, 3*, 491–562.

Leo, R. A. (1996). Inside the interrogation room. *Journal of Criminal Law &Criminology, 86*, 266–303.

Leo, R. A. (2008). *Police interrogation in America.* Cambridge, MA: Harvard University Press.

Maroney, T. A. (2009). The false promise of adolescent brain science in juvenile justice. *Notre Dame Law Review, 85*, 89–176.

McCord, J. & Spatz-Widom, C. (2001). *Juvenile crime, juvenile justice.* National Research Council, Washington DC.: National Acadamy Press.

*McKeiver v. Pennsylvania*, 403 U.S. 528 (1971).

Mears, D. P. (2012). The front end of the juvenile court: Intake and informal versus formal processing. In B. C. Feld & D. M. Bishop (Eds.), *Oxford Handbook of Juvenile Crime and Juvenile Justice.* New York: Oxford University Press.

*Miller v. Alabama,* 132 S.Ct. 2455 (2012).

*Miranda v. Arizona,* 384 U.S. 436 (1966).

Morse, S. J. (1997). Immaturity and irresponsibility. *Journal of Criminal Law & Criminology, 88*, 15–67.

Note. (1966). Juvenile delinquents: The police, state courts and individualized justice. *Harvard Law Review, 79*, 775–810.

Owen-Kostelnik, J., et al. (2006). Testimony and interrogation of minors: Assumptions about maturity and morality. *American Psychologist, 61*, 286–304.

Poe-Yamagata, E. & Jones, M. A. (2000). *And justice for some.* Davis, CA: National Council on Crime and Delinquency.

Puritz, P. & Shang, W. (2000). Juvenile indigent defense: Crisis and solutions. *Criminal Justice, 15*, 22–28.

Puritz, P. & Broks, K. (2002). *Kentucky: Advancing justice: An assessment of access to counsel and quality of representation in delinquency proceedings.* Washington, DC: American Bar Association Juvenile Justice Center.

Puritz, P., Scali, M. A., & Picou, I. (2002). *Virginia: An assessment of access to counsel and quality of representation in delinquency proceedings.* Washington, DC: American Bar Association Juvenile Justice Center.

Redlich, A. D., Silverman, M., Chen, J., & Steiner, H. (2004). The police interrogation of children and adolescents. In G. D. Lassiter (Ed.), *Interrogations, confessions, and entrapment.* New York: Springer Science.

Redlich, A. D., & Drizin, S. (2007). Police interrogation of youth. In C. L. Kessler & L. J. Kraus (Eds.), *The mental health needs of young offenders: Forging paths toward reintegration and rehabilitation.* Cambridge, MA: Cambridge University Press.

*RLR v. State*, 487 P. 2d 27 (Alaska 1971).

*Roper v. Simmons,* 543 U.S. 551 (2005).

Rosenberg, I. M. (1993). Leaving bad enough alone: A response to the juvenile court abolitionists. *Wisconsin Law Review, 1993*, 163–188.

Rubin, H. T. (1980). The emerging prosecutor dominance of the juvenile court intake process. *Crime & Delinquency, 26*, 299–318.

Saks, M. J. (1997). What do jury experiments tell us about how juries (should) make decisions? *Southern California Interdisciplinary Law Journal, 6*, 1–53.

Sanborn, J. B., Jr. (1992). Pleading guilty in juvenile court: Minimal ado about something very important to young defendants. *Justice Quarterly, 9*, 127–149.

Sanborn J. B., Jr. (1993). Philosophical, legal, and systemic aspects of juvenile court plea bargaining. *Crime & Delinquency, 39*, 509–527.

Scott, E. S. (1992). Judgment and reasoning in adolescent decisionmaking. *Villanova Law Review, 37*, 1607–1669.

Scott, E. S. (2000). The legal construction of adolescence. *Hofstra Law Review, 29*, 541–588.

Scott, E. S., Reppucci, N. D., & Woolard, J. L. (1995). Evaluating adolescent decision making in legal contexts. *Law & Human Behavior, 19*, 221–244.

Scott, E. S. & Grisso, T. (1997). The evolution of adolescence: A developmental perspective on juvenile justice reform. *Journal of Criminal Law & Criminology, 88*, 137–189.

Scott, E. S. & Grisso, T. (2005). Developmental incompetence, due process, and juvenile justice policy. *North Carolina Law Review, 83*, 793–846.

Scott, E. S. & Steinberg, L. (2003). Blaming youth. *Texas Law Review, 81*, 799–840.

Scott, E. S. & Steinberg, L. (2008). *Rethinking juvenile justice*. Cambridge, MA: Harvard University Press.

*Scott v. Illinois*, 440 U.S. 367 (1979).

Spear, L.P. (2000). The adolescent brain and age-related behavioral manifestations. *Neuroscience and Biobehavioral Reviews, 24*, 417–463.

Singleton, L. C. (2007). Say 'pleas': Juveniles' competence to enter plea agreements. *Journal of Law & Family Studies, 9*, 439–455.

Sowell, E. R., Thompson, P. M., Holmes, C. J., Jernigan, T. L., & Toga, A. W. (1999). In vivo evidence for post-adolescent brain maturation in frontal and striatal regions. *Nature Neuroscience, 2*, 859–861.

Sowell, E. R., Thompson, P. M., Tessner, K. D., & Toga, A. W. (2001). Mapping continued brain growth and gray matter density reduction in dorsal frontal cortex: Inverse relationships during postadolescent brain maturation. *Journal of Neuroscience, 21*, 8819–8829.

Stapleton, V. & Teitelbaum, L. (1972). *In defense of youth: A study of the role of counsel in American juvenile courts*. New York: Russell Sage Foundation.

*State v. Hezzie R.*, 580 N.W.2d 660 (Wis. 1998]).

*State v. Presha*, 748 A.2d 1108 (N.J. 2000).

Steinberg, L. & Cauffman, E. (1996). Maturity of judgment in adolescence: Psychosocial factors in adolescent decision making. *Law & Human Behavior 20*, 249–272.

Steinberg, L. & Cauffman, E. (1999). The elephant in the courtroom: A developmental perspective on the adjudication of youthful offenders. *Virginia Journal of Social Policy & the Law, 6*, 389–417.

Tanenhaus, D. S. (2004). *Juvenile justice in the making*. New York: Oxford University Press.

Tanenhaus, D. S. & Drizin, S. A. (2003). Owing to the extreme youth of the accused: The changing legal response to juvenile homicide. *Journal of Criminal Law & Criminology, 92*, 641–705.

Tepfer, J. A., Nirider, L.H., & Tricarico, L. M. (2010). Arresting development: Convictions of innocent youth. *Rutgers Law Review, 62*, 887–941.

Torbet, P, Gable, R., Hurst, H. IV, Montgomery, I., Szymanski, L., & Thomas, D. (1996). *State responses to serious and violent juvenile crime: Research report*. Washington, D.C.: U.S. Department of Justice, Office of Juvenile Justice and Delinquency Prevention.

Woolard, J. L., Cleary, H. M. D., Harvell, S. A. S., & Chen, R. (2008). Examining adolescents' and their parents' conceptual and practical knowledge of police interrogation: A family dyad approach. *Journal of Youth Adolescence, 37*, 685-698.

# Section II

## The Criminal Justice System: Producing, Detecting, and Remedying Wrongful Convictions

## Part Two

### Detecting and Remedying Wrongful Convictions

# Chapter Thirteen

# Judicial Review: Appeals and Postconviction Proceedings

Nancy J. King, *Vanderbilt University*

Judicial review has provided at best an incomplete remedy for individuals convicted of crimes they did not commit. In a groundbreaking study, Professor Brandon Garrett (2011) examined whether and how judicial remedies helped 250 of the first DNA exonerees. By tracking these wrongfully convicted individuals' attempts to challenge their convictions in the courts *before* they obtained the DNA test results that ultimately led to their exonerations, his study provides a glimpse of what judicial review offers the wrongfully convicted who lack DNA evidence to prove their innocence. Of those who challenged their non-capital convictions, more than 90% failed—a success rate not significantly different from that of judicial challenges brought by similar defendants convicted of similar crimes who were not exonerated. Those who succeeded in securing a judicial order reversing their initial convictions often faced continued prosecution. Garrett's research "demonstrates that normal legal mechanisms were incapable of detecting innocence in these (now indisputable) innocence cases" (Aronson & Cole, 2009, p. 614). In another study comparing the cases of 260 defendants exonerated after conviction for committing violent felonies with the cases of 200 similar defendants who avoided conviction, Professor Jon Gould and his colleagues also noted that most of the wrongfully convicted individuals were freed only after action by prosecutors and pardoning authorities (Gould, Carrano, Leo, & Young, 2013a, p. 22). Judicial review may have played an indirect role in these exonerations by attracting the attention of advocates who helped to collect and present new evidence of innocence. Only rarely, however, did the judicial system correct its own mistakes.

This chapter examines the major forms of judicial review after conviction, the reasons why these remedies have served such a limited role in past exonerations, and various reforms that may increase the ability of judicial review to correct miscarriages of justice. A primary reason that judicial remedies have not provided a direct path to relief for the wrongfully convicted is that they were never intended to serve this purpose. Asking a judge to decide whether a conviction is factually accurate is like trying to fit a square peg in a round hole. Appeals and postconviction remedies in the United States were designed to ensure that police, lawyers, and judges follow the legal rules during the investigation or prosecution of the case. So long as the rules are followed, the adversarial process is presumed to produce reliable results. Adding exoneration of the factually innocent to the function of judicial review is a significant challenge, one that states are addressing incrementally. A discussion of the newer state remedies follows an explanation of conventional judicial review and its shortcomings in cases of wrongful conviction.

# Traditional Judicial Remedies and Their Limitations for the Wrongfully Convicted

## Motions for New Trial

Every state permits a person convicted at a criminal trial to file a motion for a new trial based on newly discovered evidence, but these motions have not been particularly helpful to the wrongfully convicted. The proof that exonerees need to successfully demonstrate their innocence—undisclosed testimony and evidence, witness recantations, new scientific methods or discoveries, new evidence of another's guilt—tends to surface long after trial and only with investigation assistance. In many states, new trial motions must be filed within a designated period ranging from a month to three years after sentencing. Even in states that have removed time restrictions for filing claims of innocence based on new evidence, the standard for relief is daunting, requiring that the evidence could not have been discovered earlier and is persuasive enough to convince the judge that retrial would probably end in acquittal. A judge who just sentenced a defendant understandably may be "skeptical of claims that a defendant, fairly convicted, with proper representation by counsel, should now be given a second opportunity because of new information that has suddenly been acquired" (LaFave, Israel, King, & Kerr, 2007, § 24.11(d)).

## Direct Appeal

The form of judicial review most commonly employed by the exonerees in Garrett's (2011) study was the direct appeal—all of the 165 individuals later exonerated by DNA analysis for whom written opinions could be located challenged their convictions on appeal. Appellate review in a few states is granted at the discretion of a court; but in most states, all convicted defendants have an opportunity to attempt to overturn their convictions on appeal. States are required to provide a transcript of the trial court proceedings and a defense attorney to assist if the defendant is indigent. Yet the direct appeal has proven to be of limited utility for wrongfully convicted defendants.

**Guilty pleas and appeals.** First, appeals are essentially useless to a person who seeks to overturn his conviction after pleading guilty to a crime he did not commit. As Professor Stephanos Bibas explains in this volume, people sometimes do admit committing crimes that they never committed, and research has helped to explain why this may happen. False pleas are especially difficult to overturn on appeal because one of the legal consequences of a guilty plea is waiving the right to appeal the very errors that might have led a defendant to decide that pleading guilty was his best or only option. For example, once a defendant pleads guilty, appellate courts will not hear arguments that his confession was coerced, that a witness lied to police, or that forensic evidence was unreliable. In some cases, a defendant may waive all judicial review as part of his plea agreement, barring appeal of any claim (King, 2013a). In order to overturn such a waiver or conviction based on a guilty plea, a defendant must usually show that his plea was involuntary or uninformed. Such claims are unlikely to succeed. After a defendant has stated in open court to the trial judge that he is pleading voluntarily, appellate judges are reluctant to credit a prisoner's claim that he lied then but is not lying now. In some states there are additional barriers to appeal for those who plead guilty, such as a certification from the trial judge that the appeal is not frivolous (LaFave, *et al.*, 2007, § 27.1(a)).

**Record-based claims only.** Even for those wrongfully convicted after trial, the major shortcoming of the direct appeal remedy is that it corrects only flaws in the process by which the defendant's guilt was determined. Appellate judges will not second-guess the factual accuracy of a conviction (Findley, 2009, pp. 601–608). Unlike trial courts, where judges and juries evaluate testimony and other evidence first-hand, appellate judges lack the capacity to consider new evidence. Instead, they review only the existing trial court record. If a claim of error relies on evidence that is not in the record, the appellate court will not hear it. Most wrongful convictions are not traceable to mistakes evident from trial transcripts. Instead, as noted above, evidence that has exonerated the wrongfully convicted is typically new, discovered long after the defendant was sentenced. These mistakes are invisible to the judge or jury deciding a defendant's guilt. Because they involve proof that was never introduced in the trial court, they will remain invisible to appellate courts. If a claim rests on new evidence, it must await postconviction review, where new evidence can be introduced.

**Preserved, recognized claims only.** A wrongfully convicted defendant may be able to point to some errors in the existing trial record on appeal, such as: claims that the government's evidence should have been excluded; the judge unduly restricted defense counsel's ability to challenge that evidence; jury instructions were misleading; or the prosecutor engaged in misconduct. But some features of criminal trials that we now know contribute to wrongful convictions will not be grounds for appeal, because they may not violate state or federal law. For example, the Supreme Court recently held that the Constitution does not bar juries from considering eyewitness identification testimony procured under unduly suggestive circumstances, so long as those circumstances were not arranged by police (*Perry v. New Hampshire*, 2012). Trial and appellate courts continue to credit eyewitness testimony with more reliability than it deserves (Thompson, 2009).

Even when a convicted defendant can point to a recognized error in the record, an appellate court will consider it only if the defendant's trial attorney promptly objected when the error occurred. If not, the error will be ignored by an appellate court, unless the defendant can demonstrate (again, using only the trial court record) that the error was obvious, and failure to grant appellate relief would result in a miscarriage of justice. These well-established rules regarding "contemporaneous objections" and "plain error" are designed to encourage trial attorneys to bring errors to the attention of the trial judge when they can be addressed fully by both sides, when evidence needed to resolve the matter can be introduced and considered, and when any error can be corrected efficiently with the least interruption of the proceedings. In practice, these rules mean that defendants whose lawyers fail to raise viable objections miss their chance at appellate relief.

**Demanding standards of review.** For errors evident in the record and properly preserved by objection at trial, the legal standards that govern relief also make it difficult for a defendant to persuade a judge to overturn his conviction. A defendant convicted of a crime he did not commit may claim on appeal that the totality of evidence introduced by the government at trial was insufficient to establish guilt beyond a reasonable doubt. Garrett found that more than 40% of the exonerees who sought judicial relief from their convictions before obtaining DNA tests raised an insufficiency claim, yet all of them lost (Garrett, 2011, p. 204). Appellate courts are reluctant to second-guess jurors on the basis of a "cold" record, with no access to the witness's demeanor, tone of voice, halting or nervous speech, nor to the reactions of the defendant. The insufficiency standard reflects this deference to jurors: Judges must reject these claims unless the prisoner shows that when viewing the evidence presented at trial in the light most favorable to the prosecution, no rational juror could find that the government proved guilt beyond a reasonable doubt (*Jackson v. Virginia*, 1979). After studying cases applying this standard, one scholar concluded that in practice, courts "uphold convictions unless there is essentially no evidence supporting an element of the crime" (Findley, 2009, p. 602). In addition, "trial errors" such as the introduction of inadmissible evidence, are often considered "harmless" if, on balance, all of the other evidence supports guilt. Garrett reported that when the innocent individuals in his study challenged their convictions on appeal, they often lost, because judges decided the errors that had occurred at trial were harmless in light of other proof that the defendant clearly committed the crime (2011, pp. 200–202). For example, he found that 124 of the exonerees with appeals decided by written decisions had been convicted after faulty eyewitness identification. Although 70 of them challenged the identification evidence used against them, only five received any sort of relief. One-third of the 112 exonerees convicted with faulty forensic evidence challenged its admission after conviction, but only six succeeded (pp. 187–190). In summing up the remedy of direct appeal for the wrongfully convicted, one scholar commented that "the chances of a reversal on direct appeal bear no relation to the chances that the wrong person has been convicted" (Anderson, 2011, p. 391).

## Postconviction Review

The other major category of judicial review, provided in every state, is postconviction review, a judicial proceeding that allows a person to challenge his conviction using grounds that could not have been raised on direct appeal. Postconviction review is sometimes termed "collateral review" because it is often pursued as a new case challenging the conviction. It can encompass several different kinds of state remedies, including writs of habeas corpus and *coram nobis*, and various challenges to sentences. In every state, however, one all-purpose postconviction remedy serves as the primary judicial route for challenging criminal convictions other than direct appeal. In all but a handful of states, an application or petition for relief must be filed in the trial court where the petitioner was convicted. The available grounds for relief are usually defined by statute, and include claims under both state law and federal constitutional law.

When appeal and postconviction remedies in state court fail, a state prisoner may also challenge his conviction by filing a petition in federal court seeking a writ of habeas corpus under 28 U.S.C. § 2254. This federal postconviction remedy — essentially an order that the state release or retry the petitioner — is available only if the petitioner can prove that a federal constitutional violation affected his case. A similar remedy is available to federal prisoners.

**Limited access.** Not all prisoners will be able to use postconviction remedies. In federal court and in just over half of the states, postconviction review is limited to prisoners who are still incarcerated or on parole after their direct appeals have been completed. The mean sentence to incarceration for felony offenders in state courts is just over three years (Rosenmerkel, Durose, & Farole, Jr., 2009), a sentence that is barely long enough to complete the appellate process. Federal habeas review, which is available only to petitioners who have already completed state appeals and postconviction proceedings, is even more inaccessible. As a practical matter, it is out of reach for all but those serving the most serious sentences (King & Hoffmann, 2011, p. 73). Some defendants who plead guilty waive their right to challenge their conviction in postconviction proceedings as part of a plea agreement, and will be unable to use postconviction remedies without first proving that their plea was not voluntary (King, 2013a).

**Barriers to review.** A prisoner who does file a postconviction petition in either state or federal court may find his claim summarily dismissed if he missed the filing deadline (usually a complex calculation that varies with the facts), of if he had a chance to raise the error earlier but failed to do so. These pitfalls are a considerable risk because unlike the direct appeal, where the Constitution guarantees counsel, most states do not routinely provide attorneys to help investigate, compose, or litigate postconviction petitions, not even to prisoners who are illiterate or suffering from mental illness (King, 2013b). About half of the cases filed by noncapital prisoners in federal habeas proceedings and an unknown proportion of those in state postconviction proceedings are dismissed without merits review (King & Hoffmann, 2011, p. 78).

   **Challenges in securing relief.** Even when claims are considered and not dismissed, review is usually brief. Although postconviction courts have the capacity to consider new evidence, in most states evidentiary hearings are granted in only a small percentage of cases, and hardly ever in federal court (King, 2013b; King & Hoffmann, 2011, p. 79). Harmless error rules and deferential standards of review also make it difficult to secure postconviction relief. Consider for example, a claim of ineffective assistance of counsel, a claim raised by a third to a half of all postconviction petitioners and by many of those in Garrett's study. This claim may be one of the only claims available to a petitioner whose lawyer's failure to object at trial forfeited appellate review of what would have been a viable claim of error. But the standard for proving ineffective assistance requires a petitioner to demonstrate not only incompetent performance by his lawyer, but also that there is a reasonable probability he would not have been convicted had his lawyer acted competently. Success rates for these claims by all prisoners are estimated to be roughly 1%–5% for non-capital cases generally in state court, and far less than that in federal habeas proceedings (King, 2013b; 2012). For the innocent individuals in Garrett's (2011) study, the rate of relief was only slightly higher — only 4 of the 52 (7.7%) prisoners who raised a claim of ineffective assistance of counsel succeeded, and two of those were capital cases (p. 206). Even when judges reviewing these claims concluded that defense attorneys had been incompetent, they typically were so convinced by the evidence of guilt or so hesitant to disturb the verdict that they concluded competent assistance would not have made any difference in the jury's decision (pp. 206–207). For the exonerees who managed to file postconviction petitions, postconviction judges, like appellate judges, proved incapable of recognizing, much less remedying, their unreliable convictions.

# Stepping Back: Judicial Review as Process Enforcement—Why It Fails the Wrongfully Convicted

   In addition to the various obstacles to relief examined above, the fundamental reason that judicial review has failed so many of the wrongfully convicted is that it was not designed to help them. Judicial review corrects process errors, not factual inaccuracy. A judicial order vacating a conviction is at most a step along the way to exoneration; it does not itself establish innocence.

   We have seen that a key barrier to appellate relief for the wrongfully convicted is the inability of appellate judges to consider any evidence other than what is already in the trial record. By contrast, postconviction proceedings take place in the trial court, where judges can consider new evidence. Nevertheless, traditionally petitioners have not been permitted to use new evidence to relitigate factual guilt or innocence in postconviction proceedings. Until very recently, new evidence has been admissible only to support a claim that the trial was flawed, not that the result was false. The history of these remedies helps to explain why.

# The Origins of Process Review

The postconviction remedies available to convicted criminals today were first created in the middle decades of the 20th century for a specific purpose: to enforce constitutional rules of procedure newly recognized by the Supreme Court. Until that time, most of the rights granted to the accused by the Fourth, Fifth, Sixth, and Eighth Amendments in the Bill of Rights applied only to individuals charged with federal crimes in federal court. In the 1950s and '60s this changed. In a series of decisions, the Supreme Court declared that the Due Process Clause of the Fourteenth Amendment required states to provide a long list of constitutional procedural protections before depriving an accused of his liberty. States for the first time were ordered to enforce new procedural rules in their criminal cases, including the Fourth Amendment's exclusionary rule for unreasonable searches and seizures, *Miranda* protections for the Fifth Amendment's privilege against self-incrimination, and rights to appointed counsel and a jury drawn from a representative cross-section of the community under the Sixth Amendment.

Federal courts became a battleground over state autonomy in criminal justice. Federal judges used the writ of habeas corpus to vacate convictions and order new trials for state prisoners who demonstrated that state courts had failed to honor the new constitutional rules. If a federal judge concluded that a constitutional rule had been violated, the judge would vacate the tainted conviction and order the state to release the defendant or to re-prosecute him using constitutionally valid procedures.

State postconviction remedies evolved in response. At first, many of the new constitutional claims, such as the failure of the prosecutor to disclose exculpatory evidence for trial, ended up in federal court, because states had no judicial proceeding in which they could be considered. Claims based on non-record evidence could not be considered on direct appeal in the state courts, and these new constitutional claims did not fit within the narrow category of challenges allowed as grounds for relief under existing collateral writs. By the 1970s, however, every state had adopted a new, primary postconviction remedy—a means for petitioners to enforce these new constitutional procedural rules in state court (King & Hoffmann, 2011, pp. 70–72). Many states replaced older remedies, modeling their new postconviction statutes after either the federal statutory remedy for federal prisoners adopted by Congress in the late 1940s, or the model statute of the National Conference of Commissioners on Uniform State Laws (LaFave, *et al.,* 2007, §28.11(b); Wilkes, 2012–2013, §2.5).

During the 1970s, shortly after these new judicial remedies had taken hold in the states, the number of people prosecuted in state courts increased dramatically. Federal and state courts consequently faced an unprecedented increase in the number of applications for relief from state prisoners. Aware of the progress that states had made in providing judicial review for constitutional violations in criminal cases, the Supreme Court began to scale back federal habeas review. In 1976 it barred review of almost all claims of illegal searches or illegal arrests. By the end of the 1980s it was much more difficult for a state prisoner to obtain review of any claim in a second or successive petition, any claim that could have been but was not raised in state court, and any claim based on rules announced after the direct appeal was complete (King & Hoffmann, 2011).

It was during the Court's rollback of federal habeas review that DNA analysis made its appearance, and brought with it credible claims that apparently lawful proceedings could end in the conviction of a person who had nothing to do with the crime. As scholars, advocates and judges called for judicial review to focus on the innocent, the Court built into its many restrictions on federal habeas review exceptions for those who could show they were probably innocent, sometimes termed "innocence gateways." For example, a petitioner could avoid summary dismissal of a belated claim that he should have raised earlier if he could show "probable" innocence. But proof of innocence persuasive enough to make it through this gateway meant only that the petitioner's claim of procedural error would be considered and not summarily dismissed. As the Supreme Court has emphasized repeatedly since it first created these innocence gateways, federal judges lack authority to vacate a state conviction unless a petitioner can show that a *constitutional* rule has been violated (*McQuiggin v. Perkins*, 2013). If the federal court does find that the state courts failed to enforce a constitutional rule of procedure, the conviction will be vacated, but the prosecution will have the option to try again to convict the probably innocent petitioner (*House v. Bell*, 2006; *Schlup v. Delo*, 1995).

Many states adopted restrictions similar to those the Supreme Court imposed on habeas review, also including similar innocence gateways. With only a few exceptions, state post-conviction review retained its initial focus on enforcing the procedural protections for criminal defendants in the Bill of Rights. In other words, even after DNA began to expose how horribly wrong the results of constitutionally flawless criminal prosecutions could be, judicial review remained restricted to determining whether the investigation, pretrial, trial, plea, or sentencing *proceedings* were flawed, not whether a conviction was correct as a factual matter.

Attempts to change this procedural focus have met with limited success only in the past twenty years, and only in state courts. One argument that advocates have advanced is that the right not to be punished if actually innocent is itself a constitutional right, and like other constitutional rights, postconviction courts should be able to review and remedy its violation. The Supreme Court, however, rejected this proposition, declining to hold that a defendant who has been convicted fairly, but inaccurately, has a constitutional right to be free from punishment, even execution. It explained in 1993, "federal habeas courts sit to ensure that individuals are not imprisoned in violation of the Constitution—not to correct errors of fact." Habeas cases "are not forums in which to relitigate state trials" (*Herrera v. Collins*, 1993, pp. 400–401) (internal quotations omitted). Many continue to urge the Court to reconsider and recognize such a "bare innocence," "actual innocence," or "stand-alone innocence" claim as a viable basis for relief under existing postconviction remedies, but the Court has not done so (Hoffmann, 2012). Nor has it interpreted the Constitution to guarantee state defendants a right of access to appellate or postconviction review at all, stating instead that states have great "flexibility in deciding what procedures are needed in the context of postconviction relief" (*District Attorney's Office for Third Judicial District v. Osborne*, 2009, p. 69). The Court also has rejected a constitutional right of access to DNA testing through the courts, although judicial procedures to seek DNA testing must be fairly administered if a state provides them. As long as the Supreme Court avoids recognizing factual innocence as a federal constitutional error warranting relief, the states will not have to do so either.

In a recent divided decision, the Court did transfer to a federal trial court a stand-alone claim of innocence raised by a capital petitioner using an unusual procedure filed directly with the Supreme Court itself. After assuming that a sufficiently convincing showing of innocence would mandate relief, the lower courts in that case held that the petitioner's showing was not sufficient (*In re Davis*, 2009). Although some believe the Supreme Court's action in the case could be a first step toward recognizing a stand-alone claim of innocence as a basis for relief under the habeas statute, others have concluded that the Court's unusual order portends no such change. Nor has Congress modified the habeas statute to add a showing of actual innocence to the grounds warranting relief. Instead, its last reform of federal habeas review for state prisoners — the 1996 Antiterrorism and Effective Death Penalty Act — significantly restricted review by codifying and raising further the procedural hurdles earlier erected by the Court. That Act also barred federal courts from disrupting a state criminal judgment unless the state court's decision, based on the evidence it had at the time of its decision, and ignoring any new evidence or changes in the law since that time, was not only wrong but also objectively unreasonable (*Cullen v. Pinholster*, 2011; *Greene v. Fisher*, 2011).

As discussed below, the states have stepped into the breach here, beginning in recent years to expand their postconviction remedies to accommodate claims of actual innocence. Today state postconviction proceedings are better able to identify and correct at least some wrongful convictions. The changes have been limited and hard fought. Before turning to the reasons that courts and legislatures have been reluctant to expand judicial review beyond the correction of procedural error, it is helpful to examine how this unwavering procedural focus of appellate and postconviction review failed so many of those ultimately exonerated by other means, and why it will continue to handicap judicial review as a remedy for the wrongfully convicted.

## Why Process Review Falls Short

When judicial review is limited to enforcing rules of procedure, it is useless to a prisoner with new evidence of innocence but no viable procedural claim. For example, consider a person convicted on the basis of scientific evidence that was valid at the time of trial but was later discredited. She has new evidence of innocence — the new science showing the evidence against her was unreliable — but is unable to point to any error at trial. At trial, the lawyers, the judge, and the jury followed the rules (Plummer & Syed, 2012). It is not surprising that courts rejected all stand-alone claims of innocence raised by exonerees in Garrett's (2011) study; these petitioners did not yet have DNA evidence, and the claim itself was unrecognized (pp. 202–203).

Not only does the procedural focus of traditional judicial review exclude those with no claim of procedural error, it means that judicial review is necessarily an incomplete remedy for those factually innocent defendants who do have winning procedural claims. Those defendants still must convince prosecutors or paroling authorities of their innocence even after winning their claims in court. The remedy for procedural error on appeal or postconviction is not exoneration. Indeed, it is rarely even a final dismissal of the charges. Only if a reviewing court finds that the government violated one of the few rules that bar prosecution, or that the government's evidence was so grossly insufficient that no juror could have found guilt beyond a reasonable doubt, will a successful challenge end the prosecution. Instead, a win demonstrates only that the conviction was the result of a flawed process, not that the defendant did not commit the crime. A conviction may be vacated, but the prosecutor can try again to comply with the rules. One of three additional actions, besides appellate or postconviction relief, must occur before the defendant no longer faces prosecution: (1) The defendant must be *acquitted* after a new trial; (2) the prosecutor must move to *dismiss* the charge and a judge must grant the motion; or (3) the state's pardoning authority must *pardon* the defendant. As Garrett (2011) found, for the innocent individuals in his study, "obtaining a reversal did not usually end their ordeal. Juries wrongfully convicted them multiple times" (p. 197). Gould *et al.* (2013a) also noted that "the vast majority of exonerations were achieved not because the courts stepped in and ordered a new trial or habeas corpus relief, but because governors or other political leaders, including parole boards, intervened," often with "the active support of prosecutors" (p. 22).

Even when an acquittal or dismissal ends a prosecution, it will not necessarily establish factual innocence. After all, an acquittal means that the proof fell short of proving guilt "beyond a reasonable doubt" and may be entirely consistent with *probable* guilt, or with a conclusion that the defendant actually committed the prohibited acts but lacked the requisite intent. A dismissal or pardon, even when preceded by the discovery of evidence raising doubts about guilt, may also be motivated or explained by reasons other than innocence, including the difficulty of retrying a "guilty" defendant decades after the crime, resource allocation (especially when the defendant has already served a significant sentence), the wishes of the victim, or political pressure. Because of the ambiguous meaning of relief produced by judicial review, innocent individuals cleared of charges have had to wait years for exoneration, often until the real culprits were convicted or confessed (Garrett, 2011, p. 180; Gross & Shaffer, 2012, pp. 99–100). For the same reason, researchers studying wrongful convictions have been careful to include cases of dismissal or acquittal in their studies only if there was *additional* convincing evidence of innocence (Gould et al., 2013a, p. 39; Gross & Shaffer, 2012, p. 7). As the chapter by Griffiths and Owens in this volume details, many states limit compensation for the wrongfully convicted to those who have not only received judicial relief but who, in addition, have been pardoned or can meet stringent tests for proving factual innocence (Kahn, 2010). In sum, the process focus of judicial review deprives courts of the ability to bring an end to the nightmare suffered by the wrongfully convicted. Judicial remedies cannot be obtained except by forcing factual challenges into process boxes, and even then, relief usually does not end a prosecution or dispel inferences of guilt.

## Barriers to Reform

Cases in which individuals lost their challenges in court only to be later exonerated by DNA testing have made it difficult to deny how miserably judicial review has failed the wrongfully convicted. Reforms to change this situation have been incremental and more modest than innocence advocates have hoped. Before discussing what has changed so far, this section reviews some of the reasons, other than the historical and functional reasons mentioned above, that help to explain the persistence of the status quo.

**Federalism.** Federal courts have special reasons to avoid recognizing new constitutional claims or remedies in criminal cases. Many federal judges turn to historical practice and original intent to help interpret the scope of the federal Constitution, and neither supports a second chance for a convicted defendant to litigate his factual guilt after conviction. Clemency, not judicial review, has historically "provided the 'fail safe'" for the wrongfully convicted (*Herrera v. Collins*, 1993, p. 415). Moreover, constitutional rights are necessarily general, applying in every state, and cumbersome to change. States do not necessarily agree about the criteria defining "actual innocence" of a crime, or by what standard innocence must be proven. A constitutional standard would require the Supreme Court to select among varied approaches. Non-constitutional rights, crafted by legislatures or state courts, can be tailored to individual jurisdictions and are much more flexible. Federal judges wary of unnecessarily interfering with state control in criminal justice matters often cite such federalism concerns when declining to enlarge constitutional obligations for state courts and officials. For example, when the Supreme Court rejected a constitutional right of access to DNA evidence for testing in state postconviction proceedings, it declined to "take the development of rules and procedures in this area out of the hands of legislatures and state courts shaping policy in a focused manner and turn it over to federal courts applying the broad parameters of the Due Process Clause. There is no reason," the Chief Justice wrote for the Court, "to constitutionalize the issue in this way" (*District Attorney's Office for Third Judicial District v. Osborne*, 2009, p. 55).

**Skepticism.** Other concerns for state and federal legislators and for state and federal judges stand in the way of efforts to expand judicial relief for the wrongfully convicted. Confidence of lawmakers and judges in the reliability of judgments produced by the adversary system is well documented. Many also believe that the existing avenues for correcting these judgments—combining judicial review, prosecutorial discretion, and clemency—are already catching most errors, so there is no need to strengthen the safety net. For example, a recent study by Smith and colleagues (2011) confirmed that police, judges and prosecutors—key constituencies for any criminal justice reform effort—estimate the frequency of errors such as unreliable eyewitness identification and faulty forensic evidence at a much lower rate than defense attorneys. Compared to 92 % of defense attorneys who said procedural changes are needed to address wrongful convictions, only 30% of judges and 27% of prosecutors thought so. Given "prosecutorial hegemony over criminal justice policy," the authors of the study concluded that "advancing wrongful conviction reforms will be an arduous political task" (Smith, Zalman, & Kiger, 2011, p. 681).

**Cost and efficiency.** Some judges and legislators may consider it too costly to expand judicial remedies sufficiently to identify and correct these cases. Justice Antonin Scalia, for example, has expressed this view in several cases in which he opposed expanded remedies. He put it this way: "It would be marvelously inspiring to be able to boast that we have a criminal-justice system in which a claim of 'actual innocence' will always be heard, no matter how late it is brought forward, and no matter how much the failure to bring it forward at the proper time is the defendant's own fault." Of course, he continued, "we do not have such a system, and no society unwilling to devote unlimited resources to repetitive criminal litigation ever could" (*McQuiggin v. Perkins*, 2013, p. 1942) (internal quotations omitted).

Apprehension about increased costs looms over every decision concerning postconviction review, in part because the vast majority of existing postconviction petitions are meritless and lawmakers worry that expanding review may exacerbate this problem, making it even more difficult for judges to find the meritorious needle in the meritless haystack. Some research indicates that judges in the United States are more concerned about the cost of expansive postconviction review than judges in other countries, where imprisonment rates are much lower (Johnson, 2012, pp. 473–474; Roach, 2013, pp. 304–305). Even with only a fraction of convicts seeking appellate and postconviction relief in the United States, the volume of cases is staggering. And most of these cases are meritless, contributing to distrust of claims of innocence generally, particularly those based on recantations (Gross & Gross, 2013). Lawmakers who are willing to invest significant resources in the problem of false convictions may also prefer to opt for investing in reforms at the front end of the criminal justice system to prevent wrongful convictions before they occur rather than attempting to identify and rectify mistakes after they occur.

**Finality and other concerns.** Opponents of expanded chances to litigate factual innocence after conviction have also expressed concern that defense counsel, judges, and juries will have less incentive to "get it right" the first time at trial if they know the defendant will have multiple chances to correct a mistake later (Wolitz, 2010, p. 1066). By weakening the finality of convictions, some have argued, additional avenues for review also may reduce the ability of the criminal justice system to deter crime and provide repose to crime victims. Prosecutors may worry that reforms to correct false convictions may end up benefiting some who are actually guilty, while defenders may worry that reforms privileging claims of innocence will make it even more difficult to ensure that the factually guilty are treated fairly (Risinger & Risinger, 2012, pp. 870–873).

Judicial reluctance to reopen convictions is not limited to cases alleging actual innocence. Forcing relitigation when evidence is stale and memories have faded may actually risk a less reliable outcome. Political pressure may make it more difficult for some judges facing reelection to reverse convictions, especially in serious cases (Steiker & Steiker, 2010). Judges generally have enormous respect for jury judgments, and may feel no more competent to assess factual guilt than the jurors. Judges who have come to trust the adversarial system and believe that the most accurate verdict is the one produced by sound and fair procedures, may decide that without some indication of unfair procedures, there is no basis for mistrusting a jury's judgment. Similarly, judges, whose expertise is in legal rules, may believe that pardoning authorities are as good or better than they are at sorting the innocent from the guilty after the conclusion of legally fair proceedings.

Finally, judges who do attempt to reconsider factual guilt after conviction may sometimes have a difficult time recognizing when a mistake has been made. Research has suggested that cognitive biases may distort a judge's ability to identify or admit that the wrong person may have been convicted (Findley, 2009, pp. 605–606). These unconscious effects may be exacerbated when a claim of innocence is made to the very same judge that presided at trial, as it is in most states.

## New and Expanded Judicial Remedies

Despite this catalogue of impediments to expanded judicial relief for those claiming innocence, every state in recent years has made some changes to judicial review to accommodate actual innocence claims. Indeed, as Garrett (2011) notes, "states have themselves revisited many of the legal obstacles that so substantially delayed exoneration" of the innocent people whose cases he examined (p. 239).

**DNA testing statutes.** The most popular reform has been to help petitioners to obtain DNA testing of biological evidence through the courts. New York adopted the first postconviction DNA testing statute in 1994, and every other state has followed suit. Congress helped by making funds available to states that pass DNA testing statutes (Ginsburg & Hunt, 2010). Lawmakers also may have taken to heart arguments that the price of providing some prisoners with DNA tests is a good investment when compared to the combined cost of unwarranted incarceration of the innocent, continued litigation to resist their court challenges, and the harm to public safety if real offenders remain at large (Garrett, 2011, p. 233; Medwed, 2012, p. 153).

Most of these new statutes provide a means for a convicted person to obtain DNA testing of biological material tied to his case if he can demonstrate a reasonable probability that he would not have been convicted if an exculpatory test result had been presented at trial, although some have lower or higher standards (*District Attorney's Office for the Third Judicial District v. Osborne*, 2009; Wilkes, 2012–2013, §1:8). Some of these statutes not only authorize courts to order tests, but also to consider the test results and decide what relief, if any, might be appropriate. Many simply provide a means of procuring tests, and leave it to the petitioner to decide whether to file a postconviction petition using the test results as new evidence in support of a claim.

The speed with which state legislatures passed testing statutes is impressive. But DNA analysis is relevant in only a small percentage of cases, and is possible only in the subset of those cases where biological evidence has been collected and not lost (Garrett, 2011, pp. 263–265). In one-third of the states, testing is only available to those who contested their guilt at trial, not to those who have pleaded guilty. Some prosecutors have reportedly obtained waivers of the right to seek DNA testing as part of a plea bargain, just as some plea bargains waive other forms of postconviction review (Wiseman, 2012, pp. 961–967). All but five states exclude juveniles (Tepfer & Nirider, 2012), most exclude those convicted of all but the most serious crimes, and many bar those who did not request testing at trial (*District Attorney's Office for the Third Judicial District v. Osborne*, 2009). More than a dozen states limit testing applications to petitioners who contested identity at trial. All but a few require that applications be filed within a certain time frame, and some do not provide an appeal if testing is denied (Gabel & Wilkinson, 2008; Wilkes, 2012–2013, §1:8). Courts thus far have generally rejected challenges that these restrictions are unconstitutionally unfair (LaFave *et al.*, 2007, §28.11(a)).

The narrow scope of these statutes may be linked to concerns about the burdens of dealing with testing requests filed by guilty defendants who deny their guilt or hope for a mismatch or inconclusive result (Carroll, 2007). Indeed, among all the DNA tests procured by Innocence Projects, organizations that screen cases and accept only the most viable claims of innocence, an estimated 50–60% actually *confirm* guilt (Jacobi & Carroll, 2008, p. 270). To deter frivolous requests, some statutes require that if testing confirms guilt, petitioners must pay for the costs of testing, and paroling and pardoning authorities must be informed of the adverse result. In at least one state, a prisoner whose tests confirm guilt will have to wait in prison two extra months before becoming eligible for parole. Another state requires that applicants must waive the statute of limitations for any felony offense matched through later DNA database comparison (Jacobi & Carroll, 2008; Medwed, 2012, p. 154).

**Innocence as a ground for relief in postconviction.** In addition to providing a limited route to DNA *testing* after conviction, states are beginning to expand their all-purpose postconviction remedies to permit consideration of claims of innocence based on new evidence (Norris, Bonventre, Redlich, & Acker, 2011; Smith, 2012). In most states today, a petitioner may use the primary postconviction remedy to seek relief based on newly discovered evidence of innocence, although in some states the only authority for raising an innocence claim is set out in the DNA testing statute (Wilkes, 2012–2013, §1:4). Among states that do not limit innocence claims to those with new DNA evidence, approximately six limit the type of new evidence to some sort or scientific evidence. Most states continue to require that, like other postconviction claims, the challenge be filed within a certain time frame and while the petitioner is still incarcerated or on supervised release. Statutes may bar or limit use by defendants who have pleaded guilty, or permit only claims backed up by DNA tests or new scientific evidence. If a state does not normally provide a right to a hearing in postconviction cases, or does not provide appointed counsel or expert assistance for those who cannot afford them, petitioners who raise actual innocence claims will go without as well. The burden of proof for a claim of innocence based on new evidence varies among states. Standards include a showing of probable innocence, clear and convincing evidence of innocence, "affirmative" proof, or evidence that "unquestionably" establishes innocence—burdens which some critics say are too high (Medwed, 2012, p. 125; Simon, 2012, pp. 205, 212).

**Special innocence remedies.** Rather than use existing postconviction remedies, a few states have adopted new separate judicial remedies for innocence claims, and have not experienced a flood of claims. In Virginia, a "writ of actual innocence" is available in the court of appeals for those seeking exoneration based on non-DNA evidence; about two-dozen applications are filed each year (State of the Judiciary Report, 2012). In Utah, even fewer applications are filed each year seeking relief under a new remedy also designed for prisoners with non-

DNA evidence of innocence (Higgenbottom, 2013). Maryland and Washington D.C. have also adopted special "innocence" postconviction remedies for petitioners with new evidence.

Perhaps the most well-known innovation is the Innocence Inquiry Commission in North Carolina. Drawn from similar commissions in Canada and the United Kingdom (Thompson, Hopgood, & Valderrama, 2012, pp. 401–447), the eight-member commission reviews claims of innocence and investigates those that meet specified criteria. Following investigation, the Commission determines whether to transfer the claim to a three-judge panel for a hearing and a decision about whether to vacate the conviction and dismiss the charge. Between 2007 and April 2013, the Commission has held five hearings, and exonerated four claimants (North Carolina Innocence Inquiry Commission, 2013). The Commission has federal grant funding for staff and other costs related to DNA testing, as well as state funding. It receives about 245 claims annually, most of which are rejected because the claimant has no new evidence, has no way to prove innocence, or did not claim complete factual innocence. Similar commissions have been proposed in several states, and advocates have argued that with more legislative control over the commission's budget and expenditures, an innocence commission is a more cost effective and manageable alternative for addressing postconviction claims of innocence than expanding existing judicial remedies or recognizing new constitutional claims (Wolitz, 2010).

# Moving Forward

With the Supreme Court taking a back seat to state experimentation, the next decades are certain to produce even more innovative approaches for identifying and correcting wrongful convictions, as well as more information about the cost and effectiveness of various options. The experiences of past exonerees also suggest that a range of reforms would be helpful, not limited to revising judicial review procedures themselves.

## Ensure Adequate Indigent Defense Before Conviction

To improve the ability of any judicial remedy to catch and correct factual error in criminal cases *after* conviction, it is essential to improve the representation of defendants in trial courts *before* conviction. As the recent study of "near-miss" wrongful convictions most recently confirmed, effective defense at the outset can reveal weaknesses in a state's evidence and prevent wrongful convictions from occurring (Gould, Carrano, Leo, & Hail-Jares, 2013b). Moreover, when trial lawyers overlook errors, identifying and correcting those errors becomes much more difficult after conviction. Reviewing courts generally will not consider claims that a defendant's trial attorney could have raised but did not. For example, Garrett noted that many exonerees in his study who had been convicted on the basis of flawed expert testimony lost their best opportunities to challenge that testimony on judicial review because their trial attorneys failed to recognize its invalidity and attack it before conviction (2011, p. 189). Because effective judicial review depends upon effective assistance at trial, a discussion of how to improve judicial review of wrongful convictions at the back end of the criminal justice process must begin with providing adequate resources for the representation of the accused at the front end.

# Improve Judicial Review Mechanisms for the Wrongfully Convicted

There has been no shortage of proposals for changing judicial review in criminal cases to make it less difficult for innocent people to prove they have been wrongfully convicted. The reforms easiest to achieve politically probably are those that are narrowly focused on cases in which claims of innocence can be scientifically verified, such as provisions eliminating restrictions on access to DNA testing, and that permit courts administering existing remedies to consider claims of actual innocence based on DNA analysis or other new scientific evidence (Gabel & Wilkinson, 2008). Decisions recognizing stand-alone innocence claims under state constitutions, or changes that selectively set aside barriers and restrictions on relief for these particular claims, may also be more politically palatable than more sweeping modifications.

Another set of proposals is directed at overcoming barriers to state postconviction remedies generally, not necessarily limited to actual innocence claimants. Reforms such as providing postconviction petitioners with appointed counsel and resources for investigation, greater access to hearings, a judge other than the one who presided over the conviction, less deferential harmless error rules for unreliable eyewitness identification or informant testimony (Anderson, 2011; Findley, 2009, p. 633), and less onerous standards for relief (Simon, 2012) would probably make it easier for those with viable claims of actual innocence to secure judicial relief. But lawmakers, judges, and prosecutors concerned about the cost of applying these reforms to petitioners who raise frivolous claims are likely to continue to resist these more universal changes. An even more fundamental reform would be changing the traditional judicial review structure itself to allow claims that require fact finding to be litigated and resolved during direct appeal instead of only later during postconviction review, a model already followed in a few states. Advocates point out this procedure would be especially helpful to the wrongfully convicted because it would provide counsel to assist them in gathering and presenting new evidence of innocence (Findley, 2009; Primus, 2010), but structural changes of this magnitude would face stronger political headwinds.

# Beyond Judicial Review

Past exonerations show that judicial proceedings alone are often not enough to secure either wrongfully convicted individuals' release from incarceration or an official statement of actual innocence. Even if every jurisdiction loosened restrictions on judicial remedies for challenging convictions with DNA and new scientific evidence, the shortcomings of traditional judicial review examined above would remain for those without such evidence. Improving judicial review for claims of actual innocence is not likely to eliminate the essential functions that non-judicial actors can and will continue to serve in securing exonerations.

**Prosecutors.** The most important of these non-judicial actors is the prosecutor. Professor Daniel Medwed, who has written extensively about the role of prosecutors in cases of actual innocence, summed up why: It is "difficult for the defense to get courts to examine the accuracy of [a conviction] without the prosecution's help" (Medwed, 2012, p. 125). Plenty of criticism has been heaped on prosecutors for resisting attempts at exoneration (Green & Yaroshefsky, 2009; Medwed, 2004; Orenstein, 2011; Zacharias, 2005). Prosecutors opposed DNA testing in about one-fifth of the first 250 DNA exonerations, and in some of these cases prosecutors continued to fight exoneration even after DNA results favorable to the defendant were returned (Garrett, 2011, p. 227). The list of explanations for prosecutorial resistance range from the sinister (racism, or deliberate cover-up) to the sympathetic (good faith disputes about the relevance of test results, or lack of sufficient resources). Prosecutors, like all humans, are susceptible to cognitive biases and tunnel vision (Medwed, 2012, p. 128). In most states, they lack clear ethical guidance addressing appropriate responses to postconviction claims or evidence of innocence (Ginsburg & Hunt, 2010; Zacahrias, 2005) and may have difficulty navigating the sometimes conflicting roles of advocate and minister of justice (Swisher, 2013). Prosecutors may work in offices where there are few incentives to expose or admit error, but plenty of disincentives: Admitting that an innocent person was prosecuted can carry significant professional, political, and psychological costs (Medwed, 2012, pp. 127–131). A prosecutor may also act out of concern for the victim of the crime, or concerns for future victims if the prosecutor believes that the person seeking exoneration is dangerous. A prosecutor may defer to the jury's judgment, or worry about encouraging frivolous claims, or hope to spare taxpayers the cost of large damage awards (Medwed, 2004).

Not only do prosecutors decide when further investigation is required, once doubts about guilt have been raised, they also choose whether to support exoneration, or settle instead for a remedy such as dismissal or a negotiated settlement that ends incarceration with less fanfare, leaves some ambiguity regarding factual guilt, and avoids accepting blame for a bungled prosecution (Gross & Shaffer, 2012, pp. 95–98). Attractive alternatives include a release dismissal agreement that trades the dismissal of charges for the release of civil claims, or a sentence of time served combined with an *Alford* plea in which the defendant pleads guilty while maintaining his innocence. Medwed (2012, p. 131) argues that the only cases in which prosecutors will be eager to champion exoneration are cases where investigative reporting by the media threatens reputational harm to the prosecutor, where the exoneration would harm a political adversary, where there is evidence implicating the actual perpetrator, or where the defendant is already serving a prison term for a different crime so exoneration would not release him (Medwed, 2004, p. 159).

Despite this criticism, prosecutors have cooperated in many cases of exoneration, and there is reason to believe that the percentage of exonerations in which prosecutors have been instrumental is increasing. Prosecutors are more likely now than they once were to investigate and present evidence of innocence after conviction, and advocate on behalf of the wrongfully convicted party. They sometimes complete the exoneration process that has begun with judicial review, or provide relief when judicial review is unavailable (National Registry of Exonerations, 2013). Because changing the way that prosecutors address these issues not only can help correct but also can help *prevent* wrongful convictions, a focus on prosecutors is at least as important as judicial remedies.

The most widely applauded reform is the creation of an innocence or postconviction unit, or "innocence wing" in the offices of urban prosecutors and state attorneys general (Scheck, 2010). So far, chief prosecutors in Arizona, and the cities of Dallas, Houston, Brooklyn, and Chicago are among those who have tasked staff with revisiting credible cases of innocence, sometimes with a DNA focus (National Registry of Exonerations, 2013). Incentives to reward efforts by prosecutors to join in or refrain from contesting legitimate postconviction claims of innocence are also promising (Medwed, 2012, pp. 133–134).

**Pardoning authorities.** Unlike a judicial order dismissing a charge or vacating a conviction for procedural error, clemency has the capacity to settle the innocence question, at least when it takes the form of an official statement that the conviction was factually erroneous. As a result, clemency has played a key role in remedying wrongful convictions, supplementing and substituting for judicial review. Even some recently enacted wrongful conviction compensation statutes require a pardon as proof of exoneration, in addition to an acquittal or dismissal (Texas Civil Code § 103.001). These developments suggest that efforts to improve relief for the wrongfully convicted should include attention to the clemency process.

As unregulated mercy, clemency can be denied for any or no reason, and without explanation. In some states a governor shares her pardon power with a board, which must join in or recommend relief (Barkow, 2009; 2008; LaFave et al., 2007, § 26.2(c)). Researchers have suggested that the reasons boards and governors may decline to grant relief include doubts about their capacity to assess the facts any more accurately than the judicial system, fear of undermining public confidence in the criminal justice process, and above all, concern that a person once released may commit another crime, harming public safety as well as their own political careers. Although there are a few recent examples of governors who have exercised their pardon power more generously out of personal moral or religious conviction, there is also some evidence that shifting clemency power from the governor's office to an independent board "gives the executive some distance from the decision-making process so that decisions can be made without fear that one bad case will undercut the entire process" (Barkow, 2013, p. 338). More political independence may also prompt fewer decisions that end incarceration but leave open the question of factual guilt or innocence, forcing the individual to establish innocence in some other forum (Garrett, 2011, p. 234).

**Private attorneys, journalists, Innocence Projects.** Finally, to find and secure evidence of innocence to present to the judges, prosecutors, and pardoning authorities who have the capacity to grant relief, a wrongfully convicted person needs help reviewing and analyzing existing evidence, finding and interviewing witnesses, and working with experts. For many exonerees that help has come from volunteer investigators, journalists, and attorneys, including those now working with more than 70 Innocence Projects around the country. Innocence Projects, often based in law schools and supported by grants and donations, also identify and screen claims of innocence and provide representation and advocacy for those seeking exoneration. It is estimated that these organizations have played a substantial role in one of every five DNA exonerations so far (Gould, et al., 2013a; National Registry of Exonerations, 2013). Nearly 80% of the exonerees in Garrett's study initially sought DNA tests through Innocence Projects and postconviction attorneys (Garrett, 2011, p. 225).

States are unlikely to willingly take over the entire cost of conducting investigations that presently are funded privately, particularly if they decide that devoting more resources to *prevent* wrongful convictions might have a higher pay off in terms of saving taxpayer dollars than attempting to fix them later. Some have argued that states should authorize contingency fees for wrongful conviction litigation (Robertson, 2012; Tetelbaum, 2010). Alternatively, some state funding for existing Innocence Projects could help to provide the evidence and advocacy that is needed for judicial review to function. The Texas legislature, for example, provides funding to several Innocence Projects around the state. An advisory commission on wrongful convictions in Texas recently concluded that increasing this funding would be a more effective approach for identifying and correcting these cases than establishing a separate Innocence Commission with investigatory power like that in North Carolina (Timothy Cole Advisory Panel, 2012, pp. 34–35).

**Innocence commissions.** An independent commission like the North Carolina Innocence Inquiry Commission has the capacity to investigate, adjudicate, and grant complete relief to the wrongfully convicted. Although it involves some judges as members of the commission and on the panels that ultimately decide whether to grant relief, the Commission operates as a separate agency, outside of the judicial branch. Indeed, the Commission's departure from the relentlessly adversarial method of decision making present at every phase of the judicial system may be one of its greatest assets. Creating an entirely new path to relief, rather than transforming or tinkering with existing adversarial proceedings in the courts, is an important option that other states are considering and many commentators support.

# Conclusion

Judicial review has proven to be an incomplete remedy for the wrongfully convicted in part because it was developed to make sure that the proceedings leading to criminal punishment complied with procedural rules, not to make sure that the right person was convicted. Finding effective remedies to correct the mistakes that result from lawful proceedings will take time and experimentation. Fortunately, this undertaking has already begun. When innocent people are convicted, we can hope that these reforms will help make their quest for exoneration less onerous in the future.

# References

Associated Press (2013, March 12). DNA Evidence Clears Virginia Man in 1976 Abductions. *NBC Washington.* Retrieved from http://www.nbcwashington.com/news/local/DNA-Evidence-Clears-Va-Man-in-1976-Abductions-197287271.html.

Anderson, H. A. (2011). Revising harmless error: Making innocence relevant to direct appeals. *Texas Wesleyan Law Review, 17,* 391–402.

Aronson, J. D. & Cole, S. A. (2009). Science and the death penalty: DNA, innocence, and the debate over capital punishment in the United States. *Law & Social Inquiry, 34,* 603–624.

Barkow, R.E. (2013). Prosecutorial administration: Prosecutor bias and the department of justice. *Virginia Law Review, 99,* 271–342.

Barkow, R.E. (2009). The politics of forgiveness: Reconceptualizing clemency. *Federal Sentencing Reporter, 21,* 153–163.

Barkow, R.E. (2008). The ascent of the administrative state and the demise of mercy. *Harvard Law Review, 121,* 1332–1365.

Bibas, [THIS VOLUME].

Carroll, G. (2007). Proven guilty: An Examination of the penalty-free world of post-conviction DNA testing. *Journal of Criminal Law and Criminology, 97,* 665–698.

*Cullen v. Pinholster,* 131 S. Ct. 1388 (2011).

*District Attorney's Office for Third Judicial District v. Osborne,* 557 U.S. 52 (2009).

*Establishing conviction integrity programs in prosecutors' offices: A report on the Center on the Administration of Criminal Law's Conviction Integrity Project* (2012). Retrieved from New York University School of Law, Center on the Administration of Criminal Law website: http://www.law.nyu.edu/ecm_dlv2/groups/public/@nyu_law_website__centers__center_on_administration_of_criminal_law/documents/documents/ecm_pro_073583.pdf.

Findley, K. A. (2009). Innocence protection in the appellate process. *Marquette Law Review, 93,* 591–638.

Gabel, J. D. & Wilkinson, M. D. (2008). Good science gone bad: How the criminal justice system can redress the impact of flawed forensics. *Hastings Law Journal, 59,* 1001–1030.

Garrett, B. L. (2011). *Convicting the innocent: Where criminal prosecutions go wrong.* Cambridge, MA: Harvard University Press.

Ginsburg, D. H. & Hunt, H. (2010). The prosecutor and post-conviction claims of innocence: DNA and beyond? *Ohio State Journal of Criminal Law, 7,* 771–793.

Gould, J. B., Carrano, J., Leo, R. A., & Young, J. (2013a). *Predicting erroneous convictions: A social science approach to miscarriages of justice.* National Institute of Justice, Office of Justice Programs, United States Department of Justice. Retrieved from https://ncjrs.gov/pdffiles1/nij/grants/241389.pdf.

Gould, J. B., Carrano, J., Leo, R. A., & Hail-Jares, K. (2013b). Predicting erroneous convictions. *Iowa Law Review* (forthcoming). Advance online publication. University of San Francisco Law Research Paper No. 2013–19. Retrieved from: http://ssrn.com/abstract=2231740.

Green, B. A., & Yaroshefsky, E. (2009). Prosecutorial discretion and post-conviction evidence of innocence. *Ohio State Journal of Criminal Law, 6,* 467–517.

*Greene v. Fisher,* 132 S. Ct. 38 (2011).

Gross, S. R., & Gross, A. E. (2013, May). *Witness recantation study: Preliminary findings.* Retrieved from The University of Michigan Law School & Northwestern University Law School, The National Registry of Exonerations website: https://www.law.umich.edu/special/exoneration/Documents/RecantationUpdate_5_2013.pdf.

Gross, S. R., & Shaffer, M. (2012). *Exonerations in the United States, 1989–2012.* Retrieved from The University of Michigan Law School & Northwestern University Law School, The National Registry of Exonerations website: https://www.law.umich.edu/special/exoneration/Documents/exonerations_us_1989_2012_full_report.pdf.

*Herrera v. Collins,* 506 U.S. 390 (1993).

Higginbottom, J. (2013, May 8). Shadow of guilt: Until the Utah Supreme Court weighs in on her factual innocence, Debra Brown lives one day at a time. *Salt Lake City News.* Retrieved from http://www.cityweekly.net/utah/article-17508-shadow-of-guilt.html.

Hoffmann, J. L.,(2012). Innocence and federal habeas after AEDPA: Time for the Supreme Court to act. *Federal Sentencing Reporter, 24,* 300–305.

*House v. Bell,* 547 U.S. 518 (2006).

*In re Davis,* 130 S. Ct. 1 (2009).

*Jackson v. Virginia,* 443 U.S. 307 (1979).

Jacobi, T., & Carroll, G. (2008). Acknowledging guilt: Forcing self-identification in post-conviction DNA testing. *Northwestern University Law Review, 102,* 263–306.

Johnson, C. M. (2012). Post-trial judicial review of criminal convictions: A comparative study of the United States and Finland. *Maine Law Review, 64,* 425–477.

Kahn, D. S. (2010). Presumed guilty until proven innocent: The burden of proof in wrongful conviction claims under state compensation statutes. *University of Michigan Journal of Law Reform, 44,* 123–168.

King, N. J. (2013a). Plea bargains that waive claims of ineffective assistance—Waiving *Frye* and *Padilla. Duquesne Law Review, 51* (forthcoming). Advance online publication. Vanderbilt University Law School Public Law and Legal Theory Working Paper No. 13–25. Retrieved from http://papers.ssrn.com/sol3/papers.cfm?abstract_id=2259694##.

King, N. J. (2013b). Enforcing effective assistance after *Martinez. Yale Law Journal, 122,* 2428–2458.

King, N. J. (2012). Non-capital habeas cases after appellate review: An empirical analysis. *Federal Sentencing Reporter, 24,* 308–317.

King, N. J., & Hoffmann, J. L. (2011). *Habeas for the twenty-first century: Uses, abuses and the future of the great writ.* Chicago, IL: University of Chicago Press.

LaFave, W. R., Israel, J. H., King, N. J., & Kerr, O. S. (2007). *Criminal procedure* (3rd ed. & 2012 Suppl.). Eagan, MN: Thomson Reuters.

*McQuiggin v. Perkins,* 133 S. Ct. 1294 (2013).

Medwed, D. S. (2012). *Prosecution complex: America's race to convict and its impact on the innocent.* New York, NY: New York University Press.

Medwed, D. S. (2004). The zeal deal: Prosecutorial resistance to postconviction claims of innocence. *Boston University Law Review, 84,* 125–183.

*National Registry of Exonerations, UPDATE: 2012* (2013, April 3). Retrieved from The University of Michigan Law School & Northwestern University Law School, The National Registry of Exonerations website: https://www.law.umich.edu/special/ exoneration/Documents/NRE2012UPDATE4_1_13_FINAL.pdf.

Norris, R. J., Bonventre, C. L., Redlich, A. D., & Acker, J. R. (2011). "Than that one innocent suffer": Evaluating state safeguards against wrongful convictions. *Albany Law Review, 74,* 1301–1362.

Orenstein, A. (2011). Facing the unfaceable: Dealing with prosecutorial denial in postconviction cases of actual innocence. *San Diego Law Review, 48,* 401–446.

*Perry v. New Hampshire,* 132 S. Ct. 716 (2012).

Plummer, C. M., & Syed, I. J. (2012). "Shifted science" and postconviction relief. *Stanford Journal of Civil Rights and Criminal Law, 8* (forthcoming). Retrieved from http:// papers.ssrn.com/sol3/papers.cfm?abstract_id=1989683.

Primus, E.B. (2010). A structural vision of habeas corpus. *California Law Review, 98,* 1–57.

*Report to the Regular Session of the 2013–14 General Assembly of North Carolina and the State Judicial Council* (2013). Retrieved from North Carolina Innocence Inquiry Commission website http://www.innocencecommission-nc.gov/gar.html.

Risinger, D. M., & Risinger, L. C. (2012). Innocence is different: Taking innocence into account in reforming criminal procedure. *New York Law School Law Review, 56,* 869–909.

Roach, K. (2013). More procedure and concern about innocence but less justice? Remedies for wrongful convictions in the United States and Canada. In C. R. Huff & M. Killias (eds.), *Wrongful convictions and miscarriage of justice: Causes and remedies in North American and European criminal justice systems.* New York, NY: Routledge.

Robertson, C. T. (2012). Contingent compensation of post-conviction counsel: A modest proposal to identify meritorious claims and reduce wasteful government spending. *Maine Law Review, 64,* 513–529.

Rosenmerkel, S. P., Durose, M. R., & Farole, D. F. Jr. (2009). Felony sentences in state courts, 2006 — Statistical tables. Washington, DC: Bureau of Justice Statistics.

Scheck, B. (2010). Professional and conviction integrity programs: Why we need them, why they will work, and models for creating them. *Cardozo Law Review, 31,* 2215–2256.

*Schlup v. Delo,* 513 U.S. 298 (1995).

Simon, D. (2012). *In doubt: The psychology of the criminal justice process.* Cambridge: MA, Harvard University Press.

Smith, B., Zalman, M., & Kiger, A. (2011). How justice system officials view wrongful convictions. *Crime & Delinquency, 57*(5), 663–685.

Smith, R. J. (2012). Recalibrating constitutional innocence protection. *Washington Law Review, 87,* 139–204.

*State of the Judiciary Report* (2012). Court of Appeals of Virginia. Retrieved from http:// www.courts.state.va.us/courtadmin/aoc/judpln/csi/stats/cav_caseload_rpt_2012.pdf.

Steiker, C. S., & Steiker, J. M. (2010). Report to the ALI concerning capital punishment. *Texas Law Review, 89,* 367–421.

Swisher, K. (2013). Prosecutorial conflicts of interest in postconviction practice. *Hofstra Law Review, 41*, 181–215.

Tepfer, J. A., & Nirider, L. H. (2012). Adjudicated juveniles and collateral relief. *Maine Law Review, 64*, 553–574.

Tetelbaum, E. (2010). Remedying a lose-lose situation: How 'no win, no fee' can incentivize post-conviction relief for the wrongly convicted. *Connecticut Public Interest Law Journal, 9*, 301–342.

Texas Civil Practice & Remedies Code Annotated § 103.001 (2011).

Thompson, S. G., Hopgood, J. L., & Valderrama, H. K. (2012). *American justice in the age of innocence: Understanding the causes of wrongful convictions and how to prevent them.* Bloomington, IL: iUniverse, Inc.

Thompson, S.G. (2009). Judicial blindness to eyewitness misidentification. *Marquette Law Review, 93*, 639–669.

Timothy Cole Advisory Panel on Wrongful Convictions (2012, August). Report to the Texas Task Force on Indigent Defense. Retrieved from http://www.txcourts.gov/tidc/tcap.asp.

Wilkes, D. E., Jr. (2012–2013). *State postconviction remedies and relief handbook with forms: Volume 3.* Eagan, MN: Thomson Reuters.

Wiseman, S. R. (2012). Waiving innocence. *Minnesota Law Review, 96*, 952–1017.

Wolitz, D. (2010). Innocence commissions and the future of post-conviction review. *Arizona Law Review, 52*, 1027–1082.

Zacharias, F. C. (2005). The role of prosecutors in serving justice after convictions. *Vanderbilt Law Review, 58*, 171–239.

# Chapter Fourteen

# The Problem of Fit: Parolees, Exonerees, and Prisoner Reentry

Kimberly J. Cook, *University of North Carolina at Wilmington*
Saundra D. Westervelt, *University of North Carolina at Greensboro*
Shadd Maruna, *Queens University Belfast*

In discussions of prisoner reentry, the question of "fit" most typically revolves around issues of prisoner reintegration—how do parolees fit back into their communities and families after release? When broadening that discussion to include exonerees (those wrongly convicted of crimes), the same question remains—how do exonerees fit back into their communities and families after release? Yet, adding exonerees to the mix of ex-prisoners seeking reintegration after release from prison raises other questions of fit. How do exonerees' post-release needs fit with what we know about parolees' post-release needs? How does our knowledge about prisoner reentry fit for exonerees? This chapter examines this problem of fit when applying the lessons from prisoner reentry research to exonerees. We draw on the more extensive research literature that explores the purposes, impact, and inadequacies of post-release services for paroled ex-prisoners who have not been exonerated and are presumed to have been guilty of the crimes for which they were convicted. The unique position occupied by exonerees also helps illuminate the broader problem of fit for prisoner reintegration in general.

By virtue of their incarceration experience, exonerees and parolees emerge from prison with many shared practical and emotional hurdles to confront and overcome: difficulties finding employment and housing, challenges of remaking relationships and rebuilding families, and ongoing battles with disorientation, depression, and post-traumatic stress (Grounds, 2004; Westervelt & Cook, 2012). Yet, after their release, they also find themselves in fundamentally different relationships with the state. When correctional systems release ordinary prisoners, it is rarely with the imprimatur that they are free to go without continuing obligations to the state. Former inmates are often required to report their activities to state officials on a regular basis; failure to do so can result in re-incarceration, depending on the conditions of release (Simon, 1993). In addition, the state provides some limited post-release services to assist with job skill development, vocational training, and housing and employment location (though such services vary tremendously by state and jurisdiction) (Petersilia, 2003). Thus, the ex-prisoner typically has a continuing obligation to the state; and the state, in some cases, recognizes a continuing obligation to the ex-prisoner to assist this difficult process of reentry created by the use of incarceration as punishment (Travis, 2005).

On the other hand, once exonerated and released from prison, wrongfully convicted former prisoners are "free" in the sense that they have no continuing obligations to the state. Nor, however, does the state assume a continuing obligation to them. In most cases, for example, the state that prosecuted the wrongful conviction does not provide reparations to the exoneree, as compensation statutes are widely varied, grossly inadequate, and often even non-existent (Norris, 2012). The state typically is not held responsible for the infliction of this harm, and the exoneree most often is released without supports or programs that may be available to prisoners released on parole (Westervelt & Cook, 2012). In this sense, the wrongfully convicted exoneree may be victimized in multiple ways by the state (Westervelt & Cook, 2010).

These differences in the structural relationships between parolees, exonerees, and the state create gaps in our knowledge about the application of traditional prisoner reentry principles to exonerees. They raise questions such as: What can we learn from the research on prisoner reentry to better understand and assist exonerees? How might the discussion around reentry be broadened to better accommodate the needs and experiences of exonerees? In this chapter, we rely on our combined knowledge and experience about related matters to address these issues.

# Stepping Back: The Pains of Imprisonment and Barriers to Reentry

The experience of incarceration is painful and traumatizing for parolees and exonerees alike (for a fuller review of this literature as it relates to death row exonerees, see Westervelt & Cook, 2012; and more generally, Cohen & Taylor, 1972; Crewe, 2010; Haney, 2003a, 2003b; Liebling & Maruna, 2005; Sykes, 1958; Zamble & Porporino, 1988). The authors of the most famous study of the effects of imprisonment, the "Stanford Prison Experiment," summarize this literature thusly: "Prisons are places that demean humanity, destroy the nobility of human nature, and bring out the worst in social relations among people. They are as bad for the guards as the prisoners in terms of their destructive impact on self-esteem, sense of justice, and human compassion" (Zimbardo, Maslach, & Haney, 2000, p. 209). As Irwin and Owen (2005, p. 98) explain, "[l]ong imprisonment assaults and disorganizes the personality in ... insidious and subtle ways, including loss of agency, assaults on the self and damage to sexual orientation." Jamieson and Grounds (2005, p. 58) observe that "studies of victims of disaster [are] relevant [to the study of the effects of long-term incarceration] because such studies are similarly concerned with the consequences of sudden and overwhelming dislocations that affect the individual's total life."

Lee Bowker (1982, pp. 63-64) refers to the struggles of life in prison as a "controlled war" among inmates. Death row exoneree Kirk Bloodsworth says of his incarceration experience, "it's so damn depressing in there. Hell, you're peeling paint on the walls, rats running around, people getting stabbed every hour of the day, people screaming 'cause they're getting raped right down the hallway, you know.... I mean, it's the most brutal existence you could live in under *any* circumstance" (Westervelt & Cook, 2012, p. 113). Prisoners must deftly defend themselves against this emotionally and physically hostile world by barricading themselves as much as possible. As a consequence, inmates report experiencing problems of depression, helplessness, stress, and extreme loneliness which can lead to self-destructive patterns that "increase[] difficulties in adjusting to life after release" (Bowker, 1982, p. 69).

Given that death row confinement is "different from all other criminal punishments" (Haney, 2005, p. 243), the trauma of incarceration is even more pronounced. Individuals convicted of capital crimes are, in essence, "expelled from humanity" (Westervelt & Cook,

2012, p. 171) and not expected to return to society or recover from the pains of imprisonment. They confront daily the real possibility of their executions as well as the loneliness, boredom and frequent brutality that comes with death row confinement. Juan Melendez, an exoneree who endured death row in Florida for more than 17 years, reflects on the impact of executions occurring around him: "[T]hat was one of the hardest parts of being there, was when they kill somebody.... you think 'I'll probably be next'" (Westervelt & Cook, 2012, pp. 115-116). Delbert Tibbs, another Florida death row exoneree, says, "each day is pretty much the same as the next and to the one before" (Westervelt & Cook, 2012, p. 111). Ray Krone describes his response to this routine and boredom while on death row in Arizona, "you almost become automated then, where you don't have to have emotional responses" (Westervelt & Cook, 2012, p. 110). Finally, North Carolina death row exoneree Alfred Rivera makes clear that "on death row you truly die even before death, mentally. You have nothing to look forward to ..." (Westervelt & Cook, 2012, p. 112).

Added to the trauma caused by incarceration, exonerees confront anger, bitterness, and the unjust nature of their conviction and incarceration on top of the daily struggle for survival behind bars. Alfred Rivera addresses this layer of trauma when he says, "[I] looked around daily and said to myself, 'I don't belong here' and why am I amongst this guy or that guy, guys who maybe said or pleaded to their guilt and did not have a care in the world about it. I often expressed to my family that it didn't seem real that I was there on death row" (Westervelt & Cook 2012, p. 110). Having been incarcerated for crimes they did not commit, they battle the emotional desperation of proving their innocence over and above their daily struggle to survive. In some cases, they spend their time inside trying frantically to get anyone on the outside to listen to and believe them. Gary Gauger, Illinois death row exoneree, calls this his "message in a bottle" period, saying, "I ... was just writing anybody and everybody I thought could possibly help me. All the newspapers, magazines, TV talk shows, anything ... law firms. I thought all I gotta do is get in touch with Connie Chung or somebody and I'd be out within two weeks. I was very naïve" (Westervelt & Cook, 2012, p. 121).

The trauma of incarceration is real for prisoners whether they are rightly or wrongly convicted. Consequently, they all must develop strategies for coping with that trauma (for extensive discussion of exoneree coping strategies, see Westervelt & Cook, 2012). For parolees, the quest to assert the "real me" to the world requires that they have a platform to demonstrate that they are a "good person"—albeit one who has made some mistakes (Maruna, 2001, p. 88). For exonerees, that quest is to demonstrate they are a "good person" in order to reclaim their innocence. This process is not straightforward or easy for either group. By asserting their "real selves" publicly, they may aim to turn their experiences into object lessons for social change, creating what Judith Herman calls a "survivor mission" (1997, p. 207):

> Most survivors seek the resolution of their traumatic experience within the confines of their personal lives. But a significant minority, as a result of the trauma, feel called upon to engage in the wider world. These survivors recognize a political or religious dimension to their misfortune and discover that they can transform the meaning of their personal tragedy by making it the basis for social action. While there is no way to compensate for an atrocity, there is a way to transcend it, by making it a gift to others.

Maruna (2001, p. 103) notes that "[t]his urge to 'give people my life' appears repeatedly in the interviews with desisting people." One ex-prisoner said: "If I could stop even one person taking drugs again, it would be enough." Exoneree Delbert Tibbs says something quite similar about his wrongful capital conviction: "I believe that [the Great Spirit] took me to death row so that I could be a witness and a voice against it" (Westervelt & Cook,

2012, p. 145). By putting their hard-earned wisdom into the cause of creating social change, parolees and exonerees find healing in helping others.

Transitioning from the emotional despair and anxiety of imprisonment into a job, a family, and community is a struggle for parolees as well as exonerees, who often face similar obstacles to reentry after release. As bluntly stated in the book *Coming Out Cold: Community Reentry from a State Reformatory,* "[t]he released offender confronts a situation at release that virtually ensures his failure" (McArthur, 1974, p. 1; for empirical support for this stark argument, see Bales & Piquero, 2013; Bernburg, Krohn, & Rivera, 2006; Chiricos, Barrick, & Bales, 2007; Western, 2002). The lethal combination of stigma, social exclusion, social learning, temptation, addiction, lack of social bonds, and dangerously low levels of human and social capital (not to mention financial capital) conspire to ensure that over half of all ex-prisoners typically return to prison within a few years of their release (Langan & Levin, 2002). The problems of reintegration may be exacerbated by the enormous growth in the numbers of individuals being processed through probation and the prison system in the United States since the 1970s. Discrimination against ex-prisoners is not only facilitated *de facto* but officially sanctioned (Jacobs, 2006), and these *de jure* consequences have increased "in number, scope and severity since the 1980s" (Pinard, 2010, p 461). Indeed, in the past three decades, Congress "took collateral consequences to a new level of irrationality, making a single criminal conviction grounds for automatic exclusion from a whole range of welfare benefits" at the federal level (Love, 2003, p. 112). American citizens with even a single conviction for drug offenses and other charges can be denied housing assistance, food stamps, education loans, and the right to vote (see e.g., Alexander, 2012; Allard, 2002).

This is another area of overlap between exonerees and ordinary ex-prisoners. Because exonerees most often do not get their records expunged or sealed after release, those on the outside may see them as no different from parolees. Exonerees often report trying to explain the wrongfulness of their convictions on job applications, only for employers to reject their attempts (Westervelt & Cook, 2012). They find themselves in a double-bind: if they respond affirmatively (and truthfully) to the question "have you ever been convicted of a felony?" the application provides no room to explain a wrongful capital murder conviction; if they respond negatively to that question, the background check will reveal that they falsified an employment application. One exoneree experimented with the answer "not applicable" but that produced no better results (Westervelt & Cook, 2012). In some ways, the visibility of their exoneration can work against them, increasing their profile in the community and thus their stigma. When exonerated death row survivor Sabrina Butler applied for jobs in her hometown, she was rejected repeatedly because most people believed she was that "heinous monster" who had killed her own child. Because her case had been front-page news in her small hometown, few people gave her a chance.

Being barred from legitimate employment perpetuates a vicious cycle of economic insecurity and frustration in efforts to "make good" and be self-supporting. Restrictions on employment opportunities for ex-prisoners erect barricades that help prevent successful reintegration (Alexander, 2012; Petersilia, 2003; Travis, 2005). Unwelcoming communities then create additional frustrations and resentments, which can result in former prisoners developing depression, isolation, and emotional numbing, and thus increase the viability of crime as a mechanism for self-support (Maruna, 2001).

Having been exposed to excessive media coverage about crime in general and high-profile cases in particular, neighbors are prone to be guarded at best and openly hostile at worst to former prisoners. This is no less true for exonerees, who often still carry the stigma of incarceration and whom many believe are factually guilty. This fertilizes the community with a potent mixture of fear, suspicion, and self-protective reactions to the newly released prisoner—irrespective of whether parole or exoneration was the basis of release. Negative community sentiment makes difficult the progress any released prisoners might make toward developing a "coherent, prosocial identity for themselves," which is necessary for successful reentry (Maruna, 2001, p. 7).

Thus, parolees and exonerees have many commonalities of experience both during and after incarceration. Both groups face barriers in finding housing and employment; they lack relevant job skills and have long gaps between jobs to explain to potential employers; they struggle to rebuild family relationships and overcome drug and alcohol problems; they battle stigma within their communities; and they lack basic health, dental, and mental health care (LeBel, Burnett, Maruna, & Bushway, 2008; LeBel & Maruna, 2012; Maruna & LeBel, 2003; Westervelt & Cook, 2012, 2013).

At the same time, several differences also exist between the experiences of exonerees and ordinary ex-prisoners, and these differences must be accounted for when considering the fit of prisoner reentry paradigms to exoneree reentry and reintegration. One such difference, for example, is the ability of exonerees to plan for their impending release. As LeBel and Maruna (2012, p. 658) note about parolee reentry: "[P]risoner reentry includes many processes that begin before the individual is released from prison, experiences at the moment of release and during the first month out, and during the ... reintegration process of the first few years in the community." Many (but not all) ordinary parolees can begin to plan for reentry before release because they know they will be released and typically know approximately when. The same cannot be said for exonerees, who more often have at most a few days', or maybe a few weeks' notice of their impending release. Death row exonerees, of course, do not know if they will ever be released. Most often, prisoner reentry for exonerees begins on their day of release, when they confront two questions needing immediate answers: Who will pick me up from prison, and where will I sleep tonight? Other differences of experience that must be accounted for when applying parolee reentry to exonerees include differences in the role of stigma in shaping their lives after release, and differences in the centrality of the state in de-labeling and reintegration processes.

However, the most substantial difference that needs to be accommodated between the two groups is the fit of exonerees into a reentry model based almost entirely on rehabilitative goals of reducing recidivism and the related differences in access to post-release services between exonerees and ordinary ex-prisoners. Post-release support services for prisoners emerged in the early 20th century in the welfarist spirit of what has since become known as the "rehabilitative ideal." According to Petersilia (2003, p. 58), "the beliefs that criminals could be reformed and that every prisoner's treatment should be individualized" reflected the guiding principle of parole through the first three-quarters of the century. Reforming prisoners originally included release on parole (with several variations), work houses, half-way houses, and life skill treatment programs, known as the "Irish System" (Petersilia, 2003, pp. 57-58). This so-called "rehabilitative ideal," however, was challenged on both empirical and normative grounds during the late 1970s in the United States, and an unusual left-right coalition of critics emerged to call for the wholesale dismantling of the machinery of rehabilitation (Simon, 1993). By the end of the century, many of the post-release support services that had been taken for granted in previous decades had been substantially reduced. Petersilia (2003, p. 101) observes, "we have stopped funding transitional work and residential programs and now release the vast majority of prisoners without needed housing and social supports."

The recognition of the short-sightedness of this approach—and its role in consistently high rates of recidivism—led to a re-discovery and renewal of the rehabilitative ideal in the last decade under the banner of the "reentry movement" in the United States. The growing interest in "reentry" was largely triggered by a somewhat modest, 10-page document published in 2000 by the then director of the National Institute of Justice with the evocative title: "But They All Come Back: Rethinking Prisoner Reentry" (Travis, 2000). Travis's brief bulletin describes the scale of the resettlement project in the United States in clear terms and outlines how little attention the subject had received despite its potentially central role in community safety and recidivism reduction:

> The explosive, continuing growth of the Nation's prison population is a well-known fact.... Less well recognized is one of the consequences of this extraordinarily high figure: ... If current trends continue, this year more than half a million people will leave prison and return to neighborhoods across the country (p. 1).

In other words, locking two million people up in prisons and jails, as the United States has done, creates an enormous number of ex-convicts, so be prepared. Although this was a fairly unremarkable observation, the reaction among policy-makers, criminologists and research foundations internationally has been nothing short of remarkable. Since the NIJ published this call to arms, literally countless conferences, commissions, reports, articles, books, research projects, and government initiatives have been launched around the issue of returning ex-prisoners (for reviews, see Maruna & LeBel, 2003; Petersilia, 2003; Travis, 2005), culminating in the remarkably weighty, 650-page *Report of the Re-Entry Policy Council* from the Department of Justice (2005).[1]

Driving much of the programming for released prisoners has been a concern to improve the chances of "desistance" from criminal activity post-release, which is "the long-term abstinence from crime among individuals who had previously engaged in persistent patterns of criminal offending" (Maruna, 2001, p. 26). Desistance research explores cognitive, behavioral, structural and socio-cultural dynamics that promote and impede efforts to avoid criminal behavior. Researchers acknowledge that desistance from crime is a long process punctuated with instances of gains and setbacks among released prisoners (McNeill, 2009; Porporino, 2010). Exonerees have not been included in this research on desistance, for the obvious reason that they were wrongfully convicted in the first instance. More importantly, however, the wider policy discussion around prisoner reentry has generally overlooked the special case of exonerees. This is partly because public and official recognition that wrongful convictions are a "problem" and occur with some frequency is relatively new. Significant attention to this issue did not emerge in force until the end of the 20th century (Baumgartner, De Boef, & Boydstun, 2008; Leo, 2005; Scheck, Neufeld, & Dwyer, 2000; Westervelt & Cook, 2012). This recognition coincides with the increase in the number of exonerations, due in part to the use of DNA testing (Leo, 2005). Thus, before the turn of the last century, the problem of reentry for exonerees was most certainly flying under the radar, if not being off the grid altogether.

The assumption, then, that the state has a continuing obligation to assist exonerees with reentry does not exist in the same way it does for parolees. Further, of course, the basis of such an obligation for exonerees would be different than it is for parolees. Whereas parolee assistance is premised on the goal of reform to increase desistance for guilty offenders, the same cannot be said for exonerees (unless one assumes that the criminogenic forces of incarceration make the need for reform an equally viable need for exonerees). For exonerees, the purpose of reintegration services has less to do with the pragmatics of reducing recidivism than the more normative-based necessity to provide reparation

---

1. Available online at: http://csgjusticecenter.org/reentry/publications/the-report-of-the-re-entry-policy-council-charting-the-safe-and-successful-return-of-prisoners-to-the-community/.

for a wrong done to individuals by the state, and to assist them in managing their frustrations and needs as they rebuild their lives.

For exonerees, the problems with confronting a fearful community are compounded by the frustration that they are not guilty of the crime for which they were convicted. The stigma they carry is a false stigma, and they try openly to distance themselves from it (Westervelt & Cook, 2012). In many instances, the stigma is reinforced by representatives of the criminal justice system who often publicly admit doubt as to the exonerees' factual innocence, or worse, openly proclaim their guilt. Unlike parolees, the release of an exoneree, in particular in these more recent times, is a widely covered media event, thus amplifying any condemning statements made by officials. For instance, when Kirk Bloodworth was released from his wrongful capital conviction for the rape and murder of a nine-year-old girl in 1993, he was the first death row inmate released based on DNA evidence. He returned to his hometown in Maryland. People in his hometown who knew him from childhood believed he "got out on a technicality" and was in fact guilty of the murder (Junkin, 2004; Westervelt & Cook, 2010, 2012). Because this was a high-profile case, the media covered his release and included statements from system officials who maintained their belief in his guilt. Bloodsworth experienced painful social isolation, and few people gave him a chance to be a productive member of the community. As a consequence of this extremely difficult reentry experience, Bloodsworth developed avoidance coping strategies (Westervelt & Cook, 2012, pp. 137-139) that included withdrawal from society and numbing through excessive use of drugs and alcohol.

Resisting the toxic and painful social dynamic of such stigmatic attitudes requires enormous willpower. In spite of efforts to help them create positive self-concepts, ex-prisoners still will likely confront a hostile community that continues to see them as pariahs or bogeymen. This is possibly even more so for exonerees because they are exempt from most prisoner reentry programs where such positive reflection techniques are used. Thus, unless buoyed by family and friends providing a counterbalance to public stigma, exonerees do not have access to the positive scripts through which to reconstruct their identities.

Indeed, the avenues in the desistance research that create the most tension with the post-release experiences of exonerees revolve around the centrality of personal reform to the prisoner reentry literature. Because exonerees have been wrongly convicted, the desistance foundation for addressing their reentry is inappropriate. Rather than pursuing personal reform, exonerees pursue reparations from the entity who stole so much from them: the state.

# Moving Forward: Merging Strengths, Finding Solutions

To apply Nils Christie's (1977) famous observation to the reality of a wrongful conviction, the state stole the "conflict" from the wrong person, thus we argue that the state owes restitution and remedy to the exoneree.[2] In the case of exonerees, the reparation is not

---

2. It bears pointing out that victim-survivors of the original crime where a wrongful conviction has occurred also need remedy from the state. Unfortunately, it is beyond the scope of this chapter to delve more deeply into this aspect. Interested readers may wish to consult a special issue of the *Albany Law Review* (Volume 75, Issue 3) which presents some personal reflections, including that of victim-survivor Jennifer Thompson (2012).

due from the ex-prisoner (the exoneree) because, unlike parolees, the exoneree is not responsible for the original harm. Instead, reparation is due from the state, which is responsible for the harm of the wrongful conviction. Thus, while the community must certainly play a key role in successful reentry for exonerees, the state has a more central role to play. To repair harm, the state must recognize and "own" the harm done and take responsibility for assisting exonerees with their attempts to rebuild their lives (Westervelt & Cook, 2010).

More specifically, state reparations for exonerees must include providing automatic expungement or sealing of the record and the provision of meaningful compensation and transitional services for reentry. Other important aspects of reparations for exonerees include a meaningful apology from the system official[s] responsible for the wrongful conviction and, whenever possible, an acknowledgment of the continued injury endured by the original victim's survivor[s]. We address each of these issues.[3]

First, the large majority of exonerees who are released from prison do not have the wrongful conviction expunged automatically. As such, it is incumbent upon the exoneree to work with an attorney who is willing to represent him/her *pro bono*. The process for filing an expungement request is lengthy with no guarantee of success. Some exonerees have neither access nor funds to affect this process, which results in an immediate and (almost complete) ban from legitimate employment given the criminal background checks most employers now require. In a broader vein, however, some exonerees resent that they should be required to go through this expungement process; they believe it should be automatically entered when they are released. It is, to them, a matter of fairness. As long as that conviction stays on their records, they remain trapped in economic isolation, making it increasingly difficult to achieve self-sufficiency. (Several exonerees have opined that the state purposefully makes reentry difficult for them to increase the likelihood that they will offend in order to get by. The state then can justify its earlier mistake by saying, "see, we told you they were truly guilty.")

Second, compensation, like expungement, is not automatically generated upon release. Regardless of the mechanism through which compensation is pursued (through state statute, lawsuit, or private legislative bill), it takes years to materialize (on average 3-4 years) (Innocence Project, 2009), during which time the exoneree continues to have housing, food, transportation, medical care, psychological and/or drug counseling, clothing, and other transitional needs. While parolee reentry programs in their areas may provide modest and limited access to transitional services to address these needs, exonerees most often are exempt from these programs. In fact, one exoneree who was released from death row in Texas was actually sued by the state for back child support during the time that he was wrongly incarcerated.[4] Currently in the United States, only 29 states have compensation statutes, and they vary in the legal requirements to procure a settlement (Innocence Project, n.d.; Norris, 2012). Some requirements are written in such a way as to make it virtually impossible for compensation ever to be awarded. For instance, Oklahoma exoneree Greg Wilhoit shared his experience with pursuing compensation:

> You ought to see this application for compensation! And, the first hoop you gotta jump through to be eligible for this money ... is you gotta be pardoned by the governor, get an official pardon. So [my attorney Mark Barrett] went in front of this board and all this stuff. And they said that they don't have the authority

---

3. For more detailed discussion, see Innocence Project, 2009; Lonergan, 2008; Westervelt & Cook, 2012.

4. Clarence Brandley describes his experiences, including the state pursuing $56,000 in back child support from him upon release: see http://www.oneforten.com/clarence-brandley.

to pardon somebody who hasn't been convicted of anything. See I got acquitted in [my second trial]; I got a directed verdict. I'm not eligible for a pardon because I'm not guilty of anything. Now what kind of shit is that? ... I'm convinced they did it on purpose; they knew what they were doing (Westervelt & Cook, 2012, pp. 225–226).

Thus, compensation and transitional services for some exonerees are neither available nor possible.

Furthermore, while compensation is a necessary aspect of making reparations, it is not sufficient and can never restore the lost years, the lost loved ones, the lost productivity, and the damaged families. Some exonerees had been wrongly convicted of killing their own family members. They struggled to grieve the deaths of their parents, their children, and their spouses while simultaneously suffering the shame of being wrongly accused, tried, convicted, and sentenced to death for their murders. Some languished on death row for 15, 20, or 25 years, during which time they lost family members whom they could not adequately mourn, as well as other death row inmates, by now their friends, who were executed. They lost opportunities to build a nest egg, a family, and develop financial security (Westervelt & Cook, 2012). Compensation alone cannot repair this emotional damage and return these lost opportunities. But it can ease transition and reintegration and serve as a symbol that the offender, in this case the state, is taking responsibility for the harm done.

Third, only a few exonerees have received apologies for the harm they have endured. More typically, state officials refuse to acknowledge that the original conviction was incorrect and instead make statements to the media indicating their continued belief in the exonerees' guilt. This can cause two related problems: first, this refusal can frustrate exonerees to the extreme, increasing resentment, anger and hostility; and second, it can feed public fear and suspicion, increasing stigma and making reintegration that much more difficult. According to one exoneree, a genuine public apology "would erase from the mind of those that think that I just had a smart lawyer that got me off by coming up with some legal technicality" (Westervelt & Cook, 2012, p. 217). Another exoneree follows up with, "[an apology] carries a lot of weight right there to the public [so] that it would be something you could hold out as a proof of your innocence" (Westervelt & Cook, 2012, p. 217). Among the most coveted apologies an exoneree would hope to receive is from the original homicide victim's survivors (or the victim, in non-capital cases): "that's the only thing that really that [sic] used to bother me, that they [the victim's family] thought ... you know, that I did it. And now that he [a family member] wrote that letter [apologizing], I see what his family really thinks ..." (Westervelt & Cook, 2012, p. 220).

Fourth, exonerees acknowledge and worry about the treatment of victims and victims' survivors in the criminal justice system. They know that victims and victims' survivors are grieving their losses and at the same time are feeling overwhelming anger towards them (the exonerees) whom they typically believe to be guilty. Couple this with the grief and pain that is reopened whenever victims or their families go through another trial or hearing or intense media coverage (particularly in high-profile cases), and it is obvious that they have years of agony and frustration of their own to manage. Possibly quite different from parolees, exonerees often see themselves on the same side as the victims and victims' survivors in their shared desire to find out the truth about what really happened. Reentry research conceptualizes ex-prisoners and victims as being on opposite sides of the table, so to speak, with opposing interests and needs. Exonerees, on the other hand, see themselves as aligned with victims in a common quest for truth and justice. Reentry efforts that include exonerees must recognize this fundamental difference.

Thus, in some cases, the reentry literature provides a good foundation for approaching exoneree reintegration, albeit with a bit of tweaking here and there, but in other instances, the problem of fit looms large, particularly in those arenas where the reentry literature rests on the concepts of desistance and reform by the ex-prisoner.

We are not neutral on these normative issues (see Westervelt & Cook, 2012; Maruna and LeBel, 2003). For both rightly and wrongly convicted ex-prisoners, we support reintegration work that promotes the social acceptance of the ex-prisoner as a full-fledged member of the moral community. We also hypothesize that such reintegration efforts work best if premised on de-labeling rituals that involve the family, community, and state in creating public recognition of the ex-prisoners' identity as law-abiding citizens (see Maruna, 2011).

For parolees, de-labeling may be most successful when "some recognized member(s) of the conventional community ... publicly announce and certify that the offender has changed and that he is now to be considered essentially noncriminal" (Meisenhelder, 1977, p. 329). When this happens, the possibilities for desistance are maximized. For exonerees, desistance is not necessarily at issue. But de-labeling is still essential to reveal to the community that the exoneree is noncriminal. The focus of de-labeling for parolees is on altering their self-concept, affirming their intentions and abilities to "go straight." The focus of de-labeling for exonerees is less on changing their subjective self-concept and more on asserting and affirming their identity as innocent people to external constituencies (Westervelt & Cook, 2012). To accomplish de-labeling for exonerees, Westervelt and Cook (2012) recommend participation in community reintegration forums that bring together exonerees with public and community officials, justice system officials, family members, victims and victims' survivors (if possible), and media to, as Lofland (1969, p. 227) suggested decades ago, "publicly and formally ... announce, sell and spread the fact" of the exoneree's innocence.

In 1985, Professor Stan Cohen published what has become a classic, *Visions of Social Control*, in which he thoroughly reviewed and critiqued modern strategies of addressing crime control. No strategy was spared his keen insights, from the movement to incarcerate, to the movement to decarcerate and other debates among scholars—all was laid bare. Finally, Professor Cohen outlined his thoughts for moving forward, which he called "moral pragmatism" (1985, p. 252). He outlined three parts to moral pragmatism:

1. Doing good: "a commitment to the socialist reform of the public issues which cause these troubles."
2. Doing justice: "not equity or retribution but the sense of the rightness and fairness of punishment for the collective good."
3. Making a difference: "if the guiding values of social intervention are made clear (justice, good or whatever else might be offered) then the only question is: what difference does this particular policy make?" (pp. 252–253).

In order to "do good" in Cohen's framework, reintegration work with ex-prisoners should address the community and socio-economic conditions in which prisoners are returning. Moreover, "[t]he desistance paradigm suggests that we might be better off if we allowed offenders to *guide us* instead, listened to what they think might best fit their individual struggles out of crime, rather than continue to insist that our solutions are their salvation" (Porporino, 2010, p. 80). We agree that, like corrections in general, reentry policies and scholarship should be "reoriented towards sense and sensitivity that seriously allows and supports skilled staff to become truly skilled helpers" (Porporino, 2010, p. 80). However, for exonerees, the task of doing good is a bit different. For the wrongly convicted, Cohen's version of doing good would require taking the hard lessons of their ordeals and creating important social change. Allowing exonerees' voices to be heard and their experiences to provide direction would promote a range of significant criminal justice reforms, such as abolishing the death penalty in the United States; providing better and more effective legal representation to all indigent defendants throughout the criminal justice system; significantly reforming police and prosecutors' strategies for investigating and prosecuting cases to reduce the possibility of wrongful convictions; and recognizing the needs exonerees have following their exoneration and providing them with recognition and meaningful assistance to rebuild their lives.

"Doing justice" in reintegration would require accountability from the state. When Nils Christie (1977) first identified the state as a thief who steals conflicts from the stakeholders, he did not consider what happens when the state steals from the wrong person. Christie (1977, p. 4) argues that as thief, the state will "use the criminal case for personal gain," and as such what is most important to the state is that the criminal case is proceeding, not that it is proceeding *accurately*. The "personal gain" is secured when the prosecutors and police can assure the fearful public that they have a suspect in custody, a trial is imminent, and a conviction is sure to be followed by a prison sentence. The state wins, even though the people affected by it lose so much. The state has stolen the injury that the victim has experienced and acts to address that injury without consulting or involving the victim in the process. The state snatches a culprit and imposes a sanction on the culprit without needing to consult or involve the victim or others affected. The state speaks on behalf of the victim (without necessarily gaining her/his consent); the state publicly brands the accused culprit and her/his motives while going through processes. Christie outlines a remedy to restore the victims, offenders, and stakeholders to more prominent and influential roles in repairing the harm of crime, but he does not tackle the question of the state's accuracy. That is left to us in the developing area of wrongful conviction research.

As such, when the state gets it wrong, victims of that injury should be provided a just remedy to their harm (Westervelt & Cook, 2010). Doing justice, in this instance, includes a review of the case to identify where mistakes occurred. It means engaging in real, meaningful attempts to remedy the mistakes that lead to wrongful convictions: mistaken eyewitness identification, suppression of exculpatory evidence, knowing use of false snitch testimony, coercion of false confessions, racially motivated jury selection, and the like. For those injured by wrongful convictions—exonerees—doing justice means finding ways to recognize the wrong done to them—through formal public apology—and providing voluntary reparations by way of expungement, compensation, transitional services and holding public officials accountable when appropriate.

Finally, "making a difference," using Cohen's scheme, might involve providing remedies and assistance for parolees and exonerees, such as we have outlined elsewhere (Bazemore & Maruna, 2009; Maruna, 2001, 2006; Westervelt & Cook, 2012). In particular, we have recommended implementing state remedies driven by restorative justice principles, especially opportunities for accountability, material and practical efforts to make amends (holistically inclusive of crimes *and* punishments that inflict trauma), and inclusion of victims' needs (defined broadly) as much as possible. For all returning prisoners, we also urge a massive overhaul of the background check policies used by so many employers (see Love, 2003; Pinard, 2010).[5] For all returning prisoners, we recommend reintegration services that help them navigate their new social world more successfully upon release. For parolees, providing opportunity for them to make amends to the people they injured

---

5. The Ban the Box campaign in the USA is emblematic of this goal: http://bantheboxcampaign.org/.

(if the injured parties are willing to participate) might result in a more successful reintegration experience. For exonerated ex-prisoners, we recommend a complex array of services that will help them to fit into society, including immediate health care, housing, assistance with clothes and grocery shopping, banking, education and employment skills. Furthermore, we strongly recommend that the state which perpetrated the wrongful conviction should have some "skin in the game" to provide assistance and reparations (Westervelt & Cook, 2010). Automatic expungement of the record of wrongful conviction seems obvious, as does adequate financial compensation. In addition, we recommend reintegration ceremonies, with as many key people as possible (including victims of the original crime whenever possible) participating in a community forum that formally welcomes the exonerated inmate back to their communities (see Maruna, 2011).

Of course, none of these measures would erase the harms that have been done by wrongful conviction and nothing can compensate for the lost years and loss of trust many exonerees (and, indeed, other ex-prisoners) experience. There is no turning back of the clock in this way. However, such responses would go some way toward helping our criminal justice systems live up to the "justice" in their name.

# References

Allard, P. (2002). *Life sentences: Denying welfare benefits to women convicted of drug offenses.* Washington, DC: Sentencing Project.

Alexander, M. (2012). *The new Jim Crow: Mass incarceration in the age of colorblindness* (Revised ed.). New York, NY: The New Press.

Bales, W. D., & Piquero, A. R. (2012). Assessing the impact of imprisonment on recidivism. *Journal of Experimental Criminology, 8*(1), 71–101.

Baumgartner, F., De Boef, S., & Boydstun, A. (2008). *The decline of the death penalty and the discovery of innocence.* New York: Cambridge University Press.

Bazemore, G., & Maruna, S. (2009). Restorative justice in the reentry context: Building new theory and expanding the evidence base. *Victims and Offenders, 4,* 375–84.

Bernburg, J.G., Krohn, M. D., & Rivera, C. J. (2006). Official labelling, criminal embeddedness, and subsequent delinquency: A longitudinal test of labelling theory. *Journal of Research in Crime and Delinquency, 43*(1), 67–88.

Bowker, L. (1982). Victimizers and victims in American correctional institutions. In R. Johnson & H. Toch (Eds.), *Pains of imprisonment* (pp. 63–76). Beverly Hills, CA: Sage.

Christie, N. (1977). Conflicts as property. *British Journal of Criminology, 17*(1), 1–15.

Chiricos, T., Barrick, K., & Bales, W. (2007). The labelling of convicted felons and its consequences for recidivism. *Criminology, 45*(3), 547–581.

Cohen, S. (1985). *Visions of social control.* London: Polity Press.

Cohen, S., & Taylor, L. (1972). *Psychological survival.* New York: Pantheon.

Crewe, B. (2010). *The prisoner society.* Oxford: Oxford.

Departments of Justice, Labor, and Health and Human Services. (2005). *Report of the Re-entry Policy Council: Charting the safe and successful return of prisoners to the community.* Washington, DC: U.S. Department of Justice.

Grounds, A. (2004). The psychological consequences of wrongful conviction and imprisonment. *Canadian Journal of Criminology and Criminal Justice, 46*(2), 165–182.

Haney, C. (2003a). Mental health issues in long-term solitary and 'supermax' confinement. *Crime and Delinquency, 49*(1), 124–156.

Haney, C. (2003b). The psychological impact of incarceration: implications for postprison adjustment. In J. Travis & M. Waul (Eds.), *Prisoners once removed*. (pp. 33–66). Washington, DC: Urban Institute Press.

Haney, C. (2005). *Death by design*. Oxford: Oxford University Press.

Herman, J. (1997). *Trauma and recovery*. New York: Basic Books.

Innocence Project. http://www.innocenceproject.org.

Innocence Project. (2009). *Making up for lost time: What the wrongfully convicted endure and how to provide fair compensation*. Retrieved from http://www.innocenceproject.org/docs/Innocence_Project_Compensation_Report.pdf.

Irwin, J., & Owen, B. (1995). Harm and the contemporary prison. In A. Liebling & S. Maruna (Eds.), *The effects of imprisonment*. (pp. 94–117). Portland, OR: Willan.

Jacobs, J. B. (2006). Mass incarceration and the proliferation of criminal records. *University of St. Thomas Law Journal, 3*(3), 387–420.

Jamieson, R., & Grounds, A. (2005). Release and adjustment: perspectives from studies of wrongly convicted and politically motivated prisoners. In A. Liebling & S. Maruna (Eds.), *The effects of imprisonment*. (pp. 33–65), Portland, OR: Willan.

Junkin, T. (2004). *Bloodsworth*. Chapel Hill, NC: Algonquin.

Langan, P. A., & Levin, D. J. (2002). *Recidivism of prisoners released in 1994* (NCJ 193427). Washington, D.C.: U.S. Department of Justice, Bureau of Justice Statistics.

LeBel, T., & Maruna, S. (2012). Life on the outside: Transitioning from prison to the community. In J. Petersilia & K. Reitz (Eds.), *The Oxford handbook of sentencing and corrections*. (pp. 657–683). Oxford: Oxford University Press.

LeBel, T., Burnett, R., Maruna, S., and Bushway, S. (2008). The 'chicken and egg' of subjective social factors in desistance from crime. *European Journal of Criminology, 5*(2), 131–159.

Leo, R. (2005). Rethinking the study of miscarriages of justice: developing a criminology of wrongful convictions. *Journal of Contemporary Criminal Justice, 21*(3), 201–223.

Liebling, A. & Maruna, S. (Eds.). (2005). *The effects of imprisonment*. Portland, OR: Willan.

Lofland, J. (1969). *Deviance and identity*. Englewood, CA: Prentice Hall.

Lonergan, J. (2008). Protecting the innocent: A model for comprehensive, individualized compensation of the exonerated. *Legislation and Public Policy, 11*, 405–452.

Love, M. C. (2003). Starting over with a clean slate: In praise of a forgotten section of the model penal code. *Fordham Urban Law Journal, 30*, 101–136.

Maruna, S. (2001). *Making good: How ex-convicts reform and rebuild their lives.* Washington, DC: American Psychological Association.

Maruna, S. (2006). Who owns resettlement? Towards restorative re-integration. *British Journal of Criminology, 4*(2), 23–33.

Maruna, S. (2011). Reentry as a rite of passage. *Punishment & Society, 13*(1), 3–27.

Maruna, S., & LeBel, T. P., (2003). Welcome home?: Examining the reentry court concept from a strengths-based perspective. *Western Criminology Review, 4*(2), 91–107.

McArthur, A.V. (1974). *Coming out cold: Community reentry from a state reformatory*. Lexington, MA: Lexington Books.

McNeill, F. (2006). A desistance paradigm for offender management. *Criminology & Criminal Justice, 6*(1), 39–62.

Meisenhelder, T. (1977). An exploratory study of exiting from criminal careers. *Criminology, 15*(3), 319–334.

Norris, R. J. (2012). Assessing compensation statutes for the wrongly convicted. *Criminal Justice Policy Review, 23*(3), 352–374.

Petersilia, J. (2003). *When prisoners come home: Parole and prisoner reentry*. New York: Oxford University Press.

Pinard, M. (2010). Collateral consequences of criminal convictions: Confronting issues of race and dignity. *New York University Law Review, 85*(2), 457–534.

Porporino, F. (2010). Bringing sense and sensitivity to corrections: From programmes to 'fix' offenders to services to support desistance. In J. Brayford, F. Cowe & J. Deering (Eds.), *What else works? Creative work with offenders* (pp. 61–85). Cullompton: Willan Publishing.

Scheck, B., Neufeld, P., & Dwyer, J. (2000). *Actual innocence: Five days from execution, and other dispatches from the wrongly convicted*. New York: Doubleday.

Simon, J. (1993). *Poor Discipline: Parole and the social control of the underclass, 1890–1990*. Chicago: University of Chicago Press.

Sykes, G. (1958). *The society of captives*. Princeton, NJ, Princeton University Press.

Thompson, J. (2012). The unpredictable journey. *Albany Law Review, 75*(3), 1529–1533.

Travis, J. (2000). *But they all come back: Rethinking prisoner reentry, research in brief — sentencing and corrections: Issues for the 21st Century* (NCJ 181413). Washington, DC: U.S. Department of Justice, National Institute of Justice.

Travis, J. (2005). *But they all come back: Facing the challenges of prisoner reentry*. New York: Urban Institute.

Western, B. (2002). The impact of incarceration on wage mobility and inequality. *American Sociological Review, 67*(4), 526–546.

Westervelt, S. D. & Cook, K. J. (2010). Framing innocents: The wrongly convicted as victims of state harm. *Crime, Law, and Social Change, 53*(3), 259–275.

Westervelt, S. D. & Cook, K. J. (2012). *Life after death row: Exonerees' search for community and identity*. New Brunswick, NJ: Rutgers University Press.

Westervelt, S. D. & Cook, K. J. (2013). Life after exoneration: Examining the aftermath of a wrongful capital conviction. In C.R. Huff & M. (Eds.), *Wrongful conviction and miscarriages of justice: Causes & remedies in North America and European criminal justice systems* (pp. 261–281). New York: Routledge.

Zamble, E., & Porporino, F. (1988). *Coping, behavior, and adaptation in prison inmates*. New York: Springer-Verlag.

Zimbardo, P. G., Maslach, C., & Haney, C. (2000). Reflections on the Stanford prison experiment: Genesis, transformations, consequences. In T. Blass (Ed.), *Obedience to authority: Current perspectives on the Milgram paradigm* (pp. 193–237). Mahwah, NJ: Lawrence Erlbaum Associates.

# Chapter Fifteen

# Public Policy Responses to Wrongful Convictions

Frank R. Baumgartner, *University of North Carolina at Chapel Hill*
Saundra D. Westervelt, *University of North Carolina at Greensboro*
Kimberly J. Cook, *University of North Carolina at Wilmington*

## Introduction

From the Salem Witch trials onwards, Americans have long experienced wrongful conviction. The Death Penalty Information Center (DPIC) lists 143 death row exonerations from 1973 through 2013, and the newly created National Registry of Exonerations enumerates 1,307 cases from 1989 through early 2014 (not limited to inmates sentenced to death). Until recently, public concern with exonerations, like with the criminal justice system in general, could perhaps best be described as "out of sight, out of mind" — there was little concern about wrongful convictions and little recognition of related issues, and little desire to know more about this topic which, for most Americans, is personally irrelevant. This has changed dramatically. Beginning in the 1980s but rapidly expanding around the turn of the 21st century, recognition of the issues of innocence and wrongful conviction have become perhaps the dominant way of discussing the death penalty in America. The public understanding of capital punishment has been transformed, largely due to the public's "discovery of innocence" (Baumgartner, DeBoef, & Boydstun, 2008). Death sentences have declined, state legislatures across the country have restricted the use of capital punishment, and five states have abolished capital punishment through legislative action (New Jersey, 2007; New Mexico, 2009; Illinois, 2011; Connecticut, 2012; Maryland, 2013) while a sixth (New York, 2007) did so through judicial decision, a decision which was not later reversed by the elected leadership.

The discovery of innocence also has propelled criminal justice reforms aimed at reducing the likelihood of future wrongful convictions. Policy reforms regarding eyewitness identification, false and coerced confessions, evidence preservation, and forensic oversight are aimed at curbing wrongful convictions. While reforms in these areas are ongoing and uneven, concerns about convicting innocent people have inspired reforms within the criminal justice system.

While legislative and public policy reforms restricting the use of the death penalty have been dramatic and criminal justice reforms significant, reforms to aid exonerated former prisoners have been rare. Some states have adopted legislation allowing for compensation, but these often have provisions making actual awards surprisingly rare (see Norris, 2012 for a detailed review of the limited reach of state compensation policies). So we see a paradox. Exonerations have inspired a new public attitude towards the death penalty, because they demonstrate vividly that a human-designed institution cannot be free from error. Imposition of new death sentences has plummeted. Legislative reforms have consistently restricted the conditions for which the death penalty is applied, and have created more safeguards against wrongful conviction. On the other hand, support for the individuals exonerated has been woefully inadequate. Exonerees continue to benefit from even less support than those on parole or probation. Public officials, driven by fear of supporting individuals who may have prior criminal records or by pressure from prosecutors, oppose compensation and refuse to apologize to most exonerees. Members of the public wrongly assume that these individuals so grievously harmed by the justice system are automatically and substantially compensated.

## Stepping Back: Public Recognition of the Problem of Wrongful Conviction

In *The Decline of the Death Penalty and the Discovery of Innocence*, Baumgartner and his coauthors (2008) review news coverage of capital punishment from 1960 through 2006. They use the phrase "discovery of innocence" in the title for two reasons. First, it is a strange "discovery" since it was simply to recognize something that so concerned the framers of the U.S. Constitution that they required careful due process to prevent convicting the innocent. But more importantly, Baumgartner et al. observe that this new "discovery" was the most important driver in a historic shift in attitudes and public policies toward the death penalty. Figure 1 shows the rise in the number of *New York Times* stories on innocence, exonerations, DNA, and similar topics between 1960 and 2005.

**Figure 1. *New York Times* stories on Innocence.**

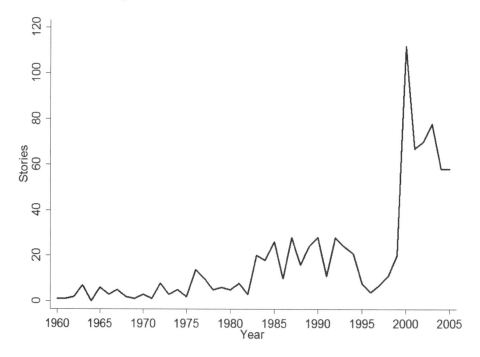

Source: adopted from Baumgartner et al. 2008, Figure 4.6.

Of course, the number of individuals found factually innocent did not surge into the criminal justice system suddenly in the year 2000. Small but steady numbers of people had been exonerated consistently since the 1970s (Death Penalty Information Center, 2013). According to DPIC, the increase in attention to innocence at the turn of the 21st century is related to several factors. First is the creation of various centers and projects focusing on exonerating wrongfully convicted persons. Starting with Centurion Ministries in 1983 and then the Innocence Project in 1992, scores of university-based innocence projects across the country emerged, creating opportunities for law and journalism students to investigate local cases for wrongful convictions. High profile police brutality and forced confession cases drew attention. Northwestern University students uncovered a massive corruption scandal in the Chicago Police Department, leading Illinois Governor George Ryan to empty the state's 167-person death row just before leaving office in 2003. As attention to such issues increased, more university-based clinics were created, more students got interested in them, more cases were investigated, and more exonerations occurred. Others, of course, have studied these trends, and the publication of some of these studies had a significant effect on the debate (see Bedau, 1987; Bedau & Radelet, 1987; Garland, 2010; Gross et al., 2005; Radelet, Bedau, & Putnam, 1994; Radelet & Borg, 2000; Scheck, Neufeld , & Dwyer, 2000; Warden & Radelet, 2008; Westervelt & Humphrey, 2001). Documenting innocence brought attention and these studies had scholarly, legal, and policy impacts. High profile cases, such as that of Kirk Bloodsworth, the first death row DNA exoneree, brought awareness of "exonerations" into the public and cultural consciousness. Following the OJ Simpson trial, popular TV shows focusing on forensic evidence, especially DNA and other factors, contributed to these trends.[1] This self-reinforcing process generated a national social cascade in which something that had always been there "suddenly" leaped to our collective consciousness. Figure 2 shows each of the 124 death row exonerations from 1973 through 2005 along with the amount of newspaper coverage generated by a Lexis-Nexis search on the name of the exonerated inmate.

Figure 2 makes clear that the same event—a death row exoneration—may or may not be newsworthy. Most of the exonerations listed generated no news coverage at all. However, several received substantial national attention, and the trend is strongly positive. Those exonerated after 1995 generated substantially more news coverage, on average, than before. Consequently, an event which was once considered "some inmate's lucky day" with no broader social importance became an indicator of a broken system. Journalists found a story-line pre-formatted for publication: *The Xth exoneration, the growing awareness of an imperfect system, the revelation of available yet overlooked, ignored, or suppressed exculpatory evidence.* Journalists referenced experts such as Richard Dieter from the Death Penalty Information Center or innocence project leaders to provide useful material for media coverage of their cases. The positive feedback process associated with the search and discovery of innocent inmates on death row transformed the debate and has put a new face, or number of faces, to the issue—that of Anthony Porter or Rolando Cruz (two Illinois exonerees), for example.

Personalizing the discussion of innocence has been fundamental to the shift in debate about the death penalty. In fact, Baumgartner and his colleagues (2008) found that newspaper coverage about the death penalty had shifted from a preoccupation with crime victims to a focus on the exonerated. From 1960 through 1993, 69 percent of the mentions of exonerees or victims focused on victims. From 1994 through 2005, it declined to 38 percent (see Baumgartner et al., 2008, figures 4.11 and 4.12). As the attention moved from the gruesome and heinous nature of the crimes to the possibility that errors had

---

1. It is not our purpose here to provide a complex discussion explaining the reasons for the discovery of innocence. For our purposes, documenting its discovery is the primary concern.

Figure 2. Newspaper coverage of 124 death row exonerees, 1973 to 2005.

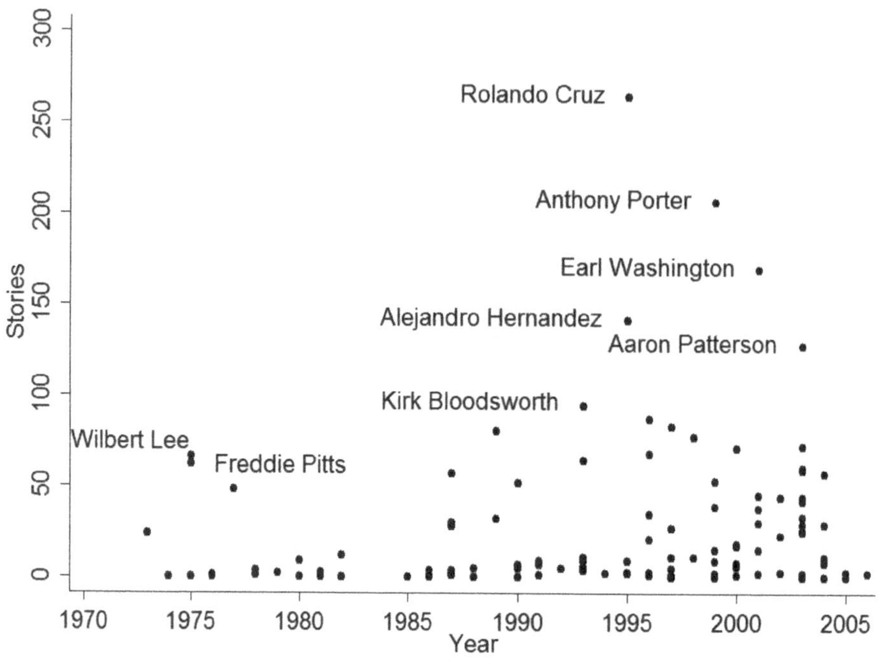

Source: adopted from Baumgartner et al., 2008, Figure 3.2.

been made in the investigation and trial, exonerees were humanized, and doubts were raised. As more exonerations occurred, so too were more doubts raised in the next cases. These shifts have affected juries, public opinion, and policymakers. So far, however, they have not substantially and directly benefitted many of those who have suffered the most.

## The Public Policy Response to Innocence

Baumgartner et al. (2008) use the "net tone" of media coverage of the death penalty to explain both the rise and the fall of death sentencing over the 1960 to 2006 period. As attention focused on morality or constitutionality arguments, or on simple explanations that the death penalty in fact was being expanded during the 1970s and 1980s, this pro-death penalty media coverage made the death penalty seem increasingly "normal," resulting in greater public support for its use. When the tone shifted in the late 1990s, largely because of the rise of the innocence frame, public opinion and public policy both shifted in return. Here, we document these trends in a new way. The point is to show that attention to wrongful convictions has had a significant impact nationally, especially on public opinion about the death penalty. Unfortunately for those who were the victims of wrongful incarceration, the benefits of this attention have been in the form of diffuse policy reforms restricting or eliminating the death penalty or increasing safeguards against future wrongful convictions. We have yet to see substantial policy efforts to address the consequences that wrongful convictions have for those most directly affected—exonerees, their families and wider networks—what Westervelt and Cook (2012b) call the "aftermath" of a wrongful conviction.

**Figure 3. Exonerations over time.**

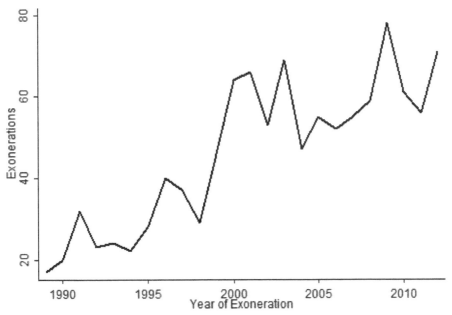

Source: data from National Registry of Exonerations.

Figure 3 shows the number of exonerations listed in the National Registry of Exonerations (2013), a project of the University of Michigan Law School and Center on Wrongful Convictions of Northwestern University School of Law that lists every exoneration known in the US since 1989.

Figure 3 makes clear a substantial surge in exonerations in the late 1990s, moving from an average of about 30 per year before 1998 to one of about 60 per year after 2000. At about this same time, state legislatures "discovered" innocence as well. Figure 4 shows the correspondence between the exoneration data and the number of state legislative bills introduced to restrict or eliminate the use of the death penalty over the same time period. The number of bills passed, and their effectiveness, is of course a different matter. But the figure shows a strong correspondence between the legislative agendas in the states and the number of death-row exonerations.

The coding process began with a Lexis-Nexis search on all state legislative bills containing the words "death penalty" or "capital punishment" from 1990 through 2011, resulting in 1,223 pieces of legislation (Loyal, 2013). Each bill was coded for whether the proposed bill would expand or restrict the use of capital punishment. The analysis documents a dramatic shift in trends in the late 1990s away from a tendency to expand the use of capital punishment and toward new restrictions. Such restrictions include reducing the number of crimes eligible for death; reducing the number of aggravating factors; increasing the number of mitigating factors; enhancing the resources available to defense attorneys; eliminating the death penalty altogether; or any other reform that would have the impact of reducing, rather than expanding, the use of capital punishment. Loyal (2013) found

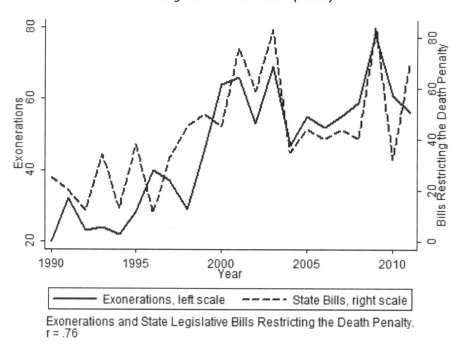

Figure 4. Exonerations and state legislative bills
restricting the use of the death penalty.

Exonerations and State Legislative Bills Restricting the Death Penalty.
r = .76

Note: Bills data come from Lexis-Nexis State Legislative Universe and were coded by Alex Loyal of UNC
for restricting or expanding the use of the death penalty. The graph shows the total number of bills
about the death penalty that restricted its use in any way.

few differences by geographic region; these trends affected the entire country at about
the same time.[2]

Figure 4 makes clear the high correspondence between exonerations and proposed legislative reforms. Figure 5 shows a similar pattern, looking at the number of death sentences
imposed across the country over the same period.

Nationally, death sentences were being imposed at the rate of about 287 per year
from 1990 through 1999 but declined to fewer than 100 by 2010. The number of
executions, of course, is far lower: After a peak of 98 executions in 1999, the number
fell to less than half (43) of that in 2012. In any case, Figure 5 clearly shows that as exonerations increase, death sentences decline dramatically. Both time series analyses document a dramatic shift in public policy around the turn of the century, exactly the time
when we see a surge in exonerations. Baumgartner et al. (2008) also identify the period
around 1998–2000 as a key moment in the discovery of innocence, such that increased
attention to the wrongfully convicted has changed the national debate surrounding
capital punishment.

---

2. As innocence drove much of the growth in restrictive legislation, significant numbers of bills
focused specifically on eliminating wrongful convictions mandating greater resources for defense
attorneys, restricting certain prosecutorial practices, and so on. Very few of these bills, however,
focused on providing resources to individual exonerees. See Norris (2012) for a detailed study of compensation policies across the states.

## Figure 5. Exonerations and death sentences.

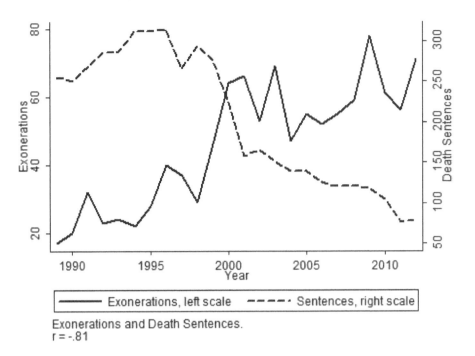

Exonerations and Death Sentences.
r = -.81

Sources: Exonerations: National Registry of Exonerations. Death Sentences: DPIC.

This connection between the discovery of innocence and decreased support for capital punishment is supported as well by public opinion polls. These polls show that concerns about wrongful convictions have contributed to reducing popular support for the death penalty. Public support for the death penalty peaked at 80% approval in 1994 (Cook, 1998), prior to the "discovery" of innocence. More recently, a CNN/ORC (2011) poll showed that 72% of respondents believed that "a person has been executed under the death penalty who was, in fact, innocent of the crime" in the preceding five years. A Pew Research Center (2012) poll found that 54% of respondents opposed the death penalty either for moral reasons (27%) or for "concerns about flaws in the system and the possibility that innocent people could be put to death" (27%).

North Carolina serves as a good microcosm of the national debate surrounding issues of innocence, the death penalty, and criminal justice reform. In the past, North Carolina has been one of the most enthusiastic users of the death penalty. In response to the U.S. Supreme Court's mandate in *Furman v. Georgia* (1972) that states move away from potentially biased forms of prosecutorial discretion, the state simply adopted a mandatory death sentence for all those charged with eligible homicide. More recently though, the state has enacted a series of reforms that have steadily restricted the use of capital punishment. As in other states, this has been due in large part to high-profile media coverage of local cases of wrongful convictions. Table 1 lists North Carolina exonerations in recent years.

## Table 1. North Carolina Exonerations

| Exoneree | Date | Exoneree | Date |
|---|---|---|---|
| Lesly Jean | 1991 | Jonathon Hoffman* | 2007 |
| Ronald Cotton | 1995 | Glen Edward Chapman* | 2008 |
| Robert Kelly | 1997 | Erick Daniels | 2008 |
| Kathryn Dawn Wilson | 1997 | Levon Junior Jones* | 2008 |
| Keith Brown | 1999 | Joseph Lamont Abbitt | 2009 |
| Alfred Rivera* | 1999 | Shawn Giovanni Massey | 2010 |
| Terence Garner | 2002 | Jonathan Scott Pierpoint | 2010 |
| Steve E. Snipes | 2003 | Gregory Taylor | 2010 |
| Leo Waters | 2003 | Kenneth Kagonyera | 2011 |
| Alan Gell* | 2004 | Robert Wilcoxson | 2011 |
| Darryl Hunt | 2004 | Willie Grimes | 2012 |
| Sylvester Smith | 2004 | Noe Moreno | 2012 |
| Dwayne Allen Dail | 2007 | LaMonte Armstrong | 2013 |

Note: The cases come from the National Registry of Exonerations and do not include the death row cases of Charles Munsey (1996, posthumous), Samuel Poole (1974), or Christopher Spicer (1975). * indicates a death row case.

Significant legislative attention followed from the cases of Ronald Cotton and Darryl Hunt, both African-American men wrongfully found guilty of rape (and murder in Hunt's case) of white women. The death row exonerations of Alan Gell, Jonathon Hoffman, Glen "Ed" Chapman, and Levon "Bo" Jones, over four years, and all but Gell being African-American men, drew particular attention to the issue of racial bias contributing to wrongful convictions and death sentencing. In 2009, North Carolina passed the Racial Justice Act (RJA), which allowed the use of statistical evidence relating to the application of the death penalty. A photo of Darryl Hunt, Jonathon Hoffman, Ed Chapman, and Bo Jones lobbying for the law, and the personal appearances of many local exonerees, likely played a key role in developing support for the RJA (for background on trends in North Carolina, see Kotch & Mosteller, 2010; O'Brien & Gross, 2011).

A review of death penalty reforms in North Carolina makes clear the rapid developments leading to the reduction in its use:

> 1994: Life Without Parole adopted as an alternative punishment to death
> 2000: Creation of Indigent Defense Services, centralizing and professionalizing legal services for capital defendants state-wide
> 2001: Discretion given to prosecutors concerning whether to proceed capitally
> 2002: Elimination of capital punishment for the mentally retarded (pre-*Atkins*)
> 2002: Creation of the NC Commission on Actual Innocence
> 2003: Best practices adopted for eyewitness testimony, police line-up procedures
> 2006: De-facto moratorium on executions based on legal and medical concerns over lethal injection
> 2006: Creation of the NC Innocence Inquiry Commission
> 2009: Publication of a widely publicized study showing that the death penalty in North Carolina costs approximately $11 million per year (Cook, 2009)
> 2009: Passage of Racial Justice Act
> 2010: Investigative series from the *Raleigh News and Observer* documents scandals affecting hundreds of cases in the State Bureau of Investigation

As a result of these reforms, capital trials in North Carolina decreased from about 60 per year before 2000 to fewer than 20; death sentences declined from over 20 per year to none in 2012; and executions have been on hold since 2006. These trends, while remarkable, are only somewhat stronger than similar trends in other states. (As readers may be aware, the governor of North Carolina signed into law a bill that repealed the Racial Justice Act in 2013; as these are pending legislative and judicial actions, it is unclear whether they will have the desired impact of reversing the recent anti-death penalty trends.)

There can be no doubt, whether we look nationally or focus our attention more specifically on a particular state, that exonerations, and more specifically public and media attention to them, have transformed the debate around capital punishment. So, it is fair to conclude that the public policy response to wrongful convictions, at least as regards the death penalty, has been substantial, relatively swift, and very progressive. Attention to the innocence issue also has affected policies governing criminal justice procedure, though the overall impact is not as pronounced as we see with capital punishment. But the criminal justice reforms created to prevent future wrongful convictions are not to be overlooked and draw their breath directly from the discovery of innocence.

Increased attention to cases of innocence has led many to ask what can be done to ensure that wrongful convictions do not occur in the future. Several areas of criminal justice procedure have been subject to reform since attention to issues of innocence dramatically increased in the late 1990s (see Figure 1 earlier) — policies governing eyewitness identification and interrogation procedures, evidence preservation, and forensic oversight, to name of few.[3] According to data gathered by Norris, Bonventre, Redlich, and Acker (2010/2011) and the Innocence Project (2013), most reforms in these areas occurred after the rise in the innocence frame, and a review of the substance of these reforms reveals a concern for preventing future wrongful convictions.

For example, all of the thirteen states that have implemented eyewitness identification reforms have done so since 2001. Most incorporate new procedures advocated by the Innocence Project and recommended by researchers who have concerns over the role of misidentifications in producing wrongful convictions (e.g., Lindsay & Wells, 1985; Wells & Bradfield, 1998; Wells et al., 1998). Similarly, of the 21 states enacting reforms around police interrogations to reduce coerced confessions, 20 states passed the reforms after 2001, and many incorporate procedures advocated by the Innocence Project. Similarly, in states implementing reforms around evidence preservation and forensic oversight, most reforms were enacted after 2000 and follow Innocence Project recommendations. Thus, while not universal across the United States, many states have responded to the increased concern over innocence with attempts to improve criminal justice procedures and decrease wrongful convictions. While possibly not as substantive as the changes in death penalty policies noted earlier, these reforms are substantial, and the trajectory is for these areas to continue to receive attention in those states that have not yet implemented new policies.

In spite of the significant impact on death penalty and criminal justice policies, the growth of the innocence frame has not had a similar impact on policies that directly affect exonerees after their release. They struggle to rebuild their lives, often without as much as an apology from the system that so grievously wronged them.

---

3. Other areas of reform aimed at preventing wrongful convictions include: DNA access laws, procedures governing informant use, and the establishment of innocence commissions (see Innocence Project website and Norris et al., 2010/2011).

# Moving Forward: Compensation, Reparation, and the Mythology of Exoneration

Official policy reform to address the needs of exonerees is limited, restrictive, and inadequate. Exonerees receive little assistance with their reintegration needs. Some innocence projects, attorneys, and advocates assist exonerees in immediate post-release transition. A few non-profit organizations around the country do their best to assist exonerees and their families after release.[4] And some states have passed new compensation statutes to provide financial assistance to those wrongly convicted. However, in comparison to the magnitude of the policy shift in regards to the death penalty and criminal justice reform, policy reform aimed at assisting exonerees is more of a tiny tremor than a seismic shift.

Regarding aftermath assistance, a common misperception is that compensation is provided automatically by the state. States can provide three primary mechanisms for exonerees to pursue compensation: private bills, litigation, and compensation statutes (for more detailed consideration of the costs and benefits of each of these, see Bernhard 2004; Innocence Project 2009; Westervelt and Cook 2012a). Once initiated by the exoneree, the processes of pursuing litigation and private bills through state legislatures are typically costly, time-consuming, and rife with political difficulties, all hurdles that frustrate the average exoneree. For example, the Innocence Project (2009) reports that of their DNA exonerees, only 9% successfully secured compensation through a private bill and 28% through litigation, after several years of effort. As a result, these exonerees had no official assistance available to them in the immediate months and years after release. They had to depend on the ability of family/friends to assist with whatever serendipitous resources they could muster, and for extended periods of time, they went without health coverage, employment, housing, and dependable transportation. (It is worth noting that clients of the Innocence Project are better positioned to succeed with these measures than most exonerees due to additional support and credibility provided to Innocence Project clients.)

Given the problems associated with these two mechanisms, many advocates agree that compensation statutes hold the most promise for providing the wrongly convicted with meaningful, timely financial assistance. Before 2000, 12 states plus the District of Columbia had established some form of compensation for wrongful conviction or wrongful incarceration (Innocence Project; Norris, 2012). Since then, most have amended their earlier policies, and 17 more states have enacted compensation statutes (Innocence Project; Norris, 2012). By August 1, 2013, 29 states plus the District of Columbia had enacted compensation statutes for individuals wrongly convicted and exonerated. Certainly, this shift over only a 13-year period is significant, and is related to the increased awareness of wrongful convictions. Still, 21 other states have not enacted compensation statutes and thus provide no mechanism to exonerees to seek compensation post-release. Individuals who are exonerated in these states are simply arbitrarily barred from statutory compensation based solely on location. A federal compensation mechanism may be helpful to address this gap in eligibility.[5]

---

4. In doing research for *Life after Death Row*, Westervelt and Cook (2012a) were able to locate 10 non-profit organizations dedicated, at least in part, to assisting exonerees post-release. See pp. 250–251 for more information.

5. Another gap in eligibility concerns compensation for American citizens wrongly convicted of crimes outside of the United States. For instance, Jason Puracal is an American citizen who was wrongly convicted and incarcerated in Nicaragua (while working in the Peace Corps). After two years,

Of course, the existence of compensation statutes does not mean that all exonerees in that state receive appropriate compensation automatically. In fact, in many states, it is likely that few who have been exonerated of crimes based on substantial evidence of factual innocence actually receive the compensation that appears to be promised to them by statute. For example, a recent overview of compensation provisions in North Carolina revealed that of those individuals exonerated prior to 2008, fewer than 40% had been compensated. In 2008, the compensation statute in North Carolina was amended to include more services and provide more compensation, making the North Carolina statute, on paper, quite progressive. However, since 2008, only 15% of North Carolina exonerees have received compensation under the newly amended statute (Westervelt & Cook, 2013). Among the eight death row exonerees in North Carolina, none have been compensated as a result of the compensation statute. Thus, it is important to remember that even though 29 states and Washington, D.C., have compensation statutes of some kind, this does not mean that exonerees are receiving the compensation, resulting in even fewer exonerees receiving assistance of any kind.

This gap between principle and practice typically results from an array of limitations and eligibility restrictions added onto compensation statutes. First, the request for compensation is triggered by the exoneree, who must work with an attorney to prove eligibility, thus placing the onus of responsibility on the exoneree him/herself to pursue this type of reparation. Second, the restrictions often attached to statutes, in some circumstances, could preclude almost any exoneree from receiving compensation. For example, North Carolina is one of only four states to require the exonerated individual to petition the Governor for a "pardon for innocence" (Norris, 2012). The exoneree must find the resources to hire an attorney to submit this complex paperwork on his/her behalf, unless lucky enough to have an advocate willing to work pro bono. Once submitted, the Governor re-reviews the case, although it has been thoroughly litigated in the courts, typically with more than one court noting evidence of factual innocence. The Governor can deny a petition without explanation, leaving the exoneree with no information with which to move forward with a reply or resubmission. Such a restriction on the provision of compensation makes a legal process an overtly political one and has resulted in few exonerees receiving compensation. Restrictions attached to compensation statutes in other states include denying compensation to any exoneree with a prior felony or subsequent felony conviction, to exonerees serving concurrent sentences, and to those said to have "contributed" to their own wrongful conviction (by way, say, of giving a false confession because of police brutality or coercion) (Norris, 2012). Other states have statutes of limitation in place that begin as soon as the exoneree is released and still others only provide compensation to DNA exonerees or to those wrongly convicted of certain crimes (Norris, 2012). So, again, while the number of states passing compensation statutes has certainly increased since 2000, this is not reason to believe that the number of exonerees actually receiving state-provided financial assistance has substantially increased.

As Westervelt and Cook (2012a) reveal in their examination of the reintegration experiences of eighteen death row exonerees, the difficulties facing exonerees when they are released are multi-dimensional and cannot be reduced to a monetary fix. This is not to say that the meaningful provision of compensation by the state to someone wrongly convicted is not important. It is very important, but the assistance that exonerees need in rebuilding their lives cannot be boiled down only to compensation. They face difficult

---

he was exonerated, released and returned to the United States. He has no known options for pursuing compensation in Nicaragua, and no American authorities or resources seem available to assist him.

short-term problems, such as finding immediate housing and transportation, adjusting to life outside of prison, improving deteriorated job skills, getting reacquainted with family. And they face frustrating long-term problems, such as securing record expungement and employment, and locating physical and psychological healthcare. In many states, parolees, who often confront some of these same problems, are offered services to help them find housing, employment, and substance abuse treatment. But, the services offered to parolees are typically not available to exonerees. Only eleven states include any kind of social service provision for exonerees within their compensation statute, and again, there is no reason to assume that these are actually provided just because they are included in the policy. Only ten non-profit organizations exist to address the specifics of life after exoneration, and these are scattered rather randomly around the country. Again, whether an exoneree can receive assistance from such a group is arbitrary and depends on their location.

Therefore, we know that most individuals who are wrongly convicted in the United States receive very little, if any, assistance from the state, or any other type of organization, in rebuilding their lives once they are exonerated and released. The significant policy reforms that have occurred with the death penalty and with regard to criminal justice procedure as a result of the "discovery of innocence" have yet to translate into meaningful assistance programs for exonerees. Public policy in this area remains fairly undeveloped, or maybe more precisely under-developed, relative to the other two areas. We conclude this section with a few thoughts as to why this might be.

We argue that the limited public policy reform addressing "aftermath" results from widespread belief in three myths: the "myth of full compensation," the "myth of actual guilt," and the "myth of the complicit victim." We wish we had a nickel for every time someone has said to us something like the following during a conversation about a wrongful conviction case, "It is terrible what happened to that person. I can't imagine being convicted and put in prison for a crime I did not commit. But, at least we give them a lot of money when they get out to help them get back on their feet." As should be clear from the preceding discussion, the reality is that most exonerees receive neither compensation nor assistance, and those few who do are not receiving lots of it (Innocence Project, 2009). However, the general public is only made aware of compensation issues when someone in their state or local area actually receives it, and more particularly receives a large amount by virtue of a generous compensation statute or winning a large lawsuit. Cases such as this typically make the news (see, for example, Elliott, 2003 on the $5 million won by Alberto Ramos or Babwin, 2007 on the $20 million won by four Illinois death row exonerees). Exonerees who receive no compensation or assistance do not receive any media attention. Consequently, the public image of exoneration is tilted towards those few cases that happen the most infrequently. But, because of this myth, policymakers and the public do not press for changes to compensation policies or provisions because they believe, mistakenly, that they are adequate and working well.

Furthermore, the general public also is led to believe in the "myth of actual guilt." This myth often is generated and maintained publicly by the legal officials—police and prosecutors—responsible for the wrongful conviction. During the exoneration process, public statements by legal officials most typically maintain the exoneree's guilt. Police and prosecutors state that, in spite of recently unearthed evidence to the contrary, they are confident in the factual guilt of the exoneree and strenuously fight against the exoneration (Westervelt & Cook, 2010; 2012a; for a recent example in the case of Larry Lamb in North Carolina, see Mims, 2013). Because they refuse to take responsibility for mistakes that may have been made that led to the wrongful conviction, state officials rarely apologize to the exoneree (something that they often desperately want), leaving the public and community suspicious of their legal status. This resistance on the part of state officials only exacerbates the trauma exonerees experience (Westervelt & Cook, 2010).

Without a study of legal officials, it is difficult to know why they so often resist recognition of the factual innocence of exonerees. It could be that tunnel vision has led them to truly believe in the exoneree's guilt, and it is just too difficult to readjust the lens at this point in the case. It could be that public recognition exposes the state to liability which they want to avoid. It could be that knowing they participated in nearly taking someone's life, and stealing away years of someone's life, is just too psychologically troubling to accept. It could be all of these or none of these. But, their insistence on actual guilt, often in the face of overwhelming evidence to the contrary, leaves enough lingering doubt in the minds of the public and policymakers that they, in turn, are not anxious to enact policies that may, even on the outside chance, help someone who is actually guilty.

And, it is true that in some cases exonerees may be easy targets for belief in this myth because of prior experience in the criminal justice system. Many exonerees have had prior contact with police; some have actually committed crimes and served time in prison before their wrongful conviction. After all, among the people most likely to be seized upon by police after a serious crime has been committed are those already known to the police and the criminal justice system. Once details of the personal histories of some exonerees are exposed, the public and policymakers may not be anxious to award compensation or assistance to them. In some cases, compensation and services may benefit what Schneider and Ingram (1993) call a "deviant population," and we are not accustomed as a society to giving monetary awards and significant assistance to people with criminal records. The cases of those exonerees with prior records may be those made most visible to the public and those most protested by legal officials. In any case, the "myth of actual guilt" works against public policy reform in favor of exonerees.

Related to this idea is the third myth, the "myth of the complicit victim" where the victim is the wrongly convicted individual. Just as there may be resistance to giving assistance to someone with a criminal record, there may be resistance to giving assistance to someone who in some way contributed to their own victimization, someone who was complicit in their victimization. Some may believe that exonerees contributed to their wrongful conviction, perhaps by participating in other criminal activity, and they just got caught for the wrong thing: "if they didn't do this, they probably did something else to deserve the punishment they got." Or maybe they were in with the wrong crowd or had shady associates; or maybe they drank too much or did drugs and so were just "bad people" anyway. Whatever the specific justification, some people may believe that the exoneree deserved the punishment they got, just maybe not for the behavior they got it for. In this way, they are not true victims, and thus are not deserving of assistance or compensation. Some believe that they got themselves into the mess so they should be responsible for getting themselves out it.

On the one hand, the public has discovered the issue of innocence over the past twenty years, leading to support for reforms in criminal justice practice and a decline in support for the death penalty. On the other hand, it seems that the public has yet to understand and embrace the belief in the actual innocence of each exoneree in every case, especially when powerful voices within the system appear to be saying the opposite. This lack of awareness and ambivalence over an actual person's innocence may explain the dearth of policy reform in the area of aftermath. With greater awareness and understanding, perhaps remedies (compensation, expungement, additional supports) will become more available (see Westervelt & Cook, 2012 for a discussion of these remedies; see also Cook, Westervelt, & Maruna, this volume).

# Conclusion

Increased public awareness of wrongful capital convictions has transformed the U.S. criminal justice system. The greatest impact has been in the realm of capital punishment where universal revulsion at the idea of executing an innocent person has transformed the terms of debate on an issue that was previously seen in terms of abstract morality. This has contributed to a reduction in use of the death penalty by over two-thirds; a reversal in the trend of increased use; abolition in several states; and a new political environment where being anti-death penalty is no longer seen as a death-knell for ambitious politicians of either party. This is a major accomplishment.

Public officials also have responded to the new politics of criminal justice based on the discovery of innocence by enacting reforms designed to prevent errors in the future. Many states have adopted new procedures to increase the accuracy of eyewitness identifications, reduce the possibility of coerced confessions, and ensure that evidence is adequately and accurately preserved. Paradoxically, the exonerees themselves have been left largely out of the picture. Reform advocates have, understandably, focused on those currently in prison, attempting to get them out. But those who work with exonerees know, as Westervelt and Cook (2012a) have recently documented, that these individuals have been traumatized by a system they may no longer be able to trust. They often reenter society with few job skills, little education, and few resources to allow them to find a place to live, get a job, or acquire the skills they need to succeed. Public officials are notably skittish about providing resources to anyone who may have other convictions. Judicial system actors may not like to draw attention to their own mistakes, or may believe the individuals are not "truly innocent" in spite of the state's decision to drop all charges. So while members of the public are outraged at the possibility of error, so too do they assume that exonerees walk from prison into a jackpot of lucrative state support. Nothing could be further from the truth. In the end, wrongful convictions have led to massive reforms in some important areas of policy, but to precious few reforms that directly affect thousands of individuals so grievously wronged by errors in our system of justice.

# References

Babwin, D. (2007). Chicago pays $20M to settle lawsuits alleging police tortured death-row inmates. *Associated Press*, December 7.

Baumgartner, F. R., De Boef, S. L., & Boydstun A. E. (2008). *The decline of the death penalty and the discovery of innocence.* New York: Cambridge University Press.

Bedau, H. A. (Ed.). (1987). *The death penalty in America: Current controversies.* New York, N.Y.: Oxford University Press.

Bedau, H. A. & Radelet, M. L. (1987). Miscarriages of justice in potentially capital cases. *Stanford Law Review, 40*(1), 21–179.

Bernhard, A. (2004). Justice still fails: A review of recent efforts to compensate individuals who have been unjustly convicted and later exonerated. *Drake Law Review, 52,* 703–738.

CNN/ORC Poll. (2011, Oct. 12). Retrieved from http://www.deathpenaltyinfo.org/documents/rel16j.pdf.

Cook, K. J. (1998). *Divided passions: Public opinions on abortion and the death penalty.* Boston, MA: Northeastern University Press.

Cook, P. J. (2009). Potential savings from abolition of the death penalty in North Carolina. *American Law and Economics Review, 11*(2), 498–529.

Death Penalty Information Center. (n.d.). http://www.deathpenaltyinfo.org/.

Elliott, A. (2003). City gives $5 million to man wrongly imprisoned in child's rape. *New York Times,* December 16.

Garland, D. (2010). *Peculiar institution: America's death penalty in an age of abolition.* Cambridge: Harvard University Press.

Gross, S. R., Jacoby, K., Matheson, D. J., Montgomery, N., & Patil, P. (2005). Exonerations in the United States 1989 through 2003. *Journal of Criminal Law and Criminology, 95*(2), 523–560.

*Furman v. Georgia,* 408 U.S. 238, (1972).

Innocence Project. (2009). Making up for lost time: What the wrongfully convicted endure and how to provide fair compensation. Retrieved from: http://www.innocence project.org/docs/Innocence_Project_Compensation_Report.pdf.

Innocence Project. (2013). http://www.innocenceproject.org.

Kotch, S. & Mosteller, R. P. (2010). The Racial Justice Act and the long struggle with race and the death penalty in North Carolina. *UNC Law Review, 88,* 2031–2132.

Lindsay, R.C.L., & Wells, G. (1985). Improving eyewitness identifications from lineups: Simultaneous versus sequential lineup presentation. *Journal of Applied Psychology, 70,* 556–564.

Loyal, A. D. (2013). The decline of the death penalty as seen through a Legislative Perspective. Senior Thesis. Department of Political Science, University of North Carolina at Chapel Hill. Available at: http://www.unc.edu/~fbaum/teaching/Misc/Loyal_Thesis_2013.pdf.

Mims, B. (2013). Ex-prosecutor stands by murder conviction of exonerated man. WRAL.com. Available at http://www.wral.com/ex-prosecutor-stands-by-murder-conviction-of-exonerated-man/12781871/. Posted August 15.

National Registry of Exonerations. (n.d.). http://www.law.umich.edu/special/exoneration/Pages/about.aspx.

Norris, R. J., Bonventre, C. L., Redlich, A. D., & Acker, J. A. (2010/2011). "Than that one innocent suffer": Evaluating state safeguards against wrongful convictions. *Albany Law Review, 74*(3), 1301–1364.

Norris, R. J. (2012). Assessing compensation statutes for the wrongly convicted. *Criminal Justice Policy Review, 23*(3), 352–374.

O'Brien, B. & Grosso, C. M. (2011). Confronting race: How a confluence of social movements convinced North Carolina to go where the McCleskey Court wouldn't. *Michigan State Law Review, 2011,* 463–504.

Pew Research Center for the People and the Press. (2012, Jan. 6), *Continued majority support for the death penalty: More concern among opponents about wrongful convictions.* Retrieved from http://www.people-press.org/2012/01/06/continued-majority-support-for-death-penalty/.

Radelet, M. L., Bedau, H. A., & Putnam, C. (1994). *In spite of innocence.* Boston: Northeastern University Press.

Radelet, M. L., & Borg, M. J. (2000). The changing nature of the death penalty debates. *Annual Review of Sociology, 26,* 43–61.

Scheck, B., Neufeld, P. & Dwyer, J. (2000). *Actual innocence: Five days to execution, and other dispatches from the wrongly convicted.* New York, N.Y.: Doubleday.

Schneider, A. & Ingram, H. (1993). Social construction of target populations: Implications for politics and policy. *American Political Science Review, 87*(2), 334–347.

Warden, R., & Radelet, M. L. (2008). *Encyclopedia of wrongful convictions.* Evanston, Ill.: Northwestern University Press.

Wells, G. & Bradfield, A. (1998). 'Good, you identified the suspect': Feedback to eyewitnesses distorts their reports of the witnessing experience. *Journal of Applied Psychology, 83*, 360–376.

Wells, G., Small, M., Penrod, S., Malpass, R., Fulero, S. & Brimacombe, C. A. E. (1998). Eyewitness identification procedures: Recommendations for lineups and photospreads. *Law and Human Behavior, 22*, 603–647.

Westervelt, S. D. & Cook, K. J. (2013). Policy implications of wrongful convictions and the impact on the accused. Presentation given at North Carolina Central University School of Law, Raleigh, NC. April 17.

Westervelt, S. D. & Cook, K. J. (2012a). *Life after death row: Exonerees' search for community and identity.* New Brunswick, NJ: Rutgers University Press.

Westervelt, S. D. & Cook, K. J. (Eds.). (2012b). *Albany Law Review: Revealing the impact & aftermath of miscarriages of justice, 73*(3).

Westervelt, S. D. & Cook, K. J. (2010). Framing innocents: The wrongly convicted as victims of state harm. *Crime, Law and Social Change, 53*(3), 259–275.

Westervelt, S. D., & Humphrey, J. A. (Eds.). (2001). *Wrongly convicted: Perspectives on failed justice.* New Brunswick, NJ: Rutgers University Press.

# Chapter Sixteen

# Remedying Wrongful Convictions: Societal Obligations to Exonerees

Elizabeth Griffiths, *Rutgers University*
Michael Leo Owens, *Emory University*

Wrongful convictions occur in the United States, albeit it to an undetermined degree (Gross et al., 2005; Gross, 2013). Fortunately, technologies like DNA and effective advocacy by interest groups like the Innocence Project have been involved in securing the exonerations of nearly 1,200 wrongly convicted persons, although many more await opportunities for post-conviction relief.[1] As the set of exonerations grows, acknowledgement of criminal justice error and "the discovery of innocence" root more firmly in the mind of the body politic (Baumgartner, De Boef, & Boydstun, 2008). Exonerations also raise the civic issue of societal obligations to the wrongfully convicted.

Most Americans probably assume that the wrongfully convicted receive compensation and extra help to reintegrate into society after imprisonment. But, curiously, at a time when the fifty states spend many millions of dollars per year to encourage the successful reentry into society of legitimately convicted prisoners, the unjustly convicted must often wage protracted battles to get even a fraction of what society owes them for wrongly taking away their liberty. Narratives by the exonerated and empirical studies by scholars detail how life after wrongful conviction is difficult for men and women with records of wrongful convictions, perhaps more difficult than the lives of those justly convicted of crimes (Vollen & Eggers, 2008; Westervelt & Cook, 2010). Beyond memories and pains of the loss of liberty itself, wrongfully convicted people must contend with disrupted work profiles, lost and limited earning power, stunted educational attainment, strained or broken relationships, and the confusion and ambivalence of the public regarding their innocence. Some of the exonerated also experience traumatic stress disorders that disrupt work and social life after they leave prison (Grounds, 2005).

Calls for public/governmental acknowledgment and fulfillment of societal obligations, especially reparations, for wrongful convictions in the United States are longstanding (Borchard, 1913). The rationale is simple—society owes a civic debt to exonerees for unjustly taking their freedom (and sometimes labor), be it intentionally or accidentally. Fulfillment of societal obligations to the wrongfully convicted by states (and the federal government) seeks to repair and compensate them for the damages of the miscarriages

---

1. The National Registry of Exonerations reports a total of 1,180 exonerations as of August 2013 (http://www.law.umich.edu/special/exoneration/Pages/about.aspx). In terms of DNA exonerations aided specifically by Innocence Project attorneys, the 300th person to have his conviction overturned in September of 2012 was a fifteen-year inmate of death row named Damon Thibodeaux.

of justice. Without compensation, penal harm endures against those undeserving of retribution.

Nonetheless, political disagreement exists in many states over the degree to which governments have and should fulfill societal obligations to the wrongfully convicted, particularly for unintentional damages. Consequently, restitution for wrongful convictions by states is spotty and unpredictable. The Innocence Project finds, for instance, that even when DNA evidence has led to overturned convictions, two out of five remain without compensation from their state governments. This statistic is more troubling when we consider that Innocence Project exonerees are often more able than non-DNA exonerees to be in a position to prove "innocence" by a standard meeting or exceeding many state eligibility requirements (Kahn, 2010). Even when consensus exists that states have a societal obligation to remedy wrongful convictions, political dissensus characterizes debates about how to best meet and balance the individual interests of the wrongfully convicted and the collective interests of governments. Ideally, a package for meeting societal obligations for wrongful convictions would address all dimensions of loss and the varied expectations for wholeness by the wrongfully convicted. Apologies, social welfare benefits, employment, education, expungement of records, reforms of criminal justice procedures, and monetary compensation, for example, would demonstrate substantial effort to fulfill societal obligations for their loss of liberty and opportunities due to wrongful conviction. But when compensation occurs, it grossly varies by quantity, quality, and method (Norris, 2012; Owens & Griffiths, 2011/2012).

We focus on compensation as a means of remedying wrongful convictions, particularly by expressing and fulfilling societal obligations to the exonerated. The first part of our chapter identifies a starting point for thinking about such obligations—current methods for compensating exonerees. Following a deeper look at the best of the current methods, namely statutory compensation, this chapter presents evidence of a curious relationship—the correlation between the number of DNA exonerations in state courts and the quality of statutory compensation offered by state governments, which has consequences for how we think about what states do and why they do it when it comes to meeting societal obligations to the exonerated. Beyond providing an empirical example of how the quantity of wrongful convictions may influence the quality of compensation designs, we use the relationship to consider and rank a small set of plausible explanations. Our exercise leads us to claim that movement to better remedy wrongful convictions requires that more states acknowledge and expand their social obligations to the exonerated. It is a civic imperative. We advocate, however, for a newer, better method of compensating for wrongful convictions, one that would parallel the worker's compensation system. We conclude with ideas for deepening research into societal obligations to the wrongfully convicted.

# Starting Point: Varied and Unequal Compensation

Where compensation is permissible among the states to fulfill societal obligations to the wrongfully convicted, there is no single system for determining and distributing reparations for miscarriages of justice. At present, there are three methods for compensating the wrongfully convicted in the United States—civil litigation, private legislation, and statutory compensation. From the beginning, however, the design of compensation for wrongful convictions in the United States could have been different—it could have been universal rather than particularistic. As Borchard (1932, p. xxiv) rightly contended, "if ... an innocent man is convicted of a crime, and it is later established that he had no connection with it, the least that the state can do to vindicate itself and make restitution to the innocent victim is to grant him an indemnity, not as a matter of grace and favor but as a matter of right." Our current designs for compensating the wrongly convicted, however, continue to elevate "favor" via private legislation and "grace" via civil litigation (and, to a lesser extent, statutory compensation) above "right" in terms of an automatic scheme with low barriers to access and broad benefits for compensating the wrongfully convicted. In that way, each is flawed.

## Civil Litigation

The wrongfully convicted may use the courts to acquire compensation. They may file common law tort claims or a civil rights claim under 42 U.S.C § 1983 against state governments and criminal justice institutions for it. But "civil rights and common law tort claims," as Kahn (2010, p. 124) notes, "require a showing of culpability on the part of the government, which is often either not present or extremely difficult for claimants to establish." Successful claims often require the identification of a malicious criminal justice actor or action, recognized as the "cause" of wrongful conviction. Exonerees, however, often due to their lower socioeconomic status, are hard-pressed to investigate and identify culpable sources linked directly to intentional wrongdoing. Finding a target for litigation is difficult too because police, prosecutors, and other criminal justice actors possess degrees of immunity that limit their exposure to lawsuits regarding discretionary decisions made in the performance of their work (De Geest, 2012).[2] Thus, civil suits are unlikely to yield compensation for the average or typical exoneree.

## Private Legislation

Beyond the courts, state legislatures are forums for the wrongfully convicted to seek compensation. Exonerees may lobby the legislature to pass private compensation bills, if states permit it. Success comes by identifying a legislator willing to introduce a bill calling for the state to compensate a specific exoneree, along with a majority vote in favor of the bill by a legislature and gubernatorial support for the legislation. In short, there must be political will for states to enact private legislation on behalf of specific exonerees.

Given that wrongful convictions are a form of penal harm by political institutions, private legislation perhaps is a reasonable method for compensation, particularly for states with few exonerations. However, this method burdens exonerees to mobilize political support for themselves while bearing the stigma of imprisonment and possessing limited political or economic resources, factors that may undermine their lobbying efforts. Plus, successful lobbying by exonerees yields differing contents of legislative bills in terms of

---

2. De Geest (2012) suggests that those who enjoy qualified immunity are more likely to externalize, rather than internalize, the precaution costs associated with their actions or decisions. When precaution costs are externalized, reliance on strict liability standards—wherein the injurer is legally obliged to fully compensate the injured—can lead to overprecaution (or chilling effects) in the regular performance of their duties. De Geest argues, instead, for a gross negligence or good-faith liability standard for those actors who enjoy some form of qualified or full immunity (such as police officers or prosecutors, respectively), for discretionary decisions in the performance of their duties.

compensation, even when wrongful criminal convictions, durations of imprisonment, and reentry needs are similar across exonerees.[3] Additionally, legislative (and gubernatorial) support for private bills may come at the cost of amendments that discipline exonerees. For example, private bills have occasionally included stipulations akin to parole/probation regulation that require recipients to obtain employment and submit to drug testing.

## Statutory Compensation

Some state legislatures provide additional forums for the wrongfully convicted to seek compensation in a form other than private legislation. Exonerees may seek recompense through statutory compensation, enacted by legislatures and regulating government behavior regarding compensation. Currently, 29 states, along with the District of Columbia and the federal government, provide for statutory compensation for wrongful convictions. Typically, they offer the exonerated monetary payments, sometimes nontaxable, based on set dollar amounts for each year of wrongful imprisonment. States may supplement monetary compensation with social services (e.g., job training, psychotherapy, medical coverage, and educational scholarships), and reimburse for legal expenses incurred securing exonerations.

Most legal scholars and wrongful conviction policy advocates prefer statutory compensation over civil suits and private legislation (e.g., Huff et al., 1996; Norris, 2012; Owens & Griffiths, 2011/2012; Scheck et al., 2000). Yet statutory compensation is an imperfect method of providing reparations to exonerees. Too often it erects high barriers to compensation (e.g., requiring clear and convincing evidence of innocence via DNA or gubernatorial pardons). It also bars many exonerees from compensation for having prior or current records of "rightful" conviction/imprisonment or contributing to their wrongful convictions by providing fabricated evidence (e.g., false confessions) or pleading guilty, all of which may be rational behaviors under some circumstances for persons facing wrongful charges carrying long sentences (Vollen & Eggers, 2008). Statutory compensation may come too with time limitations for filing claims and prohibitions of future litigation by the wrongfully convicted. Nevertheless, it remains the method most likely to foster intrastate fairness in compensation for the exonerated.

## Stepping Back: Dynamics of the Quality of Statutory Compensation

The quality of statutory compensation varies across the states that have adopted it. Analyzing statutory compensation in the 27 states that had enacted it by 2011,[4] Norris

---

3. For instance, between 2005 and 2010, legislators in Georgia introduced three private bills to compensate three individuals for their wrongful convictions for similar crimes (i.e., rape and robbery) and wrongful imprisonment (averaging approximately 23 years among them). The bills proposed compensation from $1.2 million to $3 million and actual recompense ranged from $500,000 to $1.2 million.

4. As of June 5, 2013, two more states—Colorado and Washington—have adopted statutory compensation. States without statutory compensation include: Alaska, Arizona, Arkansas, Delaware, Georgia, Hawaii, Idaho, Indiana, Kansas, Kentucky, Michigan, Minnesota, Nevada, New Mexico, North Dakota, Oregon, Pennsylvania, Rhode Island, South Carolina, South Dakota, and Wyoming.

(2012) found that monetary compensation is near universal, except for Montana. However, approximately 50 percent of states with statutory compensation cap total recompense for wrongful convictions; these range from a low of $20,000 to a high of $2,000,000, with a median of $400,000 (Norris, 2012). Additionally, only 57 percent of states with statutory compensation supplement monetary restitution with non-monetary compensation like subsidized medical care, job training, and tuition waivers.

Although statutory compensation may come closest to an ideal means of fulfilling the societal obligations to the wrongfully convicted, it yields grossly uneven generosity in compensation packages for exonerees across the states that have enacted it.[5] In other words, the quality of compensation is higher in some states than other states. Why?[6] To start to answer the question, we rely on the Quality of Statutory Compensation Index (Norris, 2012) to evaluate the extent to which statutory compensation improves as the rate of exonerations increases, using the 275 DNA-based exonerations facilitated by the Innocence Project from the late 1980s through November 30, 2011. The index measures, as of 2011, various dimensions of statutory compensation for wrongful convictions: amounts of monetary compensation; classes of social assistance such as employment assistance, mental health services, attorney fees, and the like; criminal record expungement; eligibility criteria; disqualifications for assistance; statutes of limitations; tax provisions; availability of civil redress; and upon-death provisions. The index also scores the quality of statutory compensation by states against the model compensation legislation crafted by the Innocence Project. A state with statutory compensation meeting the standard of the model legislation would receive a score of 60. Of the 27 states covered by the index, which is a relatively and normally distributed scale (mean=28.9; s.d. = 5.6), the highest score is 43 (Texas).

When we consider the zero order correlation between the number of exonerees and the quality of statutory compensation, we find a positive but nonsignificant relationship ($r = .232$; $p = .244$). This suggests that the quality of compensation and the quantity of exonerations are unrelated. Yet results from a non-linear least squares regression model yield a different interpretation. The estimated equation is $\hat{Y} = 31.418 - .719X + .022X^2$, where $\hat{Y}$ is the predicted quality of statutory compensation and X is the number of DNA-based exonerations in a state. An adjusted R2 of .252 indicates that the quantity of state-level exonerations strongly predicts the quality of state-level statutory compensation. Put another way, the number of exonerations facilitated by the Innocence Project explains approximately one-quarter of the variance in the quality of statutory compensation by states that have adopted that method of recompense. Furthermore, the finding of a significant squared term ($b = .022$; $p = .006$) means that the relationship between the quality of compensation and the quantity of exonerations is concave and curvilinear. Figure 1 illustrates that at lower levels of exonerations the predicted quality of statutory compensation score is negative. This is true for states with 15 or fewer DNA-based exonerations. As the number of DNA-based exonerations increases beyond 15, however, the quality of statutory compensation for wrongful convictions rises. Indeed, the state with the largest number of exonerees (Texas) also has the highest score on the Quality of Statutory Compensation Index.

---

5. Texas, for instance, compensated Randolph Arledge $2.4 million for his wrongful 30-year imprisonment for rape and robbery, while Wisconsin compensated Robert Lee Stinson a mere $25,000 for his wrongful 23-year imprisonment (Bonpasse, 2013).

6. Elsewhere we examine the determinants of states adopting statutory compensation, focusing on the potential effects of interest group pressure, penal regime types, and ideological composition of state governments (see Owens & Griffiths, 2011/2012). Those findings show that the major predictor of the adoption of statutory compensation is the quantity of exonerations in states.

**Figure 1. Predicted regression line in equation regressing the quality of compensation legislation on the number of exonerees in states with statutory compensation (N=27)**

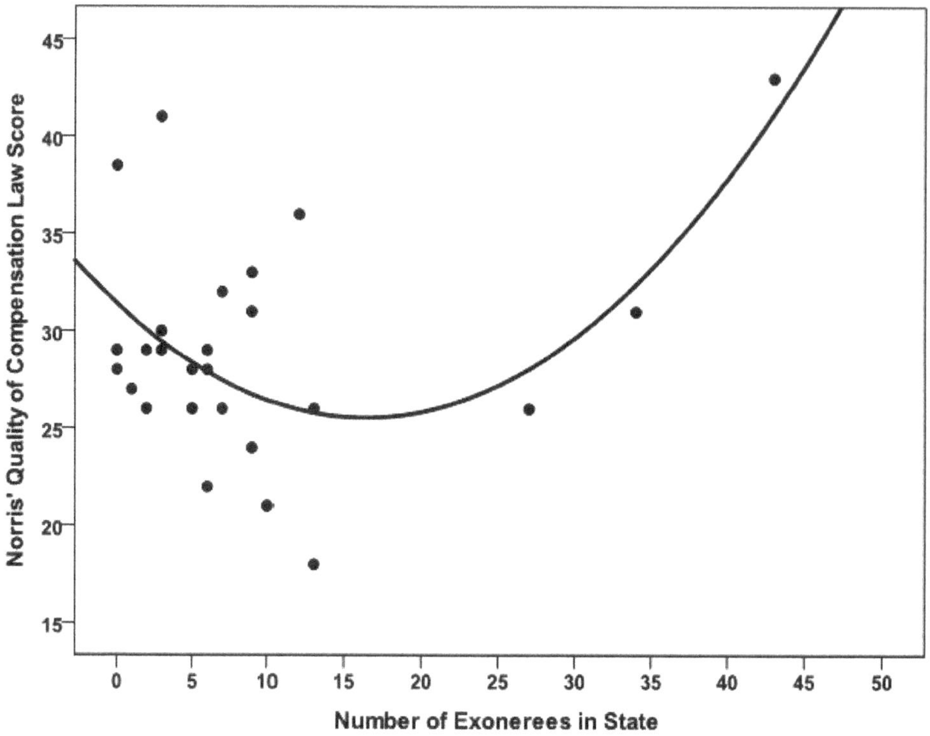

Data Source: Innocence Project website list of exonerees to November 30, 2011 (N=275).

The nature of the relationship between the quantity of exonerations and the quality of statutory compensation is instructive. At few exonerations (i.e., less than five), the quality of state compensation for wrongful convictions via statute is generally higher than that of states with between five and 15 exonerations. This finding reflects a legislative logic Callahan (2002, p.1) observed when studying the 2005 legislative debates surrounding a proposed statutory compensation bill in the Michigan House of Representatives — "no one seems to have a huge problem with the dollar amounts involved, given the fact that to date only two men in Michigan have been exonerated through DNA testing." It is noteworthy, however, that the Michigan House failed to pass that compensation statute (HB 5509, 2005 session) and is presently considering another such bill eight years later (HB 4451, 2013 session). One would expect in a case like Michigan, or similar states, that the budgetary consequences of enacting legislation to compensate the wrongfully convicted are limited because of low demand for recompense as a consequence of few exonerations.

As the number of exonerations in a state increases, however, statutory compensation shifts from symbolic expressions of a state-level commitment to fulfill societal obligations to the wrongfully convicted to substantial capital outlays from state budgets. For, as Figure 1 also shows, there is a systematic decline in the quality of statutory compensation associated with moderate increases in the number of exonerations. Yet as the number of known wrongful convictions increases beyond 15, the quality of compensation legislation changes direction and becomes positive, driven especially by Texas. Explanations for the positive relationship between the number of exonerations and the quality of statutory compensation at higher levels of recognized wrongful convictions may reflect a greater willingness of states to admit error, to investigate potential errors, and to provide reasonable remedies as appropriate. Thus, the null relationship between levels of recognized wrongful convictions and quality of statutory restitution packages shown at a bivariate level is belied by a more complicated U-shaped pattern in a non-linear least squares regression model. What may best explain the pattern of our results?

# Morality

The central premise for statutory compensation is the moral imperative to help to restore victims of state harm and provide recompense for errors that resulted in their unjust conviction and incarceration (Michelman, 1967; Rawls, 1999 [1971]). Such an argument coheres with our evidence of a positive, albeit insignificant, linear relationship between the quantity of exonerations and the quality of state recompense for wrongful convictions. That small increases in compensatory quality may result from increased exonerations suggests that states recognize the scope of wrongful convictions and work to repair the harm visited on the victims of the miscarriage of justice. Like the "just compensation" clause of the Fifth Amendment of the U.S. Constitution, which focuses on compensation for governmental taking of private property rather than the taking of liberty through wrongful imprisonment and was fueled by a liberal ideology that "sought to create a large sphere within which the individual could exercise privileges and enjoy immunities free from state interference" (Treanor, 1985, p. 705), the underlying moral premise, even the specific constitutional protection, could—should—philosophically extend to compensating those for whom state interference has been most intrusive—the wrongfully convicted (Master, 2004).[7]

Compensation, especially if coupled with other official public acknowledgements of error such as an apology, would dramatically signal societal obligation to the exonerated and desire to provide clear routes to recompense for injured parties. Yet morality-based explanations are insufficient to explain the empirical pattern in the data on quality of statutory compensation. If morality-based explanations held, we would expect to see a positive and significant relationship between the quality of compensation statute and the number of victims of state harm eligible for recompense. This is because the states are arguably instituting more generous and comprehensive restitution packages as they discover the widening the scale of error in criminal justice. We do not find evidence consistent with this premise, however. Instead, at low to moderate levels of exonerations, the effect is actually negative. For this reason, morality-based explanations may make citizens feel more confident in the "justness" of the criminal justice system, but they do not effectively explain the actions of legislatures when it comes to statutory compensation.

---

7. But see Rosenthal (2010, p. 132-3) for an argument against the use of the Constitution's Takings Clause as a rationale for restitution in the case of wrongful conviction. The Fifth Amendment's just compensation clause is intended to provide compensation for the public taking of private property. By contrast, the Fourth Amendment, which is concerned with deprivations of "life, liberty, or property," requires due process protections and is not concerned with compensatory restitution. Thus, Rosenthal (2010) argues that the extension of the just compensation premise to concerns better addressed by the Fourth Amendment are inappropriately applied.

## Utilitarianism

Public policy should, on the whole, maximize public satisfaction with the outcomes of governmental decisions (Bentham, 1988 [1781]). This utilitarian principle suggests that policymaking should simply employ cost-benefit analysis to maximize societal benefits and minimize aggregate costs. If true, state legislators, who may be attentive to the zero-sum nature of budgets, should pass legislation that benefits the greatest number of residents. As compensation claims for wrongful convictions rises, the likelihood that state legislators restrict access to recompense or reduce its quality should increase. In other words, if we expect that legislatures are concerned with limiting liability and managing state budgets efficiently, we can begin to understand why the quality of statutory compensation tends to fall as exonerations rise. The pattern of results is consistent with traditional cost-benefit explanations, and seemingly provides a better fit than morality-based explanations to the evidence presented in Figure 1.

Higher quality compensation requires greater financial outlays, which directly compete with other state budget allocations that some may deem more important (see Rosenthal, 2010). Further, states with statutory compensation effectively obligate themselves to future expenditures in the form of compensation for undiscovered wrongful convictions. As more wrongful convictions are recognized, and the possibility of detecting more error in criminal convictions increases, states hedge their bets by keeping quality of compensation lower. Still, the cost-benefit perspective, at least alone, is unable to explain the subsequent increases in quality of statutory compensation that we observe when the number of ex-onerations exceeds 15. Some caution should be exercised, however, in interpreting the upswing in quality of compensation evidenced in Figure 1, as very few states have 15 or more DNA exonerations to date. Nonetheless, these initial findings are at least suggestive of elite responsiveness to increasing public awareness of criminal justice error.

## Elite Responsiveness

Perhaps we may better understand the patterns in the quality of statutory compensation across the states by focusing on changes in societal attitudes about the welfare state and the deservedness of its beneficiaries (Priel, 2013). Perhaps public opinion regarding the "role of government in alleviating social injustices" influences support for and encourages greater quality of statutory compensation, growing largely from civic ideas about social rights, duty of care, and the soundness of government intervention (Hasenfeld & Rafferty, 1989, p. 1042; see also Priel, 2013). In the case of states compensating for wrongful convictions, we might expect the public to be ambivalent, even skeptical, about the deservedness of exonerees at first. For instance, the public may question the actual innocence of exonerees, seeing them as "getting off" rather than being truly innocent, which is a commonly expressed sentiment (Westervelt & Cook, 2010; Vollen & Eggers, 2008). As ex-onerations increase, however, especially if they spike, public opinion may favor arguments about the fallibility of criminal justice and become more accepting of the "innocence frame" (Baumgartner, De Boef, & Boydstun, 2008). The public may then be more likely to support higher quality compensation for wrongful convictions. Consequently, if policy elites seek to be responsive to their constituents, we would expect state legislators to act in ways consistent with public attitudes about reparation. Connecting that logic to wrongful convictions, we would expect legislatures in states with statutory compensation to adopt (or improve by reform) the quality of recompense for the exonerated. This argument seems most consistent with the apparent curvilinear relationship we observe between the quantity of exonerations and the quality statutory compensation for wrongful convictions.

# Moving Forward: Towards a Better Method of Compensation

Statutory compensation is better than civil litigation and private legislation as a method of meeting societal obligations for wrongful convictions. This is true despite its flaws, and a greater number of states are recognizing it: Of the 29 states with statutory compensation, 25 of them adopted it within the past decade (six states adopted statutory compensation between 2000 and 2006, and another 19 adopted it since then) (Owens & Griffiths, 2011/2012). This pace of policy diffusion is noteworthy. Nearly three decades after Wisconsin first enacted statutory compensation in 1913, for example, a second state (California) followed suit. Thereafter, state adoptions of statutory compensation were near zero until the 1980s, wherein we see a rapid cascade of policy adoptions. This pattern illustrates the sharply "punctuated equilibrium" of states adopting statutory compensation (Owens & Griffiths, 2011/2012, p. 1286). At the same time, the quality of statutory compensation across the states remains well below what the exonerated and reformers like the Innocence Project contend is adequate. At least, however, states are moving in a direction that more squarely recognizes societal obligations to the wrongfully convicted. Still, we could imagine a better method of compensation, one manifesting the clearest recognition of states that they must meet societal obligations for wrongful convictions.

A system of no-fault exoneration insurance akin to worker's compensation—whereby compensation is awarded to injured parties irrespective of any self-contribution to their harm—would be a more reasonable remedy for those harmed by wrongful conviction, which is the gravest deprivation of rights and liberties by a society. Yet statutory compensation, as it works today, fails to mimic the rationale and evolution of workers' compensation legislation.

Workers' compensation schemes emerged in the United States early in the twentieth century, following adoption of such legislation in countries like Germany (1884) and England (1897).

> [T]he basic principle underlying workers' compensation programs was that benefits would be provided to injured workers without regard to fault and, in return, employers would face limited liability. In other words, workers would be entitled to benefits if the injury was caused by their employment, regardless of who caused the injury, and employers would be responsible for specific benefits itemized in the statute in exchange for the elimination of lawsuits for negligence (Clayton, 2003/2004, p. 7).

This system effectively reduced the uncertainties associated with torts or civil suits for employers and provided protections to employees injured in the course of their employment.

The implementation of workers' compensation marked the initiation of the first social insurance scheme in the United States and all but six states rapidly adopted it between 1910 and 1921 (Clayton, 2003/2004). Despite considerable interstate variation, joint support from employers and labor unions fostered the adoption of workers' compensation schemes. Employers supported them because statutory compensation yielded more predictable outcomes by forecasting costs and limiting liability, reducing accidental insurance premiums, and virtually eliminating court costs. Labor unions supported statutory compensation because it removed from employees the burden of proving employer negligence for damages sustained in the workplace. It also ensured workers' basic and timely compensation for injuries sustained at work, even when the employee arguably contributed to them.

In contrast to workers, policy sentiment has remained that exonerees must prove that their actions did not influence the harm they experienced. This is true for statutory compensation, civil litigations, and private legislation methods of compensation. In each instance, exonerees must prove their innocence via post-conviction relief prior to restitution, and the standards of relief are uniformly high. Nearly 90 percent of states employing statutory compensation, for instance, impose a "preponderance of evidence" standard, requiring exonerees prove their factual innocence, and almost 75 percent of states with statutory compensation maintain disqualifications for recompense associated with acts by the wrongfully convicted (Norris, 2012, p. 364). That is, exonerees must prove their innocence and/or lack of responsibility for being wrongfully convicted, which is a nearly impossible feat that requires exonerees to prove a negative (Bennardo, 2007; Norris, 2012).[8]

Procedures for statutory compensation for exonerees generally consider "fault" in eligibility for recompense, which is akin to the "contributory negligence" argument employers introduced in civil suits prior to the enactment of workers' compensation programs (Clayton, 2003/2004).[9] Fault-based systems, however, undermine opportunities for compensating the wrongly convicted given that state and federal laws, backed by judicial precedent, provide varied levels of immunity for law enforcement actors. Unless exonerees can prove bad faith, or malicious or unconstitutional conduct on the part of law enforcement, fault-based liability schemes, which are common in statutory compensation, are moot. Even in cases where malicious intent on the part of law enforcement investigators is uncovered, "if the accused receives a fair trial, even if evidence obtained by investigators is wrongfully admitted in evidence, they have not deprived prosecutors of the opportunity to evaluate the evidence, the accused of a fair opportunity to seek exclusion of the evidence, the trial judge to evaluate its admissibility, and the jury to assess its probative weight, which is all the Constitution ordinarily requires" (Rosenthal, 2010, p. 151). Plus, only a small proportion of exonerees have the resources to investigate and prove malicious or unconstitutional conduct on the part of law enforcement and/or the state, and this is coupled with the fact that many of the wrongfully convicted lack resources to fight for exonerations. In sum, statutory compensation for the wrongly convicted yields significantly less benefit to its injured parties than that of workers' compensation.

A no-fault statutory compensation law may offer the best odds of distributive justice and reasonably timely recompense for the injured party (Tyler et al., 1997). It is only when the process provides some added or symbolic advantage, such as a finding of fault

---

8. Kaplan (2008) argues for a "comparative fault" approach to compensation for wrongful conviction. In this case, proof of innocence would not be a disqualifier from seeking restitution through statutory compensation. Rather, self-contribution to wrongful conviction via a guilty plea, a false confession, or other fabricated evidence would be a factor in assessing the quantity of compensation awarded.

9. Employers could mount a number of legal defenses in law suits aimed at recovering for medical expenses, lost wages, and ancillary damages upon workplace accidents. Three of the most common defenses were *contributory negligence* wherein employees were said to have contributed to the accident, the *fellow-servant* doctrine that laid blame for the accident on other employees rather than the employer, and the *assumption-of-risk* doctrine which held that employees who were aware of the dangers in the workplace were believed to have assumed those risks voluntarily by reporting for work (Clayton, 2003/2004).

and/or an apology, that civil litigation or private legislation could represent a better remedy than a no-fault compensation scheme (Shuman, 1994). By contrast, a no-fault scheme negates the burden on the wrongly convicted to prove fault on the part of the system or its actors, a difficult or impossible hurdle to overcome for most "victims of state harm" (Westervelt & Cook, 2010; Kahn, 2010).

There are critiques, of course, of no-fault approaches for wrongful conviction compensation (Rosenthal, 2010). If the objective of strict liability is to create an economically efficient rationale for prospective tortfeasors (in this case, system actors) to internalize precautionary costs during the course of hazardous enterprises, the case of wrongful conviction is ill suited to this objective. This is because "scaling back or otherwise rendering law enforcement less aggressive in order to reduce the government's potential liability for wrongful prosecutions or convictions may have substantial political costs" that considerably exceed the benefits associated with reduced liability (Rosenthal, 2010, p. 129). Additionally, the government is less concerned with efficiency and cost-benefit calculations than is the private sector and the level of error in the criminal justice system may be substantially lower than is the case for other hazardous enterprises covered under strict liability doctrines. Furthermore, even when error cannot be expected to decline as a consequence of strict liability schemes, arguments for compensation via strict liability on moral grounds treat compensation as a "loss-spreading, ... mandatory, publicly-funded wrongful conviction insurance" (Rosenthal, 2010, p. 134). In the zero-sum context of state budgets, wrongful conviction compensation would reduce spending for other public programs (or necessitate increased borrowing by states).

A no-fault compensation scheme would not necessarily provide exonerees with an official apology either (Shuman, 1994), which is something that many exonerees desire (Cook, Westervelt, & Maruna, this volume; Vollen & Eggers, 2008). There is also discontent among at least some exonerees when compensation schemes, even no-fault options, prohibit further civil litigation. After all, not all wrongful convictions have the same identifiable causes or effects for their victims; yet the uniform schedule of payments associated with no-fault types of compensation schemes may inadequately and unevenly repair the individualized sui generis damages of wrongful convictions. It is noteworthy, however, that most of these criticisms may be levied at the current "fault-based" systems of statutory compensation.

While these arguments are worthy of consideration and debate, it is substantively unjust to deprive the wrongfully convicted of compensation after exoneration on the grounds that some level of error in criminal justice processing is unavoidable and that restitution financially burdens the government and, by extension, taxpayers. Moreover, the number of errors in criminal justice processing is potentially large, albeit unknown. As the numbers of exonerations grow, we may rightly characterize the criminal justice system as an *ultra-hazardous* enterprise worthy of strict liability standards of compensation.

In the end, the costs to states adopting no-fault exoneration insurance for wrongful convictions would depend on the number of recognized wrongful convictions over time. In states without recognized wrongful convictions, adoption costs for the state governments would be low and benefits for the wrongfully convicted would largely be symbolic. In states with large numbers of recognized wrongful convictions, adoption costs for state governments would be higher and benefits for the wrongfully convicted would be relatively substantial. States with no-fault exoneration insurance could bear heavy financial burdens, which they would place on their annual budgets, effectively transferring funds from other public programs. That, however, would be a fundamental and necessary price for operating fallible criminal justice systems.

If we begin to conceptualize wrongful convictions as "normal accidents" (Lofquist, 2001) and the criminal justice system as an ultrahazardous enterprise that may err far more often than we anticipate, then swift and comprehensive compensation post-release is justified. To avoid the delays and court costs associated with civil litigation, the favoritism and partisan disagreements of private legislation, the inequities in the extent and nature of statutory compensation for the victims of state harm, and loss of public confidence in the criminal justice system, states should adopt a no-fault compensation system. Doing so would more efficiently, effectively, and equitably fulfill the civic obligation of states to remedy the harms of wrongful convictions.

# Conclusion

Exonerees ultimately require economic and social support to rebuild their lives after wrongful convictions. Although no one can restore the months and years of freedom taken away from the wrongfully imprisoned, monetary and non-monetary forms of compensation can help. Financial payments can assist the wrongfully convicted person in making up for economic losses. Both financial payments and other forms of compensation such as free tuition or job training can reduce economic vulnerability during the reentry to society and increase the person's self-sufficiency for the future. Compensation carries a moral message, too. It allows government and citizens to make amends to the wrongly convicted person; and, more generally, helps to repair damage to the state's public legitimacy and boost public faith in the good judgment and fairness of criminal justice institutions. Our current compensation schemes, however, vary too substantially by state in terms of quantity, quality, and method to satisfy these aims on a large scale.

In stepping back to think about remedying wrongful convictions, we focused on compensation as a means of meeting societal obligations to the exonerated. We identified the three means by which states distribute reparations for miscarriages of justice, highlighting their flaws as adequate means of providing recompense. Additionally, we began to explore an interesting finding about the most favored means of compensating for wrongful convictions, namely the relationship between the quality of statutory compensation and the quantity of exonerations. We showed a concave, curvilinear effect of the number of exonerations on the quality of statutory compensation for the wrongfully convicted: In particular, states with the lowest number of exonerations tend to provide higher quality statutory compensation than do states with five to fifteen exonerations but the relationship reverses and quality improves after the number of exonerations exceeds 15. From there we entertained a small set of plausible explanations for this finding, concluding that a utilitarian rationale may explain why states initially limit compensation for wrongful convictions and that elite responsiveness to public opinion may explain why quality improves as exonerations continue to climb.

Seeking to move forward the conversation and study of fulfilling societal obligations to the wrongfully convicted, we proposed what we consider a better system for compensating the wrongfully convicted, namely a no-fault system of compensation akin to worker's compensation insurance. Such a system, at minimum, would reduce interstate inequalities in the availability of compensation and move states closer towards meeting model compensation schemes (Norris, 2012). Yet adopting such a system would be difficult. Unlike unions and employers agreeing that a workers' compensation system is necessary and valuable to both parties, there is a lack of broad support on the part of law enforcement, the public, legislators, and even certain exonerees for such a system, which may hinder further progress by the states to adopt more generous statutory compensation schemes in the short-run and a no-fault system in the long-run.

As we learn more about the challenges and possibilities of remedying wrongful convictions by studying current means of fulfilling societal obligations to the exonerated, one guiding principle must be kept front and center: Society owes a civic debt when people are unjustly deprived of their liberty, and compensation is the only way to repair as much of the miscarriage of justice as possible. Moreover, it should trouble the spirit of the American body politic that the wrongly convicted so often go uncompensated. All of us should seek the fulfillment of societal obligations to them.

# References

Baumgartner, F., De Boef, S., & Boydstun, A. E. (2008). *The decline of the death penalty and the discovery of innocence.* New York: Cambridge University Press.

Bennardo, K. (2007). A defense bar: The 'proof of innocence' requirement in criminal malpractice claims. *Ohio State Journal of Criminal Law, 5,* 341–366.

Bentham, J. (1988 [1781]). *The principles of morals and legislation.* New York: Prometheus Books.

Bonpasse, M. (2013-02-06). Low payout limits can hinder wrongfully convicted. *Citizens for Criminal Justice Reform.* Retrieved from http://www.ccjrnh.org/outside_articles/low_payout_limits_can_hinder_wrongfully_convicted.

Borchard, E. M. (1914). State indemnity for errors of criminal justice. *Annals of the American Academy of Political and Social Science, 52(1),* 108–114.

Borchard, E. M. (1932). *Convicting the innocent: Errors of criminal justice.* New Haven: Yale University Press.

Callahan, D. G. (2006, February 20). Bill seeks to compensate wrongly convicted individuals in Michigan. *Michigan Lawyers Weekly.*

Clayton, A. (2003/2004). Workers' compensation: A background for social security professionals. *Social Security Bulletin, 65(4),* 7–15.

Cook, K.J., Westevelt, S.D., & Maruna, S. (2014). The problem of fit: Parolees, exonerees, and prisoner reentry. (This Volume).

De Geest, G. (2012). Who should be immune from tort liability? *The Journal of Legal Studies, 41(2),* 291–319.

Franklin, M. A. (1967). Replacing the negligence lottery: Compensation and selective reimbursement. *Virginia Law Review, 53(4),* 774–814.

Gross, S. (2013). How many false convictions are there? How many exonerations are there? In C. R. Huff & M. Killias (Eds.), *Wrongful convictions and miscarriages of justice: Causes and remedies in North American and European criminal justice systems* (pp. 45–59). New York: Routledge.

Gross, S. R., Jacoby, K., Matheson, D. J., Montgomery, N., & Patil, S. (2005). Exonerations in the United States 1980 through 2003. *Journal of Criminal Law & Criminology, 95(2),* 523–560.

Grounds, A. (2005). Understanding the effects of wrongful imprisonment. In M. Tonry (Ed.), *Crime and justice: A review of research (Volume 32)* (pp. 1–58). Chicago: University of Chicago Press.

Hasenfeld, Y., & Rafferty, J. A. (1989). The determinants of public attitudes toward the welfare state. *Social Forces, 67(4),* 1027–1048.

Huff, C. R., Rattner, A., & Sagarin, E. (1996). *Convicted but innocent*. Thousand Oaks: Sage Publications.

Kahn, D. S. (2010). Presumed guilty until proven innocent: The burden of proof in wrongful conviction claims under state compensation statutes. *University of Michigan Journal of Law Reform, 44(1)*, 123–168.

Kaplan, A. I. (2008). The case for comparative fault in compensating the wrongfully convicted. *UCLA Law Review, 56*, 227–269.

Lofquist, W. S. (2001). Whodunit? An examination of the production of wrongful convictions. In S. D. Westervelt, & J. A. Humphreys (Eds.), *Wrongly convicted: Perspectives on failed justice* (pp. 174–196). New Brunswick: Rutgers University Press.

Master, H. (2004). Revisiting the takings-based argument for compensating the wrongfully convicted. *NYU Annual Survey of American Law, 60*, 97–148.

Michelman, F. I. (1967). Property, utility, and fairness: Comments on the ethical foundations of 'just compensation' law. *Harvard Law Review, 80(6)*, 1165–1258.

Norris, R. J. (2012). Assessing compensation statutes for the wrongly convicted. *Criminal Justice Policy Review, 23(3)*, 352–374.

Owens, M. L., & Griffiths, E. (2011/2012). Uneven reparations for wrongful convictions: Examining the state politics of statutory compensation legislation. *Albany Law Review, 75(3)*, 1283–1327.

Priel, D. (2013). The indirect influence of politics on tort liability of public authorities in English law. *Law & Society Review, 47(1)*, 169–198.

Rawls, J. (1999 [1971]). *A theory of justice*. Cambridge: Harvard University Press.

Rosenthal, L. (2010). Second thoughts on damages for wrongful convictions. *Chicago-Kent Law Review, 85(1)*, 127–161.

Scheck, B., Neufeld, P., & Dwyer, J. (2000). *Actual innocence: When justice goes wrong and how to make it right*. New York: New American Library.

Shuman, D. W. (1994). The psychology of compensation in tort law. *University of Kansas Law Review, 43(1)*, 39–77.

Treanor, W. M. (1985). The origins and original significance of the just compensation clause of the fifth amendment. *Yale Law Journal, 94*, 694–716.

Tyler, T. R., Boeckmann, R. J., Smith, H. J., & Huo, Y. J. (1997). *Social justice in a diverse society*. Colorado: Westview Press.

Vollen, L., & Eggers, D. (2008). *Surviving justice: America's wrongfully convicted and exonerated*. San Francisco: McSweeny's Books.

Westervelt, S. D., & Cook, K. J. (2010). Framing innocents: The wrongly convicted as victims of state harm. *Crime, Law & Social Change, 53(3)*, 259–275.

# Section III

## Moving Forward: Advancing the Study of Wrongful Convictions

# Chapter Seventeen

# Theorizing Wrongful Conviction

Marvin Zalman,[1] *Wayne State University*

## Introduction

The task of advancing theory related to wrongful conviction is especially challenging because (i) the field of wrongful conviction studies is sprawling; (ii) the central wrongful conviction literature is extensive and the peripheral literature is huge; and (iii) very little has been written explicitly about wrongful conviction from a theoretical perspective— whether about causes, effects, uncovering error, or policy responses to wrongful convictions. Given this state of affairs, I will suggest a number of theoretical approaches that can help improve our understanding of wrongful conviction, and perhaps contribute to the goal of reducing the number of wrongful convictions through better detection and error-reduction policies. The term theory will be used herein both as used in the natural and social sciences, and in a more general way denoting abstract reasoning or systematic knowledge not necessarily supported by empirical scientific research.

Before placing specific theoretical "dishes" selected by your chef on the smorgasbord table, several preliminary issues are discussed. First, I briefly examine what is meant by theory, its uses, and the idea of theoretical orientations. Next I support the assertion that wrongful conviction literature is diverse and extensive, not to prove an obvious point, but to provide a broad canvas suggesting several areas from which theoretical orientations will be drawn. The chapter then discusses several theoretical orientations to the study of wrongful conviction before concluding.

## Theory and Theoretical Orientations

Theory construction and testing is the holy grail of scientists. This desideratum animated Richard Leo's critique of the legal literature and his call for a "criminology of wrongful conviction," arguing that the "scholarly study of miscarriages of justice ... is theoretically impoverished" (Leo, 2005, p. 213). Instead, "scholars need to seek out root causes, not legal causes, of wrongful conviction" in order "to develop theories, frameworks, or paradigms for better understanding the general patterns, logics, and characteristics of wrongful conviction cases" (Leo, 2005, p. 213). Leo was critical also of social scientists who, although studying wrongful convictions more systematically than lawyers or journalists, "have mostly avoided the construction, development, or application of theory to the study of miscarriages of justice" (2005, p. 214).

---

1. *Acknowledgements*: I wish to thank Julia Carrano for her helpful review of an earlier draft.

Leo was surely thinking about the way in which "theory" is used in empirical sociology and criminology, adapted from the natural sciences. In this perspective, theory generation and testing is integral to the research process; without theory scientific knowledge (i.e., knowledge validated by scientific procedures) is not possible. Reynolds (1971, p. 4) summarized five goals of scientific theory: (1) organizing facts into typologies; (2) predicting future events; (3) explaining past events; (4) providing a sense of understanding about facts and events, and (5) creating a potential to control events (although this may not be possible in sciences like astronomy or geology). In the scientific process, designed to produce reliable and valid explanations of phenomena (focusing on "how" questions rather than the "why" questions of religion, values, and metaphysics), scientific theory construction is needed to focus the concentration of scientists on a narrow range of phenomena (i.e., it is impossible to study "everything"), and theory *testing* is necessary to providing a satisfactory explanation of the world around us (Blalock, 1970).

Without getting into the complexities surrounding the meaning of science and the scientific method, it is worth mentioning that the key to prediction, explanation, and control consists of rigorous methods of data gathering and analysis (e.g., applied statistical tests; mathematical modeling) (see Hirschi & Selvin, 1967). This was emphasized in a recent social scientific study designed to predict wrongful convictions:

> Social science, of course, is primarily concerned with understanding the world as it is rather than as it ought to be. The goal of traditional social science is generalizable knowledge. Empirical social scientists draw on five primary methods of data gathering—experiments, field observation, surveys, interviews, and analysis of documents—to produce valid and reliable knowledge about social phenomena (Gould, Carrano, Leo, & Young, 2013, pp. 24–25).

This specific focus on theory as a component of empirical research is narrow in that it focuses only on questions that interest social scientists concerned with establishing generalizable statements. If the only question asked by a social scientist regarding wrongful convictions is how to predict them via the statistical analysis of measurable variables, then the prime methods emphasized in research methodology texts are sufficient (Maxfield & Babbie, 2008).

However, there are other important questions about wrongful conviction that can be addressed by rigorous and theoretically-oriented non-scientific scholarship that utilizes "theory" in different ways. An interesting symposium, for example, dealt with the challenges to conventional comparative politics (a combination of social scientific and historical work) from "postmodern or culturally relativistic claims" on one end of the methodological spectrum, and, at the other end, from the nomothetic claims of scholars applying deductive logic and microeconomic and game-theoretic models seeking overarching explanations of political life (Kohli et al., 1995, pp. 1–2). Peter Evans, defending the "eclectic messy center" of how comparative politics scholars approach theory, offered a model that I find attractive. The social science paradigms in his field were generated, first, by specific cases that interested scholars, which required the "ideographic [sic] knowledge that understanding specific sequences of events entails" (Evans in Kohli et al., 1995, p. 3). Next, there is a desire to predict, "not because we are positivists but because social scientists share with everyone else the desire to know what is likely to happen to them and how they might be able to improve prospective outcomes" (Evans in Kohli et al., 1995, p. 3). The kind of social science described by Leo's criminology of wrongful conviction would terminate inquiry at this point. But since comparative politics must discuss the application of issues to entire nations, another step, writing history, becomes necessary. As a result, Evans' "eclectic messy center" is work that draws on general theories whenever it can but also cares deeply about particular historical outcomes. It sees particular cases as the building blocks for general theories and theories as lenses to identify what is interesting and significant about particular cases. Neither theories nor cases are sacrosanct. Cases are always too complicated to vindicate a single theory. So scholars who work in this tradition are likely to draw on a mélange of theoretical traditions in hopes of gaining greater purchase on cases they care about (Evans, in Kohli et al., 1995, p.4).

In this spirit, I will examine the small body of social scientific work on wrongful convictions and also suggest an eclectic mix of theoretic approaches to the study of wrongful conviction.[2]

Peter Kraska (2004, 2006; see Kraska & Brent, 2011), observing that criminal justice processes can be explained by a number of theories, developed an eclectic approach which he labeled "theorizing" criminal justice.[3] Given the "inherently multi-theoretic" nature and lack of "an overarching or comprehensive theory" of the criminal justice discipline, Kraska's eight theoretic orientations "do the work of scientific theory — they organize data about criminal justice, provide a cascading *sense of understanding* of how the criminal justice system works, and guide further research" (Zalman, 2007, pp. 168, 170, 173, emphasis added). In a new paper, Norris and Bonventre (2013) applied Kraska's criminal justice theoretical orientations to wrongful convictions, in contrast to "a logical positivist view of theory," to suggest that criminal justice theoretic approaches to wrongful conviction scholarship can deepen our understanding of miscarriages of justice. Their paper compressed Kraska's categories and examined wrongful conviction through five theoretical orientations. First, viewing criminal justice as a "forced reaction" to crime (combining Kraska's "rational/legal" and "systems" orientations), wrongful convictions can be seen as normal byproducts of a criminal justice system. From this perspective, an excessive concern with errors could upset the equilibrium and efficiency of crime control mechanisms. This perspective can also frame the innocence movement as a necessary reaction to the increased number of exonerations, and force closer attention to cost/benefit issues (see Allen & Laudan, 2008). Second, understanding wrongful convictions and society's reaction to them through the value-preference lens of Packer's (1968) "crime control" and "due process" models, adopted as a theoretical orientation by Kraska, requires analysis of "the political climate of a particular period" (Norris & Bonventre, 2013). Such an ideological perspective leads to historical and legal-theoretic rather than empirical analysis (Aviram, 2011). Third, a political orientation suggests examining wrongful convictions through the lens of interests, political party orientations, and symbolic politics (Zalman, 2011). Fourth, a social constructionist understanding of criminal justice can lead researchers to examine wrongful convictions and the innocence movement's legitimacy from a moral panic perspective; such study could focus attention on the organizational and cultural environments ("bad barrels" rather than "bad apples") that generate and respond to wrongful convictions. Finally, a view of criminal justice as oppression leads to the study of wrongful convictions from a state-harms framework (Westervelt & Cook, 2010). Norris and Bonventre (2013) also suggest that "connecting classic criminal justice scholarship

---

2. Much rigorous scientific research based on scientific theory, even if not designed to generate theory, has been essential to wrongful conviction studies, but will not be addressed in this chapter. These include all the work on DNA profiling, on the chemistry of fires, forensic medicine studies of shaken baby syndrome, psychological experiments of eyewitness identification, and more.

3. I have written positively about his approach (Zalman, 2007); hence, "theorizing wrongful conviction."

with psychology and law research might provide a better understanding of interrogations and false confessions, one of the leading contributing factors to wrongful convictions." This insightful theoretic overview suggests paths of analysis that can deepen our understanding of how wrongful conviction is expressed in the criminal justice system and in American society.[4]

# The Sprawling Field of Wrongful Conviction

A reason to favor a "theoretical orientation" strategy is that while wrongful conviction study needs greater theoretical sophistication, the field (like criminal justice) is so diverse as to defy "a" theory, making diverse theoretical orientations more á propos than one grand theory. The field of wrongful conviction encompasses virtually every justice agency and process and a good part of civil society that is involved in the production of and reaction to wrongful convictions. A theory of the innocence movement, for example, would address "a related set of activities by lawyers, cognitive and social psychologists, other social scientists, legal scholars, government personnel, journalists, documentarians, freelance writers, and citizen-activists who, since the mid-1990s, have worked to free innocent prisoners and rectify perceived causes of miscarriages of justice in the United States" (Zalman, 2011, p. 1468). Theoretical understanding of wrongful convictions or exonerations as events or processes could encompass knowledge of genetics and DNA profiling (Aronson, 2007; Lynch, Cole, McNally & Jordan, 2008); the strengths and weaknesses of forensic sciences in general (National Research Council, 2009); and the psychological theories of mind that underlie studies of eyewitness identification and interrogation. Such study has deepened our understanding of where prosecutions go wrong and how to reduce errors. But this is only the beginning of knowledge.

How do the many people who administer and are caught up in the criminal justice system and its component agencies function in the production, rectification, and response to wrongful conviction? This requires knowledge of law (e.g., criminal, criminal procedure, evidence, appellate, constitutional); a "law & society" understanding of how law intersects the judicial process; and of how agencies function. To better understand the actors' motivations we need to identify the ideals, theories, professional working knowledge, and core activities of personnel in all agencies. In the face of such complexity, descriptions can be repeated ad infinitum without providing the kind of theoretical knowledge that will help analysts get below the surface to deepen understanding and fashion lasting error-reduction solutions.

# Wrongful Conviction Theoretical Orientations

Like comparative politics scholars who generate explanations of national behaviors in a messy, eclectic mix of social scientific theory, description, and historical analysis, those who seek to explain the complexity of criminal justice may be more successful in establishing a sense of understanding about facts and events with mixed methods. A skeptic may properly ask whether theoretical orientations will be subjective, in contrast to the reliable

---

4. I have previously written about a "criminal justice research agenda" for the study of wrongful conviction focusing on innocence *policy* that had theoretical elements (Zalman, 2006).

and valid knowledge produced by scientific data collection and analytic methods. The answer is that statements about wrongful conviction derived from theoretical orientations need to be tested against verified facts in future applications of the orientation; acceptance of theoretical orientations should depend on intersubjective judgments of experts who have considered and worked on the same issue, rather than idiosyncratic judgments. This is ultimately how judgments are accepted in science and nonscientific scholarship. Although conclusions drawn from theoretical orientations may not be as rigorously supported as those from social scientific research, they may be strengthened by seeking theoretical orientations of the "middle range" and adhering, to the degree possible, on "grounded theory" approaches (Lazarsfeld, 1970, pp. 37–40; Glaser & Strauss, 1967).

I begin by examining social scientific studies of wrongful conviction causes, a central issue, for their theory-generating potential, followed by other kinds of questions, including detecting wrongful convictions in single cases via idiographic approaches and exploring a few innocence reforms in light of criminological. justice and policy making theories.

# From a Criminology of Wrongful Conviction to a Criminal Justice of Wrongful Conviction — Empirically Explaining Causes

Only five published or completed studies have evaluated wrongful conviction causes by applying standard social science empirical/quantitative analysis. That so few quantitative studies exist reflects the latecomer status of criminologists to wrongful conviction studies and the substantial challenges of data collection in a field without official wrongful conviction data bases. Thus, NIJ funding was required to support the recent study by Gould et al. (2013), which did not utilize the relatively accessible death penalty data accessed by other quantitative studies. It is noteworthy that three of the studies were authored or co-authored by legal scholars (two of whom also hold Ph.D. degrees) who are also well-known wrongful conviction scholars (Garrett, 2008; Gould et al., 2013; Gross & O'Brien, 2008), and two by social scientists (Harmon, 2001; Harmon & Lofquist, 2005). It is also helpful to know that these five studies do not explore the same issue but, instead, answer four different research questions: (i) predicting death row exonerations by comparing exonerees to executed prisoners (Harmon, 2001; Gross and O'Brien, 2008); (ii) explaining why putatively innocent prisoners were executed, by comparing them to death row exonerees (Harmon & Lofquist, 2005); (iii) explaining how the appellate process failed to screen wrongful convictions and then handled exonerating DNA evidence by comparing exoneration and non-exoneration cases (Garrett, 2008); and (iv) predicting which initial justice system errors lead to (later exonerated) wrongful convictions, and which resulted in release or acquittal after indictment ("near misses") (Gould et al., 2013). Thus, whatever knowledge has been obtained from these excellent research articles has to be accounted as very thin, a point acknowledged in Gould et al. (2013, p. 30), which refers to social science research on wrongful conviction as "still too young to have evidenced a pattern of interest when employing a control group."

Only Gould et al. (2013) is examined here in detail. That study found that three sets of variables help to explain the critical phases of (i) prosecution and conviction, (ii) exoneration before final verdict, and (iii) post-conviction exoneration. As to the first, "false confession, official misconduct and some sort of identification (either an anonymous tip or a misidentification) are among the errors that bring innocent defendants into the criminal justice system," regardless of the later disposition of the case. These variables may be said to explain false indictments. Next, a second set of variables *intervene* to prevent a wrongful conviction: a strong defense, an older innocent defendant who can better withstand pressures to falsely confess and is better able to assist in his defense, a defendant without a prior criminal history, prosecutors who disclose evidence, and deliberate eyewitness misidentification (which is easier to see through than the testimony of an honestly mistaken witness). A third set of variables explain false convictions, including a state's punitiveness (i.e., whether it maintains the death penalty), forensic error, mistaken eyewitnesses, other witnesses who lie, and weak prosecution cases (a counterintuitive factor, explained by tunnel vision and the prosecutor's commitment to the case) (Gould et al., 2013).

The authors generated interesting general conclusions from these empirical findings, based in part on observations made by a panel of experts that supplemented the quantitative data analysis. This is a good strategy where the subject has not been extensively studied and the research is more exploratory than explanatory (Gould et al., 2013). Gould et al. (2013, pp. 95–96) concluded that the overarching explanation for innocent defendants getting to the prosecution stage, and then being convicted rather than exonerated, is "system failure." While this conclusion is not entirely new (see Doyle, 2010; Lofquist, 2001), they supported it with quantitative findings. Although they did not generate a theory of wrongful conviction causation, their findings suggest that additional work could generate some kind of system process theory.

What kind of theory would that be? Gould et al. (2013, p. 174, Fig. 7), and similar work, can lead to *justice process* theories, as suggested in a figure depicting an adversarial process black box at the point that wrongfully prosecuted cases diverge to near misses and later-exonerated wrongful convictions. Lofquist (2001) examined a wrongful conviction through the lens of organizational theory. And, as noted above, Norris and Bonventre (2013) drew on theoretic orientations to propose approaches for studying wrongful conviction. However valuable, these works do not include *methodologies*; as a way forward I propose that the grounded theory approach is well suited to the task of generating theories of wrongful conviction.

In *The Discovery of Grounded Theory*, Glaser and Strauss (1967) described a qualitative research approach by selecting comparison groups to the group being studied and subjecting them to *constant comparison*, with the goal of generating sociological process theories based on data evaluation rather than on logical deduction. Groups for comparison can be selected for theoretical sampling from among interview subjects, or from "historical documents, or other library materials" (Glaser & Strauss, 1967, p. 53). Once selected by a researcher sensitive to the field, various techniques can be applied to generate *conceptual categories* and their properties. These form the building blocks of *hypotheses* (generalized relationships), which are then integrated into *theories* of social behavior. My emphasis is on *substantive theory*, which applies to social areas or processes rather than *formal theory* applied to "conceptual" areas (Glaser & Strauss, 1967, pp. 33–35). Glaser and Strauss (1967) focused on "sociological" theories to explicate social interactions, using data drawn from ethnomethodological field work. My use of grounded theory may stray from this specific focus, as it applies to aspects of the justice process.

Applying the grounded theory approach to wrongful convictions with the goal of generating more satisfactory causal hypotheses and theories can take a number of paths, depending on available data. One could imagine grounded theories that better explain the dynamics of police or prosecutors that lead to wrongful convictions. Having begun with the findings of Gould et al. (2013), which established an empirical foundation to distinguish wrongful convictions from near misses causes, I will sketch a potential theory by focusing on the court processes that explain these results in the jury trial. The sociological areas analyzed by Glaser and Strauss (1967) to expand grounded theories included a wealth of data, prior studies, and examples to draw on as they applied the constant comparative method of qualitative analysis). In contrast, fewer such data, prior studies, and appropriate case studies exist regarding wrongful convictions.

A grounded theory of wrongful convictions versus near miss causation, using available published material, draws first on Givelber and Farrell's (2012) empirical study of acquittals. Past research on the criminal jury's factual accuracy raised concerns that juries acquitted guilty defendants in cases where close facts "liberated" jurors to rely more on their feelings or values in resolving questions of fact (hence the "liberation hypothesis") (Givelber & Farrell, 2012, pp. 20–39). The implication of the liberation hypothesis was that jury acquittals were likely incorrect in cases where judges would have convicted, although "a mounting body of research" now finds that professional judges and jurors perform fact-finding tasks similarly (Simon, 2012, p. 145). The liberation hypothesis tends to undermine the estimates that exonerations are the tip of a wrongful conviction iceberg that may be as high as 1 to 2% of all felony prosecutions (Gross, Jacoby, Matheson, Montgomery, & Patil, 2005; Zalman, 2012). Yet, based on new data, Givelber and Farrell (2012) demonstrated that the variables of testimony by defendant *and* defense witness, defendant's lack of criminal record, and the defendant claiming innocence to his or her defense lawyer were statistically related to a higher proportion of acquittals. Careful reasoning by the authors refuted the idea that all innocent defendants are initially screened out and that acquittals are windfalls to guilty defendants. Although their analysis could not prove the rates at which such acquitted defendants were factually innocent — when combined with Gould et al.'s (2013) finding that age, strong defense, no prior history, prosecutors who disclose evidence, and deliberate eyewitness misidentification predict near misses — a theoretical perspective begins to emerge.

The overlap of innocence-propensity (if not innocence-predictive) variables in these two studies suggests a grounded theory of the criminal jury *trial* as a *functional*, and not simply a symbolic, *due process, error-prevention mechanism*. It refutes the liberation hypothesis and directs future theory testing strategies to better measure jury accuracy. In Gould et al. (2013), the jury is treated as a black box. This is also the case in Givelber and Farrell (2012), but their variables get closer to jury deliberation by examining the type of testimony (no witness, defendant only, or both witness and defendant), and prior record (which affects whether the defendant testifies). They also suggest behavioral possibilities that shore up Gould et al.'s (2013) finding that a strong defense predicts near misses.

> Thus, it is intriguing that the defendants' insistence on their innocence as the reason why plea bargaining failed was significantly related to both jury acquittals and judges being prepared to find for the defense....
>
> One possible explanation is that defendants only insist upon innocence when they have strong evidentiary bases for doing so. Defense lawyers will probably challenge more aggressively their defendants' insistence on going to trial if there is not much in the way of the defense that can be mounted. Moreover, defense lawyers with clients insisting on innocence and witnesses to help prove it may be more energized and effective lawyers than ones forced to rely solely on poking holes in the state's cases. It is also possible, of course, that defendants claim innocence and have supportive witnesses because they are, in fact, innocent. (Givelber & Farrell, 2012, pp. 109–110)

Grounded theory also encompasses data that *qualifies* an initial hypothesis. Although jury accuracy is lionized by official legal system accounts (Simon, 2012), much skepticism about jury accuracy abounds. Dan Simon (2012) amassed a wealth of information based on psychological science that explains the ways in which juries may err. It would not be helpful in developing a grounded theory of how juries cause or prevent miscarriages of justice to generalize from these findings the conclusion that juries are invariably wrong. Instead, data drawn experimentally or from published narratives could be applied to examine the problematic areas of jury fact-finding to find whether the problematic variables are coded in favor of accuracy or inaccuracy in specific cases, just as an effective defense tends to produce near misses/acquittals and ineffective defense tends to cause wrongful convictions.

The reasons why truth can slip away during a criminal jury trial are many. A grounded theory of whether the trial is a functional due process, error-reducing mechanism needs to ask the following questions (drawn from Simon's review): Was the evidence presented at trial based on faulty police investigation? Was original evidence or synthesized evidence admitted (e.g., videotape of a confession vs. the detective's testimony)? Was witness preparation suggestive or fair? Was the in-court identification the only way in which the defendant was identified and was it conducted in a particularly damning way? Was a witness's memory-based testimony suspiciously overdetermined? Was an alibi witness likely to be believed? Corroborated? Did the quality of a litigator's storytelling overwhelm the truth? Was one litigator a far superior storyteller than the other? Were there emotional appeals? Did cross-examination appear to inject factual inaccuracy into the case? Were racial stereotypes in play? Did the coherence effect smother an exculpatory fact? Did the trial judge instruct jurors about logical traps and particularly untrustworthy evidence? Were the judge's instructions clear? Understood? Did curative instructions allow prejudicial facts to enter the case? Was a capital jury death-qualified? Was there extensive pretrial publicity?

The list of potential impediments to jury accuracy seems overwhelming, but for purposes of developing a grounded functional due process theory they should be tested. One method would be to develop accuracy-oriented and inaccuracy-oriented jury trial scenarios and subject them to mock juries. Another method would be to draw these variables from wrongful conviction narratives, from wrongful acquittal narratives (e.g., Fletcher, 1995), and from narratives of cases believed to have been accurately decided. Upward of a hundred book-length wrongful conviction narratives present a wealth of data regarding the process by which miscarriages of justice occurred, which could be applied to qualifying a functional due process theory. So too do the more than one thousand short case narratives in the National Registry of Exonerations (n.d.). While raw narrative information was properly critiqued by Leo (2005) as lacking theoretical import, such narratives might be useful for their data about trial attorney behaviors and the evidentiary posture of cases, to support or qualify a grounded theory of functional due process as a factor in wrongful conviction causation. Thus, for example, John Thompson's notorious wrongful conviction was discussed by Givelber and Farrell (2012) as anecdotal support for their hypothesis. But in an exercise to generate grounded theory, cases[5] are continuously compared to the initial hypothesis to see if they qualify or amplify the initially hypothesized theory.

Thus, for example, Kerry Max Cook (2007) did not testify at his first trial; his only witnesses were shackled jail inmates called to refute the jailhouse snitch testimony of

---

5. Glaser & Strauss (1967) examined the theoretical sampling of *groups* to generate theories of social behavior in groups; I would examine cases to generate theories of jury behavior.

"Shyster" Jackson, who wore street clothes; and the prosecution included highly prejudicial evidence of sexual acts with another man. Kirk Bloodsworth did testify in his first trial and had one defense witness to refute footprint evidence, as well as alibi and character witnesses (Junkin, 2004). Earl Washington testified at his trial, but the prosecution had read his signed confession into evidence and his only witness was a sister who did his laundry and testified that a shirt introduced into evidence was not his.[6] The defense did not enter evidence that mentally retarded persons tend to agree with an interrogator (Edds, 2003). Lawyers for the Norfolk Four believed that their clients were guilty (Wells & Leo, 2008). The prosecutor set up John Thompson for a wrongful robbery conviction to weaken his decision to testify at his murder trial (Hollway & Gauthier, 2010). Developing a more complete *functional due process jury trial* grounded theory could draw on these and many other case narratives to qualify and flesh out the dynamics of what went on at trials.

Comparing exonerations to apparently accurate convictions (admittedly a tall order) proved to be problematic for Garrett (2008), but such cases may be better suited to generating grounded theory. The plausibility of theory based on such cases would depend on the analyst's ability to draw a good theoretical sample. Glaser and Strauss (1967) emphasize that exhaustive data need not be developed for generating grounded theory. It is likely that the combination of quantitative data analysis and the insightful systematic use of narrative information would produce a better sense of understanding about how the facts and events of trials (and perhaps guilty pleas) can generate wrongful convictions and near misses.

A grounded adversary-system functional due process theory of wrongful convictions/ exonerations need not be limited to jury trials, but can encompass the process that generates more numerous guilty pleas (Leipold, 2005). Although the empirical research that explicitly links wrongful convictions to plea bargaining is scarce, an examination of the few DNA exonerations in which defendants pleaded guilty, and considerations of relevant psychological research, point to a coercive process that generates many wrongful convictions (Redlich, 2010). In addition, voluminous speculation by legal scholars (see Bowers, 2008) has generated a wealth of material, which along with narrative and film (Bikel, 2004) could provide sufficient material to apply the grounded theory methodology for an adversarial process theory related to wrongful convictions.

This does not exhaust the possibilities for theoretical inquiry surrounding the justice process regarding wrongful conviction. My exploration focused on a suggested functional due process theory of the *jury trial*. Given the availability of data, grounded theories related to police work (Zalman, 2013) or prosecution may be possible. Comparative theory may also be possible, as convictions occur in a distinctly national legal context. The American adversary process differs in many ways from adversary processes in the United Kingdom or other English-speaking nations (Colvin, 2009) and from inquisitorial system countries. Beginning with Risinger (2004), a number of scholars have begun to propose inquisitorial tinkering with the adversary trial (Bakken, 2011/2012; Gross, 2011/ 2012) and to combine the best elements of both (Findley, 2011/2012). Given the insightful theoretical examinations of trial systems by Damaška (1986), one could imagine the development of either a grounded or a *normative* theory of trial systems and wrongful conviction. Such theories would ask whether adversary or inquisitorial systems better prevent wrongful convictions. Since experiments are out of the question, base data (of

---

6. Gould et al. found that "having a family witness is associated with an *increase* in the likelihood of an erroneous conviction" (2013, p. 68, emphasis in original; see p.154, Table 21).

wrongful convictions) are unavailable, and national trial systems are extremely complex entities involving multiple agencies, procedures, traditions and relationships, I suspect that scholarship and theory building along these lines will be conducted at the level of informed speculation.

## Detecting a Wrongful Conviction

Research methodology textbooks distinguish between nomothetic and idiographic explanations, and then ignore the latter to serve the scientific goal of seeking generalizable knowledge (Maxfield & Babbie, 2011; see Gould et al., 2013). In disciplines like comparative politics, however, cases matter: "As long as we care about particular cases, we are compelled to do history, to try to understand specific sequences of events and to acquire the ideographic [sic] knowledge that understanding specific sequences of events entails" (Evans in Kohli, et al., 1995, p. 3). The efforts of Gould et al. (2013) to understand wrongful conviction generalities by the statistical analysis of case variables is sensible in large part because those interested in the study are familiar with narratives that have presented fine-grained depictions of wrongful conviction cases (e.g., Wells & Leo, 2008). I have suggested above that narratives could be mined for data to generate grounded theory. I now ask whether an idiographic research strategy can yield theoretically interesting analysis that expands our understanding of the general through the case? Most wrongful conviction narratives are literary enterprises that are uneven in their content and approaches, making them uncertain sources for idiographic research. Scholarly case studies might be another thing (see Bonventre, Norris, & West, this volume).

Current wrongful conviction literature pays little attention to general criminal investigation, in comparison to high interest in lineups, interrogations, and handling confidential informants. While these critical investigatory procedures occur in most serious investigations, they are framed by the total investigation which involves questioning ordinary witnesses, collecting physical evidence, observing the crime scene, canvassing an array of information sources, framing hypotheses about the case, and making records of the investigation. Dan Simon (2012, p. 21) has written about investigation dynamics and the wide discretion given to investigators, "much of which is not readily teachable." Investigators "have discretion in deciding whether a crime occurred, which leads to pursue, what physical evidence to collect, which witnesses to question, which testimonies to trust, when to make an arrest, when to declare the case solved, and when to give up on it." As a result, unlike the conduct of a discrete event like a lineup for which specific procedures have been shown to be error-reducing based on substantial psychological research (Cutler, 2012), it is impossible to reduce an investigator's handling of a case to a specific checklist. This does not mean that the voluminous information in standard investigation texts, training courses, and from experience are irrelevant. But, for example, a detective cannot direct a fingerprint technician to dust every square inch of every crime scene; such excess in time, effort, and cost would impede the officer's efficiency and would surely create dysfunctional information overload. Instead, the detective directs evidence collection based on her *hypothesis* of the event leading to the investigation.

The process by which detectives form hypotheses is largely unexplored and often chalked up to a combination of instinct and experience. In this process, however, lies a logical process known as abduction. Investigation, "the process of winnowing the field of possible hypotheses to the single substantiated conclusion, entails a conceptual problem" (Simon, 2012, p. 21, punctuation added). Detectives need supporting or disconfirming evidence to test a case hypothesis, but "because it is impossible to seek and test the infinite amount of evidence that might have any bearing on the case, one needs a hypothesis in order to decide which evidence to test" (Simon, 2012, p. 21). This circular nature of "investigative reasoning" involves going back and forth between evidence and hypotheses. "This dialectical tension makes the investigator's task a most delicate cognitive effort. A form of bootstrapping, known as *abductive* reasoning, is probably the only feasible method suited for conducting criminal investigations" (Simon, 2012, p. 22, emphasis in original).

Abductive reasoning is "a recursive process of generating and testing hypotheses, geared toward eliminating invalid hypotheses and substantiating the correct one" (Simon, 2012, p. 22).[7] An interpretation by philosopher Daniel McKaughan, which he calls a Pursuit-worthiness Interpretation, has relevance for criminal investigation. In this view, "[a]bduction … is merely preparatory. It is the first step of scientific reasoning, as induction is the concluding step" (Pierce, quoted in McKaughan, 2008, p. 451). Theory testing "comes *after* judgments have been made about which hypotheses are worth pursuing" (McKaughan, 2008, p. 451, emphasis in original). In a telling analogy, Pierce likens the "intelligent guessing" of abductive reasoning to playing 20 questions, in which a skillful question that tests a reasonable but possibly untrue hypothesis will set aside many false leads and direct attention to more fruitful and useful inquiry (McKaughan, 2008, pp. 457–458). In any serious inquiry (scientific study, criminal investigation) a host of likely hypotheses will spring to mind and the researcher or detective has limited resources to explore them. Abductive reasoning, then, does not itself lead to the truth, but "makes practically grounded comparative recommendations about which available hypotheses are to be tested"; therefore, "the better abduction is the one which is likely to lead to the truth with the lesser expenditure of time, vitality, etc." (McKaughan, quoting Pierce, 2008, p. 452). Abduction, then, is a research or problem-solving strategy in which the "question of Economy—Economy of money, time, thought, and energy" is central (McKaughan, quoting Pierce, 2008, p. 453).

How does abduction work in the world of criminal investigation? Jay Nordby, a philosopher and forensic scientist, explored death investigation cases through the twin lenses of abductive logic and various forensic sciences. A central insight is that unlike certain natural events that can be explored by theoretical bodies of knowledge (earthquake—geological theory) there is no "available body of generalized 'death theory' to explain particular cases in this theoretical sense." The reason for an unexplained death (e.g., a woman apparently stabbed to death by an unknown assailant in a parking garage) is not a particular instance of a body of natural laws. To solve the crime, the death investigator must "reason backward analytically [from signs] to identify the mechanics of the crime and link them with its perpetrator." Although the investigative task of satisfactorily explaining a single event is at the opposite pole of the scientific task of explicating general laws of nature, "[i]f Pierce is right theoretical scientists behave like death investigators" (Nordby, 2000, p. 122). Both begin with an interesting fact but in ignorance of an explanation. Both are fallibilists, knowing that they could be wrong, and that the search for truth rests on "a high faith in the reality of knowledge, and an intense desire to find things out" (Pierce, quoted in Nordby, 2000, p. 82). Logical tests may help to resolve cases once different hypotheses have been tested and sufficient available evidence gathered, but before this can be achieved, investigators shuttle between hypotheses and facts.

Specific tests based on scientific principles and knowledge can help. In one case the drunken female partner of a couple living in sordid circumstances was arrested for

---

7. Abduction as a logical process was conceived by pragmatist philosopher Charles S. Pierce to supplement induction and deduction (Nordby, 2000, pp. 42–43).

murdering her man. He was thrown off a porch and killed by an apparent shotgun blast to his midsection. The shotgun lay in the living room pointing outward; the glass between the living room and porch was shattered; the woman was too inebriated to recall evidence. The medical examiner patiently reasoned backward from the physical signs (interpreted through scientific principles) to convince the arresting detectives that the scene most probably depicted a drunken, out-of-control man, swinging the shotgun like a sledgehammer at everything in sight, smashing the window, tugging on the gun stuck on a smashed window frame toward himself when the trigger caught on the debris of the window frame and set off the blast that propelled him off the porch to the ground below and propelled the shotgun back into the living room (Nordby, 2000). The *apparent* scene presented to the detectives as a murder. But a careful reading of signs by the medical examiner led to hypotheses that were then tested by scientific and logical analysis of the evidence, which then led to other hypotheses, and so on until a satisfactory resolution of the case was achieved, even convincing the initially skeptical detectives, who were given a demonstration of abductive logic at work showing that no crime had been committed and the death was accidental.

Nordby's case examinations, rich in dense examination of facts (signs), larded with recondite knowledge of forensic medicine and pathology and death investigation technology, sprinkled with insights about logical reasoning from sources as diverse as Pierce, Mills, and Sherlock Holmes, and written with the skill of a master detective fiction author, are hard to summarize. But his work suggests one way toward theorizing wrongful conviction cases by reconstructing known exoneration cases with abductive approaches taken by detectives. With a sufficient number of cases it may be possible to construct a more satisfactory grounded explanation of where detectives are accurate and where inaccurate. A recent review of the detective's role in wrongful conviction examined the types of literature about criminal investigation that could provide sources for such exploration. In contrast to the general lack of interest in criminal investigation within American criminal justice scholarship, extensive criminal investigation research in the United Kingdom has led to a systematic program of improving investigation by applying cognitive interviewing techniques (Zalman, 2013).

Another idiographic approach is for innocence project investigators and lawyers to draw on abductive logic to more closely (and theoretically) examine their own work in deconstructing convictions. Medwed discussed "the innate problem of determining whether the prisoner is, in fact, innocent" (2003, p. 1107). Cases selected by innocence projects pass through a detailed process with highly ramified criteria, but with the exception of DNA cases there is no magical test to determine innocence in advance. Like a detective, the innocence project lawyer seeks signs — in this case "Signs of Innocence" (Medwed, 2003, p. 1123). Acknowledging the imperfection and possibility of error, the innocence project procedures described by Medwed included a provision to drop cases that were later thought to be guilty (2003). Findley confirmed this by noting that more than other law school clinical programs, innocence projects "involv[e] students in extensive fact litigation" (2006, p. 235). While "the traditional law school curriculum pays scant attention to the importance of facts and fact-development," innocence project students are immersed in "a fact-based story-telling perspective," in which they "examin[e] the cases to determine what went wrong, what *feels* wrong about the case, and what new evidence (facts) might be developed to prove innocence" (Findley, 2006, p. 242-243, emphasis in original). Like Pierce's fallibilists, innocence project students are taught "the importance of keeping an open mind" (Findley, 2006, p. 250). These otherwise informative articles lacked specific case analysis that disclosed the reasoning process by which innocence project faculty and students came to a satisfactory conclusion that a case is one of actual innocence. These accounts of "re-detective work" strongly suggest abductive reasoning at work.

One might argue that time- and resource-constrained innocence projects, just like time- and resource-constrained detectives, do not have the luxury of generating case studies to inspect the logic that led to conclusions of innocence. What is the practical benefit of such an exercise? First, it could produce logically stronger innocence scenarios to convince reluctant prosecutors to dismiss cases. Next, it could produce better wrongful conviction reconstructions for policy goals. In 2002 Scheck and Neufeld argued that innocence commissions, like the National Transportation Safety Board, should investigate wrongful conviction cases to uncover the underlying causes and lead to corrective recommendations. They referred to referred to Canada's Morin Commission, which examined problems with hair and fiber evidence, and the Sophonow Commission, which dealt with eyewitness testimony, police tunnel vision, alibi evidence, jailhouse snitches, and exoneree compensation. My sense is that more could be learned about wrongful convictions by carefully constructed wrongful conviction case studies that go beyond surface description and explicate the exculpatory logic embedded in the reconstructions of cases.

# Wrongful Conviction through other Theoretical Lenses

Two recent works have drawn on and analyzed various theoretical constructs to amplify our understanding of wrongful conviction. Mandery, Shlosberg, West, and Callaghan (2013) found a significant relationship between adequate exoneree compensation and re-offending. The study built explicitly on two theoretical perspectives. The first is the extensive body of work that links successful (i.e., crime free) reentry of prison inmates into society to available resources, and also draws on informed speculation that even innocent inmates have been subjected to a process of prisonization that makes them challenged by the requirements of ordinary life outside of prison. The second theoretical perspective is the procedural justice paradigm expanded by Tom Tyler and based specifically on Lind and Tyler's (1988) "group value theory" of procedural justice by which people judge institutions by instrumental and non-instrumental fairness-based criteria. It provided "a second viable explanation for the link between compensation and offending." Having been treated with consummate unfairness, "[c]ompensation can ameliorate perceptions of unfairness" for exonerees (Mandery et al., 2013, p. 131-132). Previous reviews of limited compensation for exonerees and the slow and uneven growth of adequate compensation policies tended to decry such patent unfairness.[8] Mandery et al. (2013) demonstrated the way in which empirical research combined with theoretical application advances satisfactory explanation of the relationship between compensation and reoffending.

A second study assessed three innocence policy reforms, based on published information, in light of policy making theories and models developed by political and policy scientists (Zalman & Marion, forthcoming). The three reform programs were (i) state legislation following publication of the Illinois Governor's Commission on Capital Punishment, (ii) the federal Innocence Protection Act of 2004, and (iii) Ohio legislation in 2010 regarding access to exculpatory evidence. The models drawn on were grounded in the examination of other policy processes; the most prominent models related to policy making at the

---

8. The issue of "no-fault" compensation may also generate theoretical debate from an abstract law and economics perspective. One proponent argued that exoneree compensation will produce no net social value and should be avoided (Rosenthal, 2010). Such work provides an area for legal-economic-ideological theorizing.

federal level, involving Congress and administrative agencies. The authors asked whether these extant theoretic models from the realms of political science and public policy fit the three innocence policy reforms. Centralized, top-down, structural theories such as the policy elite or iron triangle models were not good fits to information about innocence reform. In contrast to models focusing on key Congressional power holders or on long-term relationships between congressional committees, interest groups, and federal administrative agencies, innocence reform has been generated by outsiders. Temporal theories—the issue attention cycles and punctuated equilibrium models—could not fit as descriptions of innocence reform because they tracked fluctuations of interest in policy issues over decades. This makes no sense in regard to a policy area that has been in ferment for no more than twenty years and has not fallen into abeyance.[9]

Other policy theories that better fit the observed reality of innocence projects and their reformist efforts included the issue network and advocacy coalition models. Issue networks involve large numbers of interested parties with expertise in the policy area who fluidly enter or leave a policy issue for a number of reasons, and which dissolve when an issue is resolved. A model describing more structured approaches—the advocacy coalition model—involves diverse groups with shared values that cooperate over time to influence changes in policy subsystems requiring intergovernmental cooperation. Another model that held promise for helping to explain innocence policy reform was the so-called "garbage can" model which posits that policy ambiguity and unpredictability surround government agencies resulting in chaotic policy making. We found these theories of the policy making process to be closer to the three innocence reforms we tracked. Nevertheless, we needed to closely describe the contours of innocence policy reform to align the observed facts to established theories drawn from political science and public administration scholarship. Thus, Zalman and Marion (forthcoming) did not seek to develop a grounded theory of innocence policy making, although their effort could be seen as elaborating existing theories. The study of the innocence reform movement and its unusual features by policy analysts, nevertheless, can generate grounded theories of innocence movement policy making.

# Conclusion

Theorizing about wrongful conviction builds on accumulated knowledge gained by reportage, legal writing, research by psychological and other scientists, and a small number of empirical social studies of wrongful convictions. In this chapter I sketched a potential theory of error causation at the jury trial level to distinguish wrongful convictions from near-misses—a functional due-process error-reduction jury model, based on the grounded theory methodology of qualitative sociology. I then proposed that idiographic examination of single cases, applying Pierce's abductive logic construct, could expand our appreciation of wrongful conviction and help explain how innocence project "re-detectives" satisfactorily conclude that convictions in which DNA evidence is absent, were nonetheless wrongful. Also discussed were examples of the use of criminological, justice, and policy theories applied to wrongful conviction issues.

The few sketches of theorizing wrongful conviction found in this chapter do not begin to canvass potential social scientific, political, legal, and other kinds of theorizing that

---

9. In contrast, the miscarriage of justice issue has been in play in the United Kingdom for nearly two centuries and has had periods of activity and quietude (Nobles & Schiff, 2000).

could illuminate wrongful conviction. The English social scientist and innocence project leader Michael Naughton (2007) has expanded and enriched the study of "zemiology," a theory of social harms advanced in critical criminology and socio-legal studies. English legal scholars Richard Nobles and David Schiff (2000), discussing the long-term and highly legalistic approach to miscarriages of justice in Great Britain, have examined the interplay of the media and public opinion with the courts through autopoietic systems theory, a recondite theory of the autonomy of law (Jacobson, 1989; Kornhauser, 1998). Forst (2004) stressed that wrongful convictions challenge the accuracy of vital government work, opening the way to inquiry based on the social scientific and political theoretic work on political legitimacy. An inquiry by my colleague Yuning Wu and me regarding wrongful convictions in China, the United Kingdom, and the United States has us delving into comparative politics theory. Doyle (2010; 2013) has generated a concept of a wrongful conviction as an "ordinary accident," building on organizational-theory based scholarship concerning the studies of accidents in aviation, medicine, and industry.[10] Cole (2013) has applied policy models to a call for establishing ongoing forensic science reform. Historical studies like Aronson's (2007) work on the "DNA wars" expand our understanding of the innocence movement, as does scholarship in the field of science and technology studies (Lynch et al., 2008). Finally, the extensive legal literature on wrongful conviction is grounded in concepts of legal and/or constitutional theory, even if most such studies are not explicitly geared to producing jurisprudential theory. In short, wrongful conviction scholarship has built a sufficient body of data and is a sufficiently serious subject to attract the attention of social and legal scholars and direct their attention to theorizing wrongful conviction.

Having said this, I would admit that theorizing wrongful conviction may not be the most urgent task confronting scholars interested in exploring themes regarding wrongful conviction and innocence policy. Empirical researchers will likely find theorizing their results a congenial and career-boosting effort. For most American legal scholars, educated in a common-law tradition that avoids jurisprudence or treats it as a frill, theorizing wrongful conviction will be beside the point. Policy makers and agency administrators have enough to think about without being distracted by extended or involved theoretical analyses. It is instructive that the panel of experts in the near-miss study made recommendations to prevent the occurrence of wrongful convictions that went beyond the study's findings but were grounded in the many recommendations found in wrongful conviction literature over the past two decades and based on sound common sense (Gould et al., 2013). Yet, despite these caveats, a few examples demonstrate that theorizing wrongful conviction often provides a more satisfying explanation of the facts and may hold the promise of offering better support for innocence reforms.

---

10. He has been instrumental in advancing this notion to the stage of practice through ongoing work at the National Institute of Justice.

# References

Allen, R. J. & Laudan, L. (2008). Deadly dilemmas. *Texas Tech Law Review, 41*, 65–92.

Aronson, J. (2007). *Genetic witness: Science, law, and controversy in the making of DNA profiling*. New Brunswick, NJ: Rutgers University Press.

Aviram, H. (2011). Packer in context: Formalism and fairness in the Due Process Model. *Law & Social Inquiry, 36*(1), 237–261.

Bakken, T. (2011/2012). Models of justice to protect innocent persons. *New York Law School Law Review, 56*, 836–867.

Bikel, O. (2004). The plea. [video]. PBS-Frontline. Transcript retrieved from http://www.pbs.org/wgbh/pages/frontline/shows/plea/etc/synopsis.html

Blalock, H. M., Jr. (1970). *An introduction to social research*. Englewood Cliffs, NY: Prentice Hall.

Bowers, J. (2008). Punishing the innocent. *University of Pennsylvania Law Review, 156*, 1117–1179.

Cole, S. (2013). The innocence crisis and forensic science reform. In Zalman, M. & Carrano, J. (Eds.). *Wrongful conviction and criminal justice reform: Making justice*. New York: Routledge.

Colvin, E. (2009). Convicting the innocent: A critique of theories of wrongful convictions. *Criminal Law Forum, 20*, 173–192.

Cook, K. M. (2007). *Chasing justice: My story of freeing myself after two decades on death row for a crime I didn't commit*. New York: HarperCollins/William Morrow.

Cutler, B. L. (Ed.). (2012). *Conviction of the innocent: Lessons from psychological research*. Washington: American Psychological Association.

Damaška, M. (1986). *The faces of justice and state authority*. New Haven: Yale University Press.

Doyle, J. M. (2010). Learning from error in the American criminal justice system. *Journal of Criminal Law & Criminology, 100*, 109–47.

Doyle, J. M. (2013). An etiology of wrongful convictions: Error, safety, and forward-looking accountability in criminal justice. In Zalman, M. & Carrano, J. (Eds.). *Wrongful conviction and criminal justice reform: Making justice*. New York: Routledge.

Edds, M. (2003). *An expendable man: The near-execution of Earl Washington, Jr.* New York: New York University Press.

Findley, K. A. 2006. The pedagogy of innocence: Teflections on the role of innocence projects in clinical legal education. *Clinical Law Review, 13*, 231–278.

Findley, K. A. (2011/2012) Adversarial inquisitions: Rethinking the search for the truth. *New York Law School Law Review, 56*(3), 911–941.

Fletcher, G. P. (1995). *With justice for some: Protecting victims' rights in criminal trials*. Reading, MA: Addison-Wesley.

Forst, B. (2004). *Errors of justice: Nature, sources, and remedies*. Cambridge, UK: Cambridge University Press.

Garrett, B. L. (2008). Judging innocence. *Columbia Law Review, 108*, 55–141.

Givelber, D. & Farrell, A. (2012). *Not guilty: Are the acquitted innocent?* New York and London: New York University Press.

Gould, J. B., Carrano, J., Leo, R., & Young, J. (2013, February). Predicting erroneous convictions: A social science approach to miscarriages of justice. National Institute of Justice, #241389 (Award Number: 2009-IJ-CX-4110).

Gross, S. R. (2011/2012). Pretrial incentives, post-conviction review, and sorting criminal prosecutions by guilt or innocence. *New York Law School Law Review, 56*(3), 1009–1030.

Gross, S. R., Jacoby, K., Matheson, D. J., Montgomery, N., & Patil, S. (2005). Exonerations in the United States, 1989 through 2003. *Journal of Criminal Law & Criminology*, 95(2), 523–60.

Gross, S. R. & O'Brien, B. (2008). Frequency and predictors of false conviction: Why we know so little, and new data on capital cases. *Journal of Empirical Legal Studies*, 5(4), 927–962.

Harmon, T. R. (2001). Predictors of Miscarriages of Justice in Capital Cases. *Justice Quarterly 18*(4), 949–68.

Harmon, T. R. &. Lofquist, W.S. (2005). Too late for luck: A comparison of post-Furman exonerations and executions of the innocent. *Crime & Delinquency*, 51, 498–520.

Hollway, J. & Gauthier, R. M. (2010). *Killing time: An 18-year odyssey from death row to freedom*. New York: Sky Course Publishing

Jacobson, A. J. (1989). Autopoietic law: The new science of Niklas Luhman. *Michigan Law Review*, 87, 1647–1689.

Junkin, T. (2004). *Bloodsworth: The true story of the first death row inmate exonerated by DNA*. Chapel Hill: Algonquin Books.

Kohli, A., Evans, P., Katzenstein, P. J., Przeworski, A., Hoeber Rudolph, S., Scott, J. C., & Skocpol, T. (1995). The role of theory in comparative politics: A symposium. *World Politics*, 48(1), 1–49.

Kornhauser, L.A. (1998). A world apart? An essay on the autonomy of the law. *Boston University Law Review*, 78, 747–772.

Kraska, P. B. (2004). *Theorizing criminal justice: Eight essential orientations*. Long Grove, IL: Waveland Press.

Kraska, P. B. (2006). Criminal justice theory: Toward legitimacy and an infrastructure. *Justice Quarterly*, 23(2), 167–85.

Kraska, P. B. & Brent, J. J. (2011). *Theorizing criminal justice: Eight essential orientations, second edition* . Long Grove, IL: Waveland Press.

Lazarsfeld, P. (1970). *Main trends in sociology*. New York: Harper Torchbooks.

Leipold, A. D. (2005). How the pretrial process contributes to wrongful convictions. *American Criminal Law Review*, 42, 1123–65.

Leo, R. A. (2005). Rethinking the study of wrongful convictions: Developing a criminology of wrongful conviction. *Journal of Contemporary Criminal Justice*, 21(3), 201–223.

Lind, E. A. & Tyler, T. R. (1988). *The social psychology of procedural justice*. N.Y.: Plenum.

Lofquist, W. S. (2001). Whodunit? An Examination of the Production of Wrongful Convictions. In S D. Westervelt and J. A. Humphrey, (Eds.). *Wrongly convicted: Perspectives on failed justice* (pp. 174–196). New Brunswick: Rutgers University Press.

Lynch, M., Cole, S.A., McNally, R., & Jordan, K. (2008). *Truth machine: The contentious history of DNA fingerprinting*. Chicago: University of Chicago Press.

McKaughan, D. J. (2008). From ugly duckling to swan: C.S. Peirce, abduction, and the pursuit of scientific theories. *Transactions of the Charles S. Pierce Society*, 44(3), 436–468.

Mandery, E. J., Shlosberg, A., West, V., & Callaghan, B. (2013). Compensation statutes and post-exoneration offending. *Journal of Criminal Law & Criminology, 103(2)*, 553–583.

Maxfield, M. G. & Babbie, E. R. (2011). *Research methods for criminal justice and criminology, sixth edition*. Belmont, CA: Wadsworth.

Medwed, D. S. (2003). Actual innocents: Considerations in selecting cases for a new innocence project. *Nebraska Law Review 81*, 1097–1151.

Naughton, M. (2007). *Rethinking miscarriages of justice: Beyond the tip of the iceberg*. Basingstoke, Hampshire; New York: Palgrave Macmillan.

National Registry of Exonerations (n.d.). Retrieved from http://www.law.umich.edu/special/exoneration/Pages/about.aspx

National Research Council (2009). *Strengthening forensic science in the United States: A path forward*. Washington, D.C.: National Academies Press.

Nobles, Richard & David Schiff (2000). *Understanding miscarriages of justice: Law, the media and the inevitability of a crisis*. Oxford University Press.

Nordby, J. J. (2000). *Dead reckoning: The art of forensic detection*. Boca Raton, FL: CRC Press.

Norris, R. J. & Bonventre, C. L. (2013). Advancing wrongful conviction scholarship: Toward new conceptual frameworks. *Justice Quarterly*.

Packer, H. (1968). *The limits of the criminal sanction*. Stanford, CA: Stanford University Press.

Redlich, A. D. (2010). False confessions and false guilty pleas. In G. D. Lassiter, & C. A. Meissner (Eds.), *Interrogations and confessions: Current research, practice and policy* (pp. 49–66). Washington, DC: APA Books.

Reynolds, P. D. (1971). *A primer in theory construction*. Indianapolis & New York: Bobbs-Merrill.

Risinger, D. M. (2004). Unsafe verdicts: The need for reformed standards for the trial and review of factual innocence claims. *Houston Law Review, 41*, 1281–1336.

Rosenthal, L. (2010). Second thoughts on damages for wrongful convictions. *Chicago-Kent Law Review, 85*, 127–161.

Scheck, B. C. & Neufeld, P. J. (2002, Sept.– Oct.). Toward the formation of 'Innocence Commissions' in America. *Judicature, 86*(2), 98–105.

Simon, D. (2012). *In doubt: The psychology of the criminal process*. Cambridge, MA and London, Eng.: Harvard University Press.

Wells, T. & Leo, R. A. (2008). *The wrong guys: Murder, false confessions, and the Norfolk Four*. New York: The New Press.

Westervelt, S.D. & Cook, K.J. (2010). Framing innocents: The wrongly convicted as victims of state harm. *Crime, Law, and Social Change, 53*, 259–275.

Zalman, M. (2006). Criminal justice system reform and wrongful conviction: A research agenda. *Criminal Justice Policy Review, 17*(4), 468–92.

Zalman, M. (2007). The search for criminal justice theory: Reflections on Kraska's *Theorizing Criminal Justice*. *Journal of Criminal Justice Education, 18*(1), 163–181.

Zalman, M. (2011). An integrated justice model of wrongful convictions. *Albany Law Review, 73*(3), 1465–1524.

Zalman, M. (2012). Qualitatively estimating the incidence of wrongful convictions. *Criminal Law Bulletin, 48*(2), 221–279.

Zalman, M. (2013). The detective and wrongful conviction. In Zalman, M. & Carrano, J. (Eds.). *Wrongful conviction and criminal justice reform: Making justice*. New York: Routledge.

Zalman, M. & Marion, N. (forthcoming). Towards a theory of innocence policy reform. In S. Cooper, (Ed.). *Controversies in innocence cases in America*. Ashgate Publishing.

# Chapter Eighteen

# Studying Innocence: Advancing Methods and Data

Catherine L. Bonventre, *University at Albany*
Robert J. Norris, *University at Albany*
Emily West, *The Innocence Project*

## Introduction

As the preceding chapters in this volume reveal, the study of wrongful convictions raises numerous questions that are ripe for empirical investigation. It is a fundamental precept in social science that the research objective should dictate what data to collect and what analytical strategy to use. For example, the researcher exploring a phenomenon about which no conceptual frameworks or theories have been developed might find that direct observation is the most fruitful way to begin to describe and understand it. On the other hand, if one wishes to know if X causes Y, the ideal way to determine that relationship is through a controlled experiment (Shadish, Cook, & Campbell, 2002). The methodological approaches to the study of wrongful convictions in general have ranged from descriptive exploration (Bedau & Radelet, 1987; Borchard, 1932; Scheck, Neufeld, & Dwyer, 2003) to quasi-experimental designs (Gould, Carrano, Leo, & Young, 2013). More targeted research has included experimental designs such as psychology laboratory experiments (for reviews, see, e.g., Kassin, et al. 2010 and Wells et al., 1998 discussing false confessions and eyewitness identification, respectively). Borrowing language from this volume, the primary research inquiries have concerned the production of wrongful convictions and the detection and remedy of wrongful convictions. In this chapter, we discuss the extant methodological approaches for addressing these inquiries, identify gaps in them, and suggest ways to bridge those gaps, thereby "advancing methods and data collection."

We begin by discussing current approaches to understanding the correlates of wrongful convictions and their detection, as well as the gaps in such study. Next we describe the methods employed in research focusing on the consequences of, and policy responses to, wrongful conviction and the corresponding literature gaps in that domain. Finally, we "move forward" by suggesting ways in which future research might benefit from multidisciplinary collaborations among social scientists, legal scholars, and criminal justice practitioners. It is important to note from the outset that our discussion is not meant to describe every published wrongful conviction study, or provide a comprehensive review of findings, but rather to illustrate the kinds of methodologies and sources of data used and suggest how they might be supplemented or improved.[1]

---

1. Another line of inquiry that is beyond the scope of this chapter includes the establishment of actual error rates in the criminal justice system. Identifying all wrongful convictions is an extremely

# Research Methods Regarding the Production and Detection of Wrongful Convictions

In the production and detection domain of wrongful conviction research, the primary concerns have been: (1) identifying wrongful conviction cases and establishing rates; (2) examining known cases to establish the correlates of their causation and detection; and (3) focusing on established factors, such as confessions, to better understand their relationship with wrongful convictions and to improve practices. Although all three represent important lines of inquiry, our primary focus in the first part of this chapter is on the second domain. We limit our discussion in this way mainly as a matter of economy—a comprehensive discussion of the methodological approaches employed in all three lines of inquiry would consume more than a single chapter. Consequently, we have chosen to focus on the correlates of wrongful convictions in the first part because research in this domain is critically important to the prevention of wrongful convictions.

Research that aims to identify and understand the immediate correlates of wrongful convictions and their detection has primarily relied on the exonerated case—and all of its attendant circumstances at the trial or appellate level—as the unit of analysis. In contrast, research within specific disciplinary domains, such as psychology, seeks to understand the underlying causes of specific wrongful conviction correlates, such as, for example, when social psychologists examine the cognitive factors associated with forensic science errors (e.g., Dror, Charlton, & Peron, 2006), false confessions (see Kassin et al., 2010 for a review; Redlich & Goodman, 2003) or eyewitness misidentification (e.g., Wells & Olson, 2003). In this latter body of research, the unit of analysis is typically the individual criminal justice actor of interest, such as the forensic analyst, the suspect, or the eyewitness, rather than the exoneration itself. The studies discussed below have provided a wealth of information on the correlates of wrongful convictions using several methodological approaches including case studies, content analyses, descriptive statistics of aggregated data, comparison/control studies, and experimental approaches.

## Methods Employed

**Descriptive case studies.** A predominant critique of the scholarship on the production of wrongful convictions concerns using the case "narrative methodology" (Harmon, 2001, p. 951) to identify the contributing causes of wrongful convictions (Harmon, 2001; Leo, 2005; Leo & Gould, 2009). Under the narrative method, the writer describes known wrongful convictions and identifies the legal factors present at the conviction stage (Garrett, 2011; Leo, 2005; Leo & Gould, 2009; see, Borchard, 1932 and Scheck, Neufeld, & Dwyer, 2003 as examples). Beginning with Borchard (1932), scholars have scrutinized case after case of wrongful conviction using the narrative method to understand what went wrong. As a result, a general list of common correlates has emerged from these efforts, including mistaken eyewitness identification, false confessions, forensic science errors, governmental misconduct, and misplaced reliance on informants, among others. Other scholars have attempted to move beyond simple descriptions of the contributing factors and offer a deeper analysis. Case studies of individual wrongful convictions, such as Wells and Leo's

---

complex if not impossible mission. For an in-depth analysis of this complicated issue, please see Gross (2008).

(2008) treatment of the Norfolk Four case in which four Navy sailors were wrongly convicted of rape and murder, have provided a more in-depth understanding of the intricacies of individual cases, and how various factors often work together to produce the ultimate error of a wrongful conviction.

According to its critics, the "categorizing project" (Cole, 2012) fails to capture the underlying sources, or root causes (see Leo, 2005), of wrongful convictions or to appreciate the multiple complex ways that the factors can influence or interact with one another (Castelle & Loftus, 2008; Cole, 2012; Leo & Gould, 2009). For example, the factors present in wrongful convictions—mistaken eyewitnesses or false confessions—also are sometimes present in cases that do not result in conviction (Gould, et al., 2013, Leo & Gould, 2009). Thus, some scholars have called upon the wrongful conviction research community to move beyond simple qualitative case descriptions in the study of wrongful convictions and to employ social science methods for a deeper understanding of the correlates (e.g., Leo, 2005) or, as the authors in the present volume do, to examine the systemic social, structural, and institutional factors that might contribute to wrongful convictions (see also, Siegel, 2005).

**Content analysis.** Content analysis involves the systematic coding of text or other media to identify patterns, themes, or specific categories of information (see, e.g., Spencer, Ritchie, & O'Connor, 2003). Though there are numerous definitions, the classic definition is "a research technique for the objective, systematic, and quantitative description of the manifest content of communication" (Lewis, Zamith, & Hermida, 2013, p. 36, quoting Berelson, 1952). Typical steps in content analysis are as follows: "First, the research questions and/ or hypotheses are formulated; second, the sample is selected; third, categories are defined for coding; fourth, coders are trained, the content is coded, and reliability is assessed; and fifth, the coded data are analyzed and interpreted" (Lewis, Zamith, & Hermida, 2013, p. 36). The coded data can be presented in quantitative form, such as the frequency with which themes occur. Although they did not explicitly identify their method as content analysis, this is essentially the method Garrett and Neufeld (2009) used in their analysis of forensic science testimony in trial transcripts. Garrett and Neufeld (2009) collected trial transcripts from the first 232 DNA exonerations that had forensic evidence at trial, developed a coding protocol including categories for evaluating each transcript, trained research assistants on the coding protocol, and coded the transcripts to identify whether the forensic analyst who testified provided invalid testimony. Using this method, they found that 60% of the analysts provided invalid testimony at trial. In addition to reporting the frequency of invalid testimony, the authors provided rich descriptions and excerpts from the transcripts as illustrations. To the extent that content analysis involves the systematic coding of documents, many of the studies discussed below that analyze case-related materials, such as trial transcripts, police reports, media accounts, appellate documents, and so forth, may also be characterized as employing content analysis.

**Descriptive statistics of aggregate data.** Rather than describing the correlates of a handful of wrongful convictions, some scholars have employed more systematic approaches to culling information from aggregate data. These approaches identify several variables associated with known wrongful convictions and report them using descriptive statistics. For example, Gross and colleagues (2005) compiled a database of 340 exonerations that occurred from 1989 through 2003 (some of which were secured through the use of DNA evidence and some of which were not) to learn about the "overall patterns in the exonerations" and to learn "something about the causes of false convictions, and about the operation of our criminal justice system in general" (Gross et al., 2005, p. 527). In addition to the legal correlates of the cases such as mistaken eyewitnesses or false confessions, Gross et al. (2005) reported statistics on extralegal correlates such as the race, age, and mental health status of the defendants. More recently, the National Registry of Exonerations has extended the number of cases in the original Gross dataset to approximately 1,300 through February 2014 (The National Registry of Exonerations, n.d.) and continues to provide descriptive statistics on numerous legal and extralegal variables. Garrett (2011) coded trial materials from the first 250 DNA exonerations and reported descriptive statistics on several trial and post-conviction factors including the prosecution's evidence (and its associated problems) presented at trial, the type of defense attorney and defense case at trial, post-conviction challenges to the evidence, the length of time to exoneration and many more. Earlier, Drizin and Leo (2004) examined several sources of data, including police reports, trial transcripts, interrogation transcripts, media reports, and more, from 125 police-induced false confession cases and reported several demographic and case-related statistics.

**Comparison/control studies.** Adding an additional level of methodological rigor, some scholars have used comparison groups to discover what differences exist between known wrongful conviction cases and other cases. Garrett (2008) compared the noncapital cases among the first 200 DNA exonerations with a randomly selected group of putatively rightful noncapital convictions that matched the DNA exonerations by year, state, and type of crime. Using descriptive statistics, he captured the similarities and differences between the two groups by comparing them on several dimensions, for example, the type of evidence supporting their convictions, conviction reversal rates, and the types of claims raised on appeal (Garrett, 2008). Although there was less information available for the matched comparison group, Garrett (2008) demonstrated that the matched comparison group was similar to the group of exonerees in many respects, including, for example, the types of evidence supporting their convictions and appellate reversal rates. But the two groups differed in the extent to which they pursued post-conviction review with the exoneree group seeking such review at a significantly higher rate than the comparison group.

A handful of researchers have conducted comparison studies using capital cases. Harmon (2001) compared a group of inmates released from death row based on doubts about their guilt to executed inmates, matching the two groups by year of conviction and jurisdiction. She then used logistic regression to identify variables (e.g., allegations of perjury, multiple types of evidence at trial, and type of appellate attorney) that predicted whether the inmate was released from death row or executed and found that the discovery of new evidence, the type of appellate attorney, or allegations of perjury at trial increased the odds of being released from death row (see also Harmon & Lofquist, 2005). Using cross-tabulated data and a case comparison design, Gross and O'Brien (2008) compared exonerated (and presumably innocent) capital defendants to a set of executed (and presumably guilty) capital defendants matched on crime and conviction dates as well as defendant/victim race. They then reported summary statistics on several trial-stage variables to identify the factors that helped predict wrongful convictions in capital cases.

In their recent large-scale study, Gould and colleagues (2013) used logistic regression to compare wrongful convictions to cases in which innocent persons were indicted for crimes, but errors were caught prior to conviction (what they called, "near misses"). They identified 10 factors unique to wrongful convictions including state punitiveness, defendant age and criminal history, strength of the prosecution's case, intentional misidentification, and forensic evidence error. And while the authors acknowledge that their findings are largely exploratory in nature and limited by methodological issues, their study represents an important first step in addressing causes rather than simple correlates of wrongful conviction. It also highlights the complexities of finding an appropriate comparison group and the case documentation needed to support analyses—an insight that is crucial for pursuing future controlled studies on erroneous convictions.

**Experimental studies.** In addition to the more general wrongful conviction studies, a large number of psychological studies have shed light on specific factors that contribute to justice errors, primarily in eyewitness identification, false confessions, and errors in forensic science analysis. This research, which began more than 40 years ago and has prompted significant policy and legal change, has resulted in two scientific consensus papers, one on eyewitness identification (Wells et al., 1998) and one on police interrogations and confessions (Kassin et al., 2010). The unit of analysis in these studies varies according to the wrongful conviction correlate under study. For example, Dror and colleagues (2006) conducted cognitive psychology experiments with experienced fingerprint examiners and showed that case-related contextual information can skew the conclusions drawn by the examiners in their analysis of latent prints. In laboratory experiments with participants of varying ages ranging from adolescent to young adult, Redlich and Goodman (2003) demonstrated that younger participants were more likely to take responsibility for an act not committed — an experiment with implications for false confessions. The experimental literature on eyewitnesses — an ongoing enterprise since the 1970s — is vast and has identified numerous variables related to witnesses, events, and lineups that affect the accuracy of eyewitness identification (for a review, see Wells & Olson, 2003).[2] As a result of this body of research, several jurisdictions have adopted changes in law and procedure to ensure such accuracy (see Norris et al., 2010/2011; *State v. Henderson*, 2011).

# Current Gaps and Future Research

**Qualitative/ethnographic studies.** Research on the correlates of wrongful conviction has continued to expand. The most common unit of analysis in the study of wrongful convictions (outside of the psychological literature) has been the exonerated case — sometimes as a narrative study, sometimes studied in the aggregate, and sometimes compared to other cases. There is, however, room for growth in terms of units of analysis, methods, and data. Qualitative research methods, including observational studies and interviews, can provide a rich source of data to help understand processes that might not be apparent from court materials, such as hearings or trial transcripts and appellate decisions. Indeed, "[q]ualitative interview study may well be the method of choice if our aim is to describe how a system works or fails to work" (Weiss, 1994, p. 10).

As discussed in the second part of this chapter, qualitative research methods, particularly in-depth interviews, have been used extensively in the studies and literature that focus on the aftermath of wrongful convictions. Yet, qualitative methods are generally under-used in the study of the correlates and detection of wrongful convictions. Although qualitative research studies of legal actors in criminal courts are not new, such studies, to our knowledge, are seldom used to explore and shed light on the implications for wrongful convictions. Indeed, researchers have spent months in court interviewing judges, defense attorneys, and prosecutors, and observing legal proceedings (see, e.g., Eisenstein & Jacob, 1977; Feeley, 1992 [1979]; Heumann, 1977; Ulmer, 1994). As Ulmer (1994) noted:

> The classic court ethnographies of the 1960s, 1970s, and early 1980s illustrate the role of political contexts, organizational arrangements, and interaction strategies in case processing and sentencing. The most definitive of these studies conceptualize courts as *communities* in which sponsoring agencies (e.g., judges'

---

2. It is worth noting that these studies may not be wrongful conviction studies per se, and the authors may not consider themselves innocence scholars. They nevertheless have contributed immensely to our understanding of justice system errors, and thus merit discussion here.

bench, prosecutor's office, the defense bar, probation officers, etc.) and their representatives in courtroom workgroups interact around the shared tasks of case processing and sentencing. The advantage of the court community framework is that it forces researchers to go beyond statistical modeling and to take seriously the influence of political environments on court organizational relations, the influence of these organizational relations on court actors' strategies, and how these strategies in turn maintain or modify organizational arrangements and shape aggregate sentencing patterns (p. 80, emphasis in the original, internal citations omitted).

Placing the passage quoted from Ulmer (1994) above in the present context, we might substitute "shape aggregate sentencing patterns" with "have implications for wrongful convictions." Although some scholars are more optimistic (e.g., Gould & Leo, 2010) than others (e.g., Gross & O'Brien, 2008) about our current state of knowledge on the correlates of wrongful convictions, given what we *do* know, researchers can go into the field armed with that knowledge to explore the real-world contexts in which the correlates arise. Such qualitative and ethnographic endeavors are not without challenges — it is often difficult to gain intimate access to subjects of interest and to be able to invest the needed time to pursue such studies. However, the insight that such studies can produce is often invaluable, especially in helping to place quantitative findings in perspective.

**Expansion of factors and subjects involved in wrongful convictions.** All of the methods discussed above can be applied to units of analysis that have received less attention in the wrongful conviction context, including actors such as judges, juries, and victims. They also can be used to examine previously studied units of analysis in different ways. In the latter context, for example, the role of prosecutors in creating and remedying wrongful convictions has been discussed extensively in the literature. However, systematic, in-depth qualitative interviews with prosecutors could profitably explore the psychological, personal, and institutional factors that bear on prosecutors' efforts to resist or remedy post-conviction claims of innocence (Medwed, 2004), or that increase the risk of wrongful conviction (Gershman, this volume). Jurors have received less scrutiny than other legal actors in wrongful conviction research. Content analysis of jury instructions as well as interviews with actual jurors to learn "about the ways in which jurors process and respond to the myriad formulations of common charges" could shed light on whether "common jury charges breed randomness and error" (Siegel, 2005, p. 1225).

Finally, while false confession cases have been the focus of much research, guilty plea cases have not received as much attention (Redlich, 2010). While we now know considerably more about why someone might falsely confess, it is less clear why someone would plead guilty to a crime. In fact, some states have enacted or are contemplating enacting statutes that limit post-conviction access to DNA and compensation for wrongful conviction to those who did not contribute to their conviction (i.e., plead guilty). Educating policy makers about why and how false guilty pleas can happen is important.

Encouragingly, there is growing interest and research activity in this area. For example, Redlich, Summers, and Hoover (2010) surveyed more than 1000 offenders with mental disorders from six sites, finding self-reported false guilty plea rates of between 27 and 41 percent. Another study by Dervan and Edkins (2013) recruited college students to participate in a logic game exercise. Afterwards, the students were accused of cheating. They were told that if they admitted doing so, they would only lose their participant compensation, but if they did not admit it, an academic review board would review the case and if they were found to have cheated, the students would not be compensated and would have to attend an ethics course. More than half of the innocent students admitted to cheating when they had not. These studies help demonstrate that innocent people do plead guilty and that incentives play a role in the process. However, more research in this area is needed—especially for understanding individuals' decision-making processes when life and liberty are at stake.

**Expanding opportunities to share data.** It is encouraging that as wrongful conviction research grows and databases expand (see National Registry of Exonerations, n.d.), more data have become available for researchers to use. In fact, trial transcripts and other case documents are now available for DNA exonerations via the website innocencerecord.org— an online searchable document repository developed by Winston & Strawn, LLC, in collaboration with the Innocence Project. However, it is important for researchers to make their methods explicit and continue to make their data available (when feasible) so that others can replicate their work or analyze the data in different ways or apply their methods to new datasets. Although it is the convention in the social science and experimental psychology literature—as well as empirical legal scholarship—to include a detailed description of the research methodology, such descriptions are found less frequently (although not rarely) in traditional legal scholarship. In that regard, Garrett's (2011) *Convicting the Innocent* is an exemplary form of empirical legal scholarship in that the book includes an appendix which describes at length the author's data collection and analysis. Moreover, the trial transcripts coded in Garrett and Neufeld's (2009) forensic testimony study along with an appendix enumerating the coding for each transcript are available on the University of Virginia School of Law library website for other researchers to use, as are the materials analyzed in *Convicting the Innocent*. The value of researchers making their trial transcripts as a data source available cannot be understated because access to them otherwise can be difficult to achieve.

# Research on the Aftermath and Policy Responses to Wrongful Convictions

Like many aspects of criminal justice, the effects of wrongful convictions extend far beyond the cases themselves. The past several years have seen a large increase in research exploring what happens *after* a wrongful conviction and exoneration occurs.[3] No discussion of wrongful conviction research would be complete without addressing the data and methods scholars have used to examine what happens after an erroneous conviction has been produced and detected.

## Methods Employed: Aftermath

Recent scholarship on the aftermath and consequences of wrongful convictions has highlighted the far-reaching impact of system errors. Most research in this area has dealt

---

3. At least one entire law review volume has been dedicated to this precise topic (Albany Law Review, 75(3), 2012).

with the social and psychological effects on exonerees themselves, while some has emphasized the impact of errors on public attitudes, including the stigmatization associated with individuals who have been wrongfully convicted and exonerated. Methodologically, explorations of important aspects of the aftermath of wrongful conviction have included individual case descriptions, qualitative interviews, and experimental designs.

**Descriptive case studies.** As with our understanding of the causes of wrongful conviction, some of what we know about their aftermath is derived from descriptive examinations of individual cases. In Tim Junkin's (2004) coverage of Kirk Bloodsworth's case, for instance, we learn about some of the obstacles that Bloodsworth faced after he was exonerated: struggles with finances, relationships, and substance use; members of the community shying away from him in public; someone even going so far as to write "Child Killer" on Bloodsworth's truck.

While this information may seem anecdotal and case-specific, it actually highlights one of the benefits of detailed, descriptive case studies. Although such studies may lack the breadth and generalizability of other social scientific methods, they allow for a depth of understanding that may be missed in those other approaches. Indeed, simply having a detailed understanding of what happened in a case and what the exoneree experienced allows readers to more fully appreciate how others' lives might be affected following exoneration. Still, it is important to attempt to gain insights more systematically, and scholars have worked to do so using more traditional social scientific methods.

**In-depth interviews.** Through the use of qualitative research methods, scholars have explored the aftermath of wrongful convictions beyond individual cases. Doing so has allowed them to provide broader analyses and draw more general conclusions than is possible from a descriptive case study, while still developing a fairly deep understanding of the issues. Various researchers have conducted in-depth interviews with exonerees to understand the myriad difficulties associated with the aftermath of wrongful conviction (Campbell & Denov, 2004; Grounds, 2004; Westervelt & Cook, 2010, 2012; Wildeman, Costelloe, & Schehr, 2011). These studies have generally found that exonerees experience a wealth of difficulties upon release, including monetary struggles, personality change, post-traumatic stress and other psychiatric disorders, difficulties coping with grief and loss, stigmatization, familial struggles, physical and mental health problems, practical struggles, and more.

This type of inquiry provides a unique combination of depth and theoretical analysis. But it is important to address the aftermath of wrongful convictions in a variety of ways, including the use of quantitative methods.

**Experimental studies.** Although qualitative studies, particularly interviews, have been the main method used to examine the aftermath of wrongful convictions, at least one recent study used an experimental design and quantitative analysis to assess the stigma faced by individuals who have been wrongly convicted and exonerated (Thompson, Molina, & Levett, 2012). Through two studies in which student participants were randomly assigned to read a simulated news article involving either an exoneree, a guilty ex-convict, or an individual with no contact with the criminal justice system, the authors found that while guilty criminals face the highest level of stigma, innocent exonerees are still stigmatized relative to average, ordinary citizens on multiple dimensions. To our knowledge, this study represents the first true attempt to quantify one of the consequences of wrongful conviction.

The aftermath studies described in this section contribute greatly to our understanding of the lasting effects of wrongful conviction. Such studies—both qualitative and quantitative—have the potential not only to help us understand the devastating consequences of wrongful conviction, but to influence reform efforts in the criminal justice system that call for various assistance, services, and restitution for exonerees.

## Methods Employed: Policy Responses

Several scholars and advocates have suggested that a full-blown Innocence Movement has emerged, with a related agenda that has come to have an impact on public policy (Medwed, 2008; Zalman, 2010/2011). Studies using various methodologies have examined innocence-related policies, ranging from eyewitness identification and interrogation reforms, to compensation statutes for exonerees, in the United States and abroad.

**State case studies.** Norris (2014) examined statutory reforms for compensating the wrongfully convicted in Florida and Texas by studying legislative histories, newspaper reports, information from innocence advocacy groups and other research and non-profit organizations, and U.S. Census data.[4] After describing the policy reform process in each state, he drew upon the diffusion of innovations (see generally, Wejnert, 2002) framework to identify factors that influence such efforts. He concluded that there appears to be little about the policies themselves that makes them unpopular; indeed, compensation for exonerees is often framed as a moral obligation of the state. Further, the statutes do not appear to be closely tied to political leanings, although some differential voting patterns between Republicans and Democrats did appear in Florida. An important aspect of all of the reform efforts, however, seems to be the involvement of organized advocates and the use of individual cases to highlight specific reform needs. Norris did note, however, that the nature of his study is exploratory and conclusions should be drawn with caution.

**Counts, descriptions, and content analyses.** The simplest and most common studies of innocence-related policies have been straightforward counts and descriptions. These studies aim to provide a sense of how widespread the reforms are and their current form. Some have focused on reform policies at the local level. For example, using methods that the author acknowledged did not conform to rigorous social scientific standards, Sullivan (2010) found that law enforcement agencies in more than 300 jurisdictions record custodial interrogations. Combined with all of the departments in Alaska and Minnesota, where recording is required statewide, the total increases to more than 500 agencies (Sullivan, 2005; Sullivan & Vail, 2009). In a more methodologically rigorous study, the Police Executive Research Forum (PERF, 2013) conducted a survey of law enforcement agencies to determine the extent to which eyewitness procedural reforms have been adopted. These researchers surveyed 619 agencies and found, among other things, that only about one-third of the agencies had written policies for photo lineups (despite the fact that 94% of them used such procedures), and less than one-third of them video-recorded the procedure.

The innocence reform agenda is not only important at the local level, however. Several studies have examined reforms at the state level. For example, Norris, Bonventre, Redlich, and Acker (2010/2011) examined state-level reforms involving eyewitness identification procedures, forensic oversight, interrogation recording, the use of snitches, and state innocence commissions. They found that 34 states addressed at least one of the reform areas mentioned, but only 19 of those states had addressed more than one area. The most

---

4. The legislative histories used by Norris include such items as: versions of the bills from draft through passage; committee reports; bill analyses; fiscal and criminal justice impact notes; and congressional debates and hearings.

common reform area was interrogation recording, while the least common was the use of informants. The authors also provided descriptions of the policies in each state.

In addition to the preventive reforms examined by Norris and colleagues (2010/2011), numerous scholars have focused on state compensation statutes. The leading authority on compensation statutes is Adele Bernhard who, in several articles (1999, 2004, 2009), not only has tallied the number of statutes, but has provided compelling legal and practical analyses of their strengths and weaknesses. Norris (2012) provided a more systematic breakdown of the existing compensation statutes. He collected all of the American statutes (27 states and Washington, D.C. had statutes in place at the time), and coded them across 10 dimensions. He then described his findings, and constructed a rudimentary system to score each statute based on the model provided by the Innocence Project. Although limited, this effort marks the first systematic attempt to assess and rank the quality of policy reforms.

The studies previously described have provided important information about the scope of innocence reforms in the United States. Other studies have since attempted to take the next step: to examine the reform process and determine the factors that influence reform efforts.

**Comparison/control studies.** Owens and Griffiths (2011/2012) employed a quantitative approach to analyze compensation reform in the United States. Using a logistic regression model, they analyzed the presence/absence of compensation statutes across the states. Drawing on the political science and criminological literatures, they analyzed whether interest group pressures, penal regimes, or ideology influence the passage of compensation statutes. Although expressing caution regarding the definitiveness of their conclusions, the authors suggest that the number of known wrongful convictions in a state is an important factor affecting the passage of a compensation statute, while the ideological or punitive preferences of the state do not appear to significantly affect passage. It is important to note that while this is a significant first step in examining this issue, the quality of compensation statutes varies greatly from state to state, so the mere presence of a statute does not necessarily reveal how generous a state is or how concerned lawmakers are in making sure that exonerees are properly compensated for the injustices they have suffered.

**Field studies.** Legal and social science research has identified weaknesses in the criminal justice process that may lead to erroneous convictions, thus contributing to numerous policy recommendations that are now being implemented in some states and jurisdictions. Research described earlier in this chapter suggests, for example, that certain procedural reforms can reduce the likelihood of an eyewitness misidentification or false confession. But this begs an obvious question: how effective are these reforms in practice? Answers to this question come primarily from psychological laboratory studies, some of which have been described earlier in this chapter. But additional studies also have attempted to test the effectiveness of suggested reforms in a real-world setting.

Psychological research has been ongoing for more than 40 years in the area of eyewitness identification. One of the most well documented areas has focused on how accurate eye-witnesses are in identifying the perpetrator of crimes during lineup procedures. The latest meta-analysis of laboratory research to date suggests that traditional lineups, where the eyewitness views all lineup members at the same time, produces more "false positives," or inaccurate picks (innocent suspects/fillers) than sequential lineup procedures, where the eyewitness views each subject one at a time (Steblay, Dysart & Wells, 2011). However, this body of research also tends to show modest reductions in the identification of the actual perpetrator, or "false negatives" to accompany the decrease in false positives. These results have led to a debate about the benefits and costs of switching to the sequential method (see Clark, 2012; Wells, Steblay, & Dysart, 2012). Yet the research relied upon to draw these conclusions has overwhelmingly been produced in the lab, leaving criminal justice officials and policy makers with questions about whether and how lab results translate to real-world practices.

To help respond to these concerns, researchers have begun conducting field studies examining the outcomes of identification procedures using different methods. The first high profile field study came out of Illinois, with findings contradicting what lab studies had found for years. Here they found that the blind sequential method—often revealed in lab studies to be superior in terms of accuracy and reliability—produced more false positives ("innocent picks") and fewer suspect picks (or, presumably, more false negatives) than the traditional simultaneous method (Mecklenburg, 2006). However, the research design and implementation of this study have been criticized as flawed, thus compromising the validity of the results. For instance, the researchers confounded the simultaneous-sequential comparison with the added comparison of non-blind versus blind procedures (Schacter et al., 2008). Therefore, the different rates in suspect and filler picks could not be isolated to the type of procedure itself, since all else was not equal—sequential procedures were administered blind (administrator were unaware which participant in the lineup was the actual suspect) and simultaneous procedures were administered non-blind (administrator knew the identity of the actual suspect in the lineup). Further, cases were not randomly assigned to the different types of procedures, but rather more difficult or ambiguous cases were more likely to be assigned to the blind sequential method, and some of the filler picks in simultaneous procedures were not recorded (Steblay, 2011).

To avoid the methodological problems present in the Illinois study, the American Judicature Society (AJS), in partnership with the Innocence Project, the Police Foundation, the Center for Problem-Oriented Policing, and individual social scientists, conducted a field experiment in four police departments in which they compared blind sequential procedures to blind simultaneous procedures. Cases were assigned to the respective conditions randomly. Results indicated that blind sequential procedures reduced innocent filler picks without reducing suspect picks–challenging the results of the previous Illinois study (Wells, Steblay, & Dysart, 2011).

Field studies of this nature are not limited to eyewitness procedures. False confession research has expanded to address whether videotaping affects the interrogation process. A recent field study in a mid-sized city police department examined whether videotaping an interrogation of a mock suspect affected the police interviewer's tactics/behaviors (Kassin et al., 2013). Police officers reviewed a staged crime scene and were presented with a potential suspect (random assignment ensured that half of the suspects committed the mock crime and half did not). Half of the police officers were informed that their interrogation of the suspect was going to be videotaped and half were not informed of the taping (also using random assignment). Results indicated that camera-informed officers were significantly less likely than officers who were not informed of the camera to use minimization tactics (for example, downplaying the seriousness of the crime or suggesting the crime was justified) and maximization tactics (for example, threatening the suspect with harsh penalties/consequences and exaggerating the seriousness of the crime). An unexpected result of this study was that the camera-informed officers were better able to distinguish between those who actually committed the mock crime and those who did not. The researchers suggested that additional studies would be useful to examine potential effects of video-recording interrogations on suspects' behavior, as well as studies that extend the length of the interrogation to mimic real investigations, and to examine effects of habituation (when police eventually may forget the camera is there).

While field studies related to wrongful convictions are in their infancy, there is a clear need for more research of this kind. Such studies not only represent important collaborations between practitioners and researchers, but also offer greater ecological validity by involving those who would be implementing possible reforms in their working environment (Kassin et al. 2013).

## Current Gaps and Future Research

**More multiple-case study methods.** As noted earlier, some of what we know about the consequences of wrongful conviction comes from descriptive case studies. While these works may be criticized for being anecdotal and not generalizable to a wider range of cases, they offer great depth of understanding, and allow scholars from different academic disciplines to extend the research. Indeed, case studies are a well-established and important method used in social science research (see Yin, 2013). Case studies allow researchers both to describe complex phenomena and make preliminary explanatory links between the narrative elements and theoretical propositions. Because we now are aware of more than a thousand exonerations (National Registry of Exonerations, n.d.), scholars can and should utilize multiple-case-study methods, which provide some level of replication that can lead to more complete and nuanced theories (Yin, 2013).

**Expanding sample size and population of qualitative aftermath studies.** The qualitative methods used by Campbell and Denov (2004), Grounds (2004), and Westervelt and Cook (2010, 2012) have ameliorated some of the shortcomings of the more journalistic case narratives described earlier, blending depth and detail with social scientific analysis. There is, of course, room for growth for these types of studies as well. For example, the studies noted above have relied on small samples (5, 18, and 18). Given the nature of the population—those who have been wrongly convicted and exonerated—this approach is understandable. But as the Innocence Movement continues to grow, and organizations dedicated to working with exonerees expand, researchers should attempt to make use of larger samples to increase analytical power and generalizability. In addition, scholars should attempt to reach exonerees from as wide a range of cases as possible. The most comprehensive study thus far is that by Westervelt and Cook (2012), which focused solely on death row exonerees. Researchers should next focus on other types of cases and compare the post-exoneration experiences of individuals in them with Westervelt and Cook's sample; an important next step because facing court-ordered death can be expected to be a unique experience for an innocent prisoner (Westervelt & Cook, 2012).

**More quantitative/experimental studies on aftermath.** In addition to expanding qualitative methods, it is important to explore wrongful conviction aftermath with various methodologies. As noted earlier, several studies have begun to use experimental and quantitative techniques to address aftermath issues, but these studies are still in their infancy. Like many new research areas, the early work has relied primarily on student samples. Such techniques bring with them concerns about external validity, especially if the students in question are drawn from criminology or criminal justice classes and thus may be primed to respond in a certain fashion. This is not to undermine the quality or importance of the extant literature; indeed, the studies that exist are attempting to provide a more rigorous analysis of important issues. However, next steps should expand the research questions to other populations. For instance, what types of stigma do exonerees face when they interact with the general public, among whom they will live and work once they are released? And what effects do their stories and cases have on individuals such as criminal justice practitioners and policymakers, who are in a position to make changes? These types of questions can be explored using methods similar to those currently used.

**More in-depth and multi-perspective examinations of various reforms.** While numerical tabulations and descriptive studies of policy reforms are useful for seeing how widespread reform efforts are and what they look like, future research can and should be more systematic when examining the breadth of innocence reforms. Studies similar to the one completed by Norris (2012), in which statutes were coded systematically, can provide a better sense of the breadth of policies, allow better comparisons of existing statutes, and identify gaps between statutes and recommended reforms.

It is also important to continue examining the factors that influence innocence reforms. The work on compensation by Owens and Griffiths (2011/2012) is one of the only quantitative studies assessing the factors that contribute to the passage of reforms, in this case compensation statutes. Similar studies can explore policies in addition to compensation, utilize dependent variables that measure the quality of reform efforts (rather than just their presence or absence), and rely on different theoretical traditions to identify independent variables that may be relevant to the policymaking process. And as with any area of research, it is important to assess the issue from both quantitative and qualitative perspectives. The case studies conducted by Norris (2014), while useful, are limited due to the nature of the data collection, which relied on readily accessible archival materials. More in-depth qualitative case studies should use interviews with policymakers and advocates to develop a better understanding of the policymaking process. One particularly useful approach may be to track one or more innocence reforms as they make their way through the legislative process. Methods akin to observational and ethnographic studies may be useful: spending time immersed in the legislative process, speaking with those involved, and following coverage of the bills as they work through the system. In addition, as with the quantitative assessments, researchers should go beyond examining compensation statutes to study other types of wrongful conviction reforms.

Although few who care about wrongful convictions would argue against the importance of compensation statutes, from a policy research perspective, it is also important to examine other areas. Enacting reforms that can help prevent wrongful convictions—in areas including eyewitness identification, forensic science, and interrogation—is a major goal of the innocence reform agenda. And these types of policies, more so than compensation statutes, provide a fundamental challenge to the operation of the criminal justice system. Thus, it is possible, perhaps likely, that such reforms will encounter more resistance from those who already work in the system. It nevertheless is important to examine the policymaking process to identify potential reforms that would alter the way that police, prosecutors, and other officials do their jobs.

Furthermore, to the extent that academic research has implicit policy reforms, it is important to do more to learn about the real on-the-ground efforts taken to enact those reforms. There is often a disconnect between the academic community and those who are working towards policy reforms in the area of wrongful convictions. This can lead to an incomplete analysis of what reforms are needed, how to pursue them, and why efforts are or are not successful.

Brown and Saloom (2013) provide an example illustrating the complexities of policy reform efforts, specifically securing eyewitness identification reform in Maryland. In this instance, an initial legislative push for comprehensive reform in 2007 did not succeed, largely due to the opposition of law enforcement. A later push in 2012 had more momentum, and while law enforcement representatives supported most of the reform package, they did not want reform to occur through a legislative mandate. This led to a multi-perspective stakeholder collaboration to iron out uniform protocols to be adopted by law enforcement agencies statewide. The agreed-upon guidelines were to be implemented in early 2013. However, an initial analysis of the revised policies from 50 agencies revealed that less than half included the most important recommendation of blind administration of identification line-ups and show-ups.

Brown and Saloom's (2013) article exemplifies the difficulties of getting reform measures passed and the persistence needed to continue to fight for best-practice reforms. The approaches used by those on the frontline of reform efforts are often the product of careful and pragmatic deliberation and thought. To address policy reforms without the perspective and input of those doing the work "on the ground" leaves academics without a complete picture, one that is important to promote the best research and help lead to important theoretical insights about innocence as a policy matter. Thus, finding opportunities to collaborate with and learn from important actors in the policy arena should be a priority moving forward.

**More scientifically rigorous field studies**. In addition to developing a better understanding of the policymaking process, researchers should conduct evaluation studies to determine how useful the proposed reforms actually are in practice. The studies that have established the unreliability of traditional eyewitness identification procedures, the fallibility of confessions, and the like, have proven invaluable. They have led to numerous reform recommendations that seem poised to increase the accuracy of the investigative process. The vast majority of this research, however, comes from psychological lab studies. It is possible that findings from a controlled laboratory may not translate to actual practice, and that criminal justice practitioners may be hesitant to adopt reforms based solely on such research. Thus, it is important that researchers conduct further field studies to evaluate the efficacy of investigative reforms in practical application, rather than exclusively in laboratory settings. Such studies, conducted by well-informed researchers that adhere to strict, scientifically sound methodologies, can have a great impact on evaluating suggested reforms and informing criminal justice practitioners about which policies can improve the dual aims of ensuring that innocent individuals are not erroneously prosecuted and convicted and also that the guilty do not go free.

Much of what we are suggesting in the way of future research undoubtedly will involve extensive studies that will require time, energy, and funding. But improved research and correspondingly useful results are most certainly attainable. These outcomes will only be possible, however, if we actively build working relationships between the research and practitioner communities.

# Moving Forward: Bridging the Gaps Between Research and Practice

As this chapter and others in this volume have shown, there is great interest and activity in research concerning many aspects of wrongful convictions. As this interest continues to grow, it will be important to ensure that the research does not occur solely within a particular discipline or make use of limited methodological approaches. As we attempt to "move forward" with wrongful conviction scholarship, it is imperative that we continue to increase collaboration between social scientists, legal scholars, and criminal justice practitioners. Future research would benefit greatly from more multi-disciplinary collaborations, involving academics from diverse fields, practitioners, advocacy groups, defense attorney and prosecutors' offices and organizations, law enforcement, and policymakers.

Such a blend of perspectives has the potential to create more valid, efficient, comprehensive, and meaningful research studies, the results of which can be utilized to make the criminal justice system fairer and more legitimate and accurate.

There is evidence that such cross-disciplinary collaborations are happening. For example, conferences have become important for helping bridge the gap between researchers and practitioners. Criminal justice and criminology conferences are beginning to invite various actors in the wrongful conviction arena in addition to academic researchers, while many innocence advocacy meetings now regularly include social scientists and legal scholars. Such conferences create a forum for a diverse group of people to discuss different perspectives and ideas, allowing for a more comprehensive dialogue on the relevant issues.

It is important that these connections develop into strong working relationships. Social scientists have a unique set of data analysis skills that are useful for developing a broader and more generalizable understanding of wrongful convictions. Collecting data on such cases, however, is an arduous, resource-intensive task that can be extremely difficult (if not impossible) for any individual researcher or small research team to accomplish. On the other hand, innocence projects and other criminal justice organizations have a wealth of information about cases, as well as invaluable "insider" knowledge about the criminal justice process. Such organizations, however, may not have individuals trained specifically in research design and data analysis, or may lack the resources necessary to focus on research studies. It is easy to see, then, how working relationships between such organizations and researchers would be mutually beneficial. The data from these organizations can be used by researchers, and their results, along with the intimate case knowledge of the organizations, can lead to a much more complete understanding of wrongful convictions and more informed policy recommendations.

Finally, as research in this area expands and improves, we need to examine ways of effectively sharing the results with practitioners and policymakers. Too often research remains in academic settings, leaving potentially valuable knowledge outside the reach of those who are directly engaged in criminal justice practice and reform. Finding ways to translate research into practice is crucial to making real progress in the criminal justice system, as buy-in is needed from those doing the ground work and those with the power to spearhead reforms. An important step to help bridge this gap is for researchers to participate in and contribute to conferences, newsletters, publications, websites, and organizations with which practitioners and policymakers are affiliated, both to share important, accessible research findings and to gain insights and pave the way for potential collaborations for future research.

# References

Bedau, H. A. & Radelet, M. L. (1987). Miscarriages of justice in potentially capital cases. *Stanford Law Review, 40*(1), 21–179.

Bernhard, A. (1999). When justice fails: Indemnification for unjust conviction. *University of Chicago Law School Roundtable, 6,* 73–112.

Bernhard, A. (2004). Justice still fails: A review of recent efforts to compensate individuals who have been unjustly convicted and later exonerated. *Drake Law Review, 52,* 703–738.

Bernhard, A. (2009). A short overview of the statutory remedies for the wrongly convicted: What works, what doesn't, and why. *Public Interest Law Journal, 18,* 403–425.

Borchard, E. M. (1932). *Convicting the innocent: Sixty-five actual errors of criminal justice.* Garden City, NY: Garden City Publishing Inc.

Brown, R. & Saloom, S. (2013). The Imperative of Eyewitness Identification Reform and the Role of Police Leadership. *University of Baltimore Law Review, 42*(3), 535–559.

Campbell, K. & Denov, M. (2004). The burden of innocence: Coping with a wrongful imprisonment. *Canadian Journal of Criminology and Criminal Justice, 46*, 139–164.

Castelle, G. & Loftus, E. F. (2008). Misinformation and wrongful convictions. In Westervelt, S. D. & Humphrey, J. A. (Eds.), *Wrongly convicted: Perspectives on failed justice* (17–35). New Brunswick: Rutgers University Press.

Clark, S. E. (2012). Costs and benefits of eyewitness identification reform: Psychological science and public policy. *Perspectives on Psychological Science, 7*, 238–259.

Cole, S. A. (2012). Forensic science and wrongful convictions: From exposer to contributor to corrector. *New England Law Review, 46*, 711–736.

Dervan, L.E. & Edkins, V.A. (2013). The innocent defendant's dilemma: An innovative empirical study of plea bargaining's innocence problem. *Journal of Criminal Law & Criminology, 103*(1), 1–48.

Drizin, S. A. & Leo, R. A. (2004). The problem of false confessions in the post-DNA world. *North Carolina Law Review, 82*, 891–1007.

Dror, I. E., Charlton, D., & Peron, A. E. (2006). Contextual information renders experts vulnerable to making erroneous identifications. *Forensic Science International, 156*, 74–78.

Eisenstein, J. & Jacob, H. (1977). *Felony justice: An organizational analysis of criminal courts.* Boston: Little, Brown and Company.

Feeley, M. M. (1992 [1979]). *The process is the punishment: Handling cases in a lower criminal court.* New York: Russell Sage Foundation.

Garrett, B. L. (2008). Judging innocence. *Columbia Law Review, 108*, 55–142.

Garrett, B. L. (2011). *Convicting the innocent: Where criminal prosecutions go wrong.* Cambridge: Harvard University Press.

Garrett, B. L. & Neufeld, P. J. (2009). Invalid forensic science testimony and wrongful convictions. *Virginia Law Review, 95*(1), 1–97.

Gould, J. B. & Leo, R. A. (2010). One hundred years later: Wrongful convictions after a century of research. *The Journal of Criminal Law & Criminology, 100*(3), 825–868.

Gould, J. B., Carrano, J., Leo, R., & Young, J. (2013). Predicting erroneous convictions: A social science approach to miscarriages of justice. Available at https://ncjrs.gov

Gross, S. R. (2008). Convicting the innocent. The *Annual Review of Law and Social Science, 4*, 173–192.

Gross, S. R., Jacoby, K., Matheson, D. J., Montgomery, N., & Patil, S. (2005). Exonerations in the United States 1989 through 2003. *The Journal of Criminal Law & Criminology, 95*(2), 523–560.

Gross, S. R. & O'Brien, B. (2008). Frequency and predictors of false conviction: Why we know so little and new data on capital cases. *Journal of Empirical Legal Studies, 5*(4), 927–962.

Grounds, A. (2004). Psychological consequences of wrongful conviction and imprisonment. *Canadian Journal of Criminology and Criminal Justice, 46*, 165–182.

Harmon, T. R. (2001). Predictors of miscarriages of justice in capital cases. *Justice Quarterly, 18*(4), 949–968.

Harmon, T. R. & Lofquist, W. S. (2005). Too late for luck: A comparison of post-Furman exonerations and executions of the innocent. *Crime & Delinquency, 51*(4), 498–520.

Heumann, M. (1977). *Plea bargaining: The experiences of prosecutors, judges, and defense attorneys.* Chicago: The University of Chicago Press.

Junkin, T. (2004). *Bloodsworth.* Chapel Hill, NC: Algonquin Books.

Kassin, S. M., Drizin, S. A., Grisso, T., Gudjonsson, G. H., Leo, R. A., & Redlich, A. D. (2010). Police-induced confessions: Risk factors and recommendations. *Law and Human Behavior, 34*, 3–38.

Kassin, S. M., Kukucka, J., Lawson, V. Z., & DeCarlo, J. (2013, July 22). Does video recording alter the behavior of police during interrogation? A mock crime-and-investigation study. *Law and Human Behavior.* Published in advance online at http://psycnet.apa.org/

Leo, R. A. (2005). Rethinking the study of wrongful convictions: Developing a criminology of wrongful conviction. *Journal of Contemporary Criminal Justice, 21*(3), 201–223.

Leo, R. A. & Gould, J. B. (2009). Studying wrongful convictions: Learning from social science. *Ohio State Journal of Criminal Law. 7*, 7–30.

Lewis, S. C., Zamith, R., Hermida, A. (2013). Content analysis in an era of Big Data: A hybrid approach to computational and manual methods. *Journal of Broadcasting and Electronic Media, 57*(1), 34–52.

Mecklenburg, S. H. (2006). *Report to the legislature of the State of Illinois: The Illinois pilot program on double-blind, sequential lineup procedures.* Springfield, IL: Illinois State Police.

Medwed, D. S. (2004). The zeal deal: Prosecutorial resistance to post-conviction claims of innocence. *Boston University Law Review, 84*, 125–183.

Medwed, D. S. (2008). Innocentrism. *University of Illinois Law Review, 2008*, 1549–1572.

National Registry of Exonerations. (n.d.). Retrieved from www.exonerationregistry.org

Norris, R. J. (2012). Assessing compensation statutes for the wrongly convicted. *Criminal Justice Policy Review, 23*, 352–374.

Norris, R. J. (2014). Exoneree compensation: Current policies and future outlook. In M. Zalman & J. Carrano (Eds.), *Wrongful conviction and criminal justice reform: Making justice* (289–303). New York: Routledge.

Norris, R. J., Bonventre, C. L., Redlich, A. D., & Acker, J. R. (2010/2011). "Than that one innocent suffer": Evaluating state safeguards against wrongful convictions. *Albany Law Review, 74*(3), 1301–1364.

Owens, M. L. & Griffiths, E. (2011/2012). Uneven reparations for wrongful convictions: Examining the state politics of statutory compensation legislation. *Albany Law Review, 75*(3), 1283–1327.

Police Executive Research Forum. (2013). *A national survey of eyewitness identification procedures in law enforcement agencies.* Retrieved from http://policeforum.org/library/eyewitness-identification/NIJEyewitnessReport.pdf.

Redlich, A. D. (2010). The susceptibility of juveniles to false confessions and false guilty pleas. *Rutgers Law Review, 62*, 943–957.

Redlich, A. D. & Goodman, G. S. (2003). Taking responsibility for an act not committed: The influence of age and suggestibility. *Law and Human Behavior, 27*(2), 141–156.

Redlich, A. D., Summers, A., & Hoover, S. (2010). Self-reported false confessions and false guilty pleas among offenders with mental illness. *Law and Human Behavior, 34*, 79–90.

Schacter, D. L., Dawes, R., Jacoby, L. L., Kahneman, D., Lempert, R., Roediger, H. L., et al. (2008). Policy forum: Studying eyewitness investigations in the field. *Law and Human Behavior, 32*, 3–5.

Scheck, B., Neufeld, P., & Dwyer, J. (2003). *Actual innocence: When justice goes wrong and how to make it right.* New York: New American Library.

Shadish, W. R., Cook, T. D. & Campbell, D. T. (2002). *Experimental and quasi-experimental designs for generalized causal inference.* Boston: Houghton Mifflin Company.

Siegel, A. M. (2005). Moving down the wedge of injustice: A proposal for a third generation of wrongful convictions scholarship and advocacy. *American Criminal Law Review, 42,* 1219–1237.

Spencer, L., Ritchie, J., & O'Connor, W. (2003). Analysis: Practices, principles, and processes. In Ritchie, J. & Lewis, J. (Eds.), *Qualitative research practice: A guide for social science students and researchers* (199–218). London: SAGE Publications, Ltd.

*State v. Henderson,* 27 A.3d 872 (NJ, 2011).

Steblay, N. K. (2011). What we know now: The Evanston Illinois lineups. *Law and Human Behavior, 35,* 1–12.

Steblay, N. K., Dysart, J. E., & Wells, G. L. (2011). Seventy-two tests of the sequential lineup superiority effect: A meta-analysis and policy discussion. *Psychology, Public Policy, and Law,* 17, 99–139.

Sullivan, T. P. (2005). Electronic recording of custodial interrogations: Everybody wins. *Journal of Criminal Law and Criminology, 95,* 1127–1140.

Sullivan, T. P. (2010). The wisdom of custodial recording. In G. D. Lassiter & C. A. Meissner (Eds.), *Police interrogation and false confessions: Current research, practice, and policy implications.* Washington, DC: APA Press.

Sullivan, T. P. and Vail, A. W. (2009). The consequences of law enforcement officials' failure to record custodial interviews as required by law. *Journal of Criminal Law and Criminology, 99,* 215–234.

Thompson, A. M., Molina, O. R., & Levett, L. M. (2012). After exoneration: An investigation of stigma and wrongfully convicted persons. *Albany Law Review, 75,* 1373–1413.

Ulmer, J. T. (1994). Trial judges in a rural court community: Contexts, organizational relations, and interaction strategies. *Journal of contemporary ethnography, 23*(1), 79–108.

Weiss, R. S. (1994). *Learning from strangers: The art and method of qualitative interview studies.* New York: The Free Press.

Wejnert, B. (2002). Integrating models of diffusion of innovations: A conceptual framework. *Annual Review of Sociology, 28:* 297–326.

Wells, G. L., Small, M., Penrod, S., Malpass, R. S., Fulero, S. M., & Brimacombe, C. A. E. (1998). Eyewitness identification procedures: Recommendations for lineups and photospreads. *Law and Human Behavior, 22*(6), 603–647.

Wells, G. L. & Olson, E. A. (2003). Eyewitness testimony. *Annual reviews of psychology, 54,* 277–295.

Wells, G. L., Steblay, N. M., & Dysart, J. E. (2011). *A test of the simultaneous vs. sequential lineup methods: An initial report of the AJS national eyewitness identification field studies.* Des Moines, IA: American Judicature Society.

Wells, G. L., Steblay, N. K., & Dysart, J. E. (2012). Eyewitness identification reforms: Are suggestiveness-induced hits and guesses true hits? *Perspectives on Psychological Science, 7,* 264–271.

Wells, T. & Leo, R. A. (2008). *The wrong guys: Murder, false confessions, and the Norfolk Four.* New York: The New Press.

Westervelt, S. D. & Cook, K. J. (2010). Framing innocents: The wrongly convicted as victims of state harm. *Crime, Law, and Social Change, 53,* 259–275.

Westervelt, S. D. & Cook, K. J. (2012). *Life after death row: Exonerees' search for community and identity.* New Brunswick, NJ: Rutgers University Press.

Wildeman, J., Costelloe, M., & Schehr, R. (2011). Experiencing wrongful and unlawful conviction. *Journal of Offender Rehabilitation, 50,* 411–432.

Yin, R. K. (2013). *Case study research: Design and methods* (5th Ed.). Beverly Hills, CA: Sage.

Zalman, M. (2010/2011). An integrated justice model of wrongful convictions. *Albany Law Review, 74,* 1465–1524.

# Chapter Nineteen

# International Trends and Developments: Perspectives on Wrongful Convictions from Europe

Martin Killias, *University of St. Gallen*

Countries differ in the way they select justices and magistrates, but regardless of the selection process, all judicial decision-making is subject to errors. Judges can overlook or misinterpret rules, either of procedure or of substantive criminal law. In both cases, the outcome may be that a person will be convicted or acquitted, although a correct application of law would have led to a different outcome. For those who lose their case due to such errors after having turned to the criminal justice system in the hope of finding redress or justice, the outcome will be frustrating. Worse, judicial errors make the system unpredictable and ultimately lead to a loss of confidence in the judiciary. One obvious recommendation is that judges should receive adequate training and that the selection process should ensure that only highly qualified lawyers accede to the judiciary. Thus, despite differential judicial selection processes, the quality of judicial thinking is probably much enhanced by systems that insist on "objective" and less partisan or subjective criteria.

On the other hand, legal interpretation does not allow clear-cut answers in the model of the sciences. United States Supreme Court justices rarely converge in their opinions, and neither do judges elsewhere in the world.[1] Moreover, it is likely that disagreements between judges deciding a case are more frequent the higher a court ranks in the judicial hierarchy. Such a correlation obviously results in large part from the nature of the cases that reach higher judicial levels. In all countries and under all systems, only a selection of cases is submitted to the higher courts, and they often raise difficult issues of legal interpretation.

The frequent disagreement among justices in the highest courts thus masks the fact that the vast majority of cases do not raise major difficulties of legal interpretation. Thanks to the consistency of judicial decision-making in the overwhelming majority of cases, both lay citizens and legal experts can anticipate fairly well the outcome of a case once it is brought to court. The predictability and reliability of justice systems not only encourage out-of-court settlements, but more generally permit social planning and rational ways of conducting business. If cases are still brought to courts in substantial numbers, the unresolved issues are typically factual rather than legal. Courts are needed not only to

---

1. The author has been, part-time, a judge in Switzerland's Federal Supreme Court (from 1984 to 2008) and has often experienced disagreement among the judges sitting on a particular case.

announce and apply the law, but far more often to find the truth or, more modestly phrased, to establish the relevant facts.

In this respect, factual errors are, if not more frequent, at least more difficult to prevent than misinterpretations of legal rules. Errors can occur at the expense of all parties involved in a case. Acquittals due to errors in the establishment of relevant facts are, from the system's point of view, no less disturbing than convictions of innocent defendants. The famous proverb usually attributed to Voltaire but actually originating with an anonymous advisor of Roman Emperor Traianus[2] (98-117 AC)—that it is better to acquit a hundred guilty than to convict one innocent defendant—may miss an essential point, as Brian Forst (2013) has pointed out in a brilliant essay. It overlooks the harm done by abuse of police power, as well as the failure to bring offenders to justice owing to reluctance among victims to report offenses or because of incompetent agents of the criminal justice system. In this sense, error management, as it is now in use in ever increasing sectors of modern society, should follow a broader agenda than just the prevention of convicting innocent persons. Some measures designed to prevent some errors may actually increase the risks for other errors to occur, and in the end do more harm to society (Stuntz, 2011).

Still, factual errors that result in punishing defendants who did not deserve it are more damaging for the criminal justice system than any other errors. Louis XVI, the unfortunate king who lost his throne and was executed during the French Revolution, suffered not only from the financial crises that had destabilized France at that time, but also from a serious crisis of legitimacy of the criminal justice system. A few famous cases of wrongful convictions have indeed totally discredited the criminal justice system of the Ancien Régime.[3] Factual errors leading to the conviction of innocent defendants, i.e., wrongful convictions, remain, therefore, a prominent issue of public debate.

# Stepping Back: Identified Causes of Wrongful Convictions Under Various National Systems

The search for remedies has to start with the study of causes. In a given case, many factors can lead the court to depart from the truth. Prominent causes that have to date been identified are: false confessions, testimony by lying or mistaken witnesses, errors by forensic, medical, or technical experts, incompetent defense counsel, and agents of the criminal justice system who are more inclined to settle a maximum of cases with a minimum of time and effort than to guard against committing errors.

---

2. The advisor's identity is not known. The Emperor's instruction to a local magistrate (a certain *Adsidius Severus*) reads as follows (quoted from Nogrady, 2011): "*Sed nec de suspicionibus debere aliquem damnari ... satius enim impunitum relinqui facinus nocenti quam innocentem damnari*" ("None should be convicted based on suspicions alone ... because it is preferable leaving unpunished a guilty defendant over punishing an innocent man"). This rule has been integrated by the Roman lawyer Ulpianus (170–228) into his treaty of criminal law (*de officio proconsulis*) and later into the *Corpus iuris civilis* of Emperor Justinianus I. (527–565), D. 48, 18, 5 pr.

3. The most prominent case was Jean Calas, made famous through Voltaire's pamphlet. Calas was wrongfully convicted and executed in Toulouse (France) in 1762. He had been charged with the murder of his son (who actually had committed suicide) allegedly because he wanted to prevent him from converting to Catholicism. Under torture, he confessed but immediately revoked his confessions. He was nonetheless sentenced to death. Voltaire's essay on tolerance (1763) was so successful that Calas was exonerated in 1765 and his family compensated by King Louis XV (Köppel, 2008). This was probably the first official exoneration in legal history.

# False Confessions

False confessions play a major role in wrongful convictions. This is true for the Anglo-American accusatorial systems as well as under the European continental inquisitorial system. In his analyses of exonerations, Garrett (2013) found that no less than 26 percent of the overturned wrongful convictions had been produced at least in part by false confessions obtained during police interviews or were based on the defendant's guilty plea. Motivated in part to prevent false confessions, the United States Supreme Court during Earl Warren's tenure as Chief Justice announced a number of landmark decisions designed to protect defendants during police interrogations. Behind the rule that every suspect had a right to counsel and to hear the famous *Miranda* warnings was probably the experience, as expressed in Chief Justice Warren's majority opinion,[4] that all too often confessions had been obtained through the use of deception, force, or threats (Stuntz, 2011). The presence of a defense lawyer was seen as an effective check against abusive techniques of interrogation. These safeguards were all the more justified because under American law a declaration made by a defendant during a police interrogation can be used as evidence against him in court (Zalman, 2011).

The long-term outcome of the Warren Court rules, however, was not entirely positive. For example, American defense lawyers routinely advise their clients not to make any declaration at the police station (Pizzi, 1999). Without any cooperation, the police are often left without any base to start efficient investigations. If a guilty defendant is sent home under these circumstances, justice will not be done to the victim, further offenses will not be prevented, and public security may be jeopardized (Stuntz, 2011).

Acting roughly one generation after the U.S. Supreme Court, many European countries adopted similar "*Miranda*-like" standards, often prompted by decisions of the European Court of Human Rights. However, European legislators paid very little attention to possible side-effects of these rules. Rather than copying the American rules, Europeans could have avoided new problems by imposing video-recording of police interrogations. Such video devices were not available during the Warren Court era, but could have been an option in Europe forty years later. Unfortunately, law-making in this area has not been very innovative and instead has been far more focused on adopting American standards. It currently is not known whether European defense counsel react in the same way that Pizzi (1999) described their American counterparts' practice, namely urging clients to remain silent. However, whereas the U.S. does not allow adverse inferences to be drawn from suspects' silence, some European countries, such as the England and Wales, inform suspects that their silence can harm their defense (see Criminal Justice and Public Order Act, 1994).[5] Continental legal traditions may indeed favor less antagonistic attitudes among European lawyers towards the police, but we do not know how generally this may be true and for how long. Neither is it known whether European police departments in the future will more often use "dirty tricks" to obtain information from defendants, for example by using jailhouse snitches.[6]

European studies examining false confessions in wrongful convictions point to the role of excessively long and highly suggestive police interrogations. Brants (2013) reports that in a series of highly publicized Dutch murder exonerations, long, suggestive police in-

---

4. *Miranda v. Arizona*, 384 U.S. 436 (1966).
5. http://www.legislation.gov.uk/ukpga/1994/33/section/34/enacted.
6. It seems that the Italian police tried to obtain, through a cooperating cellmate, evidence against Vittorio Emmanuele di Savoia, the late Italian king's son. So far, few instances of the use of jailhouse snitches have come to public attention in Europe.

terrogations frequently played a prominent role. Several European legislatures have explicitly outlawed deceptive or manipulative interview techniques, such as falsely pretending that co-defendants have confessed, or offering advantages (such as immediate release from jail) in exchange for a confession. A systematic review of police interrogation methods (Meissner, Redlich, Bhatt & Brandon, 2012) has found that more neutral, information-gathering interview styles produce significantly fewer false confessions than harsh, authoritarian, accusatorial interrogation methods. In other words, interview methods as they are (at least in theory) imposed by legislation and also practiced widely in Europe (Slobogin, 2003; Vrij, 2003) might efficiently help curb the problem of false confessions. It is significant that such rules are not yet fully adopted in the Netherlands, where prominent cases of false confessions have occurred (Brants, 2013).

On a different level, one may question whether a defendant should be admitted as a witness in his own trial. Under the rule of the European Convention of Human Rights, defendants are—as in America—protected against self-incrimination. Therefore, the defendant's declarations during police or prosecutorial interrogation or in court never will be qualified as testimony. Without the status of a witness, he cannot commit perjury and will never be criminally liable if, at the end of the trial, his declarations turn out to be false. This does not mean that the defendant's denial is without effect—it will be up to the court to decide whether, given all the other evidence available, his version is to be credited at least to the point to establish reasonable doubt that bars a conviction.

## Errors by Witnesses

Witnesses may lie or mistakenly misrepresent what they have seen or heard. Particularly risky are witness statements regarding offender identification. In an American sample (from Virginia), one estimate suggests that in the neighborhood of 5 percent of convictions in rape cases involving an offender unknown to the victim were erroneous based on DNA analysis of recently discovered rape kit evidence. Obviously, the victim-witness had misidentified the offender (Gross, 2013). In Europe, no data are available that allow any reasonable estimates. A study conducted in a German province (Bavaria) suggests that approximately 20 to 30 percent of all rape cases reported to the police were dismissed because police and prosecutors felt the accusations were probably wrong. The alleged victim was formally prosecuted for false accusations in approximately 7 percent of all reports (Elsner & Steffen, 2005).

From a recent systematic review of studies on police interrogation of suspects (Meissner, Redlich, Bhatt & Brandon, 2012), it may be inferred that witness testimony can be improved by a similarly neutral style of interviewing. Several rules have been developed in America that offer victims better protection against defamatory styles of questioning in court, such as being cross-examined about their previous sexual experience. Such rules have been largely adopted in Europe as well, promoted by a Council of Europe Recommendation on Victims' Rights.[7] More important than such formal bars on certain subjects, however, may be that the interview takes place in a more neutral way. In European trials, this is widely accomplished by giving the presiding judge the primary role in interviewing witnesses (as well as the defendant). Cross-examination by the prosecutor and the defense counsel takes place after all justices sitting on a case have finished their questions, and it is usually limited to exploring a few additional details.

---

7. For example, Recommendation R 87 (21) on the assistance to victims and the prevention of victimization, adopted by the Committee of Ministers on 17 September 1987.

In the light of experimental studies on the quality of witness statements (Odinot, Wolters, & van Giezen, 2012), the more relaxed atmosphere that is produced by such rules may enhance the accuracy of testimony and the wealth of information provided. Being essentially uninterrupted, witnesses have a chance to tell their story in their own words and in a coherent, intelligible way—a chance American witnesses often regret not having had in court (Pizzi, 1999). Further, having the chance to tell their story first to the police, later to the prosecutor, and finally in court, victims and other witnesses may have a better chance to recall later details that did not come to their mind during the first interview (Odinot et al., 2013), especially if the victim has been questioned on aspects of the case that he/she was not prepared for.

Despite these reforms, memory decay and inaccurate identification of faces and objects will remain hard to overcome. Therefore, the best solution may be to rely less on oral statements than on documentary or material evidence collected through forensic sciences (Egger, 1984; Ribaux & Margot, 2008). The increasing role of forensic sciences makes trials far less vulnerable to errors of identification, despite the many pitfalls in forensic work. Perhaps one of the main differences between American and European trials is the considerably greater reliance under the Anglo-Saxon accusatorial system on oral statements—of defendants, witnesses, and experts. We shall now consider ways to improve forensic evidence on both sides of the Ocean.

# Forensic Science Evidence

Forensic science labs often have a problematic role because their work, with the possible exception of psychiatric experts, is hardly understandable to prosecutors, defense counsel, and judges. This makes their conclusions widely immune against challenges by the various actors in the trial. Massive frauds, as in the case of Annie Dookhan at a Massachusetts drug lab who tampered with evidence, forged colleagues' signatures, and submitted reports purporting to have found illegal substances without conducting analyses (Seelye & Bidgood, 2013), can remain undetected for many years. Some consider a crucial reform being the opening of "independent" forensic science labs rather than having such labs being institutionally integrated into the police services.

The issue of independence may be less critical in Europe, where the police are required—at least in theory—to investigate both "against" and "in favor of" suspected offenders. Although pitfalls do exist, labs usually are sufficiently independent to resist pressure to manipulate evidence, and police officers maintain their "neutral" role as investigators. In order to understand this feature of police culture, it is essential that police officers or prosecutors who suppress evidence favorable to a suspect, or who fail to collect such evidence, are liable to criminal prosecution for "abuse of power." Virtually all European nations have provisions in their criminal codes to that end. Cases of prosecutorial misconduct, as described by Petro and Petro (2013), are hard to imagine without criminal sanctions in the end. Whenever evidence was analyzed inappropriately by police labs (as in a Dutch case reported by Brants, 2013), it was basically done in good faith although unprofessionally.

More disturbing and in all likelihood more frequent are errors that are not intentional, but result from incompetence in dealing with the collection of materials at crime scenes, inappropriate examination of fingerprints (Schiffer, 2009), or inadequate statistical interpretation (Vuille, Biedermann & Taroni, 2013). It should be possible, however, to overcome such errors by developing a culture of error management in the field of forensic sciences, following the model of surgeons in general and forensic medicine in particular (Schiffer, 2009). Whenever the defendant persists in denial (e.g., of his presence at a crime scene), or whenever the forensic evidence does not fit other plausible evidence, a second test by a different lab should be available to the defense without legal or other obstacles. Further, police labs should be allowed to communicate with the defense counsel without restrictions resulting from rules of secrecy, at or before the trial stage.

## The Role of Defense Counsel

One of the most important differences between the American accusatorial and the continental European inquisitorial system concerns the role of the defense attorney. This is directly related to the role of the courts. Under the inquisitorial system, the court is ultimately responsible for finding the "truth," and it is usually the presiding judge who leads the interrogations of the defendant and all witnesses. Whenever the court feels that the evidence presented during the hearing does not allow it to make a decision, it will collect additional evidence or send back the file to the prosecution service for an additional inquiry. If the court feels that the prosecutor's conclusions do not fit the facts and that a more serious or less serious (or simply a different) offense would be applicable, it is free to adapt the indictment to the facts provided that the parties are duly informed in advance of the hearing.

These rules sharply contrast with the passive role courts play under the accusatorial system. The difference in the role of courts affects the position of the parties and in particular of the defense counsel. For example, whenever the defense argues that a different offender might have committed the crime, it will come forward with this point during one of the preliminary hearings in the prosecutor's office. If the argument has some plausibility, the prosecutor will, as a rule, charge the police with making additional investigations that in some cases can assume considerable proportions. Since the prosecutor and the police are obliged by law to investigate against as well as in favor of the suspect, they often will examine alternative explanations of a crime and even mitigating circumstances long in advance and on their own. If an alternative explanation cannot be ruled out, prosecutors usually do not bring the case to court but decide to dismiss it.[8] Most evidence is collected and most witnesses are heard at this pre-trial stage under the responsibility of the prosecutor and in presence of the defendant and his counsel. The prosecution's file is open to the defense at least once investigations are advanced or completed and before the case goes to court. Consequently, the issue of "guilty or not" is rarely contested when the case reaches the court stage, and often court hearings serve to fix an appropriate sentence rather than to find a verdict.[9] Under the continental system, most defendants plead guilty before their case comes to trial. This cooperation is not disinterested, since cooperating defendants under all systems may have a chance to receive a more lenient sentence.

As a result of these measures, the defense does not have the burden to lead a counter-investigation, except perhaps under a few very unusual circumstances. Its role is centered on participation at all pre-trial interrogations of the defendant, witnesses, and experts, with the possibility of cross-examination in the prosecutor's office. During this stage, defense counsel has the role of a watchdog who makes sure that procedural safeguards are respected, that alternative explanations are carefully scrutinized, and that legal issues are clarified in advance. Because much of what an American trial would develop in the

---

8. In Germany, there is an informal rule according to which prosecutors should bring the case to court only if the odds of a verdict are clearly above 50 percent (Kessler, 2008). Similar standards prevail in most other countries.

9. Under the inquisitorial system, the sentence is usually decided during the same hearing as the verdict and by the same bench of justices.

courtroom takes place during the pre-trial investigation, continental courts are reluctant to hear witnesses or experts again at the trial stage. Usually, the trial will be based on the minutes of the several pre-trial hearings as well as on experts' written statements,[10] and witnesses or other evidence will be examined by the court only if some contradictions need further clarification.

All these differences in the usual course of a trial in America and Europe explain why the defense counsel plays a less decisive role under the continental system. The lack of resources that often frustrates an American lawyer's initiative to start a counter-investigation, or inadequate training and experience of the defense attorney therefore are far less critical in Europe, where the court has the ultimate responsibility of finding the "truth." Continental colleagues frequently joke that a lawyer's quality and resources are far more important in civil law trials—which are more similar to American civil proceedings—than in criminal matters, where the defendant does not risk suffering much harm from his counsel's incompetence.[11]

# Paper-trials in Europe

"Paper-trials" (in which judges decide cases almost exclusively on documents included in the files produced prior to trial rather than receiving testimony from witnesses) (Brants, 2013), as they prevail across continental Europe, allow witnesses, experts, and perhaps also defendants to make more coherent statements during pre-trial hearings, without being permanently interrupted during cross-examination (Pizzi, 1999) or exposed to embarrassing media attention.[12] A less stressful, more sober atmosphere in an office in the presence of few agents may also allow the participants easier expression of more difficult aspects of a story. On the other hand, such procedures also have clear shortcomings, as pointed out by Brants (2013) in her discussion of a few dramatic wrongful convictions in the Netherlands. Paper-trials favor what Brants (2013) calls "tunnel vision," namely a trend to accept tacitly what has been concluded at the previous stage of a procedure, and to ignore "disturbing" new evidence presented later on. In the most dramatic of her cases (a murder committed in the Schiedam Park[13]), the police pushed a vulnerable defendant through long, persistent interrogations to make a confession (which he revoked two days later and which proved to be false in the end), "streamlined" the DNA evidence from the crime scene (which did not match the suspect's) and prevented the defense and the court from learning about disturbing details regarding the DNA evidence and the fact that the lab's scientists had expressed serious doubts to the prosecution about the suspect's guilt. Convicted in three levels of the judicial hierarchy, he was ultimately (and reluctantly) exonerated after a different man, arrested for raping a young woman, spontaneously confessed to the Schiedam Park murder. In this case, all actors failed dramatically in their task to

---

10. Experts typically send the prosecutor's office a written statement. An interrogation of experts takes place whenever their conclusions do not converge or are challenged by the defense. Impartiality is guaranteed by the rule that any appointment of experts (by the prosecution service) is systematically submitted to the defense in order to allow the counsel to advance reservations regarding competence or impartiality.

11. As with all jokes, this one also is obviously excessive: an incompetent watchdog can do quite a lot of harm under any system.

12. Hearings in the prosecutor's office are not public.

13. In this case, two children were sexually assaulted by an unknown man in a park near Rotterdam. The girl was strangled, the boy seriously injured. A man who passed by called the police. As it turned out, he had a history of child abuse and rapidly became a suspect, despite the fact that the boy's description of the perpetrator did not fit.

find the truth by an excessive reliance on what had been concluded at the previous stage: The police and prosecution believed in the (retracted) confession more than in the DNA evidence, the lab's staff remained silent about their doubts during the trial,[14] the higher courts relied on the lower court's verdict, and once a new suspect confessed, the investigators first questioned that person's mental condition rather than the former verdict.[15]

How shortcomings of this kind can be prevented is not obvious. Rules exist regarding the independence of courts and labs, but the climate of consensual decision-making that prevails in Netherlands at all societal levels (Killias & Huff, 2013) discourages challenging conclusions that have previously been reached. "Tunnel vision" may, therefore, be more typical for Holland's criminal justice system than for other continental countries. For the prevention of wrongful convictions, perhaps the best option would be something like a middle ground between an aggressively accusatorial and an all too consensual inquisitorial system. A further possibility may be to make appeals really work. If the probability that a lower court's decisions will be overturned by a higher court reaches substantial proportions,[16] appeals can work as a strong deterrent to violations of due process rules, convictions despite factual uncertainties, and excessive sentences. Properly practiced, appeals can work as a system of quality control and error management.

## Plea Bargaining and Summary Procedures

It is not unusual for 95 percent or more of criminal cases to be settled through plea bargaining in American courts, i.e., without a contested trial (see Bibas, this volume). In Europe, there exist various forms of simplified procedures that, according to data from Germany, France, and Switzerland (Gilliéron, 2014), reach proportions commensurate with plea bargaining in America. These simplified procedures take different forms in many continental countries, including "penal orders" or "summary procedures." As under the American plea bargaining system, these procedures imply some form of negotiation between the prosecutor and the defendant and his counsel.

In the case of the penal order, the prosecutor issues a decision that includes a verdict and a sentence. This decision becomes final if the defendant does not decide to go to court within a short deadline. Despite these similarities, important differences exist between continental Europe and America on the limits and consequences of "negotiated" pleas. If the defendant refuses the prosecutor's offer (i.e., the penal order) and decides to bring the case to court, he does not risk being sentenced far more harshly if found guilty.[17] Indeed, a prosecutor who calls for a sentence far beyond what he had offered under the form of a penal order risks being held criminally liable for "abuse of power."[18] This makes it much

---

14. The behavior of the scientists is particularly disturbing because they continued using this case during seminars for young magistrates as an illustration on how DNA can exonerate false suspects.

15. Actually, the prosecution service persisted in its denial and the exoneration came about only after a media campaign.

16. In Switzerland, about one decision in four is brought before a higher court, and about one appeal in three is successful (Killias 2008). These rates vary across Europe as much as within the United States (Gilliéron 2014). In some countries (e.g., France and England), higher courts cannot review factual but only legal issues.

17. The dilemma, therefore, is far less dramatic for a continental defendant. In America, a defendant who refuses the prosecutor's "offer" risks a far more severe sentence if found guilty, a practice that does not violate constitutional standards according to *Bordenkircher vs. Hayes*, 434 U.S. 357 (1978).

18. If the prosecutor requires at trial (in court) a far different sentence from what he had previously offered, the suspicion would arise that either one of the two was excessive and arbitrary. Under most European legislation, this is punishable as an offense usually called "abuse of power."

easier for the defendant to take his chance and appeal to the court. At the same time, *Alford* pleas, which are possible under American law,[19] cannot be dealt with through penal orders and other summary procedures since they require the offender to recognize the factual basis of the verdict.[20] Further and most importantly, penal orders and summary procedures are available only for minor offences. If the prosecutor feels that a sanction beyond a certain threshold—varying across Europe between a few months and perhaps one year—is appropriate, he has to bring the case to court. In other words, unlike in America, plea bargaining is not available in Europe for more serious offenses (Gilliéron 2014).

As the National Registry of Exonerations and the Innocence Project have shown, exonerations also occur in cases that had been settled through plea bargaining. The proportions observed so far are probably undercounts because exonerations concern mostly very serious cases that are less often settled out of court. In cases of murder, for example, about one half of cases go to trial (Gilliéron, 2013). In addition, exonerations have occurred mostly in cases of homicide or rape where DNA and other technical evidence are more readily available (Cole & Thompson, 2013). It is plausible, therefore, that wrongful convictions through negotiated pleas are far more frequent in cases involving minor and trivial offenses. This was indeed found in an analysis of all exonerations in Switzerland from 1995 to 2004 (Killias, Gilliéron, & Dongois, 2007). The study reported that exonerations in serious crimes dealt with by courts are rare, a finding that echoes data from France, Germany, and the Netherlands. In these continental countries, the proportion of exonerations remains far below American rates (as presented by Gross, 2013), taking size of population and number of convictions into account (Killias 2008; 2013). This being said, we should not forget Zalman's (2012) warning that all estimates of wrongful convictions are ultimately questionable.

If the difference between American and European rates of exonerations exists as presumed here, it is not easy to find a convincing explanation. One reason might be that America allows plea bargaining even in very serious crimes where continental systems require a full court hearing. Further and despite the fact that the collection of evidence is widely left to the pre-trial investigation, European defendants may have more complete access to the prosecution's file. As explained, the defendant, witnesses, and experts are all heard during pre-trial hearings in the presence of the defendant and his counsel. These hearings probably offer more occasions for the defendant to present his view of the case than under the American system, where plea negotiations take place between prosecutor and defense counsel and often in the absence of the defendant, witnesses, and experts.

# Moving Forward: New Forms of Wrongful Convictions

So far, we have examined causes of and outlined some remedies to wrongful convictions. In describing risks related to witness testimony, forensic evidence, defense lawyers, prosecutors, and courts, it was presumed that these agents always act in good faith and never contribute willingly to convicting innocent defendants. Consequently, the causes

---

19. These are pleas where the defendant pleads guilty while claiming to be innocent. *North Carolina vs. Alford*, 400 U.S. 25 (1970).

20. A penal order against a defendant who claims being innocent would be considered in violation of Article 6 § 2 European Convention of Human Rights (Gilliéron, 2014).

we have identified to this point, for the most part, pertain to defects of systems rather than individuals, and so do the remedies advanced.

There are situations, however, when agents of the criminal justice system operate consistently and intentionally to bring to trial defendants who are factually innocent and have them convicted and sentenced (often to unusually harsh sentences). Such cases have existed throughout history. The trial of Jesus may serve as an example, where a judge (Pontius Pilatus) sentenced to death a man he knew was actually innocent—probably out of concern not to provoke tensions between the Roman Empire (whose representative he was) and local rulers who pushed for Jesus's elimination (Demandt, 2012). There are countless instances throughout history where other rulers have basically done the same. Beethoven's opera Fidelio is a dramatic accusation of such abuses—and an appeal to overcome arbitrary punishment in a future that he hoped would not be too distant.

We know, of course, that such abuses still occur and will have to be confronted in many countries for years to come. Despite this pessimistic outlook, we should insist that, at least in democracies with a commitment to the rule of law, intentional convictions of knowingly innocent people are eliminated. In Eastern Europe and especially in Poland (Plywaczewski et al., 2008) and Hungary (Huff, 2013), many former convicts have had their cases re-opened and have finally been exonerated following sweeping political changes after 1989. Many of these exonerated defendants had been convicted not of political crimes, but of common crimes, such as theft, fraud, sex offences, and the like in an attempt to add defamation to unjustifiable imprisonment. Similar excesses are known to have occurred extensively under the Nazi regime (Friedrich, 1983) and the Stalinist soviet system.[21] More recently, authoritarian regimes in Eastern Europe returned to similar practices by sending political opponents to prison or "work camps" for lengthy periods. The cases of Julia Timoshenko[22] in Ukraine and Michail Chodorkowski[23] in Russia, along with other opponents to those in power in Kiev or Moscow, offer recent illustrations. In one of the leading Asian democracies (Malaysia), the opposition leader (Anwar Ibrahim) has been convicted based on probably fabricated accusations of sodomy.[24]

Less well known are similar occurrences in a few Western European countries. Although the scope and particulars of such abuses may differ, a few recent court decisions in Italy are a source of concern from a Human Rights perspective. Perhaps the most prominent case concerns the recent asbestos trial in Turin where the former industrialist Stephan Schmidheiny[25] was found guilty of provocation of a disaster and sentenced to 18 years in prison. Although this case is still awaiting final settlement at the Italian Supreme Court and, eventually, the European Court of Human Rights, the circumstances of this trial reveal a number of disturbing deviations from due process under the influence of heavy political and media pressure.

---

21. For which Solzhenitsyn's Gulag Archipelago still may be one of the most telling references.

22. She and many other members of her former cabinet as prime-minister have been convicted for corruption and property offenses and sentenced to unusually long prison terms.

23. He, along with his political mate Platon Lebedew, has been convicted for tax, fraud, and other property offenses. Both have recently been pardoned, after 10 years spent in detention in a Siberian camp.

24. In 1998, he was sentenced to six years of imprisonment for an alleged affair of corruption, and to nine years for homosexuality. The trial has been severely condemned, among others by former U.S. Vice President Al Gore, due to the likely use of torture and many other irregularities.

25. The author was a fellow-student of the defendant at the Zurich University Law School in 1968–70. After 40 years without contact, the author has been consulted recently as an expert of wrongful convictions by his defense counsel's team.

The story behind this case is rather simple. Asbestos had been used over many decades in industries of all sorts and particularly in the production of asbestos-cement. At age 28, Schmidheiny came to the top of a family business that owned shares in a large number of asbestos-cement factories in 20 countries. Shortly after taking office, he summoned the managers of the entire group to a conference held in Neuss (Germany), where he advised the audience about the most current knowledge on health risks related to asbestos, and where he urged his managers in all plants to apply the most appropriate safety measures recommended at that time by the International Labor Office (ILO). By then, it was known that asbestos was dangerous, but the generally held assumption was that these risks could effectively be curbed by appropriate safety measures. Later it was discovered that there was no safe use of asbestos and that this substance had to be eliminated entirely from industrial sites. As a result, most Western countries adopted a ban on asbestos in the 1990s.

In the meantime, and due to the unusually long incubation periods of asbestos-related diseases, many people who were exposed to asbestos dust at the work place or in the environment near factories became ill and several died of mesothelioma (a particularly malign cancer). Unlike the practice followed in other countries where victims of such disasters received support through various forms of social security provisions, Italy never made this a priority but instead—as the only Western country doing so—initiated criminal proceedings against former managers of industries that produced or used asbestos. Schmidheiny's trial is the first occasion where a prosecution was extended to a shareholder who never had exercised any formal managerial role in the Italian asbestos companies.

Understandably and predictably, victims of asbestos-related diseases felt abandoned and frustrated. Their anger was rapidly exploited by political figures who transformed the prevailing sentiments into a search for "justice." A wealthy man like Schmidheiny, with an extremely successful career in several industrial sectors and important philanthropic and pro-environmentalist commitments, fit the profile of an ideal scapegoat. By allocating all the blame on that one person, the role of Ministers and public agencies who failed to set appropriate safety standards when it was time to do so, or trade unions and Mayors who were more concerned with the preservation of jobs than workers' health, largely disappeared and escaped public outrage.

Several key players cooperated in this reductionist operation. First, a victims' association soon developed its own institutional agenda and deterred many victims from accepting offers of compensation by Schmidheiny, which would have substantially deprived the association, with its full-time staff, of its "raison d'être." The victims' association was very successful in lobbying efforts directed at Ministries, prosecutors, and the media. The Italian media largely ignored arguments of the defense and instead demonized the defendant up to the point of drawing parallels between him and Hitler.

Another critical actor was the chief prosecutor, who took advantage of this case to portray himself in the image of a national hero. He campaigned for years hand in hand with the victims' association at countless rallies across Italy and abroad, and eventually even became a serious candidate for the post of Minister of Justice. Such activism would be considered absolutely inappropriate in other European countries, where prosecutors and magistrates are expected to maintain a neutral, non-partisan attitude (Gilliéron, 2014). The Schmidheiny trial became further imbalanced through the participation of some 6,000 civil plaintiffs (victims or their relatives), many of whom rallied in front of the courthouse during session days and who, along with their lawyers, attended hearings inside the courtroom while carrying flags and displaying stickers.

The culminating point in this campaign-trial was reached when the presiding judge of the Court of Appeals during his opening speech compared the Neuss meeting of asbestos-industry managers[26] with the infamous Wannsee conference where the Nazi leaders decided to exterminate millions of Jewish and other victims in gas chambers. For a presiding justice to make such prejudicial comments about a case and the defendant at the opening of a trial, when the defendant is to be presumed innocent, represents an unprecedented stain on criminal justice in Europe. This incident, widely applauded by the Italian media and with no intervention by the other justices, illustrates the type of climate in which the trial occurred. All petitions by the defense were rejected, and the defendant was found guilty of having intentionally provoked a disaster and willingly killing thousands of innocent people.[27] The sentence (18 years in prison) was significantly beyond the norm of sentences imposed in European murder cases.[28]

Despite this harsh sentence—considering that Schmidheiny certainly had not "killed" these victims intentionally and that no evidence supported the court's conclusion—it is expected that the chief prosecutor will soon start a new trial with the purpose of once again having Schmidheiny convicted, but now for first-degree murder. Such a practice is consistent with highly political trials in Russia, Ukraine, and Malaysia, where prominent defendants—such as Chorodkowski, Timoshenko, and Ibrahim—commonly face additional charges in order to make sure that they will not be released once the previous sentence has been served.[29] Such subsequent trials, if based on the same facts ("criminal conduct"), are barred under European Human Rights principles.[30]

To arrive at its extreme conclusions, the court engaged in several juridical maneuvers. First, it gave the offense of provocation of a disaster a meaning that is unique in Italy's jurisprudence. In particular, the court's conclusion that the exposure of workers to asbestos will not be time-barred until approximately 2050 is appalling. It severely compromises the defendant's ability to find witnesses, documents, or any other evidence concerning whether he ignored the inefficacy of safety measures at the time the criminal conduct allegedly occurred, i.e., before 1986 (in this case).[31] Further, the Court's conclusion that the defendant failed to produce evidence, after nearly 40 years, that the investments made in the Italian plants—roughly 300 million U.S. dollars in current value in less than 10 years—served to increase safety rather than profitability, violates principles of fair trial

---

26. This uneventful meeting, organized by Schmidheiny in 1976, served to sensitize managers to the health risks of asbestos and motivate them to take appropriate safety measures in their factories.

27. The court assumed that Schmidheiny knew that the safety measures recommended by ILO and other international bodies at that time and applied in his factories were ineffective. It concluded that, therefore, the defendant had willingly killed the victims of asbestos.

28. See the sentences imposed in murder cases across Europe in www.europeansourcebook.org, Tab. 3.2.5.3/4 pp. 257–258. For completed murder and the year 2006, the average sentence across Europe was 97 months and the median 111 months. Highest was Cyprus (162 months).

29. In the case of Timoshenko and Chodorkowski, new charges have been announced for tax fraud, and Ibrahim faced new charges of sodomy in 2008. In 2012 these proceedings ended with an acquittal for Ibrahim, and Chodorkowski has been pardoned. Timoshenko, however, continues to be detained.

30. The ban on double jeopardy is guaranteed by Article 4 of the Seventh Additional Protocol to the European Convention of Human Rights (see notably the European Court's decision in the case *Zolotukhin v. Russia* of 10 February 2009 (N° 14939/03)). Italy has reluctantly implemented rulings of the European Court of Human Rights. An Italian defendant (Dorigo) whose appeal at Strasbourg was successful in 1997 continued being detained in prison up to 2006. A resolution voted (on 2nd October 2006) by the European Parliament was required to bring the Italian courts in line with European Human Rights jurisprudence (see for details the Italian Supreme Court's decision of 4th November 2011, N. 113, E. 6 pp. 10–11).

31. The European Court of Human Rights has implicitly recognized that excessively long time-limits can violate principles of due process (see especially the decision *Stubbings and Others v. The United Kingdom*, 22 October 1996).

(Article 6 § 2 European Convention of Human Rights). The burden of proof lies with the accuser and not the defense.

# Preventing and Remedying Abusive Trials

What can be done to prevent and remedy abusive prosecutions such as the ones that continue today in Russia, Ukraine, and in a few Asian and even some Western European democracies? A common recommendation is to call for more independence of the judiciary. For Russia and other democratic countries with authoritarian regimes, such an approach seems plausible. However, Italy's judiciary probably has more independence than any other justice system in the Western world. Indeed, judges, prosecutors, and all magistrates in Italy are ultimately appointed and supervised by a supreme council of senior justices. However, magistrates are backed and promoted by highly politicized unions that result in judges not being as disinterested in a political agenda as might otherwise be expected. At the same time, the full institutional independence of the judiciary may increase organizational deficiencies of all sorts and at all levels, and prevent reforms to improve the operation of the system because many shareholders will feel little inclination to support such moves.

According to international data collected by the World Economic Forum and based on assessments made by the public in 144 countries, Italy's judicial system has one of the worst records world-wide in terms of unpredictability, delays, and inefficiency in conflict resolution, protection of property rights, and protection of business against undue government interference.[32] According to the European Court of Human Rights' annual report for 2013, Italy also has one of the highest rates of decisions found to be in violation of Human Rights by the Court among Western European nations.[33] The recent proceedings against investors after accidents[34] may further jeopardize economic redress. Perhaps a more openly "political" or "partisan" judiciary, as in the United States and in Switzerland, where judges, magistrates, and most prosecutors are elected by voters or local parliaments, would help curb excessively partisan decisions more effectively. Prosecutors and judges whose political affiliation is publicly known are apt to be careful not to be perceived as unfair or one-sided.

Beyond de-politicization of the judiciary, it should be a priority to create a more balanced media culture. Rules and policies have long existed that require the media to

---

32. World Economic Forum's 2012 report on Global Competitiveness (http://reports.weforum.org/global-competitiveness-report-2012-2013/) places Italy's justice system on the last ranks among 144 countries, behind many Asian and African countries. For example, on efficiency in dispute settlement ("how efficient is the legal framework in your country for private businesses in settling disputes?"), it ranked 139th among 144 nations. In other respects, the results are similarly appalling, e.g., regarding the efficiency in challenging government regulations/actions, or protecting property rights (rank 131). Also poor is the rank with respect to judicial independence (68). See Tables 1.01, 1.06, 1.10 and 1.11 (data for 2011–12). It should be noted that these rankings are based on how survey respondents rate their *own* national criminal justice system — the survey thus measures the degree of dissatisfaction relative to those expectations, and not in relation to other countries.

33. According to the records of the Strasbourg Court, 34 Italian court rulings were quashed in 2013, compared to 3 British, 3 German and 0 Dutch decisions (http://www.echr.coe.int, country profiles). For former years, the trend was similar or worse.

34. The Schmidheiny case is probably the most prominent, but by far not the only case. It has become customary to initiate proceedings against managers and even major shareholders whenever accidents have caused casualties in industries. Luttwack (2013), an American political analyst, ascribes (in an interview with *L'Espresso* (of May 22, 2013)), the drop of foreign investment in Italy's industries to the high risks of criminal prosecution.

make clear that a suspect is not "guilty" before declared so by a court. The European Court of Human Rights has often insisted that unduly prejudicial pre-trial media reports can infringe on fair trial principles to the point that a defendant can no longer be prosecuted.[35] A possible reform could be to create a supervisory body over all media through which any defendant can obtain the ethical condemnation of excessively one-sided media reports on his case. Although symbolic in nature, such a redress might operate as a watchdog against media campaigns that almost certainly will affect magistrates presiding over a trial. As a moral rather than material sanction, it would not conflict with the freedom of the press but would still introduce some ethical barriers against abusive media reports. Finally and in the same vein, political campaigning in front of or—even worse—inside the courtroom should be prohibited.

It remains uncertain whether such measures would prove to be successful. Ultimately, however, there is little doubt that the best guarantee of a fair trial is a political climate that allows the judiciary to function without undue pressure from the public or powerful governmental figures. The best way of achieving such a climate may be to ensure that the judiciary does not escape democratic accountability. After all, despite their different—accusatorial vs. inquisitorial—traditions, both the American and Swiss systems have rather successfully overcome the risks of politicization of the criminal justice system.

At the risk of concluding on a parochial note, a system without any form of direct democratic control over the judiciary risks being more vulnerable to political bias than a system featuring justices who have explicit and transparent political identities and hence are politically accountable. After World War I, all magistrates operating under the so-called Weimar Republic had been elected through strictly "apolitical" bodies and procedures, but were rapidly "turned around" after 1933 when a new dictatorship imposed its "new" and terrible culture. In the end, a de-politicized judiciary may be more vulnerable to undue deviations from Human Rights and fair trial principles than a system in which judges and magistrates have well-known political identities and, as a result, are controllable and more effectively controlled by the public.

# References

Bibas, S. (2014). Plea bargaining's role in wrongful convictions. (This volume.)

Brants, C. (2013). Tunnel vision, belief perseverance and bias confirmation: Only human? In C.R. Huff & M. Killias (Eds.), *Wrongful convictions and miscarriages of justice: Causes and remedies in North American and European criminal justice systems* (pp. 161–192). New York: Routledge.

Demandt, A. (2012). *Pontius Pilatus*. Munich (Germany): C.H. Beck.

Egger, S.A. (1984). Working definition of serial murder and the reduction of linkage blindness. *Journal of Police Science and Administration, 12,* 348–355.

Elsner, E., & Steffen, W. (2005*). Vergewaltigung und sexuelle Nötigung in Bayern (Rape and sexual assault in Bavaria)*. Munich (Germany): Landeskriminalamt.

---

35. Although the European Court of Human Rights has constantly recognized this in principle since 1962, it has never gone so far as to quash a decision on this ground alone (Loucaides, 2007: 209–211). See as an example the decision *Craxi v. Italy* (no. 1), no. 34896/97, 5 December 2002. Despite these reservations, a fair trial requires some balance in the way a defendant is depicted before trial, including by the media (Loucaides, 2007; Michlig, 2013; Warden, 2014).

*European Sourcebook of Crime and Criminal Justice Statistics* (2010). 4th edition. The Hague: Boom Juridische Uitgevers. www.europeansourcebook.org.

Forst, B. (2013). Wrongful convictions in a world of miscarriages of justice. In C.R. Huff & M. Killias (Eds.), *Wrongful convictions and miscarriages of justice: Causes and remedies in North American and European criminal justice systems* (pp. 15–43). New York: Routledge.

Friedrich, J. (1983). *Freispruch für die Nazi-Justiz: Die Urteile gegen NS-Richter seit 1948: Eine Dokumentation (Found not guilty: Trials against Nazi judges since 1948: A documentation)*. Reinbek/Hamburg (Germany): Rowohlt.

Garrett, B.L. (2013). Trial and error. In C.R. Huff & M. Killias (Eds.), *Wrongful convictions and miscarriages of justice: Causes and remedies in North American and European criminal justice systems* (pp. 77–90). New York: Routledge.

Gilliéron, G. (2013). The risks of summary proceedings, plea bargains and penal orders in producing wrongful convictions in the U.S. and Europe. In C.R. Huff & M. Killias (Eds.), *Wrongful convictions and miscarriages of justice: Causes and remedies in North American and European criminal justice systems* (pp. 237–258). New York: Routledge.

Gilliéron, G. (2014). *Public prosecutors in the United States and Europe: A comparative analysis with special focus on Switzerland, France and Germany*. New York: Springer.

Gross, S. (2013). How many false convictions are there? How many exonerations are there? In C.R. Huff & M. Killias (Eds.), *Wrongful convictions and miscarriages of justice. Causes and remedies in North American and European criminal justice systems* (pp. 45–59). New York: Routledge.

Huff, C.R. (2013). Wrongful convictions, miscarriages of justice and political repression: Challenges for transitional justice. In C.R. Huff & M. Killias (Eds.), *Wrongful convictions and miscarriages of justice: Causes and remedies in North American and European criminal justice systems* (pp. 357–369). New York: Routledge.

Kessler, I. (2008). A comparative analysis of prosecution in Germany and the United Kingdom: Searching for truth or getting a conviction? In C.R. Huff & M. Killias (Eds.), *Wrongful convictions: Miscarriages of justice in international perspective* (pp. 213–247). Philadelphia, PA: Temple University Press.

Killias, M. (2008). Wrongful convictions in Switzerland: The experience of a continental law country. In C.R. Huff & M. Killias (Eds.), *Wrongful convictions: Miscarriages of justice in international perspective* (pp. 139–155). Philadelphia, PA: Temple University Press.

Killias, M., Gilliéron, G., & Dongois, N. (2007). A survey of exonerations in Switzerland over ten years: Report to the Swiss National Science Foundation. Lausanne and Zurich: Universities of Lausanne and Zurich.

Killias, M., & Huff, C.R. (2013). Wrongful convictions under a consensual criminal justice system. In C. Kelk, F. Koenradt, & D. Siegel (Eds.), *Veelzijdige gedachten (Liber amicorum prof. dr. C. Brants)* (pp. 407–415). Den Haag: Boom Lemma.

Köppel, H.L. (2008). *Die affäre Calas (The Calas case)*. Berlin: Aufbau-TB-Verlag.

Loucaides, L.G. (2007). *The European Convention on Human Rights: Collected essays*. Leiden (The Netherlands): Martinus Nijhoff.

Meissner, C. A., Redlich, A. D., Bhatt, S., & Brandon, S. (2012). Interview and interrogation methods and their effects on true and false confessions. www.campbellcollaboration.org.

Michlig, M. (2013). *Öffentlichkeitskommunikation der Strafbehörden unter dem Aspekt der Amtsgeheimnisverletzung (Art. 320 StGB)*. Zurich (Switzerland): Schulthess.

Nogrady A. (2011). Zustände wie im Alten Rom?!—Römisches und heutiges Strafrecht im Vergleich (Situations as in antique Rome?!—Roman and modern criminal law compared), in: Romina Schiavone (Ed.), *Gefährliches Pflaster—Kriminalität im*

*Römischen Reich* (Dangerous streets — crime under the Roman Empire), Mainz (Germany): von Zabern.

Odinot, G., Memon, A., La Rooy, D., & Millen, A. (2013) Are two interviews better than one? Eyewitness memory across repeated cognitive interviews. *PLoS ONE, 8(10):* e76305.

Odinot, G., Wolters, G., & van Giezen, A. (2012). Repeated suggestive questioning, consistency and the accuracy-confidence relation in eyewitness event memory. *Psychology, Crime and Law, 19,* 629–642.

Petro, J., & Petro, N. (2013). The prosecutor and wrongful convictions: Misplaced priorities, misconduct, immunities and remedies. In C.R. Huff & M. Killias (Eds.), *Wrongful convictions and miscarriages of justice: Causes and remedies in North American and European criminal justice systems* (pp. 91–109). New York: Routledge.

Pizzi, W. T. (1999). *Trials without truth.* New York: New York University Press.

Plywaczewski, E., Gorski, A., & Sakowicz, A. (2008). Wrongful convictions in Poland: From the communist era to the Rechtsstaat experience. In C.R. Huff & M. Killias (Eds.), *Wrongful Conviction: International perspectives on miscarriages of justice* (pp. 273–283). Philadelphia, PA: Temple University Press.

Ribaux, O., & Margot, P.A. (2008). La trace matérielle, vecteur d'information au service du renseignement (material traces as a vector of information during investigations). In M. Cusson, B. Dupont, & F. Lemieux (Eds.). *Traité de sécurité intérieure.* Lausanne: Presses polytechniques et universitaires romandes.

Schiffer, B. (2009). The relationship between forensic science and judicial error: A study covering error sources, bias and remedies. University of Lausanne: PhD dissertation.

Seelye, K.Q. & Bidgood, J. (2013). Prison for a state chemist who faked drug evidence. *New York Times* A9 (Nov. 23).

Slobogin, C. (2003). An empirically based comparison of American and European regulatory approaches to police investigation. In P.J. van Koppen & S.D. Penrod (Eds.), *Adversarial versus inquisitorial justice: Psychological perspectives on criminal justice systems* (pp. 27–54). New York: Kluwer Academic.

Stuntz, W.J. (2011). *The collapse of American criminal justice.* Cambridge, MA: Harvard University Press.

Vrij, A. (2003). We will protect your wife and child, but only if you confess: Police interrogations in England and the Netherlands. In P.J. van Koppen & S.D. Penrod (Eds.), *Adversarial versus inquisitorial justice: Psychological perspectives on criminal justice systems* (pp. 55–79). New York: Kluwer Academic.

Vuille, J., Biedermann, A., & Taroni, F. (2013). The importance of having a logical framework for expert conclusions in forensic DNA profiling: Illustrations from the Amanda Knox case. In C.R. Huff & M. Killias (Eds.), *Wrongful convictions and miscarriages of justice: Causes and remedies in North American and European criminal justice systems.* New York: Routledge.

Warden, R. (2014). The role of the media and public opinion on innocence reform: Past and future. In M. Zalman & J. Carrano (Eds.), *Wrongful conviction and criminal justice reform: Making justice* (pp. 39–55). New York: Routledge.

World Economic Forum (2012). *The global competitiveness report 2012–2013.* Geneva (Switzerland): WEF.

Zalman, M. (2012). Qualitatively estimating the incidence of wrongful convictions. *Criminal Law Bulletin, 48,* 221–277.

# Chapter Twenty

# Wrongful Convictions: Reflections on Moving Forward

Allison D. Redlich, *University at Albany, State University of New York*

James R. Acker, *University at Albany, State University of New York*

Robert J. Norris, *University at Albany, State University of New York*

Catherine L. Bonventre, *University at Albany, State University of New York*

In 1923, Judge Learned Hand referred to instances of actually innocent persons being convicted as an "unreal dream." Around the same time, a district attorney in Massachusetts is quoted as saying, "Innocent men are never convicted. Don't worry about it, it never happens in the world. It is a physical impossibility" (Borchard, 1932; p, v). Fast forward some fifty years; then-Attorney General Edwin Meese states, "The thing is you don't have many suspects who are innocent of a crime. That's contradictory. If a person is innocent of a crime, then he is not a suspect" (as quoted in Scheck, Neufeld, & Dwyer, 2003, p. xiii). And, as recently as 2006, we see Supreme Court Justice Antonin Scalia opining that our criminal justice system is successful in convicting the "right" person 99.973 percent of the time (*Kansas v. Marsh*, 2006).

Scholars of wrongful convictions are quite familiar with the above quotes. As we noted in the introductory chapter by James Acker and colleagues, although most scholars have turned their attention away from how many individuals are wrongly convicted to gaining further insights about how and why these events occur, uncertainties about the prevalence of wrongful convictions continue to prevail. Unresolved questions about the incidence of wrongful convictions arguably impede the development of new policies and legislation designed to prevent them from happening and remedying them after they are discovered (see King's discussion of skepticism as a barrier to reform, this volume). These questions surrounding the prevalence of wrongful convictions remain despite the fact that the number of exonerations has increased dramatically over a 20-year period (see Figure 3, Baumgartner, Westervelt, & Cook, this volume).

To be sure, there is an Innocence Movement afoot (Zalman, 2011), which has served to foster change in state policies, create new post-conviction review panels (Innocence Commissions and prosecutorial conviction integrity units), and help exonerate hundreds of factually innocent individuals. However, the fact remains that the majority of localities and states have failed to adopt recommended innocence-related reforms in areas including eyewitness identification procedures, electronic recording of interrogations, guarding against faulty forensic evidence, and making use of false testimony from informants (Norris, Bonventre, Redlich, & Acker, 2010/2011).

Our goal in this volume was to "step back" in order to "move forward" in regards to theory, research, and policies surrounding miscarriages of justice. More specifically, our ambition was to take a step back from the canonical list (or the "catalog of errors," Lofquist, this volume) of wrongful conviction contributing factors (i.e., eyewitness misidentification, false confessions, forensic science errors, governmental misconduct, ineffective assistance of counsel, and informants) that in many ways has simultaneously served to stimulate and stymie advancements in our knowledge. We invited scholars from a range of disciplines (psychology, sociology, criminology/criminal justice, journalism, law, political science) to take a macro look at the research in their respective fields and use their chapters to "examine the underlying individual, institutional, systemic, and social or structural conditions that are likely to precipitate miscarriages of justice and also help explain impediments to preventing, detecting, and correcting them" (Acker et al., this volume). We also asked them to apply the lessons learned from this exercise of "stepping back" to help us "move forward" to gain a better understanding of the fundamental factors that help shape criminal justice systems and/or the behavior of criminal justice actors as relevant to the production (or detection/correction) of wrongful convictions.

In this chapter, we attempt to synthesize what authors learned through this process of stepping back and moving forward. We aim to identify common themes across chapters and discuss their implications for further developing research, scholarship, and policies concerning miscarriages of justice.

# Common Themes: Stepping Back

Despite the differing disciplinary and topical foci, several shared themes emerged when authors were asked to step back. We focus on three: stereotyping and cognitive biases/errors; structural impediments and bad policy; and the lessons of history.

## Stereotypes and Cognitive Biases/Errors

One common theme that emerged concerns stereotypes and other forms of cognitive errors. In its simplest form, a stereotype is a belief associated with a group of people. One problem associated with stereotypes arises when this belief is applied to all members of the group indiscriminately. Stereotyping is believed to be an unconscious process. Humans have a natural tendency towards social categorization (the process of placing people into groups by gender, race, social class, etc.), which then leads people to magnify the differences between members in their own group and out-group members.

In Chapter 4, Cynthia Najdowski explains the potential pernicious influence of racial stereotypes on police behavior. More specifically, she explains how common (though often erroneous) stereotypes of African American men as "criminals" influence police behavior. In turn, African American men who are under suspicion experience stereotype threat. Stereotype threat is the notion that when we perceive we are being negatively stereotyped, we react in predictable ways, particularly by demonstrating anxiety (see generally, Steele, 2010). As Najdowski elaborates, in the police interrogation situation, the anxiety experienced by wrongly targeted African American suspects could be misconstrued as evidencing guilt, setting in motion a chain of events that culminates in a false confession and a wrongful conviction (Najdowski, 2011).

As noted in several chapters, African Americans and other minorities are overrepresented among identified wrongful convictions. Indeed, in Chapter 2, William Lofquist describes the *paradigmatic* (and known) wrongful conviction as involving an African American male, charged with a capital offense or rape, who is represented by court-appointed counsel, convicted at trial, and exonerated more than a decade later. However, Lofquist surmises that the *modal* wrongful (but unknown) conviction also involves an African American male, but one charged with a felony property or drug offense who pleads guilty to avoid sitting in jail for a long time. In essence, one way to interpret Lofquist's message is that the "stereotype" of the paradigmatic wrongful conviction case leads the study of wrongful convictions to "be caught in an empirical trap." He encourages readers and researchers to "step out of the shadows" of this known but clearly incomplete paradigm (see also Bonventre, Norris, & West, this volume).

Chapter 11, by Steven Drizin, Laura Nirider, and Joshua Tepfer, also concentrates on the role of stereotypes in helping generate wrongful convictions. The authors focus on two teenage tropes popular in the 1980s and 1990s and how those tropes ultimately were instrumental in misleading the police. The first concerns the black urban teenage "super-predator," who Drizin and colleagues describe as "a remorseless, amoral, animalistic black youth who engages in violent crime sprees for the fun of it." The second trope is the angry white suburban loner, "an isolated, bullied, misanthropic white youth who exacts violent revenge on his peers." In painting pictures of these two typecast teens, the authors provide several examples of cases involving juveniles and false confessions (e.g., the Dixmoor Five, Michael Crowe) in which these tropes were first used to target the suspect and then to script the confession. For example, Michael Crowe (the angry white suburban trope) was suspected of murdering his sister in part because he liked role-playing video games (which the police perceived as violent); later, this penchant for video games was used to induce a confession (ultimately proven false) whereby Michael was the evil "Odin," a character in several video games (see Drizin et al., this volume). (This trope was also used to induce a false confession from Joshua Treadway, Michael's friend.) Drizin and his colleagues conclude that narrative contamination, or the "scripting of an entire false story, one that often relies on cultural stereotypes about why a certain type of person commits crimes," can be equally as damaging as fact contamination (Garrett, 2011).

Although the capricious application of stereotypes is its own type of cognitive error, another theme to emerge across chapters relates to more general cognitive biases. This theme perhaps is most apparent in Chapter 3, authored by Barbara O'Brien and Keith Findley. These authors step back and review psychological research on the limits of cognition and subsequent decision-making. They identify several naturally occurring biases, ones from which criminal justice decision-makers are not immune. These biases include confirmation bias (the tendency to seek out, remember, and interpret information that is consistent with a preformed belief), belief perseverance (the tendency to stick to beliefs even when confronted with contrary evidence), and cognitive dissonance (the tendency to change one's beliefs to alleviate discomfort that occurs when behavior is inconsistent with them) (see O'Brien & Findley, this volume, for more descriptions of cognitive biases). O'Brien and Findley move forward by demonstrating how such cognitive biases (as well as stereotypes and racial bias) can undermine the criminal process at all points along the continuum. Additionally, they introduce another set of biases, including groupthink, diffusion of responsibility, and belief in a just world, to help explain the phenomenon of wrongful convictions.

Also highlighting the frailties of the human mind, if you will, is Chapter 10, by Stephanos Bibas, on guilty pleas (see also, King discussing why judges cannot readily recognize errors, and Gershman in regard to prosecutors, this volume). Bibas describes the "plea bargaining mindset," one produced by conditioning that presumes guilt and equates a defendant's willingness to plead guilty with factual guilt. He also discusses how police self-interest in arresting people and providing prosecutors with sufficient evidence for conviction can lead to tunnel vision (confirmation bias as well as overconfidence). In short, Bibas points out how incentives to investigate further are all but absent, especially since the police are aware of the heavy reliance on, and prevalence of, guilty pleas. Prosecutors, who can suffer from "post-charge tunnel vision," engage in their own cognitive missteps that lead to innocence blindness and the "inevitability bias" (see also O'Brien & Findley, this volume when discussing hindsight and outcome biases). And in Chapter 19, Martin Killias describes how "paper trials," which are popular in Europe, readily lend themselves to "tunnel vision" and confirmation bias. (Paper trials are trials in which judges make decisions almost exclusively from the review of documents.)

Finally, in Chapter 9, Neil Vidmar and James Coleman highlight the biases of experts in the adversarial system. They cite recent events in North Carolina in which several cases were overturned because of the reported pro-prosecution biases of agents in the State Bureau of Investigation crime laboratory, an agency which is supposed to be independent but has close ties to law enforcement. Vidmar and Coleman also discuss a recent experiment (Murrie, Bocaccini, Guarnera, & Rufino, 2013) in which forensic psychologists and psychiatrists (i.e., potential expert witnesses) were given four cases to review; half were informed they were working for the defense and the other half were informed they were working for the prosecution. Findings indicated that those who believed they were working for the defense produced opinions more favorable to the defense, with the converse true for those who believed they were working for the prosecution (akin to commitment bias). Vidmar and Coleman point out how these biases can play out in civilian witness testimony and informants, as well.

Overall, understanding how and when people stereotype and make other errors of cognition can be instructive to understanding how and when people become wrongly targeted and convicted. The modern usage of the term "stereotype" reportedly was first employed by Walter Lippmann in 1922 in his book, *Public Opinion*. Lippmann states, "For the most part we do not first see, and then define, we define first and then see. In the great blooming, buzzing confusion of the outer world we pick out what our culture has already defined for us, and we tend to perceive that which we have picked out in the form stereotyped for us by our culture" (p. 55). In many ways, the authors in this volume have demonstrated how our natural tendency to define first and see later can lead to the wrongful arrest, incarceration, and conviction of innocent individuals.

## Structural Impediments and Bad Policy

The criminal justice system is of course a complex machine with many moving and intricate parts (Bibas, 2012). Thus, it is not surprising that one of the primary themes to emerge across chapters is that wrongful convictions are generated in part by a flawed system. Below we focus on the flaws, while many and varied, which take shape in the form of structural impediments and bad policy.

At a macro-level are the national and state policies that have direct and indirect consequences for criminal justice systems. For example, in Chapter 6, Hannah Laqueur, Stephen Rushin, and Jonathan Simon explain how declaring wars on drugs and crime, which began some 45 years ago and continues to the present day, has affected police behaviors (leading to misconduct and corruption), increased arrests and incentives to arrest (or clear cases), and related policies. Because we are engaged in a war, Laqueur et al. argue, the significance of any individual's guilt is minimized in the face of other attributes of the enemy (i.e., race, and territory). Interestingly, Lofquist (this volume) recommends removing the focus from the individual actor to the act itself as a measure to help prevent wrongful convictions. Lofquist also points to the "Southern Strategy" (as well as mass imprisonment, the plea mill, and the wars on crime and drugs) as contributing to the arrest and conviction of the innocent. He defines the "Southern Strategy" as the "manipulat[ion of] racial animus among previously core Democratic constituencies, particularly Southern white males, through racialized depictions of the criminal, the welfare dependent, and the beneficiaries of governmental support, [which] provided the essential foundation for delegitimizing and defunding social welfare programs and directing those resources toward criminal justice." In turn, this strategy has served to define an era of punitiveness, influence interpretations of law (e.g., *McCleskey v. Kemp*, 1987), expand police power and discretion, and create inequities in our adversarial system.

At a meso-level are many of the laws and practices that guide our criminal justice system. In some ways, the age-old comparison first conceptualized by Roscoe Pound in 1910 between the "law on the books" and the "law in action" comes to mind. More specifically, some chapters discuss how current laws may help generate wrongful convictions or impede righting the wrongs experienced by convicted innocent persons. Other chapters focus on problems arising from how laws or policies are carried out. For instance, regarding the "law on the books," Nancy King in Chapter 13 addresses how current judicial remedies (appeals and postconviction review) tend not to provide relief to the factually innocent because they were never intended to do so. Further, harmless error rules, and the ingrained notions of finality and *stare decisis*—which are not flawed *per se*—can obfuscate truth-seeking. In essence, these mechanisms arguably are working as they should. Actual innocence is not yet recognized as a valid constitutional claim in many jurisdictions. Like the common plaint that "the law has not caught up with science," perhaps a fitting analogy is that the "law has not caught up with the problem of actual innocence." Similarly, in Chapter 12, Barry Feld reviews the developmental and legal capabilities of juveniles across the criminal justice continuum. Here we can see how the law has not always kept pace with the neuro- and social science developments concerning juveniles, in that many legal rules and policies do not distinguish between juveniles and adults (although Feld does recognize recent U.S. Supreme Court decisions [e.g., *Roper v. Simmons*, *Miller v. Alabama*, *J.D.B. v. North Carolina*] that take into account juveniles' reduced levels of culpability and other relevant developmental differences). The failure to recognize important differences between juveniles and adults and provide juveniles with correspondingly different legal protections can increase the risk of wrongful conviction and adjudication of young persons.

Finally, in Chapter 8, Ellen Yaroshefsky and Laura Schaefer review how the standards set by the Supreme Court in *Gideon v. Wainwright* (1963) and *Strickland v. Washington* (1984) do little to prevent or remedy wrongful convictions. *Strickland*, which concerns ineffective assistance of counsel, was never meant to improve the quality of defense counsel, but rather to ensure the fundamental fairness of trials (thus inquiring whether the defendant suffered prejudice as the result of the lawyer's substandard performance; see Yaroshefsky & Schaefer, this volume). In his dissent in the *Strickland* decision, Justice Marshall notes, "The difficulties of estimating prejudice after the fact are exacerbated by the possibility that evidence of injury to the defendant may be missing from the record precisely because of the incompetence of defense counsel" (p. 466). In other words, as pointed out by Yaroshefsky and Schaefer, incompetence resulting from the omissions of defense counsel will not be reflected in the record and available for review by the judges who must rule on ineffective assistance of counsel claims. Thus, the *Strickland* standard is ill-equipped to recognize, and has contributed to the failure to identify wrongful convictions that owe in part or wholly to ineffective assistance of counsel (see also, Garrett, 2011).

Regarding the "law in action," several chapters highlight the deficiencies in our public defender system. *Gideon*, which requires that all defendants in serious criminal cases have legal representation, even if they are too poor to hire an attorney, is a good example.

Many events marking *Gideon's* 50th anniversary in 2013 concluded that the ruling's essential "promise" has not been met. As noted by Yaroshefsky and Schaefer (as well as by Bibas, Feld, and Lofquist, this volume), the indigent defense system is in a "state of perpetual crisis" and representation is "shockingly inadequate." "*Gideon's* promise," a common phrase,[1] can be interpreted in different ways. One interpretation is to view the promise as a *guarantee* to provide all defendants with representation. Another interpretation relies on promise as *potential*, as in the U.S. criminal justice system meeting its potential to ensure equality and justice under the law for all. As more than one chapter in this volume laments, *Gideon's* promise has gone unmet under both interpretations of the word. Because of *Gideon's* unmet promise, the chances that innocent defendants will secure adequate defense representation are greatly diminished.

The "plea mill" is another example of how the law in action can contribute to miscarriages of justice. Although the United States relies on an adversarial system of justice (see Vidmar & Coleman, this volume), the high prevalence of guilty pleas (producing roughly 95% of convictions in many jurisdictions) all but negates the design of this two-sided system. It is beyond dispute that innocent people plead guilty. To date, the National Registry of Exonerations has identified 129 instances of wrongful convictions resulting from guilty pleas since 1989, although, of course, the very nature of plea bargaining makes erroneous convictions extremely difficult to uncover (see Redlich, 2010). As stated by Bibas (this volume), "Plea bargaining lets harried police, prosecutors, defense counsel, and judges jump to conclusions, putting efficiency ahead of accuracy." Most of the essential safeguards to protect innocent defendants (whether used properly or not) apply to trials, not guilty pleas. For example, as noted by Bibas, and Yaroshefsky and Schaefer, discovery rules typically do not require prosecutors to provide exculpatory evidence to the defense in cases resolved through guilty pleas.

In sum, as the above discussion suggests, several authors have illuminated how laws and policies enacted years ago are having unanticipated consequences for the innocent caught up in the web of our justice system. By stepping back, we are able to see such patterns and costs, and must confront how the law on the books and the law in action do not always provide sufficient safeguards for the innocent.

## Lest History Repeat Itself

Two hundred years ago, Lord Byron stated, "History, with all her volumes vast, hath one page." This sentiment, and the related one that history will repeat itself if we do not learn the lessons she teaches us, is another common theme running throughout the volume, albeit a less dominant and more implicit one. Several authors made note of significant past actions and inactions relating to wrongful convictions. For example, Killias (this volume) reminds us of the trial of Jesus in which Pontius Pilot sentenced him to death despite knowledge of his innocence.

Perhaps the importance of history is most apparent in Chapter 5, by Martin Yant. Yant takes us on a journey over the course of two hundred years, demonstrating the media's "muddled message," or how journalists and the media assisted in perpetrating injustices while also helping to uncover them. Yant juxtaposes this message in time and space. For

---

1. For example, the Southern Public Defender Training Center is now called Gideon's Promise, https://gideonspromise.org/.

example, he describes two cases arising in the 1940s in Chicago. One case involves William Heirens, the so-called "lipstick killer," who was 17 years old and who just recently died in prison (in 2012). At the time, the *Chicago Tribune* in its pursuit to catch the killer printed a false story claiming that Heirens had confessed. The newspaper also ran the prejudicial headline, "How Heirens Slew 3." Years later, many questions remain about Heiren's actual guilt. The other case concerns Joseph Majczek and Theodore Marcinkiewicz, two persons wrongly convicted of murdering a police officer. The *Chicago Times* took up their cause in the 1940s, eventually leading to their exonerations and the making of a Hollywood movie, *Call Northside 777*. Moving forward, Yant focuses on the role of DNA and the Internet in the modern age of wrongful convictions. Unfortunately, important lessons from yesterday appear not to have been carried forward to today. Specifically, Yant describes how the Internet has played a role in assembling grassroots efforts to push through exonerations (such as the case of Clarence Elkins) but also in feeding the flames of injustice (such as in the case of Amanda Knox).

Finally, Yant notes that American journalists were slower than those in Europe to get on the "exoneration bandwagon," and some evidence suggests that they are already getting off of it. That is, Scheck et al. (2003) relay a story about the impending exoneration of Dennis Fritz, in which Fritz's lawyer had called a newsmagazine show (which had been collecting footage about Fritz for almost a year) to tell them that Fritz was soon to be released. After letting the attorney know that they were going to take a pass on the story, the executive states, "[M]y bosses think there are too many of these stories going around … He's just another one of those innocent guys getting out" (p. xvi). In other words, what once was newsworthy and notable—an innocent person imprisoned for years being exonerated—has become so commonplace that it no longer merits media attention. Yant calls for more "preventative journalism," that is, proactive efforts to investigate the claims of potentially innocent persons and to improve coverage of the criminal justice system, rather than "after-the-conviction, too-late journalism," such as is evidenced in the Fritz example, above.

The theme of history also appears in chapters reflecting on the scholarship of wrongful conviction. Of late, some have critiqued this scholarship, arguing that it is often atheoretical and stagnant, relying on "exoneration narratives" (stories about individual cases), with "the same wheel [ ] reinvented each time, more or less" (Leo, 2005, p. 206; see also Norris & Bonventre, 2013). Catherine Bonventre, Robert Norris, and Emily West (Chapter 18) review these critiques, and also identify other methodological gaps and avenues for future research. To be sure, the implicit premise of this volume is that those who study wrongful convictions need to step back and examine disciplinary perspectives and issues that (in our estimation) have not been sufficiently examined to date. These critiques, however, do not imply that history and historical cases have nothing to teach us in the present. Indeed, in Chapter 17, Marvin Zalman recommends focusing more on individual cases as a strategy for *advancing* wrongful conviction theory. That is, he urges innocence "re-detectives" (such as those working at Innocence Projects) to ideographically examine cases using abductive reasoning (especially in cases lacking DNA exculpatory evidence). Although agreeing that these exoneration narratives often lack theoretical import, Zalman also notes that "[individual] narratives might be useful for their data about trial attorney behaviors and the evidentiary posture of cases, to support or qualify a grounded theory of functional due process as a factor in wrongful conviction causation."

In sum, the history of wrongful convictions and the scholarship surrounding them, in many ways, has just begun. We have much to learn from the thousands of cases that have been unearthed as well as from the untold numbers yet to come. We also have much to learn by broadening our scope beyond the known proximate causes. The next section addresses ways to move the scholarship and redress of wrongful convictions forward.

# Common Themes: Moving Forward

Moving forward takes shape in two forms in this volume. Some authors chose to move forward by applying the lessons learned from stepping back to gain new insights about the production of wrongful convictions. Others chose to move forward by proposing reforms to help prevent, detect, or address the aftermath of wrongful convictions.

## Applying Lessons

What did we learn from stepping back about the production of wrongful convictions? Hopefully, we learned so much that it cannot be succinctly reviewed here (the entire volume must be read!). In this section, we thus provide examples of what was learned through the process of stepping back.

Above, we identified the common thread in many chapters about the overrepresentation of African American men among the wrongly convicted. In her chapter, Najdowski offers one causal chain to explain this overrepresentation: Step 1: African American men are stereotyped as criminals; Step 2: African American men experience stereotype threat when interacting with the police, and as a result, become anxious and aroused; Step 3: Police mistake the anxiety and arousal (produced by stereotype threat, and innocence) as indicators of guilt; Step 4: Police proceed with guilt-presumptive interrogation of the misidentified innocent man; Step 5: Misidentified innocent man falsely confesses; Step 6: False confessor proceeds to trial and is wrongly convicted. Thus, by stepping back and understanding the social psychology of stereotype threat and race-related attitudes, we can identify the proximate cause of mistaken deception detection and false confession, as well as the ultimate (or distal) cause of the wrongful conviction. In a similar chain of events, Drizin and colleagues walk us through how stereotyped beliefs about juvenile offenders work their way into contaminated (false) confession narratives.

What can be done about these types of human cognition errors that tend to be ingrained and unconscious? Bibas suggests forcing decision-makers to entertain alternative hypotheses, i.e., that the defendant is innocent, or consider making more macro-level changes (such as moving from an adversarial to an inquisitorial system; but see Vidmar & Coleman, and Killias, this volume, for the pros and cons of both systems). O'Brien and Findley call for more experts in the courtroom to educate judges and jurors about these phenomena (see below for a more detailed discussion). Similarly, Najdowski suggests efforts towards creating more respectful interactions between police and African American men, thus enhancing feelings of police legitimacy and procedural justice.

Another example of what can be learned by stepping back is offered in the chapter by Laqueur and colleagues. Stemming from the wars on drugs and violent crime (homicide), heightened accountability, and concomitant intense pressures to respond have helped produce police misconduct. Again, it is possible to impose a step-by-step process to understand how wrongful convictions can result. Step 1: War on drugs; Step 2: Increased pressure to arrest and be "productive," as well as organizational and institutional incentives to arrest; Step 3: Subsequent influence on law enforcement practices (e.g., "buys and busts," wiretaps), leading to more indiscriminate policing and more arrests; Step 4: Drug law enforcement corruption (bribes, stealing drugs and money) and misconduct (illegal searches and seizures, entrapment, false testimony); Step 5: Wrongful conviction of factually and legally innocent individuals. A befitting example of this chain of events is what happened in Tulia, Texas, in which a Byrne-funded (see Laqueur et al, this volume) narcotics police officer (who had been awarded "Lawman of the Year" by the Texas Department of Public Safety) appeared to have falsely accused and arrested 43 local citizens. Thirty-eight of the arrestees eventually were convicted but after questions arose, coupled with a lack of evidence and documentations of innocence (e.g., being out of the state at the alleged time of the drug sale), 35 of them were pardoned by Governor Perry. A PBS website dedicated to the Tulia scandal[2] states that the events "show how America's war on drugs and its over-zealous law enforcement, combined with racial divisions, have exposed deep-seated animosities and even starker injustices."

Relevant to the Tulia scandal is the problem of false guilty pleas. Twenty-seven of the Tulia defendants pleaded guilty to crimes they did not commit, in large part because they watched seven defendants before them be convicted at trial and receive prison sentences ranging from 12 to 99 years. Bibas (this volume) reviews how the mindset, pressures, and temptations ingrained within our justice system can generate false guilty pleas. He explains how there tends to be an automatic assumption of guilt (Step 1); how police, prosecutors, defenders, and judges are all incentivized to shepherd guilty pleas through the system quickly and with little investigation (Step 2); how the structural constraints within criminal justice systems (e.g., discovery, plea, and sentencing rules, overly generous bargains) (Step 3); and psychological errors in thinking (Step 4) conspire to create the perfect storm for innocents to plead guilty. Whereas some believe that the innocent benefit from the guilty plea option (Bowers, 2008), criminal justice systems should not allow, nor encourage, the factually innocent to accept guilt.

The authors in this volume have highlighted the amount and depth of information that can be gleaned from stepping back: stepping back to obtain a birds-eye view in the larger disciplinary perspective; stepping back to assess the impact of local, state, and federal policies; and stepping back to determine the gaps in our knowledge. In the next section, we continue to move forward and identify themes that center on possible reforms.

# Reforming the System

The above section asked, "What did we learn from stepping back?" In this section, we ask, "How can the lessons learned be applied to reduce the number of wrongful convictions?" Several authors have suggested ways to change the system in order to prevent wrongful convictions, detect them, or address them and their consequences post-exoneration. Some of the suggested reforms are not novel; they have been introduced previously. However, the point remains that these reforms, most of which simply make good sense, have yet to be widely implemented despite repeated calls for them.

Not surprisingly, several authors call for more training and education. One suggestion is for broader training in law schools to help equip prospective defense attorneys to provide more skilled representation. Yaroshefsky and Schaefer argue that most defense attorneys (especially overworked and under-resourced public defenders) are ill-equipped, for example, to recognize junk science and improper forensic testimony. Gershman calls for enhanced training of prosecutors and police to ensure that best practices are in place.

---

2. http://www.pbs.org/independentlens/tuliatexas/film.html.

And O'Brien and Findley encourage increased use of experts in the courtroom to educate judges and jurors (but see above discussion on expert bias by Vidmar and Coleman).

Gershman and Bibas discuss how prosecutors (and others) are primed to believe uncritically that defendants are guilty—an area that may be particularly ripe for education. All legal actors must understand that investigations can go awry, that innocent persons are sometimes wrongly targeted, and that no one is immune to the numerous biases so thoroughly reviewed by O'Brien and Findley. The myths introduced by Frank Baumgartner, Saundra Westervelt, and Kimberly Cook in Chapter 15 offer examples of how educational campaigns could help to debunk common misperceptions. Specifically, they discuss the myths that exonerees are fully compensated, that exonerees are actually guilty (and got off on a technicality), and that exonerees are complicit victims in the process that led to their wrongful conviction. Addressing these and other mythologies within the legal system and in the public arena can help to overcome some of the barriers faced by wrongly convicted persons as they fight to get their cases overturned and reenter society.

Another way to educate is via research and scholarship. Although not research *per se*, one appealing idea was offered in Chapter 7 by Bennett Gershman. Specifically, Gershman encourages prosecutors' offices to collect data; that is, to create databases with the ability to track *Brady* and *Giglio* information on informants, police witnesses, experts, and so on. If feasible (e.g., if identifying information could be removed), these databases could have a dual purpose for researchers, allowing much more to be analyzed about informants, compliance with *Brady* requirements, and in other areas. Bonventre et al. (this volume) emphasize the need to build bridges between research and practice and for more multi-disciplinary collaborations. Noting "the sprawling field of wrongful convictions," Zalman (this volume) identifies a non-exhaustive list of people interested in and working on wrongful convictions: "lawyers, cognitive and social psychologists, other social scientists, legal scholars, government personnel, journalists, documentarians, freelance writers, and citizen-activists" (see also King, this volume). Assembling such a variety of individuals with different backgrounds, disciplinary approaches, and purposes is not an easy task, but an important one nonetheless.

A second theme surrounding reforms concerns implementing new safeguards or simply ensuring that those already in place are effectual. For example, after reviewing the developmental capabilities of juveniles in the legal system, Feld recommends that the courts adopt a functional line separating 15 year-olds and younger juveniles from older defendants, and provide these younger individuals with greater safeguards. Several authors call for a more open and transparent justice system, particularly through more expansive discovery rules. Several also call for a restructuring our nation's indigent defense system, which by most (if not all) accounts is broken.

At a broader level, Vidmar and Coleman point out that too much faith is invested in the adversarial system (see also Bibas, this volume). The hundreds of known wrongful convictions, most resulting from cases that went to trial, demonstrate all too well that our adversarial system is capable of failing. The plea bargaining system, which eschews the adversarial process almost entirely, also is mentioned by numerous authors as an especial area of study and reform. Lofquist simply calls for an investment in justice, a long-term strategy to dismantle the current era of punitiveness and crime-centric philosophies. In general, all legal actors, including the police, attorneys, judges, governors, and policymakers, must demand justice.

Finally, three chapters in the volume are dedicated to the aftermath of wrongful convictions and reforms designed to improve reentry from prison into free society. In Chapter 14, Kimberly Cook, Saundra Westervelt, and Shadd Maruna discuss the all-too-often painful process of reentry. Exonerees frequently experience stigma, barriers to employment and access to public assistance benefits, problems with addressing basic needs (including medical and dental care), and struggle to answer even the most basic of questions (such as where to sleep at night). Cook et al. emphasize that apologies would go a long way to help overcome these difficulties, as would automatic expungement of criminal histories and better compensation. Baumgartner and colleagues also stress the need for better compensation laws. In Chapter 16, Elizabeth Griffiths and Michael Leo Owens suggest a method to improve compensation for exonerees, utilizing a worker's compensation model in which "fault" is not necessarily assigned. Through an interesting set of analyses, Griffiths and Owens demonstrate that the number of state exonerations and the quality of the state's compensation statutes have a complex U-shaped relationship (see Figure 1 in their chapter), with states with a mid-level number of exonerations (more than five but less than 15) tending to have the lowest quality compensation statutes. They conclude that the most plausible explanation for this relationship is what they label "elite responsiveness," or the propensity for policy elites to be responsive to their constituents' opinions. Thus, when exonerations are frequent, the public—and by extension, policymakers—are more likely to favor better compensation packages for exonerees. In essence, the three chapters explicating what happens to individuals in the aftermath of exoneration highlight the importance of addressing the consequences, as well as the causes of wrongful convictions.

# Conclusion

In criminal justice systems in which the police, attorneys, judges, and probation and parole officers are all overworked, conditions are ripe for arresting, adjudicating, and incarcerating the innocent. Concerted efforts must be made to identify and countermand these conditions. To do so otherwise is socially irresponsible, as our nation's jails and prisons are already overflowing. Calling attention to these issues in volumes like the current one and responding to them through the work of numerous hardworking individuals associated with Innocence Projects and related endeavors, hopefully will help prevent and redress the problems associated with wrongful convictions.

In 1941, Max Hirschberg, an eminent criminal lawyer of Germany, stated:

> Innocent men wrongfully convicted are countless. It is the duty of science to open our eye to this terrible fact. It is the duty of ethics to rouse indolent and indifferent hearts. The reasons for wrongful convictions are, despite differences in procedure, almost the same in all countries. European science has much to learn from American criminology (Hirschberg, 1941, p. 20).

Within this quote are several sentiments. First is that almost 75 years ago some believed that wrongful convictions were not rare occurrences but rather so common they could not be counted. Second is the notion that science (and ethics) has an important role to play in understanding—and helping to prevent—these miscarriages of justice. Third is that wrongful convictions are a universal problem. And fourth is that one disciplinary perspective (European science) has much to learn from another (American criminology). While, of course, we do not believe that this transfer of learning is uni-directional, we wholeheartedly endorse the notion that the scholarship of wrongful conviction must be broad, multi-disciplinary, and involve the transmission of knowledge from science to practice and back. These are the ultimate goals of this volume.

# References

Acker, J. R., Redlich, A. D., Norris, R. J., & Bonventre, C. L. (2014). *Stepping back— Moving beyond immediate causes: Criminal justice and wrongful convictions in social context.* (This volume.)

Baumgartner, F. R., Westervelt, S. D., & Cook. K. J. (2014). *Public policy responses to wrongful convictions.* (This volume.)

Bibas, S. (2014). *Plea bargaining's role in wrongful convictions.* (This volume.)

Bibas, S. (2012). *The machinery of criminal justice.* New York: Oxford University Press.

Borchard, E. M. (1932). *Convicting the innocent: Errors of criminal justice.* New Haven, CT: Yale University Press.

Bonventre, C. L., Norris, R. J., & West, E. (2014). *Studying innocence: Advancing methods and data.* (This volume.)

Bowers, J. (2008). Punishing the innocent. *University of Pennsylvania Law Review, 156,* 1117–1179.

Cook, K. J., Westervelt, S.D., & Maruna, S. (2014). *The problem of fit: Parolees, exonerees, and prisoner reentry.* (This volume.)

Drizin, S., Nirider, L., & Tepfer, J. (2014). *Juvenile justice investigation: Narrative contamination, cultural stereotypes, and the scripting of juvenile false confessions.* (This volume.)

Feld, B. C. (2014). *"The worst of both worlds": Adolescent competence and the quality of justice in juvenile courts as a prescription for wrongful convictions.* (This volume.)

Garrett, B. L. (2011). *Convicting the innocent: Where criminal prosecutions go wrong.* Cambridge, MA: Harvard University Press.

Gershman, B. (2014). *The prosecutor's contribution to wrongful convictions.* (This volume.)

*Gideon v. Wainwright,* 372 U.S. 335 (1963).

Griffiths, E., & Owens, M. L. (2014). *Remedying wrongful convictions: Societal obligations to exonerees.* (This volume.)

Hirschberg, M. (1941). Wrongful convictions. *Rocky Mountain Law Review, 13,* 20–46.

*Kansas v. Marsh,* 548 U.S. 163 (2006).

Killias, M. (2014). *International trends and developments: Perspectives on wrongful convictions from Europe.* (This volume.)

King, N. J. (2014). *Judicial review: Appeals and postconviction proceedings.* (This volume.)

Laqueur, H., Rushin, S., & Simon, J. (2014). *Wrongful conviction, policing, and the "wars on crime and drugs."* (This volume.)

Leo, R. A. (2005). Rethinking the study of wrongful convictions: Developing a criminology of wrongful conviction. *Journal of Contemporary Criminal Justice, 21*(3), 201–223.

Lippmann, W. (1921). *Public opinion.* New York: Harcourt, Brace and Company, Inc. Available at, http://wps.pearsoncustom.com/wps/media/objects/2429/2487430/pdfs/lippmann.pdf.

Lofquist, W. S. (2014). *Finding the causes in the contexts: Structural sources of wrongful conviction.* (This volume.)

*McCleskey v. Kemp,* 481 U.S. 279 (1987).

Murrie, D., Boccaccini, M. T., Guarnera, L. A., & Rufino, K. A. (2013). Are forensic experts biased by the side that retained them? *Psychological Science, 24,* 1889–1897.

Najdowski, C. J. (2014). *Interactions between African Americans and police officers: How cultural stereotypes create a wrongful conviction pipeline for African Americans.* (This volume.)

Najdowski, C. J. (2011). Stereotype threat in criminal interrogations: Why innocent Black suspects are at risk for confessing falsely. *Psychology, Public Policy, and Law, 17*, 562–591.

Norris, R. J. & Bonventre, C. L. (2013). Advancing wrongful conviction scholarship: Toward new conceptual frameworks. *Justice Quarterly*. Published online, doi: 10.1080/07418825.2013.827232.

Norris, R. J., Bonventre, C. L., Redlich, A. D., & Acker, J. R. (2010/2011). "Than that one innocent suffer": Evaluating state safeguards against wrongful convictions. *Albany Law Review, 74*, 1301–1364.

O'Brien, B., & Findley, K. (2014). *Psychological perspectives: Cognition and decision making.* (This volume.)

Pound, R. (1910). Law in books and law in action. *American Law Review, 44*, 12–36.

Redlich, A. D. (2010). False confessions and false guilty pleas: Similarities and differences. In G.D. Lassiter & C. Meissner (Eds.), *Interrogations and confessions: Current research, practice and policy* (pp. 49–66). Washington, DC: APA Books.

Scheck, B., Neufeld, P., & Dwyer, J. (2003). *Actual Innocence: When justice goes wrong and how to make it right.* New York: New American Library.

Steele, C. M. (2010). *Whistling Vivaldi: How stereotypes affect us and what we can do.* New York: W. W. Norton & Company, Inc.

*Strickland v. Washington*, 466 U.S. 668 (1984).

Vidmar, N. & Coleman, J. E. (2014). *The American adversary system: Sources of error in the criminal adjudication process.* (This volume.)

Yant, M. (2014). *The media's muddled message on wrongful convictions.* (This volume.)

Yaroshefsky. E., & Schaefer, L. (2014). *Defense lawyering and wrongful convictions.* (This volume.)

Zalman, M. (2014). *Theorizing wrongful conviction.* (This volume.)

Zalman, M. (2011). An integrated justice model of wrongful convictions. *Albany Law Review, 73*(3), 1465–1524.

# Author Biographies

**James R. Acker** is a Distinguished Teaching Professor at the University at Albany School of Criminal Justice. He earned his J.D. at Duke University and his Ph.D. in criminal justice at the University at Albany. His principal research and scholarly interests involve legal and empirical issues relating to wrongful convictions, capital punishment, criminal procedure, substantive criminal law, and the rights of children. He is co-author (with Allison D. Redlich) of *Wrongful Conviction: Law, Science, and Policy* (Carolina Academic Press 2011) and he serves on the Board of Editors of the annual Miscarriages of Justice issue of the *Albany Law Review*.

**Frank R. Baumgartner** holds the Richard J. Richardson Distinguished Professorship in Political Science at the University of North Carolina at Chapel Hill. He is the co-author of *The Decline of the Death Penalty and the Discovery of Innocence* (Cambridge 2008). His current death-penalty related research relates to racial bias, geographic arbitrariness, and the national decline in usage of the death penalty.

**Stephanos Bibas** studies the powers and incentives that shape how prosecutors, defense counsel, defendants, and judges behave in the real world of guilty pleas. He also studies the divorce between criminal procedure's focus on efficiency and criminal law's interest in healing victims, defendants, and communities. His new book (*The Machinery of Criminal Justice*, Oxford 2012) explains how criminal justice should do more to encourage acceptance of responsibility, remorse, apology, and forgiveness. As director of Penn's Supreme Court Clinic, Bibas litigates a wide range of Supreme Court cases. He and his co-counsel won a landmark victory in *Padilla v. Kentucky* in 2010, persuading the Court to recognize the right of noncitizen defendants to accurate information about deportation before they plead guilty. His academic work played a central role in the Supreme Court's landmark case of *Blakely v. Washington*.

**Catherine L. Bonventre** is a Ph.D. student in the School of Criminal Justice at the University at Albany. She holds a M.S. in forensic biology from the University at Albany. She earned her J.D., with a concentration in criminal law, from Albany Law School and is licensed to practice law in the state of New York. Prior to entering law school, she spent over a decade working in clinical and research genetics. Her research interests include wrongful convictions and miscarriages of justice; crime laboratories and forensic science; criminal court processes; and judicial decision-making and policy implementation. She has co-authored academic articles on miscarriages of justice and has done volunteer work for the Arizona Justice Project and Prisoners' Legal Services of New York. Catherine serves on the Board of Editors of the annual Miscarriages of Justice issue of the *Albany Law Review*.

**James E. Coleman** Jr. is the John S. Bradway Professor of Law, and serves as co-director of the Wrongful Convictions Clinic and director of the Center for Criminal Justice and Professional Responsibility at Duke Law School. He received his A.B. from Harvard University and J.D. from Columbia University. Coleman teaches classes relating to criminal law, wrongful convictions, and legal ethics, serves as a faculty advisor to the Innocence

Project at Duke University, and formerly chaired the American Bar Association's Section on Individual Rights and Responsibilities, and the Death Penalty Moratorium Implementation Project.

**Kimberly J. Cook** lives in Wilmington, NC. She is a Professor of Sociology and Criminology at the University of North Carolina Wilmington. With Saundra Westervelt, she is co-author of the recently released book, *Life After Death Row: Exonerees' Search for Community and Identity* (Rutgers University Press). Her areas of interest include capital punishment, restorative justice, violence against women, and social justice. Her earlier work includes *Divided Passions: Public Opinions on Abortion and the Death Penalty* (1998, Northeastern University Press). In her spare time she enjoys relaxing at the beach, reading historical fiction, birding, making pottery, spending time with friends and just about any pastime with her son Greg.

**Steven A. Drizin** is an Assistant Dean of the Bluhm Legal Clinic and a Clinical Professor at Northwestern University School of Law where he has taught since 1991. From 2005–2013, he was the Legal Director of the Law School's Center on Wrongful Convictions. In 2008, he co-founded the Center on Wrongful Convictions of Youth. Drizin is a 1983 graduate of Haverford College and a 1986 graduate of Northwestern Law School. He has published numerous articles on juvenile justice and wrongful conviction matters and he and his students have litigated cases in these areas in both state and federal court for more than two decades.

**Barry C. Feld** is Centennial Professor of Law, University of Minnesota Law School, where he has taught since 1972. He has written or edited ten books including *Kids, Cops, and Confessions: Inside the Interrogation Room* (NYU Press 2013), *Oxford Handbook of Juvenile Crime and Juvenile Justice* (OUP 2012), and *Cases and Materials on Juvenile Justice Administration* (Thomson-West 4th Ed. 2013). He has written about one hundred law review articles, book chapters, and peer-reviewed criminology articles on juvenile justice administration with emphases on race, adolescents' competence to exercise rights and procedural justice, and youths' culpability, waiver, and sentencing policy. His book, *Bad Kids: Race and the Transformation of the Juvenile Court* (Oxford University Press, 1999), received the outstanding book award from the Academy of Criminal Justice Sciences, 2001, and the Michael J. Hindelang Outstanding Book Award from the American Society of Criminology, 2002. The American Bar Association awarded him the Livingston Hall Award for "lawyers practicing in the juvenile delinquency field who have demonstrated a high degree of skill, commitment, and professionalism in representing their young clients." He was named a Fellow of the American Society of Criminology and he is an elected member of the American Law Institute.

**Keith Findley** is a 1985 graduate of the Yale Law School and a 1981 graduate of Indiana University. He is an assistant professor at the University of Wisconsin Law School, where he teaches courses on criminal procedure, wrongful convictions, and evidence, and where he is also co-founder and co-director of the Wisconsin Innocence Project. He is currently the president of the Innocence Network, an affiliation of more than 60 Innocence Projects in the United States, Canada, the United Kingdom, Ireland, Australia, New Zealand, the Netherlands, France, Italy, and South Africa. He has written and published numerous articles and book chapters on various topics related to wrongful conviction of the innocent. In addition to teaching and writing about the law, he has litigated hundreds of appeals at all levels of state and federal courts, including numerous cases that led to exoneration of a wrongly convicted individual.

**Bennett Gershman** is one of the original faculty members at Pace Law School and has taught as a visiting professor at Cornell Law School and Syracuse Law School. While in private practice he specialized in criminal defense litigation. A former prosecutor with the Manhattan District Attorney's office for six years, he is the author of numerous articles as well as two books on prosecutorial and judicial ethics. He served for four years with the Special State Prosecutor investigating corruption in the judicial system. He is one of the nation's leading experts on prosecutorial misconduct. He is active on several Bar Association committees, and is a frequent pro bono litigator. Professor Gershman has taught in the London Law Program, and was named James D. Hopkins Professor for the 2007–2009 academic years.

**Elizabeth Griffiths** is an Associate Professor in the School of Criminal Justice at Rutgers University. Her current research focuses on the community context of crime, the nature of violent altercations, public housing transformation, state reparation policies, and racial disparities in the policing and prosecution of felony drug offenses, among other topics. Some of her recent work has been published in *Criminology*, *Social Problems*, and *Race & Justice*.

**Martin Killias** holds a doctoral degree in law and a M.A. in sociology and social psychology, both from the University of Zurich. After three semesters spent as a postdoctoral fellow at the School of Criminal Justice, University at Albany, he served for over 25 years as professor of criminology and criminal law at the University of Lausanne, School of Criminal Justice. In 2006 he joined the University of Zurich and in 2013 the University of St. Gallen Law School, as a professor of criminology, criminal law and criminal procedure. From 1984 to 2008, he served part-time as a justice to the Federal Supreme Court of Switzerland. During his career, he has been visiting professor at Universities in the U.S., the Netherlands, England, Italy, China and Indonesia.

**Nancy King** is the Speir Professor of Law at Vanderbilt University Law School, where she teaches courses in criminal law and procedure. Her solo or co-authored work includes the book *Habeas for the Twenty-First Century—Uses, Abuses, and the Future of the Great Writ*; two comprehensive criminal procedure treatises; the nation's leading criminal procedure text; and dozens of articles and essays covering topics including jury selection, jury nullification, double jeopardy, plea bargaining, sentencing, appellate and post-conviction review, and ineffective assistance of counsel. Her original empirical research includes a nationwide study of federal habeas litigation with researchers from the National Center for State Courts, as well as studies of jury misconduct, jury sentencing, guideline sentencing, and appeal waivers in federal plea agreements. She has served on the Advisory Committee for the Federal Rules of Criminal Procedure for thirteen years (as a member from 2001–07; since 2007 as Assistant Reporter), and has been a frequent presenter at judicial seminars. Professor King is presently a member of the ALI, and was a member of the ABA Criminal Justice Standards Committee from 2008–2012. She served as Associate Dean of the Law School from 1999–2001, and has received multiple University awards for her research.

**Hannah Laqueur** is a Ph.D. Candidate in Jurisprudence and Social Policy at University of California, Berkeley Law, with specializations in law and economics and criminal justice policy. She holds a Master's degree in Public Policy and Administration from Columbia University, and before coming to graduate school worked as a policy analyst at the New York City Mayor's Office. Her research interests include drug policy, policing, sentencing, peer influence, and, more broadly, the application of behavioral science to questions of public policy.

**William S. Lofquist** is a Professor of Sociology at the State University of New York at Geneseo. He received his Ph.D. from the University of Delaware. His primary research interest is the death penalty, with recent publications examining wrongful convictions, executions of the innocent, and the regional patterning of the death penalty and its relationship to slavery. His present research focuses on death penalty volunteers and the history and use of the death penalty in the Caribbean.

**Shadd Maruna** is the Director of the Institute of Criminology and Criminal Justice at Queen's University Belfast. Previously, he taught at the University of Cambridge and the State University of New York. His book *Making Good: How Ex-Convicts Reform and Rebuild Their Lives* was named the Outstanding Contribution to Criminology in 2001, and he was the inaugural winner of the Research Medal from the Howard League for Penal Reform in 2011. His most recent book is *Fifty Key Thinkers in Criminology* (with Keith Hayward and Jayne Mooney).

**Cynthia Najdowski** is an Assistant Professor in the University at Albany's School of Criminal Justice. She completed her graduate studies in Social and Personality Psychology and Psychology and Law at the University of Illinois at Chicago. Cynthia studies issues at the intersection of psychology and the law, particularly those that concern vulnerable populations. For example, she conducts research on perceptions of juvenile offenders and the public policies that affect them, social influences on the recovery of sexual abuse and rape victims, and social psychological factors that contribute to racial disparities in the legal system. Her chapter in this volume is related to the last research area, and includes a review of her work on understanding how African Americans experience police encounters psychologically. Cynthia's work has been recognized with several competitive awards and grants, including the Psi Chi/American Psychological Association Edwin B. Newman Graduate Research Award and a National Science Foundation Doctoral Dissertation Research Improvement Grant. Her research has been published in journals such as *Psychology, Public Policy, and Law; Journal of Studies on Alcohol and Drugs; Psychology of Women Quarterly*; and *Behavioral Sciences and the Law*. She has also co-edited a book on children, psychology, and law.

**Laura Nirider** is an Assistant Clinical Professor of Law and Project Co-Director of the Center on Wrongful Convictions of Youth (CWCY) at Northwestern University School of Law. Nirider regularly litigates cases involving false and involuntary confessions around the country and has published several articles and op-eds on interrogations and post-conviction relief. She co-authored an amicus curiae brief that was cited by the U.S. Supreme Court in *J.D.B. v. North Carolina* (2011) for the proposition that the risk of false confession is "all the more troubling … and all the more acute … when the subject of custodial interrogation is a juvenile."

**Robert J. Norris** is currently a Ph.D. candidate in the School of Criminal Justice at the University at Albany. He earned his B.A. in Sociology from the University of North Carolina at Greensboro and his M.A. from the University at Albany. His research interests include law and society; miscarriages of justice and wrongful conviction; social change and legal reform; and decision-making in the criminal justice process. He has authored or co-authored several academic articles and book chapters on state policy responses to wrongful convictions, the decision-making of suspects under investigation and at trial, and false and coerced confessions. He is currently working on his dissertation exploring the history of the "innocence movement" in the United States.

**Barbara O'Brien** is an Associate Professor at the Michigan State University College of Law. She earned her J.D. at the University of Colorado School of law, and her A.B. in Economics from Bowdoin College. She also completed a Ph.D. in social psychology at the University of Michigan. Her scholarship examines the role of race and other extralegal factors in criminal investigations, trials, and the administration of capital punishment. Her work applies empirical methodology to legal issues, such as identifying predictors of false convictions and understanding prosecutorial decision-making.

**Michael Leo Owens** is Associate Professor of Political Science at Emory University, where he teaches courses in American politics and policy, including a seminar on politics and punishment. He chairs the governing board of the Urban Affairs Association, and is a member of the board of directors of the Prison Policy Initiative and the national advisory boards of the Georgia Justice Project and Foreverfamily, Inc. The author of *God and Government in the Ghetto: The Politics of Church-State Collaboration in Black America* (University of Chicago Press, 2007), Owens is completing a book manuscript, titled *The Prisoners of Democracy*, that examines how mass incarceration both undermines and fosters political engagement, empowerment, and efficacy in urban and racialized communities in the United States.

**Allison D. Redlich** is Associate Professor in the School of Criminal Justice at the State University of New York, University at Albany, and Executive Director of the Michael J. Hindelang Criminal Justice Research Center. Previously, she was a Senior Research Associate at Policy Research Associates and a Research Scientist at the Stanford University School of Medicine. She received her Ph.D. in Developmental Psychology from the University of California, Davis. Professor Redlich is an internationally recognized expert on police interrogations and false confessions, often being asked to present her research abroad and in courts as an expert witness. Professor Redlich also has extensive programs of research on true and false guilty pleas and mental health courts. She has authored more than 75 articles and chapters, including (with J. Acker) the case law book, *Wrongful Conviction: Law, Science, and Policy*.

**Stephen Rushin** is a Visiting Assistant Professor of Law at the University of Illinois College of Law, where he teaches criminal law and information privacy law. He received his J.D. from Berkeley Law and is currently a Ph.D. candidate in the Jurisprudence and Social Policy Program at Berkeley. Rushin has published articles on a wide range of subjects related to policing law including police misconduct, police surveillance, private policing, and custodial interrogations.

**Laura Schaefer** received her Juris Doctor degree in 2013 from the Benjamin N. Cardozo School of Law in New York City. She holds a Master's of Science Degree in Human Rights Studies from the London School of Economics and Political Science, and received her Bachelor's Degree in 2008 from the Gallatin School of Individualized Study at New York University. While in law school, Laura participated in the Human Rights & Genocide Prevention and Innocence Project clinics, where she developed her interest in wrongful convictions and post-conviction advocacy. Since September 2013, Laura has held a post-graduate public interest fellowship position with the Federal Defenders for the Southern District of New York.

**Jonathan Simon** is the Adrian A. Kragen Professor of Law at UC Berkeley. His scholarship concerns crime and governance, mass incarceration, and human rights constraints on sovereign punishment. His book, *Governing through Crime: How the War on Crime Transformed American Democracy and Created a Culture of Fear* (Oxford University Press 2009), won the Michael J. Hindelang prize of the American Society of Criminology in 2010. His most recent book, *Mass Incarceration on Trial: A Remarkable Case and the Future of American Prisons*, will be published by New Press in August 2014.

**Joshua Tepfer** is an Assistant Clinical Professor of Law and Project Co-Director of the Center on Wrongful Convictions of Youth (CWCY) at Northwestern University School of Law. Tepfer has been counsel for several men who were exonerated after they falsely confessed as teenagers, including in two cases—known as the Englewood Four and Dixmoor Five—which prompted CBS' 60 Minutes to label Chicago the False Confession Capital. Tepfer frequently conducts trainings and writes on issues related to interrogations, false confessions, and wrongful convictions of youth.

**Neil Vidmar** is Russell M. Robinson II Professor of Law at Duke Law School and Research Director in Duke Law's Center for Criminal Justice and Ethical Responsibility; and he also holds a secondary appointment in the Duke Psychology Department. Vidmar received his Ph.D. in social psychology from the University of Illinois in 1967 and joined the Psychology Department at the University of Western Ontario in Canada that year. In 1973–1974 he was a Russell Sage Resident at Yale Law School. He joined Duke Law School in 1987. Vidmar is co-author of Neil Vidmar and Valerie P. Hans, *American Juries: The Verdict* (2007); co-author of Hans and Vidmar, *Judging the Jury* (1986); author of *Medical Malpractice and the American Jury* (1995); and editor/author of *World Jury Systems* (2000). He has written approximately 200 articles and reports in both social science journals and law reviews that include the following subjects: the jury system; pretrial prejudice; procedural justice; death penalty attitudes; battered woman syndrome; and numerous topics bearing on civil litigation. Vidmar was involved as an expert in the John Walker Lindh ("American Taliban") and Sami al-Arian terrorism trials and recently co-drafted amicus briefs for litigation bearing on racial discrimination in death penalty cases under North Carolina's Racial Justice Act. Vidmar has testified or consulted as an expert on jury behavior for criminal trials in the United States, Canada, England, Australia, New Zealand, and Hong Kong.

**Emily West** is Director of Research at the Innocence Project. She is responsible for systematically organizing and utilizing internal client data as well as data on DNA exonerations nationwide in order to both support policy reform efforts aimed at improving the criminal justice system and to promote more research relating to wrongful convictions. She has more than 15 years of research and evaluation experience across a broad array of disciplines including education, youth development (teen pregnancy prevention and juvenile delinquency), and criminal justice (prisoner re-entry, reducing recidivism, restorative justice, crime prevention, and wrongful convictions). Emily holds a Ph.D. from the University of Pennsylvania in sociology and criminology, with a focus on sociology of the family and juvenile delinquency.

**Saundra D. Westervelt** lives in Greensboro, N.C. with her husband, Van, and their son, Drew. She is an Associate Professor of Sociology at the University of North Carolina Greensboro. Her broad areas of interest include criminology and the sociology of law, but her more recent work has focused on miscarriages of justice. Her most recent book, *Life after Death Row: Exonerees' Search for Community and Identity* (with Kimberly J. Cook, 2012, Rutgers University Press) examines the aftermath of a wrongful capital conviction for 18 death row exonerees in the United States. In her spare time, she enjoys traveling with her family and chasing turtles with her son.

**Martin Yant** has been investigating wrongful convictions since 1978, when he revealed that a corrupt sheriff had framed a man to keep him from running against him in the next election. A series of columns he wrote about wrongful convictions in *The Columbus Dispatch* in the 1980s culminated in his book *Presumed Guilty: When Innocent People Are Wrongly Convicted* in 1991, which *The Washington Post* later named one of the eight most-important books on miscarriages of justice ever published. Yant then left journalism to investigate wrongful convictions as a private investigator. Since then, his investigations have helped free 16 wrongly convicted individuals, and he has been called "the most successful one-man innocence project in the country." The Georgetown University graduate has written three other investigative books. He is on the board of directors of Truth in Justice, an organization that seeks to heighten public awareness of wrongful convictions through the web site www.truthinjustice.org. He is also a contributing editor of The Wrongful Convictions Blog (www.wrongfulconvictionsblog.org) sponsored by The Center for the Global Study of Wrongful Conviction.

**Ellen Yaroshefsky** is Clinical Professor of Law and the director of the Jacob Burns Ethics Center at the Benjamin N. Cardozo School of Law in New York and the director of Cardozo's Youth Justice Clinic. She teaches a range of ethics and criminal justice courses, organizes symposia, and writes and lectures in the field of legal ethics, with a focus upon criminal justice issues. She has taught Wrongful Convictions, Evidence, and Youth Justice. Ms. Yaroshefsky also counsels lawyers and law firms and serves as an expert witness on legal ethics issues. She is co-chair of the American Bar Association's Ethics, *Gideon* and Professionalism Committee of the Criminal Justice Section, chair of the Ethics Committee of the National Association of Criminal Defense Lawyers, and serves on ethics committees of state and local bar associations. Prior to joining the Cardozo faculty, she was an attorney at the Center for Constitutional Rights in New York and subsequently in private practice. She began her career as an attorney for the Puyallup Tribe in Tacoma, Washington and subsequently was a criminal defense lawyer in Seattle, Washington. She has received a number of awards for litigation and received the New York State Bar Association award for "Outstanding Contribution in the Field of Criminal Law Education."

**Marvin Zalman** is Professor of Criminal Justice at Wayne State University. He has written on criminal procedure (e.g., articles on *Miranda* rights, Fourth Amendment, and venue); criminal justice policy; wrongful conviction; criminal justice and civil liberties; and judicial sentencing. Recent publications include "Wrongful Conviction" in Oxford Bibliographies Online, (Fall 2012); "Qualitatively Estimating the Incidence of Wrongful Convictions" (*Criminal Law Bulletin*, 2012); "An Integrated Justice Model of Wrongful Convictions" (*Albany Law Review*, 2011); "Measuring Wrongful Convictions" (*Encyclopedia of Criminology and Criminal Justice*, Springer, 2014); and "Edwin Borchard and the Limits of Innocence Reform" (in Huff & Killias, eds., *Wrongful Convictions & Miscarriages of Justice*, Routledge, 2014). With Julia Carrano he has co-edited *Wrongful Conviction and Criminal Justice Reform: Making Justice* (Routledge, 2014).

# Index